Petersburg
Fin de Siècle

Petersburg Fin de Siècle

Mark D. Steinberg

Yale
UNIVERSITY PRESS
New Haven & London

Published with assistance from the foundation established in memory of James Wesley Cooper of the Class of 1865, Yale College.

Yale University Press books may be purchased in quantity for educational, business, or promotional use. For information, please e-mail sales.press@yale.edu (U.S. office) or sales@yaleup.co.uk (U.K. office).

Set in Bulmer type by Newgen North America.

Printed in the United States of America.

Library of Congress Cataloging-in-Publication Data

Steinberg, Mark D., 1953–
    Petersburg fin de siècle / Mark D. Steinberg.
       p.   cm.
    Includes bibliographical references and index.
    ISBN 978-0-300-16504-3 (hardcover : alk. paper)   1. Saint Petersburg (Russia)—Civilization—19th century.   2. Saint Petersburg (Russia)—Civilization—20th century.   3. Saint Petersburg (Russia)—Intellectual life.   4. Saint Petersburg (Russia)—Social conditions.   5. City and town life—Russia (Federation)—Saint Petersburg—History.   6. Social change—Russia (Federation)—Saint Petersburg—History.   7. Modernism (Aesthetics)—Russia (Federation)—Saint Petersburg—History.   8. Popular culture—Russia (Federation)—Saint Petersburg—History.   9. Social problems—Russia (Federation)—Saint Petersburg—History.   I. Title.
    DK557.S688 2011
    947′.21083—dc22

2011006429

A catalogue record for this book is available from the British Library.

This paper meets the requirements of ANSI/NISO Z39.48-1992 (Permanence of Paper).

10 9 8 7 6 5 4 3 2 1

For Jane and Sasha

Contents

Acknowledgments

Once again I have learned that one of the great intellectual and personal pleasures of scholarly writing is the inspiring critical conversations that have resulted from sharing my work with others. This may be why I have presented my work for criticism so often. As this book has taken shape over a number of years, I have benefited enormously from discussions at conferences, workshops, and colloquia organized by the History Workshop, the Russian Studies Kruzhok, the Illinois Program for Research in the Humanities, and the Unit for Criticism and Interpretive Theory at the University of Illinois at Urbana-Champaign (a stimulating intellectual environment where I am indebted to too many colleagues to name); the Association for Slavic, East European, and Eurasian Studies (formerly AAASS); the Institute of Russian History of the Russian Academy of Sciences in St. Petersburg; the European University of St. Petersburg; the research colloquium in eastern European history at the Humboldt University of Berlin; the research colloquium at the Osteuropa-Institut of the Free University of Berlin; the University of Cambridge (Faculty of History and Department of Slavonic Studies); the Midwest Russian History Workshop; the Research Triangle intellectual history seminar; the Department of Slavic Languages and Literatures at the University of Southern California; the Department of Slavic Languages and Literatures at the University of Pennsylvania; the German Historical Institute and Centre franco-russe en sciences humaines et sociales in Moscow (a conference on emotions); the Getty Research Institute; the Wissenschaftszentrum Berlin; and the History Department at the University of Cincinnati. I am indebted to so many participants at these gatherings and to the institutions that supported them.

I would like particularly to thank individuals who have read substantial parts of this book and whose criticisms and suggestions have been invaluable: Laurie Bernstein and Joseph Bradley (who, as temporarily anonymous readers for Yale University Press, offered sustained and insightful readings, which have much affected the final text), Jim Barrett, Ruth Hober-man, Diane Koenker, Harry Liebersohn, Louise McReynolds, Mark Micale, Jan Plamper, John Randolph, and Roshanna Sylvester. Jane Hedges and Sasha Hedges Steinberg have been essential readers and critics from first word to last; I have learned much from both of them. A number of illuminating conversations with Sasha in Petersburg cafés and restaurants, as I was working on final revisions, influenced some key choices and formulations. I must thank also the many scholars, in many fields, who have written before about so many of the questions this book engages—from issues in Russian history to overly broad questions about "modernity" to even more sweeping questions of existence. Sitting at my computer surrounded by their books and articles I knew that my words were part of a lively, even chaotic, conversation across fields and time. Of course, they cannot be blamed for my misunderstandings and misuses of their work.

I have also been much aided by my research assistants at Illinois, especially in reading through long runs of microfilmed newspapers but also as critical interlocutors: Andy Bruno, Sharyl Corrado, Maria Cristina Galmarini, and Jesse Murray. And I have benefited in many ways from stimulating discussions with students in my courses on Russian history, comparative urban history, and approaches to history. I have also relied repeatedly on the excellent reference and tracking skills of the staff of the Slavic and East European Library at the University of Illinois.

For financial support allowing many research visits to St. Petersburg, research assistance, and time to reflect and write, I am honored by and grateful for support from the John Simon Guggenheim Memorial Foundation; the International Research and Exchanges Board (IREX); and, not least, at the University of Illinois, the International Council, the Russian, East European, and Eurasian Center, the Campus Research Board, and the Illinois Program for Research in the Humanities.

At Yale University Press, essential support and critical advice was provided by Jonathan Brent and Sarah Miller. Gavin Lewis improved the text with his expert, intelligent, and sensitive editing. Kirsten Painter prepared the index with exceptional skill and knowledge.

Finally, I am grateful for permissions to draw upon articles, developed out of this project, that have previously been published:

"Melancholy and Modernity: Emotions and Social Life in Russia between the Revolutions," *Journal of Social History*, Summer 2008.

" 'Chernye Maski'; Zrelishcha, obrazy i identichnosti' na gorodskikh ulitsakh," in *Kul'tury gorodov Rossiiskoi imperii*, edited by Boris Kolonitskii and Mark Steinberg (St. Petersburg: Evropeiskii dom, 2009).

"Melankholiia novogo vremeni: Diskurs o sotsial'nykh emotsiiakh mezhdu dvumia revoliutsiiami," in *Rossiiskaia imperiia chustv: Podkhody k kul'turnoi istorii emotsii,* edited by Jan Plamper, Schamma Schahadat, and Marc Elie (Moscow: Novoe literaturnoe obozrenie, 2010).

Troubled Times

Imperial Russia's final decade was an era of possibility and crisis, marked by an often desperate search for the meaning of the present and a sense of the future. In retrospect, we know that this era was a threshold: the unsettled wake of the 1905 revolution and the eve of a still greater revolutionary upheaval in the midst of a devastating war. This destination could not be known, of course. But a recognition that these were fateful years was widely evident in public discussion of "these times." A vocabulary of sickness and crisis was used to define public life, especially by the city's newspapers, journals, and magazines. And every writer, from philosophers to physicians to professional newspaper columnists, was inclined to philosophize about the larger meanings of "these times." Only partly was the sickness that was diagnosed a sign of the dying of an old regime. Much more, especially as contemporaries saw it, this was a crisis born of what was new. Endlessly, especially in the press, writers situated these Russian "times of trouble" in an encounter with modernity that was not uniquely Russian, though it had its own shadings, its own nuances, and its own distinctive consequences.

Russians worried, as others did, that modern civilization had brought with it as much suffering as pleasure, as much sickness as health. Perhaps more. Russia's fin de siècle[1] was more pessimistic than in the west. Russians had come to share the worries of earlier western European intellectuals that the brilliant promises of modern progress were an illusion and a myth. Their vocabulary became filled with talk of catastrophic disintegration, decline, groundlessness, sickness, disenchantment, and uncertainty—echoes, if not quotations, of concerns heard earlier in western Europe. In Russia, though, these judgments unfolded with greater publicity, social reach, and intensity. And with greater consequence.[2]

St. Petersburg is a natural place for thinking about Russia and the modern experience. It was the empire's political capital and its most populous and developed metropolis—it quite literally commanded and represented Russia. But Petersburg (Russians tended to omit the sacred reference, even before the city was renamed Petrograd in 1914) also famously stood for "western civilization" in Russia. Tsar Peter the Great, everyone remembers, created the city to "cut a window through to Europe" (*V Evropu prorubit' okno*, a phrase put in Peter's mouth by the poet Aleksandr Pushkin). This implicitly violent act of constructing civilization in a conquered and primitive space was the foundation of the idea of Petersburg as standing for the new and the modern—including in opposition to the old national culture—an ideal that continued to define how the city would be constructed both literally and interpretively. Without ignoring the city's distinctiveness (including a self-image as having its own "genius loci," its unique spirit of place that made it neither truly Russian nor like London or Paris) or the relative underdevelopment of the city economically (which gave some hope that the city's maladies would be overcome with more modernity), early twentieth-century commentators focused mainly on the city as exemplary of the problems of modern life. Most writers would have agreed with a journalist writing in 1912 (about the context of a particular problem in the city at the time, an "epidemic" of suicide): "the general conditions of Petersburg life are both economically and spiritually increasingly approaching the conditions of life of western European urban centers."[3] As will be seen, few considered this to be a happy fact.

In other words, this book is ambiguous about its object and place, just as St. Petersburg was for the contemporaries whose voices I examine. Of course, this is a study within Russian history: rooted in the particularities of a national history and of a distinctive city. But I agree with my informants: this particular Russian story, especially how it was told and interpreted at the time, was also a window on the west, a signifier of a modern experience with which Russia, especially urban Russia, had become inextricably entwined. In this sense, St. Petersburg *did* represent Russia: not where it had been, but where it might be going. But it also spoke of other histories and other futures. I agree with my informants also in viewing stories about modernity, for all their variety and elusive meaning, as about bigger things still: the movement of time, the human self in the social world, truth and lies, life and death, happiness and sorrow.

Modernity—as a condition, a subjective experience, a cultural representation, an ideology—is a gigantic category surrounded by a colossal body of interpreting texts, many of them at odds. Theorists who have tried to reconcile these differences and create a coherent definition have tended to argue that modernity is characterized most by its contradictions, antinomies, and ambivalences. In particular, modernity thrives on a tension between its two faces: rationalistic modernization (which includes the administrative and aesthetic ordering of society and nature, the cult of reason, scientism, and the doctrine of progress) and dynamic discontinuity, fracturing, contingency, and flux; between, as it were, the ordering (and repressing) power of Apollonian discipline and the liberating (and destructive) force of Dionysian excess. A related dialogue juxtaposes modernity's "singularity," especially as a western and often imperial project of transformative modernization, to its multiplicity, adaptability, and usability. Likewise, modernity inspires both vivid optimism—whether based on faith in the forward march of science and industry or faith in the liberation and possibility brought by the maelstrom of modern instability—and a dark pessimism in the face of the wreckage modernity leaves behind and the falseness of its promise. Some theorists have seen ways to reconcile these opposites; some have seen paths of transcendence and redemption (revolution, for example, or religious salvation); some have seen nothing but unresolved contradiction.[4]

My aim is not to better theorize modernity but to examine it as a historical object: I argue that urban Russians were painfully aware that it was "modernity" they were experiencing; I explore what they meant by this and how they used this knowledge.[5] Of course, my arguments are based on how I read the vocabularies, themes, and interpretations of the past, which are far from self-evident. Indeed, even the word "modernity" was not, properly speaking, present. Russian-speakers lacked a word to precisely translate our "modernity." Although very occasionally they borrowed, and usually wrote in Latin letters, the word *moderne,* this was almost always to speak of architecture and art. What they mainly used instead was a term as ambiguous as modernity itself: *sovremennost'*. Throughout this book, I translate this as "modernity" (and its adjectival form as "modern"), but doing so is decidedly interpretive (and oversimplifying). Not unlike the original meaning of the French *moderne* (the source for most western and central European terms now used to define this particular historical era) *sovremennost'* literally means "of the present time." But just as *moderne* evolved to signify a particular epochal time, so *sovremennost'* was adapted, by the turn of century, to speak of the distinctive times, shared well beyond Russia's borders, of the modern age.[6] The particularities and evaluations of this condition were debated. But no one was in doubt about where its defining forms were to be found: in the industrial capitalist city, where one could most fully see and experience the hallmarks of modernity. In Russia, St. Petersburg was the capital and archetype of this *sovremennost'*—the place that most embodied and symbolized Russia's experience of modernity, where "these times" and all they represented were most palpable.

I might have translated *sovremennost'* as "contemporaneity" (and I do sometimes translate the adjective *sovremennyi* as "contemporary.") This term preserves the ambiguity of the Russian: commentators were thinking both about their particular Russian moment in time and the experience of a shared modernity. Still, "modernity" need not exclude local histories; we need not overuniversalize it. Some recent theorists have gone further and made a case for "contemporaneity" as a different temporality than "modernity": one rich in asynchronous times, jostling contingencies, "multeity, adventitiousness, and inequity." Contemporaneity, in this view, is the first half of Charles Baudelaire's definition of modernity as "the transitory, the fugitive, and the contingent, one half of art of which the other half is the eternal and the immutable" (from his 1863 essay "The Painter of Modern Life") but "bereft of the comfort of the second part." This is meant to define our own present, after the alleged passing of both modernity and postmodernity.[7] But, as I will suggest, that recognition—indeed, a troubled feeling that modern time was fractured, drifting, and sick—was already part of the experience of modernity, notably in Russia.

This book examines the relationship between words and matter. At the center of attention are words used to define experience—especially when they were voiced in the public sphere and about public problems. But these words concerned very tangible conditions. They arose and did their interpreting work in a material world. Some of these words were already concrete: the city, the street, nighttime, blood, sex, sickness, and death. In use, however, these were also often winged words for pondering matters of existence and philosophical meaning. Other common words appear already abstract: the self, truth, morality, happiness, longing, disenchantment, despair, and faith, among others. In use, however, these were often tied to quite concrete things, practices, spaces, and times.

Among these abstractions and materialities, time—more precisely, time as experienced in everyday social life—is a ubiquitous presence in this book, as it was then. If one of the promises of modernity, essential to its mythic power, has been the assurance of "progress," there was a growing anxiety by the early 1900s about whether the "improvements of civilization" were actually bringing people greater happiness. To observe that many Russians were losing faith in the vision of time as linear movement forward (itself a modern idea, of course) is to describe a familiar modern experience. Historians of temporality (time manifested in human life) have shown that the old faith in time as "absolute, true, and mathematical," flowing only "from its own nature," as Isaac Newton famously put it, began to fracture and disintegrate in the late nineteenth and early twentieth centuries in the face of new conceptions of time as relative, variable, uncertain, and perceived. By the start of the twentieth century, the concept of time had broken into a proliferation of perceived and possible temporalities. Progressive historical time of linear movement toward greater good and perfection was joined and challenged by repetitive time, in which nothing is really new; decadent time of degeneration and decline; festive and especially carnival time, in which ordinary time is halted and even broken, though only giving temporary escape and relief; sacred time in which spiritual states or the appearances of the divine can halt normal temporal movement; eschatological time in which repetition or decline (or even ordinary progress) is permanently shattered, allowing entry into some new time of permanent salvation, redemption, and perfection; and others.[8] In urban Russia, as will be seen, especially after the upheavals and disappointments of 1905, writers viewed the condition of public life through all of these temporal lenses—and often tied these closely to questions of moral, social, and philosophical judgment.

"The city" is a critically important space in all this. As the largest and most enduring creation of human imagination, will, and work, the city has long stood as a potent symbol of human capacities. The urban story has almost always been shaded with ambivalence—with a sense of the city as an unstable place of opportunity and peril, vitality and decadence, power and helplessness, creativity and perplexity. The metropolis has long been seen in western culture as a contradictory expression of human achievement (or hubris) and human inadequacy, as can be seen in images of Troy, Babel, Sodom, Babylon, and Rome. In the age of the Enlightenment and capitalism, the city acquired still deeper layers of contradiction. Most famously, this was echoed and reinforced in Baudelaire's poetic and powerful images of Paris, which helped establish and define the category *la modernité* for thinking about the city: on the one hand, the strange blending of the "rapture," "joy," and "intoxication" that can be experienced amidst the urban crowd, even the transcendent "eternity" that the "heroic" connoisseur of the modern city can find in what is most ephemeral, fugitive, and artificial; but also the "darkness," "despair," and "perpetual mourning" of the city dweller, the oppressive awareness (in the words of a poet speaking of Baudelaire's vision at his funeral) of the "sad and tragic heart of the modern city."[9] The continual repetition, to the point of cliché, of this contradictory vision of the modern city in both the west and Russia—Russians freely partook of this discourse and contributed to it—reminds us how compelling this perception has been for seeking and seeing coherent meaning in the flux of urban life. If Russian observers differed, and I believe they did, it was in viewing this "sad and tragic heart" as the greater truth, as overshadowing the heroic intoxication of living in modern time.

Sources mediate the answers to the questions a historian asks. It matters a great deal who we hear speaking—and who we cannot or choose not to hear—and how we ask and listen. My approach has been to read what could also be read by a contemporary consumer of the Petersburg press (though perhaps a rather obsessive one), for my focus is on the public experience, public reception, and public representation of the meanings of urban life—on the "public sphere" as both an object of cultural imagination and the social space where this occurs. The variety of texts I have used is wide: daily newspapers, ranging from "respectable" dailies like *Novoe vremia* (New Times) on the political and cultural right and *Rech'* (Speech) on the liberal left, to mass-circulation "boulevard" papers like *Gazeta-kopeika* (Kopeck Gazette) and *Peterburgskii listok* (Petersburg News Sheet); popular magazines like *Vesna* (Spring) and *Zhizn' dlia vsekh* (Life for Everyone);

intellectual "thick journals" like *Sovremennyi mir* (The Modern/Contemporary World); literary and artistic journals such as *Apollon* and *Argus;* and, to a lesser extent, contemporary books and brochures about contemporary culture and society.

The authors are also diverse: ranging from obscure reporters and columnists to famous writers and critics; and from full-time professional reporters, to regular essayists working under contract, to a large pool of individuals who submitted occasional articles (for the chance to be heard and for the fee paid). Socially, they ranged from working journalists (whose individual biographies, sometimes even their names, are largely undocumented), to professionals in medicine and other scientific fields, to well-educated critics and philosophers. They included men and (in much smaller numbers) women. Ideologically, they ran the gamut from monarchists to socialists and from religious to secular.

Critics of my work—presented as talks or conference papers—have argued that I underemphasize the differences between authors. Indeed, I present a great many quotations in this book, but I do not always specify in the text who is speaking (though the notes duly document every word). I do this purposefully. For all their differences, what strikes me most is the extent to which these writers shared similar concerns, used similar vocabularies and images, and arrived at similar conclusions. Given the long historiography of emphasizing how polarized Russia was by class, culture, and politics, this may seem surprising. Part of their common argument, however, was how polarized Russia was, indeed how catastrophically unhappy. These writers were not the whole population, of course. They were a type of elite: literate, concerned, and outspoken, believing in their capacities to inform, instruct, and influence others. As such, for all their diversity, I often speak of them as a single group: "urban writers." I use this term to emphasize both their location and the object that most captured their attention: they wrote *about* and *in* the public spaces of the city. Their voices, intertwined and sometimes mutually referential, both reflected and defined public thought and opinion about urban life in Russia, and tried to say just what, beyond this place and time, it might all mean.

One more comment about methodology. Like all interpreters, I know that every detail, nuance, and difference in these texts—even if I could access and understand them all—cannot and need not be preserved. The point of interpretation is to find patterns, to "lump" more than "split" (in the often heard academic metaphor). Or, in Isaiah Berlin's more elegant and somewhat different distinction, to be more "fox" than "hedgehog," to view the world in its (sometimes contradictory) breadth and multiplicity rather than through the focused lens of a single topic or a singular theory. Like many historians, I am not entirely comfortable with this choice. Perhaps one of the reasons I quote so many voices (and there were many more before I edited this book to a more readable and publishable size) is to enable the reader to hear not only my own voice, but the many untidy fragments, splinters, and dissonant tones in urban writing. Still, I have deliberately organized all this into the patterns of perception and feeling I find in reading the Petersburg press. Persistent public repetition of the same images, ideas, and arguments is what is most telling. The unoriginality and cliché of so much journalistic writing reveals more of the zeitgeist than the words of the most original and talented. Still, this ordering and retelling is itself an argument. I am convinced that the patterns I highlight really were widespread and often dominant in the public discourse—and I offer a great many citations, perhaps too many, to defend this conclusion. But this remains, ultimately, interpretation and simplification.

A leitmotif in my argument is darkness—social, temporal, epistemological. Modern metropolises like Berlin, Paris, London, and New York were typically viewed as places of intertwined dread and delight.[10] Urban writers in fin-de-siècle St. Petersburg mostly dwelled on the dread. A simple explanation, also heard in Russia at the time, attributes this to Russia's economic and political backwardness, and thus the greater shock of the new. But I would argue that here on the margin of Europe, Russians were exceptionally well positioned to see and understand most acutely the dark sides of modern life. They could and did experience, and rapidly, the harshness of modernization and capitalism. They had access to a rich body of European criticism as well as to their own intellectual histories of skepticism about progress. And all of this could be debated loudly in an increasingly vital public sphere. The result was a picture of modern disarray: moral transgression and disorder, illusoriness and deception, sickness and death, excess and extravagance, and moods of disorientation, uncertainty, and incomprehension, if not outright disgust and fear.

In his 1940 essay on the concept of history, Walter Benjamin famously suggested a reading of Paul Klee's watercolor *Angelus Novus* as a portrait of modern history. The angel, Benjamin imagines, is driven forward in time by a "storm" that "we call progress." But his gaze is turned backward, his eyes staring in alarm at the mounting "wreckage" and ruin that the movement of time "hurls at his feet."[11] From Benjamin's radical perspective, it seems that the angel not only recognizes the catastrophes of the past but realizes that this very act of seeing may be the means to "awaken the dead and make whole what has been smashed," in other words to end the "state of emergency" in which we live, and which we have ceased to question as anything but normal, and to "blast open the continuum of history."[12] St. Petersburg's urban writers shared the recognition of the storm called progress, but were less optimistic about transcendence. Certainly, some were socialists and some were religious believers and thus could imagine a transcending rupture in history. But most were vaguely liberal or vaguely conservative and far from certain that modern history would produce anything but more wreckage. They were not passive, though. While they defended themselves against charges that that their own reporting nurtured an atmosphere of ruin, insisting that they were only holding up a "mirror" to the real catastrophe of everyday life, this was not the whole story. They wrote for many reasons—including commercial ones: sensation sold and they were paid to sell papers. But they also wished to shed light and awaken public sensibilities. At the least, this was a heroic stance at the "edge of an abyss" (a common image at the time). Even more, this could be an act of witnessing that, by speaking of the violence of history and time, by refusing to be silently complicit, might create conditions for change, however unclear that path remained.

City

Piter [Petersburg] has an uncommon attribute: to insult everything holy
in man and force everything secret in him out onto the surface. Only in
Piter may a man really know himself—whether he is a real human being,
a half-human, or a swine. If he suffers here, he is a human being.

—Vissarion Belinskii, 1839

St. Petersburg was never only a physical city. From the moment it was
founded at the start of the eighteenth century as a new capital for a newly
westernizing and expanding empire, this city was always also a "cultural
phenomenon," a "metaphysical" space, a "myth," a "text."[1] The extent and
intensity of interpretive preoccupation with the meanings of St. Petersburg
was enormous. While this textual history is an essential context for this
book, this chapter begins with the physical history of the city. The material
and imagined histories of the city were entwined. Even the most abstract
and metaphoric representations of the city were densely constructed out of
streets, buildings, bodies, faces, wind, and fog.[2] In turn, the experience of
the material city was shaped by encounters with the city in texts, ranging
from belles-lettres to newspaper journalism.

THE PHYSICAL CITY

Rapid growth was the most obvious facet of St. Petersburg's physical history. Founded in 1703 by Tsar Peter I (later promoted to both Emperor and
"the Great"), St. Petersburg's population had reached about 100,000 when
Catherine II (also later "the Great") came to the throne in 1762 and had
doubled by the time of her death in 1796. By the time Nicholas I became
emperor in 1825 it had doubled again, reaching nearly a half-million by 1840

and 900,000 in the 1880s. And that was before industrialization stimulated a real boom in the capital's urban development. By 1900, the population reached nearly one and a half million and grew (after a slowdown during a recession lasting until 1908) to over two million on the eve of World War I (when the name of the city was Slavicized to Petrograd). Since the number of deaths almost always exceeded births in the city, it was immigration that fueled this boom. Even when the economy slowed, contemporaries observed, the city did not lose its "magnetic power" (*pritiagatel'no znachenie*) to attract newcomers.[3] These rates of growth were not merely rapid but "tumultuous."[4] Most important, on the streets, growth that appears on historical charts as steeply rising curves meant a ceaseless influx of newcomers (mostly from the countryside), constant construction (ranging from palaces to tenements, from elegant shops and arcades to massive factories), the expansion and modernization of urban transport, and a bustling public life.

As the city grew, "modernization" became a defining category and goal. In the eighteenth and early nineteenth centuries, the imperial state did all it could to lay down the foundations of a "modern" capital, starting with the city's built environment: employing architects (mostly western Europeans) to design a geometric pattern of streets and well-balanced architectural ensembles in order to both rationally organize space and deliberately demonstrate grandeur (perspective and symmetry were highly valued and widely employed); cajoling and coercing inhabitants (especially the leading classes at court and in society) to dress and behave in the manner of civilized Europeans; bringing merchants and artisans to the city for manufacture and trade; developing a police and administrative system to ensure a well-governed city according to European norms; and establishing institutions of secular education and the arts. This physical environment was meant not only to represent a changing Russia to the world but to effect change itself, including in how people acted, thought, and felt. This was, as the historical geographer James Bater characterized it, a grand "experiment in physical and social engineering" intended to "modernize an Empire."[5] This is the orderly and optimistic vision of the capital we see portrayed in contemporary engravings, which highlighted graceful prospects and broad squares, architectural ensembles, magnificent palaces and government ministries, geometrically planted parks, and rivers and canals embanked in granite.[6] This was partly a utopian vision, to be sure. Already in the eighteenth-century, behind the city's pleasing façades and regular geometries were log dwellings and kitchen gardens, crowded and muddy neighborhoods, disorder and disease.[7]

In the late nineteenth and early twentieth centuries, the era of industrialization and true urbanization, new utilitarian industrial tracts were developed on the outskirts of the old city but also new structures overlaid and filled the interstices of the baroque and neoclassical center. Factory chimneys obtruded into every view and industrial smoke thickened, and poisoned, the already famous fogs of the capital. Streets were transformed with cheap speculative building (approximately 10,000 buildings were added to the city's housing stock between 1870 and 1915).[8] Tenements and slums proliferated, including in the city center where population density was higher than on the industrial margins. Apartments were subdivided into rooms for families and individuals, rooms were divided into "corners" (*ugoli*—it was estimated that 10 percent of the city's population lived in "corners" by 1913), and even beds were shared.[9] Flophouses (*nochlezhnye doma* or simply *nochlezhki*) offered thousands of people the most meager sort of shelter (in 1910, there were 6,200 sleeping places in 34 houses, though the numbers of homeless always exceeded the number of places to sleep).[10] According to an essayist on the housing problem in the biweekly journal *Gorodskoe delo* (City Affairs), edited by members of the duma (city council) from 1908 to 1917, St. Petersburg was distinguished both in comparison to Moscow and to European industrial cities by the very high proportion of tenements (literally, *naemnye kazarmy*, or "rent barracks," from the German *Mietskaserne*), and by higher costs.[11] The very pavement on the streets made life in the industrialized capital exceptionally noisy, dirty, and unhealthy, according to an editorial in this same journal in 1913. Although the city government enacted a law in 1912 taking responsibility for "pavement reform"—replacing old cobblestones with quieter and cleaner materials—there was not only little optimism that improvements were likely any time soon but recognition that the city streets were literally disintegrating and hence the situation was getting steadily worse.[12] Worse still—and also the subject of planned and delayed reform—was the abysmal condition of the city's water supply and sewage system.[13]

This history of troubled urban development echoes the pasts of New York, London, Paris, and other western metropoles.[14] Indeed, many Russians recognized these shared histories of urbanization and its problems, though acknowledging that Russia was, as in so much else, a latecomer. As a columnist for *Gorodskoe delo* wrote, "We are now, mutatis mutandis, experiencing a process that reminds one of the western European experience of a half-century ago."[15] He was writing about population growth, but the observation could have been applied to most every aspect of the material conditions of St. Petersburg in the early twentieth century. As will be seen, many feared that precisely because Russia had entered into this history of urban modernity so late, so rapidly, and with such intensity, but also because of the larger crisis in Russian political and social life that accompanied urbanization, St. Petersburg was less susceptible to ameliorating progress. Or perhaps this ideal of modern progress was itself only an illusion.

The story was not uniformly dark. The Petersburg urban landscape also offered all the enticements of any great city, not only opportunities for work, the primary force pulling people into the city, but a vast array of stimulations and encounters. The city was a great spectacle. Not every Petersburger could afford admission to the many theaters, operas, ballets, cafés, cinemas, and museums, be invited to grand balls, purchase goods in elegant stores, or enjoy a meal in a fine restaurant. But even the working poor had access to inexpensive popular theaters and music halls, taverns, and cheap spectator sports. And anyone could walk the major streets, especially the famous Nevskii Prospect, gaze at shop windows and advertisements, stroll along the stone-clad embankments of rivers and canals, and observe the varieties of strangers. During the summer months, the northern capital's famous "white nights" kept large numbers of people on the streets and in bars, cafés, and restaurants until morning. Nostalgic memoirs and histories of prerevolutionary St. Petersburg emphasized precisely the everyday public spectacle: the diversity of people; the bustle of city transport, ranging from incoming trains to trams (including electrically powered streetcars beginning in 1907), from cabs and private carriages to boats of all sorts; the jostle of advertisements on building facades, trams, and street columns; the nighttime illumination of streets and buildings; newspapers for every taste and cultural level; the diversity of housing ranging from private townhouses

Nevskii Prospect (Central State Archive of Film, Photographic,
and Sound Documents of St. Petersburg).

to notorious, but colorful, slums; stores, shops, and peddlers; marketplaces
such as the Haymarket and the Apraksin Court; beautiful churches; restaurants and taverns; and entertainments for rich and poor. Occasional public
ceremonies and festivities associated with state and religious festivals added
special occasion to this daily world of urban spectacle.[16] The press made

the city's spectacle exceptionally accessible. The aptly dubbed "boulevard papers" like *Gazeta-kopeika* (Kopeck Gazette) and *Peterburgskii listok* (Petersburg News Sheet) especially, along with popular magazines, were filled with descriptions, sometimes accompanied by sketches and photographs, of encounters and conversations on the street, sporting events, crime, urban nightlife, balls and masquerades, cafes and restaurants, the latest in fashion, and new inventions—all rendered as entertaining as possible. And advertisements in the press offered readers a bustling visual street, as it were, filled with commercial objects and their promised pleasures: endless varieties of food and drink, fashions for all budgets, entertainments, and ways to improve body and mind.

Perhaps the richest spectacle to be had was walking amidst the city's diverse population. The cliché about the city's "many-faced street crowd" (*mnogolikaia ulichnaia tolpa*)[17] is confirmed by statistics. As we would expect of any imperial capital, port city, or center of industry and trade—and St. Petersburg was all these things—the population in the early twentieth century included both newly arrived and well-acculturated "peasants" (a legal estate), city-born workers, many *meshchane* (a petty urban estate comprised mostly of artisans and small businessmen), nobles working not only in the bureaucracy and the military but increasingly in the professions and business, and various levels of merchants, entrepreneurs, and clergy. The likelihood that these diverse individuals would cross each other's paths was high, not least because of an underdeveloped urban transport system, which meant relatively little class segregation by neighborhood. Even on the famous Millionnaia Street near the Winter Palace, along with the spacious apartments of government officials and professionals were the rooms or corners of craftsmen, factory workers, laborers, and, of course, servants.[18]

As the metropole of an empire, St. Petersburg was a multinational city, where, a demographic researcher has argued, "the ethnic multiplicity of the population reached a maximum" in the early 1900s. The diversity was indeed great: the 1897 census identified 60 ethnic groups (based on language) living in the capital. Most were not "foreigners" (only 1.2 percent in 1910) but subjects of the tsar born in the Russian empire yet claiming a non-Russian mother tongue. Apart from a majority of "Russians" (82 percent) in 1910, though some of these native Russian-speakers had

First page of the boulevard newspaper *Gazeta-kopeika*, 13 April 1910. Advertisements are for rowanberry liqueur ("beloved by the Russian public"), the collected works of Guy de Maupassant, St. Petersburg Aviation Week, "Nestor" soap, and hypnotism ("miraculous powers of the mind: how to influence people").

non-Russian ethnic backgrounds, St. Petersburg included (in descending order) Belorussians, Poles, Germans, Jews, Estonians, Latvians, Ukrainians, Finns, Lithuanians, Tatars, French, Swedes, English, and many other smaller groups. While in the nineteenth century certain groups were attracted to certain districts of the city (e.g., Jews in the trading districts in the city center and French around Nevskii), by 1910 the location of ethnic groups in the city had become less patterned and hence city spaces had become more ethnically "variegated."[19]

Twentieth-century city administrators sought to bring rational order to the management of this increasingly modern, diverse, and contradictory city. But they also recognized that they were underfunded and overwhelmed in place of the rationalist utopian dreaming of eighteenth-century urban designers and builders grew a late-empire realism colored by both high technical knowledge and a frustrated sense of the intractability of problems. Ideas were developed and money spent on scores of projects to improve the city's sanitation, schooling, charities, police and fire departments, and civic works (in declining order of expenditure). But few believed that the amounts were adequate or the organization effective. The city council journal was filled with articles about problems that the duma could not solve: the high cost of living in the city, the "housing crisis," the disintegrating conditions of streets and bridges, the traffic and tram accidents, deplorable sanitation conditions (from water supply, to dust and dirt on the streets, to filthy inner courtyards, to smells and noise), and disease.[20] With good reason, many contemporaries felt that St. Petersburg suffered both from having become so modern and from remaining not modern enough. The more pessimistic, as will be seen, doubted whether modernity could be the solution to its own problems. This sudden, intense, and uneven development of St. Petersburg was the rich soil from which interpretations of the city grew.

LITERATURE AND THE CITY

Tsar Peter I was the first to treat St. Petersburg as text and symbol, when he laid out his vision for a new city that would turn borderland marshes into a "western" imperial capital. No other Russian city, and few other world cities, would match the flood of literature and criticism that pondered the physical spaces and cultural meanings of this creation. In literature, "Petersburg" became a trope. By the 1840s, readers knew that works with titles such as "Petersburg Tales," "Petersburg Sketches," or "Petersburg Notes," were not simply about the capital but about ideas and qualities associated with it.[21] The most influential historians of Petersburg texts, Nikolai Antsiferov and Vladimir Toporov, argued that this writing was so consistent in its patterns—in its endless repetition of the same images, tropes, formulae, phrases, and clichés—that we can speak of a single "Petersburg text."[22] One of the major unifying themes in literary portrayals of St. Petersburg, as of other modern metropoles, has been contradiction and ambivalence. Vladimir Toporov has described some of the typical antitheses in the history of writing about the Russian capital:

> Petersburg is a center of evil and crime, where suffering exceeds all measure and settles irreversibly in the people's consciousness. Petersburg is an abyss, an "alien" realm, death, but Petersburg is also that place where national self-consciousness and self-awareness develop to such an extent that new horizons of life are opened, where Russian culture celebrates its greatest triumphs, and the Russian person is irreversibly changed. . . . On one pole is recognition that Petersburg is the only real (civilized, cultured, European, model, even ideal) city in Russia. On the other are declarations that nowhere does man suffer as much as in Petersburg, reviling and anathematizing, calls to renounce and flee Petersburg.[23]

Or as Iurii Lotman elegantly argued, the textual St. Petersburg was defined by water and stone, nature and artifice, the elemental and the civilized.[24]

The extravagant richness of contradictory images in writing about the city, and their function as argument, is indeed striking. Even the city's physicality was viewed as contradictory. On the one hand, the city was spacious, clean, fresh, and bright, defined by open spaces, linear streets, and flowing waters. On the other hand, Petersburg was a dirty, stuffy, cold, damp, dim, and yellowed city, visibly and sensually defined (and literally darkened) by fog, rain, snow, floods, smoke, soot, dirt, biting wind, noise, and gloom. The social and cultural landscape of the city was similarly viewed as graced by elegant architecture, gardens, and palaces, but also marked by cold stone façades and streets, stinking and rowdy taverns, hostile strangers and crowds, and every imaginable danger. Likewise, the spirit and mood of the city and those who dwelled in it could be free, joyous, energetic, renewed, and filled with dreams, but also tired, lonely, sick, feverish, tormented, depressed, melancholy, grieving, and sorrowful. This language and imagery, of course, was as much metaphoric, symbolic, and interpretive as descriptive. By the turn of the twentieth century, these characteristic dichotomies were often framed as the relationship between the essential forces of the Apollonian and the Dionysian in human culture, echoing Friedrich Nietzsche's arguments, which were very influential in Russia, about the struggle and interdependency between the spirit of light, order, and reason and the spirit of darkness, dissolution, chaos, and passion.

These dueling images served a variety of arguments. One of the most persistent was the essential difference from Russia's old capital, Moscow, and all it represented. By the 1840s, with the debates between so-called Westernizers and Slavophiles, Antsiferov observed, "Petersburg" and "Moscow" had become less places than "slogans."[25] This persisted, with the "two capitals" continually deployed as arguments built upon oppositions of all sorts. Traditionalists tended to see the differences between St. Petersburg and Moscow as marking the struggle between unnatural and natural, soulless and spiritual, artificial and historical, imitative and original, abstract and real, cold and cozy, statist and national, foreign and Russian. Progressives reversed these values and spoke of Petersburg and Moscow as representing civilized versus backward, active versus lethargic, organized versus chaotic, logical versus irrational, European versus semi-Asiatic. Some tried to view these differences as complementary and interdependent: St. Petersburg as representing state and civic life (*gosudarstvennost'* and *grazhdanstvennost'*) while Moscow represented family and private life. Petersburg was Russia's head, Moscow its heart. Petersburg as the nation's political mind, and Moscow as its moral soul. Petersburg as male and Moscow as female.[26]

These different images and debates were intensely ideological, if course. In Aleksandr Herzen's words, "to speak about Russia today means to speak about Petersburg, about this city . . . that alone lives and acts on the level of the modern [*sovremennym*]."[27]

The hubris of modern power was a key argument in the narrative of St. Petersburg, as in the story of other great cities. In Russia, this history begins with the willfulness of Peter the Great and the ordering force of the state, indeed the violence of city building. The new capital was created, it is invariably noted, as an act of war and empire. The settlement Sankt Pieter Burkh (named to honor Peter's patron saint but also to signal his love of all things Dutch) was established in 1703 as a fortified outpost for fighting the Swedes in the Great Northern War. Determined to turn this settlement into a new capital to crown his war victories and the country's emerging new identity as an "empire," Peter famously mobilized thousands of serfs, convicts, and war prisoners to drain the marshes, drive oak piles into the ground, and construct a city. The high death toll from overwork and disease formed part of the permanent narrative of the city. Thus, for the historian and poet Nikolai Karamzin, writing in 1811, "Petersburg was founded upon tears and corpses."[28] This became a well-established historical trope. But even such cautionary historians and critics could also admire the daring and heroism of the cause, the bold effort to use St. Petersburg to reposition Russia in space and time: to turn from Asia toward Europe and from the Muscovite past toward an emerging modern Russian empire.

The troubled relationship between humans and nature was entwined with this narrative. Cities have long been symbols of both the potential and the limitations of the human ability to conquer nature. The Petersburg story, from its foundational leitmotif of "building on a swamp" to its geometric street designs and classically proportioned architecture, easily lent itself to stories of this city as an antithesis to nature, even as a site of mythic struggle between human rationality and primal chaos. That the new capital was built on the margins of Russian lands and as part of an expanding empire facilitated images of a city at the edge of the world, a place of extremes, separate from the heart of the nation, perched at the edge of an "abyss," but also a city of visionary heroism. However, the obverse of notions of control and conquest was the persistent sense that just beneath the façade of stone walls, squares, streets, and buildings a primitive natural "chaos stirs," as Fedor Tiutchev famously put it,[29] threatening to overwhelm human reason and authority. Indeed, this threat was an increasingly dominant theme. Hence the endlessly repeated images in the literature of the city of wind, storms, rain, snow, dark fogs, "gloomy darkness" (*mrak*), and, especially, uncontrollable floods.

St. Petersburg was not unique in its self-reflexive ambivalence. Russian writers themselves surely knew that other cities had been judged as expressions of both heroic human capacity and fateful human presumption and perversion. And modern cities, especially, have often been treated as forces and symbols of ordering rationality and progress but also of rupture, fragmentation, uncertainty, and death, as places for faith in progress and even pleasure in the vertiginous modern condition but also for anxiety, unease, and suffering.[30] But Petersburg was distinct, I find, in the intensity and darkness of its contradictory self-perception. Its late arrival to this story, which allowed Russians to draw on a whole history of troubled representations of cities and modernities, may have been one of the reasons for difference. But the reasons were also tangibly historical: the conditions of Russian urban life, including the suddenness of its modernization and the political background in which it unfolded, also fueled a dark view of what the contradictions of the city could mean.

For many Russian writers, the contradictions of the city were part of an elegant aesthetic coherence—what Toporov called the "antinomic unity" of the Petersburg text and Antsiferov called its essential "indivisibility of opposites."[31] But I would suggest that both the literary history of St. Petersburg and especially the burgeoning urban journalism offer less antinomic harmony than unresolved tension, ambiguity, and instability. Worse, even ambivalence tended to be overshadowed by its own dark side, by its own doubts. Even Toporov noticed that the negative vocabulary was more extensive and richer than the positive one.[32] Indeed, this dark language seemed to swell and overwhelm.

Darkness did not always overshadow writing about St. Petersburg. Writers in the eighteenth and early nineteenth centuries tended to depict sunny, panegyric images of heroic and sacred accomplishment and classical beauty. For poets like Aleksandr Sumarokov and Gavrila Derzhavin, for example, St. Petersburg was a new "northern Rome" (thus, often, Petropolis), a "Palmyra of the North," a place of aesthetic harmony between artifice and nature (or heroic subordination of nature), a built landscape in which simplicity and grandeur blended perfectly, a metropole from which the vast spaces of empire could be controlled, a city whose "charms" will impress "all the distant peoples."[33]

But the literary image of St. Petersburg began to darken in the early 1800s, especially with Aleksandr Pushkin, who was also the first to make the new capital a major literary theme in his work. Already in Pushkin's early work, the joyous balls and bright elegance of society life in the capital mixed with sorrowing moods in an environment of "tedium, cold, and granite."[34] These contrasts were deepened in what many consider the ur-text of the Petersburg myth, "The Bronze Horseman" of 1833, which Pushkin characteristically subtitled a "Petersburg Tale." In the opening pages, Pushkin echoed the adoring tradition of the eighteenth-century ode to the capital: "I love you, Peter's creation / I love your stern and graceful look." But the tone quickly changed with the arrival of the flood that devastated the city in 1824. Pushkin developed the trope of the flood as the struggle between human will and the unruly elements, but the emphasis was less on the heroism of this battle than its vanity and tragedy. The poem is overcast with images of a dolorous howling wind and cold rain, a poor and lonely hero, and then such a frenzied mutiny of the waters that the emperor himself, "with mournful brooding eyes," is forced to concede that "even tsars cannot master / God's elements," and the poem's unfortunate hero, Evgenii, is driven mad.[35] St. Petersburg's susceptibility to floods—hundreds in its history and catastrophic ones in 1777, 1824, and 1924—lent itself to metaphor: to arguments about the vanity of attempting to control the elements and a sense of impending doom.[36]

Nineteenth-century writing about St. Petersburg often echoed Evgenii's gesture, at the end of Pushkin's poem, of shaking a condemning fist at the famous statue of Peter known as the Bronze Horseman. As Toporov observed, "no other city in Russia received so much abuse, denunciation, reviling, defamation, reproach, insult, regret, lament, and disenchantment as Petersburg."[37] This language was fulsome and rich and growing steadily blacker and more inclement. For Nikolai Gogol, the capital's nightmarish damp, rains, and fogs seemed always to threaten both buildings and people with obliteration, an obscuring atmosphere that could enthrall or push one toward depression and madness.[38] Above all, Gogol's St. Petersburg (notably in his famous Petersburg tale, "Nevskii Prospect," of 1835) was a fragmented and phantasmagoric city, especially at night when the city was filled with shadows and phantoms, the "deceptive light" of street lamps ("lit by the devil himself"), and alluring but deceptive visions (*snovidenie*).[39] Significantly, too, this foggy and phantasmagoric city could not be grasped: Gogol continually emphasized the inescapability of mystery, perplexity, bewilderment, and the unknown. In this city, the very boundary "between dreaming and waking, reality and nightmare," Gogol repeatedly reminded readers, was brittle and uncertain.[40]

In a feuilleton written in 1842 (though banned from publication in Russia until 1905), Herzen explored the question of "Moscow and Petersburg." Like other Westernizers, he contrasted "lethargic" Moscow, gazing backward into the past, with "active" Petersburg, living in the present. But he also saw dark complications. While life in Moscow was "dead silence" undisturbed by activity (the streets were empty after ten in the evening, he noted as an illustration), the seemingly more vital life of the northern capital was "the eternal noise of empty vain activity" (*vechnyi stuk sueta suetstvii*). Also, in turning away from the stasis of the national past toward "universal history," Petersburg became the "embodiment of a general, abstract [*otvlechennyi*] conception of a capital city." As a result, "in the fate of Petersburg there is something tragic, gloomy, and sublime." This produced an intensity of contradictory emotion about the city. People might not like Moscow, but they hated St. Petersburg: "A thousand times, Petersburg forces every decent person to curse this Babylon," even while it clearly nurtured a life that was "physically and morally" more stimulating. What could one conclude from all this contradiction but that the ultimate meaning of the city was an incomprehensible "riddle" in its "primal chaos of mutually devouring forces and antithetical tendencies." And precisely this, Herzen recognized, was "proof of its modernity."[41]

Visual representations of the city were similarly ambivalent and darkening, as Grigorii Kaganov has shown. Eighteenth-century engravings emphasized the capital's elegant lines, grand vistas, and sweeping panorama—

its architectural heroism, as it were. But by the 1820s and 1830s, artists began to see in this open spatiality a looming "emptiness" that threatened to engulf the orderly built environment.[42] By the 1840s and 1850s, artists visualized the city in still darker terms. In particular, the city seemed to be losing its integrity and coherence. Instead of portraying the city's broad squares and unified architectural ensembles, its "marvelous panoramas" and triumphal spaces, artists focused more on dark corners, back streets, dead ends, and murky encounters. By the 1860s, the city had become a visual space obscured by fog and smoke, a city of shadows and phantoms, a city defined "by its spectral fugitiveness" (*prizrachnaia mimoletnost'*).[43]

Nikolai Nekrasov's work was characteristic of how the literary image of the city developed in the middle of the nineteenth century. Seeking St. Petersburg's "secret inwardness,"[44] Nekrasov found darkness. In his unfinished autobiographical novel of the 1840s, he anatomized the everyday city, much as diverse authors did in the collection *The Physiology of Petersburg*, which Nekrasov edited. Most characteristic were the darkening doubts emerging from growing knowledge of the city. The new arrival to the capital is first entranced by the "vast and splendid city." But as urban experience deepens, the hero discovers behind the brilliant façades the city's essential truth: dark "attics and basements, where the air is dank and noxious," ubiquitous poverty, and moral decline.[45] Nekrasov's later poetry similarly highlighted this dark spirit of the city. On the one hand, he continued to admire the city: "Streets, buildings, bridges / In the magic aura of gaslight / Are marked with beauty." But he also recognized this as a façade: on closer inspection the city turned out to be "morose and putrid" (*ugriumnyi, gniloi*), "a decrepit dandy without rouge," fouled by the ubiquitous smell of "vodka, stable, and dust / The characteristic Russian mix," accompanied with a deafening cacophony of shouts, whistles, cries, and roars. The emotions such an environment evoked were to be expected: "vanity," "melancholy" (*toska* or *khandra*), "gloom," "spite," and "depression" (*unynie*).[46]

Fedor Dostoevsky brilliantly appropriated and refined these emerging interpretations of St. Petersburg, but he also emphasized, with exceptional complexity and pathos, this city's modernity—its tangible modernization, accelerating in Dostoevsky's time, as well as the philosophical significance

of this modernity.[47] In the 1840s, Dostoevsky began exploring the city's
landscape in the double role of flâneur and feuilletonist, both characteristically modern urban styles of observing and interpreting the city: the aimless
wandering of the leisurely but anatomizing observer and the informal and
personal urban journalism of the columnist.[48] In Dostoevsky's feuilletons
for the newspaper *Sanktpeterburgskie vedomosti* (St. Petersburg News) in
1847, appearing as a "Petersburg Chronicle," he explicitly noted the sense
of the modern in the city: "Here one cannot take a step without seeing, hear-
ing, and feeling the contemporary moment and the idea of the present."[49]
Dostoevsky was quite clear what this feeling of the contemporary entailed:
"Everything here is chaos, everything a mixture." It is all "life and movement," but ambiguous movement—destruction and creation, chaos and
forward progress: "even up to the present Petersburg is in dust and rubble,
it is still being created, becoming."[50] Dostoevsky saw beauty in the city, but
a beauty that reminded him of a "young girl, sickly, and ailing," who one
moment "becomes marvelously, inexpressibly beautiful," with vitality and
light in her eyes, and the next moment looks with a "sadly thoughtful and
unfocused" gaze, and moves with "fatigue, weakness, and dull melancholy"
(*glukhaia toska*).[51]

This was not simple ambivalence. Already in these early sketches,
the darker tones are strongest. As Dostoevsky strolled the city's streets in
search of stories, he was most sensitive to the city's dust, mud, "grey fog,"
"raw mists," "dismal twilight," "damp walls," "wet granite," and the "pale-
green" faces of pedestrians, and the emotions this city environment engen-
dered in those who lived there: "gloom," "melancholy," "spite," "anger,"
"sourness," "sorrow," "despair," and "doubt."[52] Like Gogol, he concluded
that this was a city of ubiquitous "duplicity, concealment, and masks," but
added that if people "appeared as they really are, my God, it would be even
worse."[53] This was "sick, strange, and gloomy Petersburg." Yet, this was
also a city that attracted people eager for life, that nurtured "dreamers." For
Dostoevsky, who would make morose and ill-fated dreamers central characters in his novels, this morbid degeneration of vital dreams was at the heart
of the "Petersburg nightmare," its "tragedy, mute, mysterious, gloomy, savage."[54] And as for the capital's defining embrace of the modern "new"—a
key theme that opened his first feuilleton—there was really nothing new: ev-

ery Petersburger is always asking "what's new?" and every journalist sought
to feed this urban obsession for "the news," but the answer, which everyone
already knows, is that nothing is new. Hence the "piercing feeling of desolation in their voices," the "utter hopelessness that lay in this Petersburg
question."[55] This perception of temporal stasis and emotional desolation
in the city would become, as we shall see, a powerful and persistent theme
and increasingly widespread in society.

Dostoevsky's novels, especially *Crime and Punishment*, deepened
these images of the city in both complexity and darkness. His characters are
"half-sick city-dwellers" who have "all been crippled, everyone of us more
or less," though also capable of fantastic dreams and flights of imagination
(indeed, the city itself was "a magical hallucination, a dream").[56] Petersburg's climate—especially its obscuring fogs, its "dull and dirty autumn"
(*The Double*, 1846), its stifling and dusty summer (*Crime and Punishment*,
1866), its damp rains and snows—seem to personify the city's "gloomy"
spirit (the word *ugriumnyi* is ubiquitous in Dostoevsky's city novels) and
to shape characters, their stories, and their emotions. Fog, in particular,
made the city not only gloomy and unhealthy but also vague and insub-
stantial.[57] The built landscape of this "most abstract and premeditated
city in the world" also shaped city dwellers. Raskolnikov felt a "vague and
ambiguous" sense that something was wrong in the city's "magnificent
panorama": an "inexplicable coldness," as if "magnificence" itself embodied a "blank and deaf spirit."[58] The streets, where Dostoevsky's characters spend a great deal of time, are as stifling as the garrets and corners in
which they live. In the summer, closeness, dust, dirt, and smells created a
"repulsive and melancholy atmosphere" and made people sickly. On winter
nights, "desolate street lamps flickered gloomily in the snowy darkness, like
torches at a funeral."[59] To be sure, this could all have a certain morbid allure. Raskolnikov is inspired by Petersburg's "stinking, dusty, city-infected
air" and deliberately goes out into the streets "to feel even more nauseated."
Likewise, the cynical Svidrigailov is in his element on empty, endless, "despondent and dirty" streets where he can best commune with the city's
strangeness, absurdity, and mad chaos.[60]

In the late nineteenth century, writers and poets both well-known
and minor, talented and conventional, endlessly portrayed the modernizing

capital in by now canonical images: a city of shadows and specters, fogs and dreams, rain and tears, ice and stone, illness and death. And they linked these material conditions to a familiar body of emotions and ideas: suffering, melancholy, mystery, dreams, desire, madness.[61] Konstantin Sluchevskii, for example, brooded over the city's "weeping and sobbing" winds, "wandering fogs," "violent shadows," "gloomy sky," "filthy sidewalks," and inescapable crowds, the dark presence of death and suicide, and the pervading feelings of sorrow (*unynie*), melancholy, and apathy. Apollon Korinfskii's poem, "In the Fog," of 1891 was as undistinguished in its imagery as in its artistry, and thus telling of the type: "again the entire day on the foggy streets / I wander, my sadness concealed in my breast," like an ailing man in a feverish "delirium," seeing but not comprehending the tormented faces and vaguely unhappy eyes all around, as if the city itself had fallen ill "and its sick delirium / Had merged with my own confused melancholy" (*mnogodumnaia toska*).[62] Nighttime—especially the long darkness of winter but also the pale "white nights" of summer—was a favorite theme, and the images predictable: the Petersburg night as "cold, shadowy, and depressed," illuminated only by the "cold rays of light" from "ice, iron, and granite," and filled with sorrow and tears.[63] One could go on with many similar examples.[64] Indeed, their continual repetition is part of their nature and force.

Yet this late nineteenth-century poetics of the city was not entirely negative. Semen Nadson, for example, recognized the possibility, amidst the coldness, sadness, and suffering of the city, of learning to "love its movement," of "finding poetry in fogs, / Rains, unceasing downpours, / Kiosks, flower-beds, and fountains."[65] Petr Iakubovich's political idealism (he was linked to the populist left) nurtured this view of the city and modernity as both brutal and progressive (Marxists would try to make this ambivalence dialectical): a "city of cold and gloom," but also of glistening granite walls, linear streets, and broad squares; a city of death and suffering but also a "cradle of freedom"; a city of torment, sorrow, tears, and "mute melancholy," but also of bold struggle and proud determination.[66] But even without populist or Marxist ideology, some writers resisted simply condemning the city. Fedor Sologub, for example, wrote Baudelairian poems about St. Petersburg in the 1890s with characteristic images of poor and sickly youths, "insanely" noisy streets, the "vague and incomprehensible crowd," "gloomy and sorrowful faces," obscuring fogs, separation from nature, and death, but also of fleeting pleasure and "strange dreams."[67]

Around the start of the twentieth century, we see a striking revival of the eighteenth-century ideal of St. Petersburg as a harmonious and orderly ensemble of built spaces and façades, though this appreciation now involved aesthetics more than ideas about national or imperial power and was explicitly linked to "Apollonism" as a cultural ideal. Not surprisingly, this ideal was reclaimed precisely when the city's harmonies were most under siege. The artist and critic Aleksandr Benua (Benois), in his influential 1902 essay, "Painterly Petersburg," called for a renewed appreciation of the capital city's cold surfaces and harsh geometric patterns—its "cold, terrible gaze"—as an appealing sign of Russia's new beauty.[68] In this spirit, a "preservationist" movement emerged that aesthetically idealized "old Petersburg," which in their eyes meant an Apollonian city of cool "harmonies," pleasing "panoramas," open "spaces," and "integrated wholes" (all favorite terms), posed quite consciously against the actual disorder of the present city. The perception of, and longing for, an obscured and vanishing purity illumined this vision of the city. This ideal was elaborated most vividly in the work of poets, critics, and artists associated with the journal *Apollon* (Apollo), established in 1909 and named as an explicit challenge to what was felt to be the dominant spirit of the era.[69]

Even Petersburg's most committed Apollonians recognized the contradictoriness and fragility of their ideal of restored order, harmony, and light. In Benua's terms, St. Petersburg's "physiognomy" was "terrible, merciless, yet beautiful and charming: . . . at one and the same time monstrous and captivating."[70] But more than acknowledging this old sense of the city's duality, they recognized that they were fighting on the ramparts of ruins. They felt that they were experiencing the "twilight" and "downfall" of Apollo's spirit in Russian culture, especially after the revolution of 1905.[71] In mythic terms, they felt that the disorderly spirit of Dionysus or the serpent Python, the threatening spirit of earth whom Apollo had once defeated, increasingly defined the spirit of this city, indeed of the whole of modern culture. In a word, the overwhelming interpretation of both the capital and "the city," and all that these stood for, in the years of uncertainty and crisis after 1905, was that this was a time of chaos, collapse, and loss. As

Anna Lisa Crone and Jennifer Day observed, the dominant mode of Petersburg poetry in these years—and not only among the explicit Apollonians and retrospectivists—was the elegy, defined by loss, absence, vain longing, and mourning.[72]

This sense of deepening darkness, perhaps approaching catastrophe or apocalypse, was especially ubiquitous and strong in the early twentieth century, particularly after 1905, and not only, as we shall see, in literature. In poems about the city by the best-known poets of the era—Viacheslav Ivanov, Innokentii Annenskii, Mikhail Kuzmin, Sergei Gorodetskii, Valerii Briusov, Georgii Ivanov, Aleksandr Blok, Andrei Belyi, Osip Mandel'shtam, Anna Akhmatova, and others—we encounter visions of the capital as shrouded in dusky light and fog and marked by cold, wind, dust, illness, and death, tormented by the street noise of trams and shrill human voices or by ominous quiet, threatened by "chaos" and the "abyss," and haunted by looming specters and shadows, dark and feverish dreams, nervous visions, and "mystery."[73] Writers such as Zinaida Gippius emphasized the malevolent quality of the capital as a "cursed city," a terrible, godless "wasteland" (*pustyn'*) marked by the cold "breath of death and corruption."[74] Some saw Petropolis (as Petersburg was sometimes poetically called) as a Necropolis or a city defined by its "unclean" spirit and even the satanic presence of evil.[75] To be sure, such visions could look through the darkness toward ideals of beauty, transcendence, salvation, and resurrection. But such hopeful faith was often obscured by the compelling weight of the darkness and chaos itself.

Aleksandr Blok was perhaps the most important modernist poet to dwell on St. Petersburg and "the city"—indeed, it was a preoccupying theme for him.[76] The characteristic spaces, objects, and people of the city proliferate in Blok's work, as in his cycle of poems published as *Gorod* (The City, written 1904–8). Blok's St. Petersburg, especially after 1904, though not without characteristic contrasts and unstable dichotomies, was overwhelmingly a dark and "troubled" (*trevozhnyi*) city of dim fogs, dust and smoke, elemental waters and winds, looming "chaos" and the "abyss," gloom and emptiness, shadows and specters, masks and deception, transgressions, dreams, illness, loneliness, madness, suffering, blood, and death.[77] The colors of Blok's city ranged from "gloomy deep blue" (*sinii mrak*) to shades of grey and black to "blood red," all blurred by fog. Emotionally, Blok's city poems speak of longing and hope, but especially of uncertainty, incomprehension, doubt, disillusionment, and despair.[78]

Blok treated the city as a landscape reflecting transcendent questions about life, death, the divine, and salvation, along with his own personal experiences of desire, illness, and suffering. But Blok's city was always a concrete and tangible place: indeed, it was precisely in the "chaotic nightmare" of the city's streets and cafés that visions arose.[79] In this light, some critics have emphasized the realism of Blok's urban poetry, its gaze at the "madness and dissonances" of these "troubled [smutno] and chaotic" times.[80] But vision did not ensure clarity. On the contrary, Blok's poetic images of St. Petersburg—not least the haunting, ineffable, "unattainable" presence of the "Neznakomka" (variously translated as the "Stranger" or "Unknown Woman," 1907)—signified a perception of the city as nepostizhimyi, as incomprehensible and unknowable, at least to the rational mind.[81] Blok's Petersburg was a dream city, a city, as Antsiferov described it, in which "the boundaries between flesh and spirit, reality and dream, life and death are erased."[82] Looming amidst all of this was a premonition of cataclysm, the sense that St. Petersburg, and all that it stood for, was doomed. Blok retained a faith in salvation, but one that emerged precisely out of rupture, ruin, and catastrophe.[83]

In 1913, the Moscow writer Andrei Belyi published what is probably the single most important modernist literary text about the Russian capital and its modernity, the novel Petersburg.[84] The materiality of the city is strongly present, indeed essential to the novel and its construction of meaning. Streets, newspapers, crowds, trams, carriages, doorways, stairs, electric lights, and the city's notorious fogs and foul weather are abundant in the text. But these objects move in a turbulent vortex of urban disorder. The novel continually reminds us of the instability and uncertainty of modern knowledge and modern reality, embodied in the novel's ubiquitous specters, shadows, phantasmata, and masks. Belyi's narrative vocabulary makes clear what these images represented: indeterminacy, ephemerality, senselessness, smutnost' (a term suggesting both trouble and indeterminacy), and chaos, a reality that persistently "blurs," "slips," "wavers," and "flickers," a landscape in which "perplexity" and "confusion" are inescapable. Literary critics have elaborated on these arguments: Belyi's Petersburg was a "catastrophic city" of ghostly uncertainty and "ephemeralness," a city where "chaos" and the "abyss" loomed everywhere, a conditional, contingent, relative, and dubious city (*uslovnyi gorod*), always on the "edge of an abyss" (*po kraiiu bezdny*),[85] a place with such "plurality" and "proliferation of meanings" that "incoherence" was its most consistent quality, a city where the "noise of time" (the title of Osip Mandel'shtam's memoir of these years in St. Petersburg) had become a Dionysian cacophony that evoked a formless "mythic chaos" and ultimately threatened the Apollonian creation of Peter the Great and the imperial state, a city where "being" is always uncertain (ephemeral and stable, shadowy and solid, real and imaginary), time is simultaneously linear and circular and thus ultimately "turbulent," and knowledge is always relative and fleeting, continually threatened with falling into an abyss of nothingness.[86]

What is most striking about all this is not what this imagery reveals about Belyi's anthroposophical theory of cognition or his beliefs in the hidden interpenetrations of various planes of existence, from earthly to astral.[87] What is more telling, for the purposes of this study, is how much this language of indeterminacy and epistemological crisis paralleled the vision of the modern urban world that the newspapers of the day described no less fulsomely.[88] For all its complex symbolic and mystical arguments and brilliant artistry, this novel shared a language with much of the everyday social criticism in the press, as did Blok's poetry and other works of literature in those years. Belyi's vision of the city, and especially of its public spaces, as the location of modern vitality and, especially, of modern disorder, danger, degeneration, illusion, death, catastrophe, and longing, would have been familiar to any reader of the daily press.

Before we turn to journalism, we should take note of the avant-gardists who tried to find in the modern a new beauty and happiness. If there were any artists who fully embraced the Dionysian side of urban life, the best candidates would be the futurists, a diffuse literary and artistic movement that arose after 1910 mainly in St. Petersburg and Moscow. Their modernism was loud and demonstrative. They demanded, in the name of "our Time," that both the literary idols of the "stifling past" and popular writers of the present be "thrown off the steamship of Modernity" (*parokhoda*

Sovremennosti).[89] They launched iconoclastic experiments with literary and artistic form. They apotheosized the heroic and creative individual. Naturally, they were preoccupied with the objects, rhythms, and significance of the city. Contemporary critics, when they were not simply mocking the futurists' wild innovations and "scandalous" public performances,[90] saw futurism as a true sign of "our times," just as futurists saw themselves, but as a dark and threatening sign. Contemporary critics regularly condemned futurism as a reflection of the "anarchy of values," "nihilism," and "chaos" in contemporary life, as "hooliganistic" "jeering" (*glumlenie*) at everything the civilized world valued, as "one of the many turbid [*mutnye*] waves of modernity" that were reaching an "almost apocalyptic" level, as "a symptom of the deep crisis" of both modern art and "modern man."[91]

On the surface, futurists did indeed seem to embrace the radical modern—reveling with "optimism" in the "insanely rapid tempos of our skyscraper-machine-automobile culture."[92] But a close look at futurist poetry, especially their perceptions of St. Petersburg and "the city," suggests more continuity than difference with other poetic representations of the urban in Russia. The poet and painter Elena Guro has often been described as the most "urbanist" of early twentieth-century Russian poets, indeed as an exemplary poetic "female flâneur," not only because of her sustained attention to the city, especially her native St. Petersburg, but in the concreteness of her gaze: verses filled with streets, signboards, and overheard conversations, and presented more in the tangible manner of impressionism than in the transcending symbolism of poets like Blok or Belyi. Like Baudelaire, Guro described the ephemeral, sensual, and fragmentary nature of the city, but she also recognized this to be a landscape of suffering and despair. In her 1910 poem "The City," for example, she described the "barking street" as a "commotion" (*sutoloka*) of trams, automobiles, moving crowds, smoke, the smell of blood, "crying eyes," grey faceless passersby, "hopeless gazes," emptiness, and mocking laughter. An unpublished prose poem written a few years earlier, "The Street," envisioned an even more hellish atmosphere of vague blotches of strangers, crowding shadows, darkness and cold light, grating noise, cruel laughter, bodies for sale, torn nerves, and madness where even "the crucified air shouts with a cruel metallic light."[93]

The most celebrated, and reviled, of futurist poets was certainly Vladimir Maiakovskii, for whom "the city" and "the street" were major themes. Maiakovskii's city was a place, not unfamiliar by now, of piercing winds, cold fogs, "dismal rains," smoke, noise, oppressive objects (smokestacks, windows, bathrooms, elevators, trams), cannibalistic desire and greed, sickness and wounds, abused souls and bodies, harsh laughter, weeping and wailing, senselessness, alienation, despondency (*unynie*), and melancholy.[94] None of this is surprising, once we set aside stereotypes about Russian futurism, which may have more to do with echoes of Italian futurism and what Genrikh Tastevin called urbanist "posing" than with actual representations and perceptions of the city. For a poet like Maiakovskii, whose poetics were profoundly shaped by a "concern with the stultifying power of things over man" and ceaseless "war against *poshlost'* and *byt*" (crass philistinism and the banalities of everyday life), the city may have been attractive in its vital possibilities, but it was also inescapably repulsive in its present reality.[95] If there was anything really new in this futurist vision, it was the stronger desire for destruction.

We see much the same "failure" to glorify the city among another group of urban artists who we might expect to have embraced the metropole: Marxist worker-poets. Marxist leaders and theorists expected, even demanded, that proletarian writers would understand and love the "modern city" for its vitality and promise of liberation.[96] And many worker-poets, especially the most ideologically committed, did indeed see the "only path" away from "sorrow" and hopelessness as running "toward the great city-giant," where life "seethes, dazzling and intoxicating" and the "embryo of a new life" was growing.[97] But far more common were images of the big city as a "city-beast" (*gorod-chudovishche*), a "hell," a devouring "vampire," a "whirlpool" of debauchery and vulgarity where the "crowd" was "gloomy and soulless," a "prison" whose walls were "high, cold, and gloomy buildings," a "cursed place" marked by "force, cruelty, and blood." And notwithstanding hope for revolutionary transfiguration, all too often it seemed that there was "no exit."[98]

In the visual arts, even the "most urbanist" Russian artist of these years, Mstislav Dobuzhinskii, portrayed "the city" and St. Petersburg, especially

in his cycle *Urban Dreams*, which he began in 1905, as a space of crush-
ing anonymity, dehumanization, depravity, surveillance, and menace, where
what little remained that was human and valuable was threatened with destruction and ruin.[99] Contemporary critics judged other modern artists—
notably those displayed in St. Petersburg at exhibitions, now famous, by the
Union of Youth—in similar terms. Rarely sympathetic to modern art, critics
either laughed at this work, dismissing it as merely absurd play, or warned
of its troubling and dangerous spirit. A review, for example, of the 1913 exhibition of the Union of Youth, complained that these artists rejected the
"charm, clarity, and purity" of real art, expressing instead only "muddle,
chaos, and absurdity."[100] Many reviews noted the elusiveness of meaning,
clarity, and reason in contemporary art.[101] Such work, another critic concluded, perfectly expressed the spirit of the street, indeed was the "*dernier
cri*" of urban culture."[102] Nikolai Berdiaev, in a public lecture in Moscow on
"the crisis of the arts" in 1917, echoed and elaborated what many critics
had been saying in less philosophical terms: in modern painting "matter itself dematerializes, becomes disembodied, and loses solidity, strength, and
form . . . destroys all the solid boundaries of existence." Futurism took this
the farthest. This could be explained philosophically, Berdiaev concluded,
by the historical conditions of modernity: the increasing tempo of life, the
modern "whirlwind" in which "everything clear and solid in life began to
dissolve."[103]

However abstract and symbolic this textual history of St. Petersburg
seemed and sought to be, it remained quite grounded in the city's physical
environment, social landscape, and political context. Literary tropes like
"chaos" and the "abyss" were not only metaphors. These images existed
in dialogue with a tangible atmosphere of uncertainty and crisis. This troubled view of the city and modernity, including the moral and philosophical
implications of this experience, was nowhere so tangible and poignant as in
the urban press.

URBAN JOURNALISM

A growing population, increasing literacy rates even among the working
class, inexpensive print technologies, eased censorship regulations after

1905, and intensified interest in civic questions helped flood St. Petersburg in the years between the revolutions with newspapers, magazines, and
journals. By 1912, five hundred journals and magazines and more than one
hundred newspapers were published in St. Petersburg (publications from
other cities, especially Moscow, also circulated in the capital). The most
popular paper in the city, the "boulevard" tabloid *Gazeta-kopeika* enjoyed a
circulation of a quarter of a million copies (and more readers, for individual
copies were shared).[104] Indeed, the proliferation of newspapers and magazines seemed itself to observers a sign of the urban modern: the spirit of
innovation, the daily stimulation and often overstimulation of the mind and
nerves, and the compression, via printed news, of space and time.[105]

City journalists naturally focused intensely on the city. While their
stories were cast in a more factual, observational, and objective style than
literary accounts—though reporters were also attracted to sensational realities such as crime and suicide that would excite readers' curiosity and
interest—the interpretive drive was strong. Indeed, the question of "the
city" was more at stake than ever. Literature and journalism approached the
city in a similar manner, especially in that final fraught decade of the imperial
order. Diverse authors, ranging from literati like Belyi and Blok to relatively
obscure journalists writing in mass-circulation boulevard newspapers like
Gazeta-kopeika, dwelled obsessively on many of the same troubling urban
images. Of course, these were intersecting voices—poets read newspapers
(indeed, they often lifted images from the daily press) and journalists were
informed by and drew upon the literary history of the city. But the question
of "influence" is less significant than the perceptual and intellectual resonance that connects these texts to one another and to the city itself, their
object and setting.

We cannot ignore the ambiguity of journalistic knowledge. Reporters
and feuilletonists were often not terribly worried about blurring the boundaries between the real and the imagined city, between the self-consciously
literary reconstruction of St. Petersburg as text and symbol and its physical
existence and experience. In fact, even in the realm of "literature," the most
widely read prose accounts of city life after Dostoevsky straddled, even
ignored, the boundaries of reportage, ethnography, and fiction: Vsevolod
Krestovskii's novel *Petersburg Slums* (*Peterburgskie trushchoby*, also trans-

latable as "Petersburg Dens"), which was serialized in the Petersburg journal *Otechestvennye zapiski* (Fatherland Notes) during 1864–66 and then published as a book; Vladimir Mikhnevich's series of sketches on the "moral life" of the capital for the journal *Nabliudatel'* (The Observer), republished as the *Sores of Petersburg* (*Iazvy Peterburga*) in 1886; Anatolii Bakhtiarov's feuilletons for Petersburg newspapers that became *The Belly of Petersburg (Briukho Peterburga)* in 1887; Nikolai Sveshnikov's feuilletons in the newspaper *Novoe vremia* in 1892 (also later gathered as a book) about the notorious Viazemskii slums; Nikolai Zhivotov's novels "from St. Petersburg life" (*iz Peterburgskogo zhizni*—a popular subtitle for serialized novels in the press by various authors), and especially reportage from his adventurous excursions into the lower depths of urban life in the guise of a cabdriver, a tramp, a funeral torchbearer, or a waiter; and N. V. Nikitin's *Petersburg by Night* (*Peterburg noch'iu*) in 1903.[106] Though these works have generally not been treated as part of the canonical "Petersburg Text," perhaps as much because of this eclecticism of genre as due to their general lack of literary sophistication,[107] their writers dwelled, in the tradition of Nekrasov and Dostoevsky, on the city's dark corners and backstreets, on poverty and "moral ruin" (*nravstevennaia porcha*), on crimes of all sorts ranging from picking pockets to inexplicable murders, and on drunkenness, domestic violence, sexual deviance and abuse, prostitution, and suicide.

For all the insistence by these authors that they were uncovering dark truths about urban life that lay just behind the capital's elegant façades—all these works claimed that real observation was at their foundation—reportage and fictionalization were mixed up and cast in tones marked as much by the traditions of melodrama and the gothic as by scientific observation. In the early twentieth century, works like M. Semenov's and Iurii Angarov's serialized book, *New Petersburg Dens/Slums* (*Novye peterburgskie trushchoby*) of 1909–10 similarly "reported" about various dark and "hidden" corners of urban life (crime, nightlife, debauchery, etc.) with little evident regard for the boundaries between factual description and imaginative reconstruction, between information and titillation. Or rather, these writers insisted on the factuality of their narrative but presented these "facts" in obviously imaginative and literary form, blending elements of the newspaper chronicle with psychological character sketches and reconstructed or imagined dialogue.

Characteristically, these stories treated facts subjectively with a combination of moral shock, a sense of the "tragic," entertained detachment, and an unabashed effort to appeal to readers' interests in "juicy stories" (*pikantnye epizody*) about life in the capital city.[108]

Newspapers and magazines ostensibly stood fully on the side of realism, though the real balance between fact and fiction, reportage and entertainment, was often far from clear. The relation between disinterested observation and strong argument—especially concerning big questions about the meaning of St. Petersburg, the city, and the modern—was no less close. The remainder of this chapter begins our exploration of these daily texts of city life precisely with some of their most general arguments.

Some reporters and commentators—especially those oriented toward the political left or cultural modernism—insisted on the progressive and liberating effects of urban life. "The modern city," an essayist wrote in 1912 in the journal *Sovremennik* (The Contemporary),[109] stimulated the mind and spirit of the most ordinary citizens with its variety of sights and experiences and the visible power of modern technology and organization, thus raising people's consciousness and nurturing a spirit freed of prejudice and inspired by growing faith in human capacity (*sila cheloveka*). This writer insisted on the inspiring dynamism of the city, the rich "complexities of city life" that awaken thought and feeling, and even the benefits of the strain on people's nerves, for "when the nervous system is stimulated—a person thinks"[110]—an argument that directly echoes the German sociologist Georg Simmel, especially his 1900 book *The Philosophy of Money* and his famous 1903 essay "The Metropolis and Mental Life." In the tradition of comparing Moscow and St. Petersburg, an essay in the liberal newspaper *Rech'* (Speech) in 1907 judged the "antagonism" between the two capitals to be a matter of two different historical "cultures," where Moscow was a naturally conservative city for it "arose from the 'land,'" whereas St. Petersburg arose from human effort and "individuality" (*individual'nost'*) and so nurtured higher levels of "culture" (*kul'turnost'*) in everyday life, including greater industriousness and labor productivity and more sophisticated "tastes." These differences were thought to be visible even in the faces of people on the street: Moscow faces were crude; Petersburg faces were cultured.[111]

Journalists highlighted stories about scientific and technical inventions. We "steal lightning from the heavens," illuminate cities with electricity, fly like birds in the sky, send our voices great distances by telephone, capture for eternity our lives on film, build great buildings and bridges, and create new ideas, one reporter fervently declared (appropriately, he wrote for a cinema newspaper).[112] The leftist writer Aleksei Gastev, in a 1913 essay in *Zhizn' dlia vsekh* (Life for Everyone), breathlessly admired the wonders of the "New Piter" that were making it more and more a European city: new trams, bridges, railroad lines, factories using the latest technologies from Europe and America, modern housing, and even plans for an underground metropolitan railroad.[113] Others enthused about a new "electric life" and even a renaissance of human bodies.[114] The technological conquest of space and time was often proclaimed to be the defining feature of twentieth-century urban modernity. Worldwide transportation networks and the modern media, it was said, had "obliterated space."[115] Flying machines had conquered the expanses above, submarines the depths of the sea, and X-rays the once hidden interior of the human body. It seemed there were no limits: the "colossal progress of modern technology" accustomed people to "considering everything possible such that almost nothing surprises us."[116] Unsympathetic journalists mocked these naive modernist enthusiasms, but also acknowledged public fascination with all things "new" and the allure for finding the fastest road toward "the fairytale 'palace of the future.'"[117]

Many commentators found it truer and more useful to emphasize the inadequacies of actual urbanization and the fundamental unevenness, inequities, and contradictions of modern progress. For some writers, this was a result of Russian backwardness—the endlessly discussed burden of Russia's history at the margins of the west. In a truly "twentieth-century city," an essayist in *Gorodskoe delo* argued, the whole of the urban population should enjoy the benefits of the sort of improvements in water supply, sewage, electricity, gas, and new building materials that were developed in the nineteenth century. A truly modern system of urban transportation would make the crowding of all classes together in the center of the city no longer necessary and allow a more hygienic separation of commercial, manufacturing, and residential sections of the city and the modernization of these districts: a business district of tall buildings with fast elevators; a factory district characterized not by "smoke and soot, deafening noise, low, end-lessly long, and monotonous factory buildings, drunken workers" but de-fined by cleanliness, glass, light, and quiet; a residential district that is more like a "luxurious park" than a cramped inner city opening only onto noisy streets and filthy courtyards.[118] St. Petersburg was clearly very far from such "twentieth-century" modernity, though so were the most advanced world cities at that time. But even by the more modest criteria of actual contempo-rary European big cities, another writer for *Gorodskoe delo* argued, Russian metropolitan civilization was "another culture." Instead of filling citizens with the joys of "modern progress" (*progress sovremennogo blagoustroistva*) by providing such essential urban services as clean water, sewage disposal, and road repair, the Russian capital, beneath its European façade, filled ob-servers with "shame" at the "neglect" of the most elementary material needs of the population.[119]

Optimistic faith that the pathologies of Petersburg life were due only to insufficient modernity was difficult to sustain. More common was a view of these contradictions as endemic. Like many theorists of the modern city before and after, Russian urban writers were likely to see in the city, at best, "the paradoxes of modernity," even its "fatal contradictoriness" (*smertonosnye protivorechie sovremennosti*).[120] A member of the State Duma writing in *Gorodskoe delo* about urban problems in 1914, for example, re-peated what had been said in the press hundreds of times before: the city was a contradictory mix of light and darkness, of "great wealth" and "ter-rible poverty," and of culture and unculture (*nekul'turnost'*) that reached levels of "the most primitive barbarity." A hopeful liberal—a zoologist by education and a Constitutional Democrat by party affiliation—he viewed the darkness as confined to the margins: as "doleful shadows" lurking be-hind the "bright array of benefits and conveniences that modern urban life has conferred upon humanity."[121] But many saw the shadows as over-whelming—in the blunt conclusion of the *Gazeta-kopeika* columnist Ol'ga Gridina, "Life in big cities has far more dark than bright sides."[122]

Even on the political left, unambiguous admiration of the modern city was rare.[123] The well-known social democratic (Menshevik) journal-ist N. Valentinov (Nikolai Vol'skii), for example, published a long essay in *Novyi zhurnal dlia vsekh* (The New Magazine for Everyone) in 1910, entitled "The City and City Dwellers," repeating most of the images typical of public discussions in those years. He began, as many did, with an image of the city from *Les Villes tentaculaires* (1895) by the Flemish writer Emile Verhaeren: "It dominates the plain like a colossal, midnight hope. . . . The rails leading to it are a deceiving path to happiness." Valentinov was certainly aware of Verhaeren's own ambivalence: his admiration for the "beauty of the modern" and "enthusiasm" for industrial and scientific progress mixed with feelings of anxiety, pessimism, and regret in the face of the aggressiveness and destructiveness of "octopus-cities" that destroyed nature and drew people into their degrading and dehumanizing clutches.[124] Valentinov's own discussion was along the same lines. On the one hand, he saw the city as a "monstrous machine" and "a greedy vampire, sucking the best blood of the countryside"; the city "rending and devouring" people "one after another in its insatiable maw"; and city streets as filled with "noise, groans, din, and roar" (*shum, ston, gam, grokhot*), where the city dweller "dances, twists, dives like a skiff on the waves." On the other hand, he admired urbanites who could thrive in this environment. All of the stimulation in the city made people, as Simmel and others argued, nervous, superficial, and blasé, while simultaneously emancipating the individual, releasing enormous human energy to develop thought, culture, society, and industry; though this too had its dark side: the modern city also let loose man's beast, reminding us that "homo homini lupus."[125]

Capitalism was central to the contradictory nature of urban modernity. Few doubted that twentieth-century St. Petersburg was a "capitalist" city, notwithstanding the large presence of the government, the military, and state-run industry. For Marxists, of course, this was an optimistic diagnosis, framing even the harshest criticism of the brutalities of the capitalist city in a rational and progressive schema of historical progress. Marxist optimism was encouraged by growing evidence, since the late 1800s, that industrial workers in St. Petersburg were the most responsive to their arguments about capitalism, class, and revolution.[126] Thus, Marxists (though intellectuals more readily than workers) easily embraced the modern industrial city—and St. Petersburg, the argument went, had reached the highest stage in this development among Russian cities—as the cradle of both progressive development and revolutionary transcendence: the site of dynamic change and technological advancement, but also, due to the natural contradictions of this progress, the revolutionary battleground where liberation and a "new world" would be won. Conservatives also recognized capitalism's blend of suffering with progress, though they were likely to be less sanguine about the historical guarantee of transcendence. Thus, for example, when Mikhail Men'shikov, the widely read right-wing columnist for *Novoe vremia*, reflected on the half-century of Russian social and economic development set in motion by the state's decision to end serfdom and modernize Russian society, he argued that a society once characterized by "natural" economy, discipline, labor, and faith had been replaced by one marked by artificiality, anarchy, and skepticism. And he was quite blunt in blaming "capitalism—the most terrible thing that the last half-century has produced." Like a "juggernaut," he argued, capitalism has crushed millions under its wheels. And yet, like Marxists, though without their revolutionary dialectic, he saw capitalism as generating its own salvation: while capitalism "enslaves" the masses of people it also disciplines and organizes them and thus overcomes anarchy.[127]

Many writers were even more skeptical than Men'shikov and they did not limit their doubts to Russia. On the one hand, a reporter commented, you cannot but admire the evidence you find daily in the newspapers of human capacity to conquer nature, space, and time. But "turn the page" and you are faced with every sort of animalistic brutality—even the United States, "the land of progress," is afflicted by racist violence, for example—and is more concerned with how to "make a million" than love of one's neighbor.[128] At the very least, the majority of urbanites were stunned and left behind by the driving force of modern change: "Life moves at a rushing tempo, and the majority cannot keep pace. The ring of telephones and roar of engines is deafening. The telegraph conveys news around the whole world, and newspapers are filled with events of world significance and the horrors of everyday life." While it may "seem" that modern life, in the Russian expression, is "like a boiling kettle," living in such conditions was painful. No wonder, this newspaper columnist concluded, moderns "go about with such empty spirits," "desperately looking for something to believe in."[129] Indeed, instead of faith that more progress would overcome these contradictions, many saw in the future only more of the same. Imagining

in 1913 what progress would have been achieved by 1963, one journalist
heard, amidst the steady march of technology, this leitmotif of the emerging
modern age: "Business, business, business / Money, money, money / Faster,
faster, faster," while people's health and spirits would continue to decline.[130]
Yet, none of this seemed to lessen the power of St. Petersburg to attract people from all corners of the empire. Images of St. Petersburg as a "lighthouse"
reaching into the darkness of the country—though many preferred the metaphor of irresistible seducer and deceiver—was a constant theme in reporting on both the achievements and the suffering in St. Petersburg.[131] "The
complex and vital [kipuchaia] life of the capital," one boulevard newspaper
columnist typically concluded, "is terrible—terrible and attractive."[132]

Most journalistic writing about St. Petersburg dwelled on the dark
sides of modern contradiction. These writers recognized the obsessive
drive in the modern to seek the ever new.[133] But most viewed this newness as destruction rather than creation. Even liberal critics complained
that while everyone talks about "new people, new perspectives, new demands," about the "revaluation of values" (pereotsenka tsennosti—a widely
used phrase associated with Nietzsche's influence) and the struggle with
"antiquated moralities," this was leading nowhere: the old was rejected but
the new remained vague and undefined.[134] Sympathetic commentators saw
in all this an "optimistic nihilism."[135] Most observers saw the nihilism but
distrusted the optimism. The critic Viktor Burenin, for example, who had
a regular column in the conservative newspaper Novoe vremia, mockingly
described the self-proclaimed heroes of the new twentieth century as "pre-
cocious [skorospelye—literally, fast-maturing] sons of the twentieth century"
who hold everything old in contempt and race after new ways of life and
new art forms. They dream they are producing a new "beauty of the modern" (krasoty moderna), but, in fact, they produce only "unnatural trash,"
which inspires not faith in modern progress but "disgust."[136]

Religious writers offered some of the most pessimistic denunciations
of modern life. They were naturally skeptical of "faith" in human "perfect-
ibility, progress, and development" and were gratified to see a cultural crisis in which many people had come to recognize the inadequacies of the
modern social order—with its endless and unequal struggles to survive, the
"bankruptcy of science" to solve human problems, the hollowness of faith in

material "progress"—and generally "the deep abnormality of a great many of the phenomena of modernity" (*iavlenie sovremennosti*).[137] Notwithstanding their evident satisfaction in describing a modern spiritual crisis, religious critics of urban modernity were dismayed that their own values were so under siege. In a long editorial essay in 1914 on futurism in *Tserkovnyi vestnik* (Church Herald), the journal of the St. Petersburg Theological Academy, the author went from the usual sort of mocking jokes about futurist artists' embrace of modern technology and speed to a sweeping attack on the whole of modern urban civilization. The modern city bears the marks of the Beast, such as electricity (fire stolen from heaven), moral corruption, and efforts to create new men. The Beast, of course, is associated with the whore of Babylon, "that great city, which reigns over the kings of the earth" (Rev. 17:18). This author glossed the contemporary relevance of the biblical passage: "Babylon is the great city of modernity [*gorod sovremennosti*], where prostitution reigns, naked in the blinding light of 'divine electricity.'" In this modern apocalypse, "we cannot see the Beast itself—we see only its reflections in the waves of modernity."[138]

Secular writers were also likely to see degeneration in the modern city. Concrete social problems, such as the conditions facing children living in St. Petersburg, could generate sweeping reflections on the state of modern progress and civilization: "there is something fatal, some deep secret of the twentieth century, a force that humanity cannot counter," which finds at its roots the "defenseless torment of cities" today, lives "full of tragedy," even the "symptoms of poisoning by the fumes of hell."[139] A newspaper essay on "The Horrors of the City" emphasized that "the city" was defiled and poisoned morally and physically: amidst the lonely and alienated crowd "man is wolf to man" and the environment is thoroughly "befouled," including air, water, soil, food, and drink.[140] The human body itself seemed to wither in the modern city. It is the "fate of residents of big cities," it was often said, to live surrounded on all sides by "stone," cut off from nature and even from the sky. People living in such an environment become "sickly, wasted, weak-willed, and listless both physically and spiritually. . . . This is the death sentence of our age."[141]

The material and moral conditions "of our dusty and foul-smelling cities"[142] debased not only city bodies but city minds and souls. Reports on urban problems—such as epidemics of crime—blamed the "psychological illness" that was a characteristic feature of "our nervous, sick age."[143] The well-known St. Petersburg psychiatrist and professor Pavel Rozenbakh, in a public lecture in 1909, argued that "the so-called modern age" (*sovremennaia epokha*), which began in western Europe in the middle of the nineteenth century, was defined by "improvements of civilization [*kul'tury*]," which produced social and economic "revolutions" (*perevoroty*), which often had dire effects on people's lives. The noise and impatient rush of electric trams and automobiles further contributed to the urban blight of "sleepless nights" and "constant wariness and nervousness when one is on the street."[144] It is likely that Rozenbakh was influenced by Simmel's argument (especially its darker sides) that metropolitan life produced not only healthy "nervous stimulation" but a brutal "tearing the nerves . . . hither and thither."[145] In any case, many urban writers in Russia were saying the same. A journalist in 1913 hyperbolically characterized the current generation of urbanites as "we children of the twentieth century, born in automobiles under the bright light of electricity," and thus desperately needing to restore our shattered and poisoned bodies, which have been "imbued in every pore with steam, soot, and smoke."[146] The moral atmosphere of the city, indeed its moral personality, contributed to this pathological environment. The "harsh struggle for existence" (*tiazhelaia bor'ba za sushchestvovanie*) in the modern big city—a phrase often used—acquired a certain existential sense as describing not merely the material struggle to survive economically but the spiritual struggle to sustain a truly human life "in such a soulless city as Petersburg."[147] Many agreed that contemporaries were living in "a soulless iron age of technology and pitiless materialism," creating an atmosphere in which decent and intellectually aware people could not bear to live.[148]

The Petersburg press frequently printed verses about urban life, mostly by relatively unknown poets. Like other writings, newspaper and magazine poetry tended to reflect on the general in the particular: not only on St. Petersburg but on "the city" as such. These texts were often titled simply "The City" (*Gorod*) or "In the City" (*V gorode*), or "On the Street" (*Na ulitse*). These poems were strikingly, even tediously, unoriginal in imagery and style, though it is precisely their unoriginality, their reliance on repeated cliché, that is most telling, for they tended to echo the growing corpus of Russian city texts. Here the boundaries between types of urban writing—between high and low literature, literature and journalism, imagination and description, symbols and facts—were especially blurred. These were tendentious pieces. Only very rarely does the city appear in these poems as a vision to admire for its vitality and drive. Far more often, the meaning of the city was embodied in noise, shadows, chaos, blood, death, dirt, iron, stone, sadness, grief, and nightmares.[149] Physically, but also spiritually, the city was "stifling and heavy." The street, the city's most urban and public space, was almost invariably "dirty, dull, and dark," filled with harsh noises, shouts, and "vain activity" (*sueta*).[150] Above all, the city possessed a "cruel" spirit, a "cold malevolent gaze of stone," and a "granite heart," apathetic toward the filth, stench, terror, and tears from which its denizens suffer.[151] At their most hyperbolic, these newspaper and magazine poets envisioned the city as a never-sleeping "stone beast" or "city-serpent" surrounded by a hellish atmosphere of whirling dust, thick smoke, and putrid fogs, insatiably devouring new victims ("sacrifices" brought by the trainload) in its "hungry jaws."[152] Urbanites, in this imagery, become crushed "slaves of the city," with "sad smiles on pale lips" and ailing bodies and souls, vainly rushing about "without purpose," or feverishly and vainly "seeking happiness" in debauched embraces and momentary forgetting. These images often concluded with a desire to flee the city for the open fields and the "expanse of open plain" (*prostor ravnin*).[153] A prose poem in *Gazeta-kopeika* comparing city life and rural life by V. Vegenov, a largely unknown poet, contained almost every trope of the genre: the city as an "unseen hell" in which millions suffer amidst cold fog, inert stone masses, grey buildings, isolating walls, ubiquitous soot, poverty, depressed feelings and thoughts, apathy, cruelty, boredom, "pale faces in the shadows."[154]

At their most extreme, the dark judgments of urban modernity that pervaded the press echoed the older literary tradition, reaching back at least to Pushkin's "Bronze Horseman," of seeing St. Petersburg as a "doomed city" (*grad obrechennyi*), not least because of its modernist hubris. In an essay in the liberal newspaper *Rech'* at the end of 1908, Dmitrii Merezhkovskii judged St. Petersburg as approaching its long-foreseen end. Entitling his essay with the legendary curse and prophecy of Peter the Great's sister Mariia Alekseevna, "Peterburgu byt' pustu" (Petersburg will be empty),

Merezhkovskii drew readers' attention to the signs of approaching doom: first the darkness and violence of the 1905 revolution—Merezhkovskii had left Russia in 1905, returning in 1908—and now reaction, cholera, suicide, and the terrible sense that "nothing changed" in the city while he was away and that "this unchangedness [*neizmennost'*] was the unchangedness of the 'face of death.'" Dostoevsky was right, he concluded, "everything teeters on the edge of an abyss."[155]

The return of revolution in 1917 seemed to provide fresh proof of this fate. The obverse of the heroic image on the radical left of Red Petrograd, cradle and citadel of the revolution, was a view that St. Petersburg's susceptibility to revolution was a sign of its fatal spirit. The fact that the Decembrist rebellion of 1825, the 1905 revolution, and both the February and October revolutions of 1917 began on the streets of St. Petersburg had to be significant. Writing in the liberal Petrograd weekly magazine *Russkaia svoboda* (Russian Freedom) in the late summer of 1917, David Arkin found explanation for the deepest meanings of the revolution precisely in familiar tropes about the city: Petersburg as "deceit, mirage, phantom," as symbolically "standing on a swamp," as gloom, dream, lie, figment, chimera, and contradiction, as marked by pervasive phantasm, unreality, vagueness, indeterminacy, and ambivalence (*prizrachnost', nereal'nost', neiasnost', neopredelennost', dvoistvennost'*). It seemed, Arkin believed, that Petersburg had finally revealed its "hidden face"—only "guessed at" before 1917 by artists and poets—and unleashed its spirit on the whole nation.[156]

Streets

Ночь, улица, фонарь, аптека,
Бессмысленный и тусклый свет.
Живи еще хоть четверть века—
Всё бдет так. Исхода нет.

Night, street, lamp, drugstore,
A dull and meaningless light.
Live another quarter-century more—
Just the same. No way out.

—Aleksandr Blok, 1912

The street may be the most characteristically urban space: an emphatically
"public" place where "the stranger" and "the crowd" dwell. As such, the
street is laden with significance. Theorists—architectural and urban historians, philosophers, poets, novelists, and painters—have interpreted the
street as marked by crucial forms of public interaction: especially power,
but also progress and disorder, pleasure and degeneration. The architectural historian Spiro Kostof defined streets as the most characteristic products of the "urban process," spaces where technical possibility, deliberate
design, the workings of power, social relationships, and individuals come
together (and clash) to give cities their distinctive form and culture. Above
all, he showed, streets are key spaces for struggles over control. The social theorist Michel de Certeau viewed the street as vividly illustrating how
"place" is transformed into "space": the stable and regularized place created by planners and builders is reinvented as an uncertain and unstable

space by "walkers," by the people who inhabit, use, and practice public life. Throughout these works, questions of public display and power are central. Streets and squares and the buildings that bound them are designed precisely to convey a message of authority, especially the "myth of order." St. Petersburg, of course, with its genesis in a ruler's hubris and planners' determination to impose a geometric grid of streets on swampy ground to create a rational and pleasing European metropolis, already lent itself well to this treatment of urban space and its meanings. So much so that a guide for visitors to the capital in 1912 observed that tourists found the city's built *spaces*—its "streets, embankments, and squares"—far more interesting than any particular buildings.[1] But street spaces, once in use, are also at odds with order and power. They can also be sites, sometimes notoriously so, of spontaneity, illusion, desire, and danger.[2]

A strong sense of the street's unstable power is captured by Walter Benjamin's influential project in the 1920s and 1930s to collect, arrange, and comment on a vast archive of text fragments about modernity, which he saw embodied in nineteenth-century Paris. The street, Benjamin showed, is a potent space for gazing, seeing, and display. But this is a contradictory and unstable sight. The street is a space for imagination, creativity, and self-realization. But it is also a space of alienation, falseness, and failure. It is a "labyrinth," where the hidden path toward enlightenment leads also toward malevolence, a space of "stifled perspective," an epistemologically troubling terrain where truth can be glimpsed and overheard but never fully grasped. Entwined with these visual and spatial instabilities is an especially knotted relation to time. On the modern street, time is so deeply present and compressed that in a fragment of time one can walk across the movements of a century. The result is the street's characteristic simultaneities, palimpsests, and ghosts. The hero of this street is the strolling flâneur, "intoxicated" by all this "voluptuous" flux as if by opium, feeling on the street an endlessly ambivalent mixture of "estrangement and surprise," daring and hesitation.[3]

Not surprisingly, modern writers and artists were drawn to the street. They were inspired by an urgent need to understand this most constructed and inhabited public space but also by a visceral attraction to its sheer physical presence and force. Thus, the street in modern literature and art is a familiar and concrete place for locating stories but also a potent symbol: for urban civilization, for the modern experience, even for human existence as a whole. The artist's and writer's street, therefore, is a space of restless movement, confusion, fragmentariness, fleeting glimpses and encounters, memories, fantasies, pleasure, display, artifice, loneliness, boredom, dirt, smells, menace, brutality, moral fall, death, and madness. And these images are rich in larger meanings: possibility, adventure, freedom, incoherence, alienation, loss, evil, tragedy, and intimations of catastrophe. That there is little coherence uniting these jumbled images and meanings is itself part of the implied argument.[4] So is the concern that on the street darkness can so easily overwhelm the light.

SEEING "THE STREET"

St. Petersburg's writers and journalists, as we partly saw in the previous chapter, dwelled obsessively on "the street" when thinking of "the city." They too treated the street as an embodiment of historical, social, and existential meaning. Their images also evoked a space where order is imposed while "chaos stirs," a vital space of intoxicating visions and "chaotic nightmares." That these images and arguments echoed those of western writers and theorists is not surprising, and not simply because of textual influence. The Petersburg street, in the view of Russian contemporaries, was a modern street, fully part of the global experience of "civilized" urban life.

The material conditions of the street—stone walls, dust and dirt, "bustle and commotion" (*sueta i sytoloka*—this *sueta*, or vain activity, was an especially common theme), and the ceaseless "drone" (*gudenie*) of the crowd, trams, and automobiles [5]—were evidence of Petersburg's modernity but also arguments about its consequences. The tumult of sights, sounds, and smells, the street's defining "cancan of spectacular sensations" (*kankan zritel'nykh oshchushchenii*) were said to bombard the "feverish" brain and hammer the nerves of the city dweller.[6] While this sensory cancan could, as Georg Simmel influentially argued, offer vital "stimulation" to energy and mind, Russian writers were inclined to see mainly the perilous effects of this modern environment: "superficiality," "nervousness," and ultimately, for many, a desire to escape through self-willed death.[7]

Urban writers also dwelled on the street as a moral space. To say "the street" implied the tastes and the psychology of "the crowd" and the moral condition of public life.[8] " 'The street,' " one critical commentator stated directly (highlighting the category with scare quotes), "is the mirror of society's mores."[9] The immorality of the street was a ubiquitous theme. "There is no deeper abyss than the sidewalk on the streets of a big city," a newspaper feuilletonist wrote.[10] Indeed, he argued in another column, every value was upturned in the chaos of the street: what we call "crime" is "in the psychology of 'the street' 'heroism,' " what we call a "virtuous person" (*dobrodetel'*) is held in contempt by the children of the street, and our "conceptions of good and evil" are on the street viewed "in reverse."[11] Many journalists argued similarly that "the Petersburg street" had become both evidence and symbol of the degradation of public life.[12] The popular and left-leaning boulevard paper *Gazeta-kopeika*, for example, after its establishment in 1908, began a regular series of articles titled "Our Street" that highlighted problems of crime, violence, prostitution, sexual predation, suicide, and other moral sores of urban life.[13] The conservative newspaper *Novoe vremia* similarly editorialized regularly against the "mores of the street" (*nravy ulitsy*) that had come to define contemporary life, such that "moral breakdown" had taken the place of the "political breakdown" of 1905, indeed was logically connected: after the wave of "troubled waters" had broken against a political wall—the failure of revolution and growing repression—it flowed into everyday life, forcing its "filth" and "street mores" into the public sphere in the form of crime, violence, and suicide.[14]

The *soblazn ulitsy*, the sinful temptation of the street, was an often-used phrase that seemed to explain many of the pathologies of modern city life. Vasilii Rozanov, writing in *Novoe vremia* in 1905 and elaborating his thoughts in a book in 1909, argued that the Russian street was more degraded than the western European street (his reflections were prompted by the spectacle of prostitutes on the main streets of St. Petersburg) and judged this to be a sign of Russia's failure to construct a healthy public sphere: "for us the street is an alien thing [*chuzhoe delo*], where we throw out our trash."[15] Different writers emphasized different examples of the decadence of the street. Many saw prostitution and hooliganism as the worst and most telling signs, as we will later see. Others viewed the crowds of "strangers" and the "cynical" and "insolent" attitudes that prevailed there to define "the streets of our capital."[16] Others noted the foul language that "hangs over the streets of the capital" like nowhere else in Russia, exemplifying the degraded condition of urban public space: it seemed that all Petersburgers, regardless of rank and "without any reason," were constantly swearing "on the street, in streetcars, in public parks, on trains, etc.—everywhere that the crowd is."[17] That street life had become a type of "animal" existence was such a cliché that one could even make jokes (at least bitter jokes) about it. Ol'ga Gridina, the well-known columnist for *Gazeta-kopeika*, mused in 1910 that the public should not worry about the temporary closing of the Petersburg zoo, for if they want to see "animal life and animal mores" they need only look at the city's streets with its beastly drunks, the "wild tigers" in public squares who bare their "teeth" (knives) when you refuse them money, or the "pack of fierce wolves" who prey on women and girls.[18] Very often in such moralizing accounts, the street was itself personified as a living creature, tempting and malevolent. Many writers blamed Petersburg's numerous "urban sores" on the "powerful" and "ruinous influence of the street."[19] Some writers even declared the street "guilty" of what occurred there.[20]

The "crowd" often stood in for "the street." This was a relationship with a long history. In Benjamin's compendium of nineteenth-century western European treatments of the city, the urban crowd, "dwelling" on the street, preoccupied writers seeking to interpret street, city, and modernity. Responses to the crowd ranged from the idealized flâneur's knowing, heroic, and joyous *épouser la foule*—embracing, espousing, becoming one with the crowd—to anxieties about this "eternally unquiet, eternally agitated being." At best, the crowd, like the city itself, was a contradictory being: to be in its presence was to experience "solitude and multitude," shadows and light, boredom and all the remedies for boredom.[21]

Petersburg surely had its flâneurs (and the imported term *flaner*) who enjoyed being surrounded by "strangers" (*neznakomtsy i neznakomki*) and happily strolled along the sidewalks of Nevskii Prospect, looking in shop windows and at passersby.[22] The bourgeois character of the flâneur, assumed in Europe, was clearly visible: they were often described as dandies (*franty*), with leisure to prowl the streets for its pleasures and spectacles while displaying their own sense of worth and fashion. But the term "flâneur" was also used much more loosely in Russian. It was applied not only to men but also to women, especially "frivolous creatures" (*legkomyslennye osoby*) who dressed themselves in "bright and garish" clothes in order "to flâneur" (*flaniruet*) in public places.[23] Indeed, the whole of the Petersburg public, at least polite society, was said "to flâneur" on occasion, as during warm weather when strolling in the Summer and Tauride gardens,[24] or during the traditional public promenade (*gulianie*) in the springtime days leading to Easter when the whole strolling crowd was described as "flâneuring" (*flaniruiushchie*).[25] But the pleasures of flâneuring in St. Petersburg were often spoiled. While many people enjoyed going "out for a stroll on Nevskii," they also recognized that the street life they were enjoying was nothing but "vanity" and "pure simulation" (*sploshnaia falsifikatsiia*).[26] The press was usually even more damning than this, describing flâneurs and dandies with moral contempt as foppish (*khlyshchevatyi*), arrogantly swaggering (*vysokomernye*), "pestering" (*pristiushchie*) women in the streets, and rude and contemptuous toward all those beneath them in perceived social rank.[27]

Writings about the street crowd emphasized, from the perspective of respectable society, feelings of estrangement and moral disgust. Alienation is a theme long familiar in western discourse on metropolitan civilization, reaching from Edgar Allan Poe's description of "feeling in solitude on account of the very denseness of the company around" in his influential "The Man of the Crowd,"[28] to Georg Simmel's arguments about the "strangeness and repulsion" separating urbanites and about being "lonely and lost in the metropolitan crowd."[29] A characteristic Russian view appeared in a 1909 popular book titled *The Pain of Loneliness*. In the "foggy, huge, stone city," the author argued, in clichéd images, "surrounded by a mass of buildings and people," individuals "do not see or take note of one another . . . but seem to one another to be incomprehensible, distant, and alien." After publishing an earlier appeal to the lonely—he hoped to found an organization on the model of societies for the lonely in England and elsewhere—he received dozens of letters, many of which included similar phrases: "finding myself in the massive stone city I was no one special to anyone and was unknown"; "standing amidst the huge crowd I am alone."[30] The physician Grigorii Gordon diagnosed the "illness of loneliness" (*bolezn' odinochestva*)—the "newest disease, characteristic of modern society"—as felt most strongly when "among people," when surrounded by the bustling crowd of the city.[31]

Worse still, the crowd was morally debased and often dangerous. The Russian crowd, it was said, was becoming more and more like the crowd of Paris or London, notorious for finding pleasure and comfort in the suffering of others. Russians too, urban writers observed with dismay, had developed a taste for "powerful sensations" (*silnye oshchushcheniia*), a "thirst for cruel spectacles, saturated with blood." At present, this was most evident in theaters and at the circus—often driving performers, such as an acrobat then at the Cinizelli Circus, to perform acts with high risks of injury and death, just to "entertain the crowd." But it was only a matter of time, commentators thought, before "this crowd seeks 'powerful sensations' on the street, on the railroad tracks at the scene of accidents, beneath the windows of prisons, etc."[32] Some newspapers already judged the crowd in this way. Writing in *Gazeta-kopeika* in 1908, a reporter mused on the tendency for curious crowds to gather when a streetcar runs someone over, when a murder has occurred, when a passerby falls to the ground sick with cholera, but also for the simplest oddities, such as a cripple trying to cross the street.[33] The crowd as debased consumer—of commodities, of spectacles—was even the subject of jokes: a humorous dictionary of Petersburg life defined "the public" as "a collection of eyes, mouths, and stomachs."[34] Of course, the crowd also harbored danger, its "animal mores" made worse by anonymity: you meet thousands of people "in theaters, in parks and gardens, in restaurants, and on the street, and you say 'the crowd,'" for they all look alike as a mass. Yet hiding among them are criminals and even murderers.[35]

The street could possess an appealing allure, but this was usually the opening act in a drama ending in disillusionment, in moral fall and death, in being devoured by the street. Numerous newspaper reports and stories— factual, fictional, and indeterminate—described provincials who looked to the capital for salvation from poverty and from their "dirty little towns." On arriving in St. Petersburg, they are astonished at the noise and bustle on city streets, the rush and impatience. They wander "the great wide streets," gazing in shop windows and at the seething crowd. But soon comes disenchantment: the failure to find work and the strain of living amidst so much

noise and dirt, drunken and crude people, hunger and desperation. So the
provincial again throws himself into the city's "alien" streets. For women,
prostitution was often the next step. For both men and women, suicide was
often the final act in this drama, and often occurred on the street—poisoning
before "The Eyes of the Crowd," as headlines often put it, or death by leaping into a canal or river.[36] The obverse of this disillusionment was the desire
to escape these ubiquitous eyes: as one suicide put it in a note explaining
his late-night drowning beside the Troitskii Bridge: "let the waters of the
Neva hide me from people's gaze" (*ot glaz liudskikh sokroiut*).[37]

Cultural critics were concerned that the "street" had made itself felt
even in modern aesthetics. First, the Petersburg street itself had changed
aesthetically, and for the worse, in the eyes of most critics. In contrast to
the "Old Petersburg" street of eighteenth- and early nineteenth-century
design—the street of "great ensembles" and "broad panoramas," which
expressed "something Roman, a stern spirit, a spirit of order, a spirit of
formally perfect life," as Aleksandr Benua described the traditional city
in 1902—more recent construction distorted and vandalized this orderly
vision with tasteless eclecticism, transforming St. Petersburg, in Benua's
terms, from a "Roman senator" into a "vulgar dandy."[38] Worse still, this new
spirit of the street extended into other aesthetic realms. Kornei Chukovskii,
for example, who regular contributed literary and cultural criticism to the
liberal daily *Rech'*, described the modern street as the most typical example
of the modern aesthetic spirit. He was not entirely hostile. Thinking about
street advertisements, he declared,

> Of all the creations of modern art I especially love advertising
> posters [*afishi*]. Their ideal is clarity. Their artistic principle:
> hit them over the head! No intermediate tones, no nuances!
> They don't know how to whisper but must eternally shout. . . .
> They are for the thousands not only for the elect, not only for
> you. They are created . . . not for museums and galleries, be-
> cause their native land [*rodina*] is the square (and oh how dia-
> bolically they shout their colors, blue, yellow, red!). For them
> every fence is a gallery and every street a museum.

Though Chukovskii seems here to echo the spirit of the futurists, he wrote with considerably more ambivalence and sense of loss. That the creative source of the new aesthetics was no longer the refined artistic imagination but the onrushing "human tide," he judged to be a new aesthetics of "motleyness, tastelessness, and vulgarity" (*pestrotu, aliapovatost' i grubost'*). The new art had to make itself noticed by the man of the crowd, always impatiently rushing off somewhere, so it had to "shout into this gale, instantly, in one moment." In the same spirit, the newspaper feuilleton, Chukovskii added, had become the new literature of the street, which cannot afford to "whisper and intimate"; instead, its "every nerve must be tense, like electricity." And the spread of this new cultural aesthetics did not stop there: "all of our art is now moving toward the poster and all literature toward the feuilleton." This, Chukovskii concluded, with increasingly less subtle hints of dismay, is our "new street civilization" (*novaia ploshchadnaia tsivilizatsiia*, literally the new civilization of the public square).[39]

Many critics felt that the whole of contemporary culture—from art and literature to spirituality and moral values—was now defined by "the street." Modern artists, critics complained (often thinking of the futurists), had replaced the "aesthetic values" that humanity had accumulated over the centuries with mere "street fashion." This was art for the street, wishing to be noisily visible "at all the intersections of the life of our capital," and art of the street, representing the culture of the "urban crowd."[40] Nikolai Gumilev defined futurist poetry as an invasion into the once separate and pure realm of the "people of the book" by the barbaric, savage, and vulgar "people of the newspaper."[41] One of the most popular of serious "literary" Russian authors, Leonid Andreev, was regularly accused of producing literature that was, in essence, an expression of the spirit of the newspaper, the cinema, advertising, and the public square—in a word, street literature. Like the street, Andreev's writing was said to "beat on the nerves with naturalistic details" swimming in "chaos."[42] In fact, Andreev himself criticized mass culture, especially popular theater, as art for and from "the street," as an expression even of "the world street."[43] Andreev's critics would have certainly agreed. "Boulevard literature" was seen as unquestionably debased, not only in the popularity of subjects like sex and death, but in fitting the everyday rhythms and styles of urban life. Some called such writing "rail-road literature," for it was perfectly suited to distract and entertain while traveling between stations: it was so fleeting and ephemeral in substance as to leave "not a trace in consciousness" after the book was finished, not a touch of lasting influence on a reader's "thoughts or feelings." This modern literature of the street and the marketplace was all about sensation, impression, and motion.[44]

Vision was a leitmotif in these accounts of the street. The street was a place for seeing—with all the sensory, cognitive, epistemological, and psychological dimensions "seeing" suggests. The street was a space for gazing and interpreting, including by the reporters who helped expand urban seeing through writing and reading. No less, the street was a space of "darkness" and "secrets." The language of describing the street was filled with the vocabulary of vision: the gaze, the glance, display, illusion, and performance. This was a space, at least in the eyes of the press, of teeming and overflowing "spectacle" (*zrelishche*)—a ubiquitous term that, in Russian, ranges in meaning from anything that attracts visual attention (*vzor*, meaning look or gaze) to public performances in theaters and parks (thus the Roman saying about "panem et circenses" becomes in Russian "bread and *zrelishcha*."). The spectacle of the street, we will see, inspired both desire and disgust and produced mixtures of pleasure, intoxication, nervousness, unease, and shock. Or, in another favorite image, the street was a "cinematograph": flickering, motley, exuberant, excessive, informative, trivial, disorderly, and debased, where "reality" and "illusion" were difficult to disentangle.

MAPPING THE CITY

The newspaper, more than any other text, mapped St. Petersburg as a social space. Of course, guidebooks showed visitors and residents where to visit and what to see and interpreted these sights, mainly as evidence of the city's accomplishments and beauty and thus as a demonstration of Russian achievement and destiny.[45] Fiction and poetry also guided readers' gaze toward significant spaces, helping readers see and know the city, including the one beneath its façades. But newspapers were the most immediate,

A worker reading the news, August 1905 (Central State Archive of
Film, Photographic, and Sound Documents of St. Petersburg).

Reading news about the outbreak of war, August 1914 (Central State Archive
of Film, Photographic, and Sound Documents of St. Petersburg).

sustained, and ubiquitous guide to the city's social landscape. As in other large modern cities, the newspaper inventoried and made readable, on a daily basis, the city's increasingly numerous and uncertain public spaces, helping readers to see, know, interpret, navigate, and use the city.[46] Newspapers constructed narrative maps of the city that marked space as social and moral as well as physical. That this topography was as likely to be seen as fragmented rather than whole and as a spectacle rather than factually real made the newspaper itself part of the street, and thus the most intimate and implicated participant in its creation.

Essential to every newspaper, whether boulevard papers like *Gazeta-kopeika* and *Peterburgskii listok* or high-minded political and cultural dailies like *Rech'* and *Novoe vremia*, were the daily chronicles of "incidents" (*proisshestviia*, also *prikliucheniia* or *sobytiia*) on the city's streets: fires, tram accidents, drownings, fights, "disorderly conduct" (*buistvo*), robberies, street scams, arrests, suicides, rapes, stabbings, shootings, missing persons, discovered bodies, and the like—what one reporter called the "deformities of life," which, he believed, as many did, so dominated the pages of the daily press as to make reading the paper itself a moral hazard of living in the city.[47] Mapping the precise locations of incidents was important. Reports almost always specified locale: on Haymarket Square, at the corner of Liteinyi and Nevskii prospects, on Voznesenskii Prospect near Kazanskaia Street, in Chubarov Alley, on Shlisselburgskii Prospect, etc., often with the precise building number and time of day recorded. That street incidents were often reported as "zrelishcha" (sights, spectacles, performances) reinforced the sense of the newspaper as a means for seeing the public street, and of the street as a type of public theater.

Papers considered it especially important to define the moral topography of the city. The industrial outskirts, with their narrow and dirty streets, feeble artificial lighting at night (or no lighting at all), and large population of poor people were portrayed in the darkest terms. The street gangs of the Petersburg Side, a largely working-class district just across the Neva River to the north, with their marked turfs and special signs of membership in clothing and color, defined that neighborhood.[48] Many writers viewed the margins of the city as located, morally and culturally, in another time and place. Thus, for example, Okhta, on the right bank of the Neva to the east

of the city center, was described as a type of "Petersburg Mexico or Peru,"
where the main activity of young people is "fisticuffs and bloodletting"
(*mordoboem da krovopuskaniem*).[49] Appropriately, while Okhta lacked such
amenities of urban life as lighting, sewage, bridges, and trams, it had no
shortage of "theaters filled with pornography, bars, taverns, hotels—and,
crowning all of this, blackmailers."[50] Concerning the industrial working-
class neighborhood along the left bank of the Neva below the Obvodnyi
Canal known as "beyond the Nevskii gate" (*za Nevskoi zastavoi*)—though
the entry gate to the city no longer existed, the designation emphasized
its location outside the city proper—a report about the treatment of young
women resembled an ethnographic tale about an exotic and "savage" culture with its distinct rites and local vocabularies.[51] A report on Donskoi
Alley, on Vasil'evskii Island, similarly observed that "mores there are such
that you don't know whether you are in Petersburg or Babylon or among
some north African savages."[52]

Ligovka, though closer to the center, and less visibly marked as a margin by the boundaries of river or canal, was perhaps the most notorious
neighborhood in the capital. Ligovka was the common designation for Ligovskaia Street, which ran from the Nikolaevskii railroad station at Nevskii
Prospect (the busiest and most central station in the city) across the Obvodnyi Canal (the boundary of the central city) into the southern margins
of the city, along with the notoriously rough neighborhood around it. This
district, especially Ligovskaia Street itself, was the subject of many reports
about both grisly crimes and colorful characters. Even at high noon, a reporter observed, the people walking about or sitting on boulevard benches
(a boulevard was created when this section of the Ligovskii Canal was put
underground in the 1890s) were right out of Maksim Gorky, a sort of "Petersburg lower depths" (a reference to Gorky's play of that name) filled with
down-and-out "former people" (the title of a Gorky story).[53] The lowest
depth of Ligovka was the neighborhood known by the old designation
Iamskaia sloboda (Coachmen's settlement), around the intersection of Ligovskaia and Chubarov Alley (near the railroad tracks and the Obvodnyi
Canal), a district known for its heavy concentration of brothels and criminal
"dens."[54] At night and well into the morning it was said to be impossible
to walk on the Ligovka near the Obvodnyi Canal without risk of robbery.[55]

Nearness and distance were similarly emphasized in a report about the Petersburg Side: you can walk across the elegant Troitskii Bridge and along the chic Kamennoostrovskii Prospect and on to the elegant dachas and homes of Krestovskii Island, yet quite nearby, at the western edge of the Petersburg Side, are the streets around the Koltovskii Embankment where "semi-savage" people live in damp and dirt, making their livings mainly by crime.[56]

The harm the city's meanest streets posed to the children of the poor was often used as a measure of the moral character of a district. The newspapers regularly reported, with great dismay, on the proliferation of children working certain streets as pickpockets, muggers, and prostitutes.[57] Few doubted that "the street" itself was to blame for the widespread criminality among children and youth.[58] The prominent and often quoted criminologist Dr. Dmitrii Dril' put it typically: for young people from the poorer classes "the street" is a "special 'university' for criminality."[59] Even children who did not turn to lives of crime were damaged by the street. In working-class neighborhoods, it was said, children have no choice but to escape into the streets from their cramped and "dingy" apartments. And contrary to stereotypes of "street children" as "debased kids" (*isporchennye rebiata*) attracted "by their own will" toward the excitement, noise, and bright lights of the city center, the real picture is "dingy and pale." The real streets where they spend their time are not "alluring" (*soblaznitel'nyi*) at all, but "cramped and dusty, thick with the smell of smoke and soot from nearby factories." And on these streets children learn to play "disgusting and harmful" games and to drink.[60] The problem of "street children" was widely discussed in the press—with arguments continually insisting that the moral dangers of the street threatened children with both physical and moral "infection," though also recognizing the street's allure for the children of the poor.[61]

Contrary to those who might take comfort in knowing that the city's mean streets were on the outskirts or in easily identifiable rough neighborhoods with distinct boundaries, poverty and its accompaniments were often difficult to contain. St. Petersburg, as we have noted, had far less spatial segregation of neighborhoods and streets by class than most European and

American cities at that time, and so the poor were everywhere. The most tangible evidence of poverty, besides poor people, was housing. While the city's population had grown dramatically in recent decades, its housing stock remained inadequate and conditions for the less prosperous were often abysmal. According to the labor economist Konstantin Pazhitnov, apartment buildings in St. Petersburg tended to be larger and more congested than in western European cities, with an average of 52 people in a single building, 8.1 persons per apartment, and 2.4 per room, with consequent negative effects on "social hygiene."[62] Many of the poor dwelled in "corners" of rooms, where, reporters observed, they lived "like rats" without light, air, or cleanliness.[63] Efforts to address the housing shortage could make conditions still worse. Many of the newest buildings were not only aesthetically offensive ("massive stone boxes") but also physically dangerous. Some were reportedly built so quickly and shoddily that they collapsed while under construction, killing and maiming workers. It seemed to one commentator in 1909 to be only a matter of time before a building filled with residents collapsed, bringing to Petersburg a catastrophe like the recent Messina earthquake, though with entirely human causes.[64]

While commentators all recognized that it is "difficult and painful for the little man to live in the big city,"[65] littleness ranged from working-class families and people with rented apartments to destitute individuals living in corners or without fixed residence. At the bottom were the homeless, estimated in 1912 at around ten thousand people. They lived everywhere in the city, sleeping on boulevard benches, under bridges, in ditches, and on trash dumps and garbage barges. Those with a few kopecks could rent a space for the night on a divided wooden platform in one of the city's scattered flophouses, though, as we have seen, these *nochlezhnye doma* never had enough spaces to satisfy the demand. In any case, *nochlezhki* were reported to be, like the street, sites of physical and moral decay. They were peopled by "suspicious types," beggars, prostitutes, and alcoholics, as well as by simply impoverished day laborers, unemployed workers and servants, widows and their children—"fallen" people in the words of a sympathetic reporter from *Rech'*. Physically, the flophouses were characterized by the most unsanitary conditions. They were said to be "breeding grounds" for typhus and other infectious diseases that easily spread to the larger city as epidemics.[66] While city officials and the press regularly worried about how to improve the horrible sanitary and moral conditions in the flophouses, police periodically raided them in search of criminal elements.[67]

Begging was tied to homelessness, though it reached much further. Beggars were not hidden on the margins of the city but gravitated onto streets where more prosperous people could be found—though the police would periodically round up both beggars and the homeless and expel them from the city. St. Petersburg was a recognized "magnet" for beggars. According to one news report, there were more than thirteen thousand of them in the capital, so many that they effectively comprised a city bigger than many provincial towns, with an annual income, received kopeck by kopeck, of a million and a half rubles.[68] But while the homeless could be pitied for the misfortunes that led them to this state and the horrible living conditions they had no choice but to endure, beggars were more likely to be condemned as immoral actors, who were at least partly to blame for the evils of the street. Newspapers regularly complained that begging had become a "profession" and that money was going not to the truly needy but to drunkards and groups of "professional beggars" led by profit-making "entrepreneurs."[69] An editorial in *Gazeta-kopeika* observed in 1911 that there were so many "idlers" and drunkards among the evening "lineup of paupers and suspicious looking types begging alms" at "every corner" that citizens were becoming wary, with the result that many honest people who had fallen on hard times were getting nothing.[70] In 1911, the Petersburg city council established a committee to gather data on begging in the capital. The language with which the report, finally issued in 1913, characterized begging echoed evaluations in the press. On the one hand, some beggars were "truly impoverished elements" and should be helped. Also, particular Russian conditions contributed to the large number of beggars: severe social, economic, and political difficulties combined with Russians' exceptional "warm-heartedness" and willingness to give alms. But none of this lessened the beggars' own moral fault: all beggars manifested a "low morality," evident in widespread drunkenness, dishonesty, disrespect for the property of others, apathy and a weak will, "moral slovenliness" (*nravst-*

vennaia neriashlivost') reflected in physical slovenliness, and, especially among the young, the "lowest instincts," evident in widespread deceit, violence, and even sexual perversion.[71] Whatever the cause, they had become degenerates and thus a public danger.

Crime, begging, and homelessness were among the evidence, in the eyes of the press, that the old boundaries supposedly dividing safe streets from mean streets had become uncertain. Criminals were everywhere. Streetwalkers paraded themselves on the best and most crowded streets of the city center: on Nevskii, Liteinyi, Vladimirskii, and Voznesenskii prospects; on Gorokhovaia, Bol'shaia, and Malaia streets; and in the Gostinnyi dvor (Merchants' Court) and Passazh (Passage) department stores. The elegant Summer Garden attracted child molesters, who gathered near the playground there.[72] Homosexuals—viewed as equivalent to criminals— gathered and met in some of the city's most central locations: along Nevskii Prospect from the Anichkov Bridge to the Public Library, in the elegant Passazh shopping arcade connecting Nevskii to Mikhailovskii Square, along the Fontanka Embankment from the Sheremet'ev Palace to the park near the circus, and in the popular Tauride and Summer gardens.[73]

Nevskii Prospect, especially the long blocks extending from the railroad station to the Admiralty, was without peer as the city's most important and symbolic street. Nevskii was Petersburg's "most populated" (*samyi liudnyi*) street, the city's "artery" and "nerve," a place marked as no other by "eternal movement."[74] People came to Nevskii to work and shop but also to stroll, see, and be seen. The sidewalks were crowded with people going about their business (ranging from officials to servants)—who interested the press very little—but also with "flâneurs," idlers, drunks, dandies, well-heeled women and men seeking pleasure, and prostitutes with their pimps and customers.[75] The homeless or depressed wandered "aimlessly" amidst these crowds.[76] Writers of all sorts were attracted to Nevskii—for its spectacle, but also because it always seemed a signifier of larger things. Boulevard feuilletonists like Ol'ga Gridina, symbolist poets like Aleksandr Blok, and philosophers like Dmitrii Merezhkovskii all walked Nevskii looking for the meaning of the age. What they found was not unlike what Nikolai Gogol had found: a bewildering phantasmagoria marked by "multiplicity,"

Nevskii Prospect, with a view from the Singer Sewing Machine
Company to the Passazh (Central State Archive of Film,
Photographic, and Sound Documents of St. Petersburg).

"motleyness," "dissonance," deceit, and decadence,[77] though the imagery
and significance had become darker and more consequential.

No other street was so associated with the spectacle of the streets
as Nevskii. It was the city's most prominent public stage with the largest
audience—extended by the special attention that newspapers paid to what
occurred there. Some reported incidents were simply curious and entertaining, such as the naked man, in late November, who, first on Ligovka and
then on Nevskii, confronted people with a tale of his daughter's elopement
with some count.[78] Some incidents were more shocking, notably women
and men swallowing poison while standing at Nevskii's most crowded intersections or leaping to their death off Nevskii's bridges into the waters
of a canal.[79] Robberies took place every day throughout the city, but it
seemed especially significant to reporters that even at the corner of Nevskii
and Sadovaia, "the most crowded place in the capital," "bold" and "fantastic" crimes were carried out, such as when one afternoon a young man

approached a women at this intersection, bowed politely, and then stole her handbag, or when a group of women thieves walked off one evening with thousands of rubles worth of women's apparel from the nearby "Viennese Chic" store right "before the eyes of passersby" and the twenty-four-hour police watch at the intersection.[80]

The salacious "mores of Nevskii Prospect" fascinated the newspapers. It seemed that Nevskii was not only the city's main artery and nerve but also (echoing Anatolii Bakhtiarov's famous series of feuilletons from the nineteenth century) its "underbelly."[81] Cafés attracted both respectable high society and a decadent demimonde. Drunks, criminals, and prostitutes walked beside bureaucrats, officers, and intellectuals. Among prostitutes themselves, Nevskii attracted both cheap and diseased streetwalkers and the high-class category known as "Nevskii ladies."[82] Even certain spaces on the street had bad reputations, such as near the Anichkov Bridge (famous for its statues of four naked young men straining to tame rearing horses) where "public men" (*publichnye muzhchiny*), presumably homosexual male prostitutes, gathered each evening; police periodically intervened to break up the "morally depraved scenes," sometimes not without resistance.[83] The definition of Nevskii Prospect, a newspaper humorist suggested, as part of an imagined "Petersburg Dictionary," was "the tree of knowledge of good and evil."[84]

Notions of public morality, here as in the histories of other modern cities, were often entwined with gender, especially with an idealized vision of female purity threatened as women strayed from the safety of the domestic sphere.[85] In this light, Nevskii was the proverbial slippery path. While the male gaze on the street was predatory, and thus a danger to women, who were the object of this gaze, the female gaze was also harmful for it led to desire, which could lead to moral fall. Of particular concern to moralizing journalists were young working-class women whose desires were awakened while walking along Nevskii and gazing at diamonds and other luxury objects displayed in store windows and worn by richer walkers.[86] The ubiquity of display on the street was seen as a moral problem for women. Nevskii was a magnet and stage for "fashion" (*moda, shik*). But fashion was seen as yet another sign of moral danger and degeneration. At best, it catered to the ephemeral and fickle tastes of the crowd.[87] At worst, in the words of Ol'ga Gridina, fashion was a cruel "tyrant" who mocks and punishes us for abandoning nature by "ruining" us, making women "stupid and ugly" with absurd hair styles and clothes.[88] In a 1906 brochure titled simply *Nevskii Prospekt,* the writer Vera Nedesheva—like Gridina one of very few women writers to take to the streets as observer and commentator on city mores—described the alluring and ambiguous phantasmagoria of Nevskii: the shop windows "sparkling with gold, silver, and diamonds and many-colored flowers both live and artificial," and "thousands of different objects of luxury that strike the eyes of passersby," creating an "electric" atmosphere for the crowds teeming there on a summer evening. But this was a dangerous atmosphere, luring women, in particular, "like moths to a fire," to this "glitter and luxury," to this "marketplace of fashion and beauty." And with the women, indeed in pursuit of them as in a "hunt," came the "Petersburg Don Juans, lions, and wolves." The effects were dire. Desire and "appetite," stimulated by a "ruinous" (*gubitel'nyi*) environment of luxury and commerce, led to moral degradation and fall. Dreams of "French hats and perfume," of "a bright future," transformed innocent country daughters into "depressed and cynical daughters of the street."[89]

The Neva River was the watery equivalent of Nevskii Prospect (including in name)—a central economic artery, a place of constant activity, a source of intertwined benefit, beauty, and danger.[90] The press tended to dwell on the dangers. A sensationalist report in 1913 on "Neva pirates" (*Nevskie piraty*) described "two Nevas." The first, flowing in granite banks beside the city center, was bordered by palaces and factories and its waters hosted elegant yachts and a refined public. Below the Smolnyi Cathedral lay the other Neva, the dirt-banked "proletarian Neva." The rich were disgusted by this Neva, but it was paradise for the children of the poor, especially in summertime. Here they could fish, swim, and play. These working-class youths were also prime recruits for the Neva pirates, allegedly organized in bands, possessing small boats from which they could attack passing boats after dark.[91] A report a few years earlier described these river pirates as drunken "hooligans" who at best simply disturbed people with their shouting, laughing, and singing, but at worst robbed boats anchored on the river, attacked and raped women, and committed murder, effectively "turning the twentieth-century Neva into the Volga of ancient times."[92]

Nighttime, as many of these stories suggest, overlaid the spatial map of the city with a temporal one. Journalists and other urban writers constructed the street at night as the day street's "other," as what Joachim Schlör has called, in his historical study of the night in Paris, Berlin, and London, a "counterworld."[93] As such, it attracted special public concern, from both police authorities and the press. At best, as in other cities, the urban night was viewed, with mixed fascination and moral shock, as a contradictory space and time: a landscape of ominous shadows and bright lights, of danger and pleasure, of loosened moral control and promised freedoms. But the tendency in St. Petersburg was to see mainly the shadows and the dangers.

The otherness of the night was always emphasized. Like Poe's famous observation in "The Man of the Crowd" that "as the night deepened . . . the general character of the crowd materially alter[ed] (its gentler features retiring in the gradual withdrawal of the more orderly portion of the people, and its harsher ones coming out into bolder relief, as the late hour brought forth every species of infamy from its den),"[94] so did Russian writers observe that it is a "special contingent of people who use the night," that "by day the city is busy with business [gorod den' delovit, suetliv], by night it drunkenly carouses," that "all of dark Petersburg, all who desired to throw themselves into the maelstrom, poured out into the streets at dusk."[95] Drawing a stark moral divide between people of the day and the people of the night, a columnist for *Gazeta-kopeika* noted that when workers were heading in the morning to their factories, the drunken nighttime revelers, with "darkened faces," were just going to bed; when the workers took their first break, these decadent sleepers were being tormented by nightmares; and when the tired laborers returned home from work, these nighttime revelers were again in the throes of debauchery in taverns, theaters, clubs, and restaurants.[96]

Public life at night was viewed as the darkest space in the city's moral landscape. Newspaper feuilletons dwelled on the quite different "spectacle" on Petersburg streets during the hours when the "capital was submerged in darkness"—a spectacle where one cannot see what dangers lurk.[97] "When the street sinks into darkness," a newspaper poet observed, this is the time for "scandals" and fights, for "heroes from the lower depths," for both "foppish dandies" and "night hooligans," for impudence (*nakhal*) toward

women (and worse).[98] At night, criminals lurked "in the shadows." Illegal
gambling parlors and other "dens" thrived at night, including legal "brothels" that doubled as illegal "night taverns."[99] Cafés chantants (*kafeshantany*
or simply *shantany*) were the night haunt of the capital's "demimonde,"
a term writers used both directly from the French but also in the Russian
translation *polusvet* ("half-world" but also "half-light") that was even more
suggestive of nighttime shadows.[100] Newspaper headlines like "Petersburg
by Night" or "The Petersburg Night" drew readers' attention to stories
about prostitutes, sexual licentiousness and abuse, hooligans, the homeless, drunks, and violence. The dark moral landscape of the night was such
a cliché that in 1914 one newspaper playfully but grimly imagined a letter to
the editor from Sherlock Holmes, who had come to the Russian capital to
make a special study of the city's "dens of iniquity." It seemed, "Holmes"
concluded, that these were all run by satanic "vampires," whose nature required they work only at night when they have power. Certain neighborhoods, he observed, were filled with these dens, but they were invisible
until the nighttime: "By day these were streets like any other. But at night!
Hoarse and drunken voices roar the most obscene things from every entry-
way."[101] Like "Holmes," newspaper reporters promised to reveal the secrets
of the street hiding under the cloak of darkness.[102] Some writers, however,
worried that their work could shed too little light: that the night would always remain "incomprehensible."[103]

The city press offered more than a mere record of public life. It was
itself part of the street: itself a public space in the social and moral landscape of the city. Its crowded pages embodied the rhythms and images of
the street in fragmentary reports about the latest crimes and accomplishments, in the clamor of advertisements for commercial products and jobs,
and in essays echoing the talk of the street. But the newspaper was more
than a "printed digest of the flâneur's roving eye."[104] The press also helped
create the city. On the positive side, as journalists sometimes proudly insisted, the press did not merely inform the public about the city's social life
but helped to create the social itself though its role as site of public narrative
and opinion. A leading columnist for *Novoe vremia* put it this way: "to the
extent that society is possible in our anarchic age" (for "society" he uses

the term "obshchestvo," which could also be translated as "a public"), this newspaper is itself "Russian society."[105]

The self-image of the newspaper as "society" also generated a good deal of self-reflexive hand-wringing and defensiveness about whether the press was, like the street, a source of danger and harm. Newspaper columnists, for example, worried about reporters' moral right to invade the private sphere with their "immodest gaze."[106] But most troubling, they worried that by reporting the dark sides of urban life—both public and private, indeed, making the private public—the newspaper became not simply an innocent "mirror" of the street, but itself a type of mean street. Reading the newspaper, some suggested, could be as dangerous as walking the street. A leading essayist for *Gazeta-kopeika*, for example, concluded that children should not be allowed to read newspapers, for they were too young to be exposed to the "horror, cold, and egoism" of urban life.[107] And the danger was not limited to children. The periodical press, many argued (in this case, the social democrat Vladimir Posse), willfully demoralizes and corrupts readers by publishing "pandering and pornographic notices," crime novels of poor literary quality but that were "captivating for the crowd," and salacious reporting of "the most disgusting crimes," making it seem that "blood is flowing without cease" on the city's streets and creating feelings of "terror" in the public imagination.[108]

DUST, NOISE, AND DANGER

Dust, Walter Benjamin observed, was a tangible and telling expression of the modern condition: the dust that stirred and settled over nineteenth-century Paris, collected in every corner, and gathered on the heavy drapes and upholstered furniture in bourgeois parlors signified decay and ruin, the lack of real movement or vitality, restricted vision, and death.[109] Russian journalists were less explicitly philosophical about the meanings of urban dust (*pyl'*), but they were no less insistent in noting its troubling ubiquity and in sensing some larger significance in it. For many, the problem of street dust in the capital was a paradoxical product of both St. Petersburg's development and its backwardness. For urban officials and planners, who often discussed the problem, the reasons were clear: the poor quality of pavement "fouled air and soil" with dirt and dust. Not only were most Petersburg streets still paved with "ordinary cobblestones" rather than a modern road surface like asphalt, but the condition of these streets was often poor, with numerous potholes, ruts, and broken stones. These surfaces not only produced a great deal of dust but nurtured bacteria and mixed with the city's ubiquitous smoke and soot (said to settle in every corner)[110] to help produce St. Petersburg's famous fogs. The hard and uneven surfaces of the street also added to high levels of "street noise."[111]

The poor suffered most from dust and other sanitary problems. To walk the streets in a working-class district meant to "swallow dust."[112] Especially in the summer. The well-off could escape to their dachas or abroad, or, if remaining in town, enjoy a stroll in the Summer Garden or the Tauride Garden or an evening's entertainment at one of the city's pleasure gardens like Luna Park or the Bouffe Theater. But the "poor working class," and especially their children, had to settle for dirty streets and courtyards filled with trash—in a word, for a summer of "dirt" and "dust."[113] Worst of all were tenements and the flophouses for the homeless poor, about which some writers could be quite graphic in detailing the filth and stink.[114] When a city council member led reporters on a "sanitary inspection" of slum buildings located between Borovaia and Voronezh streets at the southern end of the Ligovka district, just across the Obvodnyi Canal, a reporter for *Peterburgskii listok* concluded that these slums were so horrible that they made Whitechapel in London, the worst neighborhood in any European capital, look aristocratic by comparison.[115]

Smells also told a story. Journalists regularly criticized city officials for their failure to deal with the city's harmful air and water, though this was not for the want of officials worrying aloud about the city's inadequate sewer system and other sources of contamination. No other European city, the columnist Skitalets (Wanderer) commented in *Gazeta-kopeika* in 1910, had such fouled air as St. Petersburg.[116] But most often, fetid smells were treated less as a citywide problem than as an olfactory map to the city's uneven social and moral landscape. In an apartment on 26 Vitebskaia Street (at the western edge of the central city), the home of a brothel madam, the air was "so thick with such odors that one could, as it were, cut pieces with

an axe. Of what it smells is hard to define. There are so many smells. Of
hypocrisy [*khanzhoi*]. Of people. And still of something else." Above all,
it "smelled of debauchery," a smell that wafted out of every window and
door.[117] Even worse were the "dens" of madams on the notorious Ligovka,
from which a stench so foul emanated that "a person not used to it is ready
to die."[118] Nighttime flophouses for the homeless were described in similar
terms by journalist-explorers: "the walls are covered by some sort of ooz-
ing slime, the sight of which calls forth an involuntary shudder of disgust.
The atmosphere, a stinking fog, prevents you from breathing, and is like a
spider web obscuring every free space. Into this lair, like sputum, infected
with every conceivable disease, people flow together—and what people!"[119]
Somewhat less sensationalistically, but explicit in marking urban poverty as
social and moral otherness, a reporter for the liberal newspaper *Rech'*, who
accompanied an official sanitation inspection of flophouses in 1910, wrote
that the stifling and fetid air and "repulsive" smells reminded him of some
primitive Samoyed hovel or the hut of a "hungry" peasant.[120] Odor as a
moral sign could also apply to less repellant smells. Walking down Nevskii
Prospect in the evening, for example, one would encounter the smells of
luxurious, "intoxicating" perfumes and expensive cigars. For writers like
the urban explorer Vera Nedesheva, however, these smells were also, ultimately, disgusting: part of a landscape of debased urban desire and egoism,
leading ultimately to exploitation and degradation.[121]

Noise also defined the physical experience of the city street, highlighting disorder and even chaos. The "streets of the big city," Petersburg
journalists continually commented, were "filled with noise, groans, din, and
roar" (*shumom, stonom, gamom, grokhotom*).[122] In a newspaper version of
the familiar trope of the small-town provincial arriving in the capital city, a
poor petty bourgeois (*meshchanin*) is overwhelmed by the "rumble of the
trams, the noise of carriages, the movement of the crowd."[123] The experience of peasant migrants and even of permanent workers was worse, for
the noise in factory districts was a "dreadful roar."[124] As one entered the
factories, the noise (and smells), seemed literally infernal: "hellish thunder," "thunderous noise and whistles," and the air thickened with burning
fumes and stifling smoke, making the factory resemble a "beast, grinding its
teeth"—in the words of poems appearing in the trade union press.[125]

Street transport was a major source of noise. Every district, especially
in the urban center, was populated with private carriages, a growing number of private automobiles, horse cabs for passengers and goods, and public transport—which included horse-drawn streetcars (*konki*), a few steam-
powered *konki* and motorized autobuses, and, beginning in 1907, electric
trams, which were much celebrated as a modern innovation and a sign of
the city's progress.[126] Transport contributed much to the distinctive texture
of street sounds, which delighted some and dismayed many others: the din
of horseshoes and carriage wheels on cobblestones (and the shouts of drivers), the rumble and squealing of metal wheels on poorly positioned steel
tracks, constantly ringing tram bells, and the new if still infrequent roaring
and honking of automobiles.[127] That streetcars pressed together varied passengers into a rushing and noisy public box struck many observers as emblematic of modern city life: of its speed, sounds, smells, mixing of classes,
and spontaneous intimacies. Some viewed the tram crowd as part of the
adventure of the street, a place for viewing and listening in on the variety of
people and voices of the city.[128] Others turned away in disgust, especially
when faced with passengers who shoved, shouted, and threatened or who
were simply excessively voluble and smelled of vodka.[129]

The rapid pace of trams, and the relative lack of an effective system
for orderly regulation of traffic and pedestrians, also made the street host to
the sounds and sights of frequent accidents, many quite bloody. The newspapers regularly reported people maimed or killed after being hit while
crossing the tracks in front of an oncoming tram or falling while climbing
on and off trams. These accidents, and the resulting severed limbs and
even decapitations, were so frequent as to inspire a certain black humor
that defined "tramway" as "a famous surgeon specializing in separating legs
from torsos."[130] For the columnist Skitalets, such accidents (and by 1913
he added the dangers of automobiles), were "nightmares of the streets," a
dire sign of the modern development of big cities.[131] Geographically, these
accidents occurred most often on the crowded streets of the city center,
especially along Nevskii Prospect, where they were also most likely to attract large crowds of curious spectators. Some writers blamed the "public's
carelessness" for the rise in tram accidents—passengers, sometimes inebri-

ated, leaping on or off moving trams and crossing or standing too close to the tracks in front of an oncoming streetcar.[132] But the public was more likely to blame the carelessness of the drivers, even, on occasion, riotously attacking tram drivers after witnessing yet another pedestrian run over.[133] Streetcars—and gradually automobiles[134]—were such a powerful symbol of the modern street that, like so much of the reality and reportage of the city, they became a leitmotif in contemporary literature, where electric streetcars continually appeared in obviously emblematic form: their many-eyed gaze, their alien sounds and thunderous roar, their erotic thrusting and swaying, their sparks of electric fire, and their many victims.[135]

Fires were among the many other "katastrofy" (the Russian term ranges from accidents to disasters) that attracted crowds on the street and attention in the newspapers and were treated as symbolic of the spectacular dangers of the modernizing city.[136] Newspapers like *Peterburgskii listok* created a special "Chronicle of Fires"—the only other special feature, set apart from the main listing of daily "incidents," was the daily chronicle of suicides and reports on the death toll from cholera during the epidemic that began in 1908.[137] Highlighting the mythic qualities of fires—their perception as pathology, catastrophe, and malevolence—newspapers often headlined reports with the old Russian name for destructive blazes: *krasnyi petukh* (the red rooster).[138] Other frequent *katastrofy* included collapsed scaffolding or buildings at new construction sites, falling electrical and telephone lines, and elevator crashes.[139] The growing number of stray and rabid dogs in various parts of the city, and the increasing incidence of people being bitten, seemed at one with these pictures of rising disorder and danger.[140] A public lecture on the problem in 1910, by a physician from the Institute for Experimental Medicine, suggested that, like so much else, the 1905 revolution was a turning point, after which the problem of rabid dogs began to grow at a "phenomenal pace."[141] Other spectacular street catastrophes were less common, even singular, but reported widely and in detail. For example, on the night of 6 May 1910 crowds gathered in the streets late at night hoping to see Halley's comet. When a woman who had fallen asleep while waiting on a window sill woke with a start at the shouts of "Look, there's the comet!" and then fell to her death from a fifth-story window, the crowd

"Due to the Comet," *Peterburgskii listok*, 7 May 1910.

witnessed a much different and more terrible sight than they had gathered to observe. *Peterburgskii listok* emphasized the grim spectacle with a sketch of the crowd watching the woman fall.[142]

The proliferation of commercial advertisements seemed to be a visual counterpart to noise, dirt, smells, and disorder. Writers complained of the "bacchanalia of signboards" afflicting Petersburg, such that advertisements covered every building, gate, and wall, "deforming" (*uroduetsia*) architecture and destroying the visual aesthetics of city streets. Posters, pasted on buildings, walls, advertising columns, and inside trams, and, after 1910, as walking ads carried on poles, made city streets no longer markers of order and controlling power but a space defined by bacchanalian "cacophony" and "deformity" (*bezobrazie*).[143] The pages of the periodical press, appropriate to its role as a street in print, were also covered with a profusion of advertisements that pointed to the many opportunities the city offered: things to consume, businesses offering services, jobs to be had, advice for self-improvement, entertainments, and purchasable cures of every sort of ailment, especially modern ones.

CAFÉS, CINEMAS, AND OTHER DENS

"The street" was also present behind doors: especially in bars, cafés, night-clubs, brothels, gambling parlors, and other "dens" (*pritony*). In the eyes of many, these spaces traced a "map of 'dark Petersburg.'"[144] The ubiquity of *pritony* was a common theme. Even in its narrowest use, the term covered an array of illicit public spaces, including illegal brothels, gambling parlors, criminal hideouts, "fun dens" (*veselye pritony*) for carousing, and "secret" homosexual sex clubs for men and women "of all tastes."[145] What united these spaces was transgression, against morality and often against the law, but also their characteristically ambiguous blending of visibility and invisibility, publicity and secrecy, public and private. *Pritony* were necessarily "hidden from the gaze of the police,"[146] but known to those who desired them. Of course, the newspapers, like the police, took pride in enabling the public eye to gaze into these dark corners of city life. And the city's police authorities continually tried to expose and close *pritony*. A special Ministry of Internal Affairs commission on "clubs" found a strong link between *kluby-pritony*, especially gambling clubs—many clubs ostensibly organized for quite respectable purposes were really fronts for gambling, according to the government and the press—and organized "robbery, confidence rackets, forgery, and even murder." After 1907, partly as a component of the larger crackdown on civic organizations of all sorts, the city saw a campaign of raids and prosecutions. This seems to have done little to stem the growth of secret clubs, however, judging by the continuing reports in the press on new police raids and new club-*pritony*.[147] If anything, the government itself can be partly blamed for erasing the dividing line between legitimate and illicit gathering places. According to one reporter, the main result of the government's shutting down social clubs was that, once forced underground, legitimate clubs were more likely to become blurred in function with "secret gambling dens" and "dens of debauchery" (*pritony razvrata*).[148] In general, the boundaries defining a space as a "den" were imprecise. Brothels, even legal ones, especially in the late hours after most restaurants and cafés had closed, doubled as dens for "revelers, carousers, and plain old incorrigible drunks." Especially during the war, when the sale of alcohol was forbidden, many brothels did a brisk nighttime trade in both women's bodies and forti-fied wines.[149] Likewise, many legitimate spaces for dining and entertainment doubled as *pritony*. The Café de Paris, for example, in the elegant Passazh arcade on Nevskii Prospect—though on the floor below street level—was described as "a real cesspool, dark and disgusting, where audacious rob-beries and rackets were hatched" and where a brisk "daytime flesh market" (*birzha zhivogo tovara*), including a homosexual one, thrived. This was the sort of place "beloved of the street."[150]

Cafés were morally ambiguous locations. Some writers spoke with pride of the emergence in the capital of a "European" café culture, where one could find good coffee and pastries and the crowd of patrons was el-egant and "respectable."[151] But most often, newspapers dwelled on the darker, decadent sides of café life, especially at night. Of course, this side of the story was more sensational and thus more marketable; but, as always, prurient appeal was mixed with interpretive reflections on the conditions of modern existence. Many of the city's cafés, it was reported, attracted women of loose morals and men on the prowl, with female display and male gazing at "such women" essential to the whole café experience.[152] The centrally lo-cated Quisisana (Kvisisana) café, located on the corner of Nevskii Prospect and Troitskaia (now Rubinshtein) Street, was among the most famous and characteristic of the type. This café was described, with a typical mixture of sensationalist admiration and moral shock, by Iurii Angarov in an essay in the collection *New Petersburg Dens* (*Novye petersburgskie trushchoby*). On the surface, this was a "little restaurant of vile tone" with bad food and cof-fee. But people "don't come here to eat." Rather, "the public gathers here for carousing and debauchery." The food is a "front" for the real "dish du jour" (*dezhurnaia bliuda*) offered for the "night revels" of "gastronomes": women. Especially between twelve and three at night (Quisisana was one of the few major cafés on Nevskii open after midnight) all of the "scum of soci-ety" gathered here, "all of the unclean, wanton, outcast, and contaminated, all of the bachelors, loners, and playboys," all dressed in the latest fashions. The cacophony of voices created a veritable "Tower of Babel"—in Russian, the term for the Tower of Babel, *Vavilonskaia bashnia*, also emphasizes its association with Babylon and thus with that city's mythic moral symbolism. The atmosphere at Quisisana was a "monstrous spectacle" marked by "cynicism of pose and gesture," "conversations that defy description," and wild scenes of open debauchery. This was a place where innocent provincials regularly fell, "sucked into the whirlpool of the capital."[153] It was widely understood that to speak of the "philosophy of Quisisana," as one reporter did, was to speak of decadent love, sex, and debauchery.[154] Of course, the Quisisana was only one of a number of such dubiously "chic" (*shikoznyi*) cafés in the capital.[155]

"The street" was especially evident in Petersburg's cafés chantants, which were increasingly popular among the bourgeois public. The finest cafés chantants were large and well-illuminated establishments where "fashionable" Petersburg gathered after the theater, a concert, or dinner for drinking, dancing, and a show. The performances, even at the "most European of all Russian cafés chantants," Aquarium (Akvarium), tended toward the extravagant and exotic, with acts such as "Cartes Postales," with naked women posing in various locales, their skin made up to look like marble, plaster, or bronze; ballet divertissements followed by gypsy choirs and Russia folk orchestras; acrobats and dog troupes; humorous skits such as naked women bathers having their clothing stolen; or themed shows such as a series devoted to Bacchus with "living picture" processions depicting classical bacchanalian scenes.[156] The fashionably dressed patrons were themselves on display. "Gazing," especially men gazing at women, was part of the lure of the café chantant. Indeed, at the aptly named Aquarium, it was reported that men sometimes situated themselves at tables on the balconies and gazed at women on the main floor through binoculars.[157]

Yet establishments like Quisisana and Aquarium were elegant and even respectable compared to the many cheap cafés chantants around the city, where singers often doubled as illegal prostitutes and associated with criminal gangs, and where "old lechers" came to "buy female flesh."[158] But even the very best cafés, reporters observed, were frequented by customers who, though dressed in "high chic," were really low-life criminals and former convicts.[159] Indeed, in the view of urban writers like *Gazeta-kopeika*'s Skitalets, all cafés chantants were linked to prostitution; hence, he declared, the announcement of the founding of a school where girls aged eleven to fifteen could learn to be café chantant singers was a "brazen" deceit to lure the innocent: this was, in effect, a "school for debauchery."[160] Even in certain cafés on Nevskii "the trade in women's bodies" was quite open, with no attempt to "mask" it.[161]

Many of the city's theaters and entertainment parks, especially those featuring music-hall–type performances, were treated as little different from decadent cafés chantants. Petersburg's many summertime entertainment parks and "gardens" were criticized for displays of singing, wrestling, and farces featuring "unbelievably risqué [*pikantnye*] situations."[162] Many of the city's "theaters for the people," though claiming to offer "useful entertainment," were likewise criticized as actually presenting, especially in the public gardens attached to the largest people's theaters, nothing "for mind or heart." Asking rhetorically "what do they give to the people?" a columnist in *Gazeta-kopeika* answered with dismay: "spectacle," "girls of the loosest behavior," "disgraceful goings-on [*bezobrazie*] and drunkenness."[163] Along the same lines, though for a higher social class, the fashionable Roller-Skating Rink (Sketing-rink) on Mars Field (sometimes called the American Roller-Skating Rink) was regularly criticized as a typical part of the "fun life" of the city's decadent leisure class, whose members allegedly began their day waking only in the afternoon for coffee with a lover, then heading to some tavern, and then to the Skating Rink, where "the atmosphere is saturated with dust and the smell of perfumes," where wanton women and males on the make circle the rink hand in hand, with every conversation about "passion," and women's bodies on sale.[164]

Cinemas—the newest site of public assembly and pleasure in the city—were also viewed as closely bound to the street, both in reflecting the life of the street on screen and in the influence of the street on the tone, aesthetic, and atmosphere of film and its presentation. The first cinema in Russia was opened on Nevskii Prospect in 1896. By 1909, a reporter counted 250 cinemas in the capital, the largest concentration still on Nevskii, and Petersburg would remain the country's movie-watching capital (though Moscow was Russia's film-producing center).[165] Lev Kleinbort, a well-known writer on popular culture, described the cinemas that proliferated along Nevskii as this "child of our days" that beckoned passersby with "fantastic arches and colored electric lights" and elaborately decorated interior spaces. Like the modern street, the cinema was "feverish-variegated, fantastical-noisy" (*likhoradochno-pestrykh, fantasticheski-shumnykh*).[166] The cinema echoed the images and subjects of urban public life—including cab drivers, street conversations, stores, cafés, and the streets themselves—but also reflected the city in cinematic form: "nervous and flickering like life itself," one journalist described the cinema in 1912, "changing reels like we change impressions, eternally seeking new themes, roaming the world over in the pursuit of the novel, the sensational, and the fantastic."[167] The cinema's moving images seemed to embody the press of modern life toward "eternal movement."[168]

Skitalets put all this aphoristically: "Life is a cinematograph" (*zhizn' eto sinematograf*). His explanation of the phrase rehearsed familiar tropes: "modernity is enacted before us with the same rapidity, motleyness, and unexpectedness as a cinema show. The funny and the sad, the valuable and the crass, the instructive and the insignificant alternate in disorderly succession."[169] The same argument was implied when the term "cinematograph," or one of its variant forms, was used in the press not to speak of the cinema at all but as a metonym for the life of the street and the city, even for the whole "variegated cinematograph of modernity" (*pestryi kinematograf sovremennosti*).[170] Thus, an anonymous columnist for *Gazeta-kopeika*, in the role of reporter-flâneur, penned a column, "Cinematograph," that concerned people, behaviors, and conversations observed and overheard while walking the streets.[171] Similarly, a newspaper appeared in 1911 and 1912 calling itself *Capital Cinematograph*, which also was not interested in the movies but in reporting the "truth" (*pravda*) about everyday city life—its laws and crimes, street fights, suicides, accidents, and the like.[172]

Contemporary literature also recognized the spirit of the modern street in cinema, though typically with aesthetic dismay. Some writers and artists, notably futurists, celebrated the cinema as the truest expression of modern reality: a "new art" that corresponded to the "rapid tempo of modern life," the "speed of impressions," and both "new feelings" and "modern perception."[173] But for most contemporary authors the cinema was a "bar-

baric" art designed to satisfy the "crowd" with a hideous and disgusting
(*bezobraznyi*) aesthetics of "rhythm without form [*bez obraza*]—the chaos
and roar of the primitive elements in man's soul," and an alienated representation of human beings as machine-made "illuminated shadows."[174]
Cultural critics chastised the cinema for reflecting rather than improving
the crass tastes of the mass consumer and encouraging the vulgar pursuit of
personal pleasure that allegedly so characterized contemporary urban life.[175]
Historians of early silent cinema would similarly, though without the moral
and aesthetic disgust, interpret this new medium as a new way of democra-
tized seeing in which the real and its representations were interchangeable
and indistinguishable, in which reality was experienced as spectacle and
spectacle as reality, and in which both the real and the spectacular become
commodities to be produced and consumed.[176]

It was precisely the "reality" of cinema that appealed to the few journalists who had anything good to say about it. Skitalets, for example, was
impressed at the cinema's ability to record and display "life, the present life,
life as it really is." He even found the experience of watching these flashing
images in the darkness of the theater somehow "cleansing."[177] Other writers
suggested that this presentation of real life made the cinema educational.[178]
But most commentators viewed the cinema, and its relationship to the realities of the street, with contempt and anxiety. No other modern invention
inspired such "distrust and even scorn" as the cinema, especially among
intellectual and cultural elites, according to Leonid Andreev. This hostility
began with laughter: a view of movies as "empty entertainment in the manner of the skating rink," which from time to time amuses the "fickle and frivolous street" *(peremenchivaia i pustaia ulitsa)*. But more recently, dismis-
sive ridicule had given way to nervous fear: a growing view of the cinema as
an alien and incomprehensible "stranger," an "artistic Apache," threatening
to true art and "repugnant" to aesthetically cultivated people.[179]

Typical commentary on the cinema in daily newspapers and popular
magazines was marked by disdain, disgust, and fear. Journalists condemned
the cinema as "corrupting the imagination" with its "crass [*poshlye*] scenes
and stupid fantasies,"[180] as "beckoning" and "tempting" ordinary people—
"workers, stupefied by dust, suffocating air, and machines," "shop slaves,"
serving girls, and other members of the "democratic public"—to a world of

"illusion."[181] Cinema publications like *Peterburgskii kinematograf* (Petersburg Cinematograph) did not ignore the chorus of accusations that movies "corrupt the masses" with images of sex, crime, and violence. But in defense of the new art form, they insisted that the depiction of, for example, murder on the screen did not itself inspire violence. In any case, they defensively pointed out, what the cinema showed was no different than what could be found in the literature, theater, and cabarets of the day.[182]

"CHEAP SPECTACLE"

When Georg Simmel defined the "sensory," "psychological," and "emotional" foundations of the metropolitan experience as "the rapid crowding of changing images, the sharp discontinuity in the grasp of a single glance," he implicitly highlighted intense visuality as central to the experience of urban life. And he located this experience precisely on the street: one most strongly felt the difference between metropolitan and small-town and rural life, he wrote, "with each crossing of the street."[183] Walter Benjamin even more strongly emphasized vision as a defining mode for experiencing and perceiving the street, and the visual experience of the street as key to historical and philosophical truths about the modern experience. For Benjamin, the metropolis presented city dwellers with a spectacle of desire, performance, and illusion. Like both Simmel and especially Charles Baudelaire, Benjamin recognized the visual experience of the street as both thrilling and perilous—though, like both these writers and like most of the Petersburg journalists whose visions of the street we have been considering, the dominant note was the false, debased, and harmful aspects of this spectacle. Describing the experience of walking and looking on streets or in shopping arcades—public spaces marked by a proliferation of signs, images, mirrors, windows, lights, display, and performance—Benjamin highlighted the ubiquity of "dream," "desire," and "pleasure," but also interpretively situated these in a visual and psychological landscape of "illusion," "alienated gaze," "shock," and "unease."[184] More recent theorizing about the ubiquity of visuality and spectacle in modern society, as well as historical studies of modern cities, has similarly interpreted the visual experience of modern city life as hyperstimulus and hyperreality. What Simmel had called the "rapid crowding of changing images," and what the Russian press envisioned as "life as a cinematograph," has been elaborated into arguments about the turbulence and excess of sensory stimulation, the proliferation and fragmentation of signs and other images (often mechanically reproduced), and the pleasures and perils of public seeing. Reality itself, in this context, becomes unstable and disorienting: both in the quite tangible terms of a public life marked by nervousness, disorientation, and shock, and in the epistemological terms of a visual order where spectacle, performance, image, representation, and simulacra become the only "reality."[185]

I mention this comparative and theoretical writing on modern visuality to highlight themes already visible in everyday Petersburg street texts. Russian contemporaries gazed obsessively at the street and often elevated this seen place (and touched, heard, and smelled place) into a tangible signifier. "Spectacle" (*zrelishche*) was a term the press constantly used to speak of public incidents on the streets and the appetites of the "crowd," not to mention (though they sometimes did) the profitable enthusiasm of the daily press for reporting the daily "spectacle of the streets." The same sense was conveyed in other visual metaphors: the street as a "variegated kaleidoscope,"[186] a cinematograph, a mirror, a window, or a stage. Essential to this spectacle were the ubiquitous "eyes of the crowd"—which could be both oppressively inescapable and offer opportunities for displays of the self—but also the street as the chief space where individuals could gaze at strangers. This was a disorderly spectacle. Again and again, the street was described as "motley" and "dissonant," a "bacchanalia" of signs, a space of overlapping and intersecting "maps." In a word, the street was a "cheap" spectacle—democratically accessible but also aesthetically and morally debased. Certainly, many found excitement and pleasure in this "cancan of spectacular sensations." But darker interpretations predominated. Most often, observers saw something crass (*poshlyi*), repulsive (*bezobraznyi*), obscene (*nepristoinyi*), monstrous (*urodlivyi*), and corrupt (*razvratnyi*) in the spectacle of the streets. This was an uneasy vision of modern vitality as decadent decline, and of modern public spectacle as ultimately deceitful and perilous.

For many, it was simply disgusting. Disgust, we can see, was a minor but telling theme in public reactions to the street. Disgust was implied, and often named, in accounts of the urban crowd, poverty, street children, crime, homosexuality, decadent pleasures, popular entertainment, and more. Disgust was part of how observers drew the "map of dark Petersburg." Disgust, it has been argued, announces and sustains hierarchies of social power, reveals social and psychic boundaries, and is often conjoined to desire or at least to an object's "outrageous claim for desirability" and thus the anxious need to build up and police the boundaries denying that claim.[187] At the very least, disgust highlights how much troubled social and cultural feeling "the street" evoked in public talk about contemporary life.

THREE

Masks

Savages deform their faces
With layers of paint . . .
We are civilized and live in the capital,
So we wear masks.

—*Malen'kaia gazeta*, January 1917

The modern meaning of the mask: deceptive illusion, that which
does not exist, mystical fraudulence [*samozvantsvo*], even a
hint of some horror in the most casual circumstance.

—Pavel Florenskii, 1922

Masks haunted St. Petersburg in the early twentieth century. Many were
literal and visible: masks covering the faces of criminals, the black mask hiding the head and face of the mysterious wrestler at the Cinizelli Circus who
captivated the public in 1909, alluring black masks and veils obscuring the
faces of women at society masquerade balls, masks on stage, and an obsession with masks in a great deal of the symbolist literature of the day. More
troubling, though, urban space was said to swarm with metaphoric masks:
impersonation, imposture, illusion, and falsification. It seemed at times that
"masks" veiled the faces of all modern men and women, that the city teemed
with unknown and potentially dangerous strangers, that the city hid its true
nature, even that modernity itself was defined by this phantasmagoric experience. Authenticity, reality, truth—major topics of public concern at the
time—seemed frighteningly unstable and elusive. With all their visceral and
symbolic potency, masks fascinated and troubled journalists and reporters,
and presumably their readers. Of course, the press's constant reporting of

and commentary on the ubiquity of masks and masquerade contributed to their haunting presence in the city. Stories of urban masquerade were told, in part, as diverting curiosities of modern city life. Indeed, we can never entirely be sure what in news stories was pure and precise "fact": newspaper reporting too often blurred the boundaries between truth and good stories. No less, these stories were told as signs of a troubling philosophical and political problem: how to know, interpret, and control the urban public landscape and, by extension, modern civilization; indeed, how to know what is real and true in modern life?

Illegibility, uncertainty, and the unknown were leitmotifs in urban journalism, especially in the new and unstable conditions in Russia after 1905.[1] Daily, new stories were added to the phantasmagoria of urban tales of public disguise and deception. Daily, urbanites were reminded of the inadequacy of reading the external markers of city life as signs of where criminal danger may lie. And crime stories joined accounts of other phenomena of city life that seemed to hide their faces: unidentified bodies, puzzling murders and suicides, and other evidence that the city was shrouded in shadows. Seen through the lens and language of the press, St. Petersburg, and the modern experience for which it so often stood, was full of secrets and mystery, strangers and the unknown, appearance and deception, uncertainty and lack of clarity, shadowiness, illusoriness, and masquerade. At times, it all seemed to border on "chaos," both civic and epistemological. It was, in more theoretical terms, a phantasmagoria—a spectacle of illusion—and a landscape of simulacra, filled with the seemingness of appearance.

The mask is a promiscuous and unstable cultural image. Traditionally, and this point has been well developed in modernist literature, masks speak of the self (hidden, performed, uncertain), of sexual allure, of death, of boundaries and thresholds, and of the unknown. These themes all made their appearance in the public life of St. Petersburg. But my focus—for this was the greater preoccupation of the press—is on one key theme in the modern meaning of the mask: masks as a symbol of modernity's epistemological crisis, of the modern desire to make the world ordered and legible in the face of the stubborn and unruly resistance of modern life to such ordering knowledge, and the moral and political danger that this uncertainty and instability produces. Amidst the disorder of the modern city, masks were powerful symbols of the ubiquity of deception and illusion, and behind this, of the even deeper "abyss" of uncertainty and the unknown.

Theorists of masks and masquerade have emphasized this subversion of the ordering conceit of modernity. Masquerade, writes the social psychologist Efrat Tseëlon, "unsettles and disrupts the fantasy" of coherence, "replaces clarity with ambiguity," and undermines the "phantasmic constructions of containment and closure" that characterize the modern project. This can be positive and exhilarating, of course. Masks can give us feelings of power and possibility. When we disguise ourselves, at least in theory, we feel that a field of play and possibility has opened where our identities become more protean, or where, at least, we can perform alternative selves.[2] For artistic modernists, Russians included, the creativity and vitality enabled by uncertainty and instability, the mask's power to enable transformation and transgression, was indeed inspiring and liberating. As Charles Baudelaire observed, the modernist writers and artists who knew how to "bathe" in the modern flux were also imbued with an intoxicating "craving for disguises and masks."[3] Likewise, Russian writers like Andrei Belyi and Aleksandr Blok were personally and artistically drawn to images of masquerade and illusion, to this unstable world where the self could defy rules and expectations, where embracing illusion could allow creative individuals to break out of the iron cage of ordinary reality and enter into a more fertile and productive terrain.[4]

For the modern urbanites of St. Petersburg, however—especially interpreters of the public everyday, as distinct from the modernist artists who imaginatively harnessed the images of modern reality to envision new possibilities for self-invention—the unsettling ubiquity of masquerade in public life was mainly dark and threatening. The appearance of order and progress in the city was found to conceal chaos and darkness beneath. Presumed knowledge and control of the elemental, the conceit of all cities and the essence of the idea of St. Petersburg, appeared to be only a mask of superficial legibility and power. To be sure, the endless repetition of newspaper stories of disguise and the mysterious was partly an effort to unmask the unknown, to shed light into the darkness. And the darkness in these tales was also mitigated by the thrill many readers likely found in reading sensationalist news reports about disguise, even predatory and criminal disguise. Still, these unceasing stories could not but remind readers of the ubiquity of deception and the unknown in the city and the vanity of demanding full knowledge and control of modern life.

MASQUERADES

Masquerade in urban public life was often literal. Balls and parties in mask and costume, often lasting into the early hours of the morning, were increasingly popular among the middle and upper classes of St. Petersburg in the early twentieth century. In the fall of 1907, for example, at the large Aquarium café chantant, the first in a series of annual masquerade balls was held.[5] Around each New Year, varied civic organizations would organize masquerade balls for their members or the public.[6] Carnival (*maslenitsa*) and other seasonal holidays also served as occasions, if occasion was needed, to organize "society" masquerade balls, which were held in theaters such as the Malyi or at popular pleasure sites for the well-off such as the ice-skating rink in the Iusupov Gardens or the Roller-Skating Rink on Mars Field.[7] Participants might disguise themselves in simple dominos, or as characters ranging from harlequins, to European knights and ladies, to ancient Romans or Persians or Chinese. Hired performers, also usually in masks, would sing and dance on stage and cavort with the masked crowd. Masks of all sorts were to be seen: black half-masks over the top of the face, full masks presenting a new face, and (on women) black veils covering the entire face and head.[8]

In masquerade, the unknown is often a means of pleasure, play, and experimentation, including sexual. Every writer about Russian masquerade, from reporters to poets, emphasized the undercurrent of sexuality that pervaded masquerades and that arose from the allure and danger of the unseen and the unknown. An etiquette manual, for example, observed in an entry on masquerade balls that "in human nature lies a unique craving for all things secretive, unknown, and mysterious."[9] In a book on the Petersburg night, the writer N. V. Nikitin similarly noted, with both moral dismay and salacious fascination, the permeating presence of the sexual at masquerades. The "mask itself invites acquaintance," often leading to more intimate meetings in private rooms. The "secretive mask," he clearly implied, heightened sensual allure precisely by nurturing an aura of the unknown.[10] Hiding the face accentuated the body. When worn by women, who were most likely to be masked, even when many men were not, masks were said to draw the male gaze downward, especially when masked women wore low-cut, revealing dresses or other sexualized clothing. Nikitin speaks of masquerades being frequented by "babes" (*bebe*) and other "frivolous creatures" in short dresses or in exotic costumes made of loose-flowing garments that were alluring precisely in hiding a woman's figure.[11] A "modernist" (according to a journalist's definition) painting at an exhibit in 1913, reprinted in a popular illustrated magazine, made the linkage between masks and sex explicit: a woman in a black mask poses alluringly with her dress open to display her breasts.[12] The Petersburg painter and graphic artist Konstantin Somov, who may have been that unnamed "modernist," was particularly fascinated by the sexuality associated with masks and masquerades.[13] And so was the popular press, which reported on masquerade balls for the pleasure of readers not likely to be able to afford them. The whole atmosphere of masquerades, *Peterburgskii listok* reported in 1914, was pervaded by "masked intrigues and quite 'piquant' talk."[14] As one magazine writer joked, a masquerade was a "suspicious place" to bring one's wife, though not to bring someone else's wife.[15] Behind this joke were real stories that often ended in unhappiness and even tragedy, as when a woman whose fiancé was dallying with another confronted them at a masquerade ball and demonstratively swallowed poison.[16] These stories remind us of what theorists have said about modern masquerade: these were performative sites of "strangeness, transformation, and mystery," pervaded by "pleasure, women, sex, and the unknown," even a deliberately constructed "terra incognita at the heart of civilized life" that was both "delightful and pernicious" in its "association with mystification and intrigue."[17] The pleasure to be had in the darkness of uncertainty also contained a threat.

Masquerades on stage doubled the performative nature of wearing a mask. Theatricalized masquerades also tended to highlight the mixed allure and terror of the unknown. On 3 December 1908, for example, Leonid Andreev's new play *Black Masks (Chernye maski)* opened at Vera Kommis-

sarzhevskaia's influential theater on Ofitserskaia Street. Set exotically in a
old castle in Italy, the play told of a count tormented during his own masquerade ball by uninvited and unknown guests in black masks but also by
the stranger uncertainty of not being sure who was masked and who was
not.[18] The play was staged with "primitive" and "doleful" music and with
lighting so pervasively dark that some critics said they could not tell who
was who or what was going on. To be sure, this criticism was sometimes
just a complaint—one critic quipped that the theater might have saved itself
money and not bothered with makeup or costumes. But others perceived
symbolism in this, a reflection of the "darkness," uncertainties, and "masquerade" of identities often said to mark the character of modern urban life
just outside the theater walls. The symbolism of the play's constant refrain,
"Who are they?" the repeated complaints about "deception" (*obman*), and
the talk of the suspicious, sometimes "repulsive" but also often "enchant-
ing," masks on the faces of "strangers" were all tropes to be seen again and
again in stories about masks and masquerade, both in literature and, as we
shall see, in newspaper reports about the masquerades of daily life. One insightful critic viewed Andreev's play as exploring the "double nature of the
human personality" (*razdvoenie lichnosti*): seeing the "vileness" that lurks
beneath surface appearances, realizing that "in everything is lies, on everyone masks" (*vo vsem lozh', na vsem maski*)—an echo of Nikolai Gogol's
famous cry in "Nevskii Prospect" that "it is all deceit, all a dream, not at
all what it seems!" (*vse obman, vse mechta, vse ne to, chem kazhetsia!*), but
also, by then, a journalistic cliché—and recognizing that even one's own
identity was uncertain.[19] A more hostile critic judged the play as itself a
mask trying to hide mere "charlatanism, emptiness, stupid nonsense, and
pretentiousness."[20]

The influential director Vsevolod Meyerhold was especially fascinated
by masks. He hoped to create an entire "theater of masks," which, as Katerina Clark has discussed, was at the heart of his theory of modern drama, in
which visual illusion and play, set deliberately at odds with ordinary reality, raise the philosophical question of what, especially in the modern, is
real and what is illusory.[21] In 1906, Meyerhold staged Blok's *Balaganchik*
(Fairbooth Show) which blended a modernist embrace of self-conscious

artifice with the popular traditions of commedia dell'arte and Russian street theater.[22] In 1912, he began work on a new staging of Mikhail Lermontov's classic exploration of the power and peril of disguise, *Masquerade* (1835), for the Imperial Aleksandrinskii Theater, just off Nevskii Prospect.[23] The play's tropes were all keynotes in masquerade. Masks emphasize the body: masked figures "are without soul or title—there is just body." Masks set loose the emotional self: "when features are concealed by a mask / Then feelings are boldly unmasked." And masks set morality loose: masked figures revel in their "ghostly" anonymity and the power it seems to give them to play at moral transgression—"the barrier between good and evil has been pulled down," the play's hero, Arbenin, observes at the end of Act 2. But masked figures could also see more clearly and thus warn and prophesy, as does a nameless stranger ("Neizvestnyi") who remains a mystery even with his mask removed, though he insists that he is Arbenin's ghostly alternative self and spurned conscience, suggesting again that masks also reveal aspects of the self. Ultimately, the story leads to death, linked to deception. Arbenin, as hero, arrogantly believes that he can distinguish appearance and truth amidst this often amorous play of masks, and accuses his wife, mistakenly, of unfaithfulness. In the end, it is the impossibility of removing masks that remains most true. It seems that life is nothing but a "charade," that "it is all deception (*a tseloe—obman*)."[24]

   While masquerade balls and the theater were generally for people with money and position, the less privileged were also witness to the power and threat of performances in mask. The most literally performative of these were the hugely popular spectacles of masked wrestlers.[25] Here, too, we see the typical mixture of strangeness, the unknown, and the allure of the body. The most salient example was the appearance at the wrestling matches at the Cinizelli Circus in 1909 of an "elegantly dressed stranger" (*neznakomets*) wearing a black mask over his head and face proclaiming that he was ready to wrestle any and all opponents. He called himself "Black Mask" (*Chernaia Maska*) and the newspapers and the public were thrilled. "Who is he?" reporters cried. For days the circus was filled with crowds as the mysterious "Black Mask" fought and beat all challengers. Commentators agreed that the mask itself gave him power. "The mask, the mystery, the fact that his opponents don't know his name—is a great plus in combat."[26]

Hence his declared unwillingness to be unmasked and named until someone could defeat him.[27]

On the streets, wearing masks also gave people performative power,
especially when they had crime in mind. According to one newspaper, "the
appearance of people in masks on the streets or in public places is no longer news; everyone has become used to this and no longer even notices a
mask."[28] Though this was certainly an exaggeration, it was true that masked
robbers breaking into homes and businesses was increasingly common.[29]
For example, at the very moment when the public was so fascinated by the
still unknown "Black Mask" wrestler, a gangster leader (*ataman*) was being
called by the same mysterious name. This criminal "Black Mask" headed
a gang of robbers, all wearing masks, who regularly held up stores and taverns in the city. The renown of this mysterious gang leader was enhanced
by his deliberate attention to appearance—not only by the black masks his
gang wore when in action, but also by their always "respectable [*prilichno*]
attire" and by what even victims agreed was a carefully cultivated "correctness and even courtesy" toward those being robbed.[30] A journal article of
1911 titled "Black Masks" (in this case, focusing on so-called anarchist-
expropriators) highlighted the sense that masks were symbols of the illegibility of public life: "Specters roam among us," the author melodramatically
warned. "Who are they, these black masks?" We *see* them, he answered, but
we *know* little, for they are protean and constantly changing.[31]

Masquerade was also at the center of the most important literary text
from those years about St. Petersburg, Andrei Belyi's novel *Petersburg*,
which first appeared in print in 1913.[32] Masked figures, but also faces about
which it is not entirely clear whether they are masked or not, weave through
the novel's flux of images. Like other Russian modernist writers,[33] Belyi
had long been preoccupied with the cultural and psychological significance of the mask—especially concerning truth and the self (and the self's
"others," including its internal other). In poems, stories, and essays written between 1903 and 1913, including an essay simply titled "The Mask,"
masked figures appear repeatedly as symbols of sexuality, the unknown, the
troubled and divided self, danger, revolution, and, especially, death. For Belyi, masks speak philosophically about surface illusion and the threshold
beyond which lurks the "hidden unknown" (*taiashchie nevedomoe*) and the

"abyss." And, for Belyi, the mask was also personal. Belyi described himself as masked: as Boris Bugaev, which was his real name, "peering from under the mask of 'Andrei Belyi.'"[34]

These ideas and concerns were all developed in *Petersburg*. Naturally, masks appear at masquerade balls—it is ostensibly to attend such a ball that the hero, Nikolai Ableukhov, orders his notorious red domino. But more interesting are the many appearances of masked figures, including the red domino, on the city's streets, along with "unknown strangers" (*neizvestnye*), with people who were somehow "vague and indistinct," and with individuals with mask-like faces. And when such figures appear, their presence resonates with the interpretation of masks in the public press: deception, illusion, uncertainty, and moral danger, though also the pleasures of transgression. Masks in *Petersburg* signal, in the novel's own terminology, perplexity, mystery, strangeness, confusion, illusion, phantasms, the inexpressible, and chaos, especially the incomprehensible chaos of the street.[35] Visible and present reality in the novel continually "blurs" in a typical Petersburgian fog of phantasmata, shadows, and masks. As Nikolai Ableukhov puts it, "everything's real, yet not quite real."[36] Cognitive and epistemological uncertainty, the phantasmic nature of the world outside oneself and within, is inescapable. Images, thoughts, feelings, and even people are only surface phenomena. Behind them is a more essential "cerebral play" (*mozgovaia igra*). And yet, Belyi contended, "cerebral play is only a mask; beneath this mask the brain is invaded by forces unknown to us."[37] For Belyi, of course, this all grew out of a philosophy of existence and cognition influenced by theosophy, anthroposophy, and other intellectual interests. Also, like many modernists, Belyi found this world of illusion to be not without allure, as a space where imagination and possibility are liberated from conventional forms and boundaries, even as a free and inspiring Dionysian chaos like the "blurring of bodies in dance."[38] But these ideas cannot be separated from Belyi's awareness of the street-level narratives of everyday city life, especially as reported and interpreted in the daily press. The masks of *Petersburg*, the novel, and their meanings, were entwined with the masks of Petersburg, the city.

Anna Akhmatova, writing retrospectively about her native Petersburg, viewed the year 1913, which she considered emblematic of the Russian moment before the apocalypse of war and revolution, as a year in which masks were everywhere.[39] No doubt, Akhmatova's image of this year of masks—the year, appropriately, that Meyerhold declared might be the moment when a modern "theater of masks" would finally be created[40]—was drawn from the accumulation of literary images, including the imaginary masquerades of Andreev, Blok, Belyi, and others. As we have seen, the literature of St. Petersburg had long dwelled on the city's characteristic illusoriness, indeterminacy, unreality, and deceit—its essentially masked nature, or what Vladimir Toporov called its *mirazhnost'*, its "mirageness."[41] Scores of minor poets whose work appeared in newspapers and magazines also dwelled on "the city" and "the street" as marked by "shadows," "darkness," "mystery," "secrets," "vague faces," and "masks."[42] Akhmatova surely knew how pervasive masquerade and talk of masquerade was in St. Petersburg's everyday life (as did Belyi, who playfully "quoted" in his novel newspaper reports about sightings of the mysterious masked domino on the streets of the capital). And she likely knew that the press tended to view the mask as a symbol of illusion, deception, darkness, and uncertainty, as well as of moral transgression. The difference was that for most journalists—who were more moderns than modernists—the "masquerades" of public daily life were not a productive, Dionysian chaos, but a sign of tangible danger and crisis.

CONFIDENCE GAMES

The city of strangers was made stranger still, and more dangerous, by also being a city of masks, of uncertain appearance. External markings such as dress and bearing, journalists and other urban observers continually complained, had ceased to be reliable signs of identity. In particular, the symbolic code in which "proper and respectable" (*prilichnyi*) dress signified social and moral respectability—a code constantly referred to if only to express dismay at its violation and failure—seemed to be disintegrating. Every day, the press reported stories of "respectably dressed" (*prilichnye odetye*)— even elegantly dressed—men and women who turned out to be dangerous thieves, con artists, or predators. The adjective *prilichnyi* punctuates these accounts, for its moral meanings of propriety, orderliness, and worthiness were precisely what had become so elusive in city life.[43] "The most terrible thing," the commentator Skitalets wrote in *Gazeta-kopeika* in 1910, "is that there is no guide to help you, so that from a person's outer appearance you can't really say with any certainty who is before you" socially or morally.[44] Vision could no longer be trusted. Surface appearance was often a mask.

Numerous writers similarly voiced their distress at discovering that physical appearance was often a mask, that "correctness" sometimes "conceals distasteful moral murk," that refined elegance sometimes only "masks immoral purposes,"[45] that even "dandies" wearing new, tailored suits, diamond rings, and "chic" monocles, and visiting the city's very best cafés and restaurants, might be from among the city's "dark operators" (*del'tsy temnogo Peterburga*).[46] Again and again it was observed that "dark personalities" raised "no suspicions" in the eyes of their victims because their dress and manners said that they posed no danger.[47] However naive it may seem to us, early twentieth-century Russian commentators found visual and moral dissonance when decent dress did not signify real decency and saw in this a troubling symbol of the nature of modern life. Again and again urban writers declared their dismay—but also their informed and skeptical warning—that one simply could not tell who was honest and who evil just by "looking at them."[48] The same applied to the physical and social landscape of the city itself. What might look like an honest tearoom or a civic club (for bicycle enthusiasts, for instance), might in fact—once you "raised the curtain"—turn out to be an "abyss" (*bezdna*) of crime, debauchery, or prostitution.[49]

City dwellers were regularly victimized by confidence games and other swindles (*afery* and *moshennichestva*) that depended on the possibility and power of masquerade in the public sphere of strangers. Swindlers and con artists were usually "respectably dressed," part of the mask worn in a performance designed to "snare the simpletons," as one reporter put it with a telling confidence that the knowledgeable would never fall for such cons.[50] More often, however, readers were informed that the carefully cultivated visual signs of honesty ensured that that "no one suspected"—a leitmotif in these reports. The variety of swindlers who took advantage of persistent beliefs in established signs of visual display in order to masquerade as people who could be trusted, was great: thieves, burglars, pickpockets, shoplifters, beggars, bait-and-switch artists, and pretenders (*samozvantsy*) of all sorts.

Street thieves, for example, made use of the presumed semiotics of dress to disarm their victims visually and hence interpretively. In early January 1910, a merchant heading from the Finland station to a local hotel was approached by two "respectably dressed" women whom he saw no reason to fear—here, as in many cases, out-of-date assumptions about gender were entwined with assumptions about dress. One greeted him warmly and began to kiss him while the other started going through his pockets. When the man shouted for help, the woman kissed him on the mouth to silence him. After her accomplice extricated his wallet they fled.[51] Very often, such assaults on the street by "strangers" (*neznakomtsy*)—a ubiquitous formula in these reports—were less entertaining. Or, rather, the entertainment that came from reading these sensational reports was as disturbing as it was diverting. Certain street thieves targeted newcomers to the city, who were the most likely to trust naively in appearance. When two young women from Vitebsk province, for example, arrived at the train station in St. Petersburg with the purpose of looking for work, they were stopped by a "respectably dressed gentleman and lady"—also described simply as "strangers"—who offered them domestic work, promising good conditions. Taking separate cabs—with one unknown riding with each of the girls—and traveling for a long time along various "streets and alleys," they finally stopped in some "dark alley" by the gate of a "gloomy house." As soon as the girls stepped out of the carriages, however, the cab drivers whipped up their horses and sped away with the lady and gentleman as well as the newcomers' belongings, including the money with which they had planned to start new lives for themselves in Petersburg.[52]

Pickpockets were a different category of masked street thieves. They generally tried to be entirely invisible to their victims. Some, however, found it useful to draw attention to themselves, or rather to their masquerades. For example, using a modus operandi dubbed the "sham uncle" (*mnimyi diadushka*), a middle-aged man would stop a young man on the street and warmly embrace his "nephew." When the "mistake" was clear, the "uncle" politely apologized and departed, having picked the "nephew's" pocket.[53]

Similarly, according to a chronicler of urban crime, who wrote under the pseudonym Aborigine (his self-identity as knowledgeable native seems to have come from police work in St. Petersburg), a whole special category of pickpockets known in criminal slang as *marvikhery* were distinguished by their high-class dress, manner, and place of work: "If you met [a *marvikher*] at the theater, or at a ball, or in society you would invariably take him for an important gentleman [*barin*]. He dresses splendidly and conducts himself with dignity. You might encounter him at an opening night, at the opera, or at a charity bazaar." His "work" was stealing billfolds from men's pockets.[54] Sometimes, the performances of pickpockets drew too much attention. At the tram stop by the Kazan Cathedral on Nevskii Prospect, police noticed with suspicion a young man dressed in an "elegant suit" who "gave the impression of being a rich foreigner." He carried an "elegant cane made of red wood" decorated with a likeness of a deer's head with big horns. Pushing through the crowd as if to board the tram, he deftly picked pockets as he went. After his arrest, he was identified as Ivan Volynkin, a renowned pickpocket who had been recently "working" in Germany, until he was arrested and deported.[55]

Shoplifters, too, were almost invariably "well dressed," in order to pretend to be customers.[56] No one suspected, for example, a "respectably dressed lady" who entered a clothing shop, chose her purchases, and then asked the shop boy to accompany her to her furnished apartment for payment. While the boy waited outside, she fled through the back staircase (in Russian called the "black staircase"). She had rented the room that morning, promising the landlord to return later with her belongings and the rent.[57] The press regularly reported these "sham" or "imaginary" shoppers (*mnimye pokupateli*).[58] In one reported case, this con was the work of a whole "thieves' school" for girls, headed by a "professor" and "lady professor" (*professorsha*) of robbery and pickpocketing. Among other skills, girls were taught how to appear in shops "under the guise of customers."[59]

Begging could also involve a masquerade of respectability. Of course, from ancient times begging has been a practice, rooted in social need and traditions of charity, that attracted fraud. Most often masquerade in begging involved the pretense of poverty or physical handicap—a performance enhanced variously with rags, bandages, and crutches. Periodically the press would unmask such healthy "cripples" and "rich beggars."[60] At the same time, there existed a special type of beggar whose pity-evoking performance required more respectable dress. According to one account, "in most cases, he is quite well dressed, has gracious [*blagorodnyi*] manners, and with his respectable [*imponiruiushchim*] appearance deludes the trusting public." He might work by a food store, for example, where he "politely" appeals for help for his "hungry family," or by a pharmacy, where he speaks of a wife who needs medicine, or by a bakery where he tells of children without bread. Both men and women engaged in such performances. According to seasoned observers—evoking a claim to knowledge that could always unmask deceit—such types were visibly fakes, for true need is always "modest" and quiet and usually unrewarded while these aggressive masquerades of need reaped all the benefits of people's gullibility and pity.[61]

Some of these confidence games were relatively simple and classic. A bait-and-switch *afera* reported in 1909 was typical. A boy working for a shopkeeper in the Apraksin market was sent to a bank to deposit more than a hundred rubles. On the way, he was stopped on the street by young men who noticed his bundle wrapped in newspaper, as was the custom. "God has granted us happiness," the strangers declared, and said they wanted to share their good fortune. They showed the boy a wrapped bundle which was allegedly filled with money and asked about his package, which the boy showed them, saying it was not his own money. They handed it back to the boy and left him. On later opening his bundle the boy was horrified to discover that his package had been switched for one filled with newspaper and a few copper coins.[62] The papers were full of similar stories of switched packages or dropped wallets (as prelude to a switch)—all performed, of course, by "respectably dressed" men and women.[63]

Swindling was a democratic crime: swindlers came from all levels of society, so did their victims, and so did the social references and assumptions around which swindlers built their performances. In 1911, the papers described what one editor grandiosely titled "Swindle of the Twentieth Century." A certain Sigizmund Poplavskii—reportedly born a nobleman in Tiflis—developed an elaborate fraud involving first buying life insurance in his own name, which he was able to collect on (using various false documents) by pretending that a friend of his who died was in fact himself and

that he was the heir, and then taking out a new policy in the name of his
late friend, registering another dying man (somehow taken from a hospital)
in that name, and then collecting on the second policy. When he was arrested, Poplavskii was preparing to repeat this whole "dead souls" scam a
third time. After his unmasking, it was learned that he also managed, in the
course of these successive swindles, to marry two women simultaneously,
under two of his assumed identities.[64] In a similar but more brutal scheme,
the masquerade of one's own death in order to collect insurance involved
murder and the exchange of identities.[65] Another con artist, who was also
honored with the title "swindler of the twentieth century" as well as characterized as a "special Petersburg type," was a nattily dressed "dandy" (*frant*)
who focused on financial swindles of people in high society.[66] Working a
more modest social milieu, Elena Kuz'mina—legally registered as a peasant
from Pskov province, though she possessed a number of false passports, including some registering her in the urban petty-bourgeois (*meshchanskoe*)
estate—would pretend to be waiting to collect an inheritance but claimed
to need some money to help her collect it, which she said she would return along with part of the inheritance to those who "helped" her.[67] And
there were proletarian swindles, such as the "con man–laborer" (*aferist-
chernorabochii*) who took a job without turning in his passport—"I will give
it to you very soon," he promised the manager—and then disappeared with
money he was asked to change at a bank,[68] or the weeping young working
woman who approached passersby with a made-up but convincing story of
having lost a package that she was supposed to deliver for her brutal boss
and begged money to replace the lost item,[69] or the widespread "podkidka"
("finding") swindle that targeted lower-class men: when a passerby notices
a "diamond" ring, another man claims to have seen the ring at the same moment and to recognize its value, but is willing to let the first man pay a share
of the presumed value to keep the ring, which the victim discovers, when
pawning it, to be worth only kopecks.[70]

Even the police, who were responsible for knowing and controlling
urban public life, were sometimes targeted in confidence games (though
they were not always convinced by them), as in the many reported cases
of "simulated theft" (*simuliatsiia grabezha*). For example, a worker named
Aleksei Ivanov appeared at a police station at 3 A.M., his clothes torn with

knife cuts and his hand bleeding, reporting that he had been walking near 74 Obvodnyi Canal Street with a package of 79 rubles he was delivering for his employer (a candy distributor) when two "unknown men" demanded that he hand over his money, threatening him with knives. He refused and fought back, the worker testified, but lost the battle and the money was now gone.[71] There were many such cases. One "victim" even performed for the police an entire fictional dialogue between himself and some "hooligans" who attacked him and "stole" his money.[72] Of course, such performances depended on the fact that "daring street robberies" did often occur and were regularly reported in the press. Here, as was so often the case, the illusion depended on its convincing relationship to reality.

Not only theft but violence and death could approach in mask. In the summer of 1908, for example, a young man introduced himself in church to an elderly and pious former teacher and told her that he had been unemployed for months, had no money, but wished to study. Trusting, she invited him to her home, fed him, and offered him free lessons. On arriving the next day, he crushed her head with a heavy cobblestone. While the old woman lay on the floor in a pool of blood, he demanded to know where she kept her money.[73] Such violence, the newspapers regularly observed with dismay, often came at the hands of "respectably dressed" people.[74] Even murder, the papers repeatedly and melodramatically suggested, lurked behind masks of propriety. Suicide also could be a masquerade—performances echoing real stories reported daily in the press. The press regularly reported "sham suicides" (*mnimye samoubiistva*), such as that of a woman who, in 1915, stood at a crowded spot on Nevskii Prospect, crying out to passersby, "Oh Lord, how many meek doves there are in Petrograd!" then walked into a nearby pharmacy and bought liquid ammonia and drank some of it while standing on the bridge over the Ekaterininskii canal. She screamed and fell to the ground. In the hospital she told a story about being a refugee from Dvinsk (during the war the papers were full of stories of the hardships of refugees from the front), a narrative performed, the paper reported, "with a dying voice." She won the sympathy of a nurse who took her home to her apartment on Liteinaia Street to care for her until she was well. Soon, the "refugee" stole many items from the apartment and disappeared to find new victims for her performance.[75] Of course, these performances cannot always be reduced to simple deceit for the purposes of gain. Just as the "refugee" above may indeed have been a refugee, so too were other "sham suicides" real acts of despair, reflecting, for example, the desire of a hungry person to be fed while in the hospital or of a lonely and anonymous person to see their name in the paper.[76]

Even a casual reader of the "daily chronicle" columns of the newspapers would be impressed both by the endless repetition of confidence games and by the endless innovation. Commentators emphasized the familiar in these scams, sometimes adding that it is only the "brainlessness" of so many Petersburgers that lets them fall for tricks already played hundreds of times and regularly reported in the press.[77] But newspapers also noted the limitless variety and considerable skill. Reports were often titled, or used the phrase "lovkii moshennik,"[78] emphasizing the "cunning" and "deftness" involved, and newspapers clearly liked to report the more innovative and spectacular cons. Insistence that only "brainless" "simpletons" were susceptible to these confidence tricks was itself a demonstrative act of confidence in the face of the many unknowns of city life.

IDENTITY PERFORMANCES

The dangerous uncertainties of the city were especially evident in the many criminal performances of identity. Making ill-intentioned use of the epistemological mystery of urban public life, its plenitude of strangers and the unknown, and its multitude of possible situations, stories, and opportunities, numerous men and women complicated city life still further with their own simulated identities and stories. In the language of the press, the identities of these men and women were not real but "mnimye"—imaginary, seeming, pretend. They were not their real selves, but "samozvantsy"—pretenders, frauds, imposters, literally those who name themselves. Newspapers were filled with stories of "mnimye" architects, publishers, journalists, lawyers, doctors, priests, actors, businessmen, military officers, government officials, noblemen, police detectives, postmen, delivery boys, renters, solicitors of charity, servants, matchmakers, plumbers, electricians, and repairmen. The purpose of these performances was mainly to extort money from

the gullible or to enter homes for the purpose of robbery.[79] These displays
of performed identity were so ubiquitous in the years after 1905 that one
journalist described the problem as a "mass epidemic."[80]

Relatively simple and common, though quite varied, were masquerades that enabled entry to the apartments of the wealthy. *Peterburgskii listok*, in 1913, noted the appearance of a gang of "con men-pretenders"—
described ambivalently as both "very dangerous" and as impressively
"cunning"—who appear at the doors of elegant apartments in the guise of
plumbers and report a leak to the floor below. Admitted to look at the boiler,
they advise the owner that it is defective but they will return tomorrow to
replace it, which they do (suggesting skills that made their performance not
purely fictive), taking with them the old boiler as well as many valuables.[81]
Another "plumber" advised residents in expensive apartments that the
pipes in the building were damaged and that the water supply would have
to be shut off for repair, so that residents should quickly gather what water
they could in basins and buckets. Since the "outward appearance of the
stranger did not arouse suspicion," everyone followed his advice. During
the confusion of collecting water, the stranger stole as much as he could
gather.[82] The pretense of taking a job as a servant with the goal of robbery
was especially common. For example, a well-known thief named Antonina
Guseva would in this way gain entry to high-class apartments in order to
let her gang in to steal valuables. This "predator" (*khishchnitsa*) used many
names and held numerous false passports.[83] Other masquerades used for
gaining entry included friendly visitors arriving when only servants are at
home (their proper, even lordly, outer appearance arouses no suspicion and
they are let in supposedly to leave the master or mistress a note), men pretending to court young women in order to steal from their parents, prospec-
tive "renters" looking over a furnished room in an apartment (and manag-
ing to lift various items while looking around), even "monks" distributing
religious tracts.[84] A number of confidence artists made use of the modern
and anonymous device of the telephone to perform false identities: a caller
might pretend to be a well-known journalist asking for help for a certain
ailing and impoverished actor who would later arrive to collect the contribution (in this case, the "impoverished actor" identity may have been

real).[85] There seemed to be no end to the variety of such impersonations; but whatever the particular narrative, these *aferisty* with their performed identities all shared the ability to make profitable use of the mass of possible everyday narratives, and the growing uncertainties of visual knowledge, in the modern city and then, before being apprehended, disappear, as one reporter put it, "into the blue fog" of the metropolis.[86]

Masquerade gave its perpetrators power—physical and psychological power for masked wrestlers, sexual power for women at masked balls, the power to evoke pity for sham beggars, the power of access and persuasion for many types of con men and thieves. Appropriately, very many of those who made use of borrowed identities chose from among identities imbued with actual social power: representatives of the established power elite, such as government officials or aristocrats, but mostly businessmen and professionals. Of course, most of these identities were male.

The performative wearing of uniforms to which one was not entitled had grown to "epidemic" proportions, the press observed in 1910, reflected sometimes in several arrests a day.[87] Here the hierarchical traditionalism of Russian society, where uniforms were still ubiquitous as markers of occupation and rank, clashed directly with the flux of modern life. Military uniforms were especially useful for criminal masquerades. For example, one peasant with no connection to the military was arrested on Nevskii Prospect after he repeatedly used his uniform to avoid paying at restaurants.[88] Other "pretenders" acted the parts of various government officials, also often in the appropriate uniforms. One "dangerous pretender," for example, carefully reads the newspapers for reports of lost or stolen items and then appears before the victim as a police detective to report that the items have been found but that a reward has to be paid to the finder, which he will deliver. The victim happily pays the officer, but upon arriving at the police station to collect the goods, learns that nothing has been found and the "officer" is unknown to them.[89]

Pretending to be titled aristocrats was frequent. One such "sham prince" (*mnimyi kniaz'*), whose external appearance gave no cause to suspect that he was not, as he claimed, a Prince Urusov representing the moderately liberal Octobrist party's student faction, showed up at the apartments of wealthy Petersburgers, including a number of Octobrist deputies to the Duma, offering tickets for a charity concert. Only when several Duma deputies and other supporters of the party showed up at the concert hall to be told by the porter that there was no such event did they discover that they had fallen for a confidence trick just like any other gullible "ordinary citizens" (*obyvateli*).[90] Another "prince-*aferist*" led a whole "gang, whose members, by their external appearance, appeared to be very impressive gentlemen" and conducted their activities solely in "high society" (*svetskoe obshchestvo*). Visiting "fashionable restaurants," they deviously collected signatures with which to forge promissory notes.[91]

These identity frauds were mainly played out in the public sphere—indeed, it was the increasing flux and multiplicity of public life that gave these *aferisty* their countless narratives, places to perform them, and ways to disappear. Appropriately, most "pretenders" chose their fraudulent identities from occupations that were on the rise in public life, especially business and the professions. Establishing fictive businesses in order to extort money from gullible investors was a commonly reported method of operation. One Nikolai Maklakov, for example, was finally arrested in 1912 and charged with ninety-three counts of confidence games (*moshennichestvo*) and embezzlement, involving varied identities over several years. He repeatedly pretended to be opening some new business—a theater, an encyclopedia publishing house, a grain exporting firm, a business consulting bureau, among others—and he advertised in newspapers seeking to hire managers and employees. From each investor he collected a security deposit before vanishing. Ending up for a time in western Europe, having fled Russia to avoid arrest, he pretended to be the influential Duma deputy Nikolai Maklakov as a way of getting out of paying his hotel bill but eventually was deported.[92] Another fraudulent business "married" hundreds of couples whose legal right to wed had been questioned by the official authorities for various reasons. This firm, which advertised in newspapers, offered the services of a (crooked divorce) lawyer and a (defrocked) priest, provided convincing documents, and even had its own wedding chapel.[93] Another sham business, organized during the war, offered burial services: "morticians" would read obituaries in the newspapers and then show up at the homes of people in mourning and pretend to be from a funeral bureau, accepting an advance and promising to take care of all burial needs.[94] Just as there were sham government officials and sham businessmen, there was also at least one "sham revolutionary": in 1908, a woman, whose family faced eviction for not paying rent, had a friend pose as a member of a secret committee of the Socialist Revolutionary Party and warn the landlord, the owner of a tailoring shop, that a bomb would be thrown into his store if he evicted the family.[95] Again, like so many of these performances, this one drew its narrative structure and plausibility from real stories from the newspapers, which in turn reported these masquerades.

Publishing, especially since the easing of censorship after 1905, was one of the most important sites of Russia's developing public life, full of new opportunities as well as of political significance for the country's modernization. Appropriately, fictive publishing ventures were a popular scam. One "*aferist*-publisher" impressed his victims with his long hair, dark glasses, and general "outward appearance" that gave him the look of a proper "literary type." He rented a furnished office where he met with investors who each gave him between 75 and 300 rubles to start up a new book publishing house.[96] Another "pretender-*aferist*" claimed to be the editor of a Moscow sports magazine, *K sportu*—also invented—for which he had stationery printed. This imposture was made all the deeper and more sinister in the eyes of those who reported this story by the fact that the "editor" was a Jew named Itska Lur'e, pretending to be one Nikolai Solov'ev. He had come to St. Petersburg from Mogilev, in the Jewish Pale of Settlement, readers were told, "under the mask of a journalist-editor" for various "dark dealings" in the capital.[97]

The trope of the hidden Jew was an occasional subtheme in these stories of masked public selves.[98] Whenever a criminal was ethnically Jewish, special note of this fact was made in the newspaper reports, implicitly suggesting an aggravating aspect to his or her deception. An example was the "gang of cunning con men–Jews" who pretended to operate an international wholesale company in St. Petersburg known grandly as the Austrian-French Commercial Society, which promised to sell grain products abroad at a price better than could be obtained on the domestic market. Taking grain deliveries from trusting farmers with the promise to deliver payment when the grain sold, they in fact sold the grain immediately and kept the money, then closed up shop and moved on to another city.[99] The conventional and widely believed anti-Semitic stereotypes of Jewish cosmopolitanism, rootlessness, greed, and dishonesty all seemed to be confirmed by such stories, adding to their potency as signs of the dangers released by an increasingly open and fluid public life.

Money seemed to be the motive, at least on the surface, for most of these masquerades. But not always. In 1909, *Peterburgskii listok* reported the case of a "music teacher" who dressed in a pedagogical uniform, called himself "director," "titular councilor" (*titularnyi sovetnik*, a position in the official Table of Ranks that carried personal nobility), and "department head." His "St. Petersburg Department for Aid in the Provision of Musical Education to the Underprivileged" had no teachers or music but "hired" (though failed to pay) poor young women to work as clerks, whom the "teacher" would relate to "far from correctly."[100] Here, the evident pleasure of creating for oneself a new and prestigious identity, mixed with predatory sexuality, seems to have been enough of a reason for the performance.

Other cases similarly suggest masquerade for the sake of masquerade. One night in June 1910, amidst a huge fire in several apartment buildings on Ligovskaia Street—part of the wave of summer fires that afflicted the city annually—a "young man of educated appearance" (*intelligentnyi na vid*) appeared at one of the burning buildings and declared himself to be "an official on special assignment representing the inspector general [*revizor*], Senator Garin." He gave orders to firemen during the fire and then remained on site for several days, for which he insisted on free lodging, dispensing advice on insurance and other matters. He was arrested as a fraud only when the building caretaker (*dvornik*) grew suspicious—after being sent out for herring and vodka and not being paid back—and checked on his identity.[101]

Cases like this suggest an element that may well have been present in all identity masquerades: the pleasure of pretending to be someone else, especially someone with power over others. Even when material gain was the most obvious benefit of a scam, we need not assume that financial need was the only motive. The pleasure of transgressive play with alternative identities and the enjoyment of the power that disguise brought to its wearer were also part of the game.

NIGHT

Nighttime, illuminated only by artificial light, was a world of the "mirage."[102] Urban writers viewed the alluring, flickering, and false phantasmagoria of the city at night as the city's darkest mask. This was a distinctive temporal landscape. At night, the identities and rules of the day were especially unstable, allowing for greater adventure and experimentation, but also greater danger. The night was a "dark, mysterious world" in which moral hazards were both more numerous and harder to recognize: it was more difficult at night to see the "dark, slippery path" down which one might slide or to know that harm lay behind "mysterious smiles" and other temptations. Instead of the constant and relatively reasoned movement on the streets of St. Petersburg by day, it was said, the streets at night became a space filled with shadows and the unknown and a time that "conceals in itself every sort of secret." Particularly ominous was Nevskii Prospect at night. Men and women on Nevskii "masked themselves" to seduce one another. The darkness hid "mysterious professions" and "secret refuges." In the "half dark" of its electrically lit night, Nevskii swarmed with "pale masks of hungry beasts" and "blackened masks of vice and crime."[103]

The night was especially associated with the sexual dangers that lurked behind masks in the city. The men and women who preyed on young girls on the night streets did not look dangerous, it was said, with their nice clothes and friendly faces.[104] Very common, the press reported, were masquerades performed to lure innocent girls and young women into prostitution. Newspapers regularly reported cases—sometimes revealed in suicide notes—of kindly, "respectable ladies" (*pochtennye damy*) who, "under the guise" of offering work or a loan, "force" young women to participate in "loathsome orgies" in their "dens of iniquity" (*pritony*).[105] In 1910, *Peterburgskii listok* reported a characteristic story about the recently unmasked "salon" of "Madame X and Mr. Y." The proprietors played the "role" of running a " 'respectable' establishment." They would search the papers for advertisements such as "governess seeks work" or "desperately seeking work" (*ishchu mesto bol'no*), particularly for ads that mentioned that the job seekers spoke French or German or were graduates of good schools, and send these women letters inviting them to interview for a position. When the young woman arrived, she would be told that this was a large "salon" hosting guests every evening, some of them very rich, mostly artists seeking women to paint or sculpt. If a woman accepted (though some walked out, feeling insulted at the suggestion that they might pose nude for an artist) she would be paid an advance and invited to begin work the next evening. But when she arrived, she might be told that tonight was a musical evening with dancing and wine. The apartment, she learned, had many rooms with many "secrets." The young woman soon figured out what sort of a salon this was, but by then the advance had already been spent and she was trapped. A "new victim" had been caught, the reporter melodramatically concluded.[106] A similar operation offered girls work as apprentices in shops that were really only "screens" (*shirmy*) hiding upstairs "dens," where girls were sent on errands, forced to get drunk, undressed, and made to dance for the guests.[107] The place of newspaper ads in these stories was characteristic. *Gorodskoe delo*, the journal associated with the St. Petersburg city council, noted the likelihood that an answer to a girl's advertisement seeking work will lead to her "fall." Honest people rarely answer such ads, it was said, but sexual predators do, for they know the desperation of young women alone in the city and know that their disguises will not be noticed by these innocents until it is too late.[108]

Prostitutes were not always viewed as victims in these masquerades of illusion and deception. Behind their masks of service and submission— images linked to their profession but also to assumptions about gender— they could be quite predatory. Criminal slang had a special term for one such category of prostitute-cum-swindler: "khipesnits."[109] A story in *Gazeta-kopeika* in 1908 told a typical tale of male misfortune in the company of prostitutes. A man visiting St. Petersburg from the provinces sought out the company of the city's loose women. Accompanied by two "night fairies" (*nochnye fei*), singers at a café chantant, he spent the evening carousing at the Metropol restaurant on Ligovka Street before taking a room with the women. When he woke in the morning, the "fairies" and fifteen hundred rubles were missing.[110] According to Aborigine, the specialist on city crime, true examples of the "khipes" con were not women taking advantage of sexual liaisons with strange men by robbing them and disappearing while they slept,[111] but elaborately planned masquerades: a male "tomcat" (*kot*) would seek out rich married men as victims (for they would be unlikely to report the robbery so as to avoid personal scandal), having already rented a furnished apartment in which a chair for the customer's clothing had been placed near a locked door, which was perhaps hidden behind a curtain; while the victim and the "pussycat" (*koshka*) slept, he would slip out from behind the door and steal the man's money.[112]

Prostitutes were said to wear masks to lure customers, deluding men's "naive eyes" with "painted faces," "bought lips," false teeth, and alluring looks.[113] Their "eyes beckon and their smiles lie."[114] Most obvious was the mask of gaiety and pleasure. But there were also more instrumental masks, masks that gave a measure of power, especially those of unregistered, "secret" (*tainye*) prostitutes. "In recent years," one account noted, illegal prostitutes had begun to use all sorts of tricks and masquerades to lure susceptible men into liaisons that would lead to gifts, meals in restaurants, money for rent, and other payments: a "modest stranger" seeming innocently to drop a scarf on the street; "ladies dressed in mourning" seeking trusting men who would offer them "comfort"; ostensibly chance meetings with "elegant, stylish, and stimulating creatures" in railway cars; women deceptively advertising interest in marriage or romance in the personal columns of newspapers; and street "intrigues," often played out in the vicinity of the shopping complexes of Gostinnyi dvor or the Nevskii passazh at the hour when bankers and officials were leaving work, by women pretending to be the wives of poor officials or poor widows dreaming of being able to afford some item in a shop window.[115]

GENDER DISORDER

These stories of public masquerade were often entwined with disturbing signs of a new instability in gendered identity and power. To be sure, masks could reinforce and even enhance stereotypical attributes of gendered sexuality. When faces were covered, we have seen, the gendered body took on a new centrality. Women's "shapely figures" became all the more alluring when their faces were masked.[116] This applied to men as well. In press accounts of masked wrestlers, the mask seemed to draw particular attention to the wrestler's masculine physique: "his Herculean back, chest, and arms ... excited general amazement"; "his mammoth figure, wide shoulders, and long musculature built for combat—a remarkable body."[117] But masking also revealed "gender trouble"—an anxious awareness that the characteristics of male and female are malleable and performed.[118] We have already seen some of its signs: women criminals said to use assumptions about gender to disarm their victims, and women wearing various stereotypical masks to "lure" men into sex for money (though questions of agency and victimization remain ambiguous in these relations).

One of the most talked-about new phenomena were women dressed as men and men dressed as women—though here the masquerade was designed not to divert the gaze from something hidden, nor to pretend to be the opposite sex, but to unsettle normative assumptions about gender itself. Sometimes cross-dressing was a literal performance in costume and dependent on, though playing with, traditional models. At the Cinizelli Circus, for example, demonstration dancers included pairs of women, the "male" with short hair and outfitted in a tuxedo.[119] Cabarets featured cross-dressing "transformatory."[120] And, of course, in the realm of fin-de-siècle "high culture," the androgyne had become a cultural and spiritual ideal. Perhaps the most publicly visible performance of elite gender play was the cross-dressing of the poet Zinaida Gippius.[121] There were also everyday street performances of cross-dressing. Women wearing pants may seem a rather modest gesture, but it excited much public comment. The two leading columnists at *Gazeta-kopeika* both made particular note of the new fashion of women appearing in public in loose trousers (*sharovary*). People were shocked and protested, Skitalets noted, but why? Because skirts, like the different garments worn by people in India, marked women as part of a "different caste." Trousers, he implied, subverted and transgressed this gendered caste order. He predicted that this fashion would soon spread from the elite to other classes. Skitalets tried to defuse the dangerous transgression that others saw in women in pants by suggesting that trousers were simply more comfortable and, for certain occupations, more rational. Ol'ga

Gridina also recognized and then tried to deflect the anxieties evoked by women in trousers. Most newspaper feuilletonists and most of the public, she admitted, reacted to the image of women in pants with nervous "jokes and piquant laughter." But really, she argued rationalistically, people ought to be concerned about the harmful economic effect this new fashion would have on people producing women's clothing.[122]

The press did indeed enjoy treating gender confusion as a joke. Characteristic was this imagined "modern" calling card: "A. A. Zeus. Modernist Writer. He is a She."[123] Like much humor, of course, the jokes reflected a certain anxiety. Women dressed as men, even partially, stimulated concerns about the changing place of women in public life. All over the world, a reporter noted in an article simply titled "Woman-Man," women are seeking to work in previously male domains, for which they sometimes go so far as to pretend to be men.[124] In a telling rumor (which turned out to be false), it was reported that the killers of Marianna Time in 1913—one of the most notorious murder cases in the city in these years—were two young women dressed as men "to mask their traces."[125] Particularly worrisome were men wearing the clothing and cosmetics of women, especially when this suggested transgressions of sexual as well as gender norms. In his 1908 book on the homosexual subculture of St. Petersburg, V. P. Ruadze offered the example of the well-known homosexual Kurochkin, who headed a gay "den" located on the elegant Furshtadtskaia Street and could be seen walking along city streets "masquerading" in "extravagant" women's fashions.[126] Of course, such masquerade was not a disguise but a performance, a visible transgression, a proclamation of difference. What was threatening was what the mask revealed, not what it hid. At one time, all "gomoseksualizm" had been hidden, and much of it still was. But now, Ruadze wrote with dismay, it walks about the city streets extravagantly advertising itself.[127]

While masks were seen to enhance women's sexual power, much ambivalence remained in these stories. We see this, for example, in a serialized newspaper novel given the ambiguous title *Ch'ia zhertva* ("Whose Sacrifice?" or "Whose Victim?"). Written by an author who claimed to be a woman and an aristocrat, it told the melodramatic tale of a beautiful young Russian woman named Mariia who entered the demimonde of loose pleasures and money under the ambiguously foreign name of Mary Bel'skaia.

Everyone asked, with an evident thrill, "Who is she? From where?" This
stranger insisted that she was none other than her new, created self: "Why
do you need to know who I am or where I'm from. For you I am simply
Mary Bel'skaia, a cheerful singer from the garden of happiness." Men found
this performance alluring: as one admiring count declared, she was "a miraculous fairy, who has just flown in from some fairytale world in order to
delight the eye." Clearly, power was constructed out of mystery, though not
far removed from gender norms. But this forged identity and its gendered
power also masked a quite different female experience. Embedded in this
performance of delighting femininity was darkness and tragedy—the "reality" of her life in this fictional narrative but constructed of well-known stories from daily life. "Mary" masked a female experience that Mariia wished
to discard but could not deny: a brutal childhood of cold and hunger with
a violent drunken father and an unknown mother, escape into no less abusive conditions as an apprentice seamstress, and then life on the streets as
a prostitute until she found escape of sorts in the high-class sexual role of
Mary Bel'skaia. When she revealed this true self to a man she loved, removing for once the "mask of innocence and moral decency" that hid this
real history and its wounds, he rejected her. He "loved" only her mask, she
learned.[128]

MODERNITY IN MASK

The whole of the modern city, writers intoned, was dominated by a "spirit
of deceit" (*dukh obmana*).[129] St. Petersburg, in particular, was viewed as a
masked city. A guidebook for visitors and residents of the capital described
the city as the most beautiful of European capitals but warned that this
elegant display hid real conditions—swampy soils, polluted waters, and a
harmful climate—that made every resident physically ill. A writer in *Gorodskoe delo* went further and described the backwardness "hidden" behind
the city's "external tinsel," which made it only a "likeness of a western European" city. And he blamed the city's modern rulers and residents, not its
natural conditions or its founder: a lack of concern by the powers that be for
sanitary needs or for the lives of the majority of the population, chaos and
disorder rather than any planned development, and the "apathy" of most

city residents.[130] Numerous writers about St. Petersburg said the same. Older critiques of Russia's new capital as a performance of westernization, a façade, a mask falsely signifying Europe and civilization,[131] intensified amidst the crises and uncertainties of the early twentieth century. This was a city that merely looked the part of a European city, Dmitrii Merezhkovskii bitingly wrote in the newspaper *Rech'* in 1908, in the way Smerdiakov, the illegitimate son in *The Brothers Karamazov*, looked, in Dostoevsky's words, "like a most respectable foreigner."[132]

The mask that St. Petersburg wore, however, was recognized to be a feature of its modernity, not just of a distinctive Petersburgian narrative. At the very least, it was said, city dwellers all "wear masks on their souls."[133] Indeed, the whole city should be defined by its characteristic "urban deceit."[134] The street, in particular, was a site of continual masquerade: by day, a smiling but existentially bored crowd that could only "simulate happiness and satisfaction"; by night pervasive illusion and "self-deception."[135] Others looked at the whole of contemporary modernity and saw masks: "the twentieth century is the age of the mask, the age of hidden experiences and the secret face."[136] In "the times in which we live," a journalist argued, contemporary life had become a protracted "gloomy masquerade of gay despair" (*mrachnyi maskarad veselogo otchaianiia*), a feverish "feast" of pleasure embraced in order to hide and forget our doubt and uncertainty.[137]

The popular boulevard columnist Ol'ga Gridina elaborated on these themes by regularly warning her readers that the city is a cruel "deceiver" (*obmanshchik*). Young provincials, she acknowledged, come to the capital from their dark corners of "age-old silence" expecting to feel the "pulse of the age" amidst the city's rich and varied life. They come as if entering a "bright temple," and not just for superficial pleasure but to partake of the city's "inward richness." The city answers these dreams harshly. In time, the "brilliant" appearance of the city's lively streets, theaters, and stores, with its electric lights shining like suns, is seen for the mask it really is, hiding "indifference and the harsh and bitter struggle to survive—nothing else."[138] Like the many "strangers" who turned out not to be what they appeared, the city also betrayed naive faith in appearance. The shattering of this illusion meant seeing the city's mask for what it was and thus partly removing it—even if this meant only looking nakedly at the darkness beneath.

The "spirit of deceit" pervaded every corner of city life. The "average" modern man, a journalist noted, wakes up in the morning and washes with soap made of chemicals, cleans his teeth with a celluloid brush, drinks ersatz coffee with "milk" that has mainly a "symbolic relation" to the real thing, eats artificial foods, wears clothes made of artificial materials. He goes to work in an office where he keeps accounts of falsified goods, or in a factory where they make falsified products, or for a newspaper "dedicated to falsifying the news of life." He eats a half-artificial lunch, drinks poisonous beverages, and then goes home at day's end on machine-made paths. Even his leisure is surrounded by "false and surrogate" mechanically produced music, mechanically reproduced art, and "surrogate" literature"—none of which can satisfy his spiritual needs any more than artificial foods can satisfy his body.[139]

The falsification of commercial products with the intent of deceiving consumers seemed to be the equivalent of bait-and-switch confidence tricks played out on the more elevated stage of the commercial marketplace. Milk, it was reported, was sometimes made with borax, soda, and water; coffee was made with grain and bread but few coffee beans; medicines, especially widely advertised patent medicines, contained nothing that could heal; butter was created out of various cheap ingredients (the subject of a huge trial in St. Petersburg in 1910); and sand and even pieces of metal were used to increase the sold weight of a product. Sometimes these were simple and old-fashioned falsifications; sometimes quite "scientifically" complex processes were used.[140] Commercial advertisements, which appeared in large numbers in newspapers and popular magazines and were posted along every major city street, were the intimate partner in falsification and deception. Commentators were especially disturbed by the proliferation of print ads by "charlatans" promising cures or prevention for various ailments associated with city life, such as cholera, consumption, and venereal disease, or promising to reveal (if you purchase this book) the keys to happiness and success.[141] Victims of fictive business investment opportunities were usually recruited through newspaper advertisements—adding them to the list of "victims of advertisement."[142]

The list of falsifications seemed endless. Even science could not be trusted. Responding to controversies undermining Frederick Cook's claim to have been the first to reach the North Pole in 1908, a columnist in *Novoe vremia* compared Cook to Russia's most notorious fraud and provocateur, the double agent Evno Azev, who was also unmasked in 1909, declaring with dismay, "What times we live in! 'Everything is deception, everything is untrue' [*vse obmanchivo, vse neverno*—yet another paraphrase of Gogol's famous line], all the way up to the North Pole. Even this fixed point of the globe turns out to be precarious, a falsification, and a provocation."[143] The cinema, the most modern form of cultural consumption, was also imbued with "falsification," not least in its moral content.[144] As for today's women, a newspaper feuilletonist wrote, in the name of the "modern pursuit of beauty" the contemporary woman has falsified real beauty behind a mask of "artificiality and counterfeit," behind "false teeth, false locks, corsets, cosmetics, and makeup," behind which she can hardly feel happy.[145] Many respected intellectuals and writers, some critics complained, were "pretenders" (*simulianty*) who felt and believed nothing authentic but only offered readers "stylized presentations" of ideas, concerns, and even emotions.[146]

Not even religion was to be trusted, at least not the many new currents of alternative religiosity that were so pervasive in urban Russia during these years. The press, and the Orthodox Church, had little doubt that many if not all of these new movements were confidence games and swindles (*moshennichestvo* was the term repeatedly used) perpetrated by "charlatans," no different from other falsified products competing in the marketplace. Critics accused members of an unofficial movement, the Ioannity, that venerated the recently deceased Father Ioann of Kronstadt as a new saint of acting "under the mask of religion" to engage in various illegal trade practices.[147] The leaders of the "*brattsy*" (brethren), also known as "*trezvenniki*" (teetotalers), a movement that attracted a huge lower-class following, were said to be obvious "charlatans" who pretend to be prophets, but whose real goals are "material profit," and who preach a pure life to the common folk, but themselves lead lives of "debauchery."[148] Critics said the same about the leaders of a Petersburg branch of the *khlyst* religious "sect." The so-called Okhta (a neighborhood in Petersburg) Mother of God, King Solomon, and Apostle Peter, three *khlyst* leaders put on trial in 1914 in what became a public spectacle, were accused of exploiting the common people of the capital city for "dark" purposes.[149] Some, especially in the church, suggested that these masquerades had their parallel among the very high-est elite of St. Petersburg in the "charlatan" Grigorii Rasputin, who had even (though this could only be implied in print) deceived the royal family with his performance of piety and saintliness.[150] Skeptics similarly branded spiritualism—especially séances claiming to be able to open the bound-ary between the world of the spirits and the physical world, which were increasingly popular in St. Petersburg—as charlatanism, along with palm-istry, fortune telling, and other forms of "sorcery," such as the "sorceress-gypsy" who claimed to be able, for a large fee, to find stolen property with the help of amulets, snake skins, drugs, and steam baths filled with smoke from burning herbs. Without doubt, it was reported, these were all criminal "deceptions" and "swindles."[151]

"If the nineteenth century was the age of steam and electricity," one journalist concluded, "the twentieth century deserves the honored title of the age of falsification" (*vek fal'sifikatsiia*).[152] And St. Petersburg was its Russian capital. While the term "falsification" was properly reserved for deceptive consumer practices, it stood for a deeper spirit of falsification thought to define modern public life. It seemed that "counterfeit can be seen in everything." "Honor, conscience, science, and love are also falsi-fied."[153] Truth itself became illusory.

Newspapers were complicit in all this. Ideally, the press was the citi-zen's essential guide to life in the city, including to its lies. And yet, as some newspaper columnists themselves admitted, the commercial press was also often a performance and a disguise. "What is truth?" Ol'ga Gridina asked rhetorically. To illustrate this ancient question "in its application to mod-ern times," she suggested that it was enough to "picture the ordinary city dweller [*obyvatel'*] with a newspaper in front of him." In the face of the daily fabrications and inventions that appeared in the paper, how can one know any longer what is truth? Even leaving aside political news—where, on top of the normal failures of accurate reporting, censorship (though she could not mention this) distorted the truth—the papers are filled with falsifica-tion. Concerning the everyday accidents, crimes, and other events that the press so extensively reported—including the many stories of masquerade explored here—how can one discern the real amidst all the "contradictory news"? Reports of the notorious Gilevich murder case, for example, were

a "confused mess" (*putanitsa*), with some reporters openly "fantasizing."
Of course, Gridina acknowledged, there will always be "inaccuracies" and
"mistakes" in reporting, given the speed required in preparing a modern
newspaper. But this was not what worried her. The greater concern was the
intended fabrications and inventions: "false news, events that never happened, made-up stories." All as part of the spectacle of urban life: "to please
the crowd."[154] Or as her colleague Skitalets at *Gazeta-kopeika* put it, the
press told stories to fill the "inner emptiness" in people's lives: "we greedily
throw ourselves on the newspapers as at a spectacle."[155]

Uncertainty and unknowability, and the moral danger lurking in this
darkness, were pervasive themes in these stories of urban disguise and
simulation. As we have seen, the *neznakomets*—the stranger, the unknown
one—was everywhere: thieves, pickpockets, muggers, confidence men,
and other perpetrators of everyday crimes in the public sphere were often
described as "*neznakomye*" or "*neizvestnye*" (unknown). But surrounding
these figures was the much greater strangeness and unknowability of the
city itself, of what could be seen but not understood, or seen only vaguely
and in shadow. Modern city life appeared to be a dark theater of deception,
imposture, and masquerade. At its most far reaching, this was an existential reading of the whole of human "fate" as a shadowy and unknowable
"stranger in hood and mask" (*neznakomets v kapiushone i maske*).[156] Russian urban writers would have understood very well what Walter Benjamin
later had in mind when he defined modernity as "the world dominated by
its phantasmagorias" and the modern metropolis as a dark spectacle of deception and self-deception, of simulacra, illusions, and masks.[157]

UNMASKING

Most journalistic writing about masks in everyday life sought to unmask
the mysteries of the city. Newspapers reported masquerades and mysteries partly to shed light on the many dark corners of the city, to give readers
knowledge of what was hidden. By publishing stories of "masked" performance and deceit, the press sought to make the city legible, to disenchant
it, to map its moral landscape. These stories were told often as melodramas,
the conventions of which include not only emotional excess but also a tidy

Manichean dualism between good and evil. In melodrama, stories of deception and mistaken identities are ubiquitous, but they are always resolved by
unmasking.[158] Frequent and often detailed reports on criminal trials were
similarly said to "lift the curtain hiding grotesque mores and monstrous
ways of thinking."[159] The police and the judiciary, of course, were on the
front lines of the effort to unmask deceit. Many urban writers set themselves
the same mission. "Off with the mask!" proclaimed the author of "true life
novels" (romany-byli) about masked seducers of young girls and other
moral sores of everyday Petersburg life.[160] "Off with the mask!" proclaimed
the author of a book on the homosexual subculture of St. Petersburg.[161] The
writers' self-proclaimed goal was to "lift slightly the curtain covering the
surface appearances of decency [vneshnei blagopristroinosti], to open for a
moment the hermetic seal on the Petrograd cesspit," and to reveal (changing metaphors again) the backstage realities of the "dirty skirts and torn
stockings" of pretty actresses.[162] In seeking to expose the "unvarnished
truth,"[163] of course, these writers also sought moral clarity. Removing masks
was an ethical act both in its insistence on truth and in uncovering hidden
evil. In this hopeful vision, masquerade was a simple performance of deceit:
people were hiding their true selves behind false masks. There was nothing
ambiguous about this concealment: the surfaces were made respectable in
order to hide intent that was malevolent and criminal.

But lifting the veil and removing the masks covering the city's mysteries did not always bring a sense of mastery. Often, it seemed, one's gaze
could not penetrate the "blue fog" of the metropolis. As both police and
journalists so often concluded, much remained hidden and dark—too many
aferisty remained unmasked and free, too many suicides and murders remained unexplained, too many "unknown strangers" wandered the streets
with their secrets still hidden. The "power of illusion" was overwhelming.[164]
Moral clarity was just as elusive. Even anxious reporters and essayists could
recognize the allure of transgression that masquerade allowed. For all their
dismay, they could not but notice the power that masked performances
possessed. Some reporters grudgingly admired (as likely did their readers)
the "cunning" of these criminals, the impressiveness of their appearance
and performance, their constant innovation. In the city of strangers, the
right appearance gave people real power over others. And pleasure, too. It

mattered, of course, that these tales unfolded in tsarist Russia. Transgressive public display could be especially potent and pleasurable in a society where the individual still had limited rights and opportunities.

Russian contemporaries, however, rarely found this landscape of unsettled and ambiguous public display alluring or liberating. If reporters and commentators seemed at times to see the power and pleasure of masquerade—the empowering pleasure of performing identities, the benefit of illicit material gain, and the enjoyment in writing and reading these stories—they seemed even more certain that this was dark power and immoral pleasure. Again and again this was read as emblematic of Russia's experience of modern disorder and crisis. The constant presence of strangers and of the experience of being a stranger, the elusiveness and ambiguity of all appearance, the endless parade of masking and unmasking, and the many obstacles to knowledge and legibility revealed a troubling moral map of St. Petersburg as a modern city, where strangers continually slid in and out of the shadows of city life. Beyond this, it suggested something troubling about the nature of "our times," perhaps of human existence itself. Worse still, when masks *were* removed, the truth that was revealed might be darker than the masks themselves: black truths about the human personality and human morality that were better left hidden and unknown. Even worse—though this deepest anxiety was only gestured at in most texts— appearance may have been the only truth. Perhaps no better truth was hidden behind the illusion and performance. Or as Benjamin asked, echoing a concern evident in many city texts, "where in the new does the boundary run between reality and appearance?"[165]

Death

Something different forced me to . . . see in the face of Petersburg
what doctors call *facies Hippocratica*, the "face of death."

—Dmitrii Merezhkovskii, 1908

Death in St. Petersburg was a critical social question that helped to constitute the experience of public life in the city. Newspapers were filled with
daily stories of death by disease, accident, violence, or by one's own hand.
As Skitalets, the columnist for *Gazeta-kopeika*, commented in 1913: "Newspapers are printed on white paper, but, really, in our times their pages seem
covered with blood."[1] "Abnormal" death seemed a normal part of everyday
city life. Of course, the inevitability of death has produced, in many times
and places, a cultural awareness, often a cultural anguish, that this world is
a veil of appearances, transience, futility, and loss.[2] But the daily stories of
death in St. Petersburg produced an anguish that was less abstract and existential. For one thing, these deaths were not the inevitable conclusion of a
natural life but the sudden interruption of time's normal passage. Also, this
was an intensely social narrative: individual tragedies so accumulated, and
were so visible, as to become a societal catastrophe, even a sign that society
itself was dying. In "these times," it seemed that the body and the self suffered as never before, the tragic appeared at every step, excess abounded,
and comprehension was impossible.

Excess and abnormality were literally visible in mortality statistics,
which were often reported and discussed in the press. According to the
reports of the statistical commission of the city government (*gorodskaia up-
rava*), the mortality rate in the capital fluctuated between 24 and 28 deaths
per thousand in the years 1906 to 1910 (declining somewhat to around 21
in the years leading to the war, when the rate again began to climb). This

compared, for example, to contemporary death rates of 14–15 per thousand in London and Paris in 1909, a difference that was regularly noted.[3] (What was not mentioned was that London and Paris in the mid-nineteenth century had suffered mortality rates, even leaving aside cholera years, identical to St. Petersburg's in the early 1900s.)[4] Commentators continually expressed shock at the "colossal scale" of death in St. Petersburg, which put the city far ahead of European cities at the time as well as of all other cities in the Russian empire, including Moscow, Odessa, and Warsaw.[5] Symptomatically, it was reported, urban mortality rates were not only higher than rural ones, but rising in cities while declining in the countryside.[6] Infant mortality was especially high, at 25 per hundred before the age of one in St. Petersburg in 1909—more than twice the rates in contemporary Berlin, Paris, or London.[7] The Russian imperial capital seemed to have become the most deadly city in Europe. That other European capitals had suffered and overcome comparable death rates gave the more optimistic writers reason for hope that further modernization would correct the pathologies of Russia's still developing modernity. But most urban writers saw a different temporal logic here: modern progress itself seemed to have brought this suffering to both individual bodies and the social body. As is so often the case with death, these facts stimulated philosophical reflections, though less about the "eternal theme"[8] of death's ontological meaning, than about quite secular matters of self, society, nation, and progress.

"A TRAUMATIC EPIDEMIC":
DISEASE, ACCIDENTS, VIOLENCE, RAPE, MURDER

How people died was not always knowable. Newspapers were filled with reports of unidentified corpses with unknown causes of death or evidence of violent death in unknown circumstances, often marked by headlines like "mysterious corpse" (*zagadochnyi trup*) or "mysterious murder" (*tainstvennoe ubiistvo*). Dead bodies might be found lying on a street with bullet wounds to the head ("who is he?" was the typical headline),[9] or washed up in the Neva ("who are you, unknown woman in a pink skirt and white shirt, with a silver cross on your bosom?"),[10] or lying at the bottom of an apartment stairway in a building where no one recognized the corpse.[11] Some had clearly died or been killed recently; some were deliberately defaced to disguise their identity or butchered into pieces hidden in various places;[12] others were decomposed, such as the body of a man found on the banks of the Obvodnyi Canal near the railroad tracks, whose face had been partly eaten by rats.[13] Officials periodically posted photographs of corpses in public places (though they denied requests by newspapers to reprint these) or placed the bodies on display at hospital mortuaries, hoping someone might identify them—these displays, naturally, attracted "a mass of the curious."[14] In 1910, the city administration, following European trends, began planning the construction of a central morgue that would allegedly be the most advanced in the world for the display of unidentified bodies—designed also so that the police could view spectators, looking for clues to the killer that might be evident in the "play of feelings and sensation" on viewers' faces.[15] The bodies of newborn infants—perhaps stillborn, perhaps dead soon after birth, perhaps killed by a mother unable to cope—were found (sometimes several a day) on streets and sidewalks, at train stations, in hotel rooms rented for a night, or in a river or canal.[16]

Again and again, the language of mystery and the unknown—*ugadochnost'*, *tainstvennost'*—of the impossibility of knowing or understanding, was used to frame these stories. About a brutally murdered man found early one morning in 1908, *Gazeta-kopeika* characteristically inquired, "Who is he? How did he come here? Is there anyone close to him? Who killed him?—Nothing is known. The dark autumn night guards its secrets."[17] Reporters and essayists tried to imagine the "misfortunes" and "tragedies" hidden behind these "terrible finds," as the newspapers often called them. But they often admitted the persistence of mystery. What might lead a mother to the unimaginable act of killing her own newborn? a feuilletonist asked: only God can know and understand.[18]

Many deaths were explicable. Disease, especially infectious disease, was a major cause. Government surveys, regularly reported and discussed in the press, found rates of infectious disease to be much higher in St. Petersburg than "normal" rates, as determined by European comparisons.[19] Disease was a major reason reporters dramatically dubbed St. Petersburg the "capital of death."[20] A large proportion of the city's deaths were attributable to "highly infectious diseases" such as cholera, typhus, measles, and diphtheria. Tuberculosis, pneumonia, and other less virulent illnesses also played a large part, as did noninfectious ailments like gastroenteritis (especially in children) and heart disease.[21] Alcoholism was a contributing factor to many illnesses as well as to violence.[22] Cholera seemed especially to reflect the unhealthy state of Russia and its capital. A recurrent Petersburg problem since the first epidemic in 1830, cholera was depicted as a hostile invader—an "Asiatic guest" or simply the "enemy"—but one that found urban conditions welcoming. Thousands died of the disease during the terrible epidemic that struck the capital in the summer of 1908 and lingered well into 1910. Newspapers reported the daily, weekly, and monthly toll of new infections and deaths (along with pleas not to drink unboiled water). Official statistics reported nearly 6,100 deaths from cholera in the capital during the worst years, 1908 and 1909.[23]

St. Petersburg was also the capital of *katastrofy*—industrial and urban accidents that maimed and killed. The city's statistical office registered over 3,000 "accidents" (*neschastnye sluchai*) in the city in 1908, the overwhelming number occurring on public streets, squares, and waterways or along urban tram lines.[24] The press continually reported these, sometimes illustrated with drawings (photographs were still very rare) and under headlines like "Peterburgskie katastrofy." While there were exceptional incidents—a ferry sinking on the Neva with dozens of lives lost or a lion tamer killed at the circus—most were everyday occurrences, especially people falling under tram wheels while boarding and getting off or being run over when crossing the street, railroad trains killing people walking across the tracks, pedestrians run over by automobiles, collapsed buildings or scaffolds at construction sites (an "epidemic of construction" produced an epidemic of work accidents),[25] collapsed apartment buildings due to faulty construction, falling elevators, death in factory accidents, children killed playing with guns, and fires where people lived or worked.[26] Accidental deaths among unsupervised children in the city had "in recent years become an epidemic phenomenon in the capital." On a single day in May 1913, *Peterburgskii listok* noted, children died by drowning in a canal, falling under the wheels of a cart, toppling off a balcony, being run over by an automobile, and being hit by a tram.[27] Newspaper style emphasized the shocking gruesomeness and tragedy of these deaths (especially when witnessed by crowds on the street): "in only a moment all that was left of this young and bold youth was a formless bloody mass."[28]

Other people in the city were another source of deadly danger. The papers reported an "epidemic" of murderous public violence. Although the term "murder" (*ubiistvo*) was used whenever such an attack was fatal, murder proper usually involved people who knew one another, often intimately, and with some measure of intent to kill, whereas these attacks were committed by strangers, and the main intent was usually robbery not murder. And most unfolded in public places, especially on the street but also in bars, cafés, train stations, shops, and entertainment parks. The narratives were simple and similar: a perpetrator, individually or part of a group, approached a victim and demanded money, becoming violent when rebuffed. As a rule, these were stories about unruly young males—though men were also the most common victims, especially if walking alone at night. When women were victims, rape was frequently an element of the violence. Knives were the predominant weapon. Indeed, a dark public "reign of the knife" (*nozhevshchina*) was said to afflict the city in these years (the term began to appear in the Petersburg press in 1910), attributed to urban "bandits" (*razboiniki*) after money, violent sexual predators, "hooligans" (who were said to stab for no particular reason), or simply individuals overcome by momentary anger and finding a weapon at hand.[29] Besides knives, weapons included guns, iron bars, hammers, shovels, ropes, and axes, though some victims were strangled or beaten to death with hands and fists.

While many of these crimes occurred on dark back streets, numerous attacks were quite public, and were made even more so by the reporting of newspapers, which had a strong interest in publicizing the everyday spectacles of city life. The press regularly emphasized the "large crowd" (*mnogochislennaia publika*) who became the involuntary and shocked witnesses to some violent "spectacle" on a street, at a railroad station, at a bar, or in a café.[30] When guns were involved, witnesses could become victims themselves and the scene could become a spectacle of panic, screams, and blood.[31] Newspapers chronicled the many cases of public violence in the city, such as bar brawls among strangers (e.g., among rival fans of different wrestlers after a match or simply when a personal argument escalated), the belligerent man at a café who quarreled with other customers and then stabbed them; the man who chased and repeatedly stabbed a woman who ignored his "degrading suggestions" as she walked along a street; a gambler at an illegal parlor who stabbed a card dealer to death; or the drunken government official who pulled a gun on the street and began shooting at his drinking companions.[32] The persistence of older social traditions of violence—such as street battles (*poboishshe*) among rival groups of workers, occasional acts of mob justice (*samosud*) against offending foremen or shopkeepers,[33] and occasional duels among the elite—were newly framed as part of this violent urban culture.[34] Not all violence was before the eyes of others, of course. But even violence that was hidden and private was often made into a public spectacle by the newspapers. This was especially the case with domestic violence.[35]

Many cases of urban violence lay at the boundary between public violence among strangers and private histories of murder with intent: notably, violent outbursts among acquaintances and friends, which seemed to have become epidemic. Everyone seemed so nervously on edge that violence erupted with even a slight provocation, especially when alcohol loosened inhibitions. When weapons were at hand, and they often were, these fights could be lethal. Many men, it seems, carried concealed knives and occasionally pistols when out in public. Others took up whatever might lay at hand: rocks, hammers, metal rods, pots of boiling water, or simply fists and boots. The papers were full of accounts of arguments quickly degenerating into violence, often occurring in bars or on the street, frequently over "trifles," often presumed insults, and ending in the use of a weapon.[36] For instance, a couple of working-class friends were sitting around drinking vodka when one decided he needed to go home to get some sleep before work the next morning; angry, his drinking buddy shouted "I'll show you how to treat a friend" and stabbed him in the side.[37] Or, at a springtime picnic of a group of young bookkeepers after work, jokes lead to insults, which lead to a fist-fight, which leads to a stabbing.[38] The list of such doleful tales was endless. Related, though not fatal, was acid throwing: mainly women taking revenge on men who betrayed them or the rivals they had been betrayed with. These were invariably public attacks, occurring on the street, at a ball, at the skating rink, or in a café.[39]

When children and women were victims, the public was especially shocked, at least judging by the intended echo of public sentiments in the press. Rape, whether or not it concluded with murder, was among the darkest of these stories.[40] The press was filled with accounts of children and women raped by strangers, sometimes by groups of men, often in dark streets or other public places. Some victims were tortured and killed.[41] Many rapes, of course, did not reach the police, or the courts, or the news, especially when they were "domestic" crimes, unless they were fatal and particularly bestial.[42] Everyone agreed that sexual violence had never before reached "such a colossal extent"—and no one was spared, not "seventy-year-old women, not eight-month-old infants."[43] And all classes were affected: sexual abuse in the higher classes had worsened; and among the lower classes—at one time, some optimistically believed, free of such excesses—one now saw widespread sexual violence against women and children in the "most disgusting and beastly forms."[44] These reports were part of the daily chronicle of news, though some complained about this publicity and even blamed it for stimulating susceptible readers to sexual violence.[45] While we recognize today that all rape is violence and is pathological—and some Russian writers did as well—most would have agreed with the public health physician and essayist Dmitrii Zhbankov, who not only documented the exceptionally high incidence of sexual violence in these times but emphasized the newly "abnormal and pathological character of rape at the present time." "Normal rape," he believed, was fundamentally sexual: a young male cannot restrain his natural lust when seeing an attractive woman. But in these times, rape had become "cold" violence. The high incidence of gang rape was one of many signs of this new abnormality—a "normal" male does not want to share women. But nowadays, neither blood nor death dull desire, as it would for a "healthy" person, but only stimulated the rapist into a "sort of cannibal's dance among the dead."[46]

The press was especially fascinated by murder, the incidence and brutality of which seemed to be growing "by geometrical progression," "not by the day but by the hour."[47] News reports described, often in detail, the variety of stories of murder in the city. Motives were diverse. Murders occurred during robbery and rape. They were acts of vengeance (especially due to "insult" or "betrayal") or for "romantic reasons" (usually jealousy or betrayal). They ended abusive relationships or a family's poverty and hunger. They could be due to mental illness or to no evident reason at all. Victims included wives, husbands, children (including unwanted newborns), parents, lovers, prostitutes, friends, fellow students, coworkers, foremen, guards, priests, neighbors, and roommates. By class, victims and perpetrators alike ranged from the homeless poor to the social elite. And when recounted in the daily papers, often with the help of rumors, hearsay, speculation, sketches of the crime taking place (even when there were no witnesses), and commentary—repeated and elaborated when cases came to trial—violence, whether behind closed doors or in the street, became a public spectacle.[48] Many reports dwelled with special interest on the vicious extravagance of some murders, as when victims were tortured to death[49] or dismembered or mutilated, as in the famous case in 1909 of Andrei Gilevich who cut off his victim's lips, nose, and cheeks (some news reports described even worse mutilation) in order to obliterate the face of the man whose identity he intended to steal in order to claim insurance.[50] St. Petersburg even had its own "Jack the Ripper" (*Dzhek-potroshitel'*), who brutally stabbed and strangled prostitutes in hotel rooms after sex, due to his professed desire for "vengeance" against all "beautiful women," though experts argued that this was due to his degenerate sexual taste for blood.[51]

INTERPRETING DEATH AND VIOLENCE: "CRUEL AND BLOODY ARE 'OUR TIMES'"

The profusion of death and violence begged interpretation. "The capital is ailing and dying," an essayist in *Gorodskoe delo* concluded, reflecting on the evidence of death in the city, producing "the gloomiest thoughts about the fate of Petersburg, this sick head on the half-starved body known as Russia."[52] Urban writers elaborated on these gloomy thoughts, framing the statistical and narrative evidence in dramatic metaphors: an "atmosphere of death,"[53] a "traumatic epidemic of blood and violence"[54] a "bacchanalia" of death, a "bountiful harvest of death."[55] Many simply recounted with shock the numbers and stories that showed the growing excess of death by violence, accident, suicide, and disease. In the dark words of the journalist and author Mikhail Engel'gardt, writing in 1908, contemporary life had become a black and fetid place "where pools of blood are on the floor, the walls ooze pus, and the atmosphere is saturated with the exhalations of putrefying corpses. And the further you walk, the blacker becomes the darkness and the more lethal the poisoned atmosphere."[56]

The whole of contemporary culture reeked of death, it seemed. Contemporary literature was viewed as mirror and stimulus. Critics repeatedly complained of the ubiquity of death in modern Russian letters.[57] Fedor Sologub's prose, for example, was filled with a "nightmarish life" of bloodshed and death. Zinaida Gippius's work united desire and death. Aleksandr Blok's iconic "Beautiful Lady" suggested personified death.[58] Indeed, a critic complained, the dominant "tone" in literature had become that of a requiem for the dead (*panikhida*).[59] Of course, these critical readings were not merely contemporary prejudice. Literary scholars have explored the attraction of "decadent" and symbolist writers to images of illness and death.[60] Many writers specifically linked death and the city—indeed, this was a European modernist tradition that reached back at least to Baudelaire. Nonelite literature also smelled of death, critics complained. In the work of the popular novelist Mikhail Artsybashev, for example, it seemed that "death stands behind the shoulders" of all of his heroes, who continually talk of death, think of death, kill one another, and kill themselves: "murder, suicide, and shooting—that's the whole of human life as portrayed by this artist."[61] In poetry about the city in popular newspapers and magazines— usually by amateurs and hence telling as a measure of contemporary tastes and moods—death was ubiquitous: the city "spreads out like a cemetery"; factories are "hellish" settings for "torment," "suffocation," and "death"; and the only path for the poor is "the path to the cemetery where you will be forgotten by all."[62] Popular entertainment, too, critics noticed, trafficked in death. From circus acts to works of theater—not to mention sensationalist news reports in mass circulation papers—entertainment tended to be "spectacles saturated with blood."[63] Even children's games had become noticeably more violent—including popular games of war, violent robbery, and even execution—and hence, it was said, more "contemporary."[64]

Urban writers did all they could to impose usable meaning on these stories. To be sure, death often seemed to be masked. These were "mysterious attacks," "mysterious murders," "enigmatic dramas."[65] Murder, especially when emerging out of hidden private dramas, was continually reported as bewildering in cause and motive and in the frequent vicious excess of the violence.[66] Acknowledgment of the inexplicable was itself an interpretation. But most commentators found specific meanings in death. Some writers, risking political retribution, blamed the government for this atmosphere of death, which they claimed was especially due to the Russo-Japanese war of 1904–5 and widespread repression, including a large number of executions, after the revolution of 1905. "Days without a death sentence and execution have been the exception" over the past year, a journalist noted at the end of 1909, such that "human life has lost value."[67] Even more bluntly, the Marxist-turned-liberal Aleksandr Izgoev argued in the newspaper *Rech'* that the death penalty was a "disgusting epidemic," harming moral consciousness and making the human being less human and more a "cruel, cowardly, and vile animal."[68] Other writers blamed the revolutionary movement, especially terrorist acts against officials, which proliferated in these postrevolutionary years, though they were also likely to view terrorism as a product of the times. Following the assassination of prime minister Petr Stolypin in September 1911, a journalist offered a characteristic lament: "We are to blame, all of us, even the air we breathe and the thoughts and feelings we experience. For six years already we have been sowing seeds of violence, betrayal, and murder, and have been killing with knife, bullet, and bomb, and with soaped noose."[69]

Most writers, of course, blamed the modern city. The city and death were a frequent pair in newspapers, literature, and film. The trope of the newcomer, especially the stereotypically "powerless and helpless" young woman, falling into the "jaws of the big city," led to the "inexorable sentence of Death," as Nikolai Evreinov imagined theatricalizing this conventional story of the big city.[70] Another theme was the physical "atmosphere" of the industrial city, which was said to produce exceptional rates of illness. Among the "horrors of the city," a journalist argued in 1912, was its contaminated air, water, ground, and food, which made every modern city, by definition, "poisonous, deadly, and alien."[71] Why is St. Petersburg a "butcher of children," with child mortality rates higher than even Beijing, Bombay, and Calcutta, even when comparing "normal" times in the capital with epidemic

or even famine years in these eastern cities? the essayist Skitalets asked rhetorically, reporting that 40 percent of infants born in St. Petersburg died
before the age of five. He answered with a familiar list of charges: a polluted
environment due to the lack of a decent sewage system, insufficient public green spaces, unclean food and drink, abysmal hospitals ("kingdoms of
horror"), and the high cost of living.[72] Why did St. Petersburg hold "first
place" in rates of tuberculosis throughout both Russia and Europe, another
newspaperman asked: because "this disease loves the noisy city."[73] Above
all, why had cholera made St. Petersburg a world "capital of death"? The
answer: polluted water, soil, and air; foul and dirty public markets and
food establishments; the lack of an effective system of public sanitation;
the "unpreparedness, confusion, chaos, and disorganization" of the city
administration; an inadequate system of public health and hospitals; and
the "complete ignorance, carelessness, and helplessness" of the common
people.[74] These problems were so painfully familiar that newspaper writers even joked about disease feeling especially welcome in the capital. One
feuilletonist reported his "interview" in 1910 with "Cholera," who told the
reporter how much he enjoyed returning to the Russian capital: walk by any
public market, "Cholera" declared, and "your heart leaps with joy" at the
smell, and the canals are pure ambrosia.[75]

The argument that St. Petersburg was an unhealthy place was not
new or even completely associated with the city's industrial development.
Sickness was long an essential theme in the cultural narrative of St. Petersburg. The typical Petersburger, according to this tradition, was constantly
ailing. But by the early 1900s, the emphasis was less on the particularities
of St. Petersburg—its swampy foundations, its characteristic fogs, its hidden sores, its cursed history—than on the ailments shared with all large
industrial cities: fouled soil and water, crowded populations of poor people
ignorant of the rules of modern sanitation, and skies stained with dust, dirt,
and smoke that poison lungs and bodies.[76] These writers also recognized
that the malady of social and economic progress was aggravated by the political malady of Russian backwardness, by the social, political, and moral
failure of both the government (they only could explicitly criticize the local administration, of course) and organized society to ameliorate these
conditions.

The epidemic of accidents was viewed in the same light. The daily news reminded readers that the city was filled with a special panoply of deadly dangers. Many, if not most, of these accidental deaths clearly resulted from encounters with the newest features of city life: electric trams), which transformed city streets into "deathly dangerous traps,"[77] automobiles, elevators, new construction. These reports often highlighted the randomness of danger—indeed, some saw this as essential to their meaning—which also reminded one of how susceptible city people were "to the fault of others, the carelessness of others, the venality of others." This interdependence of modern individuals was itself one of the "terrors of our life."[78] Not everyone saw dark meaning in these deaths. The crowds that gathered around the scenes of accidents and the newspapers that reported bloody injuries and fatalities in gruesome detail also recognized the spectacle and entertainment they provided.

The epidemic of violent crime was also highly urban. As the chronicler of Petersburg crime who called himself Aborigine put it: "the more urban, the more crime . . . including the most terrible bloody acts."[79] This was because the city's poisoned and sick environment was as much moral and spiritual as physical. "In the crowded city," critics complained, values like respect for others and love of the good had been relegated to the "archive" and replaced by "cynical spectacles," "sexual violence," "evil," and the most horribly brutal murders.[80] Commentators linked some of most publicized murders with the urban demimonde and its decadent values of "money, money, money," its egoistic "thirst for sensual pleasures," its excess, and its "cynicism"—such as the cases of the instructor at the trendy Roller-Skating Rink on Mars Field who robbed and killed his rich pupil and lover, or the murder, for purposes of robbery, of Marianna Time by two young men of her own high social circle ("the capital's golden youth") who also met their victim at the skating rink.[81] So many murders, it seemed, were motivated by a "selfish" and "cynical" greed for money and comfort, by a "thirst for idleness and easy gain," even for only one more night of pleasure in a restaurant or "on display at the skating rink"—revealing "one of the saddest sides of the soul of modern man [*sovremennogo cheloveka*]."[82]

This environment nurtured a modern *zhestokost'*—cruelty, brutality, savagery.[83] "Savagery" was continually underscored in reports on urban violence. Perpetrators of violence exhibited "savage mores" (*dikie nravy*) and "moral ensavagement" (*nravstvennaia odichanie*).[84] "Truly African passions" seemed to burn under "Petersburg's sad and gloomy skies."[85] Killers were "human beasts" (*liudi-zveri*)—a phrase repeated constantly in newspaper reports, to the point that some complained that this cliché was insulting to animals, "among whom there is no vileness or crime."[86] Endlessly, critics interpreted violence as reflecting the "cruel" and "beastly" "mores" of the age, as mirroring the "terrible brutality" that pervaded "contemporary" life.[87] The most dramatic cases suggested still more extravagant images associated with human bloodletting: cannibals and vampires.[88] These metaphors of beast and savage were not mainly arguments about the biological atavism of individuals, although some writers did speak of abnormal and diseased individuals, when trying to explain the worst forms of violence.[89] Mostly, they spoke of a social ensavagement. We have all "become beasts" (*zveriaem*), Skitalets argued.[90] The "whole social organism," a newspaper columnist concluded, has become "infected by a terrible disease."[91] And the main cause of this illness was the urban environment in conditions of modernity. Paradoxically, it was observed, the coming of modern society made man again into an "animal."[92] This view was reinforced by evidence from the village: the countryside had its share of savage brutality, but in its extent, extremity, and complexity brutal violence was worse in the modern city.[93]

Moral numbness and apathy in the face of this social trauma seemed to prove the depth of the catastrophe.[94] Violence had become so normal that no one seemed shocked anymore. "We have become used to the smell of blood, we are accustomed to it. Cruel and bloody are 'our times'!"[95] "We have become so used to seeing scenes of the most terrible murders that it has become impossible to surprise us with the most inhuman tortures."[96] The most "terrible thing" (a common phrase in these accounts) is that "the terror of killing has lost its sharp edge."[97] Even the most extravagant brutality seemed characteristic of the times. The widely reported murder and mutilation of a student in 1909 by the engineer Andrei Gilevich in order to steal his identity and collect insurance money was judged typical: "Gilevich did not fall from the sky. He is our bone and our flesh, the child of our troubled time [*bezvremen'ia*]."[98]

Life itself in these times, critics insisted, had been cheapened. Commentators on violence and murder were continually crying out that "life has lost value!" (*zhizn' obeztsenena!*), that "human life is valued cheaply."[99] The fact that even "good, peaceable, and modest people" kill seemed a measure of "how cheap human life has become today."[100] "Life in our terrible time," a writer for *Gazeta-kopeika* agreed, is worth no more than a kopeck, so killing is now easy.[101] Whether this devaluation was cause or effect was not always clear. On the one hand, the "traumatic epidemic" of violence, murder, and rape could itself be blamed for stimulating "animal brutality and thirst for blood."[102] On the other hand, this brutality could reflect the spirit of these times, when people so lacked values and ideals that they "thirst for intense pleasures, which are often entwined with blood and violence."[103]

These were not entirely new arguments. In the 1880s, Vladimir Mikhnevich interpreted Petersburg's high levels of violence as evidence of "the abnormal conditions of modern social life," the "psychic disorder" that came with civilization (*kul'tura*)—"savages, it is well known, don't go mad"—and the "terrible cheapness of human life."[104] Likewise, professionals in the human sciences in Russia by the end of the nineteenth century, as Daniel Beer has shown, argued that violent crime and other pathologies of contemporary life were nurtured by urbanization, industrialization, and capitalism.[105] By the early 1900s, though, this had become everyday news. And the tone and logic had shifted. Especially in the wake of 1905, a rising sense of moral panic was evident in public discussions of violence and death, not least because of the nearly universal insistence that this bloody epidemic was a symptom of civilization in crisis. To be sure, even some of the writers who had helped promote social anxiety about violence tried to resist the full logic of blaming society rather than individuals. As the two leading columnists for *Gazeta-kopeika* asked rhetorically, how could one accept that a sane person would stab and kill a virtual stranger for little or no reason, as so often seemed to be the case? The only possible—or endurable—answer was individual mental illness or some exceptional "moral blindness." Otherwise "the bright world [*belyi svet*] would seem like a dark grave" and "one would have to shut oneself away deep in the earth, in an armored cave, to flee from man as from a savage plague."[106] Most of the time, though, this was precisely the conclusion they seem to have reached.

SUICIDE STORIES

The most troubling symptom of the "traumatic epidemic" of death in the
city was the particular "epidemic" of suicide that struck urban Russia, especially St. Petersburg, soon after the end of the 1905 revolution and persisted until the war.[107] Suicide preoccupied urban journalists, intellectuals,
medical and legal professionals, clergy, and other writers. The extent of the
problem was painfully evident to all who read the daily papers. And though
it was not a new problem, nor even Russia's first suicide "epidemic," the
numbers were greater than ever before.[108] Most important, like so much
else in Russia after 1905, this wave of suicides was felt to be something new
and more terrible, to be a sign of exceptionally troubled times, even of the
troubling passage of time itself. In the words of a journalist writing in 1912,
the abnormal excess of urban suicide in these years was a measure of Russia's "mournful progress."[109]

As stories of suicide multiplied in public, people sought explanations. Statisticians collected data for study. Physicians and psychiatrists devoted special meetings and sessions of national congresses to the "modern
epidemic of suicide in Russia." Experts of all sorts offered public lectures
on the problem. Special civic commissions and societies were established
to combat suicide, especially among schoolchildren and students. Government officials considered laws that might hinder and punish suicide.[110]
Above all, the periodical press overflowed with often lengthy articles by
doctors, philosophers, theologians, intellectuals, and journalists trying to
explain this plague. The metaphor of an "epidemic," with its suggestions
not only of uncontrolled danger but also of "infectious" disease, was on everyone's lips.[111] The more cynical spoke of suicide as having become "fashionable" (*modnyi*).[112] But most commentators viewed suicide with compassion and even sympathy: not as crime, sin, or deviance—the dominant older
view—but as a telling sign of tragic times.

Clear to everyone was that these private tragedies had public significance. While some commentators saw suicide as elusive and private, a disorder rooted deep in the still poorly understood world of mind and psyche,
most were certain that it was fundamentally social in both its causes and
meanings. Suicide was "one of the most crying deformities" (*vopiiushchikh*

urodlivostei) of a deformed life.[113] As such, to understand it meant to understand and perhaps correct this life. As in other modern societies, suicide became a defining measure of civic health, a barometer of progress or crisis, and a symbol and trope with which to speak of the modern experience.[114] The efforts to answer this most "painful, burning, and cursed question" of the age[115] tell us much about the mental and emotional world of the urban public in fin-de-siècle Russia.

Many sought answers in the science of numbers. As during the nineteenth-century suicide waves in both Russia and western Europe, the collection of statistical data—especially "moral statistics" (*nravstvennaia statistika*), which documented the disorders of public life[116]—was viewed optimistically as able to bring rational order and comprehensibility to every social problem. Government agencies, civic institutions, and individual specialists assiduously gathered data, which were regularly reported in the press. Official counts, especially the often quoted data of the statistical committee of the Petersburg city administration, showed that following a relatively modest number of suicides at the start of the twentieth century, at least compared to the "epidemic" that had ended after the 1880s, the problem revived violently in the wake of 1905. From a stable average of slightly more than 400 suicides a year in St. Petersburg from the late 1890s on, the numbers began steadily rising in 1906, reaching a peak of 1,538 suicides in 1909 and then remaining near this high level until the war.[117] Independent researchers, mostly physicians and public health activists such as Dmitrii Zhbankov and N. I. Grigor'ev, found that official sources invariably undercounted compared to the daily evidence of suicide in the newspapers. Doctor Grigor'ev, for example, counted 13,085 suicides in St. Petersburg between the years of 1906 and 1911, almost twice the official tally.[118] Some writers estimated even higher numbers.[119]

These figures, it was observed pointedly, testified paradoxically to St. Petersburg's progress on the modern world stage. St. Petersburg had gained through suicide a tragic preeminence in European civilization, for it could now claim the dubious honor of having the highest per capita rate of suicide in Europe.[120] As the physician Grigorii Gordon, one of Russia's leading and most outspoken specialists on suicide, declared with rhetorical flourish in 1912, thanks to our suicide rate "we Petersburgers occupy first place in the world."[121] While none of these data can be precisely relied upon, the general situation was clear, especially to readers of the daily papers (where as many as twenty-five suicides might be reported on a single day):[122] something traumatic was occurring. But the point of collecting data, of course, was to explain and thus find means to treat this illness.

Analysts used quantitative evidence to draw a social portrait of suicide, though this revealed little of useful value about the problem apart from its ubiquity. Most suicides were working-class, and most were young (63 percent were under the age of thirty), but so was the city population as a whole.[123] Indeed, what would have likely most struck readers of the daily papers about the social profile of suicides was that a suicide could be anyone. As one specialist concluded, "it seems there are no boundaries to this horrible epidemic, which spares neither age, nor sex, nor position, nor status."[124] Some of these data pointed toward obvious social-psychological conclusions, notably that young people were the most susceptible to mental and emotional distress and that their dependent and transitional place in life placed particular pressures on them. But the data offered few usable distinctions beyond this.

The newspapers offered richer evidence for analysis. The daily papers were the primary site for the public experience of suicide. Indeed the very experience of reading the press was colored by the daily toll of self-murder: "every day," essays on the subject typically began, "you read terrible reports about suicide."[125] The effect of this daily encounter concerned observers, stimulating worries that the repetition of these stories and their occasionally graphic content might inspire suicide, that newspapers were themselves sources of "infection." It is "terrible," one commentator wrote, to think of detailed news reports of suicides falling into the hands of "young girls already in the same dark mood."[126] Others blamed the press for a converse effect: the daily accumulation of new suicide reports, like the proliferation of stories of violence, made readers "used to" (*privykly*) them,[127] leaving in readers' minds only a "mechanical and indifferent attitude" to the "horror" of suicide, even "boredom." "Another unfortunate girl has poisoned herself—what of it?" readers were imagined thinking.[128] News reports on suicide were mainly terse and raw summaries of the facts, and as repetitive as they were shocking: lists of where people killed themselves (on the street, in rivers and canals, in bars and cafés, on railroad tracks, at work, at home, etc.) and of the weapons used (guns, ropes, knives, razors, vinegar essence, acid, poison, drowning, jumping from windows, etc.). They also reported, when these were known, the supposed reasons. These, too, tended to be chillingly terse and repetitive.

A major reason was poverty.[129] Newspaper reports, often headlined "Due to Hunger," regularly highlighted the suicide's unemployment, homelessness, and need.[130] The public health specialist Zhbankov was among many observers who suggested that "if the reasons for all incidents of suicide could be known, a good half of them" would be attributable to "poverty, hunger, and unemployment."[131] So common were these histories that Skitalets, the *Gazeta-kopeika* columnist, observed that stories of desperate and "despairing" unemployed men committing suicide were quite "ordinary," having "nothing special" about them that might command one's attention.[132]

Poverty was an appealing explanation. There was something satisfyingly clear and understandable in thinking of suicide as an escape from desperate material suffering (and the politically minded could use stories of "hungry suicides" as critical evidence against contemporary society).[133] Indeed, some commentators recognized that poverty was too easy an explanation. As one newspaper columnist put it, material need was only an "indirect" or "circumstantial" influence.[134] Poverty was also easy to dismiss, at least for the more secure. As Vasilii Rozanov paraphrased the attitude of the public—again suggesting how everyday traumas can produce moral numbness—"of poor people there are always so many."[135]

Another evident motive, and one of the oldest, was suicide as a defense of dignity and honor—to erase or cleanse oneself of humiliation and shame by willfully extinguishing the self. "Shame" (*pozor*) was often an explicit theme, including in suicide notes. Shame could grow within the privacy of family life.[136] But most stories of shame leading to suicide involved public dimensions of intimacy, especially sexual life. Women were viewed as especially vulnerable and susceptible. Indeed, shame was implicitly treated as a feminine emotion. Shame was the overwhelming leitmotif—both in the judgments of reporters and in the explanations that suicides themselves offered in notes left behind or when questioned if they survived—in stories of suicides by prostitutes and other "fallen women" (so widespread as to represent a special "epidemic" within the larger suicide "epidemic").[137] Many suicides told almost identical stories of coming to the city and falling onto the "slippery path of shame," abused by exploitative madams and drunken men, and recognizing the impossibility of escape.[138] A related theme were the suicides of women who had been raped and could not "bear the shame."[139] In these stories, "shame" complexly mixed with feelings of guilt for moral transgression and feelings of victimization, of moral injury to the self. Sometimes, this shaded toward muted anger and even protest.[140] This was explicit, for example, in the "drama" of three "slaves of joy" (*rabyn vesel'ia*) who, after exchanging the stories of their "bitter lives," decided to poison themselves together in a tavern with vinegar essence in their tea. One woman had suggested revenging themselves on the men who "betrayed them" by throwing acid at their faces. But they decided instead to kill themselves and "let our deaths fall on their heads."[141] Many suicides testified to a suppressed anger in the demonstrative symbolism of their suicides, like that of the "slave" of a "den of debauchery" who symbolically hanged herself from her bed or the streetwalkers who demonstratively killed themselves on the street.[142]

Related to these stories of sex and self was the paradox of suicide from love. Suicide as a response to spurned love was a common theme.[143] But the press was especially fascinated by double suicides of young couples, often enacted as private rituals in public places. A couple would typically dress well (even if poor), go to a popular restaurant (perhaps after first visiting a club or café chantant), take a private dining room (or perhaps meet even more privately in a hotel room), order fruit and wine (or champagne or liqueurs, perhaps accompanied by appetizers or even a whole meal), and then poison themselves (less often, shoot or stab themselves). Some included in the pre-death ritual a visit to a church or to a place in the city with sentimental significance in their relationship. The stated reasons for these suicides were most often the refusal of parents to agree to the couple's marriage as Russian law required—class difference was one of many reasons that families kept lovers apart—or poverty that stood in the way of an independent life together.[144] These were, it would seem, rituals of farewell and departure, though also celebrations of ill-fated love. Sometimes cast as "modern" "Petersburg" versions of the archetypal tragedy of idealistic young love hindered, these "St. Petersburg Romeos and Juliets" saw no other way to preserve love than though death.[145] Many of these couples proclaimed their happiness at dying, such as a nineteen-year-old man and a sixteen-year-old woman, who died embracing, after taking poison, leaving a note insisting "we are very happy, since we die loving one another."[146] On some occasions, two men committed suicide together for what were called "romantic" reasons.[147] In some cases we are told that the men, close friends, were rivals for the same woman and decided to die together as a "mark of their friendship."[148] Most cases offer no explanation of these "romantic histories," leaving it for readers to surmise whether these were friends and rivals, friends who shared disappointing relationships with different woman, or perhaps homosexuals in love with one another. Double suicides, of men as of women, reflected also the desire not to die alone, even the idea that it would be "cheerier" (*veselee*), as one eighteen-year-old metalworker suggested to a fellow worker and friend, if they committed suicide together.[149]

In stories of suicide by children, which were terribly common, "shame" was a frequent theme. It was said to result from harsh treatment at school or work or mistreatment at home, including beatings and parental drunkenness.[150] For young girls, among whom rates of suicide were reportedly higher than for boys, one of the most common reasons cited was sexual abuse and exploitation, including forced prostitution.[151] These stories invariably suggested the sensitivity of the young personality to insult but also the presumed innocence of the victim, all the more so when female. Child suicides, though only a fraction of the total number, were said to be the "saddest" of suicide statistics.[152] More to the point, they were viewed as a glaring sign of the times. The problem of child suicide had always existed, one commentator noted, but only "in our days has it become a part of everyday life [*bytovym iavleniem*]," no longer merely a "circumstance" but a "life trend."[153] And while all developed societies experienced this evil, it was felt to be sadly telling of Russia's crisis that this "tragedy of the child's soul" was much more common there than in other countries.[154] One might have hoped that children would have remained innocent of the problems of the age, safe from its ailments. Instead, every problem of contemporary life seemed to cut deeply into the spirits of the young.[155]

Through their deaths, many suicides seemed determined to speak to others, perhaps in ways they could not speak, or be heard, in life. This was not limited to final notes and letters; in any case, most suicides did not leave notes, and what notes they left often explained very little. Rather, the manner of the suicide itself could speak, to oneself through ritual and to others through performance. When men who had lost their jobs returned to their place of work to shoot themselves, they were clearly speaking through death.[156] So, as we have seen, were suicides by women who hoped to inspire guilt in the men who betrayed or violated them, suicides by prostitutes on the streets on which they walked in search of customers, and "romantic" suicides involving rituals of commemorating love crushed in the world of the living.

It is in this light that we should view the fact that suicides were very often, perhaps most often, carried out in crowded public places, in "the sight of others."[157] Whether these public suicides were speaking in voices of protest or resignation, or even implicitly "crying for help," it was clear that they did "not to want to leave the world unnoticed."[158] Common headlines like "Suicide in the Eyes of Passersby" or "Suicide in the Eyes of the Crowd" emphasized this public enactment.[159] Many suicides occurred on crowded streets or bridges. Passengers waiting at train station platforms became audiences for suicides under the wheels of arriving trains. And when the weather was warm, public parks were scenes for suicide before "the eyes of the crowd." Suicides in public places where people gathered to eat and drink were especially common, from the most elegant coffeehouses and restaurants to quite plebeian tearooms and taverns. These suicides sometimes took place directly in the sight of others, though frequently in private dining rooms, where they would not be seen (and prevented) but might be heard (from the gunshots or the moaning from knife or poison) or at least quickly discovered by waiters. There were suicides also in front of guests at balls or parties, suicides in theaters (making the performative most explicit, especially when, as in one case, a student shot himself in the head in the Mariinskii Theater near the climax of the opera *Queen of Spades*, which itself ends with a suicide), and even suicides in cathedrals and churches.[160]

If one of the more obvious reasons suicides chose public places to kill themselves was not to die alone and unseen, this reasoning, along with the desire for ritual in making one's own death, was strongly evident in what the press titled "suicides by agreement" (*po ugovoru*), where two or three people decided to die together. The regularity of "romantic" double suicides in restaurants led a newspaper columnist, already in 1908, to editorialize "again a tragedy in a restaurant, again the devil-may-care attitude, the flowers, the champagne, the separate room, the Browning."[161] Sometimes, poor people chose restaurants they could not afford for their suicides.[162] The most widely discussed suicide by agreement—which "everyone is talking about" according to the papers—was the highly ritualized suicide in early March 1910 of three young Jewish women. Two of the women, the sisters Mina and Sluva (also Russified as Slava) Kal'manson, aged eighteen and nineteen, were from a well-off Jewish family in Minsk and had come to the capital the previous August to study. The third suicide was a friend, fifteen-year-old Mariia Lur'e, also from Minsk, who was living in St. Petersburg with an aunt and attending a gymnasium. Almost every evening, according to the Kal'mansons' landlady, one could hear the sounds of "piano music, singing, and happy laughter" from their room. Everyone insisted on the pure lives led by these young women—no young man had even crossed their threshold, Ol'ga Gridina wrote in *Gazeta-kopeika*. Indeed, apart from Mariia Lur'e and the landlady, the sisters had no other visitors. Gradually, according to their landlady, their mood darkened. The problem was certainly not money; their parents regularly sent sufficient sums. On Tuesday, 2 March 1910, after school, the three girls gathered in white dresses, explaining to the curious servant that "today we will present ourselves to someone and God loves purity." They drank tea, talked, and laughed together. Sluva sang an aria from Wagner's *Tannhäuser*—the song was not identified in the reports, but it was likely Elizabeth's prayer before a shrine to the Virgin: "Here in the dust I bend before thee,/Now from this earth oh set me free. / Let me, a maiden, pure and white/Enter into thy kingdom bright." When the room grew quiet, apart from sounds of faint weeping, the servant peered through the keyhole, turning this private ritual into an unintended performance for others, which would allow it to be described in detail for a still larger audience of newspaper readers. She saw the girls, each in turn, face the east, hands held together, lips whispering what must have been, the servant concluded, a prayer. They embraced. Mina, a student at the conservatory, then sat at the piano and played Chopin's funeral march, crying. The servant and the landlady, who had joined the servant at the keyhole, noticed the three move toward a writing table with three small glasses and a flask. Assuming they were about to have something to drink, the watchers left. At two in the morning, when Mariia's aunt came looking for her niece, the three girls were found poisoned with what turned out to be cyanide. Two were already dead. Sluva died later in the hospital. Although the girls evidently had few close friends in St. Petersburg, their funeral, in the Jewish section of the Preobrazhenskoe (Transfiguration) Cemetery, attracted a huge crowd—around a thousand people according to one report, evidently mostly students—carrying wreaths (with "touching" inscriptions), roses, and lilies. During the chanting in Hebrew over the grave and the prayers by the parents, "loud crying and sobbing" was heard from the crowd. The authorities, worried about disorders, had ordered a police presence at the funeral.[163]

The strangest echo of these "suicides by agreement"—possibly more rumors than real facts—were regular reports that began to appear in 1909 about suicide clubs or leagues. Members of these organizations allegedly devised a ritual that poignantly echoed the randomness of modern peril: members drew lots to decide who should kill themselves next.[164] The three Jewish girls who poisoned themselves together in March 1910, a reporter claimed to have learned from interviewing people at their funeral, were members of a society that called itself "Closer to Death" (*Blizhe k smerti*), said to have about two hundred members.[165] A police report in 1912, following a special investigation, tried to debunk news reports that a "Suicide League" with several hundred members existed in the capital, though the report acknowledged that a series of smaller clubs where members held "talks [*besedy*] about suicide" may have existed.[166] These stories, and their performative elements, so fascinated the public that in 1915 one theater even staged an operetta called "The Suicide Club."[167] Even if these clubs did not really exist, one writer argued, the fact that there are such rumors is "itself terrible," a sign of the troubled times in which we live.[168]

The newspapers' role in transforming suicide into spectacle is an important aspect in these histories. By providing a wide audience for suicide, newspapers made suicide in the "eyes of passersby" into a virtual experience involving thousands. At least one suicide acknowledged what many commentators feared was all too common: she decided to kill herself "so that they would write about me" in the papers.[169] Certainly, the press made every effort to make these daily facts interesting to their readers, to make them a "sensation."[170] Headlines dramatically spoke of "bloody dramas," "mysterious suicides," and "bloody games with life." Though most reports were brief, the more compelling stories often included graphic narrative detail: the suicide's dress and behavior, the exact method of suicide used, the "terrible bloody scene" that witnesses saw, the precise location of the wounds, the moaning of the victim, the reactions of witnesses, and anything interesting in the suicide note. To help readers visualize the story within the landscape of the city, the precise location of the suicide was always noted.

This was all part of the typically modern "spectacle of the real," where the raw materials of everyday life become objects of avid public consumption, indeed, where represented and consumed reality becomes a key feature of that reality.[171] Rozanov, in one of his regular columns for the newspaper *Novoe vremia*, recognized this inevitable transformation of suicide into public spectacle. For the "crowd," he wrote in 1911, suicide is " 'a spectacle' and 'an incident' in life." The "impersonal 'crowd,' 'strangers' [*chuzhie*]," he argued, "feel a sort of special right, indeed a certain moral right, to the 'body of the suicide.' " Because relatives and close ones had evidently failed to care for the one committing suicide, the crowd feels that "he is now ours."[172]

INTERPRETING SUICIDE

Russia's urban public, at least those whose voices constituted its public sphere, had a desperate need to inscribe meanings on the body of the suicide. The modern drive to explain suicide was well established, of course. Susan Morrissey has shown in her study of Russian responses to suicide from the seventeenth to the twentieth centuries that authorities in both state and society worked vigorously and persistently to understand suicide and thus to mitigate it.[173] In the unstable and anxious years after 1905, the need to understand the inexplicable and control the disorderly acquired new urgency. With exceptional intensity, journalists, scientists, clergy, phi-

losophers, writers, and others tried, as one newspaper columnist put it in
1910, to "disperse the darkness" that obscured these tragic stories.[174] The
reported reasons for suicide were not enough. They raised as many questions as they answered: after all, many individuals suffered from poverty,
shame, and frustrated love but did not take their own lives. In any case, a
very large number of suicides were reported to be for "unknown reasons."

The most "scientific" explanation, favored by many medical and social science professionals in both Russia and the west, was that suicide is a
physical illness. This is the oldest of modern explanations and, updated, is
the prevailing view of specialists today, who generally view suicidal behavior
as having a psychobiological foundation, which creates the underlying vulnerability, while life events serve as proximate triggers.[175] During Russia's
suicide "epidemic" after 1905, many writers appealed for a "strictly scientific" and medical approach to the problem, including statistics and greater
use of the new science of psychology.[176] Medical professionals noted, for
example, that the disproportionate number of suicides between the ages
of sixteen and twenty reflected endemic "psychological particularities" in
the development of youth.[177] Influential physicians like Grigorii Gordon
were certain, notwithstanding Emile Durkheim's arguments, that psychology not sociology would ultimately offer the "final word" on the causes of
suicide.[178] At a simpler and more popular level, newspaper reports often
branded suicides "mentally ill" (*dushevnyi bol'noi*), "psychologically disturbed" (suffering from *dushevnoe rasstroistvo*), or, most bluntly, "insane"
(*sumashchedshii*).[179]

Few seemed satisfied, however, with explanations that located the
primary cause of suicide in *individual* minds and bodies. Perhaps because
Russia's social and political crisis was so much greater after 1905 than it
had been in the nineteenth century, fewer commentators were now inclined
to view mental and nervous disorders as holding the key to unlocking the
mystery of suicide. The physician Vladimir Chekhov, for example, in a
public interview in 1913, insisted that the majority of suicides were not in
any way abnormal. No doubt, he added, at the moment a person attempts
suicide he or she is "in a state of spiritual upheaval" (*dukhovnoe vozbuzhde-
nie*). But this signifies little, for "the whole of our life" is "constant spiritual
upheaval."[180] It was precisely to this "whole of our life" that most looked for

answers. Suicide was somehow a message, a symbol, and a sign, a "bloody reproach to those remaining alive,"[181] which had to be interpreted. This pointed beyond the private illnesses or sorrows of an individual's life toward social illness and sorrow. The positive reception of Emile Durkheim's 1897 book *Suicide* when it appeared in Russian translation in 1912 reflected this strong inclination to find the origins of suicide in the dysfunctions of social community, especially the modern metropolitan community.[182] The evidence of suicide, including the words suicides left in their notes, which were widely printed and discussed, was seen to document "social moods and vibrations" (*nastroenii i kolebanii*), even the "characteristics of a whole society and the conditions in which it lives."[183] Overwhelmingly, Russian public commentators tried to explain the "epidemic" of suicide in these years by substituting the ailing social body, especially its moral disorders, for dead individual ones.[184]

Some writers went quite far in deploying suicide as political and social criticism, notwithstanding the restrictive environment for public debate. Writing in the left-leaning "thick journal" *Sovremennyi mir* (Contemporary World), Dr. Zhbankov blamed "the abnormal human relations and antisocial conditions of our life" for "carrying off a huge number of victims" by suicide. He named poverty, hunger, unemployment, and a "traumatic" recent history of war, revolution, violence, and bloody repression for devaluing human life.[185] The traumatized body of the suicide became another sign of the sickness afflicting Russia's social body.[186] But this illness was not only the effect of particular social and political conditions or events. Most commentators saw the harm of the age as more fundamental—as cultural, existential, even philosophical.

Suicide, one commentator typically put it, was everywhere a concomitant of the "development of civilization."[187] And civilization, by the early twentieth century, meant the particular modernity of urban, industrial, capitalist society. It was no coincidence, writers repeatedly noted, that suicide on a large scale was mainly an urban problem.[188] Nor was it a coincidence that St. Petersburg, the symbol and avatar of Russian modernity, was the epicenter of the catastrophe. Sometimes explanations referenced old clichés about St. Petersburg's unique characteristics: "cold, gloomy Petersburg, where the climate itself inclines one to hypochondria," as one writer characterized this popular view. But this trope was evoked mainly to dismiss it, in order to focus on the deepening modernity of St. Petersburg as the source of harm.[189] Suicide rates were exceptionally high in St. Petersburg not because of the distinctly Petersburgian or even Russian peculiarities of the capital, but because Petersburg life more and more closely resembled the "conditions of life" in western European cities, both economically and in its "spirit" (*dukhovnie otnoshenii*).[190]

In the nineteenth century, in Russia as elsewhere, suicide was already attributed to modern "civilization," which was said to bring new desires and thus new disillusionments, rampant immorality, and an unprecedented disordering of the nerves.[191] As the pace of Russia's economic and social transformation accelerated to "head-spinning speed,"[192] this diagnosis of modern life's ill effects acquired a sense of catastrophic peril. Again and again in the early 1900s, writers of all ideological stripes spoke of the profound harm caused by the damaging "atmosphere" of modern social life, especially in big cities, including "feverish" tempos, lack of stability and security, an "unhealthy life" for the working majority, and endemic "individualism."[193] For those who saw mental disorder at the base of suicide, the exceptionally stressful conditions of the modern city were identified as a leading cause of mental illness.[194]

The fact that so many new arrivals to the capital took their own lives easily became a critical theme for interpreting the modern city.[195] Too many people from the provinces, Ol'ga Gridina warned in *Gazeta-kopeika*, mistakenly imagine the metropolis, especially St. Petersburg, to be "the best place in the world," a "magical" place filled with "light and culture." And so they come by the thousands to the capital, where they learn that "in fact, nowhere is a person so alone, pathetic, and unhappy as in big cities." As a result, cities like St. Petersburg and Moscow "are stained every day with the blood of dozens of suicides. If one could count the numbers who sorrow [*toskuiushchie*] and suffer in cities, humanity would shudder." Making critical use, as many did, of the suicide in 1910 of the three girls from Minsk, Gridina concluded bluntly: they would still be alive if the city's "cold stone enormity had not surrounded them."[196] The big city, journalists like Gridina warned the naive, was a fatal "mirage," a murderous "trap," a devouring "stone monster."[197] Perhaps especially when little was known about a suicide, reference to the seductive dangers of city life seemed explanation enough. Repeatedly, we hear writers imposing on these stories melodramatic images of individuals "crushed" by the city's harsh and "soulless" spirit and "violated" by its immorality and deceit.[198] The loneliness of the individual in the modern metropolis was a pervasive theme. Newspaper stories about suicide highlighted metropolitan solitariness amidst the crowd, the endemic solitude and alienation in big cities that, given the natural human need for connectedness, can develop into an "illness" (*boleznennosti*).[199] Many suicides themselves spoke of loneliness.[200] Even the refrain in many suicide notes that "no one is to blame for my death" may be seen as a marker of solitude, as may the ways suicides reached out to others when taking their own lives: suicides were performed deliberately before the eyes of the "soulless" public as a "protest" against "exclusion from life."[201]

Looking for the dark heart of suicide, observers particularly noted the ubiquity in suicide notes of the word *razocharovanie*—disillusionment, disenchantment, disappointment. Suicides spoke repeatedly of their "disillusionment with people" (*razocharovanie v liudiakh*) and "disenchantment with life" (*razocharovanie zhizn'iu* or *v zhizni*).[202] In turn, interpreters found in this sensibility, seen as characteristic of the times, suicide's most "essential" cause.[203] Sometimes, the word was not literally present but implied in other common tropes in suicide notes. A working-class wife poisoned herself because "my life has not worked out as I wanted or as I imagined it."[204] The three young Jewish women from Minsk died together because they found in St. Petersburg "no meaning in the tedium of everyday life."[205] Nineteenth-century suicides had offered similar explanations, speaking of "boredom with life" (*skuka zhizni*), especially with a life of privileged idleness, of growing "fed up" with life's emptiness.[206] By the early twentieth century, especially after 1905, such feelings had become "democratic," as it were, less tied to the privileges of class and education; anyone now, it seemed, could feel that it was "tedious to live" (*skuchno zhit'*).[207] Moreover, though "boredom" was still heard in the vocabulary of suicides and their interpreters, stronger words now predominated, pointing to a deeper disenchantment, often entwined with the deepening social, political, and cultural crisis.

Needing to deconstruct and interpret "disenchantment"—for this was a "subjective" and "ambiguous" (*neopredelennoe*) term, Dr. Gordon recognized[208]—many commentators saw clues in another phrase often heard in suicide notes: "loss of faith." The simplest interpretation of what this meant was concretely historical and political: suicide due to the collapse of hopes for political and social change in Russia in the aftermath of the revolution of 1905. In Durkheim's explanatory model, one of the major causes of suicide, perhaps its primary cause, was a condition of social and moral disintegration in which common values and common meanings are no longer understood or accepted, and new values and meanings have not developed.[209] Many Russian writers described precisely this condition in the wake of 1905. The well-known psychiatrist Vladimir Bekhterev, for example, diagnosed suicide as the result of the "disordered life" that resulted from Russia's recent history of war, revolution, and political dissatisfaction.[210] More poetically, Viacheslav Ivanov, in an essay on suicide, described a succession of recent catastrophes undermining attachment to life: "the hecatomb of war, the hecatomb of revolution, the hecatomb of reaction, so many shaken certainties, so many exposed illusions."[211]

Most writers did not find this conjunctural explanation adequate, seeing instead (or alongside it) a vaguer disenchantment—something more existential and philosophical, something closer to what Friedrich Nietzsche called, in his reflections on Fedor Dostoevsky's images of suicide, the spiritual "catastrophe" of modern man faced with the essential loss of certain meaning and truth in life.[212] In this, as in much else, there was an echo, though louder and more desperate, of nineteenth-century anxieties about disintegrating traditions, loss of faith in former certainties and ideals, and a "spiritual illness" marked by "boredom and sickness of heart"[213] that was said to afflict victims of Russia's first suicide epidemic. In the early twentieth century, this illness had become much more widespread, invasive, and perilous.

Religious writers about suicide treated "loss of faith" literally. Aleksandr Bronzov, an outspoken professor of moral theology at the St. Petersburg Theological Academy, blamed the rise of suicide on the whole of modern "European culture" with its fatal combination of religious "indifference" (*indifferentizm*) and overly stimulated conditions "of modern life as a whole," which led to dissatisfaction with and even "disgust" for life.[214] Other religious writers spoke of suicide as a consequence of the "noxious breath of modernity" (*tletvornoe dykhanie sovremennosti*), the "spiritual bankruptcy" of the age, the "emotional disenchantment" that prevented unity with anything ideal, the painful "indeterminacy" of modern "mental" life, and a "corrosive skepticism" and "disenchantment" that made it "hard to continue to exist."[215] Critics of religion, by contrast, attributed some suicides to Christian faith itself, with its interpretation of death as a true "realization of life,"[216] even, as Rozanov bitterly argued, a tendency to "dress death up in mysticism" and elevate it to the "main ideal."[217]

For most writers about suicide, however, "loss of faith" entailed a more sweeping loss than that of religious belief alone. For the Marxist philosopher Anatolii Lunacharskii, suicide is always a "philosophical moment" when a person asks himself "What is life all about? What is this strange world?"[218] In this age, it seemed, the answers were becoming darker. As Zhbankov put it, in "recent years" we have been living in one of those "dark epochs" (*besprosvetnye epokhi*) when "faith" in other people and "connections" to other lives and to one's own life "collapse," enticing one "to the abyss of self-destruction."[219] Behind this loss of faith "in people" was the philosophical and emotional loss of faith "in life itself." Or, as so many suicides remarked in their final notes, echoing a phrase widespread in public life: in these times "life is cheap."[220]

Efforts to explain the loss of faith in life led in different directions. Some writers found a political logic: life had lost value in the conditions of Russian existence because of pervasive suffering, brutality, and violence.[221] More philosophical writers like Lunacharskii saw the root of suicidal disenchantment in the essential modern discovery that the natural world was not guided by a sentient lawmaker and divine covenants with man but was "absolutely indifferent," "murderously" driven by its own inner laws, leading people to realize that they are only "slaves" of "faceless fate" (*bezlikoi fatal'nosti*), that there is no place for human dreams and hopes. This "bourgeois pessimistic materialism," which Lunacharskii judged the pervading ideology of the day, leads "logically" to suicide.[222] For Lunacharskii, of course, this was not a reason to despair: this disenchantment with old myths was a necessary step toward the truer faith that the collective and socialism would bring redemption. But many were not comforted by this new faith, especially after the failure of 1905. As one young suicide wrote, in a note found on her body: "We people of the twentieth century are without faith, without hope, without the desire to live. Neither Christ, nor socialism, nor man—nothing exists for us except thinking, and thinking leads to suicide."[223]

For most writers, loss of faith could not be explained by the loss of ideological illusions any more than by loss of religious certainty, but by something still deeper, more elusive, and less resolvable. Commentators described a fatal emotional atmosphere of "sorrow" and "despair." People had become "exhausted, worn out from thinking, at a dead end" (*izmuchenilis', izdumalis', prikhodiat v tupik*).[224] One report on the triple suicide of the three young women in 1910 noted that Mina Kal'manson, who was evidently the first to suggest suicide to her sister and friend, kept a diary filled with "pessimistic" thoughts.[225] Some writers diagnosed a deep "taedium vitae" in the contemporary mood,[226] a fatal "exhaustion from the burden of living."[227] In this "depressed social atmosphere," a newspaper columnist wrote, with its spirit of "sorrow, depression, and apathy," the "microbes of suicide grow and multiply rapidly."[228] These were what Rozanov called "cultural suicides": meaningful gestures addressing the meaninglessness of life.[229]

Some critics blamed contemporary literature, where a "suicide epidemic" was raging just as it was in real life, for nurturing suicidal moods.[230] Educators were particularly concerned with the psychological and emotional effects of literature, especially in Russia where the writer was viewed as a moral authority. That so many writers "paint Russian reality in the gloomiest colors, endow their heroes with pessimistic worldviews, sometimes to the point of despair, do not show them any bright hopes for a better future," and then suggest that the only exit is to take their own lives, was seen as a lethal combination.[231] Writers themselves insisted on their innocence—their work only reflected reality, it did not shape it. Some critics partially agreed: literature had not created the contemporary "heavy atmosphere" of "helplessness and spiritual confusion," but it was irresponsible for writers not to counter this mood, to allow themselves to be "empty, or confused, or preach death," to respond to the great question "to be or not to be" by implying that it was better not to be.[232] Along with contemporary literature, modern philosophy, science, and culture were blamed for nurturing a corrosive philosophical mood. Among the leading culprits were Charles Darwin (the theory of evolution allegedly devalued human life) and especially Nietzsche.[233] The fifteen-year-old suicide Mariia Lur'e, the press pointedly alleged, knew almost all of Nietzsche by heart.[234]

Suicide as disenchantment with life was sometimes portrayed as a positive gesture of heroic virtue and refusal, a defiant response to the tragic nature of contemporary existence. As the literary critic Nikolai Abramovich put it, in his contribution to a 1911 collection of essays on suicide by leading Russian intellectuals, the overwhelming majority of suicides died "paradoxically" from wanting so much to live, from "an unsatisfied hunger for life." The young, in particular, were filled with vital dreams and imagination but starved by actual existence. This, Abramovich concluded, was the tragic condition of the "spirit of modern man" (*dusha cheloveka sovremennosti*), "crippled" in the struggle to fully live.[235] Other writers similarly argued that modern life was marked by a fatal contradiction between heightened desires and the actual conditions of "bland and empty" "reality."[236] This reading of suicide was ambiguous: suicides were noble and heroic in refusing to give up their dreams and illusions but also emotionally crippled by life.[237] Cutting through this paradox, though, was the ultimately political condemnation of life as it actually was—at least in the interpreting voice of commentators.

Observers similarly saw a sublime disenchantment in suicides by lovers faced with obstacles to their love. Recounting the story of a gymnasium student who shot himself on the grave of a friend, a *gimnazistka*, who had died of cholera, a newspaper reporter found something "clean" and bright in this death, a love that illumines the surrounding "dark gloom of life," that proves that "crassness" (*poshlost'*) has not conquered. "Their death is poetry."[238] The same implication that there is "poetry" in suicide can be found in the framing of double love suicides among the young as classic literary tragedies, as modern Petersburg versions of the tragedy of Romeo and Juliet. "Such suicides," Iulii Aikhenval'd concluded, "like Romeo and Juliet, sing hymns of life with their deaths," they are acts of "idealism—a sacrifice on the altar of the great goddess Life, a religious act of humility and ascetic devotion [*podvizhnichestvo*]."[239] Suicides themselves sometimes encouraged such interpretations (or perhaps were encouraged by them) when they proclaimed their happiness at dying.[240]

The political implications of reading suicides as critiques of life could be explicit.[241] It was easiest to frame suicides due to poverty or other humiliations of everyday life as using the grammar of death to censure life. But even when the reasons were elusive, suicide as such could be interpreted as a "final protest against the abnormal human relations and antisocial conditions of our life," "a mass bloody protest against life as it is," a "philosophical protest" against modern dehumanization and hopelessness.[242] Many suicide notes encouraged and echoed these arguments:

> Why is there so much suffering, which we are not in a position to relieve? Why is there so much injustice in how people are treated: so many honest people, working hard all their lives, who are beaten down and suffer without good reason, while stupid and mean people do nothing and enjoy all the blessings of life? . . . Why do we live? No reason at all. Like marionettes we swing to and fro, until the darkness falls.[243]

> Our life, ladies and gentlemen [*gospoda*—he is clearly writing for an anticipated audience], is without truth or justice [*bez pravdy*]. It is empty, gloomy, and cold. . . . To change life is more than I, as a small particle in this life, have the power to do, so it is better to separate myself from this life. Most troubling of all is that being conscious of all the pettiness [*poshlosti*] of life, I myself fell into this maelstrom of lies and injustice [*nepravdy*].[244]

At its deepest level, it was widely agreed, suicide was a "catastrophe of the self" (*katastrofa lichnosti*).[245] Across the political and philosophical spectrum, urban writers agreed that individuals were perishing because of the widespread "suppression of the person" (*podavlenie lichnosti*) in everyday modern life," because of the "suffering" and "despair" of human self, spirit, and soul (*lichnost', dukh,* and *dusha*) amidst the fundamentally "catastrophic" nature of the existence, because "they lack the possibility of realizing themselves, of living with their authentic 'I'" in the "the dark pit of life."[246]

The philosophically and ideologically important category of *lichnost'*—the person, the personality, the self—was repeatedly named or implied in these interpretations. *Lichnost'* had been a critical category in Russian intellectual, political, and literary discourse for much of the preceding century. It was used not only to explore inward subjectivities but to challenge conditions of Russian, and modern European, life that violated human dignity and natural rights. Intellectuals and writers continually diagnosed a deep "antihuman" harm to the self growing out of Russia's backwardness—its political autocracy and semifeudal social inequalities—but also out of Russia's intensifying experience of urban capitalist modernity.[247] While this had mainly been a discourse among educated elites in the nineteenth century, by the early 1900s even newspapers were speaking in philosophical and moral terms about the self and existence. Suicides were often presented as morality plays in which the suffering self was the victim of contemporary social life. Newspaper writers understood the appeal of this melodramatic narrative frame, often headlining suicide reports as "tragedies of the humiliated" and "dramas of the insulted and humiliated."[248] Suicide notes, often quoted in the press, also spoke regularly of selves fatally "insulted and slandered," of the struggle to endure an age when "man [*chelovek*] is valued cheaper than trash," of existence as "humiliation" (*unizhenii*).[249] Women were key figures in these social melodramas: newer to public life and assumed to have more delicate and innocent selves than men, women were viewed as the most sensitive barometer of the antihuman conditions of social life. In particular, they were expected to be more susceptible to victimization amidst the moral disarray of the times: to feel "shame," "humiliation," and "disgust" when experiencing the "meaningless" debauchery that had become so characteristic of the age.[250] The elements of melodrama in reporting suicide—and in suicides' own public presentations of self in their notes—was interpretative: melodrama not only as excess, sensation, and emotion but structured around an essentially moral (indeed, Manichean) interpretation of reality and of the fate of the individual.[251]

Suicide as a response to humiliation and insult could be read in positive terms as a sign of a heightened "self-consciousness" (*samosoznanie*), even among the most degraded, such that the daily humiliations of life were no longer bearable.[252] Even prostitutes felt this: hence so many tales of prostitutes sitting together in "some stifling and stagnant tavern amidst rowdiness and drunken intoxication and poisoning themselves with vinegar essence" because a sense of "self-consciousness," of their own "humanity" and "dignity," had awakened within them.[253] It seemed that the modern cultural imperative to "realize your self" (*proiavlai svoiu lichnost'*) risked also nurturing feelings of insult and fatal despair, when possibilities for self-realization were restricted by the real conditions of daily life.[254]

Focus on the self in suicide also led to reflections on the will. A few commentators echoed the Romantic ideal of suicide as a positive and often defiant act of autonomous selfhood and sovereign will.[255] The natural and sacred right of every human being to control his or her own life, some commentators on suicide continued to argue, was upheld most powerfully, if most tragically, precisely by taking it.[256] Even more, suicide could be a "free and bold" act of willful reason and virtue against surrounding irrationality and evil, a "protest, written in our own blood" that declared "I will live not how I must but how I want," even if this means to willfully die.[257] The "epic serenity" (*epicheskoe spokoistvie*), calmness, even happiness, noticed among suicides on the point of taking their own lives,[258] especially in their final notes, seemed to suggest the self's transcendence of despair though an act of free agency.

Most commentators, however, saw just the opposite in suicide: not sovereignty, free will, heroic virtue, and transcendence but weakness and degradation of self and will. Psychiatrists, educators, clergy, and newspaper columnists almost all agreed: suicide was a sign of "cowardice," "weakness of will, lethargy, flabbiness," and a lack of "strength of spirit" to face the "ordeals" of modern life.[259] Suicide notes demonstrated this degeneration of the will. Rozanov wrote with disgust of the "apologetic, acquiescent, stooping" (*izviniaiushchagosia, ustupaiushchago, skloniaiushchagosia*) language and tone so typical of suicide notes. The "secret epitaph" over the graves of so many seemingly unexplained suicides, Rozanov argued, was "In my conscious mind [*soznanie*] all is bright. But in my will there is such darkness."[260] Lunacharskii believed that human will had weakened in modern times because of the "murderous" modern knowledge that "free will" is an "absurd illusion." The "seductive demon of suicide" does its work on this modern foundation.[261]

Still, so many suicides did remain unexplained. To be sure, the flood of public discourse about suicide sought to "disperse the darkness." Interpreters tried to analyze it with the help of statistics, medicine, psychology, sociology, philosophy, and ethics, as well as varied cultural and political ideologies. As Susan Morrissey has shown, many professional specialists were reasonably confident in this scientific age that they could explain most suicides. But this confidence was difficult to sustain, especially in the uncertain years after 1905. Newspaper reports continually repeated the stubborn tropes of mystery, enigma, and "the unknown."[262] Statistics confirmed that nearly half of all suicides registered by the Petersburg government were for "reasons unknown."[263] Even more perplexing was the frequency of suicide "for no particular reason." And what many suicides considered a "reason" was only "a figment of their imagination, an illusion, a phantom."[264] It was widely recognized that the motives that suicides offered for their acts, such as poverty, complications in love, or family problems, were often only the "proximate reason" (*blizhaishchii povod*) not the deeper cause.[265] As the newspaper columnist "Vadim" observed, the list of reasons usually given for suicide was not adequate to dispel the "mystery" (*taina*), for in all times and places there have been incurable diseases, hopeless poverty, shattered love, and even "disenchantment with life," but at no time and place has suicide been so ubiquitous as in Russia today.[266]

"All suicides," a witness to one case in 1908 told a reporter, are "enigmatically horrible" (*zagadochno uzhasnoi*).[267] Commentators continually returned to this epistemological darkness. Iulii Aikhenval'd, in response to an invitation to offer his thoughts for a book of essays about suicide, observed that any opinions he might offer could only be "more or less deep conjecture," for however "intensely one looks into the sorrowing soul that condemns itself to destruction," all interpretation must remain "theoretical."[268] Suicide among the young, especially, undermined faith in explanation— here one faced a solid wall of "unknowability" and "incomprehensibility"— for children were too young and inexperienced to fully know life and its disappointments.[269] A reviewer of the 1911 collection of essays by Russian philosophers and intellectuals agreed that suicide was the most perplexing issue of the day: "Suicide! . . . What a great, mysterious, terrible, and deeply intimate but at the same time alarming question!" "Fountains of words," he acknowledged, had already rained down on this topic. But "to talk" (*boltat'*) was easy. Real understanding remained elusive.[270] Russian commentators were not alone in their perplexity. Sigmund Freud told the Vienna Psychoanalytic Society in 1910 that we must "suspend our judgment" for though "we are anxious above all to know how it becomes possible for the extraordinarily powerful life instinct to be overcome . . . we have failed to answer this psychological question because we have no adequate means of approaching it."[271]

We too cannot be certain why so many Russians, and especially Petersburgers, in those years took their own lives. Perhaps, as scientific understanding today would suggest, the answer is that most suicides suffered from diagnosable mental illness and that the particular conditions of life in Russia and especially in big cities like St. Petersburg created the triggers that often push the psychologically vulnerable to this desperate act: poverty and economic insecurity, poor physical health, widespread alcohol abuse, disrupted family and personal relationships, the "contagion" effect, and political repression and tensions. Certainly, commentators in early twentieth-century Russia recognized the potentially devastating force of private and personal problems, including mental illness. But overwhelmingly they ascribed suicide to social problems. Most of all—and this is as telling as the terrible wave of suicides itself, and more surely interpretable— contemporaries blamed the spiritual environment of Russia's modernity. The modern age, it was repeated endlessly in press discussions of suicide, was "fractured," "chaotic," "confused," "deformed," "psychically abnormal," "morally decomposed," "degenerate," "rudderless," "out of joint," and at a "dead end." This vocabulary applied to both Russia's particular crisis, especially after 1905, and a more sweeping sense of a *mal du siècle*, of the malady of living in modern times.

Public discourse about suicide raised it into a social and philosophical sign but also a political one. In nineteenth-century Europe, there had been a tendency to romanticize the suicide as a sensitive soul crushed by a cruel world. As Honoré de Balzac put this, "every suicide is a poem sublime in its melancholy." [272] For most Russian commentators in the early twentieth century, this sublime melancholy was less a response to the eternal malevolence seen to define all of human existence than to its particularly modern evils. Freud argued in 1915 that suicide is always the result of turning hostility toward the outside world against oneself, against one's own wounded ego.[273] But where Freud emphasized personal loss and resentment, Russian writers saw social loss, a social catastrophe of the self.

Historians and cultural critics have long argued that modern societies seek to marginalize, control, and deny death. But it is also clear that modernity has brought an "intensifying preoccupation with death," including views of death as the ultimate proof of the mutability of everything and as inseparable from the construction of the desiring and frustrated modern self.[274] Russian urban writers shared this modern preoccupation with the meanings of death. For them, there was no doubt that the personal tragedies of individuals—whether as victims of illness, accident, and violence, or at their own hands—must be read as damning measures of "the times." The callousness and deceit of the modern metropolis, the sufferings endured by the self, the loss of clear values or ideals, were among the features of modern life that could kill. The epidemic of death, and the sometimes desperate torrent of words around it, also reminded them of the persistence of incomprehensibility, uncertainty, and the unknown.

Decadence

Human culture at its peak has an irresistible inclination
toward degeneration, decadence, and exhaustion.

—Nikolai Berdiaev, 1917

A society in which corruption spreads is accused of exhaustion. . . .
It is precisely in times of "exhaustion" that tragedy runs through
houses and streets, that great love and great hatred are born,
that the flame of knowledge flares up into the sky.

—Friedrich Nietzsche, 1882

Excess, sickness, and decline were among the key images contemporaries
used to describe the moral and spiritual condition of public life in Russia. Whether speaking of the disordered life of "the street" or of "epidemics" of violence and death, the press continually pointed to signs that the
present age was characterized by illness and decay. Most alarming of all, it
seemed that the modern myth of time as "progress"—the promise of continual change for the better—was itself falling into ruin. Indeed, "falling"
and "ruin" were common terms in what was often a melodramatic account
of modern sickness: melodramatic both in the emotional excess of presentation and in its moralizing premises. To be sure, the Petersburg press spec-
tacularized evidence of moral degeneration to sell papers, but not only to
this end: newspapers also shared their readers' troubled fascination with
the illnesses of modern society. As talk of sickness and decline became part
of the daily news, it should be noted, writers were not inclined to evoke the
traditional philosophical recognition of "the destructiveness of time and
the fatality of decline."[1] Rather, theirs was a consciously modern diagnosis

of modern public life, exemplified by St. Petersburg, as producing a quite new experience of moral and spiritual corruption.

This discourse was not unique to Russia, of course. It echoed talk of civilizational "degeneration" heard throughout Europe in the late 1800s, where the vocabulary of "degeneration" appeared in biological arguments about evolution containing paths of decline, in medicalized diagnoses of individual human degeneration by influential specialists like Benedict Morel and Cesare Lombroso, in sweeping denunciations of degenerate fin-de-siècle culture and art (most famously by the social critic Max Nordau), in sociological studies of the urban crowd and crime, and in literary accounts of corrupted individual and social bodies. Time was already at the center of attention: the Enlightenment faith in progress was displaced by a language of sickness and decline. And blame was increasingly laid at the feet of modern civilization: the view of degeneration as a pathology of individuals was "displaced . . . to society itself—crowds, masses, cities, modernity."[2] Literature and art in fin-de-siècle Europe was famously suffused with a troubled consciousness of modern corruption, sickness, decline, and ruin, and not merely as a decadent aesthetic but also as a direct response to the suffering of the individual in the conditions of modern urban life.[3] Russians shared these preoccupations. Many artists embraced decadence: illness, perversity, decline, and ruin were fulsomely explored in fin-de-siècle Russian poetry, prose, and painting, especially after 1905. And, as in the west, this was both an artistic stance and an interpretation of the world.[4] Also, Russian physicians, psychiatrists, criminologists and other professionals, as Daniel Beer has shown, knew and used European arguments about degeneration as they sought to explain criminality, violence, suicide, and other social pathologies. And they agreed—indeed, even more readily than their European colleagues—that the social environment was decisive in the etiology of degeneracy.[5]

The urban Russian encounter with degeneration was different, however. If Russians were not original in diagnosing and describing decadence—the words had all been spoken before—these worries were more widespread in society, more public, and ultimately more pessimistic. The mood in the west, in fact, was brightening up: pessimism about civilization had begun to fade in western Europe in the decade before World War I, leading observers to speak of "moral regeneration."[6] Russians, by contrast, were less sanguine. Part of the difference may be attributed to Russian "backwardness": a belated and more sudden experience of industrialization, urbanization, capitalism, and revolution. The shock was still new and the solutions less evident. Also, the Russian encounter unfolded with prepared European interpretations at hand to help frame problems as pathologies. But perhaps the most important difference was not Russian "backwardness" but the opposite. As I have suggested in other chapters, there were many ways, not least in their own perceptions, that Russians, especially in St. Petersburg, felt modernity's crisis with particular intensity and clarity. Precisely because of the rapidity and harshness of Russian modernization and the publicity surrounding both problems and critical judgments (especially after censorship loosened in 1905), Russians, especially in St. Petersburg, were exceptionally well positioned to see the wreckage that progress brought.

THE SPIRIT OF THE AGE

The metropolis inspired rhetoric about decadent decline. But concerns about particular urban pathologies led to, and were informed by, sweeping reflections on the "spirit of the age." Often this was a vague perception of some shadowy malevolence in the cultural air. A columnist for *Gazeta-kopeika* in 1913, for example, detected a pervading "spirit of evil," one of "gigantic dimensions" and "monstrous ugliness," living at the heart of "our fractured [*raz"edinennoi*] life."[7] A reader of *Zhizn' dlia vsekh* wrote to this popular journal in the same year saying he felt the presence of "something fatal" in contemporary life, evident in widespread crime, murder, hooliganism, prostitution, and other "torments" (*muki*) of urban life. But these were only the "symptoms" of the deeper illness: "poisoning by the fumes of hell."[8]

Sickness was a ubiquitous metaphor in writing about the city. Some understood it literally, to mean the many physical illnesses rampant in urban life, from venereal disease to cholera. But more common were diagnoses of spiritual, moral, and existential illness: the "general sickness from which all strata of our society suffer—the sickness of madness, the loss of faith in the future, and bewilderment and disillusionment."[9] Children were viewed as especially susceptible to falling morally and spiritually ill in these times, and their fall was viewed as especially troubling. Children were born pure, it was argued, and their young lives should be happy and "bright"—a quite modern ideal of childhood, of course. But so many children had become "infected" with the "illness" affecting modern society, that of "devalued life."[10] Poor children were at risk especially from the temptations of the street, which threatened to "infect" children with a plenitude of morally debased values and behaviors that often led to "complete moral degeneration" (*nravstvennaia porcha*), frequently accompanied by physical degeneration, evident in their "rickety heads, crooked little legs, and pale sickly faces."[11]

Urban commentators endlessly described an atmosphere, concentrated in large cities like Petersburg but spreading though the whole national body, of "decline" *(upadok)*, "disintegration" (*razlozhenie)*, "breakdown" *(razval)*, "decadence" (*dekadans*), and "degeneration" (*vyrozhdenie, degeneratsiia*)—a mixture of familiar Russian terms with a borrowed and adapted European vocabulary. Newspaper reporters and columnists applied notions like "degeneracy" to much of public life: violent criminals, sexual libertines, the demimonde, alcoholics, modern artists, and suicides, if not the whole of the urban population. One journalist typically described these as psychologically "abnormal times" marked by widespread "degeneration" (the author uses both *vyrozhdenie* and *degeneratsiia*), one of the chief signs of which is a public "mood" in which neurotic impulsiveness overwhelms the power of the rational will.[12] Other writers were even more sweeping in denouncing modern degeneration. The influential conservative critic Viktor Burenin, writing in 1910 in the newspaper *Novoe vremia*, described the "new manners [*manery*]" of the twentieth century as resembling the manners of "some sort of unstrung and undisciplined degenerates" or simply ordinary "idiots and cretins."[13] Many critics suggested that modern humanity was descending in its moral and spiritual evolution to the level of "animals," "beasts," and "savages."[14]

While many of these jeremiads came from political and cultural conservatives, left-wing and liberal writers offered almost identical judgments. Evgenii Maksimov, an activist in the cooperative movement, writing under the pseudonym M. Slobozhanin in *Zhizn' dlia vsekh* in 1913, described "the modern experience" as a mixture of "progress" and "degeneration." While "physical and moral degenerates" had existed in all times and places, he recognized, in certain conditions, as in Russia today, this degeneration was so pervasive, strong, and deep as to threaten the nation and perhaps humanity. Also, in such times, "new types of degenerates" were appearing, especially among modern writers, artists, and intellectuals, whose rejection of established moralities yielded only ruin and "zoological" values. But degenerates also filled the streets and criminal courts. These new "heroes of our time," Slobozhanin observed, appeared civilized and well-behaved and were often the "life and soul of society," but beneath this surface were all the marks of degeneracy: egoism, lack of empathy for the suffering of others, dehumanization, "animal-like cruelty," and impassive "mask-like" faces and other "physical marks of degeneration." These "heroes of our sad reality" had "lost the very likeness of human beings" (*cheloveskii obraz*). While Slobozhanin saw such degeneracy as essentially physiological, citing the noted Russian criminologist Dmitrii Dril' as authority, he believed that its sources were environmental: the "unhealthy life of modern humanity."[15]

Especially widespread was talk of "upadok"—a term suggesting a mixture of decline, decay, disintegration, breakdown, and decadence, especially of society and culture. Writers worried in the broadest terms about the "decline [*upadok*] of faith and morality," even among Christian believers.[16] Others spoke of "decline in our very civilization."[17] Above all, decline seemed intrinsic to *urban* civilization. The many horrors of public street life—such as violence, rape, and suicide—were defined in precisely these terms: "look at how far our moral decline has gone."[18] Cities were seen as generating this decadent spirit—evident in the debased mores of the urban crowd that had developed the same animal tastes as "any European crowd."[19]

These urban writers already implicitly understood later definitions of modernity as fragmentation, lost totality, and ruin. Linguistically, they repeatedly described the decadence of public mores using a host of terms marked with the prefix *raz-*, denoting fracturing, disintegration, and collapse. They wrote of widespread "disorder" (*razbrod*), "moral breakdown" (*razval nravstvennyi*), "breakdown of the spirit" (*razval dukha*), people feeling morally and physically broken and crushed (*razbityi*).[20] Above all, they spoke of pervading and deepening *razlozhenie*—a ubiquitous term usually

translated as disintegration but also containing meanings of decomposi-
tion, dissolution, and internal collapse. For a columnist in the conservative
newspaper *Novoe vremia*, the "coherence" of the past had been replaced by
a present and future defined by "more and more *razlozhenie*," specifically
the disintegration of values, ideas, and worldviews.[21] Conservative religious
writers went further and diagnosed pervasive "collapse and bewilderment"
(*raspad i rasteriannost'*) in Russian life, including a decadence of thought
attributable to the rise of materialism and positivism, which nurtured in
the human spirit only "contradiction" and "chaos."[22] Conservative and
religious reactions to modern decadence tended to be among the most impassioned, but similar concerns about moral and spiritual breakdown were
shared by the secular and liberal press. The main difference was that conservatives and religious believers had faith that there were solutions and that
they knew where the solutions lay. Secular liberals were less confident.

     Moral breakdown was a defining symptom. As one writer put it bluntly,
the twentieth century, in moral terms, was a completely "other age" when
"everything is perverted and dishonored" (*izvrashcheno, oporocheno*).[23]
Which brings us to another ubiquitous term, which both embodied the concrete forms of moral breakdown and suggested its moral meaning: *razvrat*.
A promiscuous term, translatable variously as debauchery, depravity, and
dissipation, *razvrat* embraced a range of immodest and immoral behaviors,
especially but not solely sexual. *Razvrat* was applied not merely to "dens
of debauchery" (*pritony razvrata*) but also more broadly to café life (where
so many "habitués" were judged to be *degeneraty*),[24] gambling, prostitution, pornography, drug use, the demimonde, loose women, lecherous men,
and more. In "our capital," a newspaper columnist insisted, *razvrat* had
acquired the aura of a popular "cult"—the *kul't razvrata*.[25] And it reached
from the elites to the masses. Among the latter, writers noted the harmful
influences of popular theater, described as "depravity for everyone" (*vsena-
rodnoe razvrashchenie*), and of cinema, said to "deprave the masses" (*raz-
vrashchaet massy*).[26] Metaphorically, evidence of urban *razvrat* suggested a
city drowning in its own decay. Many wrote of a "torrent" or "wave" of filth
and debauchery flooding the capital.[27] Newspaper headlines about street
crime, murders, suicides, and debauchery often represented these as part of
the "maelstrom of life" (*omut zhizni*), a term, to be sure, that suggested both

danger and allure.[28] In a related metaphor, St. Petersburg reminded many observers of a "modern Babylon," with its frenzied debauchery (*razgul i besnovanie*)[29] and mixtures of egoism, boredom, and cheap pleasure.[30] Or of a "modern Sodom" where, as Ol'ga Gridina wrote in *Gazeta-kopeika*, "goodness, guilelessness, and trustfulness" had vanished so completely that God would not be able to find even one "righteous person" for the sake of which the city might be spared (in the original Sodom, it bears recalling, one righteous person *was* found but God required at least ten).[31]

At the heart of all this public *razvrat*, many argued, was an essential "demoralization."[32] *Demoralizatsiia* was described in many ways, often echoing western European descriptions of decadence and degeneration, especially among "the crowd." Religious writers, always especially attentive to moral decline, regularly expressed dismay at rising moral "cynicism," "roughness," "cold-heartedness," and "savagery," in public life—visible to all in the daily papers, they made certain to add.[33] Secular urban writers said much the same. Many spoke of "cynicism" (*tsinizm*): the manner in which people related to one another, their modes of speech ("cynical conversations"), and the general moral atmosphere were all described as imbued with a new cynicism, with shameless contempt for cultural and moral values.[34] Others spoke of a "roughening" or "barbarizing" of mores and manners (*nravy ozhestochaiutsia, odichanie nravov*),[35] such that people were becoming more and more like savages and beasts. Many spoke of the "deformity" of public manners and morals, embodied by another ubiquitous term in this criticism of public culture: *bezobrazie*, which suggests deformity, outrage, and disgrace. Linguistically constructed not merely around notions of moral transgression but also as visible physical deformity, *bezobrazie* created a quite literal image of moral deformity.

The moral degeneration of the self was at the center of these narratives of deformity and decline. Unbounded "egoism," "individualism," and the cult of the "I" were judged to be defining values in the debased public culture.[36] For the journalist and author Mikhail Engel'gardt, for example, the greatest "specter of the times" was the "monstrous development of egoism, a general 'save yourself if you can,' the triumph of the principle of selfishness" (*torzhestvo shkurnogo nachala*) in the most "depraved forms."[37] Gridina, in surveying the widening "torrent of filth," blamed the growing cult of selfish feeling: where today, she asked, can one find "pure, tender, and good [people] able to forget their I?. . . . They don't exist. There are only brutal and morose self-lovers" for whom "nothing in the world has more value than their vicious 'I want!'"[38] Many writers defined the reigning philosophy of the day as the pathologically unrestrained pursuit of personal pleasure: "seize the moment" (*lovi moment*), "live for the present," live "intensely," always "burning the candle at both ends," with no regard for the past (which has been lost) or the future (which may never arrive). Modern urban life stimulated this desire to live intensely and passionately, while also nurturing a false belief that this was a path to personal happiness, or at least to forgetting—in reality, it was argued, this was a path to "disgust," physical and existential fatigue, and a desire for death.[39] Closely connected to egocentrism was the spreading ethos of "indifferentizm." The association of indifference with urban life was a familiar cliché: "on the street you meet and pass in an instant, gazes intersect with indifference" (*ravnodushno*).[40] This was elaborated to define the whole age as a time of spiritual and moral "hardening of the heart," "hostile suspicion toward every stranger," and widespread "apathy," cynicism, emotional coolness, and lack of empathy.[41]

Looking for the existential essence of this morally degraded age, writers continually returned to themes of breakdown, decline, and death. Nikolai Rubakin, well known for his many journalistic writings about popular reading and education, reflected in 1912 on the moral and cultural spirit he found in the many letters he had received from readers of his articles. The present age, he concluded, unlike any before, had become an "epoch of 'the suffocation of life,'" caused by the replacement of higher moral sentiments with crass material sensation, which crushes one's "soul, strength, and spirit," producing a "base" (*gnusnaia*), partial, and empty life. Ultimately this was a life that "smells of the grave."[42] In particular, every moral truth of the past had been destroyed: "We have squandered all ten commandments, thrown overboard moral dogmas. . . . Respect for the self [*uvazhenie k lichnosti*], for the value of life, for moral duty, for conscience—we have discarded like unneeded ballast, like trash."[43]

There was something reassuring, even hopeful, in the moral clarity of these accounts of degeneration. They imply a faith that, once named and examined, decadence could be cured. Like Max Nordau, many Russian critics insisted that this illness was neither incomprehensible nor fatal. "The hysteria of the present day will not last," Nordau confidently stated.[44] Similarly, biomedical specialists in Russia argued that modern science could heal these wounds and overcome "the physical and moral-mental degeneration of man."[45] As will be seen in the next chapter, social critics offered various therapies and cures, depending on belief, ideology, and taste: a new moral consciousness, a revived spirit of "will" and "reason," religion and spirituality, and liberal or revolutionary politics. Confidence that the hysteria would not last was encouraged by arguments that the decadence of the present was the result of conditions in a particular time and place. We have already seen this argument at work: to blame, the argument went, were the disorders of the 1905 revolution, the repression that followed, and the collapse of political ideals and enthusiasms. Even many liberal writers viewed unleashed freedom as a mixed blessing and a cause of decadence. Writing in the journal *Sovremennoe slovo* (Contemporary Word) in 1910, for example, S. Liubosh (Semen Liuboshits) argued that the disorder of 1905 released into the public sphere all of society's moral "trash" (*otbrosy*) and that "freedom" was used to enable more "carousing, drunken disorders, and public debauchery."[46] Others focused on the disillusionment that followed the limitations on political and civil rights, which restricted possibilities for continued public engagement, conditions that "drove everyone inward," giving rise to a great "thirst for satisfaction and pleasure."[47] But whether writers blamed the revolutionary upheavals or state repression, many who tried to define the spirit of the times agreed that the "demoralization," "fallen mores," "cynicism," and "moral collapse" of the present grew out of the conditions of this postrevolutionary era.

And yet, as we have seen before, many commentators felt that this conjunctural explanation was too easy. Rather, it seemed to be the even heavier weight of "progress" that produced so much illness and decline. As one religious journalist put it, one of the "deformities of modernity" (*urodlivye iavlenii sovremennosti*) was that "progress" turned out to be not movement forward but a "degradation of humanity," an increasing "bestialization."[48] Or as the conservative newspaper columnist Mikhail Men'shikov argued, the last half-century proved that "evolution . . . can move downward not up."[49] Liberal newspaper essayists expressed a similar anxiety about

progress: modern times seemed, at best, marked by a contradictory mixture of advancing "humanitarianism" and advancing beastliness.[50] Such
arguments were not, of course, unique to Russia. Russian urban writers
in the early twentieth century echoed—often knowingly—European commentators who had been arguing since the nineteenth century that "we are
sick with progress."[51] Or, to use a classic metaphor of decadence, modern
progress had become a wound that would not heal. It seemed especially to
fester in urban Russia.

"HEROES OF OUR TIMES"

Russian literary and intellectual life was widely described as a mirror of the
age's disintegration and demoralization. That the intelligentsia, once the
symbol of Russian civic progress and hope, suffered a crisis of faith and
commitment after 1905 has long been a familiar argument. Although roots
of a decadent turn were evident by the end of the nineteenth century—often
inspired by western European trends in philosophy, literature, and art—the
intellectual current seemed to move most dramatically after the revolution,
away from positivism and faith in progress toward a sense of displacement
and disintegration, even a foreboding, though also an imaginative anticipation, of an approaching "end." Some embraced a melancholy mood and even
dark pessimism as nurturing the sensitive and creative spirit. Some turned
to escapist aestheticism: the old world was dying, but at least it should be
a beautiful death. Some dwelled on the self as both a new source of meaning and a dark source of danger. Some nurtured a cosmopolitan "nostalgia
for world culture" or turned back to Russia's "pure" national traditions.
Some turned toward a new spirituality. Some envisioned apocalyptic transcendence out of the ruins of the old.[52] It seemed especially characteristic
of this intellectual crisis that a group of well-known intellectuals, mostly
former Marxists, should publish a collection of essays in 1909 under the
title *Vekhi* (Landmarks or Signposts, for that is where directions change),
darkly describing the intelligentsia, which had long viewed itself as Russia's
salvation, as mentally and spiritually sick—"deformed" and "crippled," in
Mikhail Gershenzon's terms. Blame was placed on the intelligentsia's tra-

ditions of materialism, atheism, social and political mission, and faith in
modern progress.[53]

Contemporary journalists spoke readily about the intelligentsia's "crisis of the spirit" (*krizis dushi*) after 1905 but expressed little sympathy. Instead of offering society new forms of faith and transcendence, these critics
complained, the intelligentsia had fallen into a maelstrom of "gloomy disenchantment" and "confusion." Or worse: "social and moral shamelessness,
the complete disintegration [*izmel'chanie*] of ideals and character," marked
by an effort to lose themselves in a whirlwind of "decadence, anarcho-
mysticism, pessimism, and pornography."[54] The leftist critic Slobozhanin
(Maksimov) criticized the intelligentsia's "revaluation of values" (most
readers would recognize the reference to Nietzsche) as ultimately a project of destruction and ruin, creating no new values or new moralities apart
from an atavistic "zoological" ideal.[55] This new spirit, critics publicly complained, was marked by a decadent cult of "ultra-egoism" that had replaced
feelings for the social.[56] Likewise, the old "passionate" debates about
politics and democracy had been pushed aside by a new passion for the
"problem" of sex and for sex itself.[57] While the *Vekhi* authors insisted that
the solution to the crisis of the intelligentsia required turning away from
obsessive "civic-mindedness" (*obshchestvennost'*) and focusing attention
on the inward, spiritual self and personality (*lichnost'*),[58] these journalists
(like many intellectuals on the left) viewed that move inward as one of the
deplorable signs of decadence. The intelligentsia was no longer viewed as
leading society upward and forward but as simply following its descent.

Contemporary Russian literature and art provided plenty of evidence
to contemporary critics of the demoralized and degenerate spirit of the
intelligentsia. As Olga Matich has shown, in her study of "the decadent
imagination in Russia's fin de siècle," literary modernists perceived, at
times obsessively, an epochal crisis of physical and mental decline, of fragmentation and fall, and of looming catastrophe and ruin. The writings (and
lives) of poets like Aleksandr Blok and Zinaida Gippius—who were often
described in the press, as Gippius was in 1912, as "modern [*sovremennaia*]
in the highest sense of this word, for she is close to our times and to our
troubled soul"[59]—were often built around images (and fears) of infected

nature, dangerous or decaying bodies, gender ambiguity, illness (especially syphilis), blood, rupture, and death. Even the imagined cure for modern fragmentation and disintegration was often decadent, especially when salvation was sought in erotic desire, however cerebral, simulated, spiritual, and transfigured.[60]

Given the traditional esteem for and influence of literature in Russian society—the nearly century-old tradition of viewing writers as moral and spiritual guides and even prophets—journalists and other public critics were concerned about the mood and message in contemporary literature. And contemporaries were much less generous in their judgment than literary and cultural historians have been. Even when critics recognized the idealism and utopianism of modernist literature, this was itself often an object of concern and contempt. The modernist search for the "new," especially for new moral and aesthetic values, for new truths and new lives, was likely to be viewed not as "life-creation" (*zhiznetvorchestvo*), a leitmotif of Russian modernism, but as existential sickness, destruction, and decline. The influential conservative critic Viktor Burenin, writing in *Novoe vremia*, sneered that contemporary writers and artists had the impudence to proclaim as some "new beauty" the ubiquitous "signs of disgusting degeneration" (*priznaki protivnoi vyrozhdennosti*).[61] The progressive critic Slobozhanin similarly viewed writers like Fedor Sologub, whose pessimistic and decadent novels and plays were popular among the urban intelligentsia in these years, as one of the "new people" with "new views" and visions of a "new beauty," who were overthrowing old values but replacing them with only narrow egoism and animal materialism.[62] The heightened attention in literature to the inner self—mocked as a "cult of one's own psychic 'I'"—was similarly criticized as producing only a "decadent" individualism that falsely sought truth in the irrational sides of the human spirit.[63] Many critics were even less sympathetic, viewing contemporary literature as lacking any ideals whatsoever, apart from indulging, along with society, in a "noisy and wild dance [*shumnaia pliaska*] of the naked and the debauched."[64]

While critics recognized that artistic and literary "decadence" was not a coherent movement but, like everything else in this age, "broken" into fragmented trends,[65] the thrust of criticism was to see an essential spiritual unity—and not only among quite varied writers but also between literature

and social life. A review of "the literature of our times" in the magazine
Novyi zhurnal dlia vsekh in 1909 by Liubov' Gurevich insisted that, for all
their differences in style and audience, the philosopher and writer Dmitrii
Merezhkovskii, the symbolist poets Valerii Briusov and Aleksandr Blok,
and the popular commercial novelist Mikhail Artsybashev (famous for his
erotic potboiler *Sanin*, first published in the Petersburg journal *Sovremennyi mir* in 1907), were all "children of one epoch," united in a common
decadent belief that truth was to be found in the inner self, pure sensation,
the irrational, and the unseen.[66] Among writers branded as adherents of
the decadent cause, Leonid Andreev was particularly savaged by critics, as
were the debased mentality and tastes that led the public to embrace him. In
the years just before 1905, Andreev had established a reputation as a writer
interested in exploring "civilization's dark side" (*oborotnaia storona tsivili-
zatsii*), as he called it in his 1902 story "In the Fog," symbolized by images
of cruelty, ugliness, destruction, death, and incomprehensibility. Critics
viewed him as at one with this dark side. Reviewing Andreev's newest play,
Anfisa, in 1909 (made into a movie in 1912), Gurevich chastised the work
as pandering to the low aesthetic and moral values of the "noisy" public,
offering the "vulgarity," "banality," and "cheap, almost boulevard romanticism" that the "crowd" desired. Even worse, Andreev offered no insights
or meaning that could illumine the "chaos" he portrayed.[67] Religious critics, like Professor A. Bronzov of the St. Petersburg Theological Academy,
who contributed frequent essays to the Academy's journal, were especially
devastating, blaming writers like Andreev for indulging and encouraging
the "senseless decadentism" (*bezsmyslennaia dekadentshchina*) of the contemporary "public," especially youth.[68]

"Futurism" (the name was given by hostile critics, but embraced by
some futurists precisely because it was provocative), which arose around
1910, was represented as a degeneration of decadence, the product of poisoning by "toxins" made in "the laboratory of decadence."[69] Futurist art
exhibits, poetry readings, and cabaret performances were favorite subjects
of sensationalist reporting and mocking humor as well as of serious critical
concern. Conservative writers were the most explicit in developing a critical interpretation. One line of argument was that futurist poets and artists
had lowered art to the level of "the street," "the crowd," and "fashion." One

religious writer saw futurists' inspiration coming not from any artistic source
but directly from the decadence of the street: "Futurism got its ideal for life
from apaches [street hooligans], the dissipated, prostitutes, and other social
scum." Their ideal was to "live for the pleasures of today and freedom for
evil."[70] This thoroughly modern spirit was evident not only in futurists'
embrace of the urban street but in their characteristic spirit of modern disintegration, disorientation, and degeneration. They embraced speed, but
with no concern for purpose or direction. Their moral ideal was the slogan
of the age: "depravity is strength" (*razvrat est' sila*). In essence, "the futurist is a Hottentot, a naked savage, in a bowler hat." Worse still, futurism
was inspired not by a vision of the future but by a "feeling of 'the end.'"[71]
In the judgment of such critics, futurism was an infectious moral disease
that needed to be fought with the same tools as consumption and plague.[72]

Journalists recognized that "decadence" in Russian literature was
part of the "whole of European modernity."[73] But in Russia the spirit of
decline went deeper. The "exotic 'Flowers of Evil' of European decadence,"
an essayist in *Novyi zhurnal dlia vsekh* argued in 1909, were transplanted
to Russia but withered in its cultural soil, leaving in their aftermath only a
mood of disgust marked by loss of belief in any objective truths, loss of the
ability to distinguish between good and evil or to recognize beauty, and so-
lipsistic despair.[74] Even more troubling, it seemed that as the intelligentsia
grew less interested in this imported decadence (a result, one critic suggested, of the "social waves" of revolution in 1905 that destroyed the "ivory
tower" in which it thrived), its poisons entered the whole of the social body,
metastasizing into "popular decadence."[75]

KHULIGANSTVO

"Hooliganism" (*khuliganstvo*) was another imported term used to cover a
multitude of sins, all on the rise, including "rowdiness, fighting, and riot
in a public place," damage to public monuments or signs, and swearing
in public, but also violent knife attacks.[76] In her insightful study of Russian hooliganism, Joan Neuberger has emphasized the relation of these behaviors and their definition under a single term to the developing public
sphere and efforts to police it. "Hooliganism" defined behaviors that inso-

lently transgressed the norms of "civilized" public life. Indeed, the growing use of the term reflected an increasingly panicked perception, especially after the upheavals of 1905, that these behaviors represented "antonyms of 'civilization.'"[77] I would go further. Hooliganism troubled the journalists and writers whose task was to map and interpret modern urban life not merely as a threat posed against social order and morality, but as a symptom of the moral breakdown of society and culture itself, of the decadence of civilization. They wrote of these street behaviors using the same diagnostic language applied to so much else in public life: depraved egoism, degenerate values, savagery. And this was not only as a definition of a threatening "other," but very often as a sign of a sickening self.

Most hooligan attacks, judging by press reports, involved violence against strangers. The vulnerability of individuals in the city of strangers was a characteristic trope of modern life. But hooliganism was special. What made muggers into "hooligans," and stimulated such anxiety and fear, was partly who they were socially and especially the moral spirit in which they acted. Socially, hooliganism was strongly associated in press reports with the "dark Petersburg" of the urban underclass, the lumpenproletariat of the homeless and unemployed, "tramps, residents of flophouses, prostitutes, and others of the Maksim Gorky type."[78] The police agreed. In trying to suppress hooliganism, the authorities organized huge raids (in one operation in September 1910, eight hundred people were rounded up) on the places where such types were believed to hole up: cheap teahouses and taverns, "dark dens," public parks on the city outskirts, and river barges. Many hooligans were picked up in the apartments of prostitutes, for quite a few lived as pimps while also working as pickpockets and thieves.[79] Hooligans tended to be young: press reports of hooligan incidents often describe the perpetrators as teenagers (podrostki). Ol'ga Gridina believed that the term "hooligan" arose precisely to give a name to the problem of large numbers of disorderly children living on the streets—the darkest aspect of big city life today, she argued.[80]

In many ways, the evidence of social distinctiveness highlighted the otherness of hooligans: they were outsiders and aliens to society. This social otherness was attached to moral difference. The most striking sign of hooligan's moral otherness, as Neuberger emphasizes, was the apparent absence of purpose or reason in their actions. At least, this was a major theme in newspaper reports. An editorial in *Gazeta-kopeika* in 1910 described a typical scenario: a decent citizen walking peacefully down the street is approached by "unknown people" who "inflict several knife wounds in the side or back without any reason and then disappear."[81] The press continually reported such occurrences. Typical was the case of two "unknown hooligans" who accosted a man on the street and, without evident cause, started an argument with him; when he tried to flee, the hooligans attacked with fists, a rock, and a dagger, wounding him severely.[82] Journalists often concluded that this was violence for violence's sake, the only purpose being aggression itself.[83] But we should not push the argument of otherness too far. The closer one looks at how these stories were framed, the more we see this uncivilized other defined as a symptom of "our times," as further evidence of society's own decline, disintegration, and degeneration. Hooliganism's otherness broke down in a context of widespread public decadence.

A key theme was hooliganism as another sign of excess. Hooligan acts strayed beyond the bounds of necessity, reason, or proportion. In an article titled "A Life for Fourteen Kopecks," *Peterburgskii listok* reported that a man was stabbed in the neck and the chest when he refused a demand for this small amount of change, needed to purchase vodka.[84] Similar reports filled the papers. Such extravagant attacks occurred in back alleys and crowded streets, by both day and night. Most of the victims, like most of the city's residents, were "little and unknown people."[85] Stabbing a stranger who refused a demand for spare change—typically to buy a drink—was treated as both an everyday story and a symbol of the time.[86] As we have seen, knife violence in public was epidemic in these years. Indeed, some hooligan knifers (*nozhevshchiki*) skipped the preliminary demands and just attacked.[87] It seemed that both reason and life had lost value. Outrageousness, lack of proportion, extravagant violation of boundaries and norms—in a word, excess—defined hooligan violence and was a key symptom of the illness of the age.

Excess was exaggerated further when hooligans united into "gangs" (*bandy, partii, shaiki*).[88] Quite typical was the report of six young males, aged between sixteen and twenty, who came upon a nineteen-year-old man walking at one in the morning through Alexander Park, near the Peter and

Paul Fortress, returning home from a performance at the People's House: the gang suddenly started whistling and shouting "beat him!" and set upon him with fists and knives.[89] Gang violence also occurred on busy streets, as when six "hooligans" came out of a restaurant one evening (presumably drunk) and beat up two printing workers who crossed their path.[90] Most often, as in these cases, working-class people were the victims, for theirs was the world out of which hooligan gangs arose and where they mainly acted. In industrial working-class neighborhoods like Okhta, groups of hooligans were said to regularly beat up randomly chosen individuals.[91] Gangs also sometimes battled one another. In 1910, a violent feud was underway between two large "hooligan parties" on Vasil'evskii Island, numbering about seventy or eighty young men, who regularly clashed, sometimes fatally. One group bore the nickname "Comrades, Don't Grieve" (*Kompaniia ne zhuris'*). The other gang was known as the "Zheleznovodskaia Street Party" or by its nickname "Seize the Moment" (*Lovi moment*), presumably borrowed, with hooligan irony, from press reports about this degenerate motto of the age.[92]

Hooligan attacks on women in the streets were treated as especially troubling signs of the degeneration of boundaries and the collapse of restraint in public life.[93] The press regularly reported "hooligans" taking advantage of the many more women now walking alone in public to brazenly offer to "accompany" them home.[94] Women who refused were fortunate if they only suffered from crass sexual propositions (*gnusnye predlozhenie*), a typical feature of these encounters, and mocking laughter when they resisted. Some women who tried to repulse these men were stabbed; some were assaulted and raped.[95] Assaults on women were viewed as more symbolically transgressive than attacks on men because of traditional notions of women as naturally more virtuous and more sensitive to insult. Also, as Neuberger has emphasized, hooligan "victimization of women" symbolically and effectively "threatened the power of respectable men to protect their womenfolk from the dangers and vices of the public streets."[96] But we need to elaborate these meanings further, as the contemporary press did, to see these attacks as perceived signs of the growing sickness of urban society itself.

Even when hooliganism was not physically violent, it was the extravagance of the public transgression of reason and morality that defined these acts. Hooligans stole hats off the heads of male pedestrians. Hooligans robbed a working-class man and then stole his clothes (the victim was so humiliated that he attempted suicide). A hooligan cut off the braids of a teenage girl on a crowded street near the Mikhailovskii Manège. A hooligan robbed a woman of all her money, and then offered her a coin for the tram, but only if she would kiss him.[97] Two "tipsy" hooligans approached a spectacled high-school (*real'noe uchilishche*) student and punched him in the face, breaking his glasses.[98] Hooligans organized a "unique entertainment": at a dark point on a street on the outskirts of the city, they stretched a wire across the sidewalk and then laughed loudly when people tripped. Another group of hooligans unscrewed a park bench in the Tauride Gardens, popular for summer strolling, and laughed with exaggerated frenzy when people sat down and the bench collapsed.[99] The examples of such extravagant attacks on "respectable" citizens out in public could be multiplied endlessly.

Commentators sometimes recognized the performativity of hooliganism. Hooligan extravagance on the public stage of the street was viewed as part of a wider decadent spectacle. Ol'ga Gridina, for example, observed that hooligans were unafraid when women whom they aggressively approached on the streets demanded their names in order to turn them in to the police; on the contrary, they hoped to see their names in the papers: "everyone, after all, is seeking fame [*izvestnost'*] in whatever way they can: some by great deeds, others with displays of talent, and still others in street scandals and by humiliating women."[100] Hooligan laughter was an important part of these street performances and was recognized as a symptom of these deranged times. Hooligans were said to laugh when humiliating people, to laugh when their demands for money or their "vile propositions" were rebuffed, to laugh at "humanitarian" efforts to resolve the conditions producing hooliganism, and to laugh at police efforts to control them.[101] Clearly, as Neuberger has argued, central to these performances was the desire to insult and humiliate people publicly, the effectiveness of which depended on accepted definitions of cultural and social respectability, class, and public decorum. But these displays of mocking defiance were not simply the acts of outsiders: they were felt to echo a degenerate disregard for established norms that had become endemic.

Public "fear," "terror," and "panic" about spreading hooliganism— terms widely used in the press—reflected this complex mix of fear of the dangerous social "other" and recognition that these were symptoms of an ailing social body. Outsiderness was emphasized in descriptions of hooligans as "Petersburg apaches,"[102] as *razboiniki* (bandits—though this term may have added a vague tinge of the romance of banditry and brigandage),[103] or, suggesting a comparison to the ancient Mongol Horde that had once destroyed Russian independence, as a "hooligan, thieving horde."[104] Many felt that the defense of public life against this alien siege was failing. "Hooliganism grows with every passing day," a report in 1908 noted, "and acquires more and more impudent and cynical forms."[105] A long essay in *Peterburgskii listok* in 1910 described "our street" as overwhelmed with growing "hooligan filth . . . threatening to engulf" city residents. While this dirt was once confined to various "Petersburg backwoods" (*zakholust'ia*), it now reached the most crowded areas of the city center. The still young public sphere had clearly degenerated. It would be pleasant, one writer mused, to return to past, happy days when Petersburgers could go out on the streets in the evening "without armed guards" and with no fear of attack by "varied dark personages."[106] But those times were gone. And the police were powerless. And anyone, anywhere and anytime, might become a victim.[107]

Hooliganism was most terrible because it was also not simply an external threat to civilized society. Hooligan moral degeneracy was also a mirror of the world in which the hooligan lived. For Gridina, writing in 1913, hooligans were typical "modern heroes" (*noveishie geroi*), exemplary of these degraded times. "Today nothing remains 'unthinkable.' Everything is possible, everything can be, everything happens." Ultimately, it was the degradation and fragmentation of modern culture that was to blame: gone were the days when young people were inspired by established ideals and values; "there are as many ways of thinking nowadays as there are heads."[108] An essay in *Novyi zhurnal dlia vsekh* in 1914 titled "What Is Hooliganism?" similarly insisted that hooliganism was marked by a decadent spirit of purposeless enmity toward the world, of being "the enemy of each and everyone."[109] A journalist of working-class origin, Aleksei Svirskii, similarly portrayed hooliganism in 1914 as a marker of moral decay, which he defined in language little different from the vocabulary in wide use in the press to describe other signs of contemporary social decadence: hooligans are people who "no longer resemble human beings," "want nothing and strive toward nothing," "have lost any taste for life," "have lost any conception of good and evil," are "apathetic" and "indifferent." Their philosophy of life is that "everything existing on this earth is rot [*tlia*] and people are shits [*gnidy*—literally, lice eggs] not worth attention." In a word, hooligans "fear nothing, value nothing, and wish for nothing—they are spiritual suicides."[110]

Religious writers readily viewed hooliganism as more than an "accidental evil" resulting from particular conditions or reflecting a particular segment of society. Instead they reflected the "fundamental evil" afflicting the whole of "our European culture," a "symptom" of the illness and disorder (*razstroistvo*) afflicting the entire social organism, which had been "poisoned" by skepticism, by the collapse of "moral boundaries," by the liberation of individuals from the restraints of responsibility and obligation, and by the unleashing of the "egoism" in human nature.[111] That hooliganism was mainly an illness of the poor reflected the particularly deep "moral corruption [*rastlenie*] of the common people, the spiritual fall of the lower strata," "the corrupting [*razlagaiushchee*] influence of the street," and "the degrading of moral foundations."[112] Hooliganism was part of the larger "illness of our era," which "harbors in itself a source of destruction, disintegration [*razlozhenie*], moral degeneracy [*marazm*], and spiritual death."[113]

Some writers, in fact, applied the category of "hooliganism" to decadent behavior in all classes. In the first issue of *Gazeta-kopeika* in 1908, for example, the editors wrote that "hooliganism of all sorts, flourishing on the shattered foundations of the past and a still not yet firmly established new civil society [*grazhdanstvennosti*]" is now ubiquitous in society "from top to bottom," and, as such, had become one of the most dire signs of these difficult times.[114] In a lengthy article on hooliganism in *Novyi zhurnal dlia vsekh* in 1913, the writer Vasilii Brusianin similarly criticized as facile the common tendency to call a hooligan any "drunken, simply dressed person," for "the fashionably dressed flâneur who pesters unknown women on the streets of the capital is also a hooligan." Hooliganism must be defined by its moral not its social structure: as the ethos of the street, especially the philosophy of "all against each and everyone, and each against all and everyone." Plebeian hooliganism was nothing but the "individualism of the upper strata of our public life [*obshchestvennosti*]" being reflected on "the bottom—a sharper reflection, without any artistic ornamentation, but more definite and understandable."[115] Some writers went even further and saw the whole of "modern reality" as characterized by "widespread hooliganism of deed, hooliganism of thought, and hooliganism of feeling."[116] Anyone could be a "hooligan"—"youths from the city's outskirts, tramps from around the Obvodnyi Canal, people dressed in the latest fashion from Nevskii Prospect, students, gymnasium students, bureaucrats." In other words, these days "everyone hooliganizes" (*khuliganstvuiut vse*).[117] While most writers preferred the narrower, socially restricted definition of hooliganism, they agreed that the hooliganism of the poor and the decadence of the rich were morally equivalent signs of the same spirit of decadent excess and degeneration.[118]

With the same reasoning, critics branded contemporary literature and the arts as evincing hooliganism.[119] "What is hooliganism?" Dmitrii Merezhkovskii asked in a journal essay in 1908, which was quoted often in the press. His answer emphasized the amoral egoism that many writers defined as the characteristic stigma of contemporary intellectual and cultural life. "In aesthetics it is no longer merely 'boots' in general [a reference to arguments that the iconoclastic "neorealism" in literature was inspired by the principle that "boots are higher than Shakespeare"] but '*my* boots are higher than Shakespeare;' in ethics it is 'everything is allowed to *me*;' in religion it is 'in *me* is everything divine, I am God and there is no other God besides me.'"[120] The leftist critic and social activist Slobozhanin similarly defined the individualism of the age—partly inspired by a misappropriation of Nietzsche, he believed—to be "hooligan individualism."[121] The label "hooliganism" was especially applied to futurism. Like hooligans, it was said, futurists heap "mockery" upon everything valued by the cultured world, harming the public with their "cynical" "outrages" (*bezobrazie*). Like hooligans, they are "against everything," they curse and fight, they are "dissatisfied with everything." Above all, "like hooliganism, they are a signifier [*pokazatel'*] of the sick condition of our civil society [*obshchestvennost'*]," a "symptom" of the "deep crisis" now being experienced by "modern man." In a word, "futurism is hooliganism," but cloaked in art and ideology.[122]

It was certainly the case that sympathy for and optimism about the urban poor had faded in the face of the huge migration of peasants to the capital in the 1890s and early 1900s and especially after the social upheavals of 1905–7.[123] No less important, anxieties about the poor reflected and fed anxieties about wider circles of societal illness and degeneracy. There were less pessimistic views, certainly. Some writers continued to feel compassion and pity for even the unruly and degenerate poor. In an essay in 1914 in the left-leaning popular paper *Malen'kaia gazeta* (Little Gazette), for example, one of paper's feuilletonists complained of the ease with which other newspapers labeled people "hooligans." If one looked more closely one would see only "unfortunate people," whose misfortune began with growing up poor on "the street, which sucks into its slimy and clinging muck the children of the city's cellars." It was the moral "abyss" of the street, not its victims, that needed correcting.[124] An even more optimistic view interpreted hooliganism as rebellion and defiance, if only slightly conscious. Scholarly studies in our own time of popular deviance and crime have inclined toward this argument, looking for signs of social self-assertion and autonomous beliefs, symbolic and ritual expressions of alternative values ("hidden transcripts"), or subversive uses of established codes, and thus reading deviance as an exercise of alternative power. Some contemporaries, though rarely, cast hooligans in the role of rebels. An essayist in *Novyi zhurnal dlia vsekh* suggested that hooligans enjoyed a vague feeling of "satisfaction" when their acts had public "effect," especially when these acts "insulted" that which "society honors and respects." Indeed, he argued, the hooligan's essential goal, though he was not conscious of this, was to "offend society" (*nadrugat'sia nad obshchestvom*). And if he could add material loss to "moral harm," all the better. As such, the hooligan was acting "as if to avenge himself on society for something."[125] More radical writers, like the Marxist worker and author Aleksei Gastev, elaborated on this "as if" and "for something." "Today in Russia," Gastev argued in a 1913 article about working-class St. Petersburg, "people label as 'hooligans' anyone who does not perform 'cultured,' which is to say lackey, duties for the large and small parasite masters."[126]

That "hooliganism" was decadence—a mixture of excess and degeneration—was a view widely shared. Excess can be defined, generally,

as crossing boundaries of custom and reason, lack of restraint or modera-
tion, intemperance and outrageous behavior, and "extravagant violations"
of law, decency, or morality.[127] Russian public opinion again and again defined hooliganism as transgression, unreason, and extravagance. And especially as degeneration: as moral depravity and spiritual fall, a philosophy of
"everything is possible" and "seize the moment," a mixture of savagery and
cynical indifference, and the loss of concern for the boundaries of good and
evil or even for the value of life itself. If these reactions to hooliganism suggest a "moral panic," this was not limited, as traditional uses of the concept
would have it, to the threat of deviance from the lower-classes or the margins. Nor was it an ephemeral mood.[128] The threat posed by hooliganism
was seen less as a savage attack on civilized life by society's foes than as an
endemic and spreading illness in a degenerate social body.

SEX IN PUBLIC

Contemporary sexual life also signified excess and degeneration. In journalistic discourse about sex—characteristically, the press was more concerned
with what occurred on the streets and other public places than with intimate and private relations—we see an increasingly nervous and panicked
view of sexual mores as marked by unhealthy extravagance, lack of restraint
and proportion, and transgression of the boundaries of reason. Metaphors
used to describe public sexual life in St. Petersburg highlighted precisely
this uncontrolled excess: an "erotic storm," a "vulgar *pliaska*" (a free and
sensual dance), a "sexual bacchanalia." Other metaphors moved this recognition of excess toward a diagnosis of illness: sexual excess as a "traumatic
epidemic" and "hysteria."[129]

Sex has often been a compelling subject for public discussion in modern societies, not only because of its intrinsic allure but because it can be
made to stand for so much else of modern interest: conceptions of the self,
especially in relation to ideals of personal dignity and individual autonomy;
the pleasures and dangers inherent in giving social freedom to the desiring individual subject; the tension between rational self-control and libidinous passion; the changing roles of men and women; control of the public
sphere; and hierarchies of public power and discipline. In urban Russia,

as Laura Engelstein has shown in her influential study of sexual discourse among educated elites in Russia from the Great Reforms to the Great War, these questions rose intensely to the surface of public life and public discourse, especially after the upheavals of 1905, which appeared to many as libidinous excess. As educated Russians became increasingly nervous about the morally corrosive effects of urban life, individualism in the pursuit of happiness, lower-class unreason and desire, and other hazards of the modern city, sex seemed both an exemplar and a cause of troubles. Desire, broadly understood, especially its public enactments, became increasingly associated—as both reflection and stimulus—with transgression, disorder, unreason, and even chaos.[130] While concerns about disorderly public sexuality, as about hooliganism, were connected to efforts to protect and police the public sphere, as Engelstein has emphasized, the drama of sex in public fed a related but deeper set of anxieties—that contemporary society was not simply under siege or out of control but sick and in decline.

Newspaper and magazine articles detailed the "bacchanalia" of the age, and not without a good deal of excess of their own. Reports endlessly described, generally with open disgust and anxiety, conditions and practices said to be characteristic of this age: looser attitudes toward premarital sexual "purity," extramarital sex, and prostitution; women sexually exploited by their own husbands and partners to a degree verging on pimping; women walking alone on the streets being harassed by "street Don Juans" and "Lovelaces" (lovelasy) who make "vile or "insulting" propositions and sometimes act violently when rebuffed; young girls stalked and seduced by pedophiles, who offer candy and then lure girls to their apartments for "vile purposes" (gnusnye zamysly); sexual tastes once reserved only for "sexual gourmands"—including pedophilia—now regular offerings in brothels; increasingly open displays of homosexuality; naked women performing on the stages of cafés chantants; the increasing popularity of expressively sexual dances, such as the tango and the maxixe; and a print marketplace flooded with sexually explicit books, magazines, pictures, postcards, and advertisements.[131] A news report in 1908 described shameless "orgies according to the taste of Roman bacchanalias of the age of Nero or Caracalla" regularly occurring in the most "fashionable houses" of the capital.[132] In 1909, an account of the "monstrous bacchanalia" taking place by night in popular cafés like the Quisisana described a "stuffy, steamy, vaporous, stinking" atmosphere, pierced by the "crude" voices of men and the "shrill" voices of women, the whole scene an "ugly [*bezobraznoe*] spectacle" of open embracing, kissing, fondling of breasts, swearing, scandals, fights, and tears by the assembled devotees of the "cult of the body."[133] The popularity in court circles of Grigorii Rasputin, viewed by many as a religious "erotomaniac," seemed just another decadent sign of "our times,"[134] and a reminder that decadence reached from the lowest depths to the heights of society.

Not everyone reacted to the unleashed sexuality of the age with disgust. In a book on the tango, the writer M. Bonch-Tomachevskii dismissed, though he could not ignore, the many "philistines and moralists" who viewed this popular dance it as another "horror of our nightmare epoch."[135] He admitted that, "yes, the tango is sexual," and he even agreed that this sexualized dance "defines the style of the first half of the twentieth century." But he insisted that the new public sexuality was a sign of liberation not moral degeneration. He embraced the movements of the tango as "modern humanity's" effort to create the "electric dance [*khorovod*] of the world city," as a "rhythmic outline of the world of factories and machines," as the "ecstasy" of possibility," as an "underground thundering that shakes the broad, flat plains of our everyday life," summoning us to something new.[136] Similarly, responding to critics of Isadora Duncan, who performed in St. Petersburg in 1907, some writers insisted on the important distinction between the "tavern" feelings (*kabatskoe vpechatlenie*) inspired by the nakedness of dancers in cafés chantants and the high "aesthetic" sense of beauty and creativity evoked by watching the near-nakedness of Duncan's free dance.[137]

But these were voices in an anxious wilderness (in any case, the admiration was limited to analogies of sex). Most often, urban writers showed that sex had become degraded in contemporary conditions. Themes of moral and spiritual decay, extravagant excess, and sickness were ubiquitous. And this was evidently not a very joyful bacchanalia, either. This picture was rendered as an unhappy, desperate, even panicked, decadence.

As always, writers sought explanations. Many blamed, as they did for many other problems of the age, the fateful conjuncture of war, revolution, and state violence that came with the 1905 revolution and its aftermath. In

A performance of the tango at the Aquarium (Akvarium), the "most
European of all Russian cafés chantants" (Central State Archive of
Film, Photographic, and Sound Documents of St. Petersburg).

particular, it was said, these events had unleashed passions and then turned
frustrated energies away from political action.[138] A newspaper columnist
in 1907, for example, writing under the headline "Politics and Eros," described a postrevolutionary cultural crisis in which political passions were
replaced with sexual ones, and the "new god" was crass egoistic pursuit of
"life's physical benefits."[139] The conclusions and attitude of the physician
and civic activist Dmitrii Zhbankov were typical. The revolution had "unleashed passions." As a liberal, however, he considered even more harmful
the restrictions on social and political institutions that followed the revolution's collapse and the new public mood in which there was felt no longer
to be any "serious purpose or reason [*smysl*] in the present life." This fatal
combination of repression and senselessness produced a spirit of *panem et
circenses*, or, in the common Russian phrase, "feast in the time of plague"
(*pir vo vremia chumy*). The new spirit of frenzied consumption and revelry

led audiences to crave farces, operettas, and cinema but also produced a "sexual bacchanalia" in which "sexual life everywhere occupies the most important place." In such an age, Zhbankov observed, people look to sex for "both satisfaction and answers to questions about the meaning of life." Thus, the shops are filled with pornographic pictures and postcards, newspaper advertisements cater to vain male anxieties about sexual potency and female desires to preserve physical beauty and youth, boulevard literature pours "filth" into the marketplace, and even serious literature is preoccupied with sex (often in the most debased forms) more than love. Sex has become such a public obsession that young men organize societies for the pursuit of "licentious" pleasure with names like "the Society of Libertines" (*obshchestvo ogarkov*—literally "candle ends," *ogarok* is slang for dissolute and licentious young men), "the League of Free Love," and "Seize the Moment" (*lovi moment*). In this "traumatic" and "epidemic" pursuit of the pleasure of the moment, Dr. Zhbankov concluded, framing his analysis characteristically in the language of illness, no one spared "body or soul."[140]

The degeneracy of values was a leitmotif in these accounts. Different writers saw different aspects and causes but agreed in their core diagnosis: decadent decline, evident in unrestrained excess and the transgression of every boundary. The essayist Slobozhanin blamed society for enabling rather than restricting the "willful male beast" (*samovolnyi samets*) who thinks of himself as superior to others (even as a Nietzschean superman), cares only about his own debased pleasures, and treats women with "animal cruelty" even in public.[141] Another journalist concluded that people today had "obliterated the boundary between good and evil" and placed the principle of "free will" (*volia*) above morality (again, allusions to Nietzsche's presumed influence). As a result, he argued, we see a "pathological" sexual morality that both reduces sexual relations to mere "moments" of sensual experience and elevates the "erotic" to "an inherent value."[142] Ol'ga Gridina agreed in her typically blunt language: contemporary sexuality was nothing but selfish, crude, and often transgressive "sensuality" (*grubaia chuvstvennost'*).[143]

Sickness was a persistent metaphor and interpretation. Sexual life in these times was "nervous," "pathological," "hysterical," and "traumatic," a virulent illness destroying the body and soul of self and society. A report on café culture described the majority of denizens of places like Quisisana as physically ill and "proud" of this fact, for sickness, it was said, had become fashionable.[144] Newspaper advertisements offering cures for sexual problems highlighted the association of sickness and sex. Commercial medicines, along with self-help pamphlets and books, promised cures for the "sickness of our age": excessive "sexual hunger," said to lead to all sorts of abnormalities, transgressions, and crimes.[145] The urban epidemic of venereal disease, of course, provided the most obvious association of unbridled sex with illness and decay.[146] Even modern science's early successes in treating syphilis—notably the widely advertised medicine "606," which some proclaimed freed modern men and women from the "fear" that had become linked to sex—was viewed by many as yet another enabler of unrestrained sexuality.[147] Psychiatrists like Pavel Rozenbakh, who regularly participated in public discussions about the conditions and spirit of the "times," saw contemporary sexual life as linked to mental illness: nervous abnormalities resulting from abnormal sex resulting from the abnormal conditions of modern civilization. Among these unhealthy conditions was a decadent culture of excess that allowed sexual activity in young people (he believed normal and healthy sex, even in marriage, was not to be expected before the age of thirty) and the harmful affects of "restaurant life."[148]

Pornography thrived in this moral atmosphere. Commenting in 1912 on a new international law designed to curb its flood, an essayist in the church journal *Tserkovnyi vestnik* excoriated pornography as a "rust" and "poison" "corroding the mind, brain, and bones of modern humanity." He saw this rot everywhere: not only in modern literature and the arts, but in the whole life of "modern man," where one sees so much "insane" attention to " 'the body' and its lusts," so many popular pornographic publications, and even the rise of ideologists, like Vasilii Rozanov, who defended pornography philosophically.[149] Many critics branded contemporary literature as little different from commercial pornography, and some openly called it such.[150] Critics condemned literature's decadent and fashionable [*modno*] obsession with "wild orgies"[151] and the preoccupation, under the banner of "aestheticism," with "the human body, flesh, and sexuality."[152] The literary "heroes" of our times, Zhbankov wrote, "think and talk only about how to possess [*obladat'*] a girl, and the heroines wait and dream about someone taking them." Worse, contemporary writers seemed either "sated or impotent," so that "normal stimuli no longer work on them," and they write not about "ordinary" sex but only "perverted" sex.[153]

In this decadent literary maelstrom, the boundaries between "high" literature and boulevard fiction were collapsing. Serious writers like Mikhail Kuzmin, Vasilii Kamenskii, Leonid Andreev, Aleksandr Kuprin, Zinaida Gippius, and Fedor Sologub were judged to be morally and philosophically little different from less talented boulevard writers like Mikhail Artsybashev: they all dwelled on the same crass and often transgressive eroticism.[154] For the right-wing critic Viktor Burenin, modern writers, especially when interpreting "modern life," all indulged in mass "belletristic masturbation"—for which they were lauded by the critics (esp. the "kike-critics" [*kriticheskie zhidy*] whom Burenin blamed for encouraging cultural degeneration) and devoured by a public that had taste for little besides pornography.[155] Of course, it was the boulevard that was most chastised for generating "pornography." Artsybashev's *Sanin* (1907) was a particular lightning rod for attacks. In the eyes of critics, Artsybashev's decadent spirit, elaborated in his later writings as well, was evident in his preoccupations not only with the sexual body but with the sick body (his favorite hero was a consumptive) and with death.[156] Another persistent target was Anastasiia Verbitskaia's novel of sexual and personal daring, transgression, and tragedy, *Keys to Happiness* (1910–13, made into a film in 1913).[157] But there were many others, usually with even less literary merit than *Sanin* and *Keys to Happiness*. Newspapers regularly featured serialized pulp fiction with strong sexual themes, such as *Peterburgskii listok*'s story of the beautiful but poor young Mariia who became, as we have seen, the exotic and decadent Mary of Petersburg high society. Describing herself as "demon . . . in hate and love" a "daughter of darkness," "a rose with thorns," she lived an ultimately exhausting and disillusioning life surrounded by the tropes of the time: "nights of love and passion," champagne, wine, food, laughter, betrayal, murder, and suicide.[158] Popular silent films also highlighted sexual decadence and also often concluded in tragedy.[159]

Homosexuality, in the anxious eyes of the press, was a ready symbol of degenerate deviation from normality. It was, by definition, depravity, and it evoked the strongest anxieties, all the more so when this "transgression" became, as it did in St. Petersburg in those years, increasingly public and visible. The Petersburg street, as in other modern metropolises, became a key site of homosexual sociality, connection, and intimacy—not simply because of the restrictions on the homosexual domestic sphere, but also as a reflection of the growing role of public space in urban sociability generally.[160] As urban writers mapped the sexual geography of the capital, they found it especially troubling to find homosexuals cruising the city's most central and elegant streets. But whether found on bright central streets or in dark corners and margins (made visible in press reports), homosexuality was treated, with disgust and outrage, as part of the city's debased moral geography, as yet another feature of "dark Petersburg."

Homosexuality's new visibility was key to the sense that proper boundaries had degraded. The most influential contemporary text on the subject, the journalist V. P. Ruadze's alternately moralizing and titillating tract on "homosexual Petersburg," complained that what was once hidden in private spaces, or hidden even more deeply in the closeted recesses of the repressed personality, now literally walked the city streets extravagantly advertising itself: only ten years ago "homosexuality hid itself away in the capital's cellars, not disturbing and debauching the street, but now when the ulcer of homosexual debauchery has been bared, when homosexuals themselves have crawled out of their hideouts, the 'lip-smacking' of these beasts of prey, hungry for fresh meat, is heard everywhere."[161] In his exposé—ostensibly, he was calling on society to treat this spreading "ulcer" with legal force, hence the title of his book, On Trial! (K sudu!)—Ruadze described the homosexual scene in the capital: cross-dressing male madams who prowled the Passazh and other gathering places, often decked out in the most "extravagant toilette" (ekstravigantnye tualety), in search of young male "recruits"; the "aunties" (tetki—a term sometimes used for all homosexual men but mainly for aging, prosperous gay men who sought young partners)[162] who could be seen sitting on benches in the Summer or Tauride gardens doing needlework and giving "unambiguous looks" at passing youths; the public bathhouses where the "homosexual sect" conducted its affairs with complete openness; gay masquerade balls and "orgies"; "hooligan" street homosexuals of the lower classes; male homosexual prostitution; and the various sartorial signs (apart from the obvious wearing of women's clothing) used to signal sexual orientation to those who knew the code, especially a bright red necktie but also a red handkerchief visible in a jacket pocket, as well as a "foppish" (*frantovato*) style.[163] Homosexuality was also much more visible in literature, for which critics berated writers. Specialists on public health like Dr. Zhbankov worried about the harmful affects of a literary culture that had increasingly turned from "normal" sensuality to "perversion," including "homosexuality, lesbianism, and even bestiality."[164] The new openness about same-sex relations in literature especially troubled critics: what had once been confined to the private lives of debauched aristocrats now flowed onto the pages of literature where it could be read by anyone.[165]

Mostly, though, the press was concerned with heterosexual depravity (*razvrat*). At the center of attention were the uncontrolled sexual excesses of men; indeed, the sick and degraded condition of modern masculinity seemed to be part of the problem. This was an illness, however, that was seen to be spreading: it suggested the depth of the decay that even women and children, conventionally presumed to be sexually passive if not innocent, could become active decadent subjects. Sexual assaults on children inspired especial moral outrage and panic. In "recent years," newspapers observed, the sexual "hunt" by adult men—"modern fauns and satyrs"—for young girls had "reached a monstrous scale," so that children unaccompanied by their parents were no longer safe anywhere in public.[166] That victimized children were sexually innocent was emphasized by the frequent use in these reports of the term *rastlenie*, or defloration—though the Russian term can refer both specifically to the sexual violation of underage virgins and, more generally, to moral corruption, decay, and decadence.[167] Newspapers regularly reported men stalking and seducing young girls (generally between the ages of ten and fourteen, though some victims were younger). These reports were often dramatically, even melodramatically, framed as stories of "Petersburg Diu-Lius," (or Diu-Lus in an alternative spelling in the press), echoing the case of a respected French teacher in St. Petersburg, known by his Russified name Karl Diu-Liu, whose sensational trial for sexual relations with underage children began in May 1908.[168] Less frequently these men were dubbed "Svidrigailovs," after the depraved character in Fedor Dostoevsky's *Crime and Punishment* who was allegedly responsible, among his many sins, for the suicide of a pregnant fourteen- or fifteen-year-old girl he had evidently raped. These stories almost always began on the street or in a square, park, or courtyard where children were playing, typically with a man, usually prosperous looking, offering a girl candy and then luring her to a dark corner, a stairwell, or his apartment.[169] Stories about men "in the footsteps of Diu-Liu," "diuliunisti," and "diulu-izm" were disturbingly common—indeed, so common that when a woman asked a yard-keeper to report to the police a man she saw leading two girls, aged eight and ten, into a bathhouse on Shpalernaia Street, known to be a "place for debauchery" though located in an upscale neighborhood, he answered "what for, this happens here everyday!"[170]

The greater visibility of degeneracy was, again, a key theme. Once rarities who hid in the shadows, these Diu-Lius and Svidrigailovs were now ubiquitous, unashamed to act in public spaces and even by the light of day.[171] Press coverage itself, of course, helped bring these acts into the open. An article in *Sovremennoe slovo* in 1910 emphasized this: in the past, stories about "the rape and *rastlenie* of minors" appeared only in specialized text-books for doctors and jurists; now one read such reports everyday in the newspapers.[172] Many of these cases were less melodramatic than the image of respectable-looking older men luring girls on the street with candy. Ordinary examples of child rape abounded, as of the nine-year-old girl raped at a locksmith's shop where she had been sent on an errand, or the ten-year-old-girl, looking for flowers in the woods with her six-year-old brother, raped by a working-class "hooligan."[173] Closely related, though secluded in private spaces until revealed in the press, were parents who sexually abused their children, such as the drunken mother and "beast-stepfather" (*zver'-otchim*) who regularly "tormented" their thirteen-year-old daughter, which she endured until the stepfather, with the mother's aid, "severely outraged" (*tiazhko nadrugalsia*) the girl, infecting her with a "terrible, evil disease" (such euphemisms were common in these stories)—a case presented in the press as characteristic of "our cruel, heartless Petersburg."[174]

Child prostitution was a related, though more multifaceted, sign of the degeneration of public life. Like other moral illnesses, child prostitution had both proliferated and become "surprisingly open," seen at "every intersection."[175] Indeed, reflecting the familiar metaphor, it had become

an "epidemic."[176] The newspaper *Peterburgskii listok* described a typical
scene in 1908. At the corner where Nevskii Prospect met the Moika Canal,
at ten in the evening, the reporter overheard a wealthy gentleman—his top
hat and a fur coat identified his social status—hiring a twelve-year-old girl
for sex. Hoping to better understand this phenomenon, he asked a physician he knew (a natural choice of expertise, for the reporter saw this as an
illness), who informed him that it was more widespread than he imagined:
in this business demand exceeded supply. When he saw the girl later on
the streets, he interviewed her, learning that her single mother beat her if
she didn't make money prostituting herself.[177] That this was an illness of
modern men was assumed—as one writer explained, so many men sought
sex with young girls because they had lost the ability to "respond to healthy
feelings."[178] Indeed, it was felt to be a sign of the times that male sexual taste
for "child freshness" (*detskaia svezhost'*) had become so rampant that hotels allegedly kept a "stock" of child prostitutes on hand and young women
"masqueraded" as underaged girls (sometimes wearing school uniforms
and carrying schoolbooks) to respond to this market demand.[179]

While these stories were mainly structured around the sickness of
men and the victimization of girls, adult women were often complicit partners in crime. Indeed, particular outrage was voiced against these mainly
older women who used guiles of various sorts to lure girls into paid sex.
The arrest on Nevskii Prospect in 1908 of fifteen girls between the ages of
seven and twelve for "engaging in the work of debauchery" revealed that
they were all under the care of a "governess" (*vospitatel'nitsa*) who sent
them into the streets to beg and sometimes sell their bodies. The reporter
voiced anger and disgust at such a "loathsome" and "shameful" phenomenon, while recognizing it to be a characteristic "ulcer of big cities."[180] Urban
writers regularly reported procuresses—and complained that the penalties
against them were too light—who lured girls into prostitution with promises of work, sometimes even operating dressmaking and other shops for
this purpose, and then corrupting them with pornography, debauched parties, and the lure of easy money.[181]

Once girls had "fallen," the story becomes more complex as they
moved from victims to actors in the city's history of urban degeneration.
The press made it clear that there were now children on the streets actively

contributing to public degeneracy; the connection to hooliganism was obvious and sometimes explicit. Child prostitutes were described walking the streets with cigarettes dangling from their lips, accompanied by their "'lover'-pimps" (*"liubovniki"-koty*), conversing with "cynical frankness," looking men directly "in the eye" and promising pleasures.[182] As Engelstein has argued, contemporaries viewed juvenile prostitution as the "ultimate pathology" of public sexual life, for "children were supposed to be innocent and dependent, not sexually active free agents," much less themselves depraved (and often diseased).[183]

Women, like children, as numerous historians have shown for Russia and other modernizing societies, were seen as disabled subjects in the public sphere—possessing weaker and more vulnerable selves, more likely to be victims than perpetrators of moral offense, and thus more sensitive to, and symbolic of, the moral decay of public life. In this light, Russian urban writers worried aloud about the sexual dangers women faced on the streets. To be sure, commentators recognized the liberating potential of the decline of "old-fashioned mores" (*dedovskie obychai*), which made it possible for women now to leave the home without a male escort. But they also recognized that emancipated women faced a new risk of abuse in these "harsh" and "cunning" times.[184] It had become "impossible for a proper young lady to walk alone even on a crowded street without being subject to humiliation at the hands of impudent street rogues [*ulichnye nakhaly*]" who pursue women on the streets, or at work, and try to lure them into trysts.[185] Of course, the dangers were not limited to "proper" ladies strolling or shopping on Nevskii Prospect. The street also posed sexual danger for working-class women. After laboring all day in a stuffy shop, a newspaper columnist observed, working girls naturally want to go out on the open and lively streets rather than home to their cramped and stuffy rooms, especially on summer nights when "maidenly dreams" are awakened. But "wolves" await these grown-up Red Riding Hoods, and unlike in that "naive" tale, there is no brave hunter to rescue them.[186] The mythologizing structure of such stories—the working woman as innocent child and the male pest as voracious wolf—was typical, and not only of urban Russia. As in so many modernizing societies, as Judith Walkowitz has argued for London, women who "transgressed the narrow boundary of home and hearth to enter public space," walked into a seductive urban "labyrinth," thick with both tangible and symbolic "sexual danger."[187]

Stories of women's "fall" after exposure to the decadent street were commonplace. The usual narrative began with a young peasant woman coming to the capital to find work, but soon falling prey to the alluring but degraded values of "the street": fashion, perfume, male "admirers," dancing, champagne. Essential to these stories was a measure of upward social mobility through men, who, in exchange for sex, rewarded willing women materially. And some of these women, it was implied, were not simple victims. But this was presented as a false path: these stories often ended in exhaustion and disillusionment with "the intoxication of life" (*chad zhizni*), prostitution, and suicide when the shame became unbearable.[188] Similar stories appeared in serialized newspaper novels, Russian silent films, and imported films (for this was certainly not a uniquely Russian tale) such as *Abyss: The History of One Woman's Fall* (*Bezdna: Istoriia padeniia odnoi zhenshchina*).[189]

Ambiguity surrounded women's increasingly public sexuality. While these narratives of women's "fall" emphasized women as innocent victims, once they had fallen, the melodrama of lost innocence shifted to the melodrama of decadent women who posed a danger to men. We see this, for example, in the euphemisms used to describe "fallen" women. Women said to engage in the "shameful trade" (*pozornoe remeslo*) or "shameful profession" were unquestionably prostitutes, but much of the language describing decadent public women could refer both to professional prostitutes and to women freely indulging in the "sexual bacchanalia" of the times: "night fairies" (*nochnye fei*), "nocturnal butterflies" (*nochnye babochki*), "free priestesses of love" (*svobodnaia zhritsa liubvi*), "slaves of joy" (*rabyni vesel'ia*), "gay maidens" (*veselye devitsy*), and the "ruined but charming creatures" of the demimonde (*pogibshee, no miloe sozdanie*—from the title of an 1862 story by Aleksandr Levitov). A paradoxical moral narrative is imbedded in these ambiguous terms and in the narratives in which they appeared: fun, pleasure, and even love were intertwined with pretense, humiliation, disenchantment, shame, and suicide.

Sympathy for women as innocent victims devolved rapidly into anxiety, disgust, contempt, and fear. Women morphed from innocent peasant

virgins to decadent urban viragos, from sweet and simple Mariias to exotic and alluring but dangerous Marys. Thus, along with texts emphasizing
the peril women faced on entering the public sphere, we find texts about
women who had become perilous for men who were not wise to female
wiles. Women of the demimonde were, at the very least, irresistible objects
of illicit desire: "Ah, such women—the mind becomes cloudy!" a writer
joked about the scene in a café chantant. "Such hands, shoulders, bust, and
legs! . . . Uh-oh, here comes my wife!"[190] Very often, such women were portrayed as actively contributing to the decadence of public life. "Goddesses"
of love and fashion prowled the evening streets in search of "victims," wrote
Vera Nedesheva in her 1906 brochure about Nevskii Prospect. Typical was
Klara, "known to all of St. Petersburg": tall and beautiful with "burning
black eyes" heavy with makeup, potent perfume, a "searching smile," "red,
joyous lips, parted to reveal two rows of sharp, white teeth," dressed "with
chic" though a bit gaudily, wearing a large hat that was elevated over the
crowd like "the victory trophy of an Australian savage," this "night vamp"
(nochnaia khishchnitsa) gazed boldly at men and attracted the attention—
ranging from desire to fascination to disgust—of both men and women on
the street. While such women, Nedesheva observed according to the familiar formula, often came to the city as country innocents, the "ruinous atmosphere of other people's luxuries" had corrupted them.[191] Many accounts
similarly highlighted women's dangerous gaze—like the "firing of a machine
gun," in the words of one, "which enchants, entices, and invites."[192] Indeed,
various writers suggested, it was in the nature of the newly emancipated
"modern lady" to use sexuality to gain power for herself and over others.[193]

The same ambiguous narrative of excess, decline, victimization, and
responsibility pervaded stories of prostitution, the most visible sign of
women's public sexuality.[194] Though prostitution was obviously not a new
problem, public discussions in these years treated it as if it were a newly
discovered sore on the social body. It was interpreted not as the "oldest
profession" or even as a universal sign of women's subordination to male
sexual desire, but as one of many marks of contemporary society's pathological decline: the "shame of our times" (pozor nashego vremeni).[195] Partly
this was a matter of perception: society's conscience had grown more sensitive to moral deformities. But observers also insisted that prostitution was

actually more widespread and more visible than ever before. In 1913, for example, the *Gazeta-kopeika* columnist Skitalets commented that a person who happened to return to St. Petersburg after not having seen the city since before the turn of the century would notice two major differences: many more buildings and many more prostitutes.[196] The numbers calculated were, indeed, astonishing. A report at the important Congress for the Struggle against the Trade in Women, held in St. Petersburg in 1910, counted fifty thousand prostitutes in St. Petersburg, which, if true, meant one out of every fourteen women.[197] The press found even more "terrible figures" than this: according to one report, one in seven women between the ages of fifteen and forty were prostitutes.[198] Like so much else in public life, prostitution was marked by the new spirit of excess and decline.

One marker of excess was the refusal to be controlled: prostitution seemed less and less confined to channels of state legalization and surveillance or even to any clear and stable category of what a "prostitute" was. As Laurie Bernstein has noted, efforts to measure unregulated prostitution produced often "extravagant" claims, making "all of the capital sound like a veritable sex market," with almost every restaurant, bar, café, teahouse, hotel, and boutique serving as a center for prostitution.[199] To be sure, from the time the state system of legalized and regulated prostitution was put in place in the 1840s most women who engaged in the sex trade did not register as legal prostitutes. But this disorder became more extensive and troubling than ever before. Journalists, social researchers, civic activists, and medical specialists intensively documented the numbers and varieties of "secret" prostitutes, including not only women who evidently preferred to avoid the restrictions imposed on registered prostitutes (or were underage and thus not allowed to register) but also café singers, waitresses in teahouses, candy sellers in entertainment parks, and others who turned tricks on the side, or women pimped on occasion by relatives or boyfriends.[200] It was difficult to fix the boundaries between full-time professional prostitutes and women who occasionally traded sex for money or even sexually active single women rewarded with gifts. The new social ubiquity of prostitution also suggested the collapse of old boundaries: depravity had "climbed the social ladder." It used to be, one newspaper essayist argued, that prostitutes were a plebeian social element, acting largely out of social need. But in these "unfortunate" times, prostitutes come even from "privileged society," even from families with "grand titles" and high position.[201]

Decline was a dominant theme in press discussions of prostitution. That prostitutes were "fallen" women, and that their moral fall resulted from the decadent conditions of the modern city, were well-established tropes.[202] Also, well before 1905, philanthropists, feminists, and other civic activists were calling on society to "save" these "fallen" women and return them to the path of "honest labor."[203] After 1905, worries about the "dirty and slippery path" that led women into prostitution became increasingly fervent, as these stories were now part of a whole panoply of signs of societal excess, transgression, and decline. The language and tone was often appropriately melodramatic, whether coming from popular journalists who blamed the "extreme and artificially stimulated appetites" of men,[204] or political activists who blamed the "essential filth" (*sushchaia gadost'*) of contemporary social and mental life, including degrading attitudes toward women.[205] Reported biographies of prostitutes, which appeared in the press as a result of street investigations by journalists, especially after a prostitute's suicide, emphasized personal histories of corruption and decline. A "typical story" (*obyknovennaia istoriia*)—a common phrase used in these reports, which were indeed often nearly identical to one another—was constructed out of letters left behind by a young woman who had poisoned herself. Two years before, she had arrived in St. Petersburg from the provinces. "Young and inexperienced," she had accepted the invitation of an elderly woman to live with her. The "lady" treated her well as first, but then the young innocent discovered that she had "fallen into a den of iniquity." In debt to the old lady, she felt she had no choice but to remain in this degraded life or to take her own life.[206] The most common variation on this theme, as we have seen, was a young woman being tricked into dependency and prostitution by accepting an offer of seemingly legitimate work. Other reported paths included girls "sold" by their parents to wealthy men who then abandoned them or women spurned by their "fiancées" when they became pregnant.[207] The most dramatic stories involved accounts of "white slavery," including reports of women lured into illegal brothels under false pretenses and then held under guard, drugged and raped, starved, and beaten and "tortured" if they refused to participate in "orgies."[208] Seduction and betrayal were common themes in these stories, as in a newspaper report about a young woman seduced and then abandoned by "one of the countless libertines [*razvra-titelei*]" in the capital city, thus depriving her of honor and hope for a decent life. Even after she became a prostitute, her decline continued: first, she worked Nevskii Prospect and the better restaurants and cafés chantants, but soon she was seeking clients mainly on rough Ligovskaia Street and eventually in the slums of "the Sands" (*Peski*).[209]

That prostitutes could be active decadent subjects was perhaps even more troubling. A characteristic story was offered by the columnist Gridina in *Gazeta-kopeika* in 1910. Though presented as fact, whether the story was actual, embellished, or completely invented does not detract from its ability to represent a certain reality. Gridina underscored this herself by titling her series of three columns about a prostitute she met named Liza "a common story" (*obyknovennaia istoriia*). Liza had been a simple maid, twenty-two years old, good-looking, and of cheery disposition. After meeting a woman who recruited prostitutes, Liza quit her job, saying "what am I, a slave or something? I will be my own mistress." Soon, she was seen promenading down Nevskii "in gaudy silk finery and a huge fashionable round hat." When her former employers—friends of Gridina—tried to warn her against this life, preaching to her about the values of "labor, honor, and modesty," she responded with arguments about the value of "finery, pleasures, wealth, and a life limited by nothing." Two months later, she was still living the life of a "carouser" (*guliashshaia*—one of many popular euphemisms for prostitutes). Her manner was bold and saucy—she was described with the same term that was often used to speak of hooligans: *nakhal* (insolence, impudence, defiance)—and she insisted, against those who viewed her with contempt (she admitted that she was even spit upon while walking down the street), that her choice was rational: with no skills and no desire to work in the dirty servitude of domestic service, selling her own body was both legitimate ("It's mine, isn't it?") and no different from what other people did, who sold whatever they had to sell in the urban marketplace. This story of a woman's choice of a debauched life ended with melodramatic logic. Time passed and one night Gridina noticed Liza again on Nevskii, on the Anichkov Bridge, but now her beauty was gone and even some of her teeth were missing, the result of beatings by men but also by her madam. Now she

admitted that she was mistaken in all she had said before, that she had fallen
into a "pit" and the people she had trusted had destroyed both her body
and her spirit. All that was left to her was to drink herself into oblivion, to
be beaten senseless by some man, or to kill herself, for "there is a life that is
worse than death."[210]

Evidence that prostitutes could be willful, brazen, aggressive, and
dangerous usually evoked much less sympathy than Gridina showed. Most
urban writers described these degenerate subjects with disgust and fear.
Having lost whatever aura of innocent victimhood they might once have
had, they had become yet one more menacing agent of moral excess, sickness, and decline. The growing association between prostitutes and hooligans was emblematic: although some accounts emphasized women as
victims of their hooligan boyfriends who beat and pimped them and kept
most of their income, others wrote of prostitutes as "hooligans in skirts,"
guilty of specially female forms of assault—such as demanding money of
male passersby, allegedly "for cigarettes," backed, in case of refusal, by a
whole "cadre of bodyguards."[211] Particularly vicious were the "witches"
and "madams"—often former prostitutes—who regularly prowled Nevskii
Prospect and other major streets, "hunting" both for customers and for
young women to recruit to the trade. They could be recognized, according
to one report, by their sickly faces and "deformed features" as they offered
up themselves or young girls.[212]

Many insisted that all prostitutes were "pathological." As Laura Engelstein and Laurie Bernstein have shown, medical and legal professionals
and civic activists publicly debated whether prostitutes were products of
social conditions or born degenerates, the latter view influenced by western
European criminal anthropology, especially the work of Cesare Lombroso.
But health professionals in Russia, as Daniel Beer has also described, were
increasingly inclined toward social explanations. An illustrative figure is
Dr. Boris Bentovin, a physician and journalist who claimed to base his observations on his own work with prostitutes interned at the Kalinkin Hospital in St. Petersburg. Bentovin was struck by the astonishing degeneracy
of these women. Not only were their bodies often so diseased that many
looked old at the age of thirty and most died young from some combination
of drunkenness, infectious diseases, including tuberculosis, and exhaus-

tion—he commented that they had lost the very "appearance of humanity" (*oblik chelovecheskogo*)—but they were morally defective as well. Many
of the prostitutes he interviewed were boisterous and foul-mouthed. Many
lacked a sense of "shame," telling him that they viewed sex work as not only
a legitimate way for women to make a living but one that gave freedom and
suited women's natural inclinations toward "easy-going fun" (*legkomyslen-
noe vesel'e*). Many associated with hooligans (though Bentovin sympatheti-
cally observed that these woman found in the degraded street an alternative
community to the society that had rejected them). But he insistently dis-
agreed with those who had argued that these were biological pathologies,
that these women, as Dr. Veniamin Tarnovskii (who had also worked at
Kalinkin) had famously argued in the 1880s, were "born with a predisposi-
tion to vice."[213] On the contrary, Bentovin argued, these women became
degenerates due to "the social conditions of life," especially the "abyss of
poverty," and to the moral conditions among the urban poor: lack of privacy, "debauchery" that was open and normalized, alcohol consumption,
profanity, immodesty, rude and sexualized treatment of women workers by
men, and the many sexual dangers (and opportunities) in the big city that
tempted girls toward their "fall."[214]

It was fitting—and understood to be so—that hooligans and prostitutes were sometimes socially linked. Although only a minority of prostitutes had hooligan boyfriends and only a minority of hooligans pimped,
these two characteristic city types were viewed as comparable exemplars of
everyday street decadence. Along with so many other problems of daily life,
especially those involving sex and violence, they represented the modern
spirit of excess, transgression, sickness, and decline. That modernist writers were seen as united in spirit with these other "heroes of our times" may
seem even more farfetched but points to the ubiquitous diagnosis of these
troubled times as decadent. The stories considered in this chapter called
to mind the same concerns evoked by street life, criminal masquerades,
and "excess" death—indeed, they were sometimes part of a single newspaper report or magazine article. These anxieties often required hyperbolic
metaphors to make sense: that urban Russians were being poisoned by the
"fumes of hell," that a "spirit of evil" loomed, that modern life was debasing
men, women, and children alike into animals, beasts, and savages.

Happiness

There vibrates in the idea of happiness . . . the idea of salvation. This happiness
is founded on the very desolation and abandonment that were ours.

—Walter Benjamin, *The Arcades Project*

Incessant talk about the maladies of the age was aimed partly at conjuring a
cure, at finding salvation. Public writing was meant not just to hold a mirror to society but to be a critical activity, to invoke the power of words to
produce change. Words appealed to practical reason (with knowledge and
effort, they implied, this can all be fixed) but also acted as an incantation
against the darkness spreading in society and in people's moods (a hopeful
or at least comforting appeal not to let the dark stories and feelings overwhelm). When the tabloid *Gazeta-kopeika* first appeared in the summer of
1908, the editors explained why they had decided to "create a new, independent, widely accessible newspaper in our difficult, transitional times."
(The commercial goal of profit was, unsurprisingly, not mentioned, for this
would hardly suggest moral legitimacy.) Addressing the sense of trouble
and crisis that this paper would often report, the editors stood for idealism and optimism: what was needed "in these times" was "close, peaceful,
constructive work and struggle against all untruth and darkness," which
can overcome the "wounds of the past" and create a "new, beautiful, and
just life, such as the late Chekhov dreamed of, along with the best minds of
humanity."[1] On the first anniversary of the newspaper, which had quickly
become one of the most widely read in the capital, the editors reiterated
their positive and optimistic purpose: a newspaper, as the "heart of public [*obshchestvennoi*] life," has a moral responsibility not simply to reflect
people's sufferings and joys but to be a friend and leader, to stimulate in

"the popular masses" an "interest in the public sphere" (*obshchestvennost'*), to nurture in them "civic feeling" (*grazhdanskoe chuvstvo*), and "to encourage them to strive for improvement, and to seek bright and pure ideals."[2] In the face of what appeared to be an age of sickness, decline, and death, these urban writers, many with wide readerships, were determined to speak redemptively of recovery and hope. In different ways, this was the emotional message proclaimed by so many public activists at the time: professionals in civically minded fields ranging from engineering to medicine; leaders of the many new voluntary societies that were building a new civic life; political activists ranging from moderate liberals to socialist revolutionaries; and active proponents of a new revival of religion and spirituality. This was also the message, in quite another way, of "fun-loving Petersburg" (*veseliashchii-sia Peterburg*). But whatever the form, many saw a certain urgent heroism in this pursuit of hope and happiness, for it was conducted at the edge of an "abyss."

THE WILL TO HAPPINESS

Sensitive to a darkening, even despairing, public mood in the face of so many troubling conditions, journalists and other urban writers continually appealed to readers to embolden themselves with positive thoughts and feelings. New Year's editorials, for example, called upon readers to push aside skepticism about the passage of time. The New Year's "toasts" from public activists, intellectuals, and artists invited by the magazine *Ogonek* (Flame) in 1913 were typical. Many expressed an identical wish: "that our social pessimism, our lack of faith in our own strength" would be replaced by "a bright faith" in the possibility of progress, by a "spiritual renaissance," by a "mood that is bold and filled with the joy of life, though sober." Or as the artist Viktor Zarubin put it in his holiday toast, "Enough darkness, long live the sun!"[3] Many New Year's writers tried to convince their readers that pessimism in the face of problems was a misunderstanding, a failure to see progress. The present is better than the past and the future will be better still, *Gazeta-kopeika* insisted on New Year's Day 1912.[4] The world is improving every year, the editors of *Peterburgskii listok* assured their readers

on 1 January 1913, for humanity is continuing to subjugate nature to its will
and organize itself socially. There is even reason to hope, the editors concluded, that with time the human race will pass from a world in which "man
is wolf to man" to a world in which "man will be friend to man."[5] The following year, which would soon bring the catastrophe of war, the New Year's
message of *Peterburgskii listok* was just as insistently optimistic: "overcast
[*khmurye*] thoughts have no place," proclaimed a poem addressed to readers, for the coming year will bring more happiness and "fewer lies and less
evil." To be sure, the failures and disappointments of the past were remem-
bered, but only to reiterate the faith that this time "the new year will not
deceive us." The accompanying editorial spoke at length about the necessary pursuit of happiness during the coming year—though cautiously ad-
vising readers that it was the pursuit itself that brought joy, no matter what
the results.[6] That this was a deliberate and performative optimism, a heroic
stance against a sea of troubles, was often quite clear. I suspect that few really believed claims such as one from the start of 1910 that "with a bright
gaze people look to the distance" with faith and hope.[7] But it was essential
to say so, and saying this was meant to make it so.

Appeals to be optimistic were often built on a belief in the power of
positive emotions. In these dark days, an essayist on urban problems argued
in 1911, we need to nurture "constructive optimism, faith in oneself, and, it
follows, faith in others" as an antidote to the prevailing "tone" of disenchantment.[8] Public language was treated as a type of necessary "speech act" (a
later concept in language and emotion theory) that could itself affect emotions and reality: what writers needed to offer in these dark times, *Gazeta-
kopeika*'s Skitalets argued in his Easter column of 1911 (Easter, naturally, was
a good occasion for talk of salvation and light), were "good words" (*dobrye
slova*) so that people would have faith in the future and believe in the possibility of happiness.[9] Failure in this effort could bring danger. Especially
as the likelihood of war increased, public figures worried that Russians not
meet this "fateful hour" in the same dark "mood" as they met the last war,
with Japan, which was the "main psychological reason" for defeat.[10]

A heroism of will was at the heart of these hopeful arguments. The
will (*volia*)[11] was often treated as the best remedy for the illness of the age.

Russians should be more like the English and less like the weak-spirited
French, Skitalets wrote after a visit of English politicians to St. Petersburg in
1912, for this "steel race" is full of "strength, plans, and hopes and lives with
courage [*polnoi grud'iu*]."[12] Other writers looked to the Americans for a
model of positive attitudes.[13] But most often, essayists argued that Russians
should look within themselves to find the needed strength of character. The
poet and novelist Fedor Sologub, for example, though critics often accused
him of nurturing a decadent and depressed sensibility among his readers,
appealed to his "contemporaries" to recognize that they are "people not
devils from some swamp," and that "with [their] own will" they can "make
life beautiful, free, and happy."[14] Numerous writers similarly looked to the
will for salvation—with many echoes of influential nineteenth-century arguments, notably by Arthur Schopenhauer and Friedrich Nietzsche, about the
importance of the will for human subjectivity and being. Is there a way out
of the "dead end" into which the "conditions of modern life" have led us? a
magazine essayist asked in January 1914: yes, he answered himself, by learning to "realize one's will" (*tvorit' svoiu voliu*), by learning to live "avidly,
deeply, and brightly."[15] Likewise, an editorial in *Peterburgskii listok*, also
at the start of 1914, insisted that whether people are happy or depressed,
whether they take joy in everything or feel that everything is "insignificant,
monotonous, and impoverished," is entirely dependent on their own inner
self: "the consciousness of happiness or unhappiness depends exclusively
on the level of our moral strengths."[16]

Most vividly, but echoing what many were saying, Vasilii Rozanov argued, in his newspaper columns in *Novoe vremia*, that what was needed
was a "heroic personality" (*geroicheskaia lichnost'*)—not in the sense of a
spirit of conquest or genius but simply in one's everyday "tone of behavior,
words, and relations." This was a heroism marked by "seriousness" about
everything and a moral "love of work."[17] This was, as it were, a "heroism of
modern life" (in Charles Baudelaire's famous phrase) built out of the power
of human reason and emotion, uniting as "will," to stand firm against, even to
find pleasure amidst, the dispiriting disorder and decadence of the modern
condition. This heroic stance could indeed be, as Rozanov suggested, quite
simple and modest, rooted in the everyday: thus, one newspaper columnist

appealed to Petersburgers—so characteristically "pale and gloomy like the Petersburg sky," so dissatisfied with everything—to make an effort to smile more.[18]

Because words themselves were felt to contain heroic power, many urban commentators looked to literature to nurture the will to believe. While most critics worried about the "crisis" in literature, and blamed modernism for producing "decadent" moods, some thought they found in literature the "good words" needed to restore health and confidence. Futurism, for example, though mocked by most critics, seemed to some an attempt to forge a new positive spirit in artistic life. Indeed, futurists claimed to believe that "the word itself" had the power to summon the vitality of life and faith in progress in order to change the world. As the poet Aleksei Kruchenykh proclaimed in an essay published in St. Petersburg in 1913, "do not yield to reprimands and 'good advice' coming from cowardly little souls whose eyes are eternally looking backward."[19] Sympathetic critics viewed futurists as representing a new "elemental awakening of optimism," a "renaissance of faith in the earth," a new "optimism of feeling."[20]

The same could be said for other modernist trends. For many new writers, the disenchantments and disarray of modernity, including the fall of the old positivist myth of time as steady linear progress, opened new spaces and opportunities for vital creativity. In place of a rigid structure of time marching inexorably forward, or its mirror image as degeneration, modernists held up an optimistic vision of modern time as a realm of possibility, openness, and becoming, at least for the inspired, vital, and creative subject. This newly dynamic, vital, and open view of time—influenced by Henri Bergson's notions of time as indeterminate "duration" and Nietzsche's ideas of flux and will—was shared by symbolists like Zinaida Gippius, acmeists like Osip Mandel'shtam, futurists like Velimir Khlebnikov, avant-garde painters like Kazimir Malevich, composers like Mikhail Matiushin, and other modernists.[21] As Vladimir Markov observed in a defense of the "new art" in 1912, the modern destruction of boundaries, the abandonment of logic and reason, and the embrace of "dissonance" and "contingency" (*sluchainost'*) opened unprecedented "possibility" for creativity.[22] Or as Matiushin wrote, the modernist spirit emphasized the unrestricted creativity of "intuitive reason" and the desire to flee from the oppressive world of objects and the objective into a "new apprehension of space and time," a new optimistic way of understanding and seeing the world.[23] Many critics, though, saw modernism as a decadent turn from the world into the inward self, to the "I" outside of which there was no reality.[24] Or as another critic put it, modernism was nothing but "audacity" (*derzost'*)—a boldness and optimism that he viewed as idiotic.[25]

Popular artists, though with less effrontery and modernist originality but also with much larger audiences, also tried to mark a creative path of confident, even heroic, will. Journalistic critics, who generally preferred popular culture to elite modernism and thus better understood the former, enthusiastically lauded popular artists for this stance. For example, writers heaped praise on the stage actress Vera Kommissarzhevskaia, one of Petersburg's theatrical stars, especially as the city mourned her death in 1910, for being "so irrepressible, impatient, full of seething energy." Unlike so many who recoiled before the conditions of modern life, her admirers declared, she "hungrily grabbed hold of the currents of modern life and pulled forward."[26] She was "our youth, our prayer," who moved audiences not with a cathartic spirit of "tragedy" but with the tender "lyricism" needed in these times.[27]

Journalists themselves tried to embolden readers not only with emotional appeals to hopefulness but by spelling out reasons to be optimistic. As "optimistic" historians have long argued about Russia before the war, the reasons to be pessimistic about Russia's progress, ranging from the problems suffered by a society still feeling the ill effects of both backwardness and modernization to the rigidity and archaism of an autocratic government, were matched and overtaken by the many signs of change and improvement, including important social and political reforms undertaken by the government in the wake of the 1905 revolution. Since politics was difficult to discuss in a censored press, writers emphasized economic and social modernization. Rejecting skepticism about modernity, a number of urban writers insisted that modern progress was itself the cure for modern maladies, that only continued modernization would overcome the problems of the present. A. Protopopov, who regularly wrote for the Petersburg city government journal *Gorodskoe delo*, appealed for "optimism" when thinking about urban problems: the growth of populations, industry,

state incomes, and, in general, "material culture," all demonstrate sources
of strength.[28] Even the "nervousness" of modern city life could be seen as
a positive energy. The tabloid columnist Skitalets, for example, appealed
to his readers to feel the positive pulse of modern life. "Life is movement,"
he declared. Telegraph wires circle the earth, allowing all human hearts to
beat with "the same common human interests." Railroads, highways, and
giant steamships bring the people of the world closer together. Life, he argued, invoking a fitting modernist metaphor, is a real "cinematograph."[29]
Appropriately, the editor of the newspaper of Petersburg cinema, which
in its opening issue insisted on its "faith" in "light, truth, and progress,"[30]
was particularly insistent on the joys of modern "culture and civilization":
in an article appropriately titled "Toward the Sun," he expressed love for
electric lights, flying machines, telephones, phonographs, the cinema, gigantic bridges, tunnels through mountains, tall buildings, the achievements
of science, and the development of new ideas. "Modern man" has much to
be proud of, he insisted.[31] As historians of Russian technology and science
have shown, such modern optimism, formed precisely in the face of widespread disintegration, much of it attributed to modernity itself, inspired
many members of Russia's educated elite to a profound faith in the power
of reason and science to restore society to health.[32]

Writers also saw signs of moral and spiritual progress. An essayist
in the newspaper *Peterburgskii listok* expressed in 1909 his "pleasure" at
the evidence of growing "consciousness" (*soznatel'nost'*)—a widely used
term denoting various forms of enlightened understanding—which was
the "best assurance of progress, of healthy, normal, reasoned progress."[33]
Others found that the age was becoming one of "intensified searching and
creative work in all areas of thought."[34] Even the everyday moral life of the
city was seen to contain signs of hope. Writing of St. Petersburg and other
"modern Sodoms," the two leading columnists for *Gazeta-kopeika*, Skitalets
and Ol'ga Gridina, both argued that unlike the original Sodom, Petersburg
would be saved, for there was in the Russian capital not just one "righteous
person" (*pravednik*), and not just the fifty God initially demanded in Genesis, but hundreds of people with warm hearts who cared about those suffering around them.[35] The essayist Ashkinazi offered a typical perspective:

even though humanity had never been as unhappy as now, a "trembling of anticipation" could be felt throughout the world, a "predawn shadow" that was both "terrible" and "tender," a sense that some "renewal" was near.[36] Even the coming of war in 1914 did not dissuade some from hope for the future. On the contrary, the more optimistic observers thought that the war could bring renewal nearer. We are "on the eve of a great turning [*perelom*]," a church editorialist argued, "an inward, spiritual revolution [*perevorot*]."[37] Some liberal and left-wing secular writers also felt that "we live now in a time of great possibilities. Under the roar of arms . . . Russia, like a living organism, full of life, has found the strength to heal its inner sores."[38]

In many respects this was a quite modest heroism of will and feeling. Optimistic talk of faith and determination was quite far from the romantic idealism that had culminated in 1905 and was said to have been lost in its wake. Idealism now, one writer suggested in 1910, was neither bold "optimism" nor a fatalistic "reconciliation with a reality that is so cruel and bloody," but "that self-possession [*samoobladanie*] without which we will not be able to survive our dark days."[39] The well-known theologian Valentin Ternavtsev similarly argued that Christianity teaches joy and rejects hopelessness but also views the "optimism" that imagines that "illness, poverty, misery, disenchantment, and evil do not exist" or can be easily overcome as a lie.[40] Faith in human "will," religious writers regularly warned, was a deceit and a delusion.[41] But secular writers also warned against the illusions of "false optimism."[42] Instead of the radical optimism of the past, the new idealism was presented as incremental, partial, modest, and, above all, pragmatic. With a sense of relief, an essayist in 1911 observed that "thank God, there is less talk about 'moods' than formerly," by which he meant the salutary decline of revolutionary moods: "There is no great progressive grandiosity [*ob"em*], none of the former enthusiasm among the lower classes, no hopes for the coming of a sudden transformation in society or in the political order."[43] While some regretted this loss, this writer was among those who felt it to be a sign of recovery and health. Even the "disillusionment" about which so many wrote could be seen, not as a loss of ideals, but as a healthy loss of faith "in the possibility of their quick and complete realization."[44] Rather than dreaming of fundamental change "at one stroke," idealists were described as now focused on gradual and "partial" change. Even the St. Petersburg intelligentsia, "their illusions dispersing," were finally beginning to understand this.[45]

Journalists tried to encourage this new mood by appealing to their readers to think practically. In a Christmas essay in 1909, Gridina complained that we "think" too much about life's difficulties and do too little. Better, she argued, "to perish while creating and doing things than to become faintly extinguished in hopeless and pitiable despondency."[46] Appeals for "fewer words and more deeds" were a refrain in these years.[47] What was needed above all in "the conditions of these times," a newspaper editor wrote, is "a practical [*delovoe*] attitude to life."[48] The editors of *Gorodskoe delo* similarly called for recognition both of the problems of everyday life and that these were resolvable with a "practical" (*prakticheskii*) approach.[49]

The ultimate goal of even this modest optimism remained the elusive ideal of "happiness." It is for "happiness" that people always and everywhere struggle, even if they are not sure what happiness is, Skitalets argued in 1911.[50] New Year's greetings, framed by the traditional wish "for a new year and new happiness" (*s novym godom, s novym schast'em*), spoke of "hope" and "faith" for such new happiness.[51] The popularity of Anastasiia Verbitskaia's boulevard novel *Keys to Happiness*, published between 1910 and 1913, and the movie version that appeared on Petersburg screens in 1913, was emblematic of this preoccupying theme in public culture. Press summaries of both the book and the film emphasized the heroine's "thirst for happiness, which so filled her soul," and the keys to happiness that various characters offered her, ranging from devotion to art to personal pleasure.[52] Even the city's commercial life marketed to the desire for happiness. Fashion and shopping, especially for women, became sites (dangerous in the eyes of critics) of exploration, pleasure, and self-fulfillment. Advertisements offered a vast array of consumer products promising personal happiness—from musical instruments and bicycles, to tobacco and alcohol, to all sorts of entertainments.[53] As Sally West has shown, advertisements promised material salvation from all the problems of modern city life, whether "nerve-shattering street traffic," severe "depression," or a vague sense of modern "unease."[54] In this same optimistic spirit, advertisements for patent medicines, printed in a wide range of newspapers and magazines, promised users "joy in life" (*zhizneradost'*),[55] strengthened nerves, renewed "life energy," and improved "moods." Responding to a society viewed as disordered and in decline, health advertising contributed to an emerging cult of health and strength as a path to renovation and happiness, an optimistic ethos that would have its most consequential effects under Bolshevik power.[56]

Again and again, the pursuit of happiness was viewed as an exercise in willpower, irrespective of any "reasons" to be happy. The conservative columnist Mikhail Men'shikov's arguments in the spring of 1910 were typical, even clichéd: happiness is something you make for yourself. "If you want to see humanity made of none but happy people . . . start with yourself." Citing Epicurus, he reminded his readers that "happiness is not a right but a duty." It is a discipline. The first step is to "expel from one's mind all worries and concerns," to learn to rid oneself of the "tragic mood." This is not easy but needs to be practiced, one day at a time, until "one makes happiness a habit." Of course, he added, happiness was easier to nurture in nature than in the "poisoned atmosphere" of the city.[57]

Closely linked to the pursuit of happiness was the pursuit of beauty, which was said to be especially desirable in these difficult times, and redemptive. Modern art was defined by sympathizers by its search for new forms of "beauty," which required, tellingly, turning away from "the real and tangible" world toward "another world" of "mystery" and "instinct."[58] Even writers like Leonid Andreev, so often criticized for his dark and decadent spirit, were harnessed to the cause of redemptive beauty: Andreev's ideal was "tragic beauty," one critic insisted, and hence ultimately not "pessimistic."[59] Most journalistic critics hated modern art, so looked instead to the classical beauty exemplified by the Venus de Milo: in contrast to art that "confuses" the viewers' spirit, "the Venus . . . communicates feelings of calm and magnificence to the soul of the sensitive viewer. For that moment, one's soul is cleansed of the triviality of everyday life."[60] In a similar spirit, if more sophisticated and modern in language and sensibility, publications like the journal *Apollon*, which revived the aestheticist traditions of the World of Art movement in these post-1905 years, promoted an Apollonian ideal of classical beauty as the highest value and greatest necessity in these times. None of this was limited to the arts. As the journalist M. Slobozhanin argued in an essay on "idealism in practical life" in 1914, "beauty as slogan, as ideal" had become the primary goal for much of society—not only for avant-garde writers and artists and their audiences (the sort, he suggested, who might visit the "Stray Dog" artistic cabaret or listen to a lecture by Sologub) but for "the majority of our 'thick' journals, advanced newspapers, theater lovers, and even . . . students, especially female ones."[61]

To be sure, many urban writers recognized that happiness and beauty, however desirable and healthy, were sadly rare in this life. Ol'ga Gridina, for example, reported in 1910 that of the huge quantity of letters she had received from readers during the past year, her first as a regular essayist in *Gazeta-kopeika*, so far only one reader claimed to have truly "found happiness."[62] Likewise, an essay in the Petersburg theosophical journal, titled "Two Years in the City of Happiness," mournfully compared the happiness to be found in America with the situation in Russia, where the main struggle was to avoid being consumed by growing "disintegration" and "chaos" and where "the work of destruction is going more quickly than the work of creation."[63] Precisely in the face of these conditions and moods, writers insisted that people needed to believe, and to act as if they believed, that one could "make life beautiful, free, and happy."[64]

POLITICAL OPTIMISM

The belief, indeed faith, that happiness was something that must and could be "made" by human will, reason, and effort was especially strong among political activists on the left. St. Petersburg's trade union and socialist publications, which proliferated after 1905, became a key platform from which to convey this spirit.[65] Marxists held to the traditional ideological faith in history as a natural force of temporal progress, though requiring both active human struggle and moments of rupture. The strongest belief in the sureness of temporal progress was to be found in the more traditionalist Menshevik wing of the Russian Social Democratic Workers' Party. Mensheviks like Iulii Martov were confident that the very conditions of social and political life would lead the working class toward consciousness of their common class identity and their historic destiny, and hence to commitment to fight for a socialist transformation of an increasingly bankrupt social, economic, and political order. The task of revolutionaries was to help along, but not force, a dialectical temporal process in which both consciousness and revolution needed to "ripen."[66] By contrast, Vladimir Lenin and the Bolsheviks were much more likely to echo contemporary discourses about the essential power of the human will, though with a revolutionary tint. Lenin's revolutionary model—called "voluntarist" by both contemporary critics and later historians—was constructed around the agency of a "conscious" and "disciplined" "vanguard." Echoing nineteenth-century intelligentsia traditions of seeing the only hope for society's redemption from suffering in the efforts of "critically thinking individuals" (Petr Lavrov's phrase) and "new people" (made famous by Nikolai Chernyshevskii), Lenin spoke of "professional revolutionaries" in the most heroic terms, especially in his influential program for a new party, *What Is to Be Done?* (1902): "Give us an organization of revolutionaries, and we shall overturn Russia."[67]

Lenin's vanguardists were ideally driven not only by rational knowledge—especially of the telos of historical movement—but also by positive emotions: confidence, boldness, optimism. Throughout his political career, Lenin voiced contempt for people who yielded, even in the most objectively difficult circumstances, to pessimism, despair, or demoralization—terms he often spoke of with disgust. After the collapse of the 1905 revolution and the rise of repression, when many socialists admitted to frustration, disillusionment, and doubt, Lenin refused to indulge such feelings and continued to insist on necessary boldness and heroism in the continuing struggle. For example, in a retrospective essay in 1910 about a Bolshevik who had fallen in the struggles of 1905, Lenin reminded readers of the values that had inspired him: heroism, consciousness, activism. Above all, such heroes are always "relentlessly, heroically firm," and act "unswervingly" (*neustannoi, geroiski-upornoi . . . neuklonno*) even at a time of "crisis."[68] Lenin's most famous plea for boldness against doubt, of course, was his famous "Letter to Comrades" in October 1917, where he endeavored to counter the hesitation of other party leaders to take the gamble of starting an insurrection to seize power. Unambiguously and in the same manner he had been arguing in for years, he warned that "vacillation" was "shameful," that talk of "hopelessness" was unforgivable, that "pessimism" was nothing but "sadness" and fear, that those who worried that the "mood of the masses" was too filled

with hopelessness and despair to allow success were only "dumping on
the masses their own personal spinelessness," and that the time had come
to advance from "complaints and begging and tears to revolutionary action," indeed to transform the "near despairing mood" of the masses into a
mood of revolutionary "hatred." [69] After 1917, Lenin would continue to find
it necessary to remind communists that "despair is impermissible," [70] that
"for us to give way to despair" or " 'desperation' " (*dukha unyniia*, which
Lenin puts in ironic quotes) is "either comical or shameful," even in times
of great difficulty and crisis, indeed especially then. [71] Marxism, emotionally,
was guided by what Antonio Gramsci would later famously call "pessimism
of the intelligence, optimism of the will." [72] Faced with the great difficulties
of the post-1905 years in Russia, political radicals would insist on willful
heroism.

Liberals similarly insisted on the need to trust in progress. As such,
they too spoke out against moods of skepticism and despair. In a public
lecture in 1910, the history professor and leader of the Constitutional Democratic Party, Pavel Miliukov, warned against the "fin-de-siècle" spirit of
"disillusionment" with previous beliefs. In particular, Miliukov was confident that the movement of time was progressive, notwithstanding the crisis
of the present. Like Lenin, he refused to see ruin and catastrophe where
there was only the normal flux of historical change. [73] In a similar spirit, a
liberal journalist writing in the newspaper *Rech'* in 1910 insisted that people
had not become dispirited in the face of so many problems, contrary to the
overwhelmingly dark picture of the public mood found in the press. Reality
was not so bad: "society, that old adversary [*protivnik*], is still quite alive
and is not thinking about death, even though its arms and legs seem to have
been broken." True, he admitted, the years following the revolution were a
bit depressing, but this was only temporary: "the dark time of the entr'acte
is passing and the spirit is opening itself up to the new." Like many liberals
and radicals, he was sure that "hope" and determination remained alive
and ready for new life. [74] Or as another liberal journalist insisted, "man is
born for happiness as a bird is born to fly." The fact that there is so little
happiness in this world should be not a source of despair but of inspiration: the "eternal dissatisfaction" of humanity is what drives it "forward"; it

is the source of "progress."[75] Again we see a pessimism of intellect and an optimism of will.

Russian conservatives, including the tsar and many officials, were less sanguine about progress. Deeply skeptical of human reason and will, they viewed tradition and organic development, guided by a restraining state, as the only safe path forward. In judging the present, they were inclined to view free-market capitalism, especially its social relationships, as morally decadent and harmful to the individual personality (*lichnost'*). They had a marked distaste for the artificiality, alienation, and fractures of urban life— especially as evident in the capital city, St. Petersburg, which conservatives especially despised. As Mikhail Luk'ianov has shown in his excellent study of Russian conservative thought, conservatives tended to view the modern present as a new "time of troubles" (*smutnoe vremia*) marked by "chaos," "disorder," "depravity," and "fragility." But they also insisted on faith in salvation through human action. Rejecting the direction of modern progress, they believed they could make reality adjust to a more ideal system of values. The very "catastrophe" of the present—a term conservatives often used—held the promise of turning onto a new and healthier path rooted in the verities of the abandoned past. Indeed, some historians have found a strong "utopian" strain in Russian conservatism, a faith that even the worst time of troubles could produce redemption.[76]

SEEKING GOD

The desire for happiness, especially in the face of the desolation of existential experience, led many to religion or spirituality. Side by side with talk of the loss of religious faith, the spread of religious "indifferentism," and the godlessness of the modern social mood,[77] especially in the modern city, was its much discussed, and no less urban, twin: the rise of religious searching and faith. This spiritual upheaval in St. Petersburg, begun around the turn of the century but greatly intensified after 1905, was variously named: a "religious awakening," a revival of "religious enthusiasm," a "new religious consciousness," an outpouring of "religious hunger," the growth of "religious mood" and "feeling," a "mystic mood," and (especially in reference

to the intelligentsia) a movement of "God-seeking" (*bogoiskatel'stvo*).[78]
Whatever it was called, all agreed that it was one of the chief "signs of the
times."[79] No less important, observers noted (and more traditional believers noted with alarm), there was something troubling and disordered in
this heightened religious mood. This seemed to be less a religious "revival"
than a "religious time of troubles" (*religioznaia smuta*).[80]

Not so long before, it was argued, in the second half of the nineteenth
century, the whole of "the advanced thinking part of Russian society," in
the spirit of Auguste Comte, Ludwig Feuerbach, and Karl Marx, was convinced that religion was finally fading into the past. But no longer. Even
the intelligentsia were said to now recognize the strength of the "thirst" for
faith—including their own need for spiritual belief.[81] Even some committed
Marxists—and not only disillusioned defectors such as the participants in
the *Vekhi* (Landmarks) essay collection in 1909—shared in the prevalent
emotional dissatisfaction with cold philosophical rationalism and sought
to link Marxism to sacred images, ideals, and moods.[82] The journal of the
St. Petersburg Theological Academy, in 1909, described the present as a
"time of religious seeking" unlike any in the recent past. It seemed that both
"educated society" and the common people had turned toward religion in
the search for "peace for their disenchanted hearts."[83]

The visible signs of this new religious spirit were ubiquitous and
were often discussed in the Petersburg press.[84] Among the intelligentsia,
private circles and salons devoted to religious discussion were held in the
homes of individuals. Literature, philosophy, and the arts, as many historians have described, were often preoccupied with questions of religious
faith and feeling. Spiritualism, which sought to reach across the apparent
boundaries between this life and the next and to comfort believers faced
with death and loss, attracted many educated Russians. The formerly left-
wing intellectuals who joined together in *Vekhi* repudiated the materialism
and atheism that had dominated intelligentsia thought for generations in
favor of a spiritual and moral awakening to sacred truths, the inward life of
the individual, and the rediscovery of a spirit of faith that was so far from
the rationalist traditions of the intelligentsia as to be ultimately "diffident,
intimate, undemonstrable."[85] Public lectures on religious topics drew large
crowds, especially, it was reported, of "young people who are always so

sensitive to questions of religion."[86] New religious organizations appeared, such as the revived Religious-Philosophical Society in 1906 (which brought together clergy and diverse intellectuals in a hopeful search for common ground), the Spiritualist Society in 1906, and the Russian Theosophical Society in 1907.

The church itself was affected by this new religious mood. The journal of the St. Petersburg Theological Academy described a growing movement within the church to free itself from state tutelage and renew the Orthodox "spiritual community" (*sobornost'*).[87] The most famous St. Petersburg clergyman who sought to restore vitality to Orthodox worship and everyday life was Father Ioann of Kronstadt, whose services at St. Andrew's Church on Kronstadt Island near St. Petersburg attracted exceptional numbers of worshipers. After his death in December 1908, he continued to be venerated. His photograph on postcards was seen everywhere, among rich and poor, simple people and the well educated, and even, it was reported, among Tatars and Jews.[88] His most extreme followers, termed by the press Ioannity (Ioannites), refused to recognize the church's authority, deified him as Christ returned and even as the Lord God Sabaoth, and saw the apocalypse as near.[89]

Among the city's lower classes, said to be "most inclined" toward new and alternative religious teachings due to the "conditions of their lives,"[90] large numbers of people were drawn to figures such as "Brother" Ivan (Ivanushka) Churikov—a "popular prophet . . . typical for our times"—a charismatic preacher who had himself been inspired to a life of religious devotion after coming to St. Petersburg to hear Father Ioann.[91] The city's urban poor were also reported to be attracted to various urban mystics and healers (such as the popular Gavriil who claimed to have returned from the Holy Land and to work cures with holy water and earth and a piece of wood from the cross of Christ's crucifixion),[92] to numerous folk healers and fortune tellers (a reporter observed that they could be found practicing their "deceit" in almost every building in the city),[93] and to growing congregations of religious dissenters and "sectarians," ranging from Baptists to small, newly established groups.

The unorthodox direction of so much of this religious revival was clear. This was especially evident in the spread of "sectarianism"

(*sektantstvo*)—a term used by writers to categorize a wide range of unorthodox trends, though "sectarians" themselves often considered themselves truer to the Orthodox faith than the church that condemned them.
St. Petersburg seemed to have become a national center of deviant religious
belief and practice. In 1907, in the opening essay of a series of newspaper
reports in *Peterburgskii listok* on sectarians in St. Petersburg, the journalist
N. Tal'nikov noted the "unusual vitality of sectarian activities in Petersburg
in recent times"—he would soon put this even more strongly, writing of a
"springtime of sectarianism" and of a "powerful wave" of sectarianism[94]—
stimulated by the troubled social and political atmosphere in the country,
as well as greater possibilities for civic organization, in the wake of the 1905
revolution. Tal'nikov's reports on the new urban sectarianism described a
richly varied picture of religious deviance. Older groups were finding new
life, notably evangelical Christians of all sorts, judged to have made great
progress among the city's lower-middle and working classes,[95] along with
older Russian sects, much persecuted over the years, such as so-called *khlysty* (flagellants) and *skoptsy* (castrates).[96] But most groups were completely
new, appearing in the capital only in the last couple of years, along with a
variety of individual "prophets," "prophetesses," and "holy men."[97]

Amidst the huge variety of "sectarian" groups Tal'nikov described in
his newspaper series, we see certain consistent patterns of belief, in particular the familiar leitmotifs of will, optimism, and the pursuit of happiness. For
many groups, the free will of individual believers was a defining principle:
sacred truth must come from within, from the soul. This was at the heart of
the protestant faith of Baptists and other evangelical Christians, but also of
many newer groups, such as the "Free Christians" who rejected all formal
rites in favor of free-form services in which people spoke when the Spirit
moved them.[98] In this same spirit, priestlessness and limited hierarchy were
common.[99] In the face of the perceived moral disorder and degeneration
of the modern world, many sectarian groups considered an ethical life, the
pursuit of "moral perfection,"[100] to be the most essential practice. This
was the chief concern, for example, of the hugely popular *trezvenniki* (teetotalers) or *brattsy*, led by "Brother" Ivan Churikov, estimated by Tal'nikov
to number fifty thousand in St. Petersburg in 1908. To the city's poor, Churikov and other Brethren preached a pure life, inspired by the Gospels, free

of drinking, smoking, and swearing.[101] *Skoptsy* (castrates) also opposed eating meat, smoking, and drinking alcohol, as well as sex.[102] For some groups, such as the *paskhal'niki*, a moral life also meant rejecting all the forms of modern technological civilization as the work of Antichrist: telephones, telegraphs, automobiles, trams, cinemas, flying machines.[103]

Seeking the fullest realization of a happy, whole, and moral life, a number of groups looked to an apocalypse, to the imminent second coming of Christ. Adventists (who first came from western Europe in the late nineteenth century) even named a date, 1932–33, for Christ's return.[104] Many new groups, such as the Children of Revelation (who even identified the spot on the Karpovka River in St. Petersburg where Christ would appear), were also convinced that the world was living through an apocalyptic "end time" and that Christ's return was imminent.[105] A "holy man" and healer named Tikhon (a former peasant named Trofim who had come to the capital from Poltava province) preached a similar gospel of preparing for the approaching end of the world with much success in the working-class Narva Gate district.[106]

Emotions, at least implicitly, were a central tenet of much new belief in these years. These movements viewed dark moods as an obstacle to salvation and "hope" for "a renewed life and the higher joys"[107] (even if only in life after death or after Christ's return) as essential to finding the path to truth and happiness. The causes of the movements were also seen to lie in the emotions. The revival of religiosity, it was said again and again, was an upheaval of "religious instincts" more than of conventional belief, a movement of *nastroennost'* (a state of mind and feeling), a "voice of unmediated feeling," and the result of emotional "disenchantment with the rationalism and superficiality" of the scientific worldview.[108]

The popularity of many new urban religious movements, even critical churchmen recognized, was largely due to their great emotionality and their emphasis on "inward religious experiences" and "creativity" (*tvorchestvo*—which in this usage was synonymous with the expression of inward feeling).[109] Churikov's *trezvenniki*, for example were said to be driven by the power of emotion. How, a church writer asked, could Brother Ivan, a former peasant and fish trader, attract thousands of followers from the Petersburg common folk? The answer lay in the "contemporary mood":

it was not that Churikov had a brilliant mind or was a beautiful speaker (in fact, Tal'nikov and others described him as barely literate)[110] but simply that "man cannot endure the darkness of unbelief and grasps at the first strong hand extended to him."[111] Or as a more sympathetic writer noted, speaking of the *trezvenniki*'s impassioned prayer meetings and charismatic preaching, " 'Brother' Ivan knew how to set fire to the emotions."[112] Churikov himself explained that his preaching was inspired not by bookish knowledge but by the Holy Spirit working within his soul.[113] Passionate preaching was said to characterize many groups, including the highly successful Baptists.[114] The noted Baptist preacher Wilhelm Fetler, for example, was said to excite large crowds, calling on listeners to "replace their old, cold heart with a new heart, a new life," and inspiring them to respond with shouts and exclamations.[115] But even in the absence of charismatic preaching, passionate feeling was seen to be central to the piety of sectarians. The worship services of many groups were marked by joyful singing and dancing.[116] The so-called *plakuny* (wailers) or *vozdykhantsy* (meaning those who yearn for something), for example, rejected the traditional sacraments in favor of a belief only in the "sacrament of tears," in the "dogma of the saving power of holy tears."[117]

The enormous popularity of Father Ioann of Kronstadt was also attributed to his understanding of people's emotional needs in modern times: "The age of progress, the age of complicated political combinations, the age of unbelief and of deepest doubt, gave us a man who knew how to heal tired people."[118] Why was he so venerated, even among non-Orthodox? a church writer asked: because of his "nastroenie," the qualities of feeling, emotion, and temperament that he brought to prayer and the liturgy, which made people feel "renewed."[119] Similarly, in the wake of Lev Tolstoy's death in 1910, a church writer asked why Tolstoy was so revered in "contemporary society" as a moral prophet. Again the answer was found in "the closeness of Tolstoy's spiritual searching" to people's "mood," to their own existential path of "inward experience," to their own journey from loss of faith to a new search for sacred meaning.[120]

While some writers and public lecturers admired such heterodox and unorthodox trends as a healthy answer to disordered and decadent times,[121] most commentators viewed this eclectic God-seeking, mysticism,

and sectarianism as itself a sign of disorder and decadence.[122] Some writers
noted how characteristically modern all this heterodoxy was: a reflection
of the "aspiration toward the new" and of the desire for spiritual "freedom" and "creativity."[123] But most worried that this modern "new" was a
decadent new. An essay in 1910 by a church writer on the "psychology of
sectarianism" found "nothing besides decadence" (*nichto inoe kak upadok,
dekadans*) in the new religious movements, evident in their ceaseless dissatisfaction and striving for the new, their inclination toward primitivism,
and, in this critic's view, the ultimate, if unintended, replacement of better
by worse—all characteristics, he did not need to emphasize, of the modern
condition.[124] Similarly, in a New Year's Day review of "new tendencies" in
Russian cultural life in the liberal newspaper *Rech'* in 1908, the philosopher
and writer Leonid Galich described the recent growth of "neo-Christianity"
and "mystical anarchism" as examples of a "revived romanticism," which
he judged to be a sign of cultural "decadence" and philosophical "hooliganism" more than of true spirituality and faith.[125]

Church writers, naturally, were especially anxious, and they filled
the pages of the journal of the St. Petersburg Theological Academy with
screeds against sectarianism and other deviant religious paths. An essay on
"contemporary God-seeking" worried that the healthy "yearning [*toska*]
for God" that so pervaded the "mood" of both the intelligentsia and the
common people in "these times" did not put people on the correct path
to truth (which, he assumed, would lead to the Orthodox Church) but led
intellectuals to "theosophical occultism" and common people to "preach-
ers of Baptism and Shtundism [a general term for revivalist Protestantism
with German origins, especially among peasants], and to various elders
and brothers."[126] The "fashionable" appeal of spiritualism and occultism
among the higher classes was viewed as a particularly disturbing sign:
as "self-deception" at best and "evil" involvement with "unclean forces"
(*nechistaia sila*) and "devilry" (*besovshchina*) at worst.[127] While church
writers tended to express satisfaction at seeing a rise of spiritual "hunger,"
and sympathized with its causes—including a healthy disillusionment with
the philosophy of "cheap materialism" and even with western civilization
as a whole, but also dissatisfaction with merely external religiosity—they
were dismayed at how "alien" so much of this new religiosity was to the true

faith, how confused its "unique theological metaphysics."[128] The church
tried to heal this rift—while also addressing the problem of unbelief—with
a special "mission to the people" in St. Petersburg, begun in 1914.[129] The
government tried to help by periodically arresting religious dissenters, notwithstanding the 1905 decree on tolerance for religious diversity.[130]

Nonchurch writers were similarly worried. Tal'nikov echoed a common view when he argued that "religious disbelief and religious sectarianism" were part of one and the same "powerful wave."[131] In much the same
language with which newspapers (including his own) spoke of street crimes,
critics like Tal'nikov (and government prosecutors in trials of religious dissenters) spoke of sectarians as engaging not in real religion but only in confidence games or swindles (*moshennichestvo*),[132] as "clever" (*lovkii*) prophets
and "sham" (*mnimyi*) healers who "exploited the religious feelings" of the
common people.[133] Newspaper critics treated spiritualism among the elite
as simply another of the many frauds in public life perpetrated on the gullible.[134] Some writers worried about the rise of "paganism" in the city: not
only Buddhism and other alien religions brought to the city by non-Russian
migrants—the fact that Buddhists were building a temple in St. Petersburg
in 1910 struck many as a dark sign of the times—but also "worshipers of
fire, worshipers of the devil who attend 'black masses,' and the like."[135]
"God-seekers" themselves could be troubled by some of the new trends in
religious life. Dmitrii Merezhkovskii, for example, though involved in his
own out-of-church religious practices and arguing that "religious civil society [*obshchestvennost'*] will save Russia,"[136] excoriated some of the new
religious trends as little more than "Black-Hundred philistine-hooligan
religion," which saw the divine not in a transcendent God but only in the
individual human "I," a faith that was destined to lead to amoral brutality
and despair.[137]

The emotional character of this upheaval of religiosity could also be
cast in a dark light. Some writers felt that the new religious mood reflected
less faith than uncertainty, less happiness than desperation. The intelligentsia's God-seeking was seen to be especially filled with discomfort and anxiety. One essayist, for example, writing in 1909, characterized God-seeking
as not the eternal human search for the meaning of "human and world existence" but a form of "self-torment" caused by a "psychological state of

spiritual instability and ruin."[138] Sectarians, too, critics argued, dwelled excessively on the dark sides of human life. For popular sects like the *plakuny*,
for example, "the world is overfull with suffering, bitterness, and evil," leading to a "permanent consciousness of weakness and helplessness," which
naturally leads to "feelings of sorrow and anguish."[139] To be sure, a few
critics went further to argue that the whole of Christianity was preoccupied
with suffering and death. Most famously, in a published talk given at the
Religious-Philosophical Society in the late fall of 1907, Vasilii Rozanov provocatively insisted that the "main ideals" of the Christian worldview are not
everyday earthly happiness, but sorrow, death, and the grave.[140]

At best, some argued, the new trends in religion marked a desperate effort, not always successful, to turn away from the terrible predica-
ment of modern life, to survive spiritually and emotionally in dark times:
an expression of an "aesthetic-psychological striving toward beauty" in
an ugly world"[141] or a renewed understanding of "suffering" as a bright
and elevated experience that can even acquire "shades of bliss" (*ottenki
blazhenstva*).[142] Sects like the "Ivanushkovtsy," as the press called followers
of "Brother" Ivan Churikov, were described as providing a spiritual "oasis"
where one could look away from the surrounding "catastrophe," "doubt,"
"fear," "horror," and "despair."[143] Intellectual God-seeking was also viewed
against a dark background of frustration and desperation. Setting this story
in a modern and global context, an essayist in a popular magazine argued
that people today seek God but cannot find Him. Though people become
disenchanted with atheism, "there is no faith in modern humanity," only
"religious thirst and religious despair." This modern truth was especially
evident in Russian God-seeking: "not a religion of heavenly joy . . . but one
of earthly despair."[144] "Many write about religion and even more talk about
it," another journal essayist observed in 1910. "They seek religion and construct religion. Around questions of religion there has developed quite noisy
and busy activity." But all this "noise" produced nothing of value or use.[145]
Or as Rozanov argued in *Novoe vremia* about the Petersburg intelligentsia,
there was much talk of God but no "religious tone of the spirit," only "cold
words."[146] Leonid Galich, writing in *Rech'*, had a different view of what was
missing but agreed there was something false and sick here. The revival
of spirituality among the Petersburg intelligentsia, so characteristic of the

times, reflected a "terribly 'modern'" desire to "overcome pessimism." The trouble was that replacing faith in positive historical progress with the thunder and lightening of miracle—some would have said the same of faith in revolution—produced no real happiness but only "a wild mystical dance [*mysticheskaia pliaska*] at the edge of the abyss."[147]

KILLING TIME

As the jostle of advertisements on the front pages of newspapers reminded every city reader, a great deal of pleasure and fun was on offer in a growing world of urban entertainment, which was accessible even to those with modest incomes and limited time free from labor. Newspaper reporting also regularly described city life, and especially nightlife, as filled with places for fun: opera, ballet, theater, concerts, balls, private parties, restaurants, cafés, cabarets, cafés chantants, and roller-skating rinks, but also sites accessible to almost everyone, including popular theaters, "pleasure gardens," the circus, cinemas, and spectator sports (from wrestling, to auto races and air shows, to football and athletic competitions). Here was "fun-loving Petersburg" (*Veseliashchiisia Peterburg*), as the press dubbed it,[148] or what Louise McReynolds called, in her excellent study of this face of urban life, "Russia at play."[149] In this world, especially among the higher classes, the old poetic ideal of "wine, song, and love" was said to have become the thoroughly "modern program" of "drunkenness, *chantants*, and women," where carefree pleasure (terms used included *prazdnost', legkomyslie, suetnost'*) was everything and the only aim was "to kill time."[150] By the eve of the war it seemed that this spirit of fun had reached new extremes: once upon a time, a reporter complained, people worked in the day and rested quietly at home with their families in the evening, but "today it is just the opposite: nothing but sheer merriment [*sploshnoe vesel'e*] . . . we no longer know how to live without entertainment [*razvlechenie*]."[151]

The variety of entertainments was great, as were the publics being entertained. Popular theaters and theater-restaurants like Villa Rode, the Aquarium, the New Farce, or the Jardin d'Hiver promised spectators amusing "divertissements." Typical performances included "musical fun evenings"; theatrical sketches; "rhythmic poses"; "living pictures" (some-

times on the racy side); performing animals; wrestling (including women
wrestlers); acrobat-comedians; *kupletisty* (singers of humorous music-hall
songs); "gypsy" singers; impersonators (*transformatory*) such as "Ambrosia" who performed as various famous people, male and female, or played
all the many characters in skits such as "Scandal in a Restaurant"; "exotic"
dance performances such as an Egyptian dance "fantaisie," belly dancers
"from the harem," the "dance of Polish apaches," or Africans doing a "national dance"; and especially "piquant" performances such as "The Venus
of Our Days" or a scene in the garden of Eden with a naked dancing Eve.
This was a cosmopolitan entertainment culture, with performers—some
already labeled "stars"—from both Russia and abroad.[152] In the summer,
"amusement parks" and "pleasure gardens" (*uveselitel'nye sady*) offered
similar fare out of doors along with dancing and buoyant socializing by
a typically "mixed, purely capital-city public." On the opening day of the
summer "amusement" season at the Nicholas II People's House, nearly
thirty thousand people crowded into the theater's garden near the Peter
and Paul Fortress, including, "alongside the usual hooligans," a mixture of
soldiers, shop clerks, minor officials," and rich men in shiny top hats.[153]

Reports insistently emphasized the mood as escapist. Descriptions of
the Aquarium, a variety garden-theater and café chantant on Kamennoostrovskii Prospect, for example, where it was said that "all Petersburg" gathered on Saturdays, emphasized the crowds of flirtatious young men and
women, the atmosphere of "witty jokes" and "friendly laughter," and the
pleasure derived from the simultaneous performances on multiple stages
of "gypsy" choirs, comedies and operettas, divertissements, dancers, acrobats, dog troupes, orchestras, and the like, accompanied by fireworks
and confetti.[154] The most popular spectator sport in the city, wrestling, was
similarly viewed as driven by the audience's intense desire for pleasure and
fun. Attracting crowds in the thousands, wrestling was said to inspire "the
crowd of the twentieth century," like the crowd of ancient Rome, with pleasurable visions of physical "power and beauty" (though it also, critics worried, catered to the crowd's tastes for cruelty).[155] For a more highbrow audience, the bohemian cabaret "The Stray Dog" (*Brodiachaia sobaka*) was
described in the press as a place where artists, actors, poets, musicians and
their guests could, until the early hours of the morning, escape "boredom"

in a "cozy" and "intimate" setting surrounded by "witty humor," a "heightened mood," a "cheery atmosphere," and laughter.[156] Here was where the Russian "bohème" (*bogema*) could, from 1911 until its closure in 1915 (allegedly for selling wine, which was illegal during the war), "amuse itself" (*veselit'sia*).[157] Similarly, if less artistically, the prosperous men and women, dressed in white, who attended the "Bal Blanc" at the American Roller-Skating Rink on Mars Field in 1913, "laughed and had fun until four in the morning."[158] New Year's parties were often said to be motivated by the "pursuit of happiness."[159] Thus, a masked ball at the Malyi Theater in January 1914—a time, with war already felt to be looming, many would view as old Russia's final days—took as its motto a phrase very much in the spirit of these times: "Down with Boredom and Spleen! Long Live Fun and Laughter" (*Doloi skuka i splin! Da zdravstvuet vesel'e i smekh*).[160]

The cinema was also a good place to escape from the ordinary worries of the day. Urbanites crowded into proliferating movie houses, which had become the most popular form of entertainment in the city by the eve of the war. Simply walking into a cinema marked entry into an escapist dream-world. Customers approached brightly illuminated façades and passed through foyers filled with palms, bay trees, and other exotic plants, sometimes accompanied by a live orchestra.[161] Theater design after 1907 was characteristically marked by "exuberance" and "excess," as the cinema historian Yuri Tsivian has described.[162] Exuberance and excess also characterized the films themselves, which tended toward strong comedy and melodrama. As a journalist who wrote under the pseudonym "Flâneur" noted in 1909, "If it's a drama, then it's got to be a particularly bloody one. If it's a comic picture, it's caricatured to the nth degree. The public enjoys the depiction of horrors, catastrophes, and of course anything even remotely to do with sex."[163]

The cinema did not ignore the realities of urban life. Audiences saw, in films created by both Russian and European filmmakers, plenty of both poverty and material excess, dysfunctional families, the decadent demimonde, erotic desire and exploitation, violence, crime, murder, rape, suicide, drunkenness, the dangers of the street, and male angst. Film tended to cast these stories, like the black and white on the screen, in stark melodramatic form. With similar extravagance, films also presented literary classics, tales from a more romantic past, and adventure travel. Fun was also part of the mix, though sometimes in decadent extremes and with tragic results. And films were often simply funny. Clearly, cinema had much in common with popular newspapers. But, from the dismayed perspective of journalists who felt that, for all the sensation on the pages of the press, their own mission was to educate and enlighten readers, film seemed mainly to provide empty pleasure and escape. Worse, some reviewers felt, the brutalities so pervasive in modern cinema were "symptomatic" of the troubled "modern public mood" and the debased tastes of the "crowd."[164] Advocates of the cinema, however, saw nothing so heavy or deep in film. At least judging by how movie houses advertised their shows, it was the pleasure to be found there that most mattered. They especially promised fun: "funny comic laughter" (*zabavnyi komicheskii khokhot*), "uninterrupted laughter," "total laughter."[165]

Other forms of popular culture also promised pleasurable escape. Some of the most widely read works of fiction, especially among the young, were adventure stories by writers like Mayne Reid and Fenimore Cooper, which were said not only to inspire dreams of escape but even to provoke some youths to literally flee the tedious everyday realities of school or work and wander the country or even go abroad to America.[166] Newspapers also offered readers entertaining diversions alongside reports of the darker sides of modern life. Most papers carried serialized boulevard novels, sensationalist news reporting, amusing anecdotes, sports news, and accounts of curiosities from all over the world, as did popular magazines, where they might be enhanced with sketches and photographs.[167] Popular music was also oriented toward pleasure. The "gypsy" romances of Anastasiia Vial'tseva, who had come to the capital at the end of the nineteenth century and became one of Russia's most popular singers—even "the most popular artist in Russia"—were said to warm the "cold" hearts of Petersburgers. She was, it was said at the time of her death in 1913, the "Petersburg Muse," a "bright meteor" illuminating the "gray, depressing sky of our petty everyday lives," who brought to cold Petersburg, in both her songs and her personality, the spirit of the "hot southern sun." Her songs were filled with "longing for beauty and happiness," and with "crystal purity," inspiring in the "cold northerner" dreams of happiness.[168] "Longing" (*toska*) was a leitmotif of her passionate songs, hundreds of which were recorded and sold in the years between 1905 and the end of 1912. This sometimes meant melancholy feelings of sad longing and loss, but it mostly meant the longing of desire and hope for happiness—expressed in her emotion-drenched style and in lyrics filled with talk of romance, desire, love, beauty, pleasure, kisses, tears, and dreams.[169] Likewise, the press explained why Petersburgers were so moved by the performances of Isadora Duncan, who regularly visited the capital, by declaring that "worn out and longing [*toskuiushchie*] for beauty, we are hungrily attracted" to her art.[170] Duncan also offered Russians an unusually (indeed, extravagantly) happy response to urban life, including that of the Russian capital. As she described her feelings—wonderfully at odds with the conventional Russian images of Petersburg—in a letter to the editor of the popular magazine *Ogonek*: "Petersburg!/Life! /Enthusiasm!/ Action!/Here all is new in spirit. Primitive/Strong/Great spaces—/Great lines—/Great flowing Neva./Inspiration!/Opportunity!/The future all here—/Great country/I greet thee/I dance here with joy."[171]

Special occasions for fun occurred periodically in the life of the city, including some that highlighted the pleasures to be found in the new and the modern. In 1910, the first annual "aviation week in St. Petersburg" was held. Aviation was described as a new "disease that had gripped all Petersburgers," who came in huge crowds of all classes to the airfield where spectators set up "bivouacs" to eat and drink while watching the show in the sky. The "elevated and delighted mood" of the crowd was revealed by their "ardent laughter and happy talk," although several crashes temporarily "spoiled the happy mood of the public."[172] These darker moments notwithstanding, aviation was said to be able to reveal human capacity and genius and bring joy to the "hearts of cold Petersburgers."[173] Similarly, auto races such as the widely watched and read-about Petersburg-Kiev-Moscow-Petersburg race in the summer of 1910 were described as "noisy celebrations" as the masses came out to greet the drivers.[174] In the winter of 1913, large crowds of all classes also found "fun" in the tercentenary celebrations of the Romanov dynasty. Especially appealing were the decorated streets, illuminated at night. "Literally all Petersburg" came to walk along the central streets of the capital, specially lit with one and a half million light bulbs, many in color, beneath a dark and cloudy sky illuminated by columns of light from a special projector on the Admiralty and other projectors shining images of Romanov rulers onto the clouds. And though the crowds of pedestrians, automobiles, and cabs were so great as to result in unmoving traffic jams (*probki*), and police were on duty in case of disturbances, the "joyous, happy crowd" never lost its holiday spirit.[175]

Observers of everyday cultural life in the capital city felt that the pursuit of pleasure and fun was understandable, if often troublingly so. Writing in *Gazeta-kopeika* on 2 January 1911, Skitalets suggested that the "carousing and frenzy" of New Year's celebrations in the city were reminiscent of the mood in ancient Babylon (a common analogy, as we have seen). All Petersburg had been "seized by a sort of madness," he observed, by a feverish thirst for "fun" (*vesel'e*). But, unlike most other critics, he pointedly refused to condemn these "modern Babylonians": who could blame Petersburgers, amidst all of the "sorrows of everyday life," under the "burden of disillusionment," for the pleasurable "self-deception" of living as if in "Babylon for an hour."[176] Other urban writers similarly recognized this need. A cinema reporter, for instance, viewed the huge growth in the popularity of movie theaters in recent years against the dark background of the times: "The monotonous depression [*unynie*] of our life, so full of worries and sorrows, demands laughter and fun [*smekh i vesel'e*]."[177] The "pursuit of pleasure," critics argued, represented a refusal—perhaps necessary, but also full of danger—to accept the realities of the present life.[178]

Illusion and escape were key themes for interpreting the public mood. Widespread drunkenness was understood as a necessary but regrettable "stimulant" (*vozbuditel'*) to make life at least temporarily cheerier—drink, it was said, was "the great deceiver."[179] Narcotics such as opium, belladonna, and cocaine—described as exotic "stimulants" (*stimulianty*)—were also in growing use, at least among the educated and well-off.[180] The cinema was treated in much the same way: as a form of desperate self-deception, which "beckoned" and "tempted" suffering toilers—"workers, stupefied by dust, suffocating air, and machines," "shop slaves," and serving girls—into a world of "forgetting," "illusions" and escape.[181] Or worse: some critics savaged the cinema for feeding the crowd mechanically produced "shadows," "illusion,"

"hypnosis," "barbarity," and "chaos."[182] The self-deluding "masquerade,"
as many saw it, of "fun-loving Petersburg," the pursuit of amusement as an
answer to anxiety and disenchantment, exemplified the metaphor of "feast
in the time of plague" (*pir vo vremia chumy*), so often heard in these years.
As a disgusted newspaper columnist described this feast in 1910, the public
"mood," especially among the young, had in recent years turned away from
the idealism of the past "and toward the circus arena and the barnyard."[183]
The image of "feast in the time of plague"—borrowed from the title of a play
by Aleksandr Pushkin from 1830—was occasionally meant literally. A report
on new acts at Villa Rode, including the arrival in Petersburg of the "first
dancer of the harem" to amuse Petersburgers with her belly dances, noted
the arrival of another "eastern guest"—cholera. "From sorrow to laughter is
less than a step," the writer sardonically commented.[184]

Some critics tried to portray this bacchanalia with sympathy. The editors of the new monthly magazine *Argus*, for example, which began publishing in St. Petersburg in 1913, described their mission as giving readers
a bit of "rest and entertainment" (*otdykh*, a term meaning both time free
from work and diversion to help one forget one's cares) from the "political
bustle" (*sueta*) of contemporary Russian life, "from the resounding cries of
the 'big questions,' from the stupefying shouting of journal and newspaper
demagogues, from the tedious publicistic writing of warriors of different social camps, from the wearying affectations of literary posers [*samozvantsy*]
and pseudo-writers with their slogans of 'new art.'" *Argus* promised readers
a magazine free from the noise of modern "social disorder," offering healthy
words that would "cure readers of their melancholy."[185] But many writers were skeptical and seem to have agreed more with the view of another
magazine author who insisted on the baleful emotional consequences of
the pursuit of pleasure in the face of suffering. The ultimate result would be
not real happiness but only "a heavy hangover of disenchantment, a longing
for unrealizable freedom, a despair resulting from the revaluation of one's
inner strength [*sily lichnosti*]."[186] Dr. Dmitrii Zhbankov, writing in the journal *Sovremennyi mir* in 1909, offered the same diagnosis: the bacchanalian
philosophy of the day, where "nothing should stand between the individual
and his happiness," leads ultimately to feelings of "disenchantment, surfeit,
complete dissatisfaction, and revulsion."[187]

LAUGHTER

After visiting St. Petersburg in 1913, the French silent film comic Max Linder, known in Russia as the "king of laughter," insisted that St. Petersburg, quite unlike other European metropolises, was a "city without fun" (*neveselyi gorod*), without "any real, sincere, joyful [*zhizneradostnyi*] laughter."[188] Linder was likely repeating what locals were telling him—the trope of Petersburg as an eternally grieving city, or even of the whole of Russia as a country where, as Aleksandr Blok wrote in 1912, people "don't know how to have fun" (*v Rossii ne umeiut veselit'sia*).[189] In the same tradition of viewing Russia through foreigners' eyes, the newspaper columnist Ol'ga Gridina, commenting on the recent death of Mark Twain, observed that, as an American, he had faced the hardships of his life with humor. Had Twain been a Russian, she wryly suggested, he would have hanged or shot himself.[190]

Russians did laugh, of course. Newspapers and magazines regularly included humor, and some publications were almost entirely devoted to it. Popular theaters, amusement gardens, night clubs, dances, festivals, and movie houses were, as we have seen, sites of "ardent laughter." Even the most downtrodden poor, such as were to be found in the infamous slum known as "Viazemskaia lavra," near the Haymarket, were described as living in an atmosphere that was neither "tragic" nor "melodramatic," but filled with "joking, sometimes caustic and sometimes good-natured and cheerful."[191] Much of this public laughter involved little more than "small, often funny, sometimes talented, anecdotes" meant simply to amuse and help one accept the problems of everyday life.[192] Newspaper humor focused most directly on urban life, often with a tone of tolerant irony. On April Fool's Day, for example, newspapers would offer wry news items such as the report that in St. Petersburg everyone was suddenly polite, there were no drunks on the streets even though it was a holiday (in this case, Easter Monday), ugly scaffolds and fences had been taken down, and only respectable-looking boats were to be seen on the river.[193] As can be seen, this amusement had its barbs.

Magazines devoted almost entirely to humor and satire appeared in great numbers after censorship eased following 1905. Highbrow "satirical" journals like *Satirikon* (1908–14) and *Lukomor'e* (The Cove, 1914–17) joined more popular publications that advertised themselves as "humor magazines," such as *Veselaia panorama* (Merry Panorama, 1907–16), *Listok-kopeika* (Kopeck Sheet, 1909–14); *Zhivaia kopeika* (Living Kopeck, 1910–13), and *Shut* (Jester, 1911). What united them was a readiness to view every aspect of contemporary urban life (including most of the problems discussed in this book) as deserving of laughter. Objects of *Satirikon*'s relatively sophisticated satire included masquerades (and Leonid Andreev's play *Black Masks*), crime, hooliganism, murder, rape, syphilis, suicide, the Duma, being run over by a tram, the cinema, wrestling, pornography, decadence, and modernist art and literature—in other words, all "the heroes of our times."[194] Even the seriousness with which newspapers analyzed and worried about these phenomena of urban life was treated as laughable.[195]

The objects of *Listok-kopeika*'s humor, which was aimed at popular readers and tended to avoid the developed satirical irony of journals like *Satirikon* in favor of a light-hearted breeziness, no matter what the topic, included merchants' deceit, advertisements, telephones, the cinema, the new craze for air shows, conversations "overheard" on the street or in other public places, urban nightlife, balls and masquerades, cafés and restaurants, the demimonde, women's fashion, shopping, rich "lords" *(bariny)* pursuing their maids, gold-digging women, marriage, adultery (in general, sexual seduction and attraction was a major theme in contemporary humor), court trials, contemporary literature and art (especially futurism, which always seemed good for a laugh), politicians, duels, sports, foreigners speaking Russian, money (and the lack of it), pickpocketing and other street crimes, begging, drunkenness, "street outrages" *(nakhaly)*, the abysmal condition of Petersburg's streets and buildings, fatal accidents, and urban loneliness. The point was to find some merriment amidst "this endlessly tedious life."[196] Even murder and suicide could become the subject of jokes. In one piece, an elegantly dressed young woman thinks: "If the tailor spoils my new dress a second time I will have no choice but to do away with myself!"[197] The editorial announcement in the first issue of *Listok-kopeika* was typical of the sentiment of many involved in producing humor for urban readers: "healthy laughter is not a luxury but a necessity for every person.

It brightens the brain exhausted from heavy work and refreshes the soul tormented by the extreme stress and disturbances of modern life."[198]

In these times, it seemed, Petersburgers were at least learning to laugh. The art historian Nikolai Vrangel', after viewing an exhibit of work produced by *Satirikon* in the editorial offices of *Apollon* in 1910, concluded that it was no longer true that "we don't know how to laugh."[199] Indeed, a magazine journalist observed in 1912, "suddenly all Russia is . . . shaking with gay, uncontrollable laughter [*khokhot*]," such that one "might think that we have finally reached the kingdom of bright joy and tranquil well-being."[200] And the same might have been said for other recent trends in art and literature, notably futurism whose performances cultivated mutual laughter and mockery between audience and artist and even made the sounds of laughter part of the effort to create a new poetic language.[201] But, as this journalist's "might think" suggests, many felt that this laughter was not all it seemed, that it was a type of performance or mask, an act (perhaps necessary) of willful self-delusion.

Indeed, what many observers felt was missing in contemporary laughter was precisely what Linder diagnosed as absent: "real, sincere, joyful laughter," *zhizneradostnyi* laughter, inspired by joy in life. The joking atmosphere that a reporter found among slum dwellers, for example, was not happy laughter, but a paradoxical "cheerful horror" (*veselyi uzhas*).[202] The same was said of the wider atmosphere of laughing St. Petersburg. An article by Kornei Chukovskii (a literary critic but also a humorist), in the liberal newspaper *Rech'*, diagnosed contemporary laughter. For Chukovskii, as for others, Mark Twain served as a rich counterexample to degraded Russian laughter. American laughter, exemplified by Twain, was "sober, healthy, and bold." There was no "*nadryv* [tormented, damaged, hysterical feelings, a concept especially associated with Dostoevsky], no tragedy or hysterics." Twain laughed at everything and everyone, but this was "not Mephistophelean laughter, not Heinean, not Gogolian." It was laughter "without half-smiles or self-flagellation." This was laughter that "exonerates" the world and was in "harmony" with the world, that was born of "love," and grounded in "freedom," "strength," and "happiness." This was what Russia lacked.[203] A week later, Chukovskii elaborated on Russian laughter in an

article titled "The Humor of the Doomed." Looking at the "psychology" of
contemporary literature, Chukovskii found plenty of smiles and laughter,
but this was a humor marked by feelings of contempt, disgust, and "nausea"
at the sight of the "ugly deformity" (*urodstvo*) of the world.[204]

Writing in the journal *Zhizn' dlia vsekh* in 1912, Leonid Logvinovich
similarly warned that the epidemic of laughter in contemporary Russia
should not be confused with the laughter of joy and happiness. In "modern
guffawing Russia," he warned, a superficial "appearance" of gaiety was an
attempt to veil a dark abyss of "suffering" and "sadness." "Suffering flows
into a smile, and a bitter smile is transformed into an outburst of trembling,
terrible, hysterical laughter." Indeed, "laughter and sadness are the two leitmotifs of the modern mood." Sadly, he felt, there was nothing redemptive in
this laughter. This was not true humor such as one found in Nikolai Gogol's
"laughter through tears," or in Mikhail Saltykov-Shchedrin's "bilious satire," or even when Anton Chekhov "smiled with quiet sorrow." Those hu-
morists laughed healthily and "boldly" in order to "chase away the spiders
of humanity's lies and crassness" (*poshlost'*). True humor, Logvinovich argued, "is a phlegmatic view of the sad incongruity between what ought to be
and what is, between ideals and reality. Humor is 'the comic sublime [*voz-
vyshennoe v komicheskom*].'" This redemptive "striving for the sublime" in
the face of a harsh reality was what Russian humor lacked. Contemporary
Russian laughter was only "pessimistic" laughter, "reactionary laughter,"
without direction or hope.[205]

Thus, ironic laughter seemed to many the most fitting way to laugh.
An ambiguous form of humor that, especially in its modern forms, treats
the dissonance between expectations and realities, and between what one
pretends to think and what one actually thinks, as deserving not anger but
a tolerant smile or modest laughter, irony can lighten the weight of disappointment with the world. Though irony risks degrading into corrosive
doubt, apathy, and detachment, or into nihilistic play and self-indulgence
in the face of modern disorder, it can also become a critical and transcending practice. But whether irony was relief and escape or a critical tool, it
seemed to grow naturally with the development of modern life. As Søren
Kierkegaard and other nineteenth-century philosophers of modernity argued, "irony seemed to have infected every life-relation. Every aspect of life

had become charged with its corrosive freedom so that nothing could be taken at face value, and in every communication there seemed to lurk some other, and perhaps sinister message. Irony, in fact, seemed to be the fundamental characteristic of modern life, an aspect of the breakdown of a fixed cosmos and a language linked to it."[206]

Irony flourished in Russian life, art, and literature, for conditions in Russia and especially the imperial capital nourished it. Quoting Heinrich Heine, who wrote that sometimes in the spring "I no longer know where irony leaves off and the heavens begin," a newspaper feuilletonist observed that in St. Petersburg, with its mists and fog, irony never ends and the heavens never begin.[207] Once a rarified mentality reserved for a few odd intellectuals and writers, in these times it had become a contemporary "style," at least among the middle and upper classes.[208] Kornei Chukovskii, in his column in the newspaper *Rech'* in 1908, was among the first of many writers to note the growing ubiquity of irony in urban public life in Russia—and to find it troubling. An "ironic smile" (*ironicheskaia usmeshka*), "worn at all times and in every situation," had become, he observed, the main psychological mechanism with which many people now coped with the world. Threatened from all sides by the conditions of existence, this "slight, ironic, typically Petersburgian" smile, filled with "sarcasm," had become a weapon of the weak: unlike the "geniuses" of humanity (he mentioned Christ, Mohammed, Tolstoy, Ibsen, and others) who always struggled against this corrosive attitude, this was the only strength possessed by the ordinary modern urbanite—a "great but terrible strength," a powerfully distancing "ha-ha" (*khi-khi*) that made life endurable. This spirit was especially evident in modern literature, where even the biggest questions—God, eternity, death—were treated with the same universal "ha-ha," the same "tone" of stylized, jaded, ironic "buffoonery" without a hint of sympathetic "pathos."[209] Writing in the same newspaper a couple of weeks earlier, Blok viewed the spread of irony among educated Russians with even greater anxiety. Irony had had become a "terrible illness" afflicting "the most alive and sensitive children of our age." Its symptoms were "fits of exhausting laughter, which begin with devilishly mocking and provoking smiles and end with riotous behavior [*buistvo*] and blasphemy." People now laugh when speaking of their mother's death, or of their own starvation, or of being betrayed by their bride, though one never knows if after laughing they will then go and poison themselves. One might fight against such a mood, but for being infected with it oneself: "I too am locked up in a fortress, in a stuffy room, where the incredibly repulsive and incredibly beautiful prostitute Irony brazenly undresses herself in front of me." This is not fiction, Blok insisted, but a fact of life, a disease we all recognize in ourselves. And this "epidemic is raging." Those not already suffering from it are infected with its no less terrible opposite: "they cannot smile and nothing seems funny to them."[210]

Commentators in newspapers and magazines tried to soften the bad news and bad moods they reported with a simpler and gentler irony than Chukovskii's or Blok's. Thinking of the Petersburg intelligentsia, a journalist writing in 1913 saw "signs of hope" in the new lack of idealism: not one new religion, not one new prophet, not one extravagant new aesthetic theory, "not one schema of general salvation or general ruin."[211] Most common were ironic reflections on the year's everyday misfortunes. "How many disappointments, how many hopes, we buried" with the old year, began a feuilleton in January 1910 in *Listok-kopeika*. True, the past year really was bad: political scandals, terrible crimes, willful and degrading treatment of people (*samodurstvo*), and so many "unneeded and early" deaths. And true, the coming year will be no better. On the other hand, we know that "the bad new is better than the bad old." So let's drink champagne to the new and the better, to the belief that politicians will be born who will "clean out our Augean stables," making St. Petersburg the "best-run" city in the world, with the best streets, trams, buses, electric company, telephone operators, and markets. "More champagne, for God's sake!"[212]

Laughter and fun ("*smekh i vesel'e*"), along with, in a different key, insistent faith in human will and in political or religious salvation, marked a heroic determination to endure, perhaps even to embrace, the uncertainties of modern life. Perhaps, as Karl Marx suggested, "gaiety" (*Heiterkeit*) is a characteristic sign of the end of a historical epoch, a means by which people are able to reconcile themselves to the tragic loss of their past.[213] In Freudian terms, though more metaphorically than Freud intended, laughter may be a way to reconcile oneself to the loss of the object of one's desire. In other words, the poignancy of all this smiling and laughing, this "epidemic" of laughter as some called it, was not simply that it was during "a time of plague" but that it was part of the plague. It was a remedy—or at least a source of relief—made of the same material as the illness. When "the melancholy city-dweller [*toskuiushchii obyvatel'*] laughed," Logvinovich wrote, he could "forget and let others forget." But this did not mean he could deny the truth of his melancholy.[214]

Faith in human will and in paths of salvation was more optimistic than laughter and fun, though it similarly embodied the illness it sought to cure. Here was an "idea of happiness," as Benjamin described, that vibrated with both "desolation" and "salvation." Whether this meant refusing to succumb to despair in the face of the awareness of suffering and loss or a complex theological or ideological dialectics of redemption emerging precisely from this awareness, these were narratives of darkness and light that depended on one another. After 1917, we know, Marxist revolutionaries would attempt to cure this sick and grieving society with their particular dialectical vision of happiness: a cure for all suffering that grew out of a faith in human political will and in historical time. They would even mobilize laughter, much as critics like Chukovskii and Logvinovich wished: "sober, healthy, and bold" laughter, filled with hatred of the old and optimism about the new, a redemptive laughter inspired by "striving for the sublime." That this striving faith and bold will would lead to a new modern catastrophe is another story.

SEVEN

Melancholy

The "modern," the time of hell.

—Walter Benjamin, *The Arcades Project*

Nausea discovers the nakedness of being.

—Emmanuel Levinas, 1935

Anxious talk of emotion filled the urban public sphere in Russia during these years of disorder, drift, and uncertainty. Questions about mood, feeling, and affect—particularly what was called the "public mood" or "social mood" (*obshchestvennoe nastroenie*)—became literally the talk of the town, concerning not only particular problems like street life or death or debauchery, but the very nature of modern times. This emotion talk was intensely social: shared, circulated, and analyzed in the periodical press and other public spaces and interpreted as having social location, causes, and effects. And talk about public emotions was itself emotional: not simply a description and interpretation of the feelings of others, but an anxious, obsessive, even panicked part of the public mood (indeed, it helped shape that mood). This ubiquitous public talk about social feeling was a defining feature, far more than historians have tended to recognize, of the social landscape of urban Russia in the years after 1905. The social locations of these discussions were widespread. Authors ranged from essayists in intellectually minded "thick journals" to reporters and columnists writing for mass-circulation newspapers, from boulevard press fiction writers to sophisticated "silver age" poets, and civic activists of all sorts. They all shared, and spoke loudly and often about, the intense emotional landscape of the age. And they often used quite similar language and arrived at quite similar conclusions.

These commentators on public life found diverse moods in society, ranging from ecstatic pleasure and bright faith to dark depression and suicidal despair. But this rich, even disorderly, emotional landscape (including within individuals) was increasingly overshadowed by a dark cloud of feelings that viewed the present and the future with dismay and alarm. This was, I suggest, a type of "modern melancholy," marked by feelings of living amidst ruins, of finding no certain exit from the "hell" of the present. Time was central to this mood: worries about the nature of the current epoch—about the spirit of "our times"—and about the possibility of improvement, but also anxieties about modern time itself as meaningful and beneficial progress.

SOCIAL EMOTIONS

The social entanglements of emotion are not the whole of their history. Affect, many scientists and scholars have shown, cannot be reduced to a social experience or a discursive construction; emotions have (in the language of some recent affect theory) a nonconscious, unnarrativized, corporeal side. Certainly, we must recognize, the binary of cognitive thinking and corporeal feeling is a false opposition.[1] Yet it is the social life of emotions that requires our attention, for it reveals the most about what we want to (and can) understand about human subjective experience and practice, especially in the past. Debates over how to grasp and interpret emotion—especially questions of social construction and neurological influences—have occupied scholars and scientists across a number of disciplines and fields of study. This has produced a rich body of new research and theorizing about affect, emotion, feeling, and mood (not necessarily synonymous).[2] For my purposes, which are to explore public discourse about the "public mood," I find most useful the approach of scholars who have emphasized emotions as entwined with the social, in the broadest sense of this term: with power, language, culture, and history. Lila Abu-Lughod and Catherine Lutz, in an influential collection of essays by anthropologists, have highlighted the ways in which emotions are about "social life" and social "problems"—and are not only interpretive but also active agents, for emotions and talk of emotions can themselves produce experience and constitute reality.

Emotion, in other words, is "a form of social action that creates effects in the world."[3] Sara Ahmed, from the perspective of cultural studies, has written of a "sociality of emotion" where emotions are "relational" and ultimately "doing" things (including things that help constitute both the psychic and the social).[4] That emotions are strongest and most visible when self and society are most troubled—a condition appropriate to Russia in these years—is suggested by the literary scholar Sianne Ngai's terse definition of emotions as intense "interpretations of predicaments."[5] My own reading of the intense talk of emotion in the Petersburg press demonstrates this working of emotions at the dense and knotted intersections of self, subjectivity, society, culture, and history, especially when these are most unstable and troubled.

Russians writing in the early twentieth century about the meaning of "these times" did not need convincing that feelings were thickly embedded in social life. They were preoccupied with the ubiquitous evidence of intense public emotion. Indeed, they felt they were living in exceptionally emotional times, in an unprecedented "epoch of moods" (*epokha nastroenii*), as one journalist called it.[6] In modern literature, critics observed (often critically, even mockingly), authors sought truth no longer in the external world but in "the irrational capacities of their souls," in their "deepest and most intimate sensations" (*oshchushcheniia*), in their inward "passions, sensations, and moods," in emotional feeling (*chuvtsvovanie*) and sensation.[7] In the visual arts, too, the representation of "this world" was abandoned in order to dwell in "the world of feelings, love, and dreams," "instinct," "intuitive perception," and the new "psychologism" said to characterize all "modern creativity." Modern art was defined precisely by its new gaze beneath the "masks" of external realism in the pursuit of deeper "psychological" truths. Indeed, critics argued, what defined modernism in Russia was not the choice of form or subject, but this common "feeling."[8] The upheaval of religion and spirituality in Russia was likewise viewed as less a phenomenon of dogma or belief than a movement of "instincts," "aesthetic-psychological" aspirations, "unmediated feeling," and *nastroennost'* (a state of mind and feeling).[9] Even public entertainments, both highbrow and common, were marked by this defining excess of affect. Popular literature was

mocked by serious critics for its extravagant emotionalism, for stories filled
with little besides passion, frenzy, madness, terror, and despair.[10] Two of
the most famous and compelling figures in the public life of St. Petersburg,
we have seen, were the actress Vera Kommissarzhevskaia and the romance
singer Anastasiia Vial'tseva, whom critics judged to be popular and "modern" precisely because their work was so defined by emotion. Kommissarzhevskaia's acting was imbued with a "subjectivism" that expressed the
"new moods" of "modern life.[11] Vial'tseva, in turn, was said to be popular
because she sang with "authenticity" (*iskrennost'*) of feeling—for truth was
the presumed goal of emotion.[12] Komissarshevskaia's funeral in 1910, and
Vial'tseva's in 1913, attracted mourners numbering in the tens of thousands
and inspired a great deal of talk about the emotions that drew people to the
two performers.[13]

Not only did commentators find that they were living in an unprecedented era of emotions, but they were interpretively sure that the deepest
and truest meaning of these times would be found precisely here: that the
contemporary experience could best be understood in people's "moods,"
"subjective and instinctive feelings," "psychological experiences," and
"feelings about the world" (*mirooshchushchenie*).[14] They viewed emotions
as signs to be read in order to diagnose the state of their society, culture, and
polity (though explicit talk of the political order was restricted by censorship). Methodologically, they did not ignore psyche and self. After all, this
was an age in which attention to the inward self—in science, the professions, literature, and public discourses—was rampant.[15] And yet, though
a more purely psychological, even neurobiological, language of analysis
was available, public "emotion talk" (a term I borrow from psychology and
anthropology) in urban Russia overwhelmingly concerned not the inward
emotional self as a separate sphere but the dialogue between self and society. Russian urban writers (whether literati, physicians, and philosophers
writing occasionally for the public or professional journalists) were determined to view emotions, even the most devastated feelings, as products of
social disorders rather than personal ones. That looking at emotions revealed truths about the psyche or the body was less compelling or useful
than that these allowed one to see social and existential truths.

MODERN MELANCHOLY

The prevailing emotionality of the age was almost universally described as anxious and disenchanted. Other feelings were present, as we have seen. But urban writers' attention was focused on a dense body of dark feelings that seemed most to define the times, a mood that I find useful to think of as "melancholy." To be sure, contemporaries did not find any single word adequate to capture the public mood. Only rarely do we hear the Russian word *melankholiia*, though the term was available and had been quite popular among educated Russians in the nineteenth century.[16] But the archaicization of "melancholy" does not make it any less apt. On the contrary, commentators on "the times" seemed to be quoting endlessly from definitions of melancholy that had been mapped in European science and culture since the malady was first observed and named in the ancient world, and especially as the diagnosis was nourished by intensified interest in the subjective self during the Renaissance, the Reformation, and the Romantic age, including in Russia. Hippocrates found patients he diagnosed as melancholic to suffer from fear or despondency. Later analysts continued to emphasize these signs of an anxious and hopeless view of the present and the future. By the sixteenth century (when melancholy became the subject of famous treatises in English by Timothie Bright and Robert Burton), interpreters of this condition invariably described defining feelings of "gloom," "futility," "fear," and "despair." Like the humoral "black bile" that gave this malady its name, melancholy was often linked to the color black and other markers of darkness and cold.[17]

Russian melancholy in the early twentieth century echoed this discursive history, but with important differences. Traditional definitions of melancholy emphasized its groundlessness: "sadness without cause," despondency "in excess of what is justified by the circumstances," *about* nothing.[18] Causation lay within—originally in the imbalance of physical "humors," later in the inward psyche (and still later in the prevailing diagnosis of depression as neurobiological illness). Classic melancholy, in other words, was a malady of individual bodies more than of social ones, a depression that arises from within and gazes within. Russian melancholy of the early twentieth century reversed these assumptions. This was overwhelmingly social and existential melancholy: in its location in the public sphere, in attributions of causation as growing out of the "modern condition," in its constant deployment as a critical affective interpretation of society. This was a melancholy felt to arise less from a disordered mind than from a disordered world, less from private loss and sorrow than from shared experience, and less to be suffered privately than expressed aloud in public.

Russians were not unique in this view, of course. Russian social melancholy was a local variation of a larger "modern" melancholy.[19] In this focus on the social, time comes to the fore as modern melancholy's darkest shadow. Examining a mood in western Europe in the wake of the French Revolution, Peter Fritzsche has described a "melancholy of history" defined by feelings of loss and ruin, a sense of irreversible loss of the past made still worse by the loss of epistemological certainty about the present. Highly educated and sensitive Europeans like François-René Chateaubriand felt like "strangers" and "exiles" in this strange "new time," wandering amidst "shapeless ruins." This new sense of dread, Madame de Staël believed, had become "the illness of a whole Continent" in the nineteenth century.[20] In early nineteenth-century Russia, as well, Romantic poets like Vasilii Zhukovskii nurtured a pensive melancholy about a sick and fragile world filled with loss.[21] As the century advanced, many intellectuals came to view the course of modern historical time with dismay as marked by more loss and suffering than gain.[22] A literary study of melancholia and modernism in late nineteenth-and early twentieth-century Europe has emphasized a defining modernist "mood"[23] "attuned to the unavoidably melancholic nature of modern life" as riven by loss, lack, and alienation (especially from the past) and by the depressing gap between modernity's optimistic and utopian promise and its realities.[24]

The emotional experience of modern time as a sense of being trapped in a temporal hell from which there is no escape, where history has no positive telos and the myth of progress is an illusion, was a leitmotif in the writings of fin-de-siècle and early twentieth-century philosophers from Friedrich Nietzsche to Walter Benjamin. They tried to unmask modernity's myth of newness (though to emancipate not depress us), an insight that reaches back at least to Charles Baudelaire and forward to postmodernism. In the 1880s, Nietzsche described a "demon" creeping up to man in his loneliness to cruelly remind him that life continually repeats, that "there will be nothing new in it."[25] In the 1930s, Benjamin described the temporality of modern life as a mythic mask, a "terrifying phantasmagoria" that deceptively promised constant newness and progress, while in fact "the face of the world never alters, . . . the newest remains, in every respect, the same." As such, "the 'modern' [is] the time of hell," with its never-ending and never-changing punishments, with its mythic echoes of Tantalus, Sisyphus, and the Danaides. Or, in a related metaphor Benjamin often used, the appearance of temporal progress turned out to be a catastrophic "storm" bringing mainly ruin and harm.[26] Other philosophers have seen not stasis or repetition but regress, the "morbid passage of history" in which time brings decline and degeneration.[27] More recently, Jean Baudrillard wrote of a late modern and postmodern temporality (though this is clearly an older experience than he seemed to acknowledge) in which linearity and purpose are replaced by instability, indirection, reversal, chaos, and catastrophe.[28]

This modern temporal dread bordered on "trauma"—an experience, often catastrophic, that overwhelms the ability to understand and cope, leading to feelings of helplessness and despair. The dominant "mood" in European high culture throughout the nineteenth century, the philosopher Robert Pippin has argued, was colored by death, loss, mourning, and melancholy, by the "Oedipal shadings of modernity as trauma" (exemplified in the writings of Friedrich Hölderlin, Stendhal, Fedor Dostoevsky, Marcel Proust, Rainer Maria Rilke, and others). Nietzsche's famous aphorism that "God is dead" can be read as an echo of this modern experience of traumatic loss.[29] Toward the end of the century, Sigmund Freud would also posit the centrality of loss in modern melancholy—the sedimentation in the developing subject of unresolved grief for objects loved and lost—which could result, he recognized, not only from private sorrows (notably the "loss of a loved person") but also from the "loss of some abstraction . . . such as one's country, liberty, an ideal, and so on."[30] Elaborating on Freud's brief essay, Julia Kristeva described melancholy arising from a traumatic "razing of symbolic values," from an upheaval in meanings and significations, such as often accompanies eras of profound "crisis."[31]

Some analysts have described this intense existential disorientation as nausea, suggesting emotion manifest as physical experience. Martin Heidegger described the modern "mood" as a sense of being "thrown" or "falling" "into the groundlessness and nullity of inauthentic everyday-ness."[32] Jean-Paul Sartre seemed to elaborate on this feeling in his account of melancholy modern experience producing "nausea."[33] Emmanuel Levi-nas developed this further in describing a mood of "nausea" in the face of "the nakedness of being in its plenitude and in its utterly binding pres-ence," revealing the "horror . . . of being as such."[34] Drawing on many of these writers, Sianne Ngai has most recently emphasized how certain con-ditions of existence produce "ugly feelings" (negative, uneasy, frightened, confused, and irresolvable emotions). These are especially the result, she argues, of an existence, and feelings about that existence, that is "unsettled," "confused," and "obstructed"—conditions that certainly obtained in early twentieth-century Russia.[35]

So many of these words foreshadow or echo emotion talk in Russia between the revolutions. Russian commentators would have recognized in these arguments (some, of course, such as Nietzsche's, were known at least to the educated) their own feelings about the morbid movement of time, or at least the "mood" they saw as so pervasive in public life. In this era of approaching ends and uncertain beginnings, of disjuncture and drift, many people felt that they were living in a landscape of ruins and fragments,[36] that they were wandering in shattered, traumatic time. Benjamin's metaphors (mostly quotations from the nineteenth-century texts he collected in his ar-cheology of modernity) would have sounded especially familiar: modern life as "pawing the ground in place," as "lingering catastrophe," as "frozen death throe."[37] They would also have felt a disturbing sense of recognition in Benjamin's descriptions of the emotional consequences of living in such times: ennui and depression, the view that "life is purposeless and ground-less and that all striving after happiness and equanimity is futile."[38] In Rus-sia, as elsewhere, modern melancholy was a sickening sensation of being lost in timeless time (*bezvremen'e*), adrift without sight of solid land.

There was, however, a significant social difference in Russia's modern social melancholy. The dread that Madame de Staël believed had been felt by "a whole Continent" had really been the illness only of an educated elite, voiced chiefly in private correspondence, diaries, memoirs, fiction, and poetry. Much of the modernist mood described in the previous paragraphs, including the famous "fin-de-siècle" mood, are found in the words of intellectuals and philosophers. In post-1905 Russia, this philosophic dread had become urgent daily "news"—and more than anywhere else in Europe, I would suggest, though this democratization of modern melancholy had made inroads into the public culture of every modern society.[39] Melancholy broke out of the confines of literature and letters—including the traditional Petersburg stance of the melancholy poet facing the emblematic damp, cold, darkness, and sorrow of the Russian capital—to become a remarkably public language reproduced by newspaper reporters, journalists, and other urban writers for an increasingly broad audience. Translated and reinvented for public discussion, and rethought against the background of Russia's own intense experience with modern loss and uncertainty, the melancholy malady of the sensitive intellectual was reborn as a dangerously popular emotional epidemic, even a psychic illness of the social body.

There was another difference. Russia's fin-de-siècle melancholy was darker—"uglier" and more "nauseating," as it were. For many Europeans in the nineteenth century, and for many modernists across Europe in the nineteenth and twentieth centuries, the loss of the past and of certain meaning opened the possibility of alternative subjectivities and itineraries in the present and into the future. "The ruins of the past," Fritzsche has written, "were taken to be the foundations for an alternative present." Loss became possibility.[40] Other western writers—nineteenth-century philosophers and poets, Freud and Benjamin, contemporary cultural theorists—have also emphasized melancholy's ennobling, inspiring, heroic, political, and redemptive potential, even a "revolutionary melancholy."[41] In early twentieth-century Russia—especially in the wake of the collapsed 1905 revolution, but even before war and revolution made catastrophe, trauma, and ruin tangible in ways yet difficult to imagine—the mood was much more pessimistic; at least, they could not convince themselves that their readers were persuaded by pleas to live boldly in the present and to look to the future with imagination and hope.

THOUGHTS OF TIME

The annual turn of the old year into the new and the rituals of reflection
and expected celebration associated with the New Year naturally evoked
thoughts of passing time. The hope that the new would bring the better,
that time's passage was forward, was explicit in the traditional New Year's
wish *S novym godom, s novym schast'em* (For a new year and new happiness). Around this time each year, editorial writers and columnists traditionally offered their thoughts and feelings about the "contemporary moment" "at the threshold" (*na poroge*) of the new. In the past, these were
mainly vague platitudes about a happy New Year. Now, amidst the ambiguous drift and vague crisis of the years after 1905, we hear of a troubled sense
of living in broken and disenchanted time. In quite dramatic, even melodramatic, terms, and with a sense of growing anxiety and panic not heard
before, New Year's commentators characterized the progressive temporal
promises of "new happiness" as an illusion, as having been replaced by a
time that moved as if crippled and lost, such that there seemed to be "no
exit" (*net vykhoda, net iskhoda*) from the "dead end" and "untimeliness"
(*bezvremen'e*) of the present.

At the turn of 1907 and 1908 editorialists and columnists regularly
complained of a newly "depressed" social mood. A review of the past year
in the journal *Vesna* (Spring) described the widespread "depression in the
social mood" (*podavlennost' obshchestvennogo nastroeniia*).[42] A New Year's
editorial in the journal of the St. Petersburg Theological Academy similarly
reflected on the "sad circumstances" in which Russian society now found
itself: "the old has been destroyed, eliminated, and condemned," but there
was no new. Thus, the hope one felt at the start of the new year repeated
the hope one felt at the start of the old year, but it was vain, for "time has
shattered the foundations" for hope.[43] These gloomy thoughts on time and
hope had plenty of company. A review of New Year's greetings throughout
the Petersburg press diagnosed a "general despondent mood" (*obshchee
unyloe nastroenie*).[44]

This continued in successive years.[45] At the end of 1909, for example,
a review of the passing year concluded that yet another year was ending

"with an extremely depressed social mood."[46] In 1910, a New Year's editorial in the newspaper *Sovremennoe slovo* echoed the judgment of many in voicing caution and skepticism about feeling too hopeful: "How many times has the specter of happiness deceived us?"[47] At the start of 1911, even normally optimistic city officials, according to the annual review of municipal projects, seem to have fallen into an overwhelmingly "despondent mood" (*unylyi ton*).[48] Many public figures felt the same. At the beginning of 1913, the popular illustrated magazine *Ogonek* asked well-known individuals to offer public toasts for the New Year. Many acknowledged, with dismay, the "heavy depression [*ugnetenie i podavlenie*] of the Russian social mood." While it was common to express a New Year's wish that this mood would dissipate in the coming year, many recognized, such as the noted psychiatrist and academic Dr. Vladimir Bekhterev, that New Year's wishes tend to remain only "desires," because "reality does not bring happiness."[49]

A certain emotional nihilism echoed through this dark mood. In the 1908 New Year's issue of the weekly *Svobodnye mysli*, the journalist and author Mikhail Engel'gardt opened an essay characteristically titled "No Exit" with an epigraph from the Lamentations of Jeremiah, "Our eyes failed, looking in vain for help." What followed was Engel'gardt's own jeremiad: "Before us lies a long, black, stinking corridor, the end of which cannot be seen."[50] Engel'gardt's "maximalism of despair," as the editors of *Svobodnye mysli* called it when expressing their "respect" for his sincere feelings but warning that they were born of unrealistic expectations,[51] became all too typical as time passed. A New Year's Day essay by Skitalets in *Gazeta-kopeika* in 1913 noted that the previous year's wishes for "new happiness" had produced not only no "new" happiness but no happiness as all, nothing besides "a bitter aftertaste and disillusionment" (*gorechi i razocharovanie*). Looking over the past year, Skitalets concluded that "our reality is dismal, the year's results are nil, and hope flew away from us." Only the economy was improving, though hesitantly at best. As for everything else—foreign relations, literature, art, theater—one word sufficed: "nothing!" (*nechego*)[52] The very idea that time brought "progress," a church essayist observed, seemed doubtful in the face of the realities of the present.[53]

The popular mood in 1913 was seen to be especially dark as a result of widespread expectations of war, which stimulated a "presentiment of misfortune" (*predchuvtsvie bedy*).[54] But this was only one more stone weighing down the social mood. An essay in the January 1914 issue of the journal *Novyi zhurnal dlia vsekh* began with the often repeated question, especially at this time of year: "Is Russian life at the present historical moment taking shape well or poorly?" The author acknowledged that everyone had the same answer, whatever their age, position, viewpoint, or politics. "One has to have a large reserve of sang-froid [*khladnokrovie*] and faith in the future in order not to lose heart in face of the bleak picture that opens before the eyes of every observer not suffering from a surfeit of optimism." To the question "is there an exit from the dead end into which the deformed [*urodlivo slozhivshiiasia*] conditions of our contemporary life have led us?" the majority answered by "waving their hands at it all" and trying to "lose themselves in trifles and minutiae." A minority, we know, answered by quitting temporal life altogether.[55] For Skitalets, the time had come to cease offering New Year's wishes for happiness—"better to be silent."[56] On the contrary, Russian melancholy in these years tended to be garrulous.

Anxieties about the passage of time were not limited, of course, to New Year's reflections. In commentaries throughout the year on the public mood, loss of faith in the progressive movement of time was defined as essential to understanding "our times." It needs to be emphasized, as these writers so often did themselves, that this was new. To be sure, journalists had spoken before of the public's "bad mood," though this was often linked to Petersburg's famous bad climate and was said to fluctuate with the weather. And writers had periodically complained of the modern urban condition of "boredom" (*skuka*), though this mainly seemed to afflict the well-educated and looked a great deal like the sadness without cause of classical melancholy.[57] It seems that the emotional landscape of public life after 1905 really had dramatically darkened, at least as journalists perceived it. "Pessimism" became a defining leitmotif. Some worries were already voiced in the midst of the disorders of 1905. Almost everyone would later recall the days leading up to the October general strike of 1905 as a period of the most heightened and hopeful enthusiasm—of vague expectation of something new. But a few writers at the time noted spreading feelings of "doubt and fear" of the future,[58] even a "pessimism—a gloomy, weighty, and dark mood, which had seized all strata of contemporary society." This took varied forms: "the pessimism of 'world sorrow' [*pessimizm 'mirovoi skorboi'*], the pessimism of failures (suicides), of atheists, of people sick of a life of pleasure," the pessimism of "complete spiritual emptiness without the slightest hint of anything bright and joyous."[59]

After the 1905 revolution—especially after the government "coup" in June 1907, but also as social fractures became more acute and economic conditions worsened—public pessimism was remarked upon much more often. Commentators in newspapers, magazines, and journals relentlessly and nearly unanimously wrote of widespread (even an "epidemic" of) "pessimism,"[60] "depression" (*unynii*),[61] "despair" (*otchaianie*),[62] "a general depressed mood" (*ugnetennoe nastroenie* or *obshchii upadok nastroeniia*),[63] feelings of "terrible, hopeless emptiness,"[64] a "sad contemporary social atmosphere" in which people feel life has become "tiresome" (*skuchno*) and "pointless."[65] A deep "pessimism" about the possibilities of escape from the problems of the present, much less progress forward, was pervasive. An essay in 1911 on the "fate" of Russian cities agreed that almost all writing about urban life now struck "sad, Chaadaevist, chords ... echoes of the general pessimism that imbues society and government."[66] Cultural and intellectual life reflected this mood perfectly, it seemed, and encouraged it. The dominant mood in literature and the arts, indeed among the whole intelligentsia after 1905, critics repeatedly wrote, was a "deep and gloomy pessimism."[67] At its extremes, this developed into a "mystical" "pessimism" that abandoned conventional hopes for progress only to hope for some saving miracle, or even a "pessimistic demonism" that simply embraced the chaos of the times.[68]

As we saw in the previous chapter, some writers voiced impatience and even disgust with this cultural mood. An editorial in January 1908 in the magazine *Vesna* (the appropriately titled "Spring") was typical: acknowledging that the past year had been "harsh and difficult" and the public mood "depressed," the editors nonetheless insisted that "there was no cause to fold one's hands and fall into despair."[69] Some writers openly ridiculed these moods, hoping that healthy mockery might help readers see their danger. One writer described people today "sitting in darkness ... in their 'beat-up washtubs,' 'without rudder and without sail.'"[70] A religious writer complained about the "universal 'moaning and groaning' [*nyt'e*]" about "helplessness and emptiness" that had become so pervasive in society that even many clergy had begun to echo this mood, which he considered especially absurd.[71] More gently, a journalist writing in 1909 treated the disenchantments and anxieties of the intelligentsia with irony: leaving a public meeting filled with "mystical" talk about the tragic and catastrophic state of the world and the coming apocalypse, the audience "put their *tragizm* in their waist pocket along with their notes" and headed home or to a restaurant, where they behave just like people "who say nothing about the tragic, feel no abyss, and neither await nor fear catastrophe."[72] Most writers, though, found nothing funny in these moods. They also recognized that their regular appeals to be more optimistic, to overcome depression with "will" or faith, to resist melancholy, were vain shouts into a gale. In any case, many commentators admitted to sharing these dark moods.

SYMPTOMATOLOGY

In seeking a vocabulary to describe the public mood, Russian writers drew upon a mixture of loosely defined, but emotionally potent, terms and categories. One of the most widely heard was *toska* (pronounced *toská*). Like melancholy, *toska* was an elusive and ambiguous category—which made it also a very usable one. Vladimir Dal"s authoritative nineteenth-century dictionary defined *toska* as a "constricting of the spirit, a languishing of the soul, tortuous sorrow; mental and emotional anxiety, unease, dread, ennui, misery, sadness, heartache, grief."[73] Translations into English typically fluctuate between melancholy, anguish, ennui, boredom, longing, and nostalgia.[74] Vladimir Nabokov, commenting on Aleksandr Pushkin's extensive use of the term in the early nineteenth century, emphasized "anguish, often without any specific cause," a "longing" that sometimes had no object, "vague restlessness," and hints of "boredom" (*skuka*).[75] That this was largely an inward psychic malaise was assumed in nineteenth-century usages. By the early 1900s, however, *toska* would become both more widespread in social discourse (and perhaps in social experience) and less a matter of intimate, personal feeling than of existential concern with the conditions of living in modern time.

Observers of the public mood in the years following 1905 were struck by the ubiquity of *toska*.[76] Dmitrii Merezhkovskii, walking the streets of

St. Petersburg after returning from abroad in 1908 (he had left at the end of 1905), perceived something new: the "terrible *toska* on people's faces."[77] The Marxist philosopher Georgii Plekhanov noticed the same in 1909: "In contemporary Russia, there are many melancholy [*toskuiushchie*] people, and still more are being led toward *toska*."[78] Observations such as this were becoming commonplace: *toska* loomed everywhere, but especially in the big city. Many writers worried about the *toska* that arose from the solitude, loneliness, and "isolation of the self" (*odinochestvo, otorvannost' lichnosti*) that characterized the modern metropolis.[79] When one writer invited his readers to send him letters in response to a proposal to create an organization for the city's lonely, he was struck by the evidence, in the flood of letters he received, of so much "pain and *toska* among us."[80] The suicide epidemic was often attributed to the "debilitating and destructive" atmosphere of "depression [*unynie*] and *toska*" pervading city life.[81] Suicides themselves used this emotional vocabulary, speaking in final notes of "*toska*, limitless *toska*."[82] Certain groups in the city suffered especially. *Toska* "loomed over" the urban poor, one journalist argued in a melodramatic feuilleton, as they struggled to survive in the face of loneliness, poverty, unemployment, melancholy memories, and thoughts of death.[83] Even working proletarians— the class whose "life-affirming feeling" and "optimism" would change the world, many Marxists believed—often viewed their lives with "dark melancholy [*bezprosvetnaia toska*] and impenetrable skepticism."[84]

Modern literature and art were said to echo the public's *toska*— and to encourage it, many added accusingly. "Pain" and "hopelessness" pervade contemporary writing, a critic wrote; "cold and decay emanates from almost everything."[85] Reading the leading modernist writers and poets, noted the poet and critic Nikolai Gumilev, one endlessly "encounters the words pain, *toska*, and death."[86] Many agreed. It seemed that the aesthetic and emotional motto of the decadent literary intelligentsia was "my—toskuiushchie," which might be rendered "we are melancholizers" (adapting Robert Burton's term "melancholising").[87] This mood was no less evident in the boulevard fiction aimed at less educated readers; indeed, it tended to be present in such popular writing in even more extravagant and melodramatic forms. The best-selling work of Mikhail Artsybashev, for example, was said to be marked by a "prevailing mood" of "cold despair,

revulsion and hatred for man, the *toska* of solitude, and the horror of death."
Artsybashev's books were suffused by "something nightmarish, painful, full
of gloom and despair," and by "the color black," indeed with a vision of the
world as a "black room, in which someone languishes and cries."[88] High
culture and street culture reflected the same essential mood. Subtle and
rarified poetry by artists like Aleksandr Blok and Anna Akhmatova, newspaper verses by amateur poets, and popular urban songs such as Mikhail
Vavich's "Sorrow and *Toska* Without End" (*Grust' i toska bezyskhodnaia*),
all spoke of ubiquitous *toska*.[89]

Entwined with *toska* was another key category, *razocharovanie*—
translatable as disillusionment, disenchantment, and disappointment—
which literally spoke of a collapse or breaking of that which enchants,
fascinates, and captivates. The public mood, it was said, was marked by
a "prevailing tone of disenchantment."[90] This notion tended to highlight
the importance of time in the public's melancholy mood, particularly disenchantment with progress. But in quite specific ways too, this mood was
a product of the times. The newness of this feeling was often noted. In the
late summer of 1907 (the summer that began with the government closing
the troublesome Duma and rewriting the electoral laws to ensure a more
compliant legislature, political acts that many viewed as marking the decisive end of the brief era of revolution and reform) a newspaper essayist
noticed the recent appearance of this "special term," *razocharovanie*, to represent the spreading "social depression." This writer implied as clearly as
censorship allowed that this was *political* disillusionment and disaffection,
reflecting the loss of the civic enthusiasms and hopes that inspired so many
in 1905.[91] Indeed, memories of 1905 were repeatedly raised as a contrast-
ing background to the new moods of the day. Since 1905, it was often said,
"despair took the place of enthusiasm, disenchantment and demoralization
took the place of deep faith and voluntary sacrifice."[92]

But this disenchantment was not confined to mourning for recently
shattered political dreams and ideologies, nor limited to the educated or
even the political left. In quite sweeping terms, observers described people,
and sometimes themselves, as "wandering lost in the darkness without any
ideals," seeing no clear perspectives, no defined hopes and dreams," and
recognizing "all the senselessness and purposelessness of life."[93] Nikolai

Rubakin, a well-known specialist on popular reading, reflecting on the many letters he received in response to his articles on self-education, professed shock at how widespread the feeling had become that life had lost meaning, sense, and purpose. People no longer truly live, it seemed, but, as his correspondents often said of themselves, watch as "life passes by" (*zhizn' prokhodit*), an expression in which Rubakin found "inward horror."[94] The physician Dmitrii Zhbankov similarly diagnosed a civic atmosphere of "emptiness," "idea-lessness, and artificiality" producing widespread "disillusionment, revulsion, and despondency."[95] This was a disenchantment born of a powerful and existential sense of loss and of being lost—loss of bearings, loss of meanings, loss of ideals, loss of faith. In a word—and note the reluctance to limit this despair to Russia alone—"humanity has lost hope," leaving in the human soul only a sense of "the emptiness and pointlessness of life."[96] This was clearly about a great deal more than 1905 and its aftermath.

Religious writers, concerned with the spiritual state of society, were especially sensitive to the spreading "disillusionment of the heart" (*razocharovanie serdtsa*).[97] The decisive evidence, for them, naturally, was loss of religious faith (or, just as bad, religious "indifference" and "apathy"),[98] including in the teleology of salvation promised by Christianity. Nonchurch writers also worried about the destructive spread of modern "godlessness."[99] A 1914 New Year's editorial in the newspaper *Peterburgskii listok*, for example, attributed contemporary *toska* to the lack of true Christian faith: if one properly understood the "high aims" of suffering, the sort of suffering that Christ taught and exemplified, "its weight falls from one's shoulders." Our *toska*, he argued, is the emotional price we moderns pay for our "disregard of the good."[100] Lack of faith was linked to a type of spiritual despair: as an essayist in *Novyi zhurnal dlia vsekh* argued in 1909, people seek God, knowing this faith to be the best assurance that happiness will arrive one day, but they cannot find Him.[101] But this spiritual crisis was linked to a still broader existential loss of faith. Even some clerical writers recognized that "loss of faith" reached beyond theological disillusionment. A thoroughgoing skepticism seemed to have infected the public mind, some thought. An editorial in the Theological Academy's journal in 1913, for example, observed that the "mood" of the present "epoch" was the most "skeptical" in the history of humanity and that this mood was at the heart of the "disorder of contemporary life." And unlike the skepticism (*skepsis*) of old, which was largely theoretical and speculative, contemporary skepticism was rooted in understandings of everyday social life and of time itself: a "deep lack of faith in anybody or anything, a complete disenchantment with everything around one, and hopelessness in what will be." This mood was the "ruling" one "for people of our epoch." For "the modern person," this was the chief way of emotionally perceiving the world (*mirooshchushchenie*), producing everywhere the "fateful mark" of "skepticism, disenchantment, and hopelessness."[102]

Contemporary culture was marked by this disenchantment. In the realm of ideas, the "dreams" and "desires" to "solve the world's problems" that had once inspired so many, especially educated youth, were in the present replaced by a "consciousness that these problems were beyond their strength to solve," and thus by intellectual "despair."[103] In literature, critics saw the same lost hopes. What had once been a productively critical attitude to Russian life, indeed a defining trait of Russian literature, had become "a negative attitude to life in general."[104] To be sure, some critics saw hints of defiance and pleasure in this nihilism. Gumilev, writing in early 1914 about the spirit of Russian youth that he saw reflected in the work of young poets, found a sort of heroic disenchantment with the world: they "cannot imagine themselves" accepting the "rules and objects of the real world," cannot "reconcile the rhythms of their own souls with those rhythms," and therefore, unable to love the world, "begin to love their own orphanhood."[105] But even he recognized the harmful passivity and isolation in this disenchantment. And it was worse in popular culture, especially mass commercial culture. A fragment from a "novel of moods," published in a cinema paper, presented, in tellingly clichéd form, a hero characteristic of the times: "tormented by the *toska* of solitude, by bitter feelings of disenchantment, by the consciousness that all is vanity and of no use, by the pettiness of everything around him."[106]

The coming of war in 1914, though it initially inspired a patriotic determination to fight harmful sentiments, also nourished disenchantment. In September 1914, a religious writer—not without satisfaction—argued that the old faith in "progress," which had been almost a "religion" for educated

Russians, had now utterly collapsed into "disillusionment," such that the warnings that were once only heard on the pages of the conservative and church press were now coming from the pens of liberals too. In the face of this new Europe-wide war, once-popular doctrines had fallen and false beliefs had been unmasked, especially "faith in the complete and undeniable progress of humanity."[107] From a different ideological perspective, the modernist director and writer Nikolai Evreinov offered his version of this era of disenchantment in a scenario for his planned "Theater for Oneself" (which envisioned a theater of ordinary people performing theatrical acts in everyday life, "like on the film of a gigantic cinematograph," following the script of real human desires): a "sentimental" picnic at a graveside with sorrowful poems by Blok, Paul Verlaine, William Blake, and others, dwelling on the notion that it would be better to lie in one's grave than endure all of life's "disenchantments."[108] This may seem maudlin, melodramatic, and tied to the mood of the intelligentsia—indeed, Evreinov's sentimental picnickers seemed to find a certain aesthetic pleasure in their melancholizing—but this emotional tone and interpretation had become ubiquitous in everyday public life, while offering redeeming pleasure to very few.

Melancholy feelings of *toska* and disenchantment were often linked to ideas about the weakening of "self" (*lichnost'*) and the "will" (*volia*). Commentators endlessly depicted the "contemporary generation" as suffering from "darkness in the will," "the fall of will, of energy," a "weakening of the will" (*obezvolen'e*—literally the loss or deprivation of will).[109] "Now at every step," observed the physician Grigorii Gordon in a magazine essay in 1909, "one meets individuals who are weak and without will, who feel alone and isolated amidst the very noise and intensity of life. They cannot find ideals to pursue. Always and everywhere they feel themselves surrounded by the emptiness of solitude."[110] A related symptom was "apathy" (*apatiia* or *ravnodushie*).[111] It seemed that "nothing besides apathy, psychological breakdown, and emptiness" remained in the soul of the modern person.[112] These arguments about the weakening of the will partly returned melancholy to its original definition as a disease of the inward self—and they often echoed contemporary medical discourses about pathologies of the will.[113] But the emphasis remained on self in society, on *obezvolen'e* as a social debility. These arguments also implied the view, given the still common notion of "will" as a masculine spirit,[114] that melancholy was a mark of social emasculation.

This decline of the will was viewed as a social sickness—a medicalizing trope common in so much talk of the maladies of modern life, we have seen. Specifically, modern life, in Russia as elsewhere, was said to produce "nervousness" (*nervoznost'*).[115] Scientific studies, public lectures by physicians and psychiatrists, and news articles on the public mood all pointed to a "contemporary atmosphere" (*atmosfera sovremennosti*) distorted by "nervousness," "nervous exhaustion," " 'social' nervous disorder," and even "hysteria."[116] A review of best-selling literature echoed this common theme: "nervous are our times and nervous are our moods."[117] Commercial advertisements, which commoditized emotions as well as products, embraced this diagnosis of the age's sick spirit—and purported to offer remedies. In a wide range of publications (for no class seemed immune), advertisements for products ranging from cocoa and perfume, to various medical "preparations" (often ostensible imports from western Europe, including treatment with preparations made from sperm), to "electro-medical devices" and other "modern" therapeutic equipment, to advice literature, all promised help in combating the "despair" and "depression" (*otchaianie, unynye, unylost'*), "weakened nerves," "physiological ruin," and "hysteria" said to result from the "conditions of modern life." "In our nervous and sick age," ads proclaimed, you need to buy our cure.[118]

Nervous sickness sometimes reached the point of real "madness" (*bezumie*). Newspapers continually reported incidents involving "deranged" and "mentally ill" people on the streets: screaming in public, gesturing strangely, speaking incomprehensible words, leaping into canals, stopping passersby with bizarre stories of persecution.[119] Such cases became so common that in 1909 *Gazeta-kopeika* grouped these reports under a regular headline: "mad people at large" (literally, "at liberty": *sumashed-shie na svobode*). Although these stories were presented mainly as diverting entertainments for readers, they were also the subject of serious concern. At a conference of psychiatrists at the end of 1909, reported in the papers, Vladimir Bekhterev contended that there were 270,000 mentally ill people "wandering free" in Russia, "living shoulder to shoulder with us."[120] These real life stories of the mentally ill in public blended with more interpretively

embracing diagnoses of social madness, of these times as "psychically abnormal," of the psychological "sickness" of "modern Russian life."[121] In
1908, writing in the newspaper *Rech'*, Merezhkovskii described "unprecedented levels of madness (though no one notices his or others' madness for
it seems that together we are all quietly losing our their minds [*vse vmeste
potikhon'ku skhodit s uma*])."[122]

LINGERING CATASTROPHE

View of the world: the universe is a site of lingering catastrophes.

—Walter Benjamin, *The Arcades Project*

The language of "crisis" was insistently applied to these times and moods.
The intelligentsia seemed lost in "confusion" and "pessimism," suffering a
deep "crisis of the spirit."[123] A key sign of this crisis was contemporary literature, which was filled with a mood of "weariness" and "nausea" (*toshnota*,
which also suggests loathing and disgust) for life, people, objects, and the
world.[124] And this crisis of the intelligentsia was understood to be an echo
of a much broader "internal crisis,"[125] which afflicted everything: science,
art, religion, and social life (politics, too, but censorship kept this theme in
the shadows).[126] And Russia's particular crisis was felt to be an echo of a still
larger existential "crisis" facing "modern man" (*sovremennyi chelovek*).[127]
As we have seen, temporal dislocation and loss was fundamental to this experience of crisis. The past, including past hopes for the future, lay in ruins.
An essayist in the "progressive" journal *Sovremennik* offered a typical description in 1912: "We are experiencing an epoch of crises," marked by "the
visible and complete collapse of principles, systems, and programs," by the
"huge gulf between what exists and what not so long ago we so fervently
believed."[128] A conservative religious commentator agreed: everything from
the past had "passed into decrepitude and worthlessness" (*driakhlost' i ne-
godnost'*) and people can find nothing satisfying in the new.[129]

    Feelings of crisis shaded easily into perceptions of "catastrophe." The
emotional effect of living in a time when "all the values by which the majority of people lived, on which they based their peace of mind," had begun

to "disappear," was devastating: "Suddenly everyone is frightened, as in a time of natural disaster such as plague, earthquake, or flood."[130] This sense of catastrophic ruin could reach mythic dimensions. As many historians have observed, the years leading to the war were a time of heightened eschatological expectations in Russia, especially among the educated public.[131] Urban intellectuals, a newspaper article in 1909 commented (mockingly, in this case), never stopped talking about "tragedy," the "abyss," "catastrophe," and the coming apocalypse.[132] Reviews of contemporary literature similarly noted that influential writers, such as Merezhkovskii, Fedor Sologub, and Leonid Andreev, constantly voiced apocalyptic moods and visions.[133] The same was said of the most influential contemporary painters, such as Kuz'ma Petrov-Vodkin and Nikolai Rërikh (Roerich).[134] Indeed, the whole creative intelligentsia, as one critic summarized its mood, was "crying out 'We are on the eve of a great shock.'"[135] Intellectuals, writers, and artists were not alone; at least, they perceived a similar apocalyptic mood all around them. Writing in *Rech'* at the end of 1908, Merezhkovskii reported feeling overwhelmed, while walking the streets of the capital, looking into people's faces, and reading the daily papers, with the "famous 'feeling of the end.'"[136] For religious believers, of course, apocalypse was more than a metaphor; nor was it entirely to be feared. Apocalypse was a hopeful view of crisis. For people of faith, catastrophic time was redemptive time. As an editorial in the church journal *Tserkovnyi vestnik* argued in early 1914, the "pessimism of Ecclesiastes 1:5–11," with its vision of the repetitiveness of time and history, where there is "nothing new under the sun," is mistaken. "New Testament eschatology" makes clear that history does not repeat or remain unchanged nor even move forward "with strict rectilinearity," but rather moves through a succession of "crises," each "stronger and deeper" than the preceding, but ending in a new heaven and a new earth.[137] Indeed, precisely in these "bitter times" of ruined "faith and morality"[138] the apocalypse promised in the Bible had become more likely than ever. In different terms, revolutionaries, especially Marxists, shared this belief that crisis itself created the conditions for its own overcoming, that salvation would arise precisely out of the ruins of the present.

Many shared this sense of deepening crisis, though they often found it difficult to have faith that it was leading to a new world. Reflections during the Easter holy days often highlighted this troubled eschatology. Just as the marking of the New Year stimulated thinking about the passage of time and promises of "new happiness," Easter was associated with thoughts of redemption and salvation, both theological and metaphorical.[139] It was troubling therefore to conclude, as a number of writers did, especially commentators skeptical of the established church, that so many Easter worshipers were only going through the motions: they were "without faith in Christ, and, in general, without faith in anything ideal, in the triumph of love and truth."[140] An Easter editorial in a theosophical journal in 1908 described the mood even more dramatically: "Now, in this time . . . under the weight of the crisis that we are all experiencing, the weak fall and the strong perish in despair before their time, and the rest . . . wander lost in the darkness."[141] Allegorically, according to an Easter essay in the newspaper *Sovremennoe slovo* in 1910 by the left-wing priest and convert to Old Belief, Bishop Mikhail, it seemed that "dust covered the earth—or not dust but some evil poisonous dew, which has fallen from some unknown place. And blinded people, and murdered life."[142]

Crisis and catastrophe were often framed by ideas of "tragedy" (*tragizm*). An article in *Sovremennik* described a "deep *tragizm*" in the air, afflicting everyone.[143] An editorial in the journal of the Theological Academy likewise argued that the "modern cultural worldview of the majority" was an essentially "tragic" one of "collapse and bewilderment" (*raspad i rasteriannost'*), a mood that reminded this writer of what Dostoevsky had called "nadryv" (tormented, damaged, hysterical feelings).[144] Mass culture was infected by this tragic mood. According to Lev Kleinbort, who wrote often about popular literature and art, "drama" in the cinema was always "melodrama," which was always "strongly tragic."[145] (Indeed, scholars have pointed out, popular Russian melodramas tended to end unhappily, unlike the happy endings characteristic of the genre internationally.)[146] The tragic was also dominant in the daily dramas of everyday life. In a newspaper essay on poverty and homelessness in St. Petersburg, for example, Ol'ga Gridina argued that ordinary metropolitan life offered greater expression of "tragizm" than any tragic actors or theater could convey. Artistic tragedy, she argued, "is only a pale shadow, only child's play before that which life creates."[147] Daily tales of suicide, of course, were also viewed as tragic signs of tragic times—the "tragic practice of our black days."[148]

The "tragic mark of the times" was strongly evident in contemporary literature, critics felt, especially among the most popular authors.[149] Reviews of new work by Leonid Andreev, an exceptionally popular author whom many critics considered "a chronicler of the social moods," saw a pervading mood of tragic beauty, tragic solitude, and tragic suffering.[150] An essay in 1909 described all intellectuals in St. Petersburg as preoccupied with feelings and talk of "the tragic" (*tragizm*).[151] To be sure, this mood had been growing among Petersburg writers and artists since the turn of the last century. The poet Zinaida Gippius recalled "a feeling of tragedy in the air" among leading Petersburg intellectuals at the turn of the century.[152] But this mood metastasized. It was now felt to afflict the whole of the urban public.

Like apocalypse, tragedy can possess a positive telos: the classic view, as defined by philosophers from Aristotle to Nietzsche, that suffering is inescapable but also elevates the human spirit and deepens the soul, perhaps even points toward transcendence. For Nietzsche, who was especially influential among educated Russians in these years, the contemplation of tragedy enabled people to see "something sublime and significant" in their "struggles, strivings, and failures," to know, in the face of the knowledge that we are all ultimately destined to extinction, that "the individual must be consecrated to something higher than himself."[153] Some Russian intellectuals similarly argued that the "pure tragedy" and "hopelessness" experienced by Russian educated society (*russkaia obshchestvennost'*) endowed society with honor and nobility (*blagorodstvo*).[154] Religious leaders were especially insistent that the only path to salvation is through "the permanent tragedy of life that Christ promised us."[155] But many saw no path to salvation, or even a source of spiritual satisfaction, in this tragic present. Too many, in Rozanov's words, saw only a permanent "hell of anxiety, torment, and perplexity."[156] *Tragizm*, in this sense, was less an aesthetic or philosophical system than another expression (and definition) of the melancholy of the era. And it was less a thing in motion carrying one through mythic anguish toward catharsis, sublime pleasure, and redemption, than a feeling of life in infernal stasis, a feeling of modern time as the traumatic "time of hell." This was mythic catastrophe, as it were, without motion, without telos, without exit.

Finally, this was a crisis of knowing and seeing, an epistemological crisis. Terrible "uncertainty" had become the "ruling mood today."[157] Again and again it was said that a key to the "tragedy of modern culture" was that in every area of "mental" life there was now "nothing vividly clear or defined," "all objective marks of truth" had vanished, leaving only "self-castigating doubt."[158] Even daily life, as the newspapers made clear, had become "something wild, frightening, and incomprehensible."[159] Nikolai Rubakin found this uncertainty in the many letters he received from readers: repeatedly the same question, "What am I living for?" came with the same answer, "For what, I don't understand . . . I can find no purpose."[160] Metaphorically, one could no longer even see clearly: there was no "clarity" (*iasnost'*) about how to proceed through life, but only "confusion" (*sumbur*) and "disorder" (*razbrod*).[161] Today, one editorialist wrote, there is no "bright clarity. . . . Everything that clearly, strongly, and powerfully gives life color, meaning, fullness, and the basis for happiness has fallen away and disappeared."[162] Instead, many saw only shadows: people today, "seeing no light," were forced to "wander in the darkness."[163]

Deepening this sense of uncertainty, and translating emotion into physical sensation, commentators repeatedly spoke of living on unstable ground. This feeling was embodied in another keyword of these years: *bezpochvennost'*—groundlessness, a sense of being uprooted from the earth or standing on a shifting foundation. The *bezpochvennost'* of the intelligentsia was an old argument—intellectuals were said (and felt themselves) to be cut off from the healthy national life of the common people, to be "dwelling in the air," and hence to feel tormented and pessimistic.[164] But now, as it were, "groundlessness" had become a democratic condition, shared by all. Having lost in modern conditions the old "objective marks of truth," a journalist argued, contemporaries found themselves in "a hopeless 'apotheosis of groundlessness'" (*beznadezhnyi "Apofeos bezpochvennosti"*).[165] The reference is to the philosopher Lev Shestov's 1905 book, *Apofeos bezpochvennosti*. But where Shestov saw liberating possibility and hope in modern "disenchantment," "indeterminacy," "lack of clarity," and "disorder,"[166] this writer, like many, saw "groundlessness" without hope. Religious writers were especially attuned to these contemporary feelings and worried about the harm to the spirit when people could find "no solid ground" to stand on (*bezpochvennoe polozhenie*).[167] Writers in the secular press saw much the same: nothing remains of the former "solidity" of worldviews, everyone feels "unstable" (*neustoichivyi*) when looking into the future,[168] the reliable values of the past have all been replaced by "uncertainty of the solidity of the ground on which they stand."[169] In 1912, the liberal Marxist Ekaterina Kuskova, writing in the journal *Sovremennik*, found these sensibilities, which she shared, reflected in the *cri de coeur* of a character in a story published the previous year in the same journal by Maksim Gorky: "Everything stands on sand, everything floats in the air, in Russia there is no spiritual foundation, no ground on which one might build temples and palaces of reason, fortresses of faith and hope—everything is unstable and crumbly, there is only sand—and it is barren."[170] All that is solid melts into air, these writers might have said, but with far greater emotional resonance and existential panic than Karl Marx ever intended in this classic trope defining the profound disruptions brought by capitalist modernity.[171] What was to be done? Gorky's hero replied with an even more depressed answer, which Kuskova preferred not to quote, "Live and die in melancholy and be silent" (*izdykhaesh' v toske—i molchish'*).[172]

As Gorky's story suggests, if one turned to literature for the truths that seemed so elusive in these times, as Russians of all classes did, one would be disappointed. Contemporary literature, critics warned, was full of the same "emptiness," "helplessness and spiritual confusion," the same "shifting chaos," as contemporary life.[173] Andreev's work, we have seen, was often viewed as a mirror of the zeitgeist—and criticized for encouraging bad moods. Andreev's stories were described as filled with "vacillation and doubt, with spiritual uncertainty, confusion, and chaos" (*sumiatitsa, putanitsa, khaos*).[174] Some critics even dubbed him a "Jewish writer" (he was not Jewish) because of his tendency "to always ask and not answer, to pose historical questions and disguised riddles."[175] Writing in the journal *Apollon*, which championed "beautiful clarity" in the arts, the writer and poet Mikhail Kuzmin noted that while some artistic eras "strived toward clarity," in the current "time of troubles" (*smutnoe vremia*) the arts did nothing but express "chaos" and "uncomprehending horror."[176] Modernist visual arts, too, offered a picture mainly of disintegration, fragmentation, and lost totality.[177] Georgii Chulkov observed that cubism, which attracted many Russian artists in these years, perfectly "answers the spirit of modernity," for it reflected in its forms "an epoch when all forms of life are teetering [*rasshatany*], when there is no thought of coherence, when there is neither certainty nor faith."[178] As so often, Russia's particular time of troubles was viewed as part of this much larger modern crisis.

Rare individuals reveled in this liberating flux, seeing radical possibility in indeterminacy. Writing in the newspaper *Novoe vremia* about questions of death and the afterlife, Vasilii Rozanov often warned against the intellectual and emotional hazards of certainty.[179] Aware that his arguments troubled many critics, he penned the following dialogue with himself for his newspaper column:

> "So how many ideas, how many thoughts, can one have about something?"
>
> "As many as you like [*skol'ko ugodno*]. As many 'ideas' as there are in the thing itself."
>
> "So, according to you, one can have as many *moral* 'views on a subject,' as many 'convictions,' as one likes?"
>
> "In my view, and in general this is the intelligent view, as much as one likes." . . .
>
> "How terrible and somehow hopeless for the reader. Where then is truth?"
>
> "In the fullness of all thoughts. All at the same time. Fearing to choose just one. In *indecision* [*kolebanie*]."
>
> "Can *indecision* really be a principle?"
>
> "The first in life. The only thing that is firm. . . . When *unwavering* begins [*nastupi-ka ustoichivost'*]—the world, as it were, begins to turn to stone, to ice over."[180]

As a cultural critic and journalist, Rozanov was notorious for his willingness to "express the most varied, even quite contradictory, points of view about one and the same problem."[181] But few public commentators shared Rozanov's attitude or approach to knowledge. On the contrary, Rozanov's contradictoriness was regularly criticized as moral, epistemological, and emotional "cynicism."[182] For most of Rozanov's contemporaries, including most intellectuals, indecision before alternatives, a relativist sense of multiple truths, a willingness to live with uncertainty was intellectually, morally, and emotionally unbearable.

MELANCHOLY EXPLANATIONS

Past, present, and future all seemed to have become frighteningly unmoored from any narrative of positive movement through time, even from solid ground. Russian commentators—whether highbrow philosophers or tabloid journalists, whether conservatives or liberals, whether secular or religious—perceived the same widespread disillusionment with time as progress, the same melancholy public mood. What is striking about this melancholy is not only that it had become intensely public and even popular but also that it was so insistently displaced from its conventional grounding in self and psyche. In the flood of talk about loss, doubt, despair, and disenchantment, commentators almost invariably diagnosed a social illness with social causes. Urban Russia's depressed mood was thought to be a consequence of, and a commentary on, the depressing condition of Russian life. Modern Russia, in Rubakin's metaphor (thinking of the evidence of the letters readers sent him) had become a "gigantic factory of senselessness" (*gigantskaia fabrika bezsmyslennosti*).[183] Commentators struggled to describe the specific machinery at work. While it was relatively easy to describe the symptoms and to recognize a crisis, explaining this emotional atmosphere produced less certainty.

Some writers, as in discussions of other maladies of public life, blamed the particular moment: the upheavals of 1905 and their repressive aftermath. The narrative of passionate hopes turning to crushed disenchantment became an established trope, we have often seen, especially on the political left.[184] These arguments were surprisingly explicit given the political restrictions on writing about the revolution or state repression. A columnist in *Peterburgskii listok*, for example, argued in 1908 that, as after the French Revolution and the "end of every revolution," Russian society was experiencing "widespread demoralization," "cynicism," and

"apathy."[185] Following the intoxication of the revolution, this was the "epoch of the hangover," wrote Ol'ga Gridina in *Gazeta-kopeika* in 1910.[186]
Conservative writers judged this hangover a useful sobering up. Where liberals and socialists viewed the aftermath of 1905 as a time of a tragic loss of
ideals, conservatives saw the "disenchantment" of these years as the healthy
loss of "revolutionary illusions."[187]

Many commentators, however, found these conjunctural explanations too narrow and superficial. While the revolution and its aftermath aggravated the moods of both intellectuals and the wider public, these moods
were not entirely new in Russian cultural life. Russian literature had long
been dwelling on feelings of *toska, tragizm*, uncertainty, confusion, death,
chaos, and catastrophe. Indeed, some writers insisted that the causes of disenchantment and depression lay deep in Russia's essential national culture,
even in the gloomy "Russian soul," rather than in any particular moment
in its history. Our folk songs are filled with "brooding and melancholy,"
the tabloid columnist Skitalets observed, and our poets have long written
of "despondency and powerlessness."[188] A writer on city politics likewise
found "in the Russian psychology" an endemic "fatalism," a traditional
view of individuals as "insignificant particles of the whole and the mere
playthings, as it were, of Providence," leading to a conviction that nothing
could be changed, that the truest wisdom was the ancient formula "vanity
of vanities, all is vanity."[189]

Most interpreters, however, viewed Russians' melancholy as neither
a reflection of the essential Russian soul nor a consequence solely of this
particular moment in Russian history, but as a symptom of what Chulkov
called "the cultural conditions of modernity."[190] The modern city was the
main locus for these conditions and hence the main source of modern melancholy. The urban environment was constantly portrayed as a breeding
ground of social pathology and emotional suffering, as we have seen in
the chapters preceding. St. Petersburg was thought to nurture melancholy
more than any other Russian city: "Petersburgers are born just the same
as the rest of us sinners—small, red, and hairless—but if you look really
closely at this small, red, and wrinkled little face you will see the first characteristics of pessimism, which, with age, will become the defining characteristic of every native Petersburger."[191] These sorts of judgments echoed

the well-worn literary tradition of viewing St. Petersburg—both as a unique place and the avatar of Russian modernity—as gloomy, depressed, sorrowful, and grieving. Julie Buckler has aptly defined the "Petersburg text" as "an obsessive melancholic utterance that refuses to complete the work of mourning."[192] And these were not only literary tropes. Already in the nineteenth century, the urban press had begun to notice the telltale marks on city dwellers of ennui, depression, meaninglessness, and melancholy.[193] Yet now it all seemed so much more widespread and public, so much darker, so much more dangerous.

The modern metropolis, of course, was only part of the terrain of the modern. And commentators repeatedly situated the public mood in the whole spiritual and emotional crisis of "modern reality," which, as a pseudonymous essayist wrote in 1909 in *Novyi zhurnal dlia vsekh*, "has filled the human soul with indescribable sorrow." Indeed, he concluded, despite all the progress human society has made in knowledge and technology, humanity has never been as "unhappy and dissatisfied as now."[194] At the heart of contemporary unhappiness was an existential crisis of modern civilization, not limited to Russia but not sparing it either. (Stereotypical western views of Russia as "youthful and barbaric" and thereby spared the "disgust with life," "inert melancholy," and "deep despair" of the tired and decadent civilizations of the west, was not a view many Russians shared, especially by the interrevolutionary years.)[195] This modern crisis was suffused with the experience of ruin and loss. Some blamed the paradoxical progress of scientific knowledge, which produced a melancholy longing (*toska*) "for meaning in life" after modern science laid down its "heavy *ignorabimus* [we will not know],"[196] shattering the possibility of belief in "a great and consoling order to the universe," leaving knowledge only that chaos and suffering were certain.[197] Some emphasized the specific loss of religious faith.[198] Some saw cause in the very pursuit of the new that defined this life as modern: it was one of the "curious" and "paradoxical" qualities of the modern age, a magazine essayist argued in 1914, that restless progress and innovation, the continual replacement of one newly discovered theory by a still newer theory, nurtured feelings not of greater faith in progress but of "disenchantment" and "weariness with 'big questions' and with the rapid, quickened tempo of mental life."[199] Others found explanation in the essential (and undesirable) contradictoriness (*protivorechie, protivopolozhnost'*) of modern civilization: so many "troubling" (*smutnye*) ideas pour into the "contradictory soul of man," one journalist argued, that while we try to walk the path of reason, we are constantly knocked off balance.[200] When Chulkov asked "What are the cultural conditions of modernity?" his own answer echoed what were becoming commonplaces: the decline in religion, the "instability of the forms of social life," political tensions, and the anarchy of production and consumption—as in many writings, capitalism was unnamed but often implicitly present—which all "give rise to accidentality and incoherence" (*sluchainost' i netselost'*).[201] These descriptions of the modern are the clichés of its European definition. But cliché did not enable distance or detachment. The ubiquity and even familiarity of modern disenchantment made it feel all the more inescapable.

The troubling movement of modern time overshadows these reflections and explanations. We have seen that some Russians held on to hope (if not certain faith) that some intervention—reform, revolution, God, the creative self—would redeem disenchanted and melancholy humanity, or at least oneself, from this hell. Some saw opportunity in the disenchantment of the old: an optimistic vision of ruptured modern time as a realm of freedom and possibility. But these emotionally hopeful avant-gardes were swimming upstream against a strong current. Judging by the evidence of the urban press, a much larger number of Russians felt little faith in time as an agent of greater happiness or even as a space for their own creative agency. If time moved at all, it seemed to drift downward into decay and degeneration. Characteristic of this mood was Merezhkovskii's feeling in 1908 that one could see in the face of city life what doctors call "*facies Hippocratica*, the 'face of death,'" or Iulii Aikhenval'd's image of temporal existence as a mere "thawing drip."[202]

In other words, the age had become a *bezvremen'e*, an untimely and troubled time, a time without time.[203] Many used this resonant term. Variously defined as a time of foul weather, misfortune, troubles, failure, and sorrow, or "a time of social and cultural stagnation, a difficult time,"[204] the word is usually translated into English, inadequately, as "untimeliness." What *bezvremen'e* meant at the time is best seen in its use. For a journalist writing in 1910, the years since 1905 had become a terrible, contradictory, nervous, even phantasmagoric, *bezvremen'e*.[205] Others spoke of an untimeliness of degeneration and decline (*upadochnoe bezvremen'e*).[206] As early as 1906, Aleksandr Blok devoted an article to this cultural phenomenon. Titled "Bezvremen'e" and published in the modernist journal *Zolotoe runo* (Golden Fleece), the article dwelt on many of the salient conditions of this troubled time, especially in "the city," and particularly in St. Petersburg: moral and spiritual sickness, decadence in both literature and the everyday moralities of the urban "marketplace," alienation and wandering, destruction and loss, elemental storms, exhaustion, *toska*, vanity, madness, despair, and death.[207] In language that these and other Russian urban writers might well have recognized as their own, Nietzsche had described existence as "without meaning or aim," as living on its own excrement, as a "world become motionless, a frozen death throe."[208] In other words, as a "catastrophe," a "hell," a "bezvremen'e." This perception was a symptom of the modern mood; but it was also its deepest explanation.

Whether we view modernity, with Max Weber, as "the demythification and disenchantment of the social world," or with Benjamin, as the oppressive and dehumanizing remythification of social forms,[209] the melancholy disenchantment so pervasive in public discourse in urban Russia can be seen as an emotionalized interpretation of this modern experience. Sadly, perhaps, this recognition was not a heroic unmasking of the mythic dreamworld of modernity's false promises, leading to a new transcendent consciousness, such as Benjamin (and many Russian political and religious believers) desired, but the painful recognition that the disenchantments and phantasmagoric reenchantments of modern life were the only reality. As a form of unresolved mourning for lost values and hopes or, at least, a yearning for the unreachable and even the unnamable, melancholy underscores with its dark signs a disillusionment with the promise, presumed in a culture influenced by the Enlightenment notion of progress, that time's passage is forward. There is a long philosophical tradition of recognizing that the "boundless spiritual longing" and "image of fulfillment" born in each human soul can never be reached, and of recognizing the emotional consequences of this discovery.[210] Russian contemporaries attached various terms to this: *toska*, disenchantment, tragedy, groundlessness, pessimism. Whatever it was called—and its elusiveness was part of its nature—this mood emanated, some European philosophers understood, not only from conditions of the mind and the self, but from the conditions of existence, particularly the conditions of modernity: the loss of old forms of authority and community, the contradictions that "reside in the world itself," the awareness that the modern age is a "perpetual chaos" of ceaseless movement without design, intention, purpose, or concern with consequences.[211] Russian urban writers, even tabloid journalists, voiced the same thought less metaphysically. In answer to critics who complained that the newspapers were demoralizing people with their dark narratives of everyday life, Ol'ga Gridina reminded readers that "the mirror is not to blame. . . . Let life become graceful, pure, and joyful—then every issue of the newspaper will become a continual hymn of joy." But "life is such as it is," full of "horror, cold, and egoism."[212]

There was little satisfaction in this mood, notwithstanding a long tradition of melancholy's pleasures. Since at least the Romantic age, melancholy could nurture and provide proof of the sensitive and creative soul; it could be a source of inspiration, of "reverie and voluptuous sadness," and of solace. Freud recognized that "the self-tormenting in melancholia . . . is without doubt enjoyable." It could also be political: writing about the melancholy public mood and its causes could be an aesthetic and ethical protest against the world as it actually was.[213] And it was newsworthy: part of the sensationalist landscape of writing and reading about the dark face of city life, such as could be found in every major city of fin-de-siècle Europe. I am convinced that such a positive reading of these voices would lead us astray. We cannot reduce most public talk of melancholy in urban Russian in those years to solace, pleasure, or defiance. This would enchant that melancholy, transforming it into something more satisfying or heroic than it was. I find relatively little reverie or pleasure in these ubiquitous public assertions of *toska, razocharovanie,* and *tragizm*. I find, instead, a great deal of anxiety and fear, pointing, if only implicitly, toward a philosophical skepticism about both the condition of Russian life on the eve of war and revolution and about the "conditions of modernity" in which Russia, for all its particularities, was deeply situated. What pleasures melancholy might have offered seem to have drained away in what Gorky called the unstable, crumbly, and barren sand of the present.

This mood was a mirror of troubled times. Russian society was, we know, fast approaching a catastrophic rupture: a devastating international war, revolution, and civil war, which would bring (though inspired by the most optimistic of motives) a great deal of suffering and renewed reason to doubt the myths of time as progress and modernization as happiness. None of this, of course, could be known in 1908 or even 1914. It was not the cataclysm to come that most troubled Russian commentators on the times, but the one they knew and were already experiencing: the erosion of ideals and faith; the ubiquitous feelings of "groundlessness," "indeterminacy," "disintegration," and "chaos"; the "hopeless" and "catastrophic" experience of both Russian life and the larger conditions of modernity; the sense that there was "no exit." This was a thoroughly modern experience of the present as a "time of hell."

Melancholy, in this sense, was wiser than happiness. It was a deeper truth. Viewing melancholy as a form of disturbed insight and knowledge has a long and rich tradition. In the west, poets echoed this in writing of melancholy as a "sage Goddess" (John Milton) or a "black sun" shining with dark brilliance (Gérard de Nerval). Shorn of poetry, Freud recognized the melancholic's "keener eye for the truth."[214] We may speak of modern social melancholy in Russia as just such a black clarity, a true but dark knowledge about the modern world of which Russia was increasingly a part. The willingness to see and recognize the harm caused by modern progress, to admit its tragedies and losses, even in the absence of optimistic faith in salvation, may have still been a type of cultural heroism: insightful and indignant, darkly true, and thus ultimately political.[215] On the other hand, the melancholy social mood in urban Russia itself may have helped weaken the foundations for positive progress, and thus have hastened the rupture.

Conclusion

Metaphors helped contemporaries make sense of the disturbing experience of urban life in Russia in the early 1900s and help us think about what they saw, believed, and felt. Sickness was the most ubiquitous image. Notions of epidemic and debilitating illness, both physical and psychological, were applied promiscuously to street life, crime, violence, and morality. These images blended with metaphors of less scientific origin: masquerade, disenchantment, the abyss, death, hell. All of these representations were driven by real, material conditions, but also used material images to speak of philosophical things. With remarkable consistency across genres, ideologies, and audiences, urban writers described the "spirit of the times"—and the social body—as sick.

There was little that was new in these Russian perceptions. To say that modernity, and especially the modern city, was marked by fragmentation, flux, loss, disenchantment, sickness, and perplexity was no longer original by the early twentieth century. The Petersburg difference is that these perceptions and judgments were shared by a broader sweep of society, marked with greater emotional and interpretive intensity, and shaded with greater darkness. More than elsewhere in Europe, including at earlier times, a wide circle of urban Russians claimed to feel that they were living on the "edge of an abyss"—a social and political abyss, but also a moral and epistemological one. This sense of the catastrophic nature of the present is especially compelling to us, of course, because we know that Russia (and western Europe, though to a lesser extent) did indeed stand on the eve of World War I on the unstable edge of an unseen abyss. But Russian commentators about "the times" were far more worried about the catastrophe they were already experiencing: the ubiquitous feelings of instability and disenchantment, the sense of time's failure to bring progress, the fear that there was "no exit" from the darkening landscape of the present.

There were good reasons for Russians to feel greater anxiety than western Europeans. The disruptions and disappointments of the 1905 revolution shattered confidence and nurtured worries about disorder among many Russians. Social conditions in St. Petersburg were also no doubt objectively worse than in contemporary European metropolises. And there was the politically unmentionable elephant in the room: the ineffective, archaic, and oppressive persistence of autocracy. Of course, western Europeans had earlier experienced autocratic states, revolutionary upheavals, and the harshness of industrial urbanization. Indeed, an easy argument, and there were Russian writers who offered this, was that Russia's problem was its insufficient modernity: what was needed was more economic development, though also more intervention into society by modern scientific professionals. Historians of the professional classes in these years have described precisely this optimistic faith that modernity was the cure for Russia's modern ailments.[1] What is remarkable, therefore, is how seldom this argument appeared on the pages of the Petersburg press. Again and again, urban writers, both liberals and conservatives, were inclined to view Russia's urban pathologies as explicable not by national backwardness (or the particularities of this Russian moment in history or the particularities of St. Petersburg as a city) but as evidence of a sickness that arose from modern civilization itself, and perhaps the human condition.

Such worries did not begin after 1905. Journalists and other writers had long documented the familiar litany of urban problems, from poverty and disease to crime and sexual excess. In his 1886 account of "moral life" in the capital, for example, Vladimir Mikhnevich described much of what I have described in this book: crime, debauchery, deceit, transgression, murder, and suicide, leading to a troubled "modern mood" of melancholy anguish (*toska*), disenchantment (*razocharovanie*), "feast in the time of plague," and loss of faith in "progress." Mikhnevich already felt that Russia had entered a new "time of troubles" (*smutnoe vremia*).[2] Nineteenth-century literature, especially about St. Petersburg we have seen, explored similar themes. Yet urban writers after 1905 continually emphasized the newness of their experience, of their crisis. There were real differences. Partly the difference was in mood and tone: Mikhnevich's melodrama and prurience, his effort to convey both shock and adventure, did not disappear as styles of newspaper narration but were overshadowed by a mode of writing about the city that was both more analytic and more akin to moral panic. Most important, and a reason for greater fear, that which in the nineteenth century seemed to be the dark corners and back alleys of urban life had become by the early twentieth century not the margins but the defining essence of modern life, not isolated "sores" (as Mikhnevich called them) but the sickness of society itself. Mikhnevich voiced confidence that the sores of Petersburg life could be cured by further progress, and many felt the same in his time.[3] Urban writers after 1905 were rarely so confident. And they insisted that this feeling of being trapped, which they saw as widespread in public opinion, was new. In truth, it was not completely new, though such skepticism about time had been mainly the domain of a segment of the literary intelligentsia. But it was more widespread and intense. Also, difference was part of the argument itself, including the loss of a more hopeful past.

This was not an entirely hopeless argument, however. All this public hand-wringing offered something optimistic, even heroic. For some, we have seen, diagnoses of maladies led to recommended cures: strengthened will and morality; the salvation to be found in art, religion, or politics; or at least the comfort of pleasurable oblivion. But there was also, even for the skeptical, a certain splenetic heroism in speaking truth to darkness. On the other hand, these judgments and moods also helped create reality—despairing evaluations of contemporary society surely helped bring about its demise. We know the outcome: power to the Bolsheviks, who were inspired by faith in modern progress and in the capacity of people to change the world, and who would try to cure society of its ills (and its troubled moods) with a radical application of the principles of modern science, development, and discipline (and mandatory socialist enthusiasm, optimism, and faith). The optimists turned out to be the victors. But the Soviet experiment in radical modernity brought renewed reason to doubt the myths of time as progress and of modernization as happiness.

So, perhaps, after all, truth belonged to the pessimists. We might return, in this light, to Walter Benjamin's reading of Paul Klee's *Angelus Novus*: while the storm of "progress" irresistibly blows us into the future, we can, indeed must, focus our gaze at the mounting "wreckage" behind us and at our feet. But Benjamin was not a pessimist. A Marxist of sorts, and a

Jew who retained a feeling for his faith, Benjamin viewed the world though a prism of revolutionary and redemptive dialectics. History, he knew, is catastrophe. But if we are attentive to the ruins, remember them, and seize hold of them with purpose, we can see "flashes" of transformative light, hints of a new "Messianic time."[4] Perhaps Russian urban writers hoped their intense attention to the wreckage of the present would provide such flashes of light. In any case, they help us to see.

Notes

INTRODUCTION

1. I use the term fin de siècle in its well-developed cultural sense denoting not mainly the literal end of a century but the end of an epoch, especially a perceived era in which crisis, sickness, decline, and threatening death accompany, perhaps overshadow, a sense of the new and possible rebirth.

2. Indications throughout this study of the European context of Russia's modern urban experience, as well as my arguments about difference, are based on a rather large comparative literature on urban modernity. For the most influential works, see the Bibliography.

3. B. Iagodin, "Samoubiistvo i bor'ba s nim," *Zhizn' dlia vsekh* 1912, no. 12 (December), 1881.

4. Among many theorists of modernity, I would mention especially Zygmunt Bauman, Walter Benjamin, Susan Buck-Morss, and Matei Calinescu. See the Bibliography for these and other works.

5. Frederick Cooper has similarly argued that scholars "should not try for a slightly better definition so that they can talk about modernity more clearly. They should instead listen to what is being said in the world. If modernity is what they hear, they should ask how it is being used and why." Frederick Cooper, *Colonialism in Question: Theory, Knowledge, History* (Berkeley, 2005), 115.

6. In more recent times, historians have used *novoe vremia* (new times) to denote European history after the Middle Ages, and some Russian scholars today use the Slavicized neologism *modernost'* or simply "modern" in Cyrillic letters. But even these imperfect solutions were then unavailable.

7. Terry Smith, "Introduction," in *Antinomies of Art and Culture; Modernity, Postmodernity, and Contemporaneity*, ed. Terry Smith, Okui Enwezor, and Nancy Condee (Durham, N.C., 2008), esp. 6–9.

8. See especially Stephen Kern, *The Culture of Time and Space, 1880–1918* (Cambridge, Mass., 1983); Reinhart Koselleck, *Futures Past: On the Semantics of Historical Time* (Cambridge, Mass., 1985); Koselleck, *The Practice of Conceptual History: Timing History, Spacing Concepts* (Stanford, 2002); Lynn Hunt, *Measuring Time, Making History* (Budapest, 2008); David Couz ens Hoy, *The Time of Our Lives: A Critical History of Temporality* (Cambridge, Mass., 2009).

9. See, especially, Charles Baudelaire, *Les Fleurs du mal* (1857), *Le Spleen de Paris* (1862), and *Le Peintre de la vie moderne* (1863), and Marshall Berman, *All That Is Solid Melts into Air: The Experience of Modernity* (New York, 1982), pt. 3.

10. The terminology is from Judith Walkowitz, *City of Dreadful Delight: Narratives of Sexual Danger in Late-Victorian London* (Chicago, 1992).

11. Walter Benjamin, "On the Concept of History" (1940), *Selected Writings*, ed. Michael Jennings et al., 4 vols. (Cambridge, Mass., 1996–2003), 4:392.

12. Ibid., 392, 396. See also other "theses" in this work as well as "Convolute N" of Benjamin's *The Arcades Project*, trans. Howard Eiland and Kevin McLaughlin (Cambridge, Mass., 1999).

CHAPTER ONE. CITY

1. *Peterburg kak fenomen kul'tury: sbornik statei* (St. Petersburg, 1994); *Metafizika Peterburga* (Peterburgskie chtenie po teorii, istorii i filosofii kul'tury, no. 1) (St. Petersburg, 1993); V. N. Toporov, *Peterburgskii tekst russkoi literatury: izbrannye trudy* (St. Petersburg, 2003—a compilation of many earlier writings); Karl Schlögel, *Petersburg: Das Laboratorium der Moderne, 1909–1921* (Munich and Vienna, 2002; originally published Berlin, 1988); Katerina Clark, *Petersburg, Crucible of Revolution* (Cambridge, Mass., 1995); Julie Buckler, *Mapping St. Petersburg: Imperial Text and Cityshape* (Princeton, 2005).

2. It is in this sense that some observers of the city's history have sought to define the city's "physiology," its intersections of *physis* and *logos*. See especially the many writings by Nikolai Antsiferov in the 1920s. For a discussion of his work, see Emily D. Johnson, *How St. Petersburg Learned to Study Itself: The Russian Idea of Kraevedenie* (University Park, 2006), passim; Buckler, *Mapping St. Petersburg*, 110–11. A recent account of St. Petersburg's historical "smells and sounds" was inspired by Antsiferov's physiological approach to the city. V. V. Lapin, *Peterburg: Zapakhi i zvuki* (St. Petersburg, 2007).

3. K. Pazhitnov, "Naselenie Peterburga," *Gorodskoe delo* 1911, no. 4 (February 15): 338–40 (quote 339); "Bol'shie goroda," ibid., 1913, no. 19 (1 October): 1316; A. I. Kopanev, *Naselenie Peterburga v pervoi polovine XIX veka* (Moscow-Leningrad, 1957); James H. Bater, *St. Petersburg: Industrialization and Change* (Montreal, 1976), 308–9; Bater, "Between Old and New: St. Petersburg in the Late Imperial Era," in *The City in Late Imperial Russia*, ed. Michael Hamm (Bloomington, 1986), 51–53; N. V. Iukhneva, *Etnicheskii sostav i etnosotsial'naia struktura naseleniia Peterburga: vtoraia polovina XIX–nachalo XX veka* (Leningrad, 1984), 24; Bruce Lincoln, *Sunlight at Midnight: St. Petersburg and the Rise of Modern Russia* (New York, 2000), 42, 51, 67, 130, 153, 214; Clemens Zimmermann, *Die*

Zeit der Metropolen: Urbanisierung und Grossstadtentwicklung, 2d ed. (Frankfurt, 2000), 72–113.

4. Bater, *St. Petersburg*, 308.

5. Bater, "Between Old and New," 43.

6. Grigorii Kaganov, *Sankt-Peterburg: obrazy prostranstva* (St. Petersburg, 2004). English translation of the 1997 Russian edition: *Images of Space: St. Petersburg in the Visual and Verbal Arts*, trans. Sidney Monas (Stanford, 1997)

7. Denis J. B. Shaw, "St. Petersburg and Geographies of Modernity in Eighteenth-Century Russia," in *St. Petersburg, 1703–1825*, ed. Anthony Cross (New York, 2003), 6–29; James Cracraft, *The Petrine Revolution in Russian Architecture* (Chicago, 1988); Kaganov, *Sankt-Peterburg*, e.g. 21.

8. Bater, *St. Petersburg*, 324.

9. Bater, "Between Old and New," 56.

10. K. V. Karaffa-Korbut, "Nochlezhnye doma v bol'shikh russkikh gorodakh," *Gorodskoe delo* 1912, no. 11–12 (1 June): 691–712; Bater, "Between Old and New," 55–57; D. Zasosov and V. Pyzin, *Povsednevnaia zhizn' Peterburga na rubezhe XIX–XX vekov* (Moscow, 2003), 107–18.

11. K. Pazhitnov, "Kvartirnyi vopros v Moskve i v Peterburge," *Gorodskoe delo* 1910, no. 19 (1 September): 1163–65.

12. *Gorodskoe delo* 1912, no. 11–12 (1–15 June): 765; 1913, no. 13–14 (1–15 June): 960.

13. Almost every issue of *Gorodskoe delo* contained articles on the inadequacies of water supply and sewage disposal. See also Bater, "Between Old and New," 60.

14. See the Bibliography.

15. "Bol'shie goroda," *Gorodskoe delo* 1913, no. 19 (1 October): 1316.

16. Zasosov and Pyzin, *Povsednevnaia zhizn'*. See also E. E. Keller, *Prazdnichnaia kul'tura Peterburga: ocherki istorii* (St. Petersburg, 2001); Lapin, *Peterburg: Zapakhi i zvuki*.

17. Zasosov and Pyzin, *Povsednevnaia zhizn'*, 7.

18. Bater, "Between Old and New," 64–72.

19. Iukhneva, *Etnicheskii sostav*. esp. 3–41, 111–13; K. Pazhitnov, "Naselenie Peterburga," *Gorodskoe delo* 1911, no. 4 (February 15): 338–40.

20. *Gorodskoe delo*, 1909–17 passim; Bater, "Between Old and New," 61–64.

21. Buckler, *Mapping St. Petersburg*, 65.

22. N. P. Antsiferov, *"Nepostizhimyi gorod . . ."*: *Dusha Peterburga. Peterburg Dostoevskogo. Peterburg Pushkina*, ed. M. B. Verblovskaia (St. Petersburg, 1991) (a collection of works originally published in the 1920s); Toporov, *Peterburgskii tekst*, esp. 7–9, 26. See also Iu. M. Lotman, "Simvolika Peterburga i problemy semiotiki goroda," in *Uchenye zapiski Tartuskogo gosudarstvennogo universiteta*, no. 664:

Semiotika goroda i gorodskoi kul'tury: Peterburg (Tartu, 1984), 30–45. For a related but more variegated account of writing about St. Petersburg, see Buckler, *Mapping St. Petersburg*. Marshall Berman, in his comparative study of the "experience of modernity," also reflects on many of the texts discussed here. Marshall Berman, *All That Is Solid Melts Into Air* (Harmondsworth, 1988), pt. 4.

23. Toporov, *Peterburgskii tekst*, 8–9. In her study of numerous and eclectic "middle prose genres" about the city, Julie Buckler also emphasizes widespread ambivalence in how the city was judged. Buckler, *Mapping St. Petersburg*.

24. Lotman, "Simvolika Peterburga," 30–39.

25. Antsiferov, *"Nepostizhimyi gorod,"* 83.

26. For some key sources and discussion see Toporov, *Peterburgskii tekst*, 16–17; A. I. Gertsen, "Moskva i Peterburg" (1842), in *Izbrannye sochineniia* (Moscow, 1937), 262–67; V. G. Belinskii, "Peterburg i Moskva," in *Fiziologiia Peterburga: Sostavlennaia iz trudov russkikh literatorov*, ed. N. Nekrasov (St. Petersburg, 1845), pt. l: 31–97; N. A. Mel'gunov, "Neskol'ko slov o Moskve i Peterburge," *Sovremennik* (1847), in *Moskva-Peterburg: Pro et contra*, ed. K. G. Isupov (St. Petersburg, 2000), 223; and other texts ibid., esp. 81–307.

27. Gertsen, "Moskva i Peterburg," 262–63.

28. N. M. Karamzin, *Zapiska o drevnei i novoi Rossii v ee politicheskom i grazhdanskom otnosheniiakh* [1811] (Moscow, 1991), 37; online at *Lib.ru: Biblioteka Maksima Moshkova* (henceforth *Lib.ru*): http://az.lib.ru/k/karamzin_n_m/text_0120 .shtml.

29. Fedor Tiutchev, "O chem ty voesh', vetr nochnoi? . . ." (early 1830s), in *Lib .ru*: http://az.lib.ru/t/tjutchew_f_i/text_0010.shtml.

30. See studies of comparative urban modernity in the Bibliography, notably by Walter Benjamin, Marshall Berman, Vanessa Schwartz, and Judith Walkowitz.

31. Toporov, *Peterburgskii tekst*, 15; Antsiferov, *"Nepostizhimyi gorod"*, 211–12.

32. See Toporov, "Peterburgskii tekst," 60–64.

33. Gavrila Derzhavin, "Videnie murzy" (1783–84) and especially "Shestvie po Volkovy Rossiiskoi Amfitrity" (1810), along with other early poems of the city in *Sankt-Peterburg, Petrograd, Leningrad v russkoi poezii: antologiia*, ed. Mikhail Sinel'nikov (St. Petersburg, 1999), 1–36. For a late example, see Petr Viazemskii, "Peterburg" (1818), ibid., 67–69. On the "Roman connotations of Petersburg," see K. G. Isupov, "Dialog stolits v istoricheskom dvizhenii," in Isupov, *Moskva-Peterburg: Pro et contra*, 10–12.

34. A. Pushkin, "Gorod pyshnyi, gorod bednyi . . ." (1828), Sinel'nikov, *Sankt-Peterburg, Petrograd, Leningrad v russkoi poezii*, 50.

35. A. S. Pushkin, "Mednyi vsadnik" (1833), from *Russkaia virtual'naia biblioteka*, http://www.rvb.ru/pushkin/.

36. See, for example, the discussion in Buckler, *Mapping St. Petersburg*, 229–35.

37. Toporov, *Peterburgskii tekst*, 11.

38. See "Dozhd' byl prodolzhitel'nyi" and "Peterburgskie zapiski 1836 goda." Quotation is from "Dozhd' byl prodolzhitel'nyi," from *Lib.ru*: http://az.lib.ru/g /gogolx_n_w/text_0410.shtml.

39. "Nevskii prospekt" (1835), in Nikolai Gogol', *Zapiski sumashedshego: Povesti* (St. Petersburg, 2004), 34, 36–38, 42, 44, 75–76. See also discussions of "Gogol's St. Petersburg" in Donald Fanger, *Dostoevsky and Romantic Realism: A Study of Dostoevsky in Relation to Balzac, Dickens, and Gogol* (Evanston, Illinois, 1998; reprint of Cambridge, Mass., 1965 edition), chap. 6; Berman, *All That Is Solid*, 195–206; Buckler, *Mapping St. Petersburg*, passim; and Dina Khapaeva, *Koshmar: Literatura i zhizn'* (Moscow, 2010), chap. 1.

40. Khapaeva, *Koshmar*, 23 (quotation); Fanger, *Dostoevsky*, 122.

41. Gertsen, "Moskva i Peterburg." See similar arguments even more strongly stated by P. I. Sumarokov, "Staryi i novyi byt," in *Maiak sovremennogo prosveshcheniia i obrazovannosti: trudy literatorov, russkikh i innostrannykh* (St. Petersburg, 1841), in Isupov, *Moskva-Peterburg: pro et contra*, 132–76.

42. Kaganov, *Sankt-Peterburg*, 90–91.

43. Ibid., 143, 147–48, 152, 154, 156.

44. The phrase is from an unsigned review by Nekrasov of his own edited collection, *Physiology of Petersburg*, in *Literaturnaia gazeta* on 5 April 1845, in N. A. Nekrasov, *Polnoe sobranie sochinenii i pisem*, 12 vols. (Moscow, 1948–53), 9:142.

45. N. A. Nekrasov, *Zhizn' i pokhozhdeniia Tikhona Trostnikova*, in *Pol'noe sobranie sochinenii i pisem v piatnadsati tomakh* (Leningrad, 1981–), vol. 8 (1984), 250–51; Buckler, *Mapping St. Petersburg*, 202–5.

46. See especially N. A. Nekrasov, "O pogode: ulichnye vpechatlenie" (1858–65). See also "Druzheskaia perepiska Moskvy s Peterburgom" (1859), and "Utro" (1872–73), in *Polnoe sobranie sochinenii v trekh tomakh* (Leningrad, 1967), vol. 2, online at *Lib.ru*: http://az.lib.ru/n/nekrasow_n_a/text_0020.shtml. See also the discussion in Antsiferev, *"Nepostizhimyi gorod,"* 97–103. For similar perceptions, see Fedor Tiutchev, "Gliadel ia, stoia nad Nevoi" (1844), in Sinel'nikov, *Sankt Peterburg, Petrograd, Leningrad v russkoi poezii*, 133–33, and A. A. Grigor'ev, "Moskva i Peterburg: zametki zevaka" (1847), in Isupov, *Moskva-Peterburg: Pro et contra*, 217–18. On the multiple meanings of *toska*, which I have translated most often as "melancholy," see Chapter 7.

47. See N. A. Berdiaev, *Mirosozertsanie Dostoevskogo* (Prague, 1923), esp. chap. 2, and Fanger, *Dostoevsky*, 211.

48. Donald Fanger emphasizes these roles in "Dostoevsky's Early Feuilletons: Approaches to a Myth of the City," *Slavic Review* 22, no. 3 (September 1963): 469–82, and Fanger, *Dostoevsky*, chap. 5. See also Joseph Frank, *Dostoevsky: The Seeds of Revolt, 1821–1849* (Princeton, 1976), chap. 16; and Buckler, *Mapping St. Petersburg*, 99–100.

49. Fedor Dostoevskii, "Peterburgskaia letopis'," 1 June 1847. I cite these feuilletons by date of publication in *Sanktpeterburgskie vedomosti* (27 April, 11 May, 1 June, and 15 June 1847). See F. M. Dostoevskii, *Sobranie sochinenii v piatnadtsati tomakh* (Leningrad-St. Petersburg, 1988–96), 2:5–33, and online version of this text at *Russkaia virtual'naia biblioteka*: http://www.rvb.ru/dostoevski/01text /vol2/07.htm.

50. Dostoevskii, "Peterburgskaia letopis'," 1 June 1847.

51. Ibid., 15 June 1847. See also ibid., 11 May 1847.

52. Ibid., 27 April and 15 June 1847.

53. Ibid., 11 May 1847.

54. Ibid., 15 June 1847. On Dostoevsky's exploration of the relationship between nightmares and realities, see Khapaeva, *Koshmar*, chap. 3.

55. Ibid., 27 April 1847.

56. Dostoevskii, *Belyie nochi: sentimental'nyi roman iz vospominaniia mechtateli* (1848): "noch' pervaia," in Dostoevskii, *Sobranie sochinenii v piatnadtsati tomakh*, 2:154, online at http://www.rvb.ru/dostoevski/01text/vol2/13.htm; Dostoevskii, *Zapiski iz podpol'ia* (1864), pt. 2, chap. 10, ibid., 4:548, online at http://www .rvb.ru/dostoevski/01text/vol4/24.htm; Dostoevskii, "Peterburgskie snovideniia v stikakh i proze" (1861), ibid., 3:483, online at http://www.rvb.ru/dostoevski/01text /vol3/20.htm.

57. For example, F. Dostoevskii, *Unizhennye i oskorblennie* (1861), epilogue, in Dostoevskii, *Sobranie sochinenii v piatnadtsati tomakh* 4:324, online at http:// www.rvb.ru/dostoevski/01text/vol4/21.htm.

58. Dostoevskii, *Zapiski iz podnol'ia*, pt. 1, chap. 2; Dostoevskii, *Prestuplenie i nakazanie*, pt. 2, chap. 2. See also F. Dostoevskii, *Dnevnik pisatelia, 1873*, XIII: "Malen'kie kartinki," in Dostoevskii, *Sobranie sochinenii v piatnadtsati tomakh*, 12:125, online at http://www.rvb.ru/dostoevski/01text/vol12/01journal_73/ 113.htm.

59. F. Dostoevskii, *Prestuplenie i nakazanie* (1866), pt. 1, chap. 6 and pt. 2, chap. 6, in Dostoevskii, *Sobranie sochinenii v piatnadtsati tomakh* 5:5, 148, online at http://www.rvb.ru/dostoevski/tocvol5.htm; Dostoevskii, *Zapiski iz podpol'ia* (1864), pt. 2, chap. 5, ibid., 4:514, online at http://www.rvb.ru/dostoevski/01text /vol4/24.htm.

60. Dostoevskii, *Prestuplenie i nakazanie*, pt. 2, chap. 6, and pt. 6, chap. 6. See also Fanger, *Dostoevsky*, 194;

61. This can be seen in the many anthologies over the years of "St. Petersburg in Russian poetry." For a recent example (in which most of the poems cited below can be found), see Sinel'nikov, *Sankt-Peterburg, Petrograd, Leningrad v russkoi poezii*. See also Antsiferov, *"Nepostizhimyi gorod,"* 119–23, and Buckler, *Mapping St. Petersburg*, 223.

62. Konstantin Sluchevskii, "Khodit veter izbochas'..." (1860), "Utro nad Ne-voiu" (1889), "Ia skazal ei: trotuary griazny..." (date unknown), "Da, trudno izbe-zhat': dlia mnozhestva liudei..." (1898); Apollon Korinfskii, "V tumane" (1891). See also Spiridon Drozhzhin, "V stolitse" (1884).

63. For example, Aleksei Apukhtin, "Peterburgskaia noch'" (1863), and Nikolai Simborskii, "Statuia" (1877).

64. The above poems, and many like them, are from Sinel'nikov, *Sankt-Peterburg, Petrograd, Leningrad v russkoi poezii*.

65. Semen Nadson, "Ditia stolitsy..." (1884).

66. Petr Iakubovich, "Skazochnyi gorod" (1883). These quotations are from two versions of this poem. See Sinel'nikov, *Sankt-Peterburg, Petrograd, Leningrad v russkoi poezii*, 202–5, and P. F. Iakubovich, *Izbrannye stikhotvoreniia* (1905) in *Lib:ru*: http://az.lib.ru/j/jakubowich_p_f/text_0050.shtml.

67. Fedor Sologub, "Vot u vitriny pokaznoi..." (1892), "Tuman ne redeet" (1892), "Na gulkikh ulitsakh stolitsy..." (1896), "Zapakh asfal'ta i grokhot koles" (1896), "K tolpe neponiatnoi i zybkoi" (1896), "Nad bezumiem shumnoi stolitsy..." (1897), in Sinel'nikov, *Sankt-Peterburg, Petrograd, Leningrad v russkoi poezii*. See also Poliksena Solov'eva (Allegro), "Peterburg" (1901).

68. Aleksandr Benua, "Zhivopisnyi Peterburg," *Mir iskusstva*, no. 1 (1902): 2.

69. Clark, *Petersburg*, chap. 2; Kaganov, *Sankt-Peterburg*, chap. 8; Toporov, "Iz istorii peterburgskogo apollonizma: ego zolotye dni i ego krushenie" (2002), in his *Peterburgskii tekst russkoi literatury*, 118–262; Gregory Stroud, "Retrospec-tive Revolution: A History of Time and Memory in Urban Russia, 1903–1923" (Ph.D. diss., University of Illinois, Urbana-Champaign, 2005), chap. 1 ("retro-spectivism"); Johnson, *How St. Petersburg Learned to Study Itself*, chap. 2 (on "preservationism").

70. Benua, "Zhivopisnyi Peterburg," 2.

71. Toporov, "Iz istorii peterburgskogo apollonizma," 151.

72. Anna Lisa Crone and Jennifer Day, *My Petersburg/Myself: Mental Architecture and Imaginative Space In Modern Russian Letters* (Bloomington, 2004), chap. 2. Antsiferov and Toporov made similar arguments in their discussions of the "Pe-tersburg text" in the early 1900s.

73. See examples in Sinel'nikov, *Sankt-Peterburg, Petrograd, Leningrad v russkoi poezii*, 255–312, and discussions in Antsiferov, *"Nepostizhimyi gorod"*, 129, 158–66, and Toporov, "Peterburgskii tekst," 29–66.

74. Zinaida Gippius, "Peterburg" (1909), in Sinel'nikov, *Sankt-Peterburg, Petrograd, Leningrad v russkoi poezii*, 254–5. See also her "'Petrograd'" (1914), in Z. N. Gippius, *Poslednie stikhi, 1914–1918* (Petersburg [*sic*], 1918), 5–6.

75. Toporov, "Peterburgskii tekst," 45–48.

76. See V. N. Orlov, *Poet i gorod: Aleksandr Blok i Peterburg* (Leningrad, 1980), esp. 47–182.

77. See A. A. Blok, "Gorod" (1904–8), in *Polnoe sobranie sochinenii i pisem*, 12 vols., (Moscow, 1997), 2:99–140 and many later poems and poem cycles such as "Snezhnaia maska" (1907), "Faina" (1908), "Vozmezdie" (1908–13), "Strashnyi mir" (1909–16), and "Pliaski smerti" (1915), some of which were published individually in Petersburg journals.

78. See also Nancy L. Cooper, "Images of Hope and Despair in the Last Part of Blok's 'Gorod'," *Slavic and East European Journal*, 35, no. 4 (Winter 1991): 513.

79. See K. Chukovskii, "Ob Aleksandre Bloke," *Svobodnye mysli* 5/18 November 1907, 3.

80. Orlov, *Poet i gorod*, 100–101.

81. See also Blok's 1907 poem "Snow Maiden" ("Snezhnaia deva"). Both Antsiferov and Orlov emphasize this theme in Blok's poetry.

82. Antsiferov, *"Nepostizhimyi gorod"*, 152. See also R. D. Timenchik, V. N. Toporov, and T. V. Tsiv'ian, "Sny Bloka i 'Peterburgskii tekst' nachala XX veka," in *Tvorchestvo A. A. Bloka i russkaia kul'tura XX veka* (Tartu, 1975), 129–35.

83. Olga Matich, *Erotic Utopia: The Decadent Imagination in Russia's Fin de Siècle* (Madison, 2005), chap. 4. In addition to studies of Blok already cited, see Ivanov-Razumnik, "Literatura i obshchestvennost': Roza i krest (Poeziia Aleksandra Bloka)," *Zavety* 1913, no. 10 (October): 114–25; Georgii Ivanov, *Peterburgskie zimy* [Paris, 1928], in *Sobraniia sochinenii v trekh tomakh* (Moscow, 1994), 3:156–57; Iu. M. Lotman, "Blok i narodnaia kul'tura goroda" (1981), in *Izbrannye stat'i v trekh tomakh* (Tallinn, 1992–93), 3:185–200; Toporov, "Peterburg i 'Peterburgskii tekst'," passim; Crone and Day, *My Petersburg/Myself*, esp. 75–80.

84. The novel was first published in 1913, though it was later revised and republished in variant forms. Andrei Belyi, *Peterburg* (St. Petersburg, 2004). This edition, a revised reprint of the Academy of Science's 1981 edition, is based on the first printed edition of the novel, published as part of three collections (*sborniki*) by the Sirin company in St. Petersburg in 1913 and 1914. In 1916, the publisher cut apart unsold copies of these collections and combined the three installments of Bely's novel into a single volume. The best-known version of the novel in English, thanks to a very fine annotated translation by Robert E. Maguire and John E. Malmstad (Andrei Belyi, *Petersburg* [Bloomington, 1978]), is based on the 1922 revision, which may be "definitive" from the literary standpoint, as the editors argue, but less well reflects the purely prerevolutionary environment in which the

novel was first created. My comments on the novel are based on the Academy of Science's edition of the 1913 text as well as the very large scholarly literature of the novel, some of which is cited below. A recent English translation of the 1916 edition is Andrei Bely, *Petersburg*, trans. by John Elsworth (London, 2009).

85. N. Berdiaev, "Astral'nyi roman (razmyshlenie po povodu romana A. Belogo 'Peterburga')," in *Krizis iskusstv* (Moscow, 1918), 36-45; Antsiferov, *"Nepostizhimyi gorod"*, 139-46; L. K. Dolgopolov, "Obraz goroda v romane A. Belogo 'Peterburg'," *Izvestiia Akademii Nauk SSSR: Seriia literatury i iazyka* 34, no. 1 (January-February 1975): 46-59; Dolgopolov, "Printsipy i priemy izobrazheniia goroda," 604-23. See also comments by Maguire and Malmstad in Belyi, *Petersburg*, 313n.

86. Robert A. Maguire and John E. Malmstad, in *Andrei Bely: Spirit of Symbolism*, ed. John Malmstad (Ithaca, 1987), 96-144 (quotations 98, 114, 117, 144); Crone and Day, *My Petersburg/Myself*, 45-49, 64-75; Timothy Langen, *The Stony Dance: Unity and Gesture in Andrei Bely's "Petersburg"* (Evanston, 2005), esp. 9, 55, 59-62, 65-66, 94-95, 119. See also Olga Matich's emphasis on modernist themes of disintegration and explosion in Belyi's novel in "Bely, Kandinsky, and Avant-Garde Aesthetics," in *Petersburg/Petersburg: Novel and City, 1900-1921*, ed. Olga Matich (Madison, 2010), 83-120. See similar themes in Belyi's essay on the city, "Gorod" (1907), in Andrei Belyi, *Arabeski* (Moscow, 1911), 353-57.

87. See, for example, Vladimir Alexandrov, *Andrei Bely: The Major Symbolist Fiction* (Cambridge, Mass., 1985), chap. 3. See also A. Belyi, "Nechto o mistike," *Trudy i dni*, 1912, no. 2 (March-April): 46-47.

88. In addition to the following, see also J. D. Elsworth, *Andrey Bely: A Critical Study of the Novels* (Cambridge, 1982), chap. 4; Berman, *All That Is Solid*, 255-70; Alexandrov, *Andrei Bely*, chap 3; Roger Keys, *The Reluctant Modernist: Andrei Bely and the Development of Russian Fiction, 1902-1914* (Oxford, 1996), chap. 20; Peter Barta, *Bely, Joyce, and Döblin: Peripatetics in the City Novel* (Gainesville, 1996), chap. 2; Olga Matich, "Backs, Suddenlys, and Surveillance in Andrej Belyj's *Petersburg*," *Russian Literature* 58 (2005): 149-65; Colleen McQuillen, "The Russian Modernist Masquerade: Deception, Rhetoric, and Theatrical Transposition," (Ph.D. diss., Columbia University, 2006); Matich, ed., *Petersburg/Petersburg* and the accompanying website "Mapping Petersburg" at http://stpetersburg.berkeley .edu/.

89. From the famous 1912 manifesto, "A Slap in the Face of Public Taste" (Poshchechina obshchestvennomu vkusu), published in a book of the same title in 1913.

90. For example, "'Pervyi v mire' spektakl' futuristov v Peterburge," *Ogonek* 1913, no. 50 (15/28 December): n.p. (mocking reports on futurism were very common in the press).

91. Genrikh Tastevin, *Futurizm (na puti k novomu simvolizmu)* (Moscow, 1914), 5-7; Sviashchennik Evgenii Sosuntsov, "Sovremennyi antinomizm," *Tserkovnyi*

vestnik 1914, no. 21 (22 May): 625–27; "Futurizm," *Tserkovnyi vestnik* 1914, no. 27 (3 July): 825; S. Isakov, "Mysli ob iskusstve (k voprosu o 'futurizme')," *Novyi zhurnal dlia vsekh* 1914, no. 1 (January): 54.

92. Tastevin, *Futurizm*, 29. See also B. Shaposhnikov, "Futurizm i teatr," *Maski*, no. 7–8 (1912–13): 29–30.

93. Elena Guro, *Sharmanka* (St. Petersburg, 1909); Guro, "Gorod" (March 1910), *Ocharovannyi strannik*, no. 10 (1916): 1 (first published in *Futuristy: Ryka-iushchii Parnas* [St. Petersburg, 1914]); Guro, "Vozliubiv bol' poruganiia . . . ," *Sovremennik* 1914, no. 9 (May): 3; Anna Ljunggren and Nils Åke Nilsson, eds., *Elena Guro: Selected Prose and Poetry* (Stockholm, 1988); Anna Ljunggren and Nina Gourianova, eds., *Elena Guro: Selected Writings from the Archives* (Stockholm, 1995), 38–41. For critical studies of Guro, see Milica Banjanin's work, especially Milica Banjanin, "Between Symbolism and Futurism: Impressions by Day and by Night in Elena Guro's City Series," *Slavic and East European Journal* 37, no. 1 (Spring 1993), 67–84; "Elena Guro: From the City's Junkyard of Images to a Poetics of Nature," *Studia Slavica Finlandensia* 16, no. 1 (1999): 43–63; "The Female 'Flâneur': Elena Guro in Petersburg," *Australian Slavonic and East European Studies* 11, no. 1/2 (1997), 47–63; and Kjeld Jensen, *Russian Futurism, Urbanism, and Elena Guro* (Arhus, 1977).

94. See especially "Iz ulitsy v ulitsu" (1913), "Koe-chto pro Peterburg" (1913), and "Posledniaia peterburgskaia skazka" (1916), also "Noch'" (1912), "Utro" (1912), "Ulichnoe" (1913), "Ia" (1913), "Liubov'" (1913), and "Shumiki, Shumy, Shumishchi" (1913), all in Vladimir Maiakovskii, *Polnoe sobranie sochinenii v trinadtsati tomakh*, 13 vols. (Moscow, 1955–61), vol. 1 (1912–17) (Moscow, 1955).

95. Paul A. Klanderud, "Maiakovskii's Myth of Man, Things and the *City*: From 'Poshlost' to the Promised Land," *Russian Review* 55, no. 1 (January 1996), 40, 44. See also discussion in Antsiferov, *"Nepostizhimyi gorod"*, 166–69, and Crone and Day, *My Petersburg/Myself*, 24–29.

96. See Mark D. Steinberg, *Proletarian Imagination: Self, Modernity, and the Sacred in Russia, 1910–1925* (Ithaca, 2002), 150–51.

97. I. Loginov, "V gorode," *Sbornik proletarskii pisatelei*, ed. M. Gor'kii, A. Serebrov, and A. Chapygin (Petrograd, 1917), 174; M. Artamonov, "Taet," *Metallist* (the newspaper of the Petersburg metalworkers' union) 1914, no. 4/41 (1 April): 5–6. See also *Pervyi sbornik proletarskikh pisatelei* (St. Petersburg, 1914).

98. See, for example, M. Gerasimov, "V gorode," in *Pervyi sbornik proletarskikh pisatelei*, 51; A. Bibik, "Bor obrechennyi," *Novaia rabochaia gazeta*, 13 October 1913; A. Pomorskii, "Zhertvam goroda," *Metallist*, 1913, no. 5/29 (July 19): 4. See discussions in Steinberg, *Proletarian Imagination*, chap. 4.

99. Kaganov, *Sankt-Peterburg*, 168–78 (who emphasizes the threat); Betsy F. Moeller-Sally, "No Exit: Piranesi, Doré, and the Transformation of the Petersburg

Myth in Mstislav Dobuzhinskii's *Urban Dreams*," *Russian Review* 57, no. 4 (October 1998): 539–67. See drawings such as *Staryi domik* (1905), *Budni* (1906), *Prazdnik* (1906), and *D'iavol* (1906).

100. "Vystavka kartin 'Soiuza molodezhi' v Peterburge," *Ogonek* 1913, no. 48 (1/14 December): n.p.

101. See, for example, the review of the "Tramway V" exhibition and Kazimir Malevich in *Ogonek* 1915, no. 11 (15/28 March): 15.

102. Mikhail Anderson, "Reaktsionnoe iskusstvo (Salon Soiuza Molodezhi)," *Sovremennik* 1914, no. 4 (February): 98.

103. Berdiaev, *Krizis iskusstv* (Moscow, 1918), 6–12. Perhaps the lapsed Marxist Berdiaev was thinking of Karl Marx's famous description of modern civilization: "all things solid melt into air."

104. Louise McReynolds, *The News Under Russia's Old Regime: The Development of a Mass-Circulation Press* (Princeton, 1991), appendixes; *Statistika proizvedenii pechati vyshedshikh v Rossii v 1912 godu* (St. Petersburg, 1913), 91–102; L. N. Beliaeva, ed., *Bibliografiia periodicheskikh izdanii Rossii, 1901–1916*, 4 vols. (Leningrad, 1958–61).

105. For example, Vadim, "Zakliucheniia (po pov . . .)," *Gazeta-kopeika*, 24 February 1913, 5.

106. Vsevolod Krestovskii, *Peterburgskie trushchoby: kniga o sytykh i golodnykh*, 4 vols. (St. Petersburg, 1867); Vladimir Mikhnevich, *Iazvy Peterburga: Opyt istoriko-statisticheskogo issledovaniia nravstvennosti stolichnogo naseleniia* (St. Petersburg, 1886); Anatolii Bakhtiarov, *Briukho Peterburga: obshchestvenno-fiziologicheskie ocherki* (St. Petersburg, 1887); N. N. Zhivotov, *Peterburgskie profili*, 4 vols (St. Petersburg, 1894–95); N. Sveshnikov, *Peterburgskie Viazemskie trushchoby i ikh obitateli: original'nyi ocherk s natury* (St. Petersburg, 1900); N. V. Nikitin, *Peterburg noch'iu: bytovye ocherki* (St. Petersburg, 1903). These works are discussed briefly as examples of "literary slumming" in Buckler, *Mapping St. Petersburg*, 171–79.

107. See Buckler, *Mapping St. Petersburg*, 179.

108. *Novye peterburgskie trushchoby: ocherki stolichnoi zhizni* (St. Petersburg, 1909–10). This was a series of sketches, alternately written by Semenov and Angarov, published in installments. See page 63 for an explicit recognition of the presence of both the tragic and the *pikantnyi*.

109. The journal was named in remembrance of the famous journal of the same name from the 1860s, to signify their shared commitment to "progress" and "realism." *Sovremennik* 1911, no. 1 (January): 1.

110. A. Karelin, "K voprosu o psikhike proletariev: eskiz," *Sovremennik* 1912, no. 3 (March): 282–95, esp. 284–86. See also A. Zorin [Gastev], "Rabochii mir: Novyi Piter," *Zhizn' dlia vsekh* 1913, no. 10 (October): 1454–62.

111. Aleks. Mertvago, "Peterburg i Moskva," *Rech'*, 26 August 1907, 3.

112. Al. Fedorov, "K solntsu!" *Peterburgskii kinematograf,* 12 February 1911, 2.

113. A. Zorin [Gastev], "Rabochii mir: Novyi Piter," *Zhizn' dlia vsekh* 1913, no. 10 (October): 1454.

114. See the, admittedly short-lived, 1907 magazine, "The Ideal Life" (*Ideal'naia zhizn'*), as described in an announcement in *Svobodnye mysli,* 17 September 1907.

115. Markov, "Printsipy novogo iskusstva," *Soiuz molodezhi,* no. 1 (April 1912): 6; L. M. "Epokha sinematografa," *Novyi zhurnal dlia vsekh* 1913, no. 12 (December): 127–34.

116. G. Tsyperovich, "Kinematograf," *Sovremennyi mir* 1912, no. 1 (January): 181.

117. Favn, "Malen'kii fel'eton: 'Neo' . . . ," *Novoe vremia,* 20 May 1909, 4. See also V. Burenin, "Kriticheskie ocherki: pri vstuplenii v novyi god," ibid., 8 January 1910, 4.

118. E. Tsuberbiller, "Gorod XX stoletiia," *Gorodskoe delo* 1909, no. 7 (25 March): 308–14.

119. D. Protopopov, "Sud'ba russkikh gorodov" *Gorodskoe delo* 1911, no. 44 (15 December): 1710–13. See also D. Protopopov, "Novyi sposob bor'by s ulichnoi pyl'iu," ibid., no. 19 (1 October): 1419.

120. P. Cher-skii. "Paradoksy sovremennosti," *Novyi zhurnal dlia vsekh* 1914, no. 4 (April): 51–53; M. S.-in, "Nrvastvennost' i dolgoletie," *Vsemirnaia panorama,* no. 31 (20 November 1909): 10.

121. Chlen Gos. Dumy M. Novikov, "Bor'ba s vlast'iu ulitsy i pomoshch' besprizornym detiam," *Gorodskoe delo* 1914, no. 9 (1 May): 526. See also K. Barantsevich, "Fiziologiia Peterburga (Nabroski karandashem): Briukho, Mozg, Serdtsa," *Zhizn' dlia vsekh* 1909, no. 12 (December): 94–111.

122. Ol'ga Gridina, "Odna zhenshchina," *Gazeta-kopeika,* 6 June 1910, 5.

123. See also Steinberg, *Proletarian Imagination,* chaps. 4–5.

124. See P. Mansell Jones, *Verhaeren* (New Haven, 1957), esp. 33–34. Verhaeren's works, in translation, appeared widely in Russian anthologies and journals as well as in individual volumes, in the early 1900s, and he visited St. Petersburg, to great acclaim, in 1913.

125. N. Valentinov, "Gorod i gorozhane," *Novyi zhurnal dlia vsekh* 1910, no. 20 (June): 91–96. See also Tastevin, *Futurizm,* 5–9.

126. The literature on proletarianization in St. Petersburg and on the revolutionary movement is vast. See, especially, Reginald Zelnik, *Labor and Society in Tsarist Russia* (Stanford, 1971); Victoria Bonnell, *Roots of Rebellion: Workers' Politics and Organizations in St. Petersburg and Moscow, 1900–1914* (Berkeley, 1983); Gerald Surh, *1905 in St. Petersburg: Labor, Society, and Revolution* (Stanford, 1989).

127. M. Men'shikov, "Za polstoletiia," *Novoe vremia,* 28 February 1909, 2.

128. Sluchainyi, "Nazad ili vpered," *Gazeta-kopeika,* 27 June 1910, 4–5.

129. Vadim, "Zakliucheniia (po pov . . .)," ibid., 24 February 1913, 5.

130. Vadim, "Cherez 50 let," ibid., 16 June 1913, 5.

131. For example, Ol'ga Gridina, "Gorod-obmanshchik," ibid., 24 December 1913, 3; Gridina, "Rokovaia oshibka," ibid., 13 March 1910.

132. Mikh. Dubrovskii, "V bor'be za sushchestvovanie," ibid., 26 September 1911, 3.

133. P. Cher-skii, "Paradoksy sovremennosti," *Novyi zhurnal dlia vsekh* 1914, no. 4 (April): 51.

134. M. Slobozhanin, "Iz sovremennykh perezhivanii," *Zhizn' dlia vsekh* 1913, no. 1 (January): 115.

135. Georgii Chulkov, "Demony i sovremennost'," *Apollon* 1914, no. 1-2 (January–February): 70-75.

136. V. Burenin, "Kriticheskie ocherki: pri vstuplenii v novyi god," *Novoe vremia*, 8 January 1910, 4. See also, from more liberal writers, V. Shirokii, "Cherty sovremennoi russkoi zhizni," *Novyi zhurnal dlia vsekh* 1914, no. 1 (January): 46; Al. Fedorov, "V nashi dni," *Peterburgskii kinematograf*, 22 January 1911, 2.

137. "Dukhovnye bluzhdaniia," ibid., 1910, no. 46 (18 November): 1426; "Osnovnaia bolezn' sovremennoi kul'tury," ibid., 1914, no. 24 (12 July): 713-14; Professor A. Bronzov, "Progress-li?" ibid., 1912, no. 1 (5 January): 4-9; "Khristianstvo i sovremennaia zhizn'," ibid., 1914, no. 20 (15 May): 594-95. See also "Sovremennaia kul'tura i khristianstvo," ibid., 1914, no. 23 (5 June): 682.

138. "Futurizm," ibid., 1914, no. 27 (3 July): 825-26. See also D. Merezhkovskii, *Griadushchii Kham* (St. Petersburg, 1906); V. Rozanov, "Kiev i Kievliane," *Novoe vremia*, 17 September 1911, 3-4, and 24 September 1911, 4.

139. Podpischik zhurnala *Zhizn' dlia vsekh*, "Golos iz nedr nevezhestva," *Novyi zhurnal dlia vsekh* 1913, no. 9 (September): 1289-96.

140. Shigaleev, "Uzhasy goroda," *Gazeta-kopeika*, 29 April 1912, 4-5.

141. Al. Fedorov, "Bez vesny," *Peterburgskii kinematograf*, 19 March 1911, 2. See also S. Arnova, "Samoubiistvo v proshlom i nastoiashchem," *Zhizn' dlia vsekh* 1911, no. 3-4 (March–April): 476; A. V. Amfiteatrov, "Zakat starogo veka" *Sovremennik* 1911, no. 1 (January): 29.

142. M. Men'shikov, "Pis'mo k blizhnym," *Novoe vremia*, 30 May 1910, 4.

143. Obozrevatel', "Sovremennyi vampir," *Peterburgskii listok*, 19 May 1909, 2.

144. P. Ia. Rozenbakh, "Prichiny sovremennoi nervoznosti i samoubiistv," *Peterburgskaia gazeta*, 26 April 1909, 3.

145. Georg Simmel, "The Metropolis and Mental Life," *The Sociology of Georg Simmel*, trans. and ed. Kurt Wolff (Glencoe, 1950; originally published 1903), 410, 414. Simmel's works were well-known in Russia in these years and regularly translated into Russian.

146. S. Gamalov, "Pod znamenem Khama," *Novyi zhurnal dlia vsekh* 1913, no. 12 (December): 110.

147. For example, Al. Fedorov, "V nashi dni," *Peterburgskii kinematograf,* 22 January 1911, 2; Mikh. Dubrovskii, "V bor'be za sushchestvovanie," *Gazeta-kopeika,* 26 September 1911, 3.

148. K. Reinbakh, "Iskanie novykh form zhizni," *Zhizn' dlia vsekh* 1916, no. 3 (March): 421.

149. Vsevolod Kozhevnikov, "Gorod," *Sovremennyi mir* 1911, no. 3 (March): 60–62; Pavel Egorov, "Kartiny goroda," ibid., 1913, no. 4 (April): 22; Vl. Kokhanovskii, "Smert'," *Novyi zhurnal dlia vsekh* 1912, no. 11 (November): 27–42; Filaret Chernov, "Gorod," *Zhizn' dlia vsekh* 1916, no. 4–5 (April-May): 502–5 and Chernov, "Gorod," ibid., 1917, no. 2 (February): 266.

150. G. Viatkin, "Iz knigi nastroenii," *Novyi zhurnal dlia vsekh* 1910, no. 18 (April): 10; Leonid Shenfel'dt, "Na ulitse," ibid., 1910, no. 20 (June): 10; Natan Vengrov, "Ulitsa," ibid., 1915, no. 5 (May): 3.

151. S. Frid, "Noch'iu," *Zhizn' dlia vsekh* 1915, no. 4 (April): 576; A. Topol'skii, "V gorode," *Novyi zhurnal dlia vsekh* 1910, no. 23 (September): 10; Rom. A-., "Granitnaia serdtsa," *Gazeta-kopeika,* 17 August 1909, 2–3.

152. V. Vegenov, "Gorod," ibid., 13 June 1911, 3; A. Luk'ianov, "Gorod," *Peterburgskii kinematograf* 1911, no. 13 (16 February): 3; Mikh. Artamonov, "Gorod," *Malen'kaia gazeta,* 30 July 1915, 4.

153. N., "Raba goroda," *Malen'kaia gazeta,* 23 July 1915, 4; Vengrov, "Ulitsa," *Novyi zhurnal dlia vsekh* 1915, no. 5 (May): 3; Leonid Shenfel'dt, "Na ulitse," ibid., 1910, no. 20 (June): 10; G. Viatkin, "Iz knigi nastroenii," ibid., no. 18 (April): 11.

154. V. Vegenov, "V gorode i v glushe," *Gazeta-kopeika,* 20 February 1909, 3.

155. D. Merezhkovskii, "Peterburgu byt' pustu," *Rech',* 21 December 1908, 2.

156. D. E. Arkin, "Grad obrechennyi" (dated 10 August 1917), *Russkaia svoboda,* no. 22/23 ([30 September] 1917): esp. 11–13. The author is probably David Efimovich Arkin, a Moscow University student who would later become a respected Soviet architecture professor. For similar arguments, see I. N. Potapenko, "Prokliatyi gorod," *Nashi vedomosti,* 3 January 1918, and N. V. Ustrialov, "Sud'ba Peterburga," *Nakanune,* 2 April/25 March 1918, both reprinted in *Peterburg kak fenomen kul'tury,* 120–26. On the theme of Petersburg as city of doom (*gorod gibeli i obitel' obrechennykh*), see also Isupov, "Dialog stolits v istoricheskom dvizhenii," in Isupov, *Moskva-Peterburg: Pro et contra,* 51–52, and Buckler, *Mapping St. Petersburg,* 229.

CHAPTER TWO. STREETS

1. N. Borovskii, "Peterburg nashikh dnei," *Peterburgskii gid,* no. 7 (December 1912): 1.

2. Spiro Kostof, *The City Assembled: The Elements of Urban Form Through History* (London, 1992), esp. chap. 4 ("The Street"); Zeynep Çelik, Diane Favro, and

Richard Ingersoll, *Streets: Critical Perspectives on Public Space* (Berkeley, 1994), esp. introduction; Michel de Certeau, *The Practice of Everyday Life* (Berkeley, 1984), esp. chap. 7 ("Walking the City") and chap. 9 ("Spatial Stories"); Lewis Mumford, *The City in History* (New York, 1961), e.g. 426; Judith Walkowitz, *City of Dreadful Delight: Narratives of Sexual Danger in Late-Victorian London* (Chicago, 1992); Elizabeth Wilson, *The Sphinx in the City: Urban Life, the Control of Disorder, and Women* (Los Angeles, 1992); Vanessa Schwartz, *Spectacular Realities: Early Mass Culture in Fin-de-Siècle Paris* (Berkeley, 1998); Joachim Schlör, *Nights in the Big City: Paris, Berlin, London, 1840–1930* (London, 1998). On the category of the public sphere—strongly associated with Jürgen Habermas, but elaborated and recast by many of his critics—see especially Craig Calhoun, ed., *Habermas and the Public Sphere* (Cambridge, Mass., 1992). A valuable set of studies of central and eastern Europe is Andreas R. Hofmann and Anna Veronika Wendland, eds., *Stadt und Öffentlichkeit in Ostmitteleuropa, 1900–1939: Beiträge zur Entstehung moderner Urbanität zwischen Berlin, Charkiv, Tallinn und Triest* (Stuttgart, 2002). On St. Petersburg, see especially Karl Schlögel, *Petersburg: Das Laboratorium der Moderne, 1909–1921* (Munich and Vienna, 2002; originally published Berlin, 1988), chap. 4. For a compelling study of the street in another Russian imperial city, see Roshanna Sylvester, *Tales of Old Odessa: Crime and Civility in a City of Thieves* (Dekalb, 2005).

3. Walter Benjamin, *The Arcades Project*, trans. Howard Eiland and Kevin McLaughlin (Cambridge, Mass., 1999), 83, 103, 416–20, 425, 431, 429, 435, 444, 518–19, 901, 905. For an important earlier exploration of the forms, culture, and meanings of the street, see Benjamin, *Einbahnstraße* (Berlin, 1928).

4. On literature, see especially Robert Alter, *Imagined Cities: Urban Experience and the Language of the Novel* (New Haven, 2005); also Burton Pike, *The Image of the City in Modern Literature* (Princeton, 1981) and Richard Lehan, *The City in Literature: An Intellectual and Cultural History* (Berkeley, 1998). On visual arts, see especially T. J. Clark, *The Painting of Modern Life: Paris in the Art of Manet and His Followers* (Princeton, 1984); and Lynda Nead, *Victorian Babylon: People, Streets and Images in Nineteenth-Century London* (New Haven, 2000).

5. S. Chernikover, *Peterburg* (Moscow, 1909), 3–7; V. Novitskii, "Zver'—v chelovek," *Peterburgskaia gazeta*, 6 April 1909, 1.

6. N. Valentinov, "Gorod i gorozhane," *Novyi zhurnal dlia vsekh* 1910, no. 20 (June): 93–94; A. Karelin, "K voprosu o psikhike proletariev: eskiz," *Sovremennik* 1912, no. 3 (March): 282–95, esp. 285.

7. N. Valentinov, "Gorod i gorozhane," *Novyi zhurnal dlia vsekh* 1910, no. 20 (June): 93–94; "Zhazhda silnykh oshchushchenii," *Tserkovnyi vestnik* 1909, no. 7 (12 February): 198–99; P. Ia. Rozenbakh, "O prichinakh sovremennoi nervoznosti i samoubiistv," *Novoe slovo* 1909, no. 11: 41–43.

8. In addition to examples below, Sangvinik, "Pritony azarta i razvrata," *Peterburgskii listok*, 15 April 1910, 5.

9. V. P. Ruadze, *K sudu!* . . . *Gomoseksual'nyi Peterburg* (St. Petersburg, 1908), 4.

10. I. V. Lebedev, "Mertvye tsvety," *Malen'kaia gazeta*, 5 September 1914, 1. The notion of "the street" as "abyss" (*bezdna*) was repeated often in Lebedev's column.

11. I. V. Lebedev (Diadia Vania), "Kto vinovat," *Malen'kaia gazeta*, 31 October 1914, 3–4.

12. A. M-., "Peterburgskaia ulitsa," *Peterburgskii listok*, 27 November 1905, 3.

13. V. Tr-ov, "Nasha ulitsa," *Gazeta-kopeika*, 14 August 1908, 3–4; 22 August 1908, 3; 24 August 1908, 2–3. See also, for example, Bova, "Nasha ulitsa," *Peterburgskii listok*, 5 September 1910.

14. "Nashi zadachi, nadezhdy, i pozhelaiia," *Novoe vremia*, 1 January 1909, 2.

15. V. Rozanov, "V katolicheskoi Germanii," ibid., 27 July 1905, 4; Rozanov, *Ital'ianskiia vpechatleniia* (St. Petersburg, 1909), 269.

16. Arnol'dov, "Svidrigailovy," *Gazeta-kopeika*, 28 February 1909, 4; V. Pr., "Ulichnyi nakhal," ibid., 3 July 1909, 3; P. Z., "Na temy dnia," ibid., 7 October 1909, 3.

17. P. Zaikin, "Petersburgskie skvernoslovie," ibid., 3 February 1909, 3.

18. O. Gridina, "Zverinye nravy," ibid., 14 May 1910, 3.

19. M. Novikov, "Bor'ba s vlast'iu ulitsy i pomoshch' besprizornym detiam," *Gorodskoe delo* 1914, no. 9 (1 May): 526.

20. For example, "Liudi-zvery," *Gazeta-kopeika*, 2 January 1909, 3. See also the street's defensive response in Valentin Gorianskii, "Molitva ulitsy," *Malen'kaia gazeta*, 21 September 1914, 1.

21. Benjamin, *The Arcades Project*, 111, 269, 286, 423, 437, 445. Charles Baudelaire, *The Parisian Prowler: Le Spleen de Paris, Petits Poèmes en prose*, 2d ed. (Athens and London, 1997), 21 ("Crowds").

22. K. Barantsevich, "Fiziologiia Peterburga (Nabroski karandashem): Briukho, Mozg, Serdtsa," *Zhizn' dlia vsekh* 1909, no. 12 (December): 99; *Malen'kaia gazeta*, 2 November 1914, 4.

23. N. V. Nikitin, *Peterburg noch'iu: bytovye ocherki* (St. Petersburg, 1903), 99.

24. Khronos, "O zeleni i gul'iane," *Gazeta-kopeika*, 29 April 1913, 3.

25. Obyvatel', "Verby," ibid., 22 March 1909. 3.

26. K. Barantsevich, "Fiziologiia Peterburga (Nabroski karandashem): Briukho, Mozg, Serdtsa," *Zhizn' dlia vsekh* 1909, no. 12 (December): 94.

27. Kavaler Foblaz, "Nevskii vo mrake," *Gazeta-kopeika*, 10 June 1910, 3; Sergei Auslender, "Narodnyi Dom Grafini Paniny," *Apollon 1910*, no. 4 (January): 76; V.

Brusianin, "O khuliganakh i khuliganstve," *Novyi zhurnal dlia vsekh* 1913, no. 4 (April): 152; Vegenov, "Kaleka (s natury)," *Gazeta-kopeika*, 19 September 1908, 3; "Zhizn' 'cheloveka'," *Malen'kaia gazeta*, 10 July 1915, 3 (on rudeness to waiters).

28. Edgar Allan Poe, "The Man of the Crowd," *Burton's Gentleman's Magazine* (December 1840): 267.

29. Georg Simmel, "The Metropolis and Mental Life," in *The Sociology of Georg Simmel*, trans. and ed. Kurt Wolff (Glencoe, 1950; originally published 1903), esp. 415–16, 418.

30. M. Liberson, *Stradanie odinochestva* (St. Petersburg, 1909), 7–8, 23.

31. G. Gordon, "Ob odinokikh," *Novyi zhurnal dlia vsekh* 1909, no. 7 (May): 85, 88.

32. V. Novitskii, "Zver'—v chelovek," *Peterburgskaia gazeta*, 6 April 1909, 1; K. Barantsevich, "Zhazhdushchie silnykh oshchushchenii," *Slovo*, 2 February 1909, 2; "Zhazhda silnykh oshchushchenii," *Tserkovnyi Vestnik* 1909, no. 7 (12 February): 198–99.

33. Vegenov, "Kaleka (s natury)," *Gazeta-kopeika*, 19 September 1908, 3.

34. Zabavnik, "Peterburgskii slovar'," ibid., 28 February 1909, 4.

35. P. Z. "Na temy dnia," ibid., 7 October 1909, 3.

36. For example, A. Petrov, "Istoriia kazhdogo dnia," ibid., 19 August 1909, 3; "Nuzhda i gore brosili ego pod kolesa," *Malen'kaia gazeta*, 2 July 1915, 3.

37. V. Tr-ov, "Nashe ulitsa: Samoubiitsa," *Gazeta-kopeika*, 24 August 1908, 2.

38. Aleksandr Benua, "Zhivopisnyi Peterburg," *Mir iskusstva*, no. 1 (1902): 1–2.

39. K. Chukovskii, "O Leonide Andreeve," *Rech'*, 6 June 1910, 2. Chukovskii cleverly uses the adjective "ploshchadnyi," which means crass and crude, but also suggests a relationship to the city square (*ploshchad'*).

40. Mikhail Anderson, "Reaktsionnoe iskusstvo (Salon Soiuza Molodezhi)," *Sovremennik* 1914, no. 4 (February): 95.

41. N. Gumilev, "Pis'mo o russkoi poezii," *Apollon* 1914, no. 1–2 (January–February): 123–25.

42. L. Gurevich in *Zaprosy zhizni* 1909, no. 1 (18 October): 29–30; Chukovskii, "O Leonide Andreeve," *Rech'*, 6 June 1910, 2.

43. Leonid Andreev, "Pis'ma o teatre," *Maski*, no. 3 ([1912]–1913): 3.

44. L. Kozlovskii, "Russkaia literatura," *Vestnik znaniia* 1910, no. 4 (April): 209–13. See also Leonid Galich, "Novye techenie," *Rech'*, 1 January 1908, 1.

45. Julie Buckler, *Mapping St. Petersburg: Imperial Text and Cityshape* (Princeton, 2005), 89–96; Emily D. Johnson, *How St. Petersburg Learned to Study Itself: The Russian Idea of Kraevedenie* (University Park, 2006), chap. 1.

46. Peter Fritzsche, *Reading Berlin 1900* (Cambridge, Mass., 1996), esp. 14–18; Schwartz, *Spectacular Realities*, esp. 26–44. On the history and content of

newspapers in Russia, see Louise McReynolds, *The News Under Russia's Old Regime: The Development of a Mass-Circulation Press* (Princeton, 1991).

47. Skitalets, "Bodrye liudi," *Gazeta-kopeika*, 10 April 1911, 4.

48. B. Bentovin, *Torguiushchiia telom* (St. Petersburg, 1910), 228.

49. "Okhtenskie 'rebiata'," *Gazeta-kopeika*, 19 June 1908, 5.

50. Ne Okhtianin, "Okhtenskie shantazhisty," *Peterburgskii listok*, 19 April 1909, 3.

51. K-n., " 'Venteriushniki': Nravy stolichnykh okrain," *Gazeta-kopeika*, 31 August 1909, 3.

52. "Zerkalo stolitsy," *Malen'kaia gazeta*, 27 October 1914, 3.

53. V. T., "Na ligovskom bul'vare," *Gazeta-Kopeika*, 23 June 1909, 3.

54. Sledopyt, " 'Krasnyi fonar' i narodnaia nravstvennost'," *Malen'kaia gazeta*, 22 November 1914, 4.

55. "Massovye buiistva khuliganov," *Peterburgskii listok*, 24 November 1905, 4.

56. S. Liubosh, "Peterburgskie zametki," *Sovremennoe slovo*, 9 May 1910, 2.

57. For example, "14-letnii ataman shaiki vorov," *Peterburgskii listok*, 11 January 1913, 3. See also Chapter 5.

58. "Detskii sud," *Peterburgskii listok*, 11 January 1910, 1; S. Liubosh, "Peterburgskie zametki: o detovodstve," *Sovremennoe slovo*, 9 May 1910, 2; N. Kholmskii, "Voina i detskaia prestupnost'," *Malen'kaia gazeta*, 6 October 1914, 4.

59. "Maloletnye apashi i blagotvoritel'nyi patronat," *Peterburgskaia gazeta*, 13 March 1910, 3. See similar views on street culture and juvenile delinquency, including by Dr. Dril' at a congress on juvenile crime, in Joan Neuberger, *Hooliganism: Crime, Culture, and Power in St. Petersburg, 1900–1914* (Berkeley, 1993), 178–98.

60. Boris Frommet, "Deti ulitsy," *Zhizn' dlia vsekh* 1914, no. 6 (May–June): 696–700.

61. For example, M. Novikov, "Bor'ba s vlast'iu ulitsy i pomoshch' besprizornym detiam," *Gorodskoe delo* 1914, no. 9 (1 May): 526–32. See also *Gazeta-kopeika*, 2 January 1909, 3.

62. K. Pazhitnov, "Kvartirnyi vopros v Moskve i v Peterburge," *Gorodskoe delo* 1910, no. 19 (1 September): 1163–65.

63. "Izgnanka Peterburga—'Uglovye'," *Ogonek* 1910, no. 35 (28 August/10 September): n.p.

64. Sergei Solomin, "Obshchestvennye prestuplenie," *Gazeta-kopeika*, 16 September 1909, 3.

65. Oko, "Stolichnye pauki (Ocherki)," *Malen'kaia gazeta*, 21 September 1914, 3–4.

66. "Bezdomnye," *Ogonek* 1910, no. 33 (14/27 August): n.p; S. Liubosh, "Na perepisi," *Rech'*, 16 December 1910, 2; K. V. Karaffa-Korbut, "Nochlezhnye doma

v bol'shikh russkikh gorodakh," *Gorodskoe delo* 1912, no. 10 (15 May): 627–28, no. 11 (1 June): 695–706; *Peterburgskii listok*, 19 May 1913, 8; "Peterburgskie trushchoby," ibid., 15 February 1914, 3; S. Kondurushkin, "Pritony sna (perepiska nochlezhnikov)," ibid., 12 September 1910, 3.

67. For example, *Peterburgskii listok*, 31 May 1913, 4,

68. N. Shigaleev, "Gorod Nishchensk," *Gazeta-kopeika*, 16 June 1911, 3.

69. For example, ibid., 6 November 1908, 3; Skitalets, "Na kladbishchakh," ibid., 15 January 1909, 3.

70. Ibid., 27 March 1911, 1.

71. *Nishchenstvo i bor'ba s nim* (St. Petersburg, 1913), esp. 58–59, 73–129. See also Adele Lindenmeyr, *Poverty Is Not a Vice: Charity, Society, and the State in Imperial Russia* (Princeton, 1996); and Hubertus Jahn, *Armes Rußland: Bettler and Notleidende in der russischen Geschichte vom Mittelalter bis in die Gegenwart* (Paderborn, 2010), chap. 6.

72. Bentovin, *Torguiushchiia telom*, 103, 150; V. Tr-ov, "Nasha ulitsa," *Gazeta-kopeika*, 22 August 1908, 3.

73. Ruadze, *K sudu!* esp. 102–9. On the geography of homosexual "streetscapes" in St. Petersburg, see also Dan Healey, *Homosexual Desire in Revolutionary Russia: The Regulation of Sexual and Gender Dissent* (Chicago, 2001), chap. 1. See also the discussion of Mikhail Kuzmin's mappings of the homosexual street by Ulla Hakanen, "Panoramas from Above and Street from Below: The Petersburg of Viacheslav Ivanov and Mikhail Kuzmin," in *Petersburg/Petersburg: Novel and City, 1900–1921*, ed. Olga Matich (Madison, 2010), 208–11.

74. These are common phrases found in many of the sources cited in this section.

75. For example, Frant s Plutalovoi, "V 'kafe' (gm!) na Nevskom," *Malen'kaia gazeta*, 5 October 1914, 4 (and other installments of this regular feuilleton).

76. *Novye peterburgskie trushchoby: ocherki stolichnoi zhizni* (St. Petersburg, 1909–10), 41–42.

77. Quotations from A. Damanskaia, "Nevskii prospekt v dni voiny," *Argus* 1916, no. 3 [no month]: 27; Graf Amori [I. P. Rapgof], *Tainy Nevskogo prospekta* (Petrograd, 1915), 3.

78. "Nagoi chelovek on Ligovke," *Peterburgskii listok*, 29 November 1908, 4.

79. For example, *Gazeta-Kopeika*, 2 June 1912, 3 (Nevskii and Sadovaia).

80. "Feericheskii razgrom 'Venskogo shika'," *Peterburgskii listok*, 28 May 1913, 5; ibid., 19 March 1909, 6.

81. K. Barantsevich, "Fiziologiia Peterburga (Nabroski karandashem): Briukho, Mozg, Serdtsa," *Zhizn' dlia vsekh* 1909, no. 12 (December): 94–99 (Briukho).

82. *Peterburgskii listok*, 20 March 1909, 5.

83. "Nravy Nevskogo prospekta," *Gazeta-kopeika*, 2 April 1910, 5.

84. Zabavnik, "Peterburgskii slovar'," ibid., 28 February 1909, 4.

85. The comparative literature is large, but see especially Walkowitz, *City of Dreadful Delight* and Wilson, *The Sphinx in the City.*

86. Kniag. O. Bebutova, "Brillianty (roman iz sovremennoi peterburgskoi zhizni)," *Peterburgskii listok*, 3 January 1914, 2.

87. See the regular fashion reports in Argus in 1914 ("Damskaia stranichka").

88. Ol'ga Gridina, "Mest' krasoty," *Gazeta-kopeika*, 23 November 1909, 2–3.

89. V. Nedesheva, *Nevskii prospekt* (St. Petersburg, 1906), 3–11. The author, Vera Ivanovna Nedesheva (meaning Faith Not-Cheap daughter of Ivan, one tends to think this is a nom de plume), was the author of a number of literary works and essays (*ocherki*), as well as a public lecturer, on matters of women, morality, and family. See also A. Damanskaia, "Nevskii prospekt v dni voiny," *Argus* 1916, no. 3 [no month]: 27. For a social and cultural history of fashion in Russia, see Christine Ruane, *The Empire's New Clothes: A History of the Russian Fashion Industry, 1700–1917* (New Haven, 2009).

90. For a history of the Neva river as a public space, see Randall Dills, "The River Neva and the Imperial Façade: Culture and Environment in Nineteenth-Century St. Petersburg, Russia" (Ph. D. diss., University of Illinois, 2010).

91. Mikh. Dubrovskii, "Nevskie piraty," *Argus* 1913, no. 9 (September): 69–79.

92. *Gazeta-kopeika*, 7 July 1909, 3.

93. Joachim Schlör, *Nights in the Big City: Paris, Berlin, London, 1840–1930* (London, 1998). See also Craig Koslofsky, *Evening's Empire: A History of the Night in Early Modern Europe* (Cambridge, 2011). On the night in Russian popular entertainment culture, see Louise McReynolds, *Russia at Play: Leisure Activities at the End of the Tsarist Era* (Ithaca, 2003), chaps. 6–7, and Sylvester, *Tales of Old Odessa*, chap. 4.

94. Poe, "The Man of the Crowd," 268.

95. Nikitin, *Peterburg noch'iu*, 3; V. Vegenov, "V gorode i v glushe," *Gazeta-kopeika*, 20 February 1909, 3; Iurii Angarov, "Nevskii vecherom," *Novye peterburgskie trushchoby*, 23.

96. Vadim, " 'Gaida, troika!' " *Gazeta-kopeika*, 7 March 1913, 3–4.

97. Pchela, "Den' za den'," *Peterburgskii listok*, 14 May 1907, 2.

98. Kavaler Foblaz, "Nevskii vo mrake," *Gazeta-kopeika*, 10 June 1910, 3. See also "Poboishche na Nevskom," *Peterburgskii listok*, 13 July 1910, 4.

99. *Peterburgskii listok*, 3 January 1910, 6; ibid., 19 May 1913, 11; *Malen'kaia gazeta*, 28 November 1914, 3.

100. For example, "Nash demi-mond," supplement to the journal *Shut*, 1911, no. 5.

101. *Malen'kaia gazeta*, 16 December 1915, 2.

102. See, for example, Nikitin, *Peterburg noch'iu* [1903]; *Peterburg noch'iu*, supplement to the journal *Shut*, 1911, no. 3 (12 November 1911); Amori, *Tainy Nevskogo prospekta*; Kolia Nespiashchii [i.e. Nick the Unsleeping], "Petrograd noch'iu (iz al'boma prazdnoshataiushchagosia cheloveka)," *Malen'kaia gazeta*, 10 December 1914, 4.

103. Zabavnik, "Peterburgskaia noch'," *Gazeta-kopeika*, 22 March 1909, 3.

104. Schwartz, *Spectacular Realities*, 16.

105. M. Men'shikov, "Pis'ma k blizhnim," *Novoe vremia*, 8 March 1909, 4. See also *Gazeta-kopeika*, 19 June 1909, 1.

106. Skitalets, "Konets spletnika," *Gazeta-kopeika*, 12 October 1911, 4–5.

107. O. Gridina, "Zerkalo ne vinovato," ibid., 31 October 1910, 3.

108. V. Posse, "Obshchestvennaia zhizn'," *Zhizn' dlia vsekh* 1910, no. 7 (July): 139.

109. Benjamin, *The Arcades Project*, 102–3, 108–9. See also Susan Buck-Morss, *The Dialectics of Seeing: Walter Benjamin and the Arcades Project* (Cambridge, Mass., 1989), 95–96.

110. V. Vegenov, "V gorode i v glushe," *Gazeta-kopeika*, 20 February 1909, 3.

111. "Peterburgskaia khronika: mostovaia reforma," *Gorodskoe delo* 1913, no. 13–14 (1–15 July): 960; ibid., 1911, no. 9 (1 May): 788–89; ibid., 1912, no. 1 (1 January): 5–18. On street surfaces as a source of noise and smell, see V. V. Lapin, *Peterburg: Zapakhi i zvuki* (St. Petersburg, 2007), 49–53.

112. K-n, " 'Venteriushniki': nravy stolichnykh okrain," *Gazeta-kopeika*, 31 August 1909, 3.

113. Khronos, "O zeleni i gul'iane," *Gazeta-kopeika*, 29 April 1913, 3.

114. K. V. Karaffa-Korbut, "Nochlezhnye doma v bol'shikh russkikh gorodakh," *Gorodskoe delo* 1912, no. 10 (15 May): 627–28.

115. "Peterburgskie trushchoby," *Peterburgskii listok*, 15 February 1914, 3.

116. Skitalets, "Ministry goroda," *Gazeta-kopeika*, 5 April 1910, 3.

117. "Stolichnye ved'my," *Malen'kaia gazeta*, 30 July 1915, 3.

118. "Stolichnye ved'my," *Malen'kaia gazeta*, 7 August 1915, 4.

119. *Peterburg noch'iu*, supplement to the journal *Shut, 1911*, no. 3 (12 November 1911): n.p.

120. S. Kondurushkin, "Pritony sna (perepiska nochlezhnikov)," *Peterburgskii listok*, 12 September 1910, 3.

121. Nedesheva, *Nevskii prospekt*, 3, 4, 7.

122. N. Valentinov, "Gorod i gorozhane," *Novyi zhurnal dlia vsekh* 1910, no. 20 (June): 93.

123. A. Petrov, "Istoriia kazhdogo dnia," *Gazeta-kopeika*, 19 August 1909, 3.

124. K-n, " 'Venteriushniki': nravy stolichnykh okrain," ibid., 31 August 1909, 3.

125. Chechenets, "Pesnia rabov," *Rabochii po metallu*, no. 22 (10 October 1907): 3; N. R-tskii, "Chego zhaleet ego?" *Edinstvo*, no. 8 (10 August 1909): 3; A. Buiko, "Na shakhtakh," *Metallist* 1913, no. 4/28 (3 July): 4–5; A. Dikii, "V rabochei slobodke," *Nash put'*, no. 13 (10 February 1911): 4; S. Obradovich, "Na zavode," *Rabochii den'*, no. 8 (11 June 1912): 1. See also Mark D. Steinberg, *Proletarian Imagination: Self, Modernity, and the Sacred in Russia, 1910–1925* (Cornell, 2002), chap. 4.

126. See D. Zasosov and V. Pyzin, *Povsednevnaia zhizn' Peterburga na rubezhe XIX–XX vekov* (Moscow, 2003), 53–65.

127. Lapin, *Peterburg*, 155–68.

128. "Kinematograf: v tramvae," *Gazeta-kopeika*, 9 October 1909, 3.

129. P. Druzhinin, "V tramvae (s natury)," ibid., 23 March 1909, 3; "Panika v vagone tramvaia," *Peterburgskii listok*, 11 September 1910, 4.

130. Zabavnik, "Letnyi slovar'," *Gazeta-kopeika*, 14 June 1911, 3.

131. Skitalets, "Koshmary ulitsy," ibid., 6 April 1913, 3.

132. D-r D. Nikol'skii, "K voprosu o neschastnykh sluchaiakh na gorodskikh rel'sovykh putiakh pri konnoi, parovoi i elektricheskoi tiage," *Gorodskoe delo*, 1909, no. 7 (25 March): 303–7. See also Skitalets, "Bez viny i bez suda," *Gazeta-kopeika*, 6 October 1909, 3; D. Nikol'skii, "Samoubiistvo i tramvai," *Rech'*, 12 July 1910, 3; *Peterburgskii listok*, 19 September 1910, 3.

133. *Peterburgskii listok*, 23 April 1909, 6.

134. On automobiles and their drivers, see Bova, "Nasha ulitsa," ibid., 5 September 1910, 5; "Ulichnyi skandal iz-za motora," ibid., 11 May 1913, 5.

135. R. D. Timenchik, "K simvolike tramvaia v russkoi poezii," *Uchenye zapiski Tartuskogo gosudarstvennogo universiteta*, no. 754: *Simvol v sisteme kul'ture* (Tartu, 1987), 135–43; Alyson Tapp, "'The Streetcar Prattle of Life': Reading and Writing St. Petersburg's Trams," in ed. Matich, *Petersburg/Petersburg*, 123–48.

136. On the meanings of fire in Russian culture before 1905, especially in the village, see Cathy A. Frierson, *All Russia Is Burning! A Cultural History of Fire and Arson in Late Imperial Russia* (Seattle, 2002).

137. *Khronika pozharov* was the title of an irregular column in *Peterburgskii listok* throughout these years.

138. For example, "'Krasnyi petukh' za Nevskoe zastava," ibid., 3 July 1910, 3; "Krasnyi petukh," ibid., 4 September 1910, 1.

139. Sergei Solomin, "Obshchestvennye prestuplenie," *Gazeta-kopeika*, 16 September 1909, 3; *Peterburgskii listok*, 27 August 1910, 2; "Novaia katastrofa s pod"emnoi mashinoi," ibid., 17 July 1910, 2.

140. Ibid., 9 April 1909, 6; 11 May 1909, 3; 6 January 1910, 7; 13 April 1910, 3; 3 September 1910, 4; *Peterburgskaia gazeta*, 6 January 1910, 5.

141. *Peterburgskaia gazeta*, 7 January 1910.

142. "Iz-za kometa," *Peterburgskii listok*, 7 May 1910, 4.

143. Ser'eznyi gid, "Vyvesochnaia vakkhanaliia v S.-Peterburge," *Peterburgskii gid*, no. 6 (December 1912): 1; E. Baumgarten, "Torzhestvo reklamy," *Gorodskoe delo* 1909, no. 4 (15 February): 35–38. See also Zasosov and Pyzin, *Povsednevnaia zhizn' Peterburga*, 43.

144. "Grandioznaia oblava na khuliganov i bezdomnikov," *Peterburgskii listok*, 17 September 1910, 2.

145. For example, "Omut zhizni: obyknovennaia istoriia," *Gazeta-kopeika*, 6 July 1908, 2–3, and "Torgovlia 'zhivym tovarom' v Peterburg," *Peterburgskii listok*, 3 March 1910, 4 (illegal and deceitful brothels); ibid., 15 March 1909, 6 (gambling dens); ibid., 5 March 1913, 4 (criminal hide-outs); *Peterburgskii listok*, 21 May 1913, 2 (veselyi priton); Ruadze, *K sudu!* 6–7, 14–15, 17–19 (homosexual dens).

146. "Arest peshchernykh obitatelei stolitsy," *Peterburgskii listok*, 5 March 1913, 4.

147. Klubmen, "Klubnaia vakhanaliia," ibid., 25 July 1910, 3; "Igornyi priton v kvartire shansonetnoi pevitsy," ibid., 19 September 1910, 6. Both *Peterburgskii listok* and *Gazeta-kopeika* regularly reported raids on illegal gambling parlors, usually in private apartments or businesses after hours. For example, *Peterburgskii listok*, 19 May 1913, 11.

148. Sangvinik, "Pritony azarta i razvrata," *Peterburgskii listok*, 15 April 1910, 5. See also "Novyi zakon o klubakh," ibid., 27 May 1910. 3.

149. Sledovatel', "'Krasnyi fonar' i narodnaia nravstvennost'," *Malen'kaia gazeta*, 28 November 1914, 3.

150. Ruadze, *K sudu!* 102.

151. N. Borovskii, "Peterburg nashikh dnei," *Peterburgskii gid*, no. 7 (December 1912): 3.

152. For example, "Nash demi-mond," supplement to the journal *Shut*, 1911, no. 5.

153. Angarov, "Kvisisana," *Novye peterburgskie trushchoby*, 11–17.

154. P.Z., "Ogarki," *Gazeta-kopeika*, 20 November 1908, 3.

155. *Malen'kaia gazeta*, 12 August 1915, 3.

156. Iurii Alianskii, *Veseliashchiisia Peterburg (Po materialam sobraniia G. A. Ivanova)*, 6 vols. (St. Petersburg, 1992–2002) 1:74, 76–77, 79, 82–82 (citing and quoting articles in *Obozrenie teatrov* of 1907 and 1911, and *Birzhevye vedomosti* from 1909).

157. P. Iuzhnyi, "Liudi v triko," *Argus* 1913, no. 2 (February): 104–5. On men's public and critical "gaze" at women, see also Nikitin, *Peterburg noch'iu*, 99.

158. For example, "Omut zhizni," *Gazeta-kopeika*, 11 July 1908, 3; O. Gridina, "Zverinye nravy," ibid., 14 May 1910, 3.

159. "Del'tsy temniago Peterburga," *Peterburgskii listok*, 20 August 1910, 4.

160. Skitalets, "Shkola razvrata," *Gazeta-kopeika*, 20 January 1913, 3.

161. Frant s Plutalovoi, "'Kafe' na Nevskom," *Malen'kaia gazeta*, 21 September 1914, 4.

162. Kavaler Foblaz, "Peterburzhets veselitsia," *Gazeta-kopeika*, 4 August 1909, 3.

163. "Teatr i zrelishcha," *Gazeta-kopeika*, 19 June 1908, 5; Sergei Auslender, "Narodnyi Dom Grafini Paniny," *Apollon 1910*, no. 4 (January): 76. See also E. Anthony Swift, *Popular Theater and Society in Tsarist Russia* (Berkeley, 2002), e.g. 235–36.

164. Vadim, "'Gaida, troika!'" *Gazeta-kopeika*, 7 March 1913, 3–4. Two famous murders were linked to the Skating Rink. See Chapter 4.

165. Skitalets in *Gazeta-kopeika*, 25 November 1909, 3; Denise Youngblood, *The Magic Mirror: Moviemaking in Russia, 1908–1919* (Madison, 1999), 8–10. See also N. A. Lebedev, *Ocherk istorii kino SSSR*, vol. 1 (Moscow, 1947); and S. Ginzburg, *Kinomatografiia dorevoliutsionnoi Rossii* (Moscow, 1963).

166. L. Kleinbort, "Kinematograf," *Novyi zhurnal dlia vsekh* 1912, no. 6 (June): 99–101. See also see Yuri Tsivian, *Early Cinema in Russia and Its Cultural Reception*, trans. Alan Bodger (London, 1994), 24–30. On the contemporary "association [of cinema] more with urban culture than with art," see also Robert Bird (Berd in the Russian), "Russkii simvolizm i razvitie kinoestetike," *Novoe literaturnoe obozrenie* 81 (2006) at *http://magazines.russ.ru/nlo/2006/81/be6.html* (accessed December 2009).

167. G. Tsyperovich, "Kinematograf," *Sovremennyi mir* 1912, no. 1 (January): 181–82.

168. L. M. "Epokha sinematografa," *Novyi zhurnal dlia vsekh* 1913, no. 12 (December): 131.

169. Skitalets, "Sinematograf," *Gazeta-kopeika*, 25 October 1909, 4.

170. Genrikh Tastevin, *Futurizm (na puti k novomy simvolizmu)* (Moscow, 1914), 7–8.

171. For example, "Kinematograf: v tramvae," *Gazeta-kopeika*, 9 October 1909, 3. Skitalets did the same in "Sinematograf," ibid., 25 October 1909, 4 (and he may have been the author).

172. *Stolichnyi kinematograf*, 6 June 1911–17 January 1912.

173. B. Shaposhnikov, "Futurizm i teatr," *Maski*, no. 7–8 (1912–13): 29–30.

174. Maksimilian Voloshin, Andrei Belyi, and others quoted in Robert Berd (Robert Bird), "Russkii simvolizm i razvitie kinoestetiki: nasledie Viach. Ivanova u A. Bakshi i Adr. Piotrovskogo," *Novoe literaturnoe obozrenie* 81 (2006): 67–98.

175. K. Chukovskii, *Nat Pinkerton i sovremennaia literatura* (a pamphlet published in two editions, in 1908 and 1910), reprinted in *Sobranie sochinenii v shesti*

tomakh, 6 vols. (Moscow, 1965–69), 6:126–27; I. Brusilovskii, "Smysl' zhizni," *Sovremennoe slovo*, 13 March 1910, 1.

176. Especially Schwartz, *Spectacular Realities*, introduction and chap. 5.

177. Skitalets in *Gazeta-kopeika*, 25 November 1909, 3.

178. *Peterburgskii kinematograf*, no. 1 (5 January 1911): izd. 1, 2.

179. Leonid Andreev, "Pis'ma o teatre," *Maski*, no. *3* ([1912]–1913): *3–4*. It was reported that one now found more students in the cinema than at the Public Library, Skitalets, "Deti vremeni," *Gazeta-kopeika*, 7 December 1913, *3–4*.

180. Skitalets in *Gazeta-kopeika*, 25 November 1909, 3.

181. L. Kleinbort, "Kinematograf," *Novyi zhurnal dlia vsekh* 1912, no. 6 (June): 99–103.

182. *Peterburgskii kinematograph*, no. 1 (5 January 1911): izd. 1, 2.

183. Simmel, "The Metropolis and Mental Life," 410.

184. Benjamin, *The Arcades Project*, esp. 40, 43, 54, 60, 71, 207, 246, 277, 281, 433, 448, 901, 911 (final quote). See also Benjamin's essay "On Some Motifs in Baudelaire," in *Illuminations*, ed. Hannah Arendt (New York, 1968), esp. 191–94; and Buck-Morss, *The Dialectics of Seeing*, esp. chaps. 4–5.

185. See, for example, Hal Foster, ed., *Vision and Visuality* (New York, 1988); Martin Jay, *Downcast Eyes: The Denigration of Vision in Twentieth-Century French Thought* (Berkeley, 1993); Leo Chaney and Vanessa R. Schwartz, *Cinema and the Invention of Modern Life* (Berkeley, 1995), esp. introduction and chap. 3 (Ben Singer, "Modernity, Hyperstimulus, and the Rise of Popular Sensationalism"); Schwartz, *Spectacular Realities*; Jonathan Crary, *Suspensions of Perception: Attention, Spectacle, and Modern Culture* (Cambridge, Mass., 2000). See also, more eccentrically but provocatively, Georges Bataille, *Visions of Excess: Selected Writings, 1927–1939*, ed. Allan Stoekl (Minneapolis, 1985); Guy Debord, *La Société du spectacle* (Paris, 1967); Jean Baudrillard, *Simulacra and Simulation* [1985], trans. Sheila Faria Glaser (Ann Arbor, 1994); Umberto Eco, *Travels in Hyperreality*, trans. William Weaver (San Diego, 1986).

186. V. Novitskii, "Zver'—v chelovek," *Peterburgskaia gazeta*, 6 April 1909, 1.

187. William Miller, *The Anatomy of Disgust* (Cambridge, Mass., 1997); Jonathan Dollimore, *Sexual Disgust: Homosexuality and Psychoanalysis* (Chicago, 2001); Sianne Ngai, *Ugly Feelings* (Cambridge, Mass., 2005), 332–54. See also essays on disgust by Olga Matich and Adi Kuntsman, in *Slavic Review* 68, no. 2 (Summer 2009): 284–328.

CHAPTER THREE. MASKS

1. A similar public preoccupation with the significance of everyday urban masquerade and imposture—indeed many similar stories, reminding us that this

is an urban phenomenon in no way distinct to St. Petersburg—is discussed by Roshanna Sylvester in *Tales of Old Odessa: Crime and Civility in a City of Thieves* (Dekalb, 2005). For an examination of Soviet-era imposture and confidence games (*samozvanshchina* and *aferi*) and their relationship to "making selves" and the uncertainties of public life—though more focused, given the different historical moment, on reinventing the social self in the wake of revolution—see Sheila Fitzpatrick, "Making a Self for the Times: Impersonation and Imposture in 20th-Century Russia," *Kritika* 2, no. 3 (Summer 2001): 469–87; Fitzpatrick, "The World of Ostap Bender: Soviet Confidence Men in the Stalin Period," *Slavic Review* 61, no. 3 (Fall 2002): 535–57; Fitzpatrick, *Tear off the Masks: Identity and Imposture in Twentieth-Century Russia* (Princeton, 2005).

2. Efrat Tseëlon, ed., *Masquerade and Identities: Essays on Gender, Sexuality, and Marginality* (London, 2001), quotation 3; Terry Castle, *Masquerade and Civilization: The Carnivalesque in Eighteenth-Century English Culture and Fiction* (Stanford, 1986).

3. Charles Baudelaire, *The Parisian Prowler: Le Spleen de Paris. Petits Poèmes en prose*, 2d ed. (Athens and London, 1997), 21 ("Crowds").

4. Thomas Seifrid, "'Illusion' and Its Workings in Modern Russian Culture," *Slavic and East European Journal* 45, no. 2 (Summer 2001): esp. 213–14; Colleen McQuillen, "The Russian Modernist Masquerade: Deception, Rhetoric, and Theatrical Transposition" (Ph.D. diss., Columbia University, 2006); Olga Soboleva, *The Silver Mask: Harlequinade in the Symbolist Poetry of Blok and Bely* (Bern, 2008).

5. Reports in *Obozrenie teatrov* cited in Iurii Alianskii, *Veseliashchiisia Peterburg (Po materialam sobraniia G. A. Ivanova)*, 6 vols. (St. Petersburg, 1992–2002) 1:76–77, 80.

6. For example, *Ogonek* 1913, no. 2 (13/26 January): n.p.

7. *Ogonek* 1910, no. 10 (6/19 March): n.p.; *Listok-kopeika* no. 171 (February 1913): 2; *Peterburgskii listok*, 5 January 1913, 4, and 7 January 1914, 2.

8. From various reports on masquerades in the press (see citations above and below) and from photographs of masquerades in the Central State Archive of Film, Photographic, and Sound Documents of St. Petersburg. For example, E-8702, E-10231, E-13186. See also McQuillen, "The Russian Modernist Masquerade," chap. 1.

9. *Khoroshii ton: sbornik pravil i sovetov*, 5th ed. (St. Petersburg, 1910), 248. Although the book was regularly if only slightly revised, this observation was unchanged from the original edition (St. Petersburg, 1881), 348.

10. N. V. Nikitin, *Peterburg noch'iu: bytovye ocherki* (St. Petersburg, 1903), 120.

11. Ibid., 118–21. About masks focusing attention on a woman's body, see also, in a humorous vein, *Listok-kopeika*, no. 171 (February 1913): 2.

12. *Ogonek* 1913, no. 41 (13 October): n.p.

13. See especially his drawings, evidently worked on between 1908 and 1918, for *Le livre de la marquise* (St. Petersburg, 1918). See Edward Kasinec and Robert H. Davis, Jr., "A Note on Konstantin Somov's Erotic Book Illustration," in *Eros i pornografiia v russkoi kul'tury*, ed. M. Levitt and A. Toporkov (Moscow, 1999), 338-95.

14. *Peterburgskii listok*, 7 January 1914, 2.

15. "V maskarade," *Listok-kopeika*, no. 4 (December 1909): 2.

16. *Gazeta-kopeika*, 29 November 1909, 4.

17. Castle, *Masquerade and Civilization*, 111, 114-16.

18. Leonid Andreev, *Chernye maski* (1907), in *P'esy* (Moscow, 1991).

19. *Birzhevye vedomosti*, vechernyi vypusk, 3 December 1908; *Birzhevye vedomosti*, vtoroe izdanie, 5 December 1908.

20. V. Burenin, "Kriticheskie ocherki," *Novoe vremia*, 11 December 1909, 4.

21. Katerina Clark, *Petersburg, Crucible of Revolution* (Cambridge, Mass., 1995), esp. 95-96.

22. See McQuillen, "The Russian Modernist Masquerade," 111-28, 166-70; Cameron Wiggins, "The Enchanted Masquerade: Alexander Blok's *The Puppet Show* from the Stage to the Streets," in *Petersburg/Petersburg: Novel and City, 1900-1921*, ed. Olga Matich (Madison, 2010), 174-193.

23. For an excellent discussion of this production in its cultural setting, see Clark, *Petersburg*, chap. 3. See also the discussions of the theme of the mask in Lermontov's play by Harriet Murav in *Russia's Legal Fictions* (Ann Arbor, 1998), 25-26; and Elizabeth Cheresh Allen, "Unmasking Lermontov's 'Masquerade': Romanticism as Ideology," *Slavic and East European Journal* 46, no. 1 (Spring 2002): 75-97.

24. Mikhail Lermontov, *Maskarad* (1835), from M. Iu. Lermontov, *Polnoe sobranie stikhotvorenii*, 2 vols. (Leningrad, 1989), vol. 1. Quotations from Act 1, Scene 1; Act 2, Scene 4; Act 3, Scene 2; Act 4, Scene 1 (414, 480, 493, 507). See also Allen, "Unmasking Lermontov's 'Masquerade'," esp. 79, 86.

25. On the popularity of wrestling in these years, and its significance as public "spectacle" focusing on the body, see Louise McReynolds, *Russia at Play: Leisure Activities at the End of the Tsarist Era* (Ithaca, 2003), 90-92, 131-43. She also briefly discusses a wrestler known as "Red Mask" on 143.

26. The power masks give in a different type of combat was emphasized in an article called "War in Masks," which described the frightening appearance of British soldiers in their large white gas masks. *Petrogradskii listok*, 20 December 1915, 3.

27. *Peterburgskii listok*, 3 April 1909, 5 (quote); *Gazeta-kopeika*, 1 April 1909, 9. When finally defeated, he removed his mask and revealed that his name was Shneider (possibly the Estonian Aleksandr Shneider, see I. V. Lebedev, *Bortsy* [Petrograd,

1917], 8). For other masked wrestlers, see ibid., 2 (the author, widely known as Diadia [uncle] Vania, claimed to have invented the idea of wrestling in a black mask),
and the articles on a wrestler in a blue mask in *Malen'kaia gazeta*, 1 July 1915, 1;
2 July 1915, 4; 4 July 1915; 5 July 1915, 4; 15 July 1915, 4; 16 July 1915, 4. On the
same subject, in 1913 a silent film appeared, produced by the Vita film studio, called
Wrestler in a Black Mask, with a script by Nikolai Breshko-Breshkovskii and starring
the aforementioned Lebedev. See Ven. E. Vishnevskii, "Khudozhestvennye fil'my
dorevoliutsionnoi Rossii: filmograficheskie opisanie (Moscow, 1945), 25; and Jay
Leyda, *Kino: A History of the Russian and Soviet Film* (New York, 1960): 62.

    28. *Peterburgskii listok*, 3 April 1909, 5.

    29. See ibid., 22 December 1907, 5; 18 October 1908, 4; 5 April 1909, 6; *Rech'*,
18 March 1908, 4; *Gazeta-kopeika*, 11 May 1910, 3, and 31 December 1911, 4.

    30. *Peterburgskii listok*, 31 March 1909, 4; *Gazeta-kopeika*, 1 April 1909, 2.
When finally captured, the leader turned out to be a Georgian-born telegraph official at the St. Petersburg station of the Nikolaevskii Railroad, named Anton Iodze.
He claimed to have developed the idea of the mask from reading books about famous bandits.

    31. Tan, "Chernye maski," *Zaprosy zhizni* 1911, no. 1 (5 October): 62.

    32. Andrei Belyi, *Peterburg* (St. Petersburg, 2004—a revised reprint of the So-
viet Academy of Science's 1981 edition, which was based on the first edition of the
novel, printed in three installments in St. Petersburg in 1913 and 1914).

    33. See especially Fedor Sologub, *Petty Demon* (1902) and Aleksandr Blok,
"Balaganchik" (1906) and "Snow Mask" (1907). And see discussions in McQuillen, "The Russian Modernist Masquerade" and Soboleva, *The Silver Mask*.

    34. For masks in Belyi's early writings, see his "Prishedshii: otryvok is nenapisan-
noi misterii," *Severnye tsvety* 3 (1903), 3-4, 7-8, 25; "Maska," *Vesy* 1 (1904), no. 6:
6-15; "Apokalipsis v russkoi poezii" (1905) in *Lug zelenyi: kniga statei* (Moscow,
1910), 222-47; "Maskarad" (1908), "Prazdnik" (1906), and "V Letnom sadu"
(1908) in *Pepel* (St. Petersburg, 1909), 123-26, 130-31, 148-49. See also Roger Keys,
*The Reluctant Modernist: Andrei Belyi and the Development of Russian Fiction,
1902-1914* (Oxford, 1996), 107-9; McQuillen, "The Russian Modernist Masquerade," 92-93; Soboleva, *The Silver Mask*, passim. It is telling that Belyi's final novel
was called *Masks* (*Maski*, 1932), and is filled with images of urban chaos, madness,
and mute and faceless figures. See John Elsworth, "*Moscow* and *Masks*," in *Andrei
Bely: Spirit of Symbolism*, ed. Robert Maguire and John Malmstad (Ithaca, 1987),
chap. 5. On Belyi's autobiographical relation to masks, see his *Mezhdu dvukh revo-
liutsii* (Moscow, 1990), 85, 286, and "Vospominaniia o Bloke," *Epopeia* 3 [Mos-
cow and Berlin, 1922], 187.

    35. For example, Belyi, *Peterburg*, 46, 54-59, 156-59, 167.

36. Ibid., 262. This is how Maguire and Malmstad translate *vse to—da ne to.* See Andrei Bely, *Petersburg,* translated, annotated, and introduced by Robert E. Maguire and John E. Malmstad (Bloomington, 1978), 183.

37. Belyi, *Peterburg,* 56.

38. For scholarly discussions of *Petersburg* that explore these questions of reality, illusion, knowledge, and masquerade, see studies, cited in Chapter 1, notes 85–88, by Vladimir Alexandrov, Peter Barta, Anna Lisa Crone and Jennifer Day, Leonid Dolgopolov, J. D. Elsworth, Roger Keys, Timothy Langen, Colleen McQuillen, Olga Matich, and Robert Maguire and John Malmstad. The quotation is from Timothy Langen, *The Stony Dance: Unity and Gesture in Andrei Bely's "Petersburg"* (Evanston, 2005), 64.

39. Clark, *Petersburg,* 98. See Anna Akhmatova, "Poema bez geroia" (1940–62), much of it set in Petersburg in 1913. In her "The Russian Modernist Masquerade," Colleen McQuillen insightfully discusses the trope of the mask in this poem.

40. See Meyerhold's New Year's toast in *Ogonek* 1913, no. 1 (6/19 June): n.p.

41. See Chapter 1; V. N. Toporov, *Peterburgskii tekst russkoi literatury: izbrannye trudy* (St. Petersburg, 2003), passim.

42. See, for example, Vsevolod Kozhevnikov, "Gorod," *Sovremennyi mir* 1911, no. 3 (March): 60–62; Kozhevnikov, "Ulitsa," ibid., 1912, no. 8 (August); L. M. Vasilevskii, "Maski," ibid., 1909, no. 5 (May): 182.

43. In *Tales of Old Odessa,* Roshanna Sylvester examines this category, which was also central to newspaper accounts of street masquerades in Odessa, and its cultural meanings.

44. Skitalets, "Mopsik i Piliulia," *Gazeta-kopeika,* 14 June 1910, 3.

45. Graf Amori [I. P. Rapgof], *Kavalery Shneider: roman-byl iz obshchestvennoi zhizni Petrograda* (St. Petersburg, n.d. [1915]), 3.

46. "Del'tsy temnogo Peterburga," *Peterburgskii listok,* 20 August 1910, 4.

47. *Novye peterburgskie trushchoby: ocherki stolichnoi zhizni* (St. Petersburg, 1909–10), 1–11.

48. "Del'tsy temnogo Peterburga," *Peterburgskii listok,* 20 August 1910, 4.

49. I. V. Lebedev (Diadia Vania), "Birzhi zhenskoi zhizni," *Malen'kaia gazeta,* 3 November 1914, 2; Klubmen, "Klubnaia vakkhanaliia," *Peterburgskii listok,* 25 July 1910, 3; *Novye peterburgskie trushchoby,* 17–22.

50. *Malen'kaia gazeta,* 22 December 1915, 3.

51. *Peterburgskii listok,* 6 January 1910, 4.

52. Ibid., 16 January 1910, 4. For a similar case—with, on this occasion, the man claiming to be a count—see "Peterburgskie shakaly," *Gazeta-kopeika,* 1 September 1909, 3.

53. *Peterburgskii listok,* 24 October 1908, 4.

54. Aborigen, *Krovavye letopisi Peterburga: prestupnyi mir i bor'ba s nim* (St. Petersburg, 1914), 5.

55. *Peterburgskii listok*, 2 June 1913, 3.

56. For example, ibid., 18 March 1909, 4.

57. Ibid., 2 January 1905, 4.

58. Ibid., 1 May 1909, 4.

59. Ibid., 6 March 1909, 4.

60. For example, "Nishchie-bogachi," *Gazeta-kopeika*, 26 March 1909, 2; "Nishchii simuliant," *Peterburgskii listok*, 29 January 1913, 4; ibid., 25 November 1908, 5; *Nishchenstvo i bor'ba s nim* (St. Petersburg, 1913), 58–59, 73, 75.

61. Nikitin, *Peterburg noch'iu*, 191–92. The problem of false beggars had a long history. See also Hubertus Jahn, *Armes Rußland: Bettler and Notleidende in der russischen Geschichte vom Mittelalter bis in die Gegenwart* (Paderborn, 2010), chap. 6.

62. *Peterburgskii listok*, 6 March 1909, 4.

63. For example, *Gazeta-kopeika*, 11 June 1911, 3; *Peterburgskii listok*, 16 May 1913, 15.

64. "Moshennichestvo XX-go veka," *Gazeta-kopeika*, 11 November 1911, 4; 12 November 1911, 3.

65. *Gazeta-kopeika*, 17 October 1909, 3.

66. Skitalets, "Kto nam nuzhen," ibid., 3 October 1909, 2–3.

67. *Peterburgskii listok*, 8 April 1909, 4.

68. Ibid., 11 May 1907, 4.

69. *Gazeta-kopeika*, 19 August 1908, 3.

70. P. Z. "Na udochku" (Swallowing the Bait), *Gazeta-kopeika*, 15 January 1909, 3. This article also describes a common bait-and-switch that targeted poor priests with a find of gold coins.

71. *Peterburgskii listok*, 13 April 1909, 4. See also ibid., 22 November 1908, 4.

72. Ibid., 26 November 1908, 4; 5 December 1908, 4.

73. *Gazeta-kopeika*, 13 July 1908, 2.

74. For example, ibid., 22 October 1911, 3; *Peterburgskii listok*, 12 January 1910, 5; 13 January 1910, 5.

75. *Malen'kaia gazeta*, 14 August 1915, 3. For other performative uses of suicide, see *Gazeta-kopeika*, 24 August 1908, 2–3; *Peterburgskii listok*, 18 September 1910, 3.

76. "Mnimye samoubiistva," *Gazeta-kopeika*, 25 November 1909, 3; 28 April 1912, 3.

77. Ol'ga Gridina, "Bezmozglye," ibid., 11 June 1911, 3.

78. For instance, *Peterburgskii listok*, 29 January 1910, 4; 1 February 1910, 4.

79. For example, in addition to the cases cited below, *Peterburgskii listok*, 21 October 1908, 5; 17 November 1908, 4; 6 December 1908, 4; 12 April 1909, 7; 19 April 1909, 8; 8 January 1910, 4; 5 March 1910, 62; 27 August 1910, 4; 5 May 1913, 10; 29 May 1913, 5; *Gazeta-kopeika*, 27 August 1908, 3; 13 November 1908, 2; 7 December 1908, 2; *Rech'*, 11 April 1908, 3.

80. *Peterburgskii listok*, 24 March 1910, 4. This article concentrates on one particular practice: the misuse of military uniforms.

81. Ibid., 7 February 1913, 13.

82. Ibid., 18 December 1915, 5.

83. Ibid., 8 January 1910, 4. For similar cases, see ibid., 19 April 1909, 8, and *Gazeta-kopeika*, 27 August 1908, 3.

84. *Peterburgskii listok*, 1 February 1910, 4 (also ibid., 21 June 1908, 3, and *Aborigen, Krovavye letopisi Peterburga*, 13); *Gazeta-kopeika*, 30 October 1908, 3; *Malen'kaia gazeta*, 1 August 1915, 4; *Gazeta-kopeika*, 30 March 1911, 3.

85. "Lovkii moshennik," *Peterburgskii listok*, 9 September 1910, 4. For another example of a telephone scam, ibid., 16 December 1915, 4.

86. *Malen'kaia gazeta*, 1 August 1915, 4.

87. "Massovoe poiavlenie samozvantsev," *Peterburgskii listok*, 24 March 1910, 4.

88. Ibid., 12 March 1910, 3.

89. Ibid., 8 March 1914, 4.

90. Ibid., 17 November 1908, 4.

91. Ibid., 3 December 1908, 5. For a "prince" who worked his scam on the railroad, see ibid., 5 March 1910, 3. For a sham "Princess Obolenskaia," ibid., March 1914, 4.

92. *Gazeta-kopeika*, 11 April 1912, 1, 3-4.

93. "Brachnye aferisty v Peterburge," *Peterburgskii listok*, 30 January 1913, 3. For a related case of a fraudulent matchmaking business, which included a sham lawyer, see ibid., 26 January 1910, 5.

94. *Malen'kaia gazeta*, 2 July 1915, 3.

95. *Gazeta-kopeika*, 28 June 1908, 3.

96. *Peterburgskii listok*, 8 January 1910, 4. For a similar case, see *Gazeta-kopeika*, 1 September 1911, 3.

97. *Peterburgskii listok*, 7 June 1913, 4.

98. It was also a concern for some Jewish writers who worried that too often Jews deliberately kept their identities hidden by writing under a pseudonym and by speaking of Jews as "they" instead of "we." See the letter of V. Zhabotinskii in *Svobodnye mysli*, 24 March 1908, 2. See also Harriet Murav, *Identity Theft: the Jew in Imperial Russia and the Case of Avraam Uri Kovner* (Stanford, 2003).

99. *Peterburgskii listok*, 13 March 1909, 8.

100. Ibid., 12 April 1909, 7.

101. Ibid., 15 June 1910, 4.

102. Graf Amori [I. P. Rapgof], *Tainy Nevskogo prospekta* (Petrograd, 1915), 3-4.

103. *Novye peterburgskie trushchoby*, 27; Nikitin, *Peterburg noch'iu*, 3, 7, 41, 50; Iv. Lukash, "Nevskii prospekt," *Sovremennoe slovo*, 4/17 April 1918, 2.

104. Maria Volgina, "Okhota na detei," *Gazeta-kopeika*, 14 August 1913, 3.

105. *Gazeta-kopeika*, 6 July 1908, 2-3; *Peterburgskii listok*, 15 February 1913, 3.

106. G. "Iz tain 'veselogo Peterburga'," *Peterburgskii listok*, 9 May 1910, 5.

107. "Torgovlia 'zhivym tovarom' v Peterburge," ibid., 3 March 1910, 4.

108. *Gorodskoe delo*, 1910, no. 2 (15 January): 116-17.

109. See Sylvester, *Tales of Old Odessa*, 94-95, for a discussion of *khipesnichestvo* in Odessa.

110. *Gazeta-kopeika*, 11 July 1908, 3.

111. For example, ibid., 19 December 1908, 3; 5 August 1911, 3.

112. Aborigen, *Krovavye letopis' Peterburga*, 24-28; *Gazeta-kopeika*, 22 July and 25 July 1913, 3-4. See also *Peterburgskii listok*, 19 February 1914, 5.

113. Nikitin, *Peterburg noch'iu*, 55; *Peterburg noch'iu*, supplement to the journal *Shut*, 1911, no. 3.

114. *Novye peterburgskie trushchoby*, 25.

115. Dr. B. Bentovin, *Torguiushchie telom: ocherki sovremennoi prostitutsii*, 3d ed. (St. Petersburg, 1910), 150-53.

116. Nikitin, *Peterburg noch'iu*, 120.

117. *Gazeta-kopeika*, 2 April 1909, 3; *Malen'kaia gazeta*, 2 July 1915, 4.

118. Judith Butler, *Gender Trouble: Feminism and the Subversion of Identity* (New York, 1990), especially 60-73, 204 n. 18.

119. See, for example, Central State Archive of Film, Photographic, and Sound Documents of St. Petersburg, G-12429, G-12431, G-12442 (1910-14).

120. McReynolds, *Russia at Play*, 150-52, 220, 280.

121. Olga Matich, *Erotic Utopia: The Decadent Imagination in Russia's Fin de Siècle* (Madison, 2005), esp. 171-79. See also *Apollon* 1910, no. 5 (February): 18.

122. *Gazeta-kopeika*, 24 March 1911, 3; 5 April 1911, 2-3.

123. *Listok-kopeika*, no. 8 (January 1910): 2.

124. This article focused on a famous case in England. "Zhenshchina-Mushchina," *Peterburgskii listok*, 21 August 1910, 2.

125. Ibid., 16 January 1913, 4.

126. V. P. Ruadze, *K sudu!... Gomoseksual'nyi Peterburg* (St. Petersburg, 1908), 14-15.

NOTES TO PAGES 110-113

127. Ibid., 113. For an excellent discussion of the homosexual subculture in St. Petersburg, see Dan Healey, *Homosexual Desire in Revolutionary Russia* (Chicago, 2001), 29–49.

128. Kn. O. B-va, "Ch'ia zhertva," *Peterburgskii listok*, 24 March 1909, 1; 26 March 1909, 2; 27 March 1909, 2; 15 April 1909, 2; 17 April 1909, 1.

129. G. Tsyperovich, "Fal'sifikatsiia i surrogat," *Sovremennyi mir* 1912, no. 1 (July): 147–81 (quotations from 175–78).

130. F. Belorus and N. Rozanov, *Tovarishch Peterburzhtsa* (St. Petersburg, 1910), 6; D. Protopopov, "Sud'ba russkikh gorodov," *Gorodskoe delo* 1911, no. 24 (15 December): 1712–13.

131. See Chapter 1.

132. D. Merezhkovskii, "Peterburgu byt' pustu," *Rech'*, 21 December 1908, 2. The passage is quoted from *Brothers Karamazov* book 5, chap. 2 ("Smerdiakov with a Guitar"). See also N. Ustrialov, "Sud'ba Peterburga," *Nakanune* [Berlin] 1918, no. 4 (2 April/25 March): 5–6; and *Peterburg kak fenomen kul'tury: sbornik statei* (St. Petersburg, 1994), 123–24.

133. Vladimir Kirillov, "Gorod," *Stikhotvoreniia 1914–1918* (St. Petersburg [*sic*], 1918), 26. See also M. Liberson, *Stradanie odinochestva* (St. Petersburg, 1909), 30. Julia Kristeva, echoing Benjamin, Baudelaire, and Poe, observed that we wear masks to hide our "interior distance" from others even in the "midst of the crowd." Julia Kristeva, *Strangers to Ourselves* (New York, 1991), 5, 27.

134. N. Liublin, "O Petrograde: stikhi: vecherom," *Novyi zhurnal dlia vsekh* 1916, no. 2–3 (February–March): 59.

135. Amori, *Tainy Nevskogo prospekta*, 3–4 (he uses the terms *fata morgana* and *samoobman*). See also 128 on city life as performance.

136. Mikhail Bonch-Tomashevskii, *Kniga o tango: iskusstvo i seksual'nost'* (Moscow, 1914), 21.

137. Kaled, "Ivanushkovtsy," *Sanktpeterburgskie vedomosti*, 9 (22) December 1910, 2.

138. Ol'ga Gridina, "Gorod-obmanshchik," *Gazeta-kopeika*, 24 December 1913, 3.

139. G. Tsyperovich, "Fal'sifikatsiia i surrogat," *Sovremennyi mir* 1912, no. 1 (July): 147–81 (quotations from 175–78).

140. Boris Frommett, "Fal'sifikatsie i bor'ba s neiu," *Sovremennik* 1914, no. 3 (February): 90–98; "Fal'sifikatsia medikamentov," *Vesna* 1910, no. 47–48: 246; *Peterburgskii listok*, 6 July 1910, 3. See also *Petrogradskii listok*, 18 December 1915, 5.

141. *Gazeta-kopeika*, 3 June 1908, 3; 5 September 1908, 3; *Vesna* 1910, no. 47–48: 246; Frommett, "Fal'sifikatsie i bor'ba s neiu," *Sovremennik* 1914, no. 3 (February): 95.

142. "Zhertvy reklamy," *Gazeta-kopeika*, 1 September 1911, 3. See also *Gazeta-kopeika*, 3 June 1908, 3.

143. "Malen'kii fel'eton: Azef ot nauki," *Novoe vremia*, 23 December 1909, 4; ibid., 8 May 1909, 4.

144. L. Kleinbort, "Kinematograf," *Novyi zhurnal dlia vsekh* 1912, no. 6 (June): 105.

145. Novator, "Muchenitsy 'krasoty'," *Gazeta-kopeika*, 23 January 1912, 3–4. See also "Zhenshchina v spal'ne," supplement to the journal *Shut*, 1911, no. 1, n.p.

146. V. Rozanov, "Literaturnye simulianty," *Novoe vremia*, 11 January 1909, 4.

147. "Pod maskoi religii (arest ioannitov)," *Gazeta-kopeika*, 23 April 1909, 2.

148. *Tserkovnyi vestnik* 1910, no. 11 (18 March): 333–34.

149. *Peterburgskii listok*, 17 March 1914, 3.

150. *Tserkovnyi vestnik* 1910, no. 22 (3 June): 667.

151. Professor A. Bronzov, "Spiritizm—zlo," ibid., 1910, no. 15–16 (15 April): 469–74; Skitalets, "Khiromanty," *Gazeta-kopeika*, 12 December 1911, 3–4; Vikt. G-llo, "U khiromanta: ocherk Peterburga," *Peterburgskii kinematograf*, 8 January 1911, 2; "Vo vlasti koldun'i-tsyganka," *Peterburgskii listok*, 6 March 1913, 4.

152. Boris Frommett, "Fal'sifikatsie i bor'ba s neiu," *Sovremennik* 1914, no. 3 (February): 90.

153. *Gazeta-kopeika*, 13 July 1908, 2.

154. Ol'ga Gridina, "Vrany," ibid., 7 January 1910, 3.

155. Skitalets, "Adskie zhmurki," ibid., 10 February 1910, 4.

156. Leonid Galich, "Mysli," *Rech'*, 8 June 1907, 1–2.

157. This theme pervades Benjamin's work, notably Walter Benjamin, *The Arcades Project*, trans. Howard Eiland and Kevin McLaughlin (Cambridge, Mass., 1999). The quotation is from the conclusion of his 1939 "Exposé," ibid., 26. See also the discussions in Susan Buck-Morss, *The Dialectics of Seeing: Walter Benjamin and the Arcades Project* (Cambridge, Mass., 1989), esp. chaps. 4 and 8 (e.g. pages 81, 92); and Graeme Gilloch, *Myth and Metropolis: Walter Benjamin and the City* (Cambridge, 1996), e.g. 149. As Buck-Morss notes (81), Benjamin was influenced by Marx's use of the term "phantasmagoria" to refer to "the deceptive appearance of commodities as 'festishes' in the marketplace." Also pertinent are Baudrillard's arguments about the simulacrum. Jean Baudrillard, *Simulacra and Simulation* (Ann Arbor, 1994). For an erudite and insightful exploration of the centrality of "illusion" as an obsessive theme in modern Russian literature, see Seifrid, "'Illusion' and Its Workings in Modern Russian Culture."

158. On melodrama in Russian culture, including its "trafficking in secrets," see Louise McReynolds and Joan Neuberger, eds., *Imitations of Life: Two Centuries of Melodrama in Russia* (Durham, N.C., 2002).

159. *Peterburgskii listok*, 1 June 1913, 1.

160. Amori, *Kavalery Shneider*, 4, and *Tainy Nevskogo prospekta*, 4.

161. Ruadze, *K sudu!* 114.

162. Amori, *Tainy Nevskogo prospekta*, 4.

163. Ibid.

164. I. Davidson, "Sila illiuzii," *Novyi zhurnal dlia vsekh* 1912, no. 7 (July): 93.

165. Walter Benjamin, *Das Passagen-Werk*, ed. Rolf Tiedemann, 2 vols. (Frankfurt am Main, 1982), 2:1217 (a different English translation is given in Benjamin, *The Arcades Project*, 911). Such an argument, of course, has been developed by a number of philosophers of the modern and postmodern. For an influential early example, see Friedrich Nietzsche, *The Gay Science* (1882), trans. Walter Kaufmann (New York, 1974), e.g. 116 (book 1, section 54).

CHAPTER FOUR. DEATH

1. Skitalets, "Ozverenie," *Gazeta-kopeika*, 16 January 1913, 3.

2. See, especially, Jonathan Dollimore, *Death, Desire and Loss in Western Culture* (London, 1998).

3. *Predvaritel'nyi svod statisticheskikh dannykh po g. S-Peterburgu za 1909 god* (St. Petersburg. n.d. [1910?]), 31; *Statisticheskii spravochnik po Petrogradu* (Petrograd, 1918), 27; N., "Kak khvoraet i umiraet stolitsa," *Gorodskoe delo* 1909, no. 11 (1 June): 544–47.

4. For London see the *Annual Reports of the Registrar-General of Birth, Deaths, and Marriages in England* (London: 1849, 1867, 1878). For Paris, see Louis Chevalier, *Labouring Classes and Dangerous Classes in Paris During the First Half of the Nineteenth Century* (London, 1973), 327.

5. "Smertnost' v Peterburge," *Gazeta-kopeika*, 1 June 1909, 3; A. Zarubin, "Statisticheskii Peterburg," *Peterburg i ego zhizn'* (St. Petersburg, 1909), 298–300.

6. L. A. Vilikhov, "Munitsipial'noe obozrenie: sravnitel'naia smertnost' gorodskogo i sel'skogo naseleniia Rossii," *Gorodskoe delo* 1911, no. 13–14 (1 July): 1045–47; Zakh. Frenkel', Narodnoe zdorov'e v gorodakh Rossii po poslednim ofitsial'nym dannym," *Gorodskoe delo* 1910, no. 5 (15 February): 275–82.

7. Vl. Budorovskii, "Detskaia smertnost' v Rossii i bor'ba s nim," *Tserkovnyi vestnik* 1908, no. 3 (17 January): 76–80; Zarubin, "Statisticheskii Peterburg," 298–300.

8. Vasilii Rozanov, "Vechnaia tema," *Novoe vremia*, 4 January 1908, 3; "Eshche o vechnoi teme," ibid., 22 February 1908, 4–5.

9. *Peterburgskii listok*, 17 November 1905, 4.

10. *Malen'kaia gazeta*, 3 August 1915, 3.

11. "Zagadochnoe ubiistvo na Peterburgskoi storonoi," *Peterburgskii listok*, 22 September 1910, 5; *Malen'kaia gazeta*, 28 December 1915, 3; "Tainstvennaia gibel'

zhenshchiny," *Petrogradskii listok*, 28 December 1915, 4; "Taina smerti," *Petrogradskaia gazeta*, 28 December 1915, 5.

12. *Peterburgskii listok*, 1 September 1910, 4; ibid., 1 June 1913, 4; 2 June 1913, 4; "Neobychainoe ubiistvo," ibid., 1 June 1913, 4.

13. "Zagodochnyi trup v improvizirovannyi nochlezhke," ibid., 27 November 1908, 4. See also ibid., 19 April 1909, 3.

14. Ibid., 4 June 1913; 4–5; "Tainstvennoe ubiistvo na Obvodnom kanale," ibid., 18 August 1910, 2; ibid., 4 June 1913, 4.

15. "Morg v Peterburge," ibid., 8 September 1910, 4.

16. *Rech'*, 21 September 1907, 4; 8 March 1908, 3; 27 April 1908, 4; 2 October 1908, 5; *Peterburgskii listok*, 6 May 1909, 4; Vadim, "Kto karat'?" *Gazeta-kopeika*, 12 July 1913, 3; *Malen'kaia gazeta*, 4 July 1915, 3.

17. *Gazeta-kopeika*, 17 September 1908, 3.

18. I. V. Lebedev (Diadia Vania), "Mat'," *Malen'kaia gazeta*, 24 August 1914, 1.

19. N., "Kak khvoraet i umiraet stolitsa," *Gorodskoe delo* 1909, no. 11 (1 June): 545.

20. M. Men'shikov, "Stolitsa smerti," *Novoe vremia*, 2 July 1909, 2.

21. *Predvaritel'nyi svod statisticheskikh dannykh po g. S-Peterburgu za 1909 god*, 32–34, table 6; *Kratkii svod statisticheskikh dannykh po g. Petrograda za 1913–1914 gg.* (Petrograd, n.d [1915?]), table 7; *Statisticheskii spravochnik po Petrogradu* (Petrograd, 1918), 27; Zarubin, "Statisticheskii Peterburg," 299.

22. Skitalets, "Starye slova," *Gazeta-kopeika*, 28 December 1910, 3–4; *Vesna* 1910, no. 1, 2.

23. *Predvaritel'nyi svod statisticheskikh dannykh po g. S-Peterburgu za 1909 god*, 32.

24. Ibid., 38.

25. "V zashchitu rabochikh i publiki," *Novoe vremia*, 19 June 1909, 2.

26. This list based on many news reports in *Gazeta-kopeika*, *Peterburgskii listok*, and *Novoe vremia*.

27. *Peterburgskii listok*, 27 May 1913, 4.

28. *Gazeta-kopeika*, 19 June 1908, 2.

29. For some typical uses of the term, see "Nozhevshchina," *Gazeta-kopeika*, 6 April 1910, 7; "Nozhevshchina," *Peterburgskii listok*, 6 April 1910, 7; "Podvigi nozhevshchikov," ibid., 30 August 1910, 5.

30. "Liudi-zveri," *Peterburgskii listok*, 13 May 1907, 4.

31. Ibid., 22 October 1908, 3.

32. Ibid., 20 April 1909, 4; 9 May 1910, 5; 27 May 1913, 4; "Troinoe ubiistvo," ibid., 14 January 1913, 3; ibid., 13 January 1910, 5; "Ubiistvo v pritone azarta," ibid., 17 September 1910, 3; "Krovavaia drama na Ligovke," ibid., 29 January 1914, 5.

33. "Grandioznoe buiistvo rabochikh za Nevskoi zastavoi," ibid., 8 June 1910, 4.

34. On street battles, *Gazeta-kopeika*, 2 July 1908, 3; *Peterburgskii listok*, 19 May 1909, 4; 2 August 1910, 4; 17 August 1910, 5; 5 January 1910, 4. On duels, *Gazeta-kopeika*, 24 June 1908, 1; 26 June 1908, 1.

35. For example, "Zhestokoe istiazanie rebenka," *Peterburgskii listok*, 11 March 1910, 6; *Novoe vremia*, 6 July 1909, 2.

36. *Gazeta-kopeika*, 2 July 1908, 3; *Peterburgskii listok*, 9 April 1909, 6; 4 February 1910, 5; 10 February, 1910, 5; 8 August 1910, 7; Skitalets, "Ochen' prosto," *Gazeta-kopeika*, 1 April 1913, 3.

37. *Gazeta-kopeika*, 26 June 1908, 2.

38. "Krovavyi piknik," *Peterburgskii listok*, 22 May 1913, 4.

39. For example, ibid., 17 January 1910, 8; "Drama v kofeinoi," 5 March 1910, 4; Skitalets, "Opasnoe pokhmel'e," *Gazeta-kopeika*, 16 November 1910, 5–6; "Tragicheskaia final flirta na katke," *Peterburgskii listok*, 22 February 1913, 6; M. Slobozhanin, "Iz sovremennikh perezhivanii," *Zhizn' dlia vsekh* 1913, no. 2 (February): *313*.

40. See Alexandra Oberländer, "Shame and Modern Subjectivities: The Rape of Elizaveta Cheremnova," in *Interpreting Emotion in Russia and Eastern Europe*, ed. Mark D. Steinberg and Valeria Sobol (DeKalb, 2011); and her "Die Provokation ging auf dem Nevskij spazieren: Die Wahrnehmung sexueller Gewalt im ausgehenden Zarenreich, 1880–1914." (Ph.D. diss., Humboldt University, Berlin, 2010).

41. *Gazeta-kopeika*, 22 July 1908, 2; 7 March 1909, 3; 9 August 1908, 2–3; 28 September 1908, 2; 24 March 1909, 5; 27 June 1910, 4; 21 August 1911, 4; 31 July 1913, 3; *Peterburgskii listok*, 9 August 1910, 3; 4 January 1913, 4; 25 January 1913, 4.

42. Skitalets, "Prestuplenie i nakazanie," *Gazeta-kopeika*, 9 July 1910, 3.

43. D., "Polovaia vakkhanaliia," ibid., 27 July 1909, 3.

44. D. Zhbankov, "Polovaia prestupnost'," *Sovremennyi mir* 1909, no. 7 (July): 69.

45. Ibid., 54; S. Liubosh, "Griaznaia volna," *Sovremennoe slovo*, 7 April 1910, 1; O. Gridina, "Zerkalo ne vinovato," *Gazeta-kopeika*, 31 October 1910, 3.

46. Zhbankov, "Polovaia prestupnost'," *Sovremennyi mir* 1909, no. 7 (July): 88–89.

47. *Peterburgskii listok*, 21 January 1913, 3; *Gazeta-kopeika*, 2 June 1913, 4.

48. Based on the newspapers *Gazeta-kopeika*, *Peterburgskii listok*, *Novoe vremia*, *and Rech'*. See also Aborigen, *Krovavye letopisi Peterburga: prestupnyi mir i bor'ba s nim* (St. Petersburg, 1914). See also Louise McReynolds, "Ubiistvo v gorode: narrativy urbanizma," in *Kul'tury gorodov rossiiskoi imperii na rubezhe XIX–XX vekov*, ed. Boris Kolonitskii and Mark Steinberg (St. Petersburg, 2009), and her forthcoming book on murder and modernity in Russia.

49. For example, "Zverskoe ubiistvo," *Gazeta-kopeika*, 8 October 1909, 3; "Chtoby chuvstvovala," *Malen'kaia gazeta*, 8 November 1914, 3.

50. For example, *Gazeta-kopeika*, 5–9, 16, 17, 26 October 1909; "Zagadochnoe prestuplenie," *Vesna* 1909, no. 40–43 (4–25 October): 272.

51. "Dzhek-potroshitel'," *Gazeta-kopeika*, 18 September 1909, 3; 19 September 1909, 3; 21 September 1909, 3; 22 September 1909, 3; "Sud'ba 'Vadima-Krovianika'," *Peterburgskii listok*, 5 June 1910, 2.

52. N., "Kak khvoraet i umiraet stolitsa," *Gorodskoe delo* 1909, no. 11 (1 June): 544–47.

53. S. Arnova, "Samoubiistvo v proshlom i nastoiashchem," *Zhizn' dlia vsekh* 1911, no. 3–4 (March–April): 476.

54. D. Zhbankov, "Itogi travmaticheskoi epidemii za noiabr'–dekabr' 1909 g.," *Novoe vremia*, 14 January 1910, 2; Zhbankov, "Sovremennye samoubiistva," *Sovremennyi mir* 1910, no. 3 (March): 40–41; Zhbankov, "Polovaia prestupnost'," ibid., 1909, no. 7 (July): 54, 69.

55. Skitalets, "Ozverenie," *Gazeta-kopeika*, 16 January 1913, 3; N. V., "Itogi minuvshago goda," *Vesna* 1908, no. 1 (6 January): 1.

56. Mikh. Al. Engel'gardt, "Bez vykhoda," *Svobodnye mysli*, 7 January 1908, 1.

57. For example, Lev Pushchin, "Kak zhit'," *Novyi zhurnal dlia vsekh* 1912, no. 5 (May): 81; N. Gumilev, "Pis'mo o russkoi poezii," *Apollon* 1914, no. 5 (May): 36.

58. V. G. Tan (Bogoraz), review of Sologub in *Svobodnye mysli*, 17/30 December 1907, 2; G. Plekhanov, "Iskusstvo i obshchestvennaia zhizn'," *Sovremennik* 1913, no. 1 (January): 142; Ivanov-Razumnik, "Literatura i obshchestvennost'," *Zavety* 1913, no. 10 (October): 119–22.

59. P. Pertsov, "Literaturnye pis'ma," *Novoe vremia*, 7 January 1909, 4. See also V. L'vov-Rogachevskii, "Simvolisty i nasledniki ikh," *Sovremennik* 1913, no. 6 (June): 267.

60. For example, Olga Matich, *Erotic Utopia: The Decadent Imagination in Russia's Fin de Siècle* (Madison, 2005).

61. V. L'vov-Rogachevskii, "M. Artsybashev," *Sovremennyi mir* 1909, no. 11 (November): pt. 2, 34.

62. Filaret Chernov, "Mertvyi son," *Zhizn' dlia vsekh* 1916, no. 4–5 (April-May): 502; N., "Raba goroda," *Malen'kaia gazeta*, 23 July 1915, 4. I discuss these themes in working-class poetry in my *Proletarian Imagination: Self, Modernity, and the Sacred in Russia, 1910–1925* (Ithaca, 2002), esp. 164–69.

63. V. Novitskii, "Zver'—v chelovek," *Peterburgskaia gazeta*, 6 April 1909, 1. See also N. Shigaleev, "Ne dovernulsia," *Gazeta-kopeika*, 6 August 1911, 3.

64. Zhbankov, "Sovremennye samoubiistva," *Sovremennyi mir* 1910, no. 3 (March), 40–41, 52, and "Polovaia prestupnost'," ibid., 1909, no. 7 (July): 54, 63.

65. Numerous articles on both street violence and murder were headlined in these ways.

66. For example, "Zagadochnoe prestuplenie," *Vesna* 1909, no. 40–43 (4–25 October): 272.

67. R. Blank, "1909-yi g.," *Zaprosy zhizni* 1909, no. 11 (29 December): 1–2.

68. A. S. Izgoev, "Literaturno-obshchestvennyi dnevnik: tri palacha," *Rech'*, 8 August 1910, 2.

69. Tan, "Chernye maski," *Zaprosy zhizni* 1911, no. 1 (5 October): 60–61.

70. N. Evreinov, "Sentimental'naia progulka (instsena 'teatra dlia sebia')," *Novyi zhurnal dlia vsekh* 1916, no. 2–3 (February-March): 53. Among the many newspaper accounts and arguments that provided Evreinov his real-life sources, see Vadim, "Taina Obvodnogo kanala," *Gazeta-kopeika*, 2 June 1913, 3–4; Gridina, "Gorod-obmanshchik," ibid., 24 December 1913, 3.

71. N. Shigaleev, "Uzhasy goroda," *Gazeta-kopeika*, 29 April 1912, 5.

72. Skitalets, "Ministry goroda," ibid., 5 April 1910, 3.

73. Borei, "Malen'kie zametki," *Novoe vremia*, 3 April 1910, 13.

74. M. Gran, "Peterburg i kholera," *Gorodskoe delo* 1909, no. 5 (1 March): 187–93 (quotation about city administration, 190); "Kholera u vorot," *Gazeta-kopeika*, 29 July 1908, 2 (quotation about the poor); M. Men'shikov, "Stolitsa smerti," *Novoe vremia*, 2 July 1909, 2; N. N., "Kholera i gorod," *Peterburgskii listok*, 14 July 1910, 2; N. Snesarev, "Kladbishche S.-Peterburgskoi gorodskoi dumy 1908–09 gg.," *Novoe vremia*, 15 July 1909, 3; Levas, "Epidemii," *Zhizn' dlia vsekh* 1911, no. 7 (July): 933–39.

75. Dobrik, "Iubilei," *Gazeta-kopeika*, 9 July 1910, 3–4.

76. Dr. V. Kashkadomov, "Dym gorodov, vrednoe deistvoe ego i bor'ba s nim," *Gorodskoe delo* 1912, no. 1 (January): 5–18; "Peterburgskaia khronika," ibid., 1913, no. 13–14 (1–15 June): 60.

77. Skitalets, "Bez viny i bez suda," *Gazeta-kopeika*, 6 October 1909, 3.

78. Skitalets, "Krugovaia poruka," ibid., 12 June 1910, 3.

79. Aborigen, *Krovavye letopisi Peterburga*, 43.

80. Professor A. Bronzov, "Progress-li?" *Tserkovnyi vestnik* 1912, no. 1 (5 January): 4–9.

81. "Peterburgskii omut," *Ogonek* 1913, no. 11 (17/30 March): n.p.; "Zagadochnoe ubiistvo na Kirochnoi ulitse," *Peterburgskii listok*, 15 January 1913, 3; Skitalets, "Chelovek umer," *Gazeta-kopeika*, 8 February 1913, 3; "Raskrytii ubiistva Time," *Peterburgskii listok*, 8 February 1913, 3; ibid., 5 March 1913, 3; Vadim, "Delo o ubiistve Time," *Gazeta-kopeika*, 29 May 1913, 3; Aborigen, *Krovavye letopisi Peterburga*, 65–68.

312 NOTES TO PAGES 130-131

82. Skitalets, "Plokhoi matematik," *Gazeta-kopeika*, 17 October 1909, 3; Skitalets, "Chelovek umer," ibid., 8 February 1913, 3; Vadim, "Koshmarnoe delo," ibid., 26 May 1913, 3–4.

83. In addition to examples below, notes 84–93, see also Skitalets, "Krugovaia poruka," ibid., 12 June 1910, 3; Nikolai Engel'gardt, "Mysli i kartinki," *Novoe vremia*, 20 July 1910, 3; Stepan Filenkin, "Koshmary zhizni," *Gazeta-kopeika*, 29 July 1911, 3; Al. Fedorov, "V shume zhizni," *Peterburgskii kinematograf*, 12 January 1911, 2.

84. "Liudi-zveri," *Peterburgskii listok*, 13 May 1907, 4; V. Novitskii, "Zver'— v chelovek," *Peterburgskaia gazeta*, 6 April 1909, 1; "Liudi-zvery," *Peterburgskii listok*, 2 May 1909, 3; "Liudi-zveri," *Gazeta-kopeika*, 2 January 1909, 3; "Dikie nravy," *Peterburgskii listok*, 7 November 1908, 3; N. Shigaleev, "Ne dovernulsia." *Gazeta-kopeika*, 6 August 1911, 3. "Nravstvennaia razrukha sovremennogo obshchestva," *Tserkovnyi vestnik* 1914, no. 7 (13 February): 205.

85. Ol'ga Gridina, "Vse khuzhe," *Gazeta-kopeika*, 10 December 1909, 4.

86. Ol'ga Gridina, "Za cheloveka strashno," ibid., 30 December 1911, 4–5.

87. V. Trofimov, "'Zhestoki u nas nravy' . . . ," ibid., 4 April 1909, 3; "Zverskoe ubiistvo," ibid., 5 October 1909, 3; V. Posse, "Zhestokost'," *Vesna* 1909, no. 11 (15 March): 83–85.

88. Zhbankov, "Polovaia prestupnost'," *Sovremennyi mir* 1909, no. 7 (July): 88–89; Obozrevatel', "Sovremennyi vampir," *Peterburgskii listok*, 19 May 1909, 2.

89. P. Z. "Na temy dnia," *Gazeta-kopeika*, 7 October 1909, 3; "Ob Lombrozo," ibid., 8 October 1909, 3. For discussion of the views of scientific professionals, including their own tendency toward social explanation, see Daniel Beer, *Renovating Russia: The Human Sciences and the Fate of Liberal Modernity, 1880–1930* (Ithaca, 2008), 103–14.

90. Skitalets, "Ozverenie," *Gazeta-kopeika*, 16 January 1913, 3.

91. Sakmarov, "Samoe uzhasnoe," ibid., 12 September 1909, 3.

92. Nikolai Engel'gardt, "Mysli i kartinki," *Novoe vremia*, 20 July 1910, 3.

93. Aborigen, *Krovavye letopisi Peterburga*, 43; N. Shchigaleev, "Zhizn' ili smert'?" *Gazeta-kopeika*, 3 June 1912, 5.

94. In recent scholarship, "moral numbness" has been seen to result from major traumatic experiences like the Holocaust, the Vietnam war, or the AIDs epidemic. See, for example, Carolyn Dean, *The Fragility of Empathy After the Holocaust* (Ithaca, 2004). It seems clear, though, that it can result from an environment of what might be called everyday catastrophe such as was felt to pervade the troubled public life of a city like St. Petersburg.

95. Smarad Gornostaev, "Geroi nashego vremeni," *Gazeta-kopeika*, 29 May 1909, 3.

96. Ol'ga Gridina, "Zhestokye nravy," ibid., 30 March 1912, 3.

97. A. Sakmarov, "Samoe uzhasnoe," ibid., 12 September 1909, 3.

98. Skitalets, "Pochemu on ubil?" ibid., 21 October 1909, 3.

99. Dukh Banko [The Ghost of Banquo], "Prodaetsia Bezsmertie," *Svobodnye mysli*, 20 August/2 September 1907, 1; *Gazeta-kopeika*, 19 October 1909, 3; Vas. Nemirovich-Danchenko, "Zhizn' deshevo! (ocherki epidemii otchaianiia)," *Zaprosy zhizni* 1910, no. 10 (7 March): 581-90; Stepan Filenkin, "Deshevaia zhizn'," *Gazeta-kopeika*, 23 August 1911, 3.

100. A. Sakmarov, "Samoe uzhasnoe," *Gazeta-kopeika*, 12 September 1909, 3.

101. N. Podol'skii, "Zhizn'—kopeika," ibid., 17 November 1909, 3.

102. D. Zhbankov, "Sovremennye samoubiistva," *Sovremennyi mir* 1910, no. 3 (March): 40.

103. Zhbankov, "Polovaia prestupnost'," ibid., 1909, no. 7 (July): 54-55.

104. Vladimir Mikhnevich, *Iazvy Peterburga: opyt istoriko-statisticheskogo issledovaniia nravstvennosti stolichnogo naseleniia* (St. Petersburg, 1886), 206-7, 222.

105. Beer, *Renovating Russia*, esp. chap. 2.

106. Ol'ga Gridina, "Za cheloveka strashno," *Gazeta-kopeika*, 30 December 1911, 4-5; Skitalets, "Ochen' prosto," ibid., 1 April 1913, 3.

107. For other discussions of suicide in Russia in these years, see Susan Morrissey, "Suicide and Civilization in Late Imperial Russia," *Jahrbücher für Geschichte Osteuropas* 43 (1995): 201-17; Morrissey, *Suicide and the Body Politic in Imperial Russia* (Cambridge, 2006), chaps. 10-11; Irina Paperno, *Suicide as a Cultural Institution in Dostoevsky's Russia* (Ithaca, 1997), 94-104, 109-10, 121-22, 158-59; and Kenneth Pinnow, *Lost to the Collective: Suicide and the Promise of Soviet Socialism, 1921-1929* (Ithaca, 2010), 25-42.

108. See Paperno, *Suicide as a Cultural Institution*, which focuses on the middle and late nineteenth century and Morrissey, *Suicide and the Body Politic*, which takes the story back to the seventeenth century and forward into the twentieth.

109. Vladimir Vol'skii, "Traurnyi progress," *Sovremennyi mir* 1912, no. 6 (June): 281-96.

110. On statistical work, see notes 117-20 below. Medical meetings: "Samoubiistvo vzroslykh i detei," *Vesna* 1911, no. 23-26: 175; R. L. "Bor'ba s samoubiistvom," *Zaprosy zhizni* 1910, no. 17 (30 April): 19-20. Public lectures: *Peterburgskaia gazeta*, 26 April 1909, 3; *Rech'*, 3 February 1910, 4; *Gazeta-kopeika*, 7 September 1911, 1; *Peterburgskii listok*, 20 January 1913, 5. Civic commissions: *Rech'*, 27 October 1910, 4; *Vesna* 1911, no. 23-26: 175; *Gazeta-kopeika*, 30 January 1912, 1; *Peterburgskii listok*, 19 January 1913, 3. Law proposals: *Gazeta-kopeika*, 5 May 1909, 3 and 6 October 1909, 3.

111. For example, V. Lavretskii, "Tragediia sovremennoi molodezhi," *Vesna* 1910, no. 14-15: 106-7 (originally a series of articles in *Rech'*, 31 March, 22 June, and 30 September 1910); *Peterburgskii listok*, 7 March 1910, 8; *Gazeta-kopeika*,

6 September 1908, 2; 31 October 1908, 3; 3 January 1909, 2; 7 September 1911, 1; *Rech'*, 8 May 1910, 2; Arnova, "Samoubiistvo v proshlom i nastoiashchem," *Zhizn' dlia vsekh* 1911, no. 3-4 (March-April): 478. On the prevalence of the "epidemic" metaphor, both in the late nineteenth century and after 1905, see Paperno, *Suicide as a Cultural Institution*, 3, 45, 75, 95-97.

112. M. P. Artsybashev in "Samoubiistvo (nasha anketa)," *Novoe slovo* 1912, no. 6: 6.

113. B. Iagodin, "Samoubiistvo i bor'ba s nim," *Zhizn' dlia vsekh* 1912, no. 12 (December): 1881.

114. Howard I. Kushner, "Suicide, Gender, and the Fear of Modernity in Nineteenth-Century Medical and Social Thought," *Journal of Social History* 26, no. 3 (Spring 1993): 461-90; Barbara Gates, *Victorian Suicide: Mad Crimes and Sad Histories* (Princeton, 1988), esp. chap. 8.

115. Vadim, "V chem taina," *Gazeta-kopeika*, 14 January 1913, 3; and Vadim, "Dukh zla (po povodu ankety o samoubiistvakh)," ibid., 16 February 1913, 3.

116. On these efforts in the nineteenth century, see Paperno, *Suicide as a Cultural Institution*, 66-73. On the development of "moral statistics" in Europe, see Jack D. Douglas, *The Social Meanings of Suicide* (Princeton, 1967), 7-12.

117. *Predvaritel'nyi svod statisticheskikh dannykh po g. S-Peterburgu za 1909 god.* See also Arnova, "Samoubiistvo v proshlom i nastoiashchem," *Zhizn' dlia vsekh* 1911, no. 3-4 (March-April): 476; *Peterburgskii listok*, 26 April 1909, 3; *Gazeta-kopeika*, 10 August 1913, 3.

118. N. I. Grigor'ev, "Samoubiistvo i pokusheniia na samoubiistvo v Peterburge," *Russkii vrach* 1913, no. 6: 187-89, quoted and discussed, along with other statistics, in L. Slonimskii, "Samoubiistvo s obshchestvennoi i nravstvennoi tochek zreniia," *Vestnik Evropy* 1914, no. 1 (January): 255; and Morrissey, "Suicide and Civilization," 207-8. For other useful discussions of suicide numbers and rates, D. Zhbankov, "Sovremennye samoubiistva," *Sovremennyi mir* 1910, no. 3 (March): 27; G. Gordon, "Sovremennye samoubiistva," *Russkaia mysl'* 1912 (May): 74-75; Vladimir Vol'skii, "Traurnyi progress," *Sovremennyi mir* 1912, no. 6 (June): 287; Arnova, "Samoubiistvo v proshlom i nastoiashchem," *Zhizn' dlia vsekh* 1911, no. 3-4 (March-April): 481. Soviet statisticians also calculated higher rates for imperial St. Petersburg than prerevolutionary government sources. See Pinnow, *Lost to the Collective*, 165.

119. Arnova, "Samoubiistvo v proshlom i nastoiashchem," *Zhizn' dlia vsekh* 1911, no. 3-4 (March-April): 481. See also *Gazeta-kopeika*, 6 April 1911, 1.

120. The Russian national rate was comparatively low, precisely, it was noticed, because this was an urban disease. For contemporary discussions of comparative suicide rates in Russia and Europe, see G. Gordon, "Sovremennye samoubiistva," *Russkaia mysl'* 1912 (May): 74-75; Vladimir Vol'skii, "Traurnyi progress," *Sovre-*

mennyi mir 1912, no. 6 (June): 285–87. See also Walter A. Lunden, "Suicides in France, 1910–43," *American Journal of Sociology*, 52, no. 4 (January 1947): 321–22.

121. G. Gordon, "Sovremennye samoubiistva," *Russkaia mysl'* 1912 (May): 75.

122. For a discussion of discrepancies, see Morrissey, *Suicide and the Body Politic*, 316 n. 17; *Gazeta-kopeika*, 30 March 1912, 2.

123. Zhbankov, "Sovremennye samoubiistva," *Sovremennyi mir* 1910, no. 3 (March): 28; *Gazeta-kopeika*, 30 March 1912, 2; *Gazeta-kopeika*, 3 June 1912, 5; *Vesna* 1911, no. 23–26: 175; *Petrograd po perepesi 15 dekabria 1910 goda* (Petrograd, 1914).

124. G. Gordon, "Samoubiistvo v nashikh tiur'makh," *Rech'*, 7 December 1910, 3.

125. For example, *Zhizn' dlia vsekh* 1910, no. 4 (April): 68; *Tserkovnyi vestnik* 1910, no. 12 (25 March): 362.

126. *Gazeta-kopeika*, 12 March 1910, 3. See also S. V-n, "Zarazitel'nost' prestuplenii," ibid., 1 December 1913, 5.

127. In addition to sources cited in note 128, see Ol'ga Gridina, "Bez rulia," *Gazeta-kopeika*, 11 April 1910, 5; B. Greidenberg, "Samoubiistvo detei," *Rech'*, 21 May 1910, 1; Skitalets, "Nichego osobennogo," *Gazeta-kopeika*, 18 August 1910, 3; Arnova, "Samoubiistvo v proshlom i nastoiashchem," *Zhizn' dlia vsekh* 1911, no. 3–4 (March–April): 478.

128. V. T., "Privykli," *Gazeta-kopeika*, 10 May 1909, 3; *Rech'*, 17 June 1910, 1–2. See also "Samoubiistvo (Nasha anketa)," *Novoe slovo* 1912, no. 6: 4; "V pautine razvrata," *Peterburgskii kinematograf*, 19 March 1911, 2.

129. Lists of the reasons for suicide almost always placed poverty at or near the top. For example, official statistics of St. Petersburg for 1909 ranked poverty as second only to "alcohol abuse," which was often connected to poverty, as the "motive" for suicide—accounting for 23.5 percent (poverty) and 37.7 percent (alcoholism) of all suicides where reasons were known (55 percent of all suicides). *Predvaritel'nyi svod statisticheskikh dannykh po g. S-Peterburgu za 1909 god*, 39.

130. For example, "Iz-za goloda," *Peterburgskii listok*, 4 March 1909, 4.

131. Zhbankov, "Sovremennye samoubiistva," *Sovremennyi mir* 1910, no. 3 (March): 29.

132. *Gazeta-kopeika*, 18 August 1910, 3.

133. G. I. Gordon, "Golodnye samoubiistva," *Zhizn' dlia vsekh* 1912, no. 4 (April): 669–80.

134. Vadim, "Chelovecheskie dokumenty," *Gazeta-kopeika*, 17 February 1913, 4.

135. V. Rozanov, "O samoubiistvakh," in *Samoubiistvo: sbornik obshchestvennykh, filosofskikh i kriticheskikh statei* (Moscow, 1911), 50–51.

136. *Peterburgskii listok*, 6 June 1913, 4; *Gazeta-kopeika*, 21 August 1908, 3.

137. Obyvatel', "Samoubiistvo," *Gazeta-kopeika*, 3 January 1909, 2; D. Zhbankov, "Polovaia prestupnost'," *Sovremennyi mir* 1909, no. 7 (July): 63; Dr. G. Gordon, "Prostitutki i samoubiistvo," *Rech'*, 23 April 1910, 1–2.

138. "Ne vynesli pozora," *Peterburgskii listok*, 7 May 1909, 4. See also V. T., "Privykli," *Gazeta-kopeika*, 10 May 1909, 3; *Peterburgskii listok*, 17 January 1913, 14; "Omut zhizni," *Gazeta-kopeika*, 2 July 1908, 3.

139. *Peterburgskii listok*, 4 January 1913, 4. For another example of suicide following rape, *Gazeta-kopeika*, 6 November 1908, 3.

140. On prostitutes' suicides as both moral suffering and "protest," see Dr. G. Gordon, "Prostitutki i samoubiistvo," *Rech'*, 23 April 1910, 2.

141. "Drama 'rabyn vesel'ia'," *Peterburgskii listok*, 16 November 1908, 7. See also Obyvatel', "Samoubiistvo," *Gazeta-kopeika*, 3 January 1909, 2.

142. "Omut zhizni," ibid., 2 July 1908, 3; *Peterburgskii listok*, 29 December 1908, 4.

143. *Peterburgskii listok*, 16 December 1908, 5; 20 May 1909, 4; 16 March 1909, 4; 16 July 1910, 3; 14 January 1910, 5; *Gazeta-kopeika*, 18 September 1908, 2; 16 October 1908, 3; 16 December 1908, 2.

144. *Gazeta-kopeika*, 21 November 1908, 2; 10 December 1908, 2–3; 24 December 1908, 3; *Peterburgskii listok*, 21 November 1908, 5; 10 December 1908, 4; 15 December 1908, 4; 29 March 1909, 3; *Peterburgskii listok*, 8 January 1910, 4. For elements of religious ritual, ibid., 24 March 1912, 3.

145. "Peterburgskie Romeo i Dzhul'etta," *Peterburgskii listok*, 20 September 1910, 3; "Sovremennoe Romeo i Dzhul'etta," *Peterburgskii listok*, 20 January 1914, 4.

146. Baron Igrok, "Dvoinye samoubiistva," ibid., 19 April 1909, 3. See also ibid., 28 March 1910, 8.

147. *Gazeta-kopeika*, 18 July 1908, 2. See also *Peterburgskii listok*, 24 March 1910, 4.

148. *Peterburgskii listok*, 19 July 1910, 3. Among many similar cases, see *Gazeta-kopeika*, 20 August 1908, 3; 11 October 1908, 3.

149. "Dvoinoe samoubiistvo," *Peterburgskii listok*, 2 March 1910, 5.

150. For example, *Gazeta-kopeika*, 19 November 1908, 1; 28 May 1909, 3; 19 December 1909, 3; *Peterburgskii listok*, 7 December 1908, 5; 19 December 1908, 5; 8 April 1909, 4; 28 April 1910, 4.

151. *Predvaritel'nyi svod statisticheskikh dannykh po g. S-Peterburgu za 1909 god*, 39; For example, Obyvatel', "Samoubiistvo," *Gazeta-kopeika*, 3 January 1909, 2; "Uzhasy zhizni," *Peterburgskii listok*, 18 April 1909, 4.

152. Zhbankov, "Sovremennye samoubiistva," *Sovremennyi mir* 1910, no. 3 (March): 52; G. Gordon, "Samoubiistvo molodezhi i eia nervno-psikhicheskaia neustoichivost'," *Novyi zhurnal dlia vsekh* 1912, no. 9 (September): 105.

153. Episkop Mikhail, "Pobezhdeniia Khristos i 'lunnye murav'i'," in *Samoubi-istvo: sbornik*, 26–29; B. Greidenberg, "Samoubiistvo detei," *Rech'*, 21 May 1910, 1.

154. Gordon, "Samoubiistvo molodezhi i eia nervno-psikhicheskaia neustoichi-vost'," *Novyi zhurnal dlia vsekh* 1912, no. 9 (September): 105 (he dated the begin-ning of the rise in child suicide rates to 1904), "P. Z.," Tragediia detskikh dushi," *Gazeta-kopeika*, 31 October 1908, 3.

155. Zhbankov, "Sovremennye samoubiistva," *Sovremennyi mir* 1910, no. 3 (March): 52–55. See also A. L., "Samoubiistvo uchashchikhsia," *Tserkovnyi vest-nik* 1909, no. 36 (3 September): 1109.

156. *Peterburgskii listok*, 3 April 1909, 4.

157. Zhbankov, "Sovremennye samoubiistva," *Sovremennyi mir* 1910, no. 3 (March): 30. See also "Razval dukha," *Tserkovnyi vestnik* 1911, no. 45 (10 Novem-ber): 1413; Nikol'skii, "Samoubiistvo i tramvai," *Rech'*, 12 July 1910, 3.

158. Zhbankov, "Sovremennye samoubiistva," *Sovremennyi mir* 1910, no. 3 (March): 30.

159. See, for example, *Gazeta-kopeika*, 2 June 1912, 3 (at the very crowded inter-section of Nevskii and Sadovaia); *Peterburgskii listok*, 7 January 1910, 4.

160. From many examples reported in *Gazeta-kopeika*, *Peterburgskii listok*, *Malen'kaia gazeta*, and *Petrogradskaia gazeta* between 1907 and 1915. On the Mariinskii suicide, *see Rech'*, 26 February 1908, 5.

161. *Gazeta-kopeika*, 22 November 1908, 3.

162. *Peterburgskii listok*, 21 January 1914, 4.

163. *Peterburgskii listok*, 4 March 1910, 6; 5 March 1910, 4; 6 March 1910, 4; 9 March 1910, 5; *Gazeta-kopeika*, 4 March 1910, 3; 5 March 1910, 3; *Sovremennoe slovo*, 4 March 1910, 2; 5 March 1910, 3; 6 March 1910, 3; *Rech'*, 4 March 1910, 4; 5 March 1910, 4. See also Morrissey, "Suicide and Civilization," 201–2, 213–17, and *Suicide and the Body Politic*, 340–41. For discussions of the representational power of funerals as street spectacles in Russia, see Thomas Trice, "The 'Body Politic': Russian Funerals and the Politics of Representation, 1841–1921" (Ph.D. diss., Uni-versity of Illinois, 1998).

164. Skitalets, "Adskie zhmurki," *Gazeta-kopeika*, 10 February 1910, 3.

165. *Peterburgskii listok*, 9 March 1910, 5. B. Greidenberg, "Samoubiistvo de-tei," *Rech'*, 21 May 1910, 1.

166. *Gazeta-kopeika*, 3 April 1912, 3. Both columnists for *Gazeta-kopeika*, Ol'ga Gridina and Skitalets, also considered reports of suicide clubs to be false rumors. Ibid., 11 February 1912, 3; 19 February 1912, 4. Police also thought these were claims made only for dramatic "effect." Ibid., 13 November 1913, 3. For reports on foreign suicide clubs—this was presented as an evil to be found in many modern cities—see ibid., 11 May 1909, 3–4; and *Peterburgskii listok*, 12 April 1909, 10. For other evidence and discussion, see G. I. Gordon, "Kluby samoubiits," *Sovremennoe*

slovo, 25 January 1911; *Peterburgskii listok*, 22 February 1914, 4; and Morrissey, *Suicide and the Body Politic*, 341-42.

167. *Malen'kaia gazeta*, 15 December 1915, 2. Of course, many Russians had long known Robert Louis Stevenson's story from 1878 of the same name.

168. I. Brusilovskii, "Smysl' zhizni," *Sovremennoe slovo*, 13 March 1910, 1.

169. "Zhazhda izvestnost'," *Gazeta-kopeika*, 4 September 1911, 5.

170. A. Zorin [Gastev], "Rabochii mir," *Zhizn' dlia vsekh* 1911, no. 8 (August): 1077.

171. Vanessa Schwartz, *Spectacular Realities: Early Mass Culture in Fin-de-Siècle Paris* (Berkeley, 1998), esp. 11-12, 190.

172. Rozanov, "O samoubiistvakh," in *Samoubiistvo: sbornik*, 48.

173. Morrissey, *Suicide and the Body Politic*.

174. I. Brusilovskii, "Trevoga," *Sovremennoe slovo*, 11 March 1910, 1.

175. On early European medical explanations, see Paperno, *Suicide as a Cultural Institution*, 20-22. On Russian studies of suicide as a medical problem, see Morrissey, *Suicide and the Body Politic*, chap. 7. On the persistence of these arguments into the 1920s, see Pinnow, *Lost to the Collective*, chap. 3. On recent science, see J. John Mann, Maria Oquendo, Mark D. Underwood, and Victoria Arango, "The Neurobiology of Suicide Risk: A Review for the Clinician," *Journal of Clinical Psychiatry*, 1999, 60 (Suppl. 2): 7-11; and Eve K. Mościcki, "Epidemiology of Completed and Attempted Suicide: Toward a Framework for Prevention," *Clinical Neuroscience Research* 1, no. 5 (November 2001): 310-23 (and other articles in this special issue).

176. *Sovremennik* 1911, no. 2 (February): 374-79.

177. "Samoubiistvo vzroslykh i detei," *Vesna* 1911, no. 23-26: 175. See also Gordon, "Samoubiistvo molodezhi i eia nervno-psikhicheskaia neustoichivost'," *Novyi zhurnal dlia vsekh* 1912, no. 9 (September): 108-10; Gordon, "Nekotorye psikhologicheskiia cherty iunykh samoubiits," *Vestnik psikhologii* 1912, no. 4-5: 109-19.

178. Dr. G. Gordon, "Predislovie," in E. Diurkgeim, *Samoubiistvo: sotsiologicheskii etiud* (St. Petersburg, 1912), xviii, xxii.

179. *Peterburgskii listok*, 12 May 1907, 4; 22 November 1908, 3; 11 December 1908, 6; *Gazeta-kopeika*, 21 March 1909, 4; 21 May 1909, 3; *Peterburgskii listok*, 7 January 1910, 4; 4 January 1913, 4; 10 May 1913, 4; 6 June 1913, 4.

180. "Prichiny sovremennogo samoubiistva (beseda s d-rom V. V. Chekhovom), *Gazeta-kopeika*, 5 December 1913, 3. Another medical specialist, Professor P. Ia. Rozenbakh, who regularly lectured on the psychology of suicide, concluded that no more than one third of suicides can be attributed to mental illness. Arnova, "Samoubiistvo v proshlom i nastoiashchem," *Zhizn' dlia vsekh* 1911, no. 3-4 (March-April): 478. See also the report on Rozenbakh's lecture, titled "Prichiny sovremennoi nervoznosti i samoubiistv," in *Peterburgskaia gazeta*, 26 April 1909,

3, and what is most likely the text, P. Ia. Rozenbakh, "O prichinakh sovremennoi nervoznosti i samoubiistv," *Novoe slovo* 1909, no. 11: 41–42.

181. Zhbankov, "Sovremennye samoubiistva," *Sovremennyi mir* 1910, no. 3 (March): 27.

182. Paperno, *Suicide as a Cultural Institution*, 99–104; Morrissey, *Suicide and the Body Politic*, 202–4. See Emile Durkheim, *Suicide: A Study in Sociology*, trans. by John Spaulding and George Simpson (Glencoe, 1951), esp. chapters on egoistic and anomic suicide. The 1912 translation was published in St. Petersburg with a preface by Dr. Grigorii Gordon.

183. Dr. G. Gordon, "Samoubiitsy i ikh pis'ma," *Novyi zhurnal dlia vsekh* 1911, no. 28 (February): 107.

184. Daniel Beer, in his *Renovating Russia*, documents a growing inclination in the biomedical sciences to view many pathologies of individual behavior, though framed in biological terms, as socially contingent (and thus correctable).

185. Zhbankov, "Sovremennye samoubiistva," *Sovremennyi mir* 1910, no. 3 (March): 27, 29, 40, 53. See also Zhbankov, "Polovaia prestupnost'," ibid., 1909, no. 7 (July): 54, 63. Particular attention was paid the harmful effects of the death penalty. In addition to Zhbankov, see Brusilovskii, "Trevoga," *Sovremennoe slovo*, 11 March 1910, 1; Gridina, "Bez rul'ia," *Gazeta-kopeika*, 11 April 1910, 5–6.

186. See also Vladimir Vagner, "Samoubiistvo i filosofskii pessimizm," *Zaprosy zhizni* 1912, no. 49 (8 December): 2811; Paperno, *Suicide as a Cultural Institution*, 94–104; Morrissey, *Suicide and the Body Politic*, passim, and "Suicide and Civilization," 205–7.

187. Rozenbakh, "Prichiny sovremennoi nervoznosti i samoubiistv," *Peterburgskaia gazeta*, 26 April 1909, 3.

188. For example, Arnova, "Samoubiistvo v proshlom i nastoiashchem," *Zhizn' dlia vsekh* 1911, no. 3–4 (March–April): 481; Professor A. Bronzov, "Samoubiistvo," *Tserkovnyi vestnik* 1912, no. 5 (2 February): 138.

189. Arnova, "Samoubiistvo v proshlom i nastoiashchem," *Zhizn' dlia vsekh* 1911, no. 3–4 (March–April): 476.

190. Iagodin, "Samoubiistvo i bor'ba s nim," *Zhizn' dlia vsekh* 1912, no. 12 (December): 1881.

191. Vladimir Mikhnevich, *Iazvy Peterburga: opyt istoriko-statisticheskogo issledovaniia nravstvennosti stolichnogo naseleniia* (St. Petersburg, 2003; originally published 1886), esp. 614–15; Paperno, *Suicide as a Cultural Institution*, 231; Morrissey, "Suicide and Civilization," 204–7, and *Suicide and the Body Politic*, 179, 189–90, 312; Beer, *Renovating Russia*, chap. 2. See also Kushner, "Suicide, Gender, and the Fear of Modernity," 462–67.

192. P. Ia. Rozenbakh, "O prichinakh sovremennoi nervoznosti i samoubiistv," *Novoe slovo* 1909, no. 11: 41–42.

193. Professor Tarnovskii, quoted in Arnova, "Samoubiistvo v proshlom i nas-toiashchem," *Zhizn' dlia vsekh* 1911, no. 3–4 (March–April): 482. On the "feverish tempo" of modern life as potentially leading to suicide, see also *Gazeta-kopeika*, 10 August 1913, 3.

194. P. Ia. Rozenbakh, "Prichiny sovremennoi nervoznosti i samoubiistv," *Peterburgskaia gazeta*, 26 April 1909, 3. Rozenbakh, "O prichinakh sovremennoi nervoznosti i samoubiistv," *Novoe slovo* 1909, no. 11: 41–47.

195. For example, in addition to references below, "Zhertva obshchestvennogo ravnodushiia," *Peterburgskii listok*, 13 December 1908, 4; "Iz-za goloda," *Peterburgskii listok*, 4 March 1909, 4; V. T., "Privykli," *Gazeta-kopeika*, 10 May 1909, 3.

196. Ol'ga Gridina, "Rokovaia oshibka," *Gazeta-kopeika*, 13 March 1910, 3. See also Ol'ga Gridina, "Smert' otvetila!" ibid., 5 March 1910, 3.

197. Ol'ga Gridina, "Prostoi vykhod," ibid., 8 May 1910, 3, and see also Ol'ga Gridina, "Prevrashchenie, grifelia," ibid., 7 October 1911, 3; Ol'ga Gridina, "Gorod-obmanshchik," ibid., 24 December 1913, 3; N. Shchigaleev, "Zhizn' ili smert'?" ibid., 3 June 1912, 5.

198. Al. Fedorov, "V shume zhizni," *Peterburgskii kinematograf*, 12 January 1911, 2; Skitalets, "Adskaia zhmurka," *Gazeta-kopeika*, 10 February 1910, 3–4; "Podzabornaia smert'," *Malen'kaia gazeta*, 31 July 1915, 3; ibid., 23 December 1915, 4.

199. Zhbankov, "Sovremennye samoubiistva," *Sovremennyi mir* 1910, no. 3 (March): 43–44; N., "Samoubiistvo uchashchikhsia," *Tserkovnyi vestnik* 1909, no. 32 (6 August): 982; "Razval dukha," ibid., 1911, no. 45 (10 November): 1413; *Peterburgskii listok*, 17 January 1910, 6; *Gazeta-kopeika*, 7 November 1908, 4; 30 January 1912, 1; Vadim, "Chelovecheskie dokumenty," ibid., 17 February 1913, 4.

200. For example, *Peterburgskii listok*, 17 January 1910, 6; *Gazeta-kopeika*, 30 January 1912, 1; *Malen'kaia gazeta*, 3 July 1915, 3.

201. Zhbankov, "Sovremennye samoubiistva," *Sovremennyi mir* 1910, no. 3 (March): 30, 51.

202. For example, *Peterburgskii listok*, 25 December 1908, 7; 5 May 1909, 5; 7 January 1910, 4; 17 January 1910, 6; 4 March 1910, 6; *Gazeta-kopeika*, 20 April 1912, 3; 17 February 1913, 4; *Peterburgskii kinematograf*, 12 January 1911, 3; *Malen'kaia gazeta*, 1 August 1915, 3. See also Liberson, *Stradaniia odinochestva*, 7, and, for a literary echo of what was found the newspapers, Z. N. Gippius, "Lunnye muravye" [Moon Ants], *Lunnye muravye* (Moscow, 1912), 19.

203. Skeptik, "Uspokoenie," *Rech'*, 4 March 1910, 1.

204. *Peterburgskii listok*, 16 January 1910, 4.

205. *Rech'*, 4 March 1910, 4; 5 March 1910, 4.

206. Morrissey, *Suicide and the Body Politic*, 160–68, 261–69; *Novoe vremia*, 27 January 1900, 3–4.

207. For example, *Novoe vremia*, 13 February 1910, 13.

208. Gordon, "Samoubiitsy i ikh pis'ma," *Novyi zhurnal dlia vsekh* 1911, no. 28 (February): 107–8.

209. Douglas, *The Social Meanings of Suicide*, esp. 41–73; Durkheim, *Suicide*, esp. chaps. 2–3 (egoistic suicide) and 5 (anomic suicide).

210. Al. Ks., "Epidemiia samoubiistv," *Novoe vremia*, 9 March 1910, 5. For other examples, Zhbankov, "Sovremennye samoubiistva," *Sovremennyi mir* 1910, no. 3 (March): 53, and "O samoubiistvakh v poslednie gody," *Russkoe bogatstvo* 1909, no. 4 (April): 29; "Prichiny sovremennogo samoubiistva (beseda s d-rom V. V. Chekhovom), *Gazeta-kopeika*, 5 December 1913, 3.

211. Viacheslav Ivanov in "Samoubiistvo (Nasha anketa)," *Novoe slovo* 1912, no. 6: 7.

212. See Nietzsche's sketch "Diary of a Nihilist" and notes on Dostoevsky's *Possessed* in Friedrich Nietzsche, *Werke: Kritische Gesamtausgabe*, vol. 8, no. 2 (Berlin, 1970), 381–83. Discussed by Paperno, *Suicide as a Cultural Institution*, 154–57.

213. Paperno, *Suicide as a Cultural Institution*, 46, 82, 83, 94, 125, 129, 138, 140–42, 157, 161, 166, 173.

214. Bronzov, "Samoubiistvo," *Tserkovnyi vestnik* 1912, no. 5 (2 February): 139–40.

215. "Sovremennost' i dumy," ibid., 1913, no. 31 (1 August): 948; "K samoubiistvam molodezhi," ibid., 1910, no. 12 (25 March): 362; Ibid., 1914, no. 5 (30 January): 137–40; "Tragediia sovremennoi kul'tury," ibid., 1914, no. 27 (3 July): 811; N., "Samoubiistvo uchashchikhsia," ibid., 1909, no. 32 (6 August): 980–83. For examples of similar arguments by secular authors, see *Samoubiistvo: sbornik*, 85, 120, and Vadim, "V chem zlo i prichiny," *Gazeta-kopeika*, 20 February 1913, 4.

216. Abramovich, "Samoubiistvo," in *Samoubiistvo: sbornik*, 107.

217. V. Rozanov, "Vechnaia tema," *Novoe vremia*, 4 January 1908, 3. V. V. Rozanov, "O sladchaishem Isuse i gor'kikh plodakh mira" (report to meeting of 21 November 1907), *Zapiski Sankt-Peterburgskogo religiozno-filosofskogo obshchestva*, no. 2 (1908): 22–25. See Dmitrii Merezhkovskii's criticism in "Misticheskie khuligany," *Svobodnye mysli*, 28 January 1908, 2. Vasilii Rozanov, *Temnyi lik: metafizika khristianstva* (St. Petersburg, 1911), e.g. 61–66. See also Paperno, *Suicide as a Cultural Institution*, 97–99.

218. A. Lunacharskii, "Samoubiistvo i filosofiia," in *Samoubiistvo: sbornik*, 72.

219. Zhbankov, "Sovremennye samoubiistva," *Sovremennyi mir* 1910, no. 3 (March): 43–44.

220. For example, "Troinoe samoubiistvo po ugovoru," *Peterburgskii listok*, 4 March 1910, 6; Rozanov, " 'Bez tseli i smysla' (o samoubiistvakh)," *Novoe vremia*, 5 March 1910, 4; Vladimir Vagner, "Samoubiistvo i filosofskii pessimizm," *Zaprosy zhizni* 1912, no. 49 (8 December): 2811–16.

221. Zhbankov, "Sovremennye samoubiistva," *Sovremennyi mir* 1910, no. 3 (March): 40; D., "V zashchitu . . . uksusnoi essentsii," *Gazeta-kopeika*, 6 October 1909, 3.

222. A. Lunacharskii, "Samoubiistvo i filosofiia," in *Samoubiistvo: sbornik*, 72, 75, 77, 78, 79–85.

223. Typically, despite this philosophical statement, evidence suggests that her suicide was mainly for more personal reasons. *Gazeta-kopeika*, 12 August 1910, 4. This letter was also quoted, with slight variation and without noting the source, by Bishop Mikhail in his essay in the collection *Samoubiistvo: sbornik*, 21.

224. Brusilovskii, "Trevoga," *Sovremennoe slovo*, 11 March 1910, 1.

225. *Sovremennoe slovo*, 4 March 1910, 2.

226. This term was also used, among others, by Gordon, "Samoubiitsy i ikh pis'ma," *Novyi zhurnal dlia vsekh* 1911, no. 28 (February): 108.

227. Rozanov, "O samoubiistvakh," in *Samoubiistvo: sbornik*, 44, 46, 55, 56.

228. Brusilovskii, "Trevoga," *Sovremennoe slovo*, 11 March 1910, 1.

229. V. Rozanov, "'Bez tseli i smysla' (o samoubiistvakh)," *Novoe vremia*, 5 March 1910, 4.

230. Kornei Chukovskii, "Samoubiitsy (ocherki sovremennyi slovesnosti)," *Rech'*, 23 December 1912, 3; Maksim Gor'kii, "O sovremennosti" (1912), *Stat'i (1905–1916)* (Petrograd, 1918), 103.

231. A. Gladkii, "Vzgliad khudozhnikov na zhizn' i samoubiistvo," *Vestnik vospitanii* 1913, no. 6: esp. 42–44.

232. Pushchin, "Kak zhit'," *Novyi zhurnal dlia vsekh* 1912, no. 5 (May): 81–82. See also Paperno, *Suicide as a Cultural Institution*, 101–2, and Morrissey, *Suicide and the Body Politic*, 336–37. The journal *Novoe slovo* invited Leonid Andreev, Fedor Sologub, and Mikhail Artsybashev—who were among the most criticized for supposedly encouraging suicide—to comment on the suicide epidemic. "Samoubiistvo (Nasha anketa)," *Novoe slovo* 1912, no. 6, 4–12.

233. N., "Samoubiistvo uchashchikhsia," *Tserkovnyi vestnik* 1909, no. 32 (6 August): 982; Vadim, "V chem zlo i prichiny," *Gazeta-kopeika*, 20 February 1913, 5.

234. *Peterburgskii listok*, 8 March 1910, 4.

235. N. Ia. Abramovich, "Samoubiistvo," in *Samoubiistvo: sbornik*, 95, 98, 103, 106, 109, 112, 113.

236. Ol'ga Gridina, "Smert' otvetila!" *Gazeta-kopeika*, 5 March 1910, 3. See also Nemirovich-Danchenko, "Zhizn' deshevo!" *Zaprosy zhizni* 1910, no. 10 (7 March): 584.

237. Morrissey sees this ambivalence throughout the history of interpreting suicide. See, for example, Morrissey, *Suicide and the Body Politic*, 75, 345.

238. P. Zaikin, "Padaiushchie zvezdy," *Gazeta-kopeika*, 16 September 1908, 3.

239. Aikhenval'd, "O samoubiistve," in *Samoubiistvo: sbornik*, 122–23.

240. For critical concern about the dangerous "apotheosis" and "poeticization" (*opoetizirovanie*) of suicide, including at funerals, see I. Brusilovskii, "Trevoga," *Sovremennoe slovo*, 11 March 1910, 1; and Rozanov, "O samoubiistvakh," in *Samoubiistvo: sbornik*, 59.

241. In addition to examples below, notes 242–44, see "Zhertva obshchestvennogo ravnodushiia," *Peterburgskii listok*, 13 December 1908, 4.

242. Zhbankov, "Sovremennye samoubiistva," *Sovremennyi mir* 1910, no. 3 (March): 27, 30; N. Ia. Abramovich, "Samoubiistvo," in *Samoubiistvo: sbornik*, 113; A. Lunacharskii, "Samoubiistvo i filosofiia," in *Samoubiistvo: sbornik*, 72.

243. Quoted by Lavretskii, "Tragediia sovremennoi molodezhi," *Vesna* 1910, no. 14–15: 107.

244. Quoted from the newspaper *Rech'* (1909) by various sources, for example, Zhbankov, "Sovremennye samoubiistva," *Sovremennyi mir* 1910, no. 3 (March): 55.

245. Rozanov, "O samoubiistvakh," in *Samoubiistvo: sbornik*, 47–48.

246. N., "Samoubiistvo uchashchikhsia," *Tserkovnyi vestnik* 1909, no. 32 (6 August): 980–83; Lunacharskii, "Samoubiistvo i filosofiia," in *Samoubiistvo: sbornik*, 72–78, 82; Abramovich, "Samoubiistvo," ibid., 104.

247. For a discussion of the meanings and uses of *lichnost'* see Mark D. Steinberg, *Proletarian Imagination: Self, Modernity, and the Sacred in Russia, 1910–1925* (Ithaca, 2002), 2–5, 62–101. See also V. V. Vinogradov, *Istoriia slov* (Moscow, 1994), 271–309; Derek Offord, "*Lichnost'*: Notions of Individual Identity," in *Constructing Russian Culture in the Age of Revolution, 1881–1940*, ed. Catriona Kelly and David Shepherd (Oxford, 1998), 13–25; Oleg Kharkhordin, *The Collective and the Individual in Russia* (Berkeley, 1999), 184–90; Laura Engelstein and Stephanie Sandler, eds., *Self and Story in Russian History* (Ithaca, 2000).

248. For example, "Tragediia oskorblennoi nevesty," *Peterburgskii listok*, 16 March 1909. 4, and "Dramy unizhennykh i oskorblennykh," ibid., 17 January 1913, 14. The phrase made famous by Dostoevsky's 1861 novel *Unizhennye i oskorblennye*, often translated as *The Insulted and the Injured*, echoes literally in much of this discourse on the moral drama of suicide.

249. *Peterburgskii listok*, 10 January 1910, 7; Skitalets, "Zimnee pal'to," *Gazeta-kopeika*, 20 October 1911, 5; *Peterburgskii listok*, 22 February 1914, 4.

250. Obyvatel', "Samoubiistvo," *Gazeta-kopeika*, 3 January 1909, 2; Zhbankov, "Sovremennye samoubiistva," *Sovremennyi mir* 1910, no. 3 (March): 47–48, and "Polovaia prestupnost'," ibid., 1909, no. 7 (July): 67–68. See also Iagodin, "Samoubiistvo i bor'ba s nim," *Zhizn' dlia vsekh* 1912, no. 12 (December): 1884.

251. Peter Brooks, *The Melodramatic Imagination: Balzac, Henry James, and the Mode of Excess* (New Haven, 1976); Ben Singer, *Melodrama and Modernity: Early Sensational Cinema and Its Contexts* (New York, 2001); Louise McReynolds

and Joan Neuberger, eds., *Imitations of Life: Two Centuries of Melodrama in Russia* (Durham, N.C., 2002).

252. Zhbankov, "Sovremennye samoubiistva," *Sovremennyi mir* 1910, no. 3 (March): 29.

253. Nemirovich-Danchenko, "Zhizn' deshevo! (ocherki epidemii otchaianiia)," *Zaprosy zhizni*, 1910, no. 10 (7 March): 581-83. See also Laurie Bernstein, *Sonia's Daughters: Prostitutes and Their Regulation in Imperial Russia* (Berkeley, 1995), 78.

254. Zhbankov, "Sovremennye samoubiistva," *Sovremennyi mir* 1910, no. 3 (March): 53. See also A. L., "Samoubiistvo uchashchikhsia," *Tserkovnyi vestnik* 1909, no. 36 (3 September): 1109.

255. For examples from the nineteenth century and earlier, see Morrissey, *Suicide and the Body Politic*, 2, 35, 49, 52-53, 75, 241; and Paperno, *Suicide as a Cultural Institution*, 9-10, 16-17, 144-46.

256. Aikhenval'd, "O samoubiistve," in *Samoubiistvo: sbornik*, 118; Andreev and Artsybashev in "Samoubiistvo (Nasha anketa)," *Novoe slovo*, 1912, no. 6: 4, 6.

257. Nemirovich-Danchenko, "Zhizn' deshevo! (ocherki epidemii otchaianiia)," *Zaprosy zhizni* 1910, no. 10 (7 March): 581; Aikhenval'd, "O samoubiistve," in *Samoubiistvo: sbornik*, 124.

258. Gordon, "Samoubiitsy i ikh pis'ma," *Novyi zhurnal dlia vsekh* 1911, no. 28 (February): 109-14; For example, *Peterburgskii listok*, 27 November 1908, 4.

259. "K samoubiistvam molodezhi," *Tserkovnyi vestnik* 1910, no. 12 (25 March): 362; N. Vysotskii, "Zadacha shkoly v bor'be s samoubiistvami uchashchikhsia," *Russkaia shkola* 1910, no. 4 (April): 54; Ol'ga Gridina, "Prostoi vykhod," *Gazeta-kopeika*, 8 May 1910, 3, and see also Gridina, "Bez rulia," ibid., 11 April 1910, 5-6; Vadim, "Chelovecheskie dokumenty," ibid., 17 February 1913, 4.

260. Rozanov, "O samoubiistvakh," in *Samoubiistvo: sbornik*, esp. 55-56.

261. Lunacharskii, "Samoubiistvo i filosofiia," ibid., 75-78, 87-89.

262. For example, *Peterburgskii listok*, 3 March 1909, 5; 4 March 1909, 4; 16 March 1909, 4; 7 January 1910, 4; 8 January 1910, 4; 14 January 1910, 5; 17 January 1910, 6; 24 March 1910, 4; 6 August 1910, 5; *Malen'kaia gazeta*, 28 November 1914, 4; 21 July 1915, 4; 28 December 1915, 3; 5 February 1917, 4.

263. *Predvaritel'nyi svod statisticheskikh dannykh po g. S-Peterburgu za 1909 god*, 39 (which identifies 44.8 percent of suicides as for unknown motives). See also Iagodin, "Samoubiistvo i bor'ba s nim," *Zhizn' dlia vsekh* 1912, no. 12 (December): 1884 (who counts 37 percent for "reasons unknown").

264. Kornei Chukovskii, "Samoubiitsy (ocherki sovremennyi slovesnosti)," *Rech'*, 23 December 1912, 3. See also Paperno, *Suicide as a Cultural Institution*, 103. On suicides "without reason," see also V. Rozanov, "'Bez tseli i smysla' (o samoubiistvakh)," *Novoe vremia*, 5 March 1910, 4.

265. Vadim, "V chem taina," *Gazeta-kopeika*, 14 January 1913, 3.

266. Iagodin, "Samoubiistvo i bor'ba s nim," *Zhizn' dlia vsekh* 1912, no. 12 (December): 1884–85.

267. *Peterburgskii listok*, 12 December 1908, 5, and update, 17 December 1908.

268. Aikhenval'd, "O samoubiistve," in *Samoubiistvo: sbornik*, 117. See also *Gazeta-kopeika*, 7 September 1911, 1.

269. Rozanov, "O samoubiistvakh," in *Samoubiistvo: sbornik*, 53; I. Brusilovskii, "Trevoga," *Sovremennoe slovo*, 11 March 1910, 1; Brusilovskii, "Smysl' zhizni," *Sovremennoe slovo*, 13 March 1910, 1; K. Lupokova, "Krasota zhizni," *Gazeta-kopeika*, 12 March 1910, 3; Skitalets, "Ne umeiut dogadat'sia," ibid., 29 April 1912, 4.

270. *Sovremennik* 1911, no. 2 (February): 374–79.

271. Sigmund Freud, "Contributions to a Discussion of Suicide" (1910), *The Standard Edition of the Complete Psychological Works of Sigmund Freud*, trans. and ed. James Strachey, vol. 11 (London, 1957), 232.

272. See Lisa Lieberman, "Romanticism and the Culture of Suicide in Nineteenth-Century France," *Comparative Studies in Society and History 33*, no. 3 (July 1991): 612.

273. Sigmund Freud, "Mourning and Melancholia" (1915, published 1917), in *The Standard Edition of the Complete Psychological Works of Sigmund Freud*, trans. and ed. James Strachey, vol. 14 (London, 1957), 252.

274. Dollimore, *Death, Desire and Loss*, esp. xxviii (quote), 84–101, 119–27, 153–60. 173–97, 231–48. See also Drew Gilpin Faust, *This Republic of Suffering: Death and the American Civil War* (New York, 2008).

CHAPTER FIVE. DECADENCE

1. Matei Calinescu, *Five Faces of Modernity* (Durham, N.C., 1987), 151.

2. Daniel Pick, *Faces of Degeneration: A European Disorder, c. 1848–1918* (Cambridge, 1989), 4. See also Robert Nye, *Crime, Madness, and Politics in Modern France: The Medical Concept of National Decline* (Princeton, 1984); Sander Gilman and J. Edwards Chamberlin, eds., *Degeneration: the Dark Side of Progress* (New York, 1985); Mark Micale, *Approaching Hysteria* (Princeton, 1994), and Micale, *Hysterical Men: The Hidden History of Male Nervous Illness* (Cambridge, Mass., 2008).

3. Sharon Hirsch, *Symbolism and Modern Urban Society* (Cambridge, 2004); and Mary Gluck, *Popular Bohemia: Modernism and Urban Culture in Nineteenth-Century Paris* (Cambridge, Mass., 2005), esp. chap. 4.

4. Olga Matich, *Erotic Utopia: The Decadent Imagination in Russia's Fin de Siècle* (Madison, 2005). See also Adrian Wanner, *Baudelaire in Russia* (Gainesville,

1996), esp. chap. 2; Kirsten Lodge, "Russian Decadence in the 1910s: Valery Briusov and the Collapse of Empire," *Russian Review* 69, no. 2 (April 2010): 276–93;
and Kirsten Lodge, ed., *The Dedalus Books of Russian Decadence: Perversity, Despair and Collapse* (Sawtry, UK, 2007), introduction.

5. Daniel Beer, *Renovating Russia: The Human Sciences and the Fate of Liberal
Modernity, 1880–1930* (Ithaca, 2008), esp. chaps. 1–2.

6. Pick, *Faces of Degeneration*, 102.

7. Vadim, "Dukh zla," *Gazeta-kopeika*, 16 February 1913, 3.

8. Podpischik zhurnala "Zhizn' dlia vsekh," "Golos iz nedr neveshestva," *Zhizn'
dlia vsekh* 1913, no. 9 (September): 1289–90.

9. Az., "Deti-nozhevshchiki," *Gazeta-kopeika*, 9 December 1908, 4. See a similar view in "Tragediia sovremennoi kul'tury," *Tserkovnyi vestnik* 1914, no. 27 (3
July): 809–12.

10. Az., "Deti-nozhevshchiki," *Gazeta-kopeika*, 9 December 1908, 4.

11. A. E., "Detskie sudy," *Vsemirnaia panorama* 1909, no. 37 (31 December): 1;
M. Novikov, "Bor'ba s vlast'iu ulitsy i pomoshch' besprizornym detiam," *Gorodskoe
delo* 1914, no. 9 (1 May): 526–32; L. L-l., "Klub gorodskikh detei," *Argus* 1915,
no. 4 [no month]: 73–78. See also *Nishchenstvo i bor'ba s nim* (St. Petersburg,
1913), esp. 58–59, 73–129.

12. Baron Igrok, "Dvoinye samoubiistva," *Peterburgskaia gazeta*, 19 April
1909, 3.

13. V. Burenin, "Kriticheskie ocherki: pri vstuplenii v novyi god," *Novoe vremia*,
8 January 1910, 4.

14. For example, O. Gridina, "Zverinye nravy," *Gazeta-kopeika*, 14 May 1910,
3; "Tragediia sovremennoi kul'tury," *Tserkovnyi vestnik* 1914, no. 27 (3 July):
809–12.

15. M. Slobozhanin, "Iz sovremennykh perezhivanii," pt. 1 ("Staraia znakomaia"), *Zhizn' dlia vsekh* 1913, no. 1 (January): 115–25, and "Iz sovremennykh
perezhivanii," pt. 2 ("'Pod-cheloveki' nashego vremeni"), ibid., no. 2 (February):
310–22. Quotations are from pt. 2, 310–20. Some of these observations echo arguments by Max Nordau, whose *Degeneration* (*Entartung*, 1892–93) had been translated and published in St. Petersburg in 1894 as *Vyrozhdenie*.

16. "Religioznoe teplokhladost'," *Tserkovnyi vestnik* 1909, no. 10 (5 March): 291;
Posse, "Obshchestvennaia zhizn'," *Zhizn' dlia vsekh* 1912, no. 4 (April): 705–6;
"Antikhrist," *Peterburgskii listok*, 12 February 1914, 4.

17. M. Men'shikov, "Genii schast'ia," *Novoe vremia*, 13 June 1909, 2.

18. *Peterburgskii listok*, 23 October 1908, 2.

19. K. Barantsevich, "Zhazhdushchie silnykh oshchushchenii," *Slovo*, 2 February 1909, 2; "Zhazhda silnykh oshchushchenii," *Tserkovnyi vestnik* 1909, no. 7
(12 February): 198–99.

20. Pritykin, "Krizis intelligentskoi dushi," *Svobodnye mysli*, 24 March 1908, 2; *Novoe vremia*, 1 January 1909, 2; "Razval dukha," *Tserkovnyi vestnik* 1911, no. 45 (10 November): 1412; A. Zorin [Gastev], "Rabochii mir," *Zhizn' dlia vsekh* 1911, no. 8 (August): 1075.

21. V. Portugalov, "V oblasti kul'tury," *Vesna* 1908, no. 1 (6 January): 3 (the article originally appeared in *Novoe vremia*).

22. "Tragediia sovremennoi kul'tury," *Tserkovnyi vestnik* 1914, no. 27 (3 July): 809–12. See a similar sense of modern vanity and chaos in *Teosoficheskoe obozrenie*, no. 2 (November 1907): 89, and no. 7 (April 1908): 487.

23. M. Semenov, "Komnata na naem," *Novye peterburgskie trushchoby: ocherki stolichnoi zhizni* (St. Petersburg, 1909–10), 72.

24. Frant s Plutalovoi, "V 'kafe' (gm!) na Nevskom," *Malen'kaia gazeta*, 5 October 1914, 4.

25. Pchela, "Kul't razvrata," *Peterburgskii listok*, 8 December 1908, 2.

26. "Teatr i zrelishcha," *Gazeta-kopeika*, 19 June 1908, 5; *Peterburgskii kinematograf*, no. 1 (5 January 1911): izd. 1, 2.

27. For example, O. Gridina, "Griaznyi potok," *Gazeta-kopeika*, 27 February 1910, 3; S. Liubosh, "Griaznaia volna," *Sovremennoe slovo*, 7 April 1910, 1.

28. This was the title of a regular column on the crimes and transgressions of Petersburg life in *Gazeta-kopeika*.

29. Skitalets, "Vavilon na chas," ibid., 2 January 1911, 4–5; "Futurizm," *Tserkovnyi vestnik* 1914, no. 27 (3 July): 825–26. See also Kn. O. F. Bebutova, "Nash Vavilon (Roman iz peterburgskoi zhizni)," *Peterburgskii listok*, 28 February 1913, 1.

30. *Ogonek* 1908, no. 17 (27 April/10 May): cover.

31. O. Gridina, "Kamni," *Gazeta-kopeika*, 18 May 1911, 3. See also Vadim, "Svet vo t'me," ibid., 3 March 1913, 5–6.

32. Pchela, "Kul't razvrata," *Peterburgskii listok*, 8 December 1908, 2.

33. "Nravstvennaia rasteriannosti russkogo obshchestva," *Tserkovnyi vestnik* 1913, no. 10 (7 March): 299–301. See also ibid., no. 3 (17 January): 75–77; no. 8 (21 February): 237–40; no. 40 (4 October): 1259.

34. For example, Pchela, "Kul't razvrata," *Peterburgskii listok*, 8 December 1908, 2; "Na ligovskom bul'vare," *Gazeta-kopeika*, 23 June 1909, 3; Graf Amori [I. P. Rapgof], *Tainy Nevskogo prospekta* (Petrograd, 1915), 19.

35. V. Trofimov, "'Zhestoki u nas nravy' . . . ," *Gazeta-kopeika*, 4 April 1909, 3; *Teosoficheskoe obozrenie*, no. 7 (April 1908): 487.

36. In addition to examples below, *Vesna* 1908, no. 5 (3 February): 35; *Teosoficheskoe obozrenie*, no. 7 (April 1908): 487. As so often, this echoes Nordau's definition of the degenerate's "hysterical" focus on "his own 'I.'" Max Nordau, *Degeneration* (New York, 1895), 26.

37. M. A. Engel'gardt, "Prizraki vremeni," *Svobodnye mysli*, 4 February 1908, 1-2.

38. O. Gridina, "Griaznyi potok," *Gazeta-kopeika*, 27 February 1910, 3.

39. Fal'ks, "Zachem my zhivem?" *Teosoficheskoe obozrenie*, no. 3 (December 1907): 130; V. L'vov-Rogachevskii, "M. Artsybashev," *Sovremennyi mir* 1909, no. 11 (November): pt. 2, 26; D. Zhbankov, "Polovaia prestupnost'," ibid., 1909, no. 7 (July): 64, and "Sovremennye samoubiistva," ibid., 1910, no. 3 (March): 50; Rozanov, "O samoubiistvakh," in *Samoubiistvo: sbornik obshchestvennykh, filosofskikh i kriticheskikh statei* (Moscow, 1911), 44, 46, 55, 56; Prof. A. Bronzov, "Samoubiistvo," *Tserkovnyi vestnik* 1912, no. 5 (2 February): 140.

40. V. Vegenov, "V gorode i v glushe," *Gazeta-kopeika*, 20 February 1909, 3.

41. Podpischik zhurnala "Zhizn' dlia vsekh," "Golos iz nedr neveshestva," *Zhizn' dlia vsekh* 1913, no. 9 (September): 1289-90; M. Liberson, *Stradanie odinochestva* (St. Petersburg, 1909), 31-32; For example, "Religioznoe teplokhladost'," *Tserkovnyi vestnik* 1909, no. 10 (5 March): 289-92; M. Liberson, *Stradanie odinochestva* (St. Petersburg, 1909), 31-32; "V pautine razvrata," *Peterburgskii kinematograf* 1911, no. 19 (19 March): 2; O. Gridina, "Kamni," *Gazeta-kopeika*, 18 May 1911, 3.

42. N. Rubakin, "Dlia chego ia zhivu na svete," *Novyi zhurnal dlia vsekh* 1912, no. 6 (June): 68-70. While Rubakin builds his argument through metaphor, other writers were blunt: in these times "higher" feelings were being "dissipated" [*razseianie*] by "low sensation" [*nizshaia sfera oshchushchenii*]." Fal'ks, "Zachem my zhivem?" *Teosoficheskoe obozrenie*, no. 3 (December 1907): 130.

43. S. Gamalov, "Pod znamenom Khama," *Novyi zhurnal dlia vsekh* 1913, no. 12 (December): 109-12.

44. Nordau, *Degeneration*, 550.

45. See Beer, *Renovating Russia*, 7. See also Irina Sirotkina, *Diagnosing Literary Genius: A Cultural History of Psychiatry in Russia, 1880-1930* (Baltimore, 2001), chap. 4.

46. S. Liubosh, "Griaznaia volna," *Sovremennoe slovo*, 7 April 1910, 1.

47. Zhbankov, "Sovremennye samoubiistva," *Sovremennyi mir* 1910, no. 3 (March): *Sovremennyi mir* 1910, no. 3 (March): 47-48, and "Polovaia prestupnost'," ibid., 1909, no. 7 (July): 67-68.

48. "Tragediia sovremennoi kul'tury," *Tserkovnyi vestnik* 1914, no. 27 (3 July): 809-12.

49. M. Men'shikov, "Za polstoletiia," *Novoe vremia*, 28 February 1909, 2.

50. For example, V. Novitskii, "Zver'—v chelovek," *Peterburgskaia gazeta*, 6 April 1909, 1.

51. Calinescu, *Five Faces of Modernity*, 167-68 (quoting Edmond and Jules Goncourt and Emile Zola); Pick, *Faces of Degeneration*.

52. See, especially, S. A. Vengerov, ed., *Russkaia literatura XX veka*, vol. 1 (Moscow, 1914), pp. 1–26; Irina Paperno and Joan Delaney Grossman, eds., *Creating Life: the Aesthetic Utopia of Russian Modernism* (Stanford, 1994); Katerina Clark, *Petersburg, Crucible of Revolution* (Cambridge, Mass., 1995); Hillary L. Fink, *Bergson and Russian Modernism, 1900–1930* (Evanston, 1999); Matich, *Erotic Utopia*.

53. *Vekhi: Sbornik statei o russkoi intelligentsii* (Moscow, 1909). Translated as *Vekhi/Landmarks: A Collection of Articles about the Russian Intelligentsia*, trans. and ed. Marshall S. Shatz and Judith E. Zimmerman (Armonk, 1994). See especially the essays of Nikolai Berdiaev, Mikhail Gershenzon, A. S. Izgoev, and Semen Frank.

54. St. Ivanovich, "Tekushchaia zhizn': Pod znakom nadezhdy," *Novyi zhurnal dlia vsekh* 1913, no. 1 (January): 109; M. Pritykin, "Krizis intelligentskoi dushi," *Svobodnye mysli*, 24 March 1908, 2; I. Zhilkin, "Dve intelligentsii," *Zaprosy zhizni* 1909, no. 3 (1 November): 2.

55. M. Slobozhanin, "Iz sovremennykh perezhivanii," pt. 1 ("Staraia znakomaia"), *Zhizn' dlia vsekh* 1913, no. 1 (January): esp. 115, 124–25.

56. "Peterburgskie 'satanisty'," *Peterburgskii listok*, 12 February 1913, 3; L. Gurevich, "Literatura nashego vremeni," *Novyi zhurnal dlia vsekh* 1909, no. 3 (January): 100. See also *Vesna* 1908, no. 5 (3 February): 35.

57. N. Mikhailovich, "Politika i erotika," *Svobodnye mysli*, 8/21 October 1907, 1–2.

58. See, especially, M. O. Gershenzon, "Tvorcheskoe samosoznanie," in *Vekhi*.

59. *Sovremennik* 1912, no. 5 (May): 364.

60. Matich, *Erotic Utopia*, esp. chaps. 3–5. See also Aleksandr Etkind, *Sodom i Psikheia: ocherki intellektual'noi istorii Serebrianogo veka* (Moscow, 1996).

61. V. Burenin, "Kriticheskie ocherki: pri vstuplenii v novyi god," *Novoe vremia*, 8 January 1910, 4.

62. M. Slobozhanin, "Iz sovremennykh perezhivanii," pt. 1 ("Staraia znakomaia"), *Zhizn' dlia vsekh* 1913, no. 1 (January): 115–25. See also the continuation of this series, ibid., no. 2 (February): 311–20; no. 3 (March–April): 461–78; no. 7 (no months): 1012–33.

63. L. Gurevich, "Literatura nashego vremeni," *Novyi zhurnal dlia vsekh* 1909, no. 3 (January): 100.

64. *Argus* 1913, no. 2 (February): 3.

65. V. Portugalov, "V oblasti kul'tury," *Vesna* 1908, no. 1 (6 January): 3 (the article originally appeared in *Novoe vremia*); K. Chukovskii, "Russkaia literatura," *Rech'*, 1 January 1910, 10.

66. L. Gurevich, "Literatura nashego vremeni," *Novyi zhurnal dlia vsekh* 1909, no. 3 (January): 100. For discussion of *Sanin* and its public reception see Laura

Engelstein, *Keys to Happiness: Sex and the Search for Modernity in Fin-de-Siècle Russia* (Ithaca, 1992), 383-88; and Eric Naiman, *Sex in Public: The Incarnation of Early Soviet Ideology* (Princeton, 1997), 47-50.

67. L. Gurevich in *Zaprosy zhizni* 1909, no. 1 (18 October): 29-30.

68. Prof. A. Bronzov, "Pisateli-razvratiteli," *Tserkovnyi vestnik* 1909, no. 44 (29 October): 1361-63.

69. Genrikh Tastevin, *Futurizm (na puti k novomy simvolizmu)* (Moscow, 1914), 30-32.

70. Sviashchennik Evgenii Sosuntsov, "Sovremennyi antinomizm," *Tserkovnyi vestnik* 1914, no. 21 (22 May): 626-27.

71. "Futurizm," ibid., no. 27 (3 July): 825-26.

72. Sosuntsov, "Sovremennyi antinomizm," ibid., no. 21 (22 May): 627.

73. Evgenii Anichkov, "Kollektivizm, sverkh-chelovek, i sverkh-liubov'," *Sovremennik* 1912, no. 10 (October): 153.

74. Ashkinazi, "Ot individualizma k bogostroitel'stvu," *Novyi zhurnal dlia vsekh* 1901, no. 6 (April): 96-105.

75. Tastevin, *Futurizm*, 16-17.

76. Vadim, "Iazva vremeni," *Gazeta-kopeika*, 31 January 1913, 3.

77. Joan Neuberger, *Hooliganism: Crime, Culture, and Power in St. Petersburg, 1900-1914* (Berkeley, 1993).

78. *Peterburgskii listok*, 12 May 1910, 4; ibid., 5 May 1907, 4; "Ulichnaia sektantskaia missiia," ibid., 23 September 1908, 2.

79. "Grandioznaia oblava na khuliganov i bezdomnikov," ibid., 17 September 1910, 2.

80. Ol'ga Gridina, "Odna zhenshchina," *Gazeta-kopeika*, 6 June 1910, 5.

81. Ibid., 6 October 1910, 1.

82. *Peterburgskii listok*, 5 May 1913, 11.

83. For example, V. Ivanov, "Chto takoe khuliganstvo?" *Novyi zhurnal dlia vsekh* 1914, no. 1 (January): 48.

84. "Zhizn' za 14 kopeek," *Peterburgskii listok*, 5 January 1912, 3.

85. *Gazeta-kopeika*, 6 October 1910, 1.

86. *Peterburgskii listok*, 3 April 1909, 1; ibid., 10 May 1913, 4.

87. For example, "Omut zhizni: khuligany," *Gazeta-kopeika*, 21 June 1908, 3; "Podvigi ulichnykh grabitelei," *Peterburgskii listok*, 2 August 1910, 3.

88. *Peterburgskii listok*, 5 May 1907, 4.

89. Ibid., 16 March 1910, 6.

90. *Gazeta-kopeika*, 3 September 1913, 3.

91. Ibid., 19 June 1908, 5.

92. "Vrazhda khuliganskikh partii," *Peterburgskii listok*, 6 April 1910, 5; ibid., 9 June 1910, 4. See also "Khuligany-mstiteli," ibid., 4 August 1910, 3.

93. Skitalets, "Neotlozhnyi zakon," *Gazeta-kopeika*, 20 July 1910, 3.

94. Ol'ga Gridina, "Noveishie geroi," ibid., 5 December 1913, 3.

95. Ibid., 18 January 1912, 4; "Lovelas-khuligan," *Peterburgskii listok*, 28 January 1913, 4; "Lovelas-nozhevik," ibid., 5 May 1909, 5. See also "Omut zhizni: khuligany-nasil'niki," *Gazeta-kopeika*, 22 July 1908, 2; "Dikoe napadenie khuliganov," *Peterburgskii listok*, 18 August 1910, 3.

96. Neuberger, *Hooliganism*, 32.

97. A. M., "Peterburgskaia ulitsa," *Peterburgskii listok*, 27 November 1905, 3; *Gazeta-kopeika*, 23 February 1911, 4; ibid., 28 February 1910, 3.

98. *Peterburgskii listok*, 14 March 1913, 14.

99. *Gazeta-kopeika*, 3 September 1913, 3; *Peterburgskii listok*, 27 July 1906, quoted in Neuberger, *Hooliganism*, 30.

100. Ol'ga Gridina, "Noveishie geroi," *Gazeta-kopeika*, 5 December 1913, 3.

101. "Omut zhizni: khuligany-nasil'niki," ibid., 22 July 1908, 2; "Gumannost' i khuliganstvo," *Tserkovnyi vestnik* 1914, no. 26 (26 June): 788-89; *Gazeta-kopeika*, 6 October 1910, 1. See also Skitalets, "Neotlozhnyi zakon," ibid., 20 July 1910, 3.

102. "Grandioznaia oblava na khuliganov i bezdomnikov," *Peterburgskii listok*, 17 September 1910, 2; "Stolichnye apashi," *Gazeta-kopeika*, 6 May 1912, 4; V. Brusianin, "O khuliganakh i khuliganstve," *Novyi zhurnal dlia vsekh* 1913, no. 4 (April): 144. The term apache was borrowed directly from the French; it was the Parisian name for muggers. See Neuberger, *Hooliganism*, 226-27.

103. *Peterburgskii listok*, 3 April 1909, 1.

104. A. M., "Peterburgskaia ulitsa," ibid., 27 November 1905, 3.

105. "Khuliganstvo," *Gazeta-kopeika*, 16 September 1908, 3.

106. Bova, "Nasha ulitsa," *Peterburgskii listok*, 5 September 1910, 5.

107. St. Filenkin, "Khuliganstvo," *Gazeta-kopeika*, 17 August 1912, 3.

108. Ol'ga Gridina, "Noveishie geroi," ibid., 5 December 1913, 3. See also Vadim, "Iazva vremeni," ibid., 31 January 1913, 3.

109. V. Ivanov, "Chto takoe khuliganstvo?" *Novyi zhurnal dlia vsekh* 1914, no. 1 (January): 47-50.

110. A. Svirskii, "Peterburgskie khuligany," in *Peterburg i ego zhizni* (St. Petersburg, 1914), 253, 258-69. On Svirskii, see McReynolds, *The News Under Russia's Old Regime*, 151-52; and Neuberger, *Hooliganism*, esp. 243-46.

111. "Tragediia sovremennoi kul'tury," *Tserkovnyi vestnik* 1914, no. 27 (3 July): 812-13; "Sovremennost' i dumy," ibid., 1913, no. 31 (1 August): 947-48.

112. "Ulichnaia sektantskaia missiia," *Peterburgskii listok*, 23 September 1908, 2; "Kham torzhestvuiushchii," *Tserkovnyi vestnik* 1913, no. 45 (7 November): 1406; P. Nikol'skii, "Odna iz mer v bor'be s khuliganstvom," ibid., no. 33 (15 August): 1030.

113. "Gumannost' i khuliganstvo," *Tserkovnyi vestnik* 1914, no. 26 (26 June): 788–89.

114. *Gazeta-kopeika*, 19 June 1908, 1.

115. V. Brusianin, "O khuliganakh i khuliganstve," *Novyi zhurnal dlia vsekh* 1913, no. 4 (April): 152–54.

116. Ashkinazi, "Ot individualizma k bogostroitel'stvu," ibid., 1909, no. 6 (April): 106.

117. "Khuliganstvo," *Gazeta-kopeika*, 16 September 1908, 3; see also "Kham torzhestvuiushchii," *Tserkovnyi vestnik* 1913, no. 45 (7 November): 1406.

118. M. Slobozhanin, "Iz sovremennykh perezhivanii," pt. 2 ("'Pod-cheloveki' nashego vremeni"), *Zhizn' dlia vsekh* 1913, no. 2 (February): 311; P. Nikol'skii, "Odna iz mer v bor'be s khuliganstvom," *Tserkovnyi vestnik* 1913, no. 33 (15 August): 1030.

119. See also K. Chukovskii, "Russkaia literatura," *Rech'*, 1 January 1910, 10.

120. D. Merezhkovskii, "Misticheskie khuligany," *Svobodnye mysli*, 28 January 1908, 2 (emphasis in original)

121. M. Slobozhanin, "Iz sovremennykh perezhivanii," pt. 4 ("'Ia' i okruzhaiushchaia sreda"), *Zhizn' dlia vsekh* 1913, no. 7 [July]: 1020.

122. Evgenii Sosuntsov, "Sovremennyi antinomizm," *Tserkovnyi vestnik* 1914, no. 21 (22 May): 626–27; S. Isakov, "Mysli ob iskusstve (k voprosu o 'futurizme')," *Novyi zhurnal dlia vsekh* 1914, no. 1 (January): 54; "Futurizm, ego ideologiia i sushchnost'," *Tserkovnyi vestnik* 1914, no. 27 (3 July): 823. Joan Neuberger explores the affinity between hooligans and futurists (though not citing such contemporary arguments), in *Hooliganism*, 142–57, and "Culture Besieged: Hooliganism and Futurism," in *Cultures in Flux: Lower-Class Values, Practices, and Resistance in Late Imperial Russia*, ed. Stephen P. Frank and Mark D. Steinberg (Princeton, 1994), 185–203.

123. See, for example, Neuberger, *Hooliganism*, esp. 235–43, 250–55.

124. I. V. Lebedev (Diadia Vania), "Kto vinovat," *Malen'kaia gazeta*, 31 October 1914, 3–4.

125. V. Ivanov, "Chto takoe khuliganstvo?" *Novyi zhurnal dlia vsekh* 1914, no. 1 (January): 47–50.

126. Zorin [Gastev], "Rabochii mir: novyi Piter," *Zhizn' dlia vsekh* 1913, no. 10 (October): 1457.

127. These are well-established definitions of "excess" in English. See *Oxford English Dictionary Online* (Oxford University Press, 2010) at http://www.oed .com/. For an important discussion of the relation of "excess" to the limits of reason, transgression of hierarchies, and deviance, see George Bataille, *Visions of Excess: Selected Writings, 1927–1939*, ed. Allan Stoekl (Minneapolis, 1985). Excess

is ubiquitous in literary decadence, evident in such foundational texts as Charles Baudelaire's poetry and especially J. K. Huysmans, *A rebours* (1884).

128. Stanley Cohen, *Folk Devils and Moral Manics: The Creation of Mods and Rockers* (London, 1972); Neuberger, *Hooliganism*, 3.

129. N. Mikhailovich, "Politika i erotika," *Svobodnye mysli*, 8/21 October 1907, 1–2; D., "Polovaia vakkhanaliia," *Gazeta-kopeika*, 27 July 1909, 3; Zhbankov, "Polovaia prestupnost'," *Sovremennyi mir* 1909, no. 7 (July): 91; V. L'vov-Rogachevskii, "M. Artsybashev," *Sovremennyi mir* 1909, no. 11 (November): pt. 2, 26; Chulkov, "Revniteli slova," *Zaprosy zhizni* 1910, no. 1 (5 January): 28.

130. Engelstein, *Keys to Happiness*. See also Etkind, *Sodom i Psikheia*. On the tensions between desire and dread in the modern city, see also Judith Walkowitz, *City of Dreadful Delight: Narratives of Sexual Danger in Late-Victorian London* (Chicago, 1992). The subtitle of this section is borrowed from Eric Naiman's study of public discourse about sex in early Soviet Russia, *Sex in Public*, though my emphasis is equally on public discourse about sex and on discourse about the public aspects of sex. For a discussion of the discourse of sexuality as anxiety-filled political and metaphysical "drama" in post-Soviet Russia, see Eliot Borenstein, *Overkill: Sex and Violence in Contemporary Russian Popular Culture* (Ithaca, 2008).

131. Attitudes: Zhbankov, "Polovaia prestupnost'," *Sovremennyi mir* 1909, no. 7 (July): 64. Exploitation: D-r B. Bentovin, *Torguiushchie telom: ocherki sovremennoi prostitutsii*, 3d ed. (St. Petersburg, 1910), 154. "Lovelaces": V. Pr., "Ulichnyi nakhal," *Gazeta-kopeika*, 3 July 1909, 3; "Lovelas-nozhevik," *Peterburgskii listok*, 5 May 1909, 5; "Dikoe napadenie lovelasa," ibid., 13 January 1910, 5. Pedophiles: *Gazeta-kopeika*, 9 June 1909, 3–4. Brothels: Bentovin, *Torguiushchie telom*, 165. Homosexuality: V. P. Ruadze, *K sudu! . . . Gomoseksual'nyi Peterburg* (St. Petersburg, 1908), 4. Naked performances: Fedor Kommissarzhevskii, "Kostium i nagota," *Maski*, no. 2 (1912): 49; *Gazeta-kopeika*, 27 November 1908, 3. Dance: Mikhail Bonch-Tomashevskii, *Kniga o tango: iskusstvo i seksual'nost'* (Moscow, 1914), 31 (on criticism); Zhbankov, "Polovaia prestupnost'," *Sovremennyi mir* 1909, no. 7 (July): 66. Print culture: ibid., 65–66; Bentovin, *Torguiushchie telom*, 153; Pchela, "Kul't razvrata," *Peterburgskii listok*, 8 December 1908, 2; Prof. A. Bronzov, "Pechal'nye znamenie vremeni," *Tserkovnyi vestnik* 1912, no. 12–13 (22 March): 372.

132. Pchela, "Kul't razvrata," *Peterburgskii listok*, 8 December 1908, 2.

133. Iurii Angarov, "Kvisisana," *Novye peterburgskie trushchoby*, 11–17. See also D., "Polovaia vakkhanaliia," *Gazeta-kopeika*, 27 July 1909, 3.

134. S. Liubosh, "Sviatoi nashego vremeni," *Zaprosy zhizni* 1910, no. 21 (6 June): 9–16.

135. In addition to the regular public criticisms the author refers to, it was the rule of some organizations, such as the Women's Polytechnic, that at organized

dances the tango was forbidden and officials would interfere when couples tried to dance it. "Intsident iz-za tango," *Peterburgskii listok*, 13 February 1914, 14.

136. Bonch-Tomashevskii, *Kniga o tango*, 5, 26–41. See also Yuri Tsivian, "Russia 1913: Cinema in the Cultural Landscape" in *Silent Film*, ed. Richard Abel (New Brunswick, N.J., 1996), 205–7.

137. Kommissarzhevskii, "Kostium i nagota," *Maski*, no. 2 (1912): 49–50. See also Engelstein, *Keys to Happiness*, 414–18; and the discussion of Duncan by Irina Sirotkina in *Rossiiskaia imperiia chuvstv: podkhody k kul'turnoi istorii emotsii*, ed. J. Plamper, S. Schahadat, and M. Elie (Moscow, 2010), 282–305.

138. In addition to works below, see also Pchela, "Kul't razvrata," *Peterburgskii listok*, 8 December 1908, 2; Pchela, "Plody pinkertonovshchina," ibid., 28 January 1910, 3; *Zhizn' dlia vsekh*, 1912, no. 1 (January): 108.

139. N. Mikhailovich, "Politika i erotika," *Svobodnye mysli*, 8/21 October 1907, 1–2.

140. Zhbankov, "Polovaia prestupnost'," *Sovremennyi mir* 1909, no. 7 (July): esp. 65–67, 91. See also Zhbankov, "Sovremennye samoubiistva," ibid., 1910, no. 3 (March): 47–48. On Zhbankov and his views, see Engelstein, *Keys to Happiness*, 266–68 and passim, and Laurie Bernstein, *Sonia's Daughters: Prostitutes and Their Regulation in Imperial Russia* (Berkeley, 1995), 241–46. For an example of the use of "*pir vo vremia chumy*," see Zorin [Gastev], "Rabochii mir," *Zhizn' dlia vsekh* 1911, no. 8 (August): 1075. See also Chapter 6.

141. Slobozhanin, "Iz sovremennykh perezhivanii," pt. 2 ("Pod-cheloveka"), *Zhizn' dlia vsekh* 1913, no. 2 (February): 311–19. These thoughts were inspired by the trial of a man who threw acid in the face of a girlfriend who had spurned him.

142. Ashkinazi, "Ot individualizma k bogostroitel'stvu," *Novyi zhurnal dlia vsekh* 1901, no. 6 (April): 96–109, quotations 105.

143. O. Gridina, "Griaznyi potok," *Gazeta-kopeika*, 27 February 1910, 3.

144. Iurii Angarov, "Kvisisana," *Novye peterburgskie trushchoby*, 11–17.

145. *Gazeta-kopeika*, 23 May 1910, 6; *Peterburgskii listok*, 11 July 1910, 10; *Peterburgskii kinematograf*, no. 12 (12 February 1911): izd. 1, 4. See also Engelstein, *Keys to Happiness*, 260–69.

146. Laura Engelstein examines in detail elite public responses to venereal disease, especially emphasizing issues of class and control. Engelstein, *Keys to Happiness*, esp. 185–211, 268–74.

147. I. Bikerman, "Sotsial'noe znachenie '606'," *Novyi zhurnal dlia vsekh* 1910, no. 24 (October): 89–95. For a humorous version of the critique, see *Ogonek* 1910, no. 31 (31 July/13 August): n.p., and Engelstein, *Keys to Happiness*, 210. "606" was arsphenamine, an arsenical compound developed by the German bacteriologist

Paul Erlich, and marketed for treatment of syphilis beginning in 1910 under the names "Salvarsan" and "606" (its development number), remaining in widespread use until the development of penicillin.

148. P. Ia. Rozenbakh, "Prichiny sovremennoi nervoznosti i samoubiistv," *Peterburgskaia gazeta*, 26 April 1909, 3.

149. Filevskii, "O bor'be s pornografiei," *Tserkovnyi vestnik* 1912, no. 17 (26 April): 510–13. See also Prof. A. Bronzov, "Pechal'nye znamenie vremeni," ibid., no. 12–13 (22 March): 372, and *Peterburgskii listok*, 24 April 1910, 4.

150. Pchela, "Kul't razvrata," *Peterburgskii listok*, 8 December 1908, 2; V. Burenin, "Kriticheskie ocherki," *Novoe vremia*, 15 May 1909, 3. See also G. S. Novopolin, *Pornograficheskii element v russkoi literature* (St. Petersburg, 1909) and Marcus Levitt and Andrei Toporkov, eds., *Eros and Pornography in Russian Culture/Eros i pornografiia v russkoi kul'ture* (Moscow, 1999).

151. Zorin, "Rabochii mir," *Zhizn' dlia vsekh* 1911, no. 8 (August): 1075.

152. Slobozhanin, "Iz sovremennykh perezhivanii," pt. 3, ibid., 1913, no. 3–4 (March–April): 461–62.

153. Zhbankov, "Polovaia prestupnost'," *Sovremennyi mir* 1909, no. 7 (July): 65.

154. Anichkov, "Kollektivizm, sverkh-chelovek, i sverkh-liubov'," *Sovremennik* 1912, no. 10 (October): 143.

155. V. Burenin, "Kriticheskie ocherki," *Novoe vremia*, 15 May 1909, 3.

156. V. L'vov-Rogachevskii, "M. Artsybashev," *Sovremennyi mir* 1909, no. 11 (November): pt. 2, 26–48.

157. See Engelstein, *Keys to Happiness*, 399–418; and Louise McReynolds, "Reading the Russian Romance: What Did the Keys to Happiness Unlock?" *Journal of Popular Culture* 31, no. 4 (1998): 95–108.

158. Kn. O. B-va, "Ch'ia zhertva?" *Peterburgskii listok*, esp. 2 April 1909, 2; 6 April 1909, 1; 7 April 1909, 2; 7 May 1909, 2; 22 May 1909, 2.

159. See Louise McReynolds, "Home Was Never Where the Heart Was: Domestic Dystopias in Russia's Silent Movie Melodrama," in *Imitations of Life: Two Centuries of Melodrama in Russia*, ed. Louise McReynolds and Joan Neuberger (Durham, N.C., 2002), 127–51.

160. Ruadze, *K sudu!*; "Nravy Nevskogo prospekta," *Gazeta-kopeika*, 2 April 1910, 5; Dan Healey, *Homosexual Desire in Revolutionary Russia: The Regulation of Sexual and Gender Dissent* (Chicago, 2001), chap. 1. On the relationship between urban public space and male homosexual identities and practices, see Matt Houlbrook, *Queer London: Perils and Pleasures in the Sexual Metropolis, 1918–1957* (Chicago, 2005).

161. Ruadze, *K sudu!* 113.

162. See Healy, *Homosexual Desire*, 41–42.

163. Ruadze, *K sudu!* esp. 6, 15, 17–25, 102–9.

164. Zhbankov, "Polovaia prestupnost'," *Sovremennyi mir* 1909, no. 7 (July): 65.

165. See the wide-ranging discussion of gender uncertainties and homosexual desire in "decadent" literature in Matich, *Erotic Utopia*. See also Engelstein, *Keys to Happiness*, 388–91, and Healey, *Homosexual Desire*, 101–2, 106.

166. Mariia Volgina, "Okhota na detei," *Gazeta-kopeika*, 14 August 1913, 3.

167. For discussion of terminology and legal issues concerning sex with minors, see Engelstein, *Keys to Happiness*, 76–80.

168. *Novoe vremia*, 28 May 1908, 13; 1 June 1908, 4. See also Alexandra Oberländer, "Die Provokation ging auf dem Nevskij spazieren: Die Wahrnehmung sexueller Gewalt im ausgehenden Zarenreich, 1880–1914." (Ph.D. diss., Humboldt University, Berlin, 2010).

169. V. Tr-ov, "Nasha ulitsa: Milyi diadia," *Gazeta-kopeika*, 22 August 1908, 4. See also L. T-k., "Diuluizm v Peterburge (torgovlia maloletnymi det'mi), *Peterburgskii listok*, 23 October 1908, 2; ibid., 9 June 1909, 3; Ol'ga Gridina, "Beregite detei!" ibid., 28 October 1909, 3; *Peterburgskii listok*, 5 July 1910, 3; "Po-stopam Diu-liu," *Gazeta-kopeika*, 17 June 1912, 3; "Po-stopam Diu-Liu," *Peterburgskii listok*, 25 January 1913, 4.

170. "Eshche odin Diu-Liu," *Peterburgskii listok*, 3 September 1910, 3.

171. Arnol'dov, "Svidrigailovy," *Gazeta-kopeika*, 28 February 1909, 4.

172. S. Liubosh, "Griaznaia volna," *Sovremennoe slovo*, 7 April 1910, 1.

173. *Gazeta-kopeika*, 7 March 1909, 3; "Uzhasnoe prestuplenie," *Peterburgskii listok*, 30 May 1913, 4.

174. "V obshchestve zashchity detei ot zhestokogo obrashcheniia," ibid., 16 September 1910, 5.

175. Bentovin, *Torguiushchie telom*, 166.

176. Amori, *Tainy Nevskogo prospekta*, 5–9.

177. L. T-k., "Diuluizm v Peterburge (torgovlia maloletnymi det'mi), *Peterburgskii listok*, 23 October 1908, 2.

178. Amori, *Tainy Nevskogo prospekta*, 5–9.

179. Bentovin, *Torguiushchie telom*, 163–67; Ol'ga Gridina, "Beregite detei!" *Gazeta-kopeika*, 28 October 1909, 3; V. T., "Uzhasy zhizni: detskaia prostitutsiia," ibid., 20 July 1912, 3. The law defined the boundary between sexual innocence and responsibility variously at fourteen or seventeen, though, after 1901, women under twenty-one could not be registered in brothels. On child prostitution, see also Bernstein, *Sonia's Daughters*, 42–46; and Engelstein, *Keys to Happiness*, 80, 89–91, 275–97.

180. "Detskii razvrat," *Gazeta-kopeika*, 17 October 1908, 3.

181. M. Semenov, "Za okonnymi zanaveskami," *Novye peterburgskie trushchoby*, 32–37. See also Rozanov, "G-zha Miliukova o s"ezde po bor'be s prostitutsiei," *Novoe vremia*, 14 May 1910, 4.

182. V. T., "Uzhasy zhizni: detskaia prostitutsiia," *Gazeta-kopeika*, 20 July 1912, 3; Bentovin, *Torguiushchie telom*, 165. See also I. V. Lebedev (Diadia Vania), "Panel'nye," *Malen'kaia gazeta*, 26 October 1914, 2–3.

183. Engelstein, *Keys to Happiness*, 291, 293–94.

184. Al. Fedorov, "Odna," *Peterburgskii kinematograf*, 16 February 1911, 2.

185. V. Pr., "Ulichnyi nakhal," *Gazeta-kopeika*, 3 July 1909, 3.

186. Vadim, "Krasnaia Shapochka," ibid., 14 July 1913, 4.

187. Walkowitz, *City of Dreadful Delight*, 3–7, 15–18, 50–52, 97–105, and passim.

188. For example, *Peterburgskii listok*, 6 May 1907, 7; "Nash demi-mond," supplement to the journal *Shut*, 1911, no. 5.

189. For example, the serialized novel "Ch'ia zhertva?" in *Peterburgskii listok* in 1909; Evgenii Bauer's film *Child of the Big City* (*Ditia bol'shogo goroda*, 1914); and other films (or stories for films), both Russian and imported, described in *Peterburgskii kinematograf*, 5 January 1911, 26 January 1911, 17 March 1911, 25 March 1911, and 27 March 1911.

190. "Nash demi-mond," *Shut: Khudozhestvennyi zhurnal s karikaturami*, 1911, no. 3, 6. The ellipses are in the original.

191. V. Nedesheva, *Nevskii prospekt* (St. Petersburg, 1906), 3–4, 10.

192. *Peterburg noch'iu*, supplement to the journal *Shut*, 1911, no. 3 (12 November 1911): n.p.; N. V. Nikitin, *Peterburg noch'iu: bytovye ocherki* (St. Petersburg, 1903), 99.

193. For example, "Zhenshchina v spal'ne," supplement to the journal *Shut*, 1911, no. 1: n.p.; P. Cher-skii, "Paradoksy sovremennosti," *Novyi zhurnal dlia vsekh* 1914, no. 4 (April): 51–52.

194. The best study of prostitution in Russia is Bernstein, *Sonia's Daughters*. Also useful are Engelstein, *Keys to Happiness*, and N. B. Lebina and M. V. Shkarovskii, *Prostitutsiia v Peterburge* (Moscow, 1994).

195. For example, Zhbankov, "Polovaia prestupnost'," *Sovremennyi mir* 1909, no. 7 (July): 63.

196. Skitalets, "Belyia baryni," *Gazeta-kopeika*, 1 November 1913, 3.

197. Ibid., 16 April 1910, 3.

198. "Strashnye tsifry," *Sovremennoe slovo*, 17 April 1910, 1.

199. Bernstein, *Sonia's Daughters*, 46–47.

200. Bentovin, *Torguiushchie telom*, chap. 5 ("Tainaia prostitutsiia"). See also Bernstein, *Sonia's Daughters*, 46–56.

201. Pchela, "Kul't razvrata," *Peterburgskii listok*, 8 December 1908, 2.

202. For example, Vladimir Mikhnevich, *Iazvy Peterburga: opyt istoriko-statisticheskogo issledovaniia nravstvennosti stolichnogo naseleniia* (St. Petersburg, 1886), 147–50; N. V. Nikitin, *Peterburg noch'iu* (St. Petersburg, 1903), 55–59.

203. See, especially, Bernstein, *Sonia's Daughters*, 191–232, 265–95.

204. Nedesheva, *Nevskii prospekt*, 11–16.

205. Zorin [Gastev], "Rabochii mir: O zhenshchine," *Zhizn' dlia vsekh* 1912, no. 3 (March): 449–57.

206. "Omut zhizni: obyknovennaia istoriia," *Gazeta-kopeika*, 6 July 1908, 2–3.

207. Obyvatel', "Samoubiistvo," ibid., 3 January 1909, 2.

208. "Sem' dnei u torgovtsev zhivym tovarom," *Peterburgskii listok*, 9 February 1913, 6; "Novaia zhertva torgovtsev zhivym tovarom," ibid., 15 February 1913, 3.

209. "Na posledniuiu stupen'," *Malen'kaia gazeta*, 23 July 1915, 3.

210. Ol'ga Gridina, "Obyknovennaia istoriia," *Gazeta-kopeika*, 4 October 1910, 3; "Po baryshu—chest'," ibid., 5 October 1910, 3–5; "Est' zhizn', kotoraia . . . ," ibid., 6 October 1910, 3. See also "Stolichnye uzhasy," *Peterburgskii listok*, 27 April 1909, 2.

211. A. M., "Peterburgskaia ulitsa," *Peterburgskii listok*, 27 November 1905, 3. See also V. Tr-ov, "Nasha ulitsa," *Gazeta-kopeika*, 14 August 1908, 3–4; "Soiuz prostitutok i khuliganov," ibid., 28 December 1911, 5; ibid., 3 September 1913, 3; and Bentovin, *Torguiushchie telom*, 225–26.

212. See the lengthy series "Stolichnye ved'ma" in the newspaper *Malen'kaia gazeta* in 1915 (esp. 10 July 1915, 3; 15 July 1915, 2–3; 16 July 1915, 3; 30 July 1915, 3; M. Semenov, "Za okonnymi zanaveskami," *Novye peterburgskie trushchoby*, 30–32. See also "Torgovlia 'zhivym tovarom' v Peterburg," *Peterburgskii listok*, 3 March 1910, 4.

213. Engelstein, *Keys to Happiness*, 130–44 (quoting from Tarnovskii's *Prostitutsiia i abolitsionizm* [St. Petersburg, 1888]). See also Bernstein, *Sonia's Daughters*, 126–28, 194–95.

214. Bentovin, *Torguiushchie telom*, esp. 1–67, 126, 140, 144, 232. An earlier version of some of this material appeared as "Torguiushhiia telom," *Russkoe bogatstvo*, nos. 11–12 (November–December 1904): 80–113; 137–76. See also Bernstein, *Sonia's Daughters*, 172–75, and Engelstein, *Keys to Happiness*, 289–90, 293–95.

CHAPTER SIX. HAPPINESS

1. *Gazeta-kopeika*, 19 June 1908, 1 (editorial in issue no. 1).

2. Ibid., 19 June 1909, 1.

3. Apart from Zarubin, the quotes are from the industrialist and Duma deputy Aleksandr Konovalov, and the psychiatrists and academics Vladimir Bekhterev and Mikhail Nizhegorodtsev. *Ogonek* 1913, no. 1 (6 January): n.p.

4. *Gazeta-kopeika*, 1 January 1912, 2 (by Skitalets).

5. "Nashim chitateliam," *Peterburgskii listok*, 1 January 1913, 1.

6. N. Nikiforov, "S novym godom" (poem) and the editorial "S novym schast'em," *Peterburgskii listok*, 1 January 1914, 2.

7. "S novym godom!" *Tserkovnyi vestnik* 1910, no. 1 (7 January): 3.

8. Protopopov, "Sud'ba russkikh gorodov," *Gorodskoe delo* 1911, no. 24 (15 December): 1715.

9. Skitalets, "Bodrye liudi," *Gazeta-kopeika*, 10 April 1911, 4.

10. Speech by Baron Pozen to the State Council, 29 January 1914, *Peterburgskii listok*, 30 January 1914, 4.

11. In a Russian context, an even more precise argument about the will is what Mikhail Bakhtin would call, in the 1920s, "emotional-volitional tone" (*emotsional'no-volevoi ton*). M. M. Bakhtin, *K filosofii postupka* (Moscow, 1986).

12. Skitalets, "Stal'naia rasa," *Gazeta-kopeika*, 16 January 1912, 4.

13. Strannik, "Dva goda v gorode Schast'ia," *Teosoficheskoe obozrenie*, no. 2 (November 1907): 89. See also responses to Mark Twain and Isabel Duncan discussed later in this chapter.

14. *Ogonek* 1913, no. 1 (6 January): n.p.

15. Shirokii, "Cherty sovremennoi russkoi zhizni," *Novyi zhurnal dlia vsekh* 1914, no. 1 (January): 45-46.

16. "S novym schast'em," *Peterburgskii listok*, 1 January 1914, 2. See also Slobozhanin, "Iz sovremennykh perezhivanii," pt. 2 (" 'Pod-cheloveki' nashego vremeni"), *Zhizn' dlia vsekh* 1913, no. 2 (February): 320.

17. V. Rozanov, "Malen'kii fel'eton: geroicheskaia lichnost'," *Novoe vremia*, 3 December 1909, 3; Rozanov, "Voprosy russkogo truda," *Novoe vremia*, 26 March 1909, 3-4.

18. V. Musin, "Ulibaites'," *Peterburgskii gid*, no. 3 (November 1912): 1.

19. Aleksei Kruchenykh, "Novye puti slova," in *Troe*, ed. A. Kruchenykh, V. Khlebnikov, and E. Guro (St. Petersburg, 1913).

20. Genrikh Tastevin, *Futurizm (na puti k novomy simvolizmu)* (Moscow, 1914), 5-6. See also V. L'vov-Rogachevskii, "Simvolisty i nasledniki ikh," *Sovremennik* 1913, no. 6 (June): 263, 271.

21. Hillary L. Fink, *Bergson and Russian Modernism, 1900-1930* (Evanston, 1999), chaps. 2-3; Frances Nethercott, *Une rencontre philosophique: Bergson en Russie (1907-1917)* (Paris, 1995).

22. Vladimir Markov, "Printsipy novogo iskusstva," *Soiuz molodezhi*, no. 1 (April 1912): 5-14.

23. M. Matiushin, "O vystavke 'poslednikh futuristov'," *Ocharovannyi strannik* (Spring 1916): 17-18.

24. For example, G. Plekhanov, "Iskusstvo i obshchestvennaia zhizn'," *Sovremennik* 1913, no. 1 (January): 130–50.

25. "Vystavka 'Soiuza molodezhi'," *Ogonek* 1913, no. 1 (6/19 January): n.p.

26. *Zhizn' dlia vsekh* 1910, no. 3 (March): 135–37; *Novyi zhurnal dlia vsekh* 1910, no. 17 (March): 114, 118.

27. Georgii Chulkov, "Pamiati V. F. Kommissarzhevskoi," *Apollon 1910*, no. 6 (March): 22–24.

28. Protopopov, "Sud'ba russkikh gorodov," *Gorodskoe delo* 1911, no. 24 (15 December): 1717.

29. Skitalets, "Dvizhenie," *Gazeta-kopeika*, 20 July 1911, 3. As seen in Chapter 2, this was not the first time he used this phrase.

30. *Peterburgskii kinematograf*, 5 January 1911, 2.

31. Al. Fedorov, "K solntsu!" ibid., 12 February 1911, 2. See also Chapters 1 and 2 for other positive representations of the modern city.

32. For a recent discussion, see Daniel Beer, *Renovating Russia: The Human Sciences and the Fate of Liberal Modernity, 1880–1930* (Ithaca, 2008).

33. Ant. Oss-ii, "Soznatel'nost'," *Peterburgskii listok*, 7 March 1909, 2.

34. Aleksandr Gizetti, review of a series of books on new ideas in philosophy, in *Sovremennik* 1912, no. 9 (September): 383.

35. Ol'ga Gridina, "Dorogie ogon'ki," *Gazeta-kopeika*, 16 December 1911, 5; Skitalets, "Vse khoroshi," ibid., 17 October 1916, 3. On other occasions, as we have seen, Gridina doubted that even one righteous person could be found. See Chapter 5.

36. Ashkinazi, "Ot individualizma k bogostroitel'stvu," *Novyi zhurnal dlia vsekh* 1909, no. 6 (April): 105.

37. "Nakanune velikogo pereloma," *Tserkovnyi vestnik* 1914, no. 44 (30 October): 1313.

38. *Gorodskoe delo* 1915, no. 15–16 (1–15 August): 799. See also V. Posse, "Obshchestvennaia zhizn'," *Zhizn' dlia vsekh* 1915, no. 8–9 (August–September): 1317.

39. Georgii Chulkov, "Revniteli slova," *Zaprosy zhizni* 1910, no. 1 (5 January): 28.

40. V. A. Ternavtsev, in discussions at the Religious-Philosophical Society (of which he was one of the founders) on 12 December 1907, *Zapiski S.-Peterburgskogo religiozno-filosofskogo obshchestva*, no. 2 (1908): 64.

41. Bishop Georgii, for example, warned that it was human folly to think that the path to "happiness" lay in living "by the will of their own hearts," rather than trusting in God's will, guided by the words of the Lord's Prayer, "Thy will be done on earth as it is in heaven." Episkop Georgii, "Slovo na Novyi god," *Tserkovnyi vestnik* 1912, no. 1 (5 January): 1–3.

42. For example, I. Davidson, "Sila illiuzii," *Novyi zhurnal dlia vsekh* 1912, no. 7 (July): 94.

43. Mikhail Kovalevskii, "Zatish'e," *Zaprosy zhizni* 1911, no. 12 (23 December): 705.

44. K. Arsen'ev in *Slovo*, reprinted in *Vesna* 1908, no. 2 (13 January): 11.

45. Protopopov, "Sud'ba russkikh gorodov," *Gorodskoe delo* 1911, no. 24 (15 December): 1715–18; "Peterburgskaia khronika," ibid., 1913, no. 24 (15 December): 1693.

46. O. Gridina, "Vpered," *Gazeta-kopeika*, 25 December 1909, 6–7.

47. For example, the New Year's toast by the art critic and journalist L. N. Benua. *Ogonek* 1913, no. 1 (6 January): n.p.

48. *Gazeta-kopeika*, 19 June 1908, 1.

49. "Ot redaktsii," *Gorodskoe delo*, 1909, no. 1 (1 January): 3.

50. Skitalets, "Dvizhenie," *Gazeta-kopeika*, 20 July 1911, 3.

51. "S novym godom!" *Tserkovnyi vestnik* 1910, no. 1 (7 January): 3.

52. Review of the first volume: ibid., 1909, no. 33 (13 August): 1013; summary of the film: "Kliuchi schast'ia," *Peterburgskie kinemoteatry*, no. 79 ([November] 1913): 1. See also Laura Engelstein, *Keys to Happiness: Sex and the Search for Modernity in Fin-de-Siècle Russia* (Ithaca, 1992), 404–14.

53. Sally West, "The Material Promised Land: Advertising's Modern Agenda in Late Imperial Russia," *Russian Review* 57, no. 3 (July 1998): 345–63; see also West, "Constructing Consumer Culture: Advertising in Imperial Russia to 1914" (Ph.D. diss., University of Illinois, 1995), and West, *I Shop in Moscow: Advertising and the Creation of Consumer Culture in Late Tsarist Russia* (DeKalb, 2011); Steve Smith and Catriona Kelly, "Commercial Culture and Consumerism," in *Constructing Russian Culture in the Age of Revolution, 1881–1940*, ed. Catriona Kelly and David Shepherd (Oxford, 1998), 106–55; Christine Ruane, *The Empire's New Clothes: A History of the Russian Fashion Industry, 1700–1917* (New Haven, 2009), esp. 143–49, 209–20.

54. West, "The Material Promised Land," esp. 362–63.

55. For example, the advertisement for Kola-Dul'ts (Kola-Dultz) in *Peterburgskii listok*, 5 June 1913, 5.

56. Susan K. Morrissey, "The Economy of Nerves: Health, Commercial Culture, and the Self in Late Imperial Russia," *Slavic Review* 69, no. 3 (Fall 2010): 645–75. See also Beer, *Renovating Russia*.

57. M. Men'shikov, "Pis'mo k bliznym," *Novoe vremia*, 30 May 1910, 4.

58. Vladimir Markov, "Printsipy novogo iskusstva," *Soiuz molodezhi*, no. 1 (April 1912): 5–6; no. 2 (June 1912): 5.

59. Speranskii, "Ideia tragicheskoi krasoty i Leonid Andreev," *Novyi zhurnal dlia vsekh* 1908, no. 1 (November): 77.

60. V. A. Posse, "Venera Milosskaia," *Zhizn' dlia vsekh* 1911, no. 8 (August): 1135. This essay was prompted by the recent theft of the Mona Lisa from the Louvre museum—for Posse, the sixteenth-century Gioconda was an example of art that "gazes into your soul and confuses it."

61. M. Slobozhanin, "Idealizm v prakticheskoi zhizni," *Zhizn' dlia vsekh* 1914, no. 1 (January): 103. See also M. Slobozhanin, "Iz sovremennykh perezhivanii," pt. 3: "Ob estetikh noveishei formatsii i estetizme voobshche," *Zhizn' dlia vsekh* 1913, no. 3–4 (MarchApril): 461.

62. Ol'ga Gridina, "V temnuiu noch'," *Gazeta-kopeika*, 17 October 1910, 4.

63. Strannik, "Dva goda v gorode Schast'ia," *Teosoficheskoe obozrenie*, no. 2 (November 1907): 89.

64. *Ogonek* 1913, no. 1 (6 January): n.p.

65. After trade unions were legalized in 1906, most produced irregular newspapers, generally edited by socialist activists. In 1912, Bolsheviks and Mensheviks were for the first time allowed to publish legal newspapers of their own; the key national papers of both parties were published in St. Petersburg. Other legal publications closely associated with the socialist movements included the magazine *Sovremennyi mir* and *Zhizn' dlia vsekh*.

66. See Martov's famous essay "On Agitation" (1894) and discussions in F. I. Dan, *Proiskhozhdenie bol'shevizma* (New York, 1946), esp. 244–45, and Leopold Haimson, *The Russian Marxists and the Origins of Bolshevism* (Boston, 1955), chap. 5.

67. V. I. Lenin, "Chto delat'? Nabolevshie voprosy nashego dvizheniia," in *Sochineniia*, 4th ed., 40 vols. (Moscow, 1954–62) 5:435.

68. Lenin, "Ivan Vasil'evich Babushkin (nekrolog)," *Rabochaia gazeta*, 18/31 December 1910, in *Sochineniia*, 16:333–34.

69. Lenin, "Pis'mo k tovarishcham" (published in *Rabochii Put'*, 19, 20, 21 October 1917), in *Sochineniia*, 26:166–84.

70. Letter to N. A. Rozhkov, 29 January 1919, in *The Unknown Lenin*, ed. Richard Pipes (New Haven, 1999), 62. Lenin used this same phrase often, for example in "Neschastnyi mir," *Pravda*, 24 February 1918, 1.

71. Letter to M. F. Sokolov, 16 May 1921 (first published in *Pravda*, 1 January 1924), in *Sochineniia*, 35:419–20. See also *The Lenin Anthology*, ed. Robert C. Tucker (New York, 1975), 717. See also Mark Steinberg, *Proletarian Imagination: Self, Modernity, and the Sacred in Russia, 1910–1925* (Ithaca, 2002), esp. 283–84; Sheila Fitzpatrick, "Happiness and *Toska*: An Essay in the History of Emotions in Pre-war Soviet Russia," *Australian Journal of Politics and History* 50, no. 3 (2004): 357–71; Kenneth Pinnow, *Lost to the Collective: Suicide and the Promise of Soviet Socialism, 1921–1929* (Ithaca, 2010).

72. Antonio Gramsci, *Prison Notebooks*, 3 vols. (New York, 1991–2007), esp. 1:474–75.

73. S. Litovtsev, "Russkaia intelligentsia i 'Vekhi': Lektsiia P. N. Miliukova," *Rech'*, 11 February 1911, 3.

74. Tan, "Nastroenie," *Rech'*, 23 October 1910, 2.

75. I. Gessen, "Kvadratura kruga," ibid., 20 September 1910, 2 (a review of a recent book on the history of utopias).

76. Mikhail Luk'ianov, *Rossiiskii konservatizm i reforma, 1907–1914* (Stuttgart, 2006). See also Mikhail Suslov, "Geopolitical Utopias in Comparative Perspective 1880–1914" (Doctoral thesis, European University Institute, Florence, 2009); and Mark Steinberg, *The Fall of the Romanovs: Political Dreams and Personal Struggles in a Time of Revolution* (New Haven, 1995), introduction.

77. See, for example, the discussion of why urban life led people away from Orthodoxy in *Tserkovnyi vestnik* 1910, no. 41 (14 October): 1279; M. Men'shikov's complaints about the "decline of faith" in both city and country and a process of secularization even within the church, in "Padenie very," *Novoe vremia*, 15 August 1910, 3; and a report on the decline of the church as the faithful and even clergy turn away from it, in "Raspad tserkovno-prikhodskoi zhizni," *Peterburgskii listok*, 14 January 1910, 2.

78. S. A. Askol'dov [Alekseev], "O starom i novom religioznom soznanii," *Zapiski S.-Peterburgskogo religiozno-filosofskogo obshchestva*, no. 1 (1908), 3 (meeting of 3 October 1907); L. S-g, "Starye i novye bogoiskateli," *Zaprosy zhizni* 1909, no. 4 (8 November): 12; "Raby svobody," *Tserkovnyi vestnik* 1911, no. 31 (4 August): 963; ibid., 1914, no. 44 (30 October): 1313–15; "Religiia i obshchestvennaia zhizn'," ibid., 1913, no. 26 (27 June): 798–99; ibid., 1914, no. 40 (2 October): 1204–5; "Religioznost' i samoubiistvo molodezhi," *Peterburgskii listok*, 19 January 1913, 3.

79. P. Pertsov, "Literaturnye pis'ma," *Novoe vremia*, 7 January 1909, 4.

80. "Sovremennoe bogoiskatel'stvo," *Tserkovnyi vestnik* 1909, no. 11 (12 March): 323. See also M. Men'shikov, "Padenie very," *Novoe vremia*, 15 August 1910, 3.

81. I. Knizhnik, "Sovremennyi progress religii," *Zhizn' dlia vsekh* 1914, no. 1 (January): 96–97.

82. See A. V. Lunacharskii, "Ateizm," *Ocherki po filosofii marksizma: filosofskii sbornik* (St. Petersburg, 1908), esp. pp. 115–116, 148–157 (and other contributions to this collection); Lunacharskii, *Religiia i sotsializm*, 2 vols. (St. Petersburg, 1908–11); and discussions of Marxist "God-building" (*bogostroitel'stvo*) by Jutta Scherrer, "'Ein gelber und ein blauer Teufel': Zur Entstehung der Begriffe 'bogostroitel'stvo' und 'bogoiskatel'stvo'," *Forschungen zur osteuropäischen Geschichte* 25 (1978): 319–329; Scherrer, "L'intelligentsia russe: sa quête da la 'vérité religieuse du socialisme'," *Le temps de la réflexion* 2 (1981): 134–151.

83. "Sovremennoe bogoiskatel'stvo," *Tserkovnyi vestnik* 1909, no. 11 (12 March): 321.

84. For general discussions of these religious movements and trends, see A. S. Pankratov, *Ishchushchie boga* (Moscow, 1911); Nicolas Zernov, *The Russian Religious Renaissance of the Twentieth Century* (New York, 1963); A. I. Klibanov, *Istoriia religioznogo sektantstva v Rossii* (Moscow, 1965); Gregory Freeze, "Subversive Piety: Religion and the Political Crisis in Late Imperial Russia," *Journal of Modern History* 68 (June 1996): 308–50; Bernice Glatzer Rosenthal, ed., *The Occult in Russian and Soviet Culture* (Ithaca, 1997); Mark Steinberg and Heather Coleman, eds., *Sacred Stories: Religion and Spirituality in Modern Russia* (Bloomington, 2007). For a study of Russian discourse about sectarianism, see Aleksandr Etkind, *Khlyst: Sekty, literatura i revoliutsiia* (Moscow, 1998).

85. Quoted in Aileen Kelly, *Toward Another Shore: Russian Thinkers between Necessity and Chance* (New Haven, 1998), p. 174. See also *Vekhi-Landmarks*, trans. and ed. Marshall Schatz and Judith Zimmerman (Armonk, 1994).

86. *Tserkovnyi vestnik* 1910, no. 14 (8 April): 436–38. See also "Dukhobory (lektsiia I. M. Tregubova)," *Peterburgskii listok*, 9 May 1907, 3; "Sovremennaia religioznye techeniia," ibid., 12 December 1908, 4.

87. "S novom godom!" *Tserkovnyi vestnik* 1910, no. 1 (1 January): 3–4.

88. A. Bronzov, ibid., 1909, no. 1 (1 January): 6–7. See also Nadieszda Kizenko, *A Prodigal Saint: Father John of Kronstadt and the Russian People* (University Park, 2000).

89. *Peterburgskii listok*, 22 December 1907, 4. See also reports ibid., 9 and 16 December 1907, and Kizenko, *A Prodigal Saint*, chap. 6, esp. 200.

90. N. Tal'nikov, "Sektanty v Peterburge," *Peterburgskii listok*, 3 March 1909, 6. See also "Sovremennoe bogoiskatel'stvo," *Tserkovnyi vestnik* 1909, no. 11 (12 March): 321–23.

91. Kaled, "Ivanushkovtsy," *Sanktpeterburgskie vedomosti*, 9 December 1910, 2–3; A. Iadrov, "'Bratets' Ivan Churikov," *Malen'kaia gazeta*, 15 December 1914, 3.

92. N., "Ioannit-Istselitel'," *Peterburgskii listok*, 7 March 1909, 2.

93. "Otgadyvatel'," *Gazeta-kopeika*, 1 June 1909, 3.

94. Tal'nikov, "Sektanty v Peterburge (iz nabliudenii i vpechatlenii)," *Peterburgskii listok*, 24 December 1907, 5; Tal'nikov, "Sektanty v Peterburge: 'Vesna' sektantstva," ibid., 3 March 1908, 5; Tal'nikov, "Sektanty v Peterburge," ibid., 20 October 1908, 2.

95. N. Tal'nikov, "Sektanty v Peterburge," ibid., 24 December 1907, 5. See also Tal'nikov, "Sektanty i kholera," ibid., 7 September 1908, 3; "Raby svobody," *Tserkovnyi vestnik* 1911, no. 31 (4 August): 959–63; K. T-i, "Sektantskaia propaganda," *Peterburgskii listok*, 5 April 1909, 2; ibid., 18 January 1910, 3. See also Heather J. Coleman, *Russian Baptists and Spiritual Revolution, 1905–1929* (Bloomington, 2005).

96. N. Tal'nikov, "Sektanty v Peterburge," *Peterburgskii listok*, 20 October 1908, 2.

97. One cannot be certain of the factuality of all of the details Tal'nikov reported, especially concerning many small sects that he investigated. He was writing for a paper more concerned with keeping readers interested than in reporting only confirmed facts, and religious deviance could be as entertaining (and troubling) as stories of violence, crime, and suicide. Still, his overall picture of spreading sectarianism is consistent with other accounts.

98. N. Tal'nikov, "Sektanty v Peterburge," *Peterburgskii listok*, 3 March 1908, 5.

99. For example, N. Tal'nikov, "Sektanty v Peterburge," ibid., 28 January 1908, 5 and 26 March 1909, 5.

100. Putnik, "P'ianstvo telesnoe i p'ianstvo dukhovnye," *Malen'kaia gazeta*, 18 December 1915, 2. Leonid Galich also emphasized the preoccupation with "perfection" among "neo-Christians." Galich, "Novye techeniia," *Rech'*, 1 January 1908, 5.

101. N. Tal'nikov, "Sektanty v Peterburge," *Peterburgskii listok*, 28 January 1908, 5. See also A. M. "U trezvennikov," *Malen'kaia gazeta*, 1 October 1914, 3; A. Iadrov, "'Bratets" Ivan Churikov," ibid., 8 December 1914, 3; ibid., 15 December 1914, 3; 22 December 1914, 3; and W. Arthur McKee, "Sobering Up the Soul of the People: The Politics of Popular Temperance in Late Imperial Russia," *Russian Review* 58, no. 2 (April 1999): 212-33.

102. N. Tal'nikov, "Sektanty v Peterburge," ibid., 20 October 1908, 2.

103. N. Tal'nikov, "Sektanty v Peterburge," ibid., 26 March 1909, 5.

104. N. Tal'nikov, "Sektanty v Peterburge," ibid., 10 April 1908, 5.

105. N. Tal'nikov, "Sektanty v Peterburge," ibid., 7 January 1908, 3. See also N. Tal'nikov, "Sektanty v Peterburge," ibid., 11 February 1908, 5,

106. N. Tal'nikov, "Sektanty v Peterburge," ibid., 5 November 1908, 1. As Tal'nikov recognized, such "self-proclaimed holy men" were part of a long tradition in Russia.

107. N. Tal'nikov, "Ulichnaia sektantskaia missiia," ibid., 23 September 1908, 2. For other discussions on the importance of "hope" in attracting people to both traditional and unorthodox religion, see *Teosoficheskoe obozrenie*, no. 3 (December 1907): 113-14; Fal'ks, "Zachem my zhivem?" ibid., 129-30; Ep. Mikhail, "Nevidimyi grad," *Sovremennoe slovo*, 18 April 1910, 1.

108. "Bludnyi syn," *Tserkovnyi vestnik* 1914, no. 22 (29 May): 652; "Religioznost' i samoubiistvo molodezhi," *Peterburgskii listok*, 19 January 1913, 3; S. A. Askol'dov, "O starom i novom religioznom soznanii," *Zapiski S.-Peterburgskogo religiozno-filosofskogo obshchestva*, no. 1 (1908): 6 (meeting of 3 October 1907); P. Cher-skii, "Paradoksy sovremennosti," *Novyi zhurnal dlia vsekh* 1914, no. 4 (April): 51.

109. For example, "V chem sila sektantstva?" *Tserkovnyi vestnik* 1911, no. 38 (22 September): 1178-79.

110. N. Tal'nikov, "Sektanty v Peterburge," *Peterburgskii listok*, 28 January 1908, 5. A church investigation also found him to be ignorant of the holy texts and even the Gospels. " 'Bratets' Chirikov u mitropolita Vladimira," *Peterburgskii listok*, 6 June 1913, 4 (reprinted from *Kolokol*).

111. *Tserkovnyi vestnik* 1910, no. 50 (16 December): 1587. Partly paraphrasing the arguments of Kaled, "Ivanushkovtsy," *Sanktpeterburgskie vedomosti*, 9 December 1910, 3.

112. *Dumy narodnye*, no. 6 ([6 March] 1910): 1. See also ibid., no. 3 (13 February 1910): 4.

113. " 'Bratets' Churikov u mitropolita Vladimira," *Peterburgskii listok*, 6 June 1913, 4 (reprinted from *Kolokol*); A. M. "V gostiakh u 'brattsa'," *Malen'kaia gazeta*, 3 October 1914, 3-4.

114. K. T-i, "Sektantskaia propaganda," *Peterburgskii listok*, 5 April 1909, 2.

115. Ibid., 18 January 1910, 3.

116. For example, N. Tal'nikov, "Sektanty v Peterburge," ibid., 26 March 1909, 5.

117. N. Tal'nikov, "Sektanty v Peterburge," ibid., 10 March 1908, 3.

118. Ibid., 21 December 1908, 5.

119. A. Bronzov in *Tserkovnyi vestnik* 1909, no. 1 (1 January): 7-9.

120. "Dukhovnye bluzhdaniia," ibid., 1910, no. 46 (18 November): 1425-28.

121. For example, "Sovremennye religioznye techeniia," *Peterburgskii listok*, 12 December 1908, 4.

122. In addition to citations following, see "Bludnyi syn," *Tserkovnyi vestnik* 1914, no. 22 (29 May): 652-53. See also ibid., 1916 (7 February): 65-66.

123. Aspiration for novelty: "Psikhologiia sektantstva," ibid., *Tserkovnyi vestnik* 1910, no. 37 (16 September): 1150. 132. Spiritual freedom: "Raby svobody," ibid., *Tserkovnyi vestnik* 1911, no. 31 (4 August): 959. This was a critical view; for a positive view of sectarianism seeking "equality, fraternity, and liberty," but "without bloodshed or the dirt of the streets," see "Sovremennye religioznye techeniia," *Peterburgskii listok*, 12 December 1908, 4. 133. Spiritual creativity: *Tserkovnyi vestnik* 1910, no. 50 (16 December): 1587; "V chem sila sektantstva?" ibid., *Tserkovnyi vestnik* 1911, no. 38 (22 September): 1179.

124. "Psikhologiia sektanstva," ibid., 1910, no. 37 (16 September): 1150-51.

125. Leonid Galich [Gabrilovich], "Novye techeniia," *Rech'*, 1 January 1908, 5. See also the discussion by D. Merezhkovskii, "Misticheskie khuligany," *Svobodnye mysli*, 28 January 1908, 2. On "mystical anarchism," see Georgii Chulkov, *O misticheskom anarkhizme* (St. Petersburg, 1906); Bernice Glatzer Rosenthal, "Mystical Anarchism and the Revolution of 1905," *Slavic Review* 36, no. 4 (December

1977): 608–27; and Rosenthal, "Political Implications of the Early Twentieth-Century Occult Revival," in Rosenthal, *The Occult in Russian and Soviet Culture*, 382–89.

126. "Sovremennoe bogoiskatel'stvo," *Tserkovnyi vestnik* 1913, no. 47 (21 November): 1471.

127. Professor A. Bronzov, "Spiritizm—zlo," ibid., 1910, no. 15–16 (15 April): 469–74. See also Bronzov, "Pechal'nye znameni vremeni," ibid., 1912, no. 12–13 (22 March): 372–73.

128. Ibid., 1914, no. 44 (30 October): 1313–15; "Bogoiskatel'stvo vne Tserkvi," ibid., 1908, no. 38 (18 September): 1169–71; "Sovremennoe bogoiskatel'stvo," ibid., 1909, no. 11 (12 March): 321.

129. P. M. "Pravoslavnaia missiia v Petrograde," ibid., 1916, no. 21–22 (12–19 June): 485.

130. "O bor'be s sektantstvom," ibid., 1912, no. 38 (20 September): 1193–94. Reports of arrests and trials, especially of St. Petersburg "Ioannity" and "khlysty," appeared in the newspapers periodically in these years.

131. N. Tal'nikov, "Sektanty v Peterburge," *Peterburgskii listok*, 20 October 1908, 2.

132. "Pod maskoi religii (arest Ioannitov)," *Gazeta-kopeika*, 23 April 1909, 2; N., "Ioannit-Istselitel'," *Peterburgskii listok*, 7 March 1909, 2; "Delo okhtenskoe bogoroditsy," ibid., 17 March 1914, 3 (quoting the prosecutor summing up the case against a group of "*khlysty*" active in St. Petersburg since 1902).

133. N. Tal'nikov, "Sektanty v Peterburge," *Peterburgskii listok*, 5 November 1908, 1.

134. See, for example, A. M., "Spiriticheskoe sharlatanstvo," ibid., 17 February 1913, 9.

135. N. Tal'nikov, "Iazychniki v Peterburge," ibid., 8 June 1910, 3.

136. D. Merezhkovskii, *Griadushchii Kham* (St. Petersburg, 1906), reprinted in Dmitrii Merezhkovskii, *Bol'naia Rossiia: Izbrannoe* (Leningrad, 1991), 44.

137. D. Merezhkovskii, "Misticheskie khuligany," *Svobodnye mysli*, 28 January 1908, 2, discussing Leonid Galich [Gabrilovich], "Novye techeniia," *Rech'*, 1 January 1908, 5. Church writers argued that emphasis on the "I" as the source of all truth was one of the errors of "sectarianism." See I. Aivazov, "Osnovy russkogo sektantstva," *Tserkovnyi vestnik* 1916, no. 2 (31 January): 45–48.

138. L. S-g, "Starye i novye bogoiskateli," *Zaprosy zhizni* 1909, no. 4 (8 November): 12. He compares "new" God-seeking to the "old" God-seeking of Gogol', the Slavophiles, and Dostoevskii, and finds the contemporary forms unoriginal and primitive.

139. N. Tal'nikov, "Sektanty v Peterburge," *Peterburgskii listok*, 10 March 1908, 3.

140. Doklad V. V. Rozanova, "O sladchaishem Isyse i gor'kikh plodakh mira" (21 November 1907), *Zapiski Sankt-Peterburgskogo religiozno-filosofskogo obshchestva*, no. 2 (1908): 20–25.

141. *Zapiski S.-Peterburgskogo religiozno-filosofskogo obshchestva*, no. 2 (1908): 6 (meeting of 3 October 1907).

142. "S novym schast'em," *Peterburgskii listok*, 1 January 1914, 2.

143. Kaled, "Ivanushkovtsy," *Sanktpeterburgskie vedomosti*, 9 December 1910, 2.

144. Ashkinazi, "Ot individualizma k bogostroitel'stvu," *Novyi zhurnal dlia vsekh* 1909, no. 6 (April): 107, 109. See also "Dukhovnye bluzhdaniia," *Tserkovnyi vestnik* 1910, no. 46 (18 November): 1425–28.

145. P. Iushkevich, "Religioznyi opyt," *Zaprosy zhizni* 1910, no. 5 (31 January): 269–70.

146. V. Rozanov, "V Religiozno-filosofskom obshchestve," *Novoe vremia*, 23 January 1909, 3. See also discussion in "Religioznost' v religiozno-filosofskom obshchestve," *Tserkovnyi vestnik* 1909, no. 5 (29 January): 134–35.

147. Galich, "Mysli: nauchnyi optimizm i meshchane," *Rech'*, 11 July 1907, 2.

148. The phrase, often used in newspaper reports, such as *Gazeta-kopeika*, 20 June 1908, 3, or *Peterburgskii listok*, 15 January 1910, 4–5, is the title of Iurii Alianskii's series of books, *Veseliashchiisia Peterburg*, 6 vols. (St. Petersburg, 1992–2002), which are based on a massive card file on prerevolutionary entertainments in St. Petersburg compiled by an amateur historian, German Ivanov (1908–91). See also texts and discussions in James von Geldern and Louise McReynolds, ed., *Entertaining Tsarist Russia* (Bloomington, 1998), pt. 5. On the establishment of Petersburg amusement parks in the nineteenth century, see Al'bin M. Konechnyi, "Shows for the People: Public Amusement Parks in Nineteenth-Century St. Petersburg," in *Cultures in Flux: Lower-Class Values, Practices, and Resistance in Late Imperial Russia*, ed. Stephen Frank and Mark Steinberg (Princeton, 1994), 121–30.

149. Louise McReynolds, *Russia at Play: Leisure Activities at the End of the Tsarist Era* (Ithaca, 2003).

150. Skitalets, "Opasnoe pokhmel'e," *Gazeta-kopeika*, 16 November 1910, 6.

151. Rabotnichek, "Bezumnaia zhizn'," *Peterburgskii listok*, 23 February 1914, 3.

152. *Peterburgskii listok*, 9 May 1907, 4; 8 March 1909, 7; 9 March 1909, 1, 3; 13 January 1910, 1; 15 January 1910, 4–5; *Gazeta-kopeika*, 27 November 1908, 3; *Peterburgskii gid*, no. 2 (November 1912): 1–3; no. 3 (November 1912): 2; *Ogonek* 1910, no. 39 (25 September): n.p.; *Argus* 1913, no. 2 (February): 104.

153. "Na otkrytii letnykh uveselenii v Narodnom Dome Imperatora Nikolaia II v S.-Peterburge," *Ogonek* 1913, no. 17 (28 April): n.p.

154. *Obozrenie teatrov*, 19 May 1911, 7. See also Alianskii, *Veseliashchiisia Peterburg*, 1:73–83; P. Iuzhnyi, "Liudi v triko," *Argus* 1913, no. 2 (February): 104–5.

155. I. V. Lebedev (Diadia Vania), *Bortsy: 375 portretov "gladiatorov nashikh dnei" s kratkimi kharakteristikami* (Petrograd, 1917), 32. See also *Ogonek* 1910, no. 14 (3/16 April): n.p.

156. Alianskii, *Veseliashchiisia Peterburg*, 2:170–78; A. E. Parnis and Roman D. Timenchik, "Programmy 'Brodiachei sobaki'," in *Pamiatniki kul'tury: novye otkrytiia. Ezhegodnik 1983* (Leningrad, 1985): 187, 196, 197, 199, 204, 222, 239 (from official announcements, news reports, and memoirs). See also *Peterburgskii gid*, no. 2 (November 1912): 1.

157. *Peterburgskii kur'er*, 19 March 1914, quoted in Parnis and Timenchik, "Programmy 'Brodiachei sobaki'," 229. On closure, ibid., 242–43.

158. *Peterburgskii listok*, 16 February 1913, 8.

159. "S novym schast'em," ibid., 1 January 1914, 2.

160. Ibid., 4 January 1914, 2. Though an imported term—notably used by Pushkin among others—"spleen" continued much longer in Russian than in English to retain the sense of "excessive dejection or depression of spirits; gloominess and irritability; moroseness; melancholia" (Oxford English Dictionary). In Russian the meaning is close to *toska*, *unynie*, and *khandra* (melancholy, sadness, depression).

161. L. Kleinbort, "Kinematograf," *Novyi zhurnal dlia vsekh* 1912, no. 6 (June): 99–101; Yuri Tsivian, *Early Cinema in Russia and its Cultural Reception*, trans. Alan Bodger (London, 1994), 24–30.

162. Tsivian, *Early Cinema in Russia*, 24, 29.

163. Flaner, "Kinematografiia," *Zhizn'*, 5 January 1909, quoted in Tsivian, *Early Cinema in Russia*, 26.

164. "Zhazhda silnykh oshchushchenii," *Tserkovnyi vestnik* 1909, no. 7 (12 February): 198–99; and K. Barantsevich, "Zhazhdushchie silnykh oshchushchenii," *Slovo*, 2 February 1909, 2. For an examination of the content and reception of films in these years, see Yuri Tsivian, "Russia 1913: Cinema in the Cultural Landscape" in *Silent Film*, ed. Richard Abel (New Brunswick, N.J., 1996), and Tsivian, *Early Cinema in Russia*; and Denise J. Youngblood, *The Magic Mirror: Moviemaking in Russia, 1908–1918* (Madison, 1999).

165. *Peterburgskii kinematograf*, 12 February 1911.

166. Gemi, "Tragediia molodogo pokoleniia (beseda s zasluzhennym professorom P. I. Kovalevskim), *Peterburgskii listok*, 27 January 1910, 6; Pchela, "Plody pinkertonovshchiny," ibid., 28 January 1910, 3. See also Jeffrey Brooks, *When Russia Learned to Read: Literacy and Popular Culture, 1861–1917* (Princeton, 1985).

167. Such as *Ogonek: ezhenedel'nyi khudozhestvenno-literaturnyi zhurnal* (St. Petersburg, 1899–18); *Vsemirnaia panorama* (St. Petersburg, 1909–18); and *Argus: ezhemesiachnyi literaturno-khudozhestvennyi zhurnal* (St. Petersburg, 1913–17).

168. *Pamiati A. D. Vial'tsevoi* (St. Petersburg, [1913]), 3; Obituary in *Peterburg-skii listok*, 5 February 1913, 3. See also Louise McReynolds, " 'The Incomparable One': Anastasia Vial'tseva and the Culture of Personality," in *Russia, Women, Culture*, ed. Helena Goscilo and Beth Holmgren (Bloomington, 1996): 273–94.

169. Published texts of her most popular songs include *Ia stepei i voli doch'* (Moscow, 1912) and *Romansy i pesni A. D. Vial'tsevoi* (no publishing information).

170. *Peterburgskii gid*, no. 9 (January 1913): 3.

171. Letter from Isadora Duncan to editor, *Ogonek*, 1908, no. 7 (17 February): 16.

172. "Peterburgskaia nedel'ia aviatsii: pervyi den'," *Rech'*, 26 April 1910, 3; "Aviatsionnaia nedelia v Peterburge," *Peterburgskii listok*, 1 May 1910, 3; 2 May 1910, 5; *Ogonek* 1910, no. 38 (18 September): n.p.; *Rech'*, 27 April 1910, 4; "Peterburgskaia nedel'ia aviatsii: piatyi den'," *Rech'*, 30 April 1910, 4.

173. "Peterburgskaia nedel'ia aviatsii: pervyi den'," *Rech'*, 26 April 1910, 3; *Peterburgskii listok*, 15 May 1913, 4. See also Scott W. Palmer, *Dictatorship of the Air: Aviation Culture and the Fate of Modern Russia* (Cambridge, 2006), chaps. 1–2.

174. *Ogonek* 1910, no. 27 (3/16 July): n.p. See also *Vsemirnaia panorama* 1910, no. 62 (25 June): 5.

175. *Peterburgskii listok*, 22 February 1913, 4–5.

176. Skitalets, "Vavilon na chas," *Gazeta-kopeika*, 2 January 1911, 4–5.

177. *Peterburgskii kinematograf*, 12 January 1911, 2.

178. "Samoubiistvo i vyrozhdeniia," *Peterburgskii listok*, 20 January 1913, 5.

179. *Vesna* 1910, no. 1: 2 (a speech by Duma deputy A. I. Shingarev at the First Russian Congress for the Struggle against Drunkenness).

180. *Zaprosy zhizni* 1909, no. 4 (8 November): 21; "Peterburgskie 'satanisty'," *Peterburgskii listok*, 12 February 1913, 3. For a fictionalized memoir of drug use on the eve of revolution and into the revolutionary years, see *Roman s kokainom* (1934), translated as *Novel with Cocaine*, trans. Michael Henry Haim (Evanston, 1998). I am grateful to Roshanna Sylvester for drawing my attention to this novel.

181. L. Kleinbort, "Kinematograf," *Novyi zhurnal dlia vsekh* 1912, no. 6 (June): 99–103.

182. See Robert Berd [Bird], "Russkii simvolizm i razvitie kinoestetiki: nasledie Viach. Ivanova u A. Bakshi i Adr. Piotrovskogo," *Novoe literaturnoe obozrenie* 81 (2006), 67–98.

183. Stepan Felenkin, "Nasha molodezh'," *Gazeta-kopeika*, 8 February 1910, 3.

184. *Ogonek*, 1910, no. 39 (25 September): n.p. Pushkin's play was based on John Wilson's poem about London, "The City of the Plague" (1816), though Pushkin also had in mind the Russian cholera epidemic of his own time.

185. Vas. Reginin, "K chitateliam," *Argus*, no. 2 (February 1913): 3.

186. Ashkinazi, "Ot individualizma k bogostroitel'stvu," *Novyi zhurnal dlia vsekh* 1909, no. 6 (April): 96.

187. Zhbankov, "Polovaia prestupnost'," *Sovremennyi mir* 1909, no. 7 (July): 67–68, and "Sovremennye samoubiistva," ibid., 1910, no. 3 (March): 48 (see also 53).

188. "Korol' smekha v Peterburge," *Gazeta-kopeika*, 21 November 1913, 3. See also Skitalets, "Deti vremeni," ibid., 7 December 1913, 3. A report in *Malen'kaia gazeta*, 12 September 1914, 4, claimed that Linder was born in Russian Poland as Mordkha (Mordechai) Gol'dshtein. In fact, he was born Gabriel-Maximilien Leuvielle in France.

189. Aleksandr Blok, "Dnevnik" (26 November 1912), *Sobranie sochinenii v vos'mi tomakh*, vol. 7 (Moscow and Leningrad, 1963), 184.

190. Ol'ga Gridina, "Bez rulia," *Gazeta-kopeika*, 11 April 1910, 5–6.

191. S. Liubosh, "Peterburgskie zametki," *Sovremennoe slovo*, 2 June 1910, 2.

192. L. Logvinovich, "Smekh i pechal'," *Zhizn' dlia vsekh* 1912, no. 1 (January): 112.

193. V. Tr[ofim]ov, "Den' chudes," *Gazeta-kopeika*, 1 April 1909, 5.

194. For example, *Satirikon*, 1908, no. 10: 4 (an article called "Geroi nashego vremeni"); no. 14: 6; no. 19: 14; no. 29: 7; no. 30: 4–5; no. 31: 3; no. 33: 9; no. 36: 8.

195. Ibid., 1908, no. 1: 3.

196. *Listok-kopeika* 1909–10, 1913, passim. Quotation no. 6 (December 1909).

197. Ibid., no. 26 (May 1910): 2.

198. Ibid., no. 1 (November 1909): cover.

199. Vrangel' blamed pre-1905 censorship. *Apollon* 1910, no. 4 (January): 56–57.

200. L. Logvinovich, "Smekh i pechal'," *Zhizn' dlia vsekh* 1912, no. 1 (January): 107.

201. Notably, Velimir Khlebnikov's "Zakliatie smekha" (Incantation by Laughter, 1908–9).

202. S. Liubosh, "Peterburgskie zametki," *Sovremennoe slovo*, 2 June 1910, 2.

203. K. Chukovskii, "Mark Tven," *Rech'*, 10 April 1910, 3.

204. K. Chukovskii, "Iumor obrechennykh," ibid., 17 April 1910, 2.

205. L. Logvinovich, "Smekh i pechal'," *Zhizn' dlia vsekh* 1912, no. 1 (January): 107–14.

206. Harvie Ferguson, *Melancholy and the Critique of Modernity: Søren Kierkegaard's Religious Psychology* (London, 1995), 34–55.

207. S. Liubosh, "Peterburgskie zametki," *Sovremennoe slovo*, 6 June 1910, 2. The Heine quote is from his *Die Harzreise* (1824). Heinrich Heine, *Historisch-kritische Gesamtausgabe der Werke*, ed. Manfred Windfuhr, vol. 6, ed. Jost Hermand

(Hamburg, 1973), 138. While I have used "heavens" to translate the Russian *nebo*, its meaning, like Heine's *Himmel*, includes both sky and Heaven.

208. Petr Struve at a meeting of the Religious-Philosophical Society, 8 November 1907, in *Zapiski S.-Peterburgskogo religiozno-filosofskogo obshchestva*, no. 2 (1908): 33.

209. K. Chukovskii, "O khikhikaiushchikh," *Rech'*, 20 December 1908, 3.

210. A. Blok, "Ironiia," ibid., 7 December 1908, 2.

211. St. Ivanovich, "Tekushchaia zhizn': pod znakom nadezhdy," *Novyi zhurnal dlia vsekh* 1913, no. 1 (January): 109–10.

212. Onseved, "Eshche shampanskoe," *Listok-kopeika*, no. 8 (January 1910): 2.

213. See Walter Benjamin, *The Arcades Project*, trans. Howard Eiland and Kevin McLaughlin (Cambridge, Mass., 1999), 467, quoting and interpreting Karl Marx, "Zur Kritik der Hegelschen *Rechtsphilosophie*" (1844).

214. L. Logvinovich, "Smekh i pechal'," *Zhizn' dlia vsekh* 1912, no. 1 (January): 107–14.

CHAPTER SEVEN. MELANCHOLY

1. See, for example, Brian Massumi, *Parables for the Virtual* (Durham, N.C., 2002); Jane Thrailkill, *Affecting Fictions: Mind, Body, and Emotion in American Literary Realism* (Cambridge, Mass., 2007); Patricia Ticineto Clough with Jean Halley, eds., *The Affective Turn: Theorizing the Social* (Durham, N.C., 2007).

2. See, especially, Richard A. Shweder and Robert A. Levine, eds., *Culture Theory: Essays on Mind, Self, and Emotion* (Cambridge, 1984); Cheshire Calhoun and Robert C. Solomon, eds., *What Is an Emotion? Classic Readings in Philosophical Psychology* (New York, 1984); Peter N. Stearns and Carol Z. Stearns, "Emotionology: Clarifying the History of Emotions and Emotional Standards," *American Historical Review*, 90, no. 4 (October 1985): 813–36; Catherine S. Lutz and Lila Abu-Lughod, eds., *Language and the Politics of Emotion* (Cambridge, 1990); Martha Nussbaum, *Upheavals of Thought: The Intelligence of Emotions* (Cambridge, 2001); William Reddy, *The Navigation of Feeling: A Framework for the History of Emotions* (Cambridge, 2001); Eve Kosofsky Sedgwick, *Touching Feeling: Affect, Pedagogy, Performativity* (Durham, N.C., 2003); Sara Ahmed, *The Cultural Politics of Emotions* (New York, 2004); Sianne Ngai, *Ugly Feelings* (Cambridge, Mass., 2005); Barbara H. Rosenwein, *Emotional Communities in the Early Middle Ages* (Ithaca, 2006); Daniel Gross, *The Secret History of Emotion: From Aristotle's "Rhetoric" to Modern Brain Science* (Chicago, 2007). On Russia, see Sheila Fitzpatrick, "Happiness and *Toska*: An Essay in the History of Emotions in Prewar Soviet Russia," *Australian Journal of Politics and History* 50, no. 3 (2004):

NOTES TO PAGES 236-237

357-58; John Randolph, *The House in the Garden: The Bakunin Family and the Romance of Russian Idealism* (Ithaca, 2007); Mark Steinberg, "Melancholy and Modernity: Emotions and Social Life in Russia Between the Revolutions," *Journal of Social History* 41, no. 4 (Summer 2008): 813-41; Jan Plamper, ed., "Emotional Turn? Feelings in Russian History and Culture," special section of *Slavic Review* 68, no. 2 (Summer 2009); Jan Plamper, Schamma Schahadat, and Marc Elie, eds., *Rossiiskaia imperiia chuvstv: podkhody k kul'turnoi istorii emotsii* (Moscow, 2010). For a more detailed discussion and bibliography, see Mark Steinberg and Valeria Sobol, eds., *Interpreting Emotions in Russia and Eastern Europe* (DeKalb, 2011).

3. Lutz and Abu-Lughod, *Language and the Politics of Emotion*, 16, 88, 12.

4. Ahmed, *The Cultural Politics of Emotions*, esp. 4-12.

5. Ngai, *Ugly Feelings*, 3.

6. Molover, "Epokha nastroenii," *Vesna* 1908, no. 6 (10 February): 44 (reprinted from *Stolichnaia pochta*).

7. L. Gurevich, "Literatura nashego vremeni," *Novyi zhurnal dlia vsekh* 1909, no. 3 (January): 100, 102; B. Shaposhnikov, "Futurizm i teatr," *Maski*, no. 7-8 (1912-13): 29-30. See also V. L'vov-Rogachevskii, "Novaia drama Leonida Andreeva," *Sovremennik* 1913, no. 10 (October): esp. 254-55.

8. Vladimir Markov, "Printsipy novogo iskusstva," *Soiuz molodezhi*, no. 1 (April 1912): 6, 10; no. 2 (June 1912): 5-6; Sergei Makovskii, "Zhenskie portrety sovremennykh russkikh khudozhnikov," *Apollon 1910*, no. 5 (February): 11, 12, 15.

9. See Chapter 6.

10. K. Chukovskii, "Intelligentnyi Pinkerton," *Rech'*, 21 February 1910, 2-3.

11. Georgii Chulkov, "Pamiati V. F. Kommissarzhevskoi," *Apollon 1910*, no. 6 (March): 23; *Zhizn' dlia vsekh* 1910, no. 3 (March): 135-37.

12. *Pamiati A. D. Vial'tsevoi* (St. Petersburg, [1913]), 3. Although he does not discuss Vial'tseva, David MacFadyen emphasizes "excessive feeling" in prerevolutionary popular song in his *Songs for Fat People: Affect, Emotion, and Celebrity in the Russian Popular Song, 1900-1955* (Montreal, 2002).

13. See *Novyi zhurnal dlia vsekh* 1910, no. 17 (March): 113-18. Louise McReynolds, "'The Incomparable One': Anastasia Vial'tseva and the Culture of Personality," in *Russia, Women, Culture*, ed. Helena Goscilo and Beth Holmgren (Bloomington, 1996): 273-94. On Kommissarzhevskaia's funeral, see Thomas Trice, "The 'Body Politic': Russian Funerals and the Politics of Representation, 1841-1921" (Ph.D. diss., University of Illinois, Urbana-Champaign, 1999), 188-96.

14. Quoted phrases are *Peterburgskii listok*, 3 October 1905, 2; Mikhailov, "Politika i erotika," *Svobodnye mysli*, 8 October 1907, 1; A. Karelin, "K voprosu o psikhike proletariev: eskiz," *Sovremennik* 1912, no. 3 (March): 282-95; "Sovremennost' i dumy," *Tserkovnyi vestnik* 1913, no. 31 (1 August): 946.

15. Laura Engelstein, *Keys to Happiness: Sex and the Search for Modernity in Fin-de-Siècle Russia* (Ithaca, 1992); Laura Engelstein and Stephanie Sandler, eds., *Self and Story in Russian History* (Ithaca, 2000); Irina Sirotkina, *Diagnosing Literary Genius: A Cultural History of Psychiatry in Russia, 1880–1930* (Baltimore, 2001); Mark Steinberg, *Proletarian Imagination: Self, Modernity, and the Sacred in Russia, 1910–1925* (Ithaca, 2002), chap. 2; Daniel Beer, *Renovating Russia: The Human Sciences and the Fate of Liberal Modernity, 1880–1930* (Ithaca, 2008).

16. I. Iu. Vinitskii, *Utekhi melankholii. Uchenye zapiski Moskovskogo kul'turologicheskogo litseia No. 1310. Seriia: Filologiia*, no. 2 (Moscow, 1997), 107–289.

17. See Jennifer Radden, ed., *The Nature of Melancholy: From Aristotle to Kristeva* (New York, 2000); Raymond Klibansky, Erwin Panofsky, and Fritz Saxl, *Saturn and Melancholy: Studies in the History of Natural Philosophy, Religion, and Art* (New York, 1964); Stanley Jackson, *Melancholy and Depression: From Hippocratic Times to Modern Times* (New Haven, 1986); Harvie Ferguson, *Melancholy and the Critique of Modernity: Søren Kierkegaard's Religious Psychology* (London, 1995), chap. 1.

18. Radden, *The Nature of Melancholy*, 10–12.

19. In addition to the references following, see Eric Gidal, "Civic Melancholy: English Gloom and French Enlightenment," *Eighteenth-Century Studies* 37, no. 1 (Fall 2003): 26; and Wolf Lepenies, *Melancholie und Gesellschaft* (Frankfurt am Main, 1969).

20. Peter Fritzsche, *Stranded in the Present: Modern Time and the Melancholy of History* (Cambridge, Mass., 2004), e.g. 8, 30, 45, 47, 75, 90.

21. Vinitskii, *Utekhi melankholii*, 165–68 and passim.

22. See, for example, N. K. Mikhailovskii, "Chto takoe progress?" (What Is Progress?) (St. Petersburg, 1869).

23. Here, as in many works, "mood" draws on Martin Heidegger's influential notion of *Stimmung* as a way of being touched, attuned, and disposed toward the world, as a result of shared existence, experience, and being. Martin Heidegger, *Sein und Zeit* (1927), as discussed in Charles Guignon, "Moods in Heidegger's *Being and Time*," in Calhoun and Solomon, *What Is an Emotion?* 230–43.

24. Jonathan Flatley, *Affective Mapping: Melancholia and the Politics of Modernism* (Cambridge, Mass., 2008), 5–6 and passim. See also evidence that loss and "the loss of bearings in time and place" were central to turn-of-the-century notions of degeneration in Daniel Pick, *Faces of Degeneration: A European Disorder, c. 1848–1918* (Cambridge, 1989), quotation 156.

25. Friedrich Nietzsche, *The Gay Science* (New York, 1974; original publication 1882): 273 (section 341). See discussion in Robert Pippin, "Nietzsche and the Melancholy of Modernity," *Social Research* 66, no. 2 (Summer 1999): 509. On

Nietzschean "eternal recurrence" and nausea, see David Couzens Hoy, *The Time of Our Lives: A Critical History of Temporality* (Cambridge, Mass., 2009), 82–89.

26. Walter Benjamin, *The Arcades Project*, trans. Howard Eiland and Kevin McLaughlin (Cambridge, Mass., 1999), esp. 101–19, 544–45; Walter Benjamin, "Paris, Capitale du XIXème siècle: Exposé," in *Das Passagen-Werk*, ed. Rolf Tiedemann, 2 vols. (Frankfurt am Main, 1982), 1:61, and *The Arcades Project*, 15; Benjamin, "On the Concept of History" (1940), in *Selected Writings*, ed. Michael Jennings et al., 4 vols. (Cambridge, Mass., 1996–2003), 4:389–411. See discussion of Benjamin's conceptions of modern time in Susan Buck-Morss, *The Dialectics of Seeing: Walter Benjamin and the Arcades Project* (Cambridge, Mass., 1989), 79, 95–97, 99, 103–9, 178; Michael Löwy, *Fire Alarm: Reading Walter Benjamin's 'On the Concept of History'*, trans. Chris Turner (London, 2005); Tyrus Miller, "Eternity No More: Walter Benjamin on Eternal Return," in *Given World and Time: Temporalities in Context*, ed. Tyrus Miller (Budapest, 2008), chap. 14.

27. Pick, *Faces of Degeneration*, quotation 67.

28. Jean Baudrillard, *L'illusion de la fin* (Paris, 1992).

29. Pippin, "Nietzsche and the Melancholy of Modernity," *Social Research* 66, no. 2 (Summer 1999): 495–520. See also Pippin, *Modernism as a Philosophical Problem: On the Dissatisfactions of European High Culture*, 2d ed. (Oxford, 1999).

30. Freud, "Mourning and Melancholia" (1915, published 1917), in *The Standard Edition of the Complete Psychological Works of Sigmund Freud*, trans. and ed. James Strachey, vol. 14 (London, 1957), 243. See also Judith Butler, *The Psychic Life of Power: Theories in Subjection* (Stanford, 1997); Rei Terada, *Feeling in Theory* (Cambridge, Mass., 2001), esp. 132–34, 167–95.

31. Julia Kristeva, *Black Sun: Depression and Melancholia* (New York, 1989), esp. 5–6, 10–14, 123, 128 (quotation), 171, 221–22.

32. Heidegger, *Being and Time* [1927], quoted and used by Ngai in developing her own arguments about "anxiety" as the agitated "modern variant" of classic male melancholia, in *Ugly Feelings*, 209–15, 226–36. See also "Moods in Heidegger's *Being and Time*," in Calhoun and Solomon, eds., *What Is an Emotion?* esp. 242.

33. Jean-Paul Sartre, *Nausea* (1938), trans. Lloyd Alexander (New York, 2007). Sartre titled the novel *Melancholia*, which the publisher revised to *Nausea*.

34. Emmanuel Levinas, *On Escape: De L'evasion* (1935), introduced and annotated by Jacques Rolland, trans. Bettina Bergo (Stanford, 2003), 34, 36, 53, 67.

35. Ngai, *Ugly Feelings*, esp. 3–14.

36. See also the forum "Ruins and Russian Culture," *Slavic Review* 65, no. 4 (Winter 2006).

37. Benjamin, *The Arcades Project*, 111, 113, 115.

38. Ibid., 105, 108. See also 104–5, 110.

39. Although most studies of the fin-de-siècle mood have focused on cultural elites, the spread of feelings of loss, doubt, and pessimism in the wider European urban public is suggested sporadically in such studies as Pick, *Faces of Degeneration*, and Mary Gluck, *Popular Bohemia: Modernism and Urban Culture in Nineteenth-Century Paris* (Cambridge, Mass., 2005).

40. Fritzsche, *Stranded in the Present*, 96, and chap. 3 passim.

41. See, especially, discussions of redemptive and political melancholy (and other negative feelings) in Flatley, *Affective Mapping* (esp. chap. 1) and Ngai, *Ugly Feelings*. See also Ahmed, *The Cultural Politics of Emotion*; Butler, *The Psychic Life of Power*; and Sedgwick, *Touching Feeling*. Dennis Hoy has emphasized the activist and revolutionary potential in many modern and postmodern theories of temporality. Hoy, *The Time of Our Lives*. Some scholars have written of Benjamin's "revolutionary melancholy." See Löwy, *Fire Alarm*, 11.

42. N. V., "Itogi minuvshago goda," *Vesna* 1908, no. 1 (6 January): 1.

43. "S novym godom," *Tserkovnyi vestnik* 1908, no. 1 (3 January): 1.

44. "Novogodnye mysli," ibid., no. 2 (10 January): 43.

45. This discussion draws on New Year's editorials and columns in various St. Petersburg dailies in addition to examples quoted.

46. R. Blank, "1909-yi god," *Zaprosy zhizni* 1909, no. 11 (29 December): 1.

47. "1910 god," *Sovremennoe slovo*, 1 January 1910, 5. See also *Rech'*, 1 January 1910, 12.

48. "Unylyi ton novogodnykh deiatel'nosti gorodskikh obshchestvennykh upravlenii za istekshchii god," *Gorodskoe delo* 1911, no. 2 (15 January): 199–200.

49. *Ogonek* 1913, no. 1 (6 January), n.p.

50. Mikh. Al. Engel'gardt, "Bez vykhoda," *Svobodnye mysli*, 7 January 1908, 1. The Bible quotation is *Plach Ieremii* 4:17, which I have translated according to *Lamentations* 4:17 (New International Version). For other uses of the phrase "no exit" (often as "net vykhoda"), see Dr. G. Gordon, "Prostitutki," *Rech'*, 23 April 1910, 2; V. Shirokii, "Cherty sovremennoi russkoi zhizni," *Novyi zhurnal dlia vsekh* 1914, no. 1 (January): 45. See also, at two ends of the literary spectrum, Aleksandr Blok's 1907 poem "Net iskhoda" (No exit) and Mikhail Vavich's popular song, recorded around 1906, *Grust' i toska bezyskhodnaia* ("sorrow and *toska* without exit.")

51. Redaktsiia, "Maksimalizm otchaianiia," ibid., 14 January 1908, 1.

52. Skitalets, "Molchanie," *Gazeta-kopeika*, 1 January 1913, 3–4.

53. A. Bronzov, "Progress-li? (Razmyshlenniia na 'Novyi god')" *Tserkovnyi vestnik* 1912, no. 1 (5 January): 4–9.

54. V. Posse, "Obshchestvennaia zhizn': v predchuvstvii bedy," *Zhizn' dlia vsekh* 1913, no. 1 (January): 171.

55. V. Shirokii, "Cherty sovremennoi russkoi zhizni," *Novyi zhurnal dlia vsekh* 1914, no. 1 (January): 45.

56. Skitalets, "Molchanie," *Gazeta-kopeika*, 1 January 1913, 3-4.

57. For example, M. Men'shikov, "Iz pisem k blizhnim," *Novoe vremia*, 27 April 1903, 203 (on the weather and mood); F. Bulgakov, "O skuke," ibid., 20 April 1900, 2 (on boredom).

58. Melankholik, "Ekho" [about the funeral of Prince S. N. Trubetskoi], *Peterburgskii listok*, 3 October 1905, 2.

59. "Pessimizm v zhizni i shkole," ibid., 9 October 1905, 3.

60. For example, Leonid Galich, "Mysli: nauchnyi optimizm i meshchane," *Rech'*, 11 July 1907, 2; Leonid Andreev, "Liudi tenovoi storony," *Svobodnye mysli*, 18 February 1908, 2; Molover, "Epokha nastroenii," *Vesna* 1908, no. 6 (10 February): 44 (reprinted from *Stolichnaia pochta)*; L. Logvinovich, "Smekh i pechal'," *Zhizn' dlia vsekh* 1912, no. 1 (January): 111.

61. B. Bazilevich, "Mnimye strakhi," *Svobodnye mysli*, 13 August 1907, 2; I. Brusilovskii, "'Smysl' zhizni," *Sovremennoe slovo*, 13 March 1910, 1.

62. "K samoubiistvam molodezhi," *Tserkovnyi vestnik* 1910, no. 12 (25 March): 362; A. Zorin [Gastev], "Rabochii mir: Vera, otchianie, opyt," *Novyi zhurnal dlia vsekh* 1911, no. 8 (August): 1075; Nemirovich-Danchenko, "Zhizn' deshevo! (ocherki epidemii otchaianiia)," *Zaprosy zhizni* 1910, no. 10 (7 March): 588.

63. V. Lavretskii, "Tragediia sovremennoi molodezhi," *Vesna* 1910, no. 14-15: 106 (a reprinting of a series of articles in *Rech'*, 31 March, 22 June, 30 September 1910); Ol'ga Gridina, "Bez rulia," *Gazeta-kopeika*, 11 April 1910, 5.

64. D. Zhbankov, "Sovremennye samoubiistva," *Sovremennyi mir* 1910, no. 3 (March): 48, 53, and "Polovaia prestupnost'," *Sovremennyi mir* 1909, no. 7 (July): 64; *Teosoficheskoe obozrenie*, no. 3 (December 1907): 113-14.

65. "Razval dukha," *Tserkovnyi vestnik* 1911, no. 45 (10 November): 1412.

66. A. Protopopov, "Sud'ba russkikh gorodov," *Gorodskoe delo* 1911, no. 24 (15 December): 1715. Petr Chaadaev, in his *First Philosophical Letter* of 1829 (published in the journal *Teleskop* in 1836), wrote about Russia as a historically uprooted and bankrupt civilization standing "outside of time."

67. M. Engel'gardt, "D. Merezhkovskii i russkaia intelligentsiia," *Svobodnye mysli*, 7 April 1908, 2; D. Ovsianiko-Kulikovskii, "Literaturnye besedy," *Rech'*, 4 October 1910, 2; L'vov-Rogachevskii, "Novaia drama Leonida Andreeva," *Sovremennik* 1913, no. 10 (October): 254.

68. Galich, "Mysli: nauchnyi optimizm i meshchane," *Rech'*, 11 July 1907, 2; Chulkov, "Demony i sovremennost'," *Apollon* 1914, no. 1-2 (January–February): 70-75.

69. N. V., "Itogi minuvshago goda," *Vesna* 1908, no. 1 (6 January): 1.

70. L. Logvinovich, "Smekh i pechal'," *Zhizn' dlia vsekh* 1912, no. 1 (January): 110–11 (these are Russian colloquial expressions).

71. "K voprosu o sovremennykh zadachakh pastyrstva," *Tserkovnyi vestnik* 1911, no. 50 (15 December): 1572–73.

72. S. Liubosh, "Boi na fontanke," *Slovo*, 22 January 1909, 2. See also discussion in "Religioznost' v religiozno-filosofskom obshchestve," *Tserkovnyi vestnik* 1909, no. 5 (29 January): 134–35.

73. Vladimir Dal', *Tolkovyi slovar' zhivago Velikorusskago iazyka*, 4 vols. (St. Petersburg, 1882), 4:422. Ushakov defined *toska* similarly as "strong mental and emotional languishing, mental and emotional anxiety united with sorrow and ennui." D. N. Ushakov, ed., *Tolkovyi slovar' Russkogo iazyka*, 4 vols. (Moscow, 1940), 4:755.

74. See, for example, *The Oxford Russian Dictionary*, ed. Marcus Wheeler, Boris Unbegaun, and Paul Falla, 3d ed. (Oxford, 2000), 517.

75. Alexander Pushkin, *Eugene Onegin*, trans. and commentary by Vladimir Nabokov, rev. ed., 4 vols. (Princeton, 1975) 2:141, 337. See also 2:151–56, and 1:25. Most recent discussions of *toska* quote Nabokov.

76. On the persistence of *toska* in the immediate postrevolutionary years, as reflected in writings by working-class authors, see Steinberg, *Proletarian Imagination*, esp. 134–35, 144, 278 (see also Flatley's discussion of *toska* in Andrei Platonov's 1927 novel *Chevengur*, in *Affective Mapping*, chap. 5). On the persistent, or revived, "omnipresence" of *toska* in the 1930s, see Fitzpatrick, "Happiness and *Toska*," 357–59, 365–71.

77. Merezhkovskii, "Peterburgu byt' pustu," *Rech'*, 21 December 1908, 2.

78. G. Plekhanov, "O tak nazyvaemykh, religioznykh iskaniiakh v Rossii," *Sovremennyi mir* 1909, no. 10 (October), 178.

79. L. Gurevich, "Literatura nashego vremeni," *Novyi zhurnal dlia vsekh*, no. 3 (January 1909): 102; G. Gordon, "Ob odinokikh," ibid., no. 7 (May 1909), 85, 88. See also I. G. Ashkinazi, "Ot individualizma k bogostroitel'stvu," ibid., no. 6 (April 1909): 106.

80. M. Liberson, *Stradanie odinochestva* (St. Petersburg, 1909), 20.

81. N. Ia. Abramovich, "Samoubiistvo," in *Samoubiistvo: sbornik obshchestvennykh, filosofskikh i kriticheskikh statei* (Moscow, 1911), 112–13.

82. V. Lavretskii, "Tragediia sovremennoi molodezhi," *Vesna* 1910, no. 14–15: 7.

83. "Umiraiushchie fialki," *Peterburgskii kinemoteatry* 1913, no. 7 (25 January): 2. See also Ol'ga Gridina, "Predel' skorbi," *Gazeta-kopeika*, 13 September 1910, 3.

84. A. Zorin [Gastev], "Sredi tramvaishchikov (nabrosok)," *Edinstvo*, no. 12 (21 December 1909), 11. See also Steinberg, *Proletarian Imagination*, esp. 100–101.

85. M. Nevedomskii, "Chto stalos' s nashei literaturoi," *Sovremennik* 1915, no. 5 (May): 254.

86. N. Gumilev, "Pis'mo o russkoi poezii," *Apollon* 1914, no. 5 (May 1914): 36.

87. V. Rozanov, "Popy, zhandarmy i Blok," *Novoe vrem'ia*, 16 February 1909, 3. See also V. Burenin, "Kriticheskie ocherki: pri vstuplenii v novyi god," ibid., 8 January 1910, 4.

88. L'vov-Rogachevskii, "M. Artsybashev," *Sovremennyi mir* 1909, no. 11 (November): pt. 2, 32, 35-36.

89. See also Steinberg, *Proletarian Imagination*, chap. 2.

90. Protopopov, "Sud'ba russkikh gorodov," *Gorodskoe delo* 1911, no. 24 (15 December): 1715. See also I. Zhilkin, "Dve intelligentsii," *Zaprosy zhizni* 1909, no. 3 (1 November): 2; "K voprosu o sovremennykh zadachakh pastyrstva," *Tserkovnyi vestnik* 1911, no. 50 (15 December): 1573.

91. B. Bazilevich, "Mnimye strakhi," *Svobodnye mysli*, 13 August 1907, 2. See also, for example, *Vesna* 1908, no. 2 (13 January): 10-11; *Tserkovnyi vestnik* 1910, no. 1 (7 January): 3 (on the *razocharovanie* of the last four years).

92. Delevskii, "Sotsial'nye antagonizmy i obshchestvennyi ideal," *Sovremennik* 1912, no. 1 (January): 252.

93. "Khristos voskrese!" *Teosoficheskoe obozrenie*, no. 7 (April 1908): 488; "K voprosu o sovremennykh zadachakh pastyrstva," *Tserkovnyi vestnik* 1911, no. 50 (15 December): 1572-73; N. Rubakin, "Dlia chego ia zhivu na svete," *Novyi zhurnal dlia vsekh* 1912, no. 6 (June): 67.

94. N. Rubakin, "Dlia chego ia zhivu na svete," *Novyi zhurnal dlia vsekh* 1912, no. 6 (June): 67.

95. Zhbankov, "Polovaia prestupnost'," *Sovremennyi mir* 1909, no. 7 (July): 90-91, and "Sovremennye samoubiistva," ibid., 1910, no. 3 (March): 29, 47-50, 53.

96. *Teosoficheskoe obozrenie*, no. 3 (December 1907): 113-14. See also *Tserkovnyi vestnik* 1914, no. 5 (30 January): 137-40.

97. "Sovremennoe bogoiskatel'stvo," *Tserkovnyi vestnik* 1909, no. 11 (12 March): 321.

98. "Religioznaia teplokhladnost'," ibid., no. 10 (5 March): 289-91.

99. Al. Fedorov, "V nashi dni," *Peterburgskii kinematograf*, 22 January 1911, 2.

100. "S novym schast'em," *Peterburgskii listok*, 1 January 1914, 2.

101. Ashkinazi, "Ot individualizma k bogostroitel'stvu," *Novyi zhurnal dlia vsekh*, no. 6 (April 1909): 107.

102. "Sovremennost' i dumy," *Tserkovnyi vestnik* 1913, no. 31 (1 August): 945-46, 948.

103. Redaktsiia, "Maksimalizma otchaianiia," *Svobodnye mysli*, 14 January 1908, 1; Stepan Filenkin, "Deshevaia zhizn'," *Gazeta-kopeika*, 23 August 1911, 3.

104. M. Engel'gardt, "D. Merezhkovskii i russkaia intelligentsiia," *Svobodnye mysli*, 7 April 1908, 2.

105. N. Gumilev, "Pis'mo o russkoi poezii," *Apollon* 1914, no. 5 (May): 36.

106. Aleksandr Lukoianov, "Ty pomnish' . . . (otvryvok iz romana nastroenii)," *Peterburgskii kinematograf*, 19 March 1911, 2. See also "Umiraiushchie fialki," *Peterburgskii kinemoteatry* 1913, no. 7 (25 January): 2.

107. "Razocharovanie v progresse," *Tserkovnyi vestnik* 1914, no. 39 (25 September): 1162.

108. N. Evreinov, "Sentimental'naia progulka (instsena 'teatra dlia sebia')," *Novyi zhurnal dlia vsekh* 1916, no. 2–3 (February–March): 53; N. Evreinov, "Kazhdaia minuta—teatr," *Teatr dlia sebia*, vol. 1 (St. Petersburg, 1915), 66–76 (quotation 71). See also Katerina Clark, *Petersburg, Crucible of Revolution* (Cambridge, Mass., 1995), 105–6.

109. P. Ia. Rozenbakh, "Prichiny sovremennoi nervoznosti i samoubiistv," *Peterburgskaia gazeta*, 26 April 1909, 3; G. Gordon, "Ob odinokikh," *Novyi zhurnal dlia vsekh*, no. 7 (May 1909): 87; "K samoubiistvam molodezhi," *Tserkovnyi vestnik* 1910, no. 12 (25 March): 362; Rozanov, "O samoubiistvakh," in *Samoubiistvo: sbornik*, 55–56; Nemirovich-Danchenko, "Zhizn' deshevo! (ocherki epidemii otchaianiia)," *Zaprosy zhizni* 1910, no. 10 (7 March): 588.

110. G. Gordon, "Ob odinokikh," *Novyi zhurnal dlia vsekh*, no. 7 (May 1909): 87.

111. For example, I. Brusilovskii, " 'Smysl" zhizni," *Sovremennoe slovo*, 13 March 1910, 1; Skitalets, "Adskie zhmurki," *Gazeta-kopeika*, 10 February 1910, 4; Blank, "1909-yi god," *Zaprosy zhizni* 1909, no. 11 (29 December): 1.

112. N., "Samoubiistvo uchashchikhsia," *Tserkovnyi vestnik* 1909, no. 32 (6 August): 981–82.

113. See Sirotkina, *Diagnosing Literary Genius*, and Beer, *Renovating Russia*.

114. See Engelstein, *The Keys to Happiness*, and Barbara Evans Clements, Rebecca Friedman, and Dan Healey, eds., *Russian Masculinities in History and Culture* (New York, 2002).

115. This term was more general than, and more often used than, the terms neurosis (*nevroz*) and neurasthenia (*nevrasteniia*). On this widespread phenomenon in other modern societies, see Marijke Gijswijt-Hofstra and Roy Porter, eds., *Cultures of Neurasthenia from Beard to the First World War* (Amsterdam, 2001); and Mark S. Micale, *Hysterical Men: The Hidden History of Male Nervous Illness* (Cambridge, Mass., 2008).

116. Gurevich, "Literatura nashego vremeni," *Novyi zhurnal dlia vsekh* 1909, no. 3 (January): 103; P. Ia. Rozenbakh, "Prichiny sovremennoi nervoznosti i samoubiistv," *Peterburgskaia gazeta*, 26 April 1909, 3 (in addition to his teaching and clinical

practices, the author was the author of many books on mental illness, including *On Neurasthenia* [1889] and *Toward the Study of Traumatic Neuroses* [1892]); Doktor meditsiny Ershov, "Zametki vrachi (vozstanovlenie nervnogo istoshcheniia) (Iz *Novogo vremeni*)," *Peterburgskii kinematograf*, 12 February 1911, 3; Vadim, "V chem taina," *Gazeta-kopeika*, 14 January 1913, 3; L'vov-Rogachevskii, "M. Artsybashev," *Sovremennyi mir* 1909, no. 11 (November): pt. 2, 26; Georgii Chulkov, "Revniteli slova," *Zaprosy zhizni* 1910, no. 1 (5 January): 28. See also Laura Goering, "'Russian Nervousness': Neurasthenia and National Identity in Nineteenth-Century Russia," *Medical History* 47, no. 1 (January 2003): 23–46; Susan K. Morrissey, "The Economy of Nerves: Health, Commercial Culture, and the Self in Late Imperial Russia," *Slavic Review* 69, no. 3 (Fall 2010): 645–75.

117. S. Adrianov, "Kuda idet Leonid Andreev," *Zhizn' dlia vsekh* 1909, no. 12 (December): 127. See also S. Gamalov, "Pod znamenem Khama (literatura i zhizn'), *Novyi zhurnal dlia vsekh* 1913, no. 12 (December): 112.

118. *Gazeta-kopeika*, 22 March 1909, 5; 26 March 1909, 4; 5 May 1909, 1; 25 May 1910, 1; 14 July 1913, 5; *Ogonek* 1910, no. 21 (22 May): n.p.; *Novyi zhurnal dlia vsekh*, no. 18 (April 1910): 7; *Peterburgskii kinematograf*, 12 February 1911, 4; *Peterburgskii listok*, 26 May 1913, 13; 5 June 1913, 5; 4 February 1913, 7. These citations represent only a fraction of similar ads that appeared repeatedly over these years. See also Engelstein, *Keys to Happiness*, 360–64; and Morrissey, "The Economy of Nerves," 645, 658–69.

119. *Gazeta-kopeika*, 21 March 1909, 4; V. Trofimov, "Sumashedshie na svobode (maniia presledovaniia)" ibid., 16 August 1909, 3; 18 August 1909, 3; 8 September 1909, 3; "Sumashedshaia na Znamenskoi ploshadi," ibid., 9 September 1909, 3,

120. Ibid., 29 December 1909, 1. See also comments by Ol'ga Gridina, "More bed," ibid., 5.

121. Baron Igrok, "Dvoinye samoubiistva," *Peterburgskii listok*, 19 April 1909, 3; "Futurizm i bezumie," ibid., 22 January 1914, 4.

122. D. Merezhkovskii, "Peterburgu byt' pustu," *Rech'*, 21 December 1908, 2.

123. M. Pritykin, "Krizis intelligentskoi dushi," *Svobodnye mysli*, 24 March 1908, 2; *Vekhi: Sbornik statei o russkoi intelligentsii* (Moscow, 1909).

124. K. Chukovskii, "Iumor obrechennykh," *Rech'*, 17 April 1910, 2.

125. Pchela, "Kul't razvrata," *Peterburgskii listok*, 8 December 1908, 2.

126. "Bludnyi syn," *Tserkovnyi vestnik* 1914, no. 22 (29 May), 649–54.

127. S. Isakov, "Mysli ob iskusstve," *Novyi zhurnal dlia vsekh* 1914, no. 1 (January): 54; "O dukhovnom krizise sovremennoi epokhi," *Tserkovnyi vestnik* 1911, no. 30 (25 July): 913–14.

128. Iu. Delevskii, "Sotsial'nye antagonizmy i obshchestvennyi ideal," *Sovremennik* 1912, no. 1 (January): 252.

129. "Bludnyi syn," *Tserkovnyi vestnik* 1914, no. 22 (29 May): 651. See also "Sovremennaia kul'tura i khristianstvo," *Tserkovnyi vestnik* 1914, no. 23 (5 June): 682.

130. Kaled, "Ivanushkovtsy," *Sanktpeterburgskie vedomosti*, 9 December 1910, 2. See discussion in *Tserkovnyi vestnik* 1910, no. 50 (16 December): 1586–87.

131. For example, Bernice Glatzer Rosenthal, "Eschatology and the Appeal of Revolution: Merezhkovsky, Bely, Blok," *California Slavic Studies* 11 (1980): 105–39; Robert C. Williams, "The Russian Revolution and the End of Time," *Jahrbücher für Geschichte Osteuropas*, 43, no. 3 (1995): 364–401; V. P. Shestakov, *Eskhatologiia i utopiia (ocherki russkoi filosofii i kul'tury)* (Moscow, 1995); M. N. Luk'ianov, "V ozhidanii katastrofy: eskhatologicheskie motivy v russkom konservatizme nakanune pervoi mirovoi voiny," *Russian History/Histoire russe* 31, no. 4 (Winter 2004): 419–61.

132. S. Liubosh, "Boi na fontanke," *Slovo*, 22 January 1909, 2. See also discussion in "Religioznost' v religiozno-filosofskom obshchestve," *Tserkovnyi vestnik* 1909, no. 5 (29 January): 134–35.

133. L. Gurevich, "Literatura nashego vremeni," *Novyi zhurnal dlia vsekh*, no. 3 (January 1909), 102; S. Isakov, "Mysli ob iskusstve," *Novyi zhurnal dlia vsekh* 1914, no. 1 (January): 53.

134. See, for example, the discussion, with photographs, of an exhibition in St. Petersburg of paintings by K. Petrov-Vodkin and N. Rerikh, in *Ogonek* 1913, no. 3 (20 January).

135. S. Isakov, "Mysli ob iskusstve," *Novyi zhurnal dlia vsekh* 1914, no. 1 (January): 53.

136. D. Merezhkovskii, "Peterburgu byt' pustu," *Rech'*, 21 December 1908, 2.

137. "Bludnyi syn," *Tserkovnyi vestnik* 1914, no. 22 (29 May): 651.

138. Ioann Filevskii, "O bor'be s pornografiei," ibid., 1912, no. 17 (26 April): 510; "Antikhrist," *Peterburgskii listok*, 12 February 1914, 4. "Bitter times," a phrase often heard, was likely a reference to Revelation 8:11: "the name of the star [which fell from the heavens] is Wormwood. A third of the waters turned bitter, and many people died from the waters that had become bitter."

139. For a discussion of Easter as a moment of public discourse about time, focused on Easter 1918, see Gregory Stroud, "Retrospective Revolution: A History of Time and Memory in Urban Russia, 1903–1923" (Ph.D. diss., University of Illinois at Urbana-Champaign, 2006), chap. 4.

140. Posse, "Obshchestvennaia zhizn'," *Zhizn' dlia vsekh* 1912, no. 4 (April): 705.

141. "Khristos Voskrese!" *Teosoficheskoe obozrenie*, no. 7 (April 1908): 487–88.

142. Ep. Mikhail, "Nevidimyi grad," *Sovremennoe slovo*, 18 April 1910, 1. Writing at the same time, Zinaida Gippius offered a similar image of poisonous dew as an

allegory for the spiritual crisis of the age. See Z. N. Gippius, "Lunnye muravye," *Lunnye muravye* (Moscow, 1912), 19 (the story was first published early in 1910 in *Novoe slovo*). Bishop Mikhail may have partly borrowed his image and its meaning from this story. See his "Pobezhdeniia Khristos i 'lunnye murav'i'," in *Samoubistvo: sbornik*, 5-40.

143. Delevskii, "Sotsial'nye antagonizmy i obshchestvennyi ideal," *Sovremennik* 1912, no. 1 (January): 252.

144. "Tragediia sovremennoi kul'tury," *Tserkovnyi vestnik* 1914, no. 27 (3 July): 809.

145. L. Kleinbort, "Kinematograf," *Novyi zhurnal dlia vsekh* 1912, no. 6 (June): 104.

146. Louise McReynolds and Joan Neuberger, eds., *Imitations of Life: Two Centuries of Melodrama in Russia* (Durham, N.C., 2002), 143-45.

147. Ol'ga Gridina, "Predel' skorbi," *Gazeta-kopeika*, 13 September 1910, 3.

148. Aikhenval'd, "O samoubiistve," in *Samoubiistvo: sbornik*, 117.

149. L. Gurevich, "Literatura nashego vremeni," *Novyi zhurnal dlia vsekh* 1909, no. 3 (January): 103.

150. L. Logvinovich, "Smekh i pechal'," *Zhizn' dlia vsekh* 1912, no. 1 (January): 107; Prof. V. P. Speranskii, "Ideia tragicheskoi krasoty i Leonid Andreev," *Novyi zhurnal dlia vsekh*, no. 1 (November 1908): 71-79. See also the review of Andreev's play, at the *Novyi teatr* in 1908, *Dni nashei zhizni* (Days of Our Lives), ibid., no. 2 (December 1908): 122; and Aleksandr Blok's criticism of Andreev's spirit of "world tragedy" in "Protivorechie," *Rech'*, 1 February 1910, 2.

151. "Religioznost' i religiozno," *Tserkovnyi vestnik* 1909, no. 5 (29 January): 135. See also D. Merezhkovskii, *Griadushchii Kham* (St. Petersburg, 1906), reprinted in Dmitrii Merezhkovskii, *Bol'naia Rossiia: izbrannoe* (Leningrad, 1991), 33; Galich, "Mysli: nauchnyi optimizm i meshchane," *Rech'*, 11 July 1907, 2.

152. Z. Gippius-Merezhkovskaia, *Dmitrii Merezhkovskii* (Paris, 1951), 79.

153. Friedrich Nietzsche, *Richard Wagner in Bayreuth* (1876), quoted in Laurence Lampert, *Nietzsche and Modern Times* (New Haven, 1993), 295-97, 417. For the influence of Nietzsche, and especially of his *Birth of Tragedy*, see Bernice Glatzer Rosenthal, ed., *Nietzsche in Russia* (Princeton, 1986); Rosenthal, *New Myth, New World: from Nietzsche to Stalinism* (University Park, 2002); Edith Clowes, *The Revolution in Moral Consciousness: Nietzsche in Russian Literature, 1890-1914* (DeKalb, 1988).

154. Merezhkovskii, *Griadushchii Kham*, 32-33. See also Galich, "Mysli: nauchnyi optimizm i meshchane," *Rech'*, 11 July 1907, 2.

155. *Zapiski S.-Peterburgskogo religiozno-filosofskogo obshchestva*, no. 2 (1908): 30 (meeting of 21 November 1907).

156. Ibid., no. 1 (1908): 44 (meeting of 15 October 1907).

157. Zhbankov, "Polovaia prestupnost'," *Sovremennyi mir* 1909, no. 7 (July): 64.

158. "Tragediia sovremennoi kul'tury," *Tserkovnyi vestnik* 1914, no. 27 (*3* July): 811; Ashkinazi, "Ot individualizma k bogostroitel'stvu," *Novyi zhurnal dlia vsekh*, no. 6 (April 1909): 105; I. Zhilkin, "Dve intelligentsii," *Zaprosy zhizni* 1909, no. 3 (1 November): 1.

159. V. Sh, "Cherty sovremennoi russkoi zhizni," *Novyi zhurnal dlia vsekh* 1914, no. 1 (January): 46.

160. Rubakin, "Dlia chego ia zhivu na svete," ibid., 1912, no. 6 (June): 65–66.

161. Pritykin, "Krizis intelligentskoi dushi," *Svobodnye mysli*, 24 March 1908, 2. See also "Tainy zhizni i bytiia," *Peterburgskii listok*, 30 April 1910, 116.

162. Al. Fedorov, "V nashi dni," *Peterburgskii kinematograf*, 22 January 1911, 2. The Russian term *iarkii*, normally translated as "bright," also means color distinguished by purity and freshness of tone and, figuratively, something convincing and certain. See also Pritykin, "Krizis intelligentskoi dushi," *Svobodnye mysli*, 24 March 1908, 2.

163. D. Zhbankov, "Itogi," *Rech'*, 14 January 1910, 2; "Khristos Voskrese!" *Teosoficheskoe obozrenie*, no. 7 (April 1908): 488.

164. For restatements in these years, see especially Merezhkovskii, *Griadushchii Kham*, 36–37; Pertsov, "Literaturnye pis'ma," *Novoe vremia*, 7 January 1909, 4.

165. Ashkinazi, "Ot individualizma k bogostroitel'stvu," *Novyi zhurnal dlia vsekh*, no. 6 (April 1909): 105.

166. Lev Shestov, *Apofeos bezpochvennosti* (St. Petersburg, 1905), passim.

167. "K voprosu o sovremennykh zadachakh pastyrstva," *Tserkovnyi vestnik* 1911, no. 50 (15 December): 1572–73. See also "S novym godom," ibid., 1908, no. 1 (*3* January): 1. See also ibid., no. 2 (10 January): 43.

168. V. Portugalov, "V oblasti kul'tury," *Vesna* 1908, no. 1 (6 January): 3 (the article originally appeared in *Novoe vremia*)

169. Kaled, "Ivanushkovtsy," *Sanktpeterburgskie vedomosti*, 9 December 1910, 2.

170. M. Gor'kii, "Zhaloba," *Sovremennik* 1911, no. 1, quoted in E. Kuskova, "Vo chto zhe verit' (nabroski i mysli)," ibid., no. 5 (May 1912): 266. See M. Gor'kii, *Polnoe sobranie sochinenii*, vol. 11 (Moscow, 1971), 12. Gorky may have been partly echoing Petr Chaadaev's famous lament about Russia. In his "First Philosophical Letter" of 1829 he wrote: "Today, say what you will, we are a blank in the intellectual order of things. . . . Look around you. Everyone seems to have one foot in the air. . . . We have nothing that binds, . . . nothing that endures, nothing that remains." In *Russian Intellectual History: An Anthology*, ed. Marc Raeff (New York, 1966), 165–73.

171. Karl Marx, *The Communist Manifesto* (1848). For an influential discussion, see Marshall Berman, *All That Is Solid Melts into Air: The Experience of Modernity* (New York, 1982).

172. Gor'kii, "Zhaloba," in *Polnoe sobranie sochinenii*, 11: 12.

173. Lev Pushchin, "Kak zhit'," *Novyi zhurnal dlia vsekh* 1912, no. 5 (May): 81; Gurevich in *Zaprosy zhizni* 1909, no. 1 (18 October): 30.

174. V. L'vov-Rogachevskii, "Novaia drama Leonida Andreeva," *Sovremennik* 1913, no. 10 (October): 254–55. See also Gurevich, "Literatura nashego vremeni," *Novyi zhurnal dlia vsekh* 1909, no. 3 (January): 102.

175. L'vov-Rogachevskii, "Novaia drama Leonida Andreeva," *Sovremennik* 1913, no. 10 (October): 254.

176. M. Kuzmin, "O prekrasnoi iasnosti: zametki o proze," *Apollon 1910*, no. 4 (January): 5.

177. For the larger context of modern art, see Linda Nochlin, *The Body in Pieces: The Fragment as a Metaphor of Modernity* (New York, 1994).

178. Georgii Chulkov, "Demony i sovremennost' (mysli o frantsuzskoi zhivopisi)," *Apollon* 1914, no. 1–2 (January–February): 66, 70–71.

179. For example, V. Rozanov, "Vechnaia tema," *Novoe vremia*, 4 January 1908, 3.

180. V. Rozanov, "Literaturnye i politicheskie aforizmy (otvet K. I. Chukovskomu i P. B. Struve)," *Novoe vremia*, 25 November 1910, 4 (emphases in original).

181. N. Iu. Kazakova, *V. V. Rozanov i gazeta A. S. Suvorina "Novoe vremia"* (avtoreferat dissertatsii) (Moscow, 2000), 15.

182. Ibid., 15–18. See also E. Gollerbakh, *V. V. Rozanov* (Paris, 1922).

183. N. Rubakin, "Dlia chego ia zhivu na svete," *Novyi zhurnal dlia vsekh* 1912, no. 6 (June): 67.

184. For example, K. Arsen'ev in *Slovo*, reprinted in *Vesna* 1908, no. 2 (13 January): 10; A. Zorin [Gastev], "Rabochii mir: Vera, otchaianie, opyt," *Novyi zhurnal dlia vsekh* 1911, no. 8 (August): 1069, 1075.

185. Pchela, "Kul't razvrata," *Peterburgskii listok*, 8 December 1908, 2.

186. Ol'ga Gridina, "Bez rulia," *Gazeta-kopeika*, 11 April 1910, 5.

187. Bazilevich, "Mnimye strakhi," *Svobodnye mysli*, 13 August 1907, 2. See also *Tserkovnyi vestnik* 1910, no. 1 (7 January): 3.

188. Skitalets, "Bodrye liudi," *Gazeta-kopeika*, 10 April 1911, 4.

189. L. A. Vilikhov, "Idealizm i material'naia kul'tura" (introduction to "Munitsipal'noe obozrenie"), *Gorodskoe delo* 1912, no. 11–12 (1–15 June): 742–43.

190. Chulkov, "Demony i sovremennost' (mysli o frantsuzskoi zhivopisi)," *Apollon* 1914, no. 1–2 (January–February): 66, 70–71.

191. K. Barantsevich, "Fiziologiia Peterburga," *Zhizn' dlia vsekh* 1909, no. 12 (December): 94.

192. Julie Buckler, *Mapping St. Petersburg: Imperial Text and Cityshape* (Princeton, 2005), 21. See also Chapter 1.

193. Irina Paperno, *Suicide as a Cultural Institution in Dostoevsky's Russia* (Ithaca, 1997), esp. 81–94, 162–202.

194. Ashkinazi, "Ot individualizma k bogostroitel'stvu," *Novyi zhurnal dlia vsekh* 1909, no. 6 (April): 105.

195. Quotations from Emile Durkheim and Henry Havelock Ellis in Sirotkina, *Diagnosing Literary Genius*, 118.

196. Ashkinazi, "Ot individualizma k bogostroitel'stvu," *Novyi zhurnal dlia vsekh* 1909, no. 6 (April): 106. The phrase "ignoramus et ignorabimus" (we do not know and will not know) was used in nineteenth-century Europe to speak pessimistically of the limits on scientific knowledge.

197. A. Lunacharskii, "Samoubiistvo i filosofiia," in *Samoubiistvo: sbornik*, 82.

198. This was a continual argument in the church journal *Tserkovnyi vestnik*. For example, "Sovremennost' i dumy," *Tserkovnyi vestnik* 1913, no. 31 (1 August): 945–48.

199. P. Cher-skii, "Paradoksy sovremennosti," *Novyi zhurnal dlia vsekh* 1914, no. 4 (April): 51.

200. S. Isakov, "Mysli ob iskusstve," *Novyi zhurnal dlia vsekh* 1914, no. 1 (January): 53. See also "Tragediia sovremennoi kul'tury," *Tserkovnyi vestnik* 1914, no. 27 (3 July): 811.

201. Chulkov, "Demony i sovremennost' (mysli o frantsuzskoi zhivopisi)," *Apollon* 1914, no. 1–2 (January–February): 66, 70–71.

202. D. Merezhkovskii, "Peterburgu byt' pustu," *Rech'*, 21 December 1908, 2; Iu. Aikhenval'd, "O samoubiistve," in *Samoubiistvo: sbornik*, 123.

203. For example, in addition to the works cited in notes 204–7, I. Brusilovskii, "Smysl' zhizni," *Sovremennoe slovo*, 13 March 1910, 1; Mikhail Kovalevskii, "Zatish'e," *Zaprosy zhizni* 1911, no. 12 (23 December): 705.

204. Dal', *Tolkovyi slovar' zhivago velikorusskago iazyka*, 1:59; Ushakov, *Tolkovyi slovar' russkogo iazyka*, 1:106.

205. V. Lavretskii, "Tragediia sovremennoi molodezhi," *Rech'*, 30 September 1910, 2.

206. M. Slobozhanin, "Iz sovremennykh perezhivanii," pt. 4: "'Ia' i okruzhaiushchaia sreda," *Zhizn' dlia vsekh* 1913, no. 7 [July]: 1019–21. Also pt. 3: "Ob estetikh noveishei formatsii i estetizme voobshche," ibid., 1913, no. 3–4 (March–April): 461.

207. Aleksandr Blok, "Bezvremen'e," *Zolotoe runo* 1906, no. 11–12, 107–14, in Blok, *Polnoe sobranie sochinenii i pisem*, vol. 7 (Moscow, 2003), 21–31, 221, 264–65.

208. Benjamin, *The Arcades Project*, 115, mainly quoting from Nietzsche's *Will to Power*, a compilation of his notebooks and other unpublished writings, first published in 1901.

209. See Susan Buck-Morss, *The Dialectics of Seeing*, 252–53.

210. See, for example, the discussion of Blaise Pascal in Ferguson, *Melancholy and the Critique of Modernity*, esp. 17–19.

211. Ibid., quotations 17–33.

212. O. Gridina, "Zerkalo ne vinovato," *Gazeta-kopeika*, 31 October 1910, 3.

213. Daniel Mornet, *Le Romantisme en France au XVIIIe siècle* (Paris, 1912), cited in Charles Taylor, *Sources of the Self: The Making of Modern Identity* (Cambridge, Mass., 1989), 296; Vinitskii, *Utekhi melankholii* (Solace/Pleasures of Melancholy—also the title of a book published in Russia in 1802, which, in turn, explicitly echoed Thomas Wharton's *Pleasures of Melancholy* [London, 1747]); Kristeva, *Black Sun*, 145, 170; Freud, "Mourning and Melancholia," 251; Ferguson, *Melancholy and the Critique of Modernity*, 20; Flatley, *Affective Mapping*, 1–10, 160.

214. Klibansky, Panofsky, and Saxl, *Saturn and Melancholy*, 229–32; Radden, *The Nature of Melancholy*, 12–17, 136, 178, 219; Gérard de Nerval, "El Desdichado (The Disinherited)" (1853), discussed in Kristeva, *Black Sun*, chap. 6; Freud, "Mourning and Melancholia," 246; Kristeva, *Black Sun*, 4. See also Ferguson, *Melancholy and the Critique of Modernity*, 12.

215. See Flatley, *Affective Mapping*, 65 (concerning Walter Benjamin).

CONCLUSION

1. Most recently, Daniel Beer, *Renovating Russia: The Human Sciences and the Fate of Liberal Modernity, 1880–1930* (Ithaca, 2008).

2. Vladimir Mikhnevich, *Iazvy Peterburga: opyt istoriko-statisticheskogo issledovaniia nravstvennosti stolichnogo naseleniia* (St. Petersburg, 2003; reprint of original 1886 edition), quotations 43–44, 554, 595, 613–15.

3. In addition to Mikhnevich, see other journalistic publications, such as Vsevolod Krestovskii, *Peterburgskie trushchoby* (St. Petersburg, 1867); Anatolii Bakhtiarov, *Briukho Peterburga* (St. Petersburg, 1887); N. Sveshnikov, *Peterburgskie Viazemskie trushchoby i ikh obitateli* (St. Petersburg, 1900); N. V. Nikitin, *Peterburg nochiu: bytovye ocherki* (St. Petersburg, 1903). I found the same greater confidence in a modern cure reading the press before 1905, notably *Novoe vremia* (read for the late 1880s and 1900 and 1903).

4. See, especially, Thesis VI in "On the Concept of History," in Walter Benjamin, *Selected Writings*, ed. Michael Jennings et al., 4 vols. (Cambridge, Mass., 1996–2003), 4:391.

Bibliography

PRIMARY SOURCES

Archives

Tsentral'nyi gosudarstvennyi arkhiv kinofotofonodokumentov Sankt-Peterburga (TsGAKFFD, Central State Archive of Film, Photographic, and Sound Documents of St. Petersburg)
Rossiiskii gosudarstvennyi arkhiv literatury i isskustva (RGALI, Russian State Archive of Literature and Art), Moscow

Petersburg Newspapers

Dates indicate years read.
Gazeta-kopeika (Kopeck Gazette), 1908–16
Malen'kaia gazeta (Little Gazette), 1914–16
Novoe vremia (New Times), 1888, 1900, 1903, 1909–10
Peterburgskaia gazeta (Petersburg Gazette), selected issues 1906–16
Peterburgskie kinemoteatry (Petersburg Cinema Theaters), 1912–14
Peterburgskii gid (Petersburg Guide), 1912–13
Peterburgskii kinematograf (Petersburg Cinematograph), 1911
Peterburgskii listok (Petersburg News Sheet), 1906–16
Rech' (Speech), 1907–11
Sovremennoe slovo (Modern/Contemporary Word), 1910
Stolichnyi kinematograf (Capital Cinematograph), 1911–12
Svobodnye mysli (Free Thoughts), 1907–8

Magazines and Journals

Dates indicate years read.
Apollon (Apollo), 1909–17
Argus, 1913–17
Dvadtsatyi vek (Twentieth Century), 1911, 1913
Gorodskoe delo (City Affairs), 1909–17
Listok-kopeika (Kopeck Sheet), 1909–11
Maski (Masks), 1912–13
Nash kinematograf (Our Cinematograph), 1913

Niva (Field), 1913
Novyi zhurnal dlia vsekh (New Magazine for Everyone), 1908–16
Ocharovannyi strannik (Enchanted Wanderer), 1913–16
Ogonek (Flame), 1908–16
Peterburgskii svetoch (Petersburg Light), 1912–13
Peterburgskii zhurnal (Petersburg Magazine), 1910–11
Satirikon, 1908
Shut (Jester), 1911
Soiuz molodezhi (Union of Youth), 1912–13
Sovremennik (The Contemporary/Modern), 1911–15
Sovremennyi mir (Contemporary/Modern World), 1906–16
Teosoficheskoe obozrenie (Theosophical Observer), 1907–8
Tserkovnyi vestnik (Church Herald), 1908–16
Vesna (Spring), 1907–1911
Vsemirnaia panorama (Universal Panorama), 1910
Zapiski Sankt-Peterburgskogo religiozno-filosofskogo obshchestva (Notes of the
      St. Petersburg Religious-Philosophical Society), 1908
Zaprosy zhizni (Problems of Life), 1909–11
Zavety (Precepts), 1912
Zhizn' dlia vsekh (Life for Everyone), 1909–17
Zhizn' za nedeliu (Life During the Week), 1913
Zhurnal-kopeika (Kopeck Magazine), 1909

Books

Aborigen [Zarin, Andrei Efimovich]. *Krovavye letopisi Peterburga*. St. Petersburg,
      1914.
Alekseev, Gleb, B., ed. *Peterburg v stikhotvoreniiakh russkikh poetov*. Berlin, 1923.
Alianskii, Iurii Lazarevich. *Veseliashchiisia Peterburg (Po materialam sobraniia
      G. A. Ivanova)*. 6 vols. St. Petersburg, 1992–2002.
Amori, Graf [I. P. Rapgof]. *Tainy Nevskogo prospekta*. Petrograd, 1915.
Anufriev, Konstantin I. *Nishchenstvo i bor'ba s nim*. St. Petersburg, 1913.
Bakhtiarov, Anatolii. *Briukho Peterburga: obshchestvenno-fiziologicheskie ocherki*.
      St. Petersburg, 1887.
Belyi, Andrei. *Peterburg* [1913] St. Petersburg, 2004.
Bentovin, Boris Il'ich [on cover: D-r B. Bentovin]. *Torguiushchie telom: ocherki
      sovremennoi prostitutsii*. 3d ed. St. Petersburg, 1910.
Berdiaev, Nikolai. *Krizis iskusstva*. Moscow, 1918.
Berman, Iak[ov A.]. *P'ianstvo i prestupnost': po dannym Svoda Stat. Sved. po delam
      ugolovym za 1906–1910*. Petrograd, 1914.

Bonch-Tomashevskii, Mikhail Mikhailovich. *Kniga o tango: iskusstvo i seksual'nost'*. Moscow, 1914.

Cherikover, S. *Peterburg*. Moscow, 1909.

Fiziologiia Peterburga [1844–45]. Moscow, 1991.

Gernet, M. N., ed. *Deti-prestupniki: sbornik statei*. Moscow, 1912.

Isupov, K. G. ed., *Moskva-Peterburg: Pro et contra*, St. Petersburg, 2000.

Khoroshii ton: sbornik pravil i sovetov. St. Petersburg, 1910.

Kratkii svod statisticheskikh dannykh po g. Petrograda za 1913–1914 gg. St. Petersburg., n.d. (1915?).

Krestovskii, Vsevolod. *Peterburgskie trushchoby: kniga o sytykh i golodnykh*, 4 vols. St. Petersburg, 1867.

Liberson, M. *Stradanie odinochestva*. St. Petersburg, 1909.

Merezhkovskii, Dmitry S. *Bol'naia Rossiia: izbrannoe*. Leningrad, 1991.

Mikhnevich, Vasilii. *Iazvy Peterburga: opyt istoriko-statisticheskogo issledovaniia nravstvennosti stolichnogo naseleniia*. St. Petersburg, 1886.

Nedesheva, V. *Nevskii prospekt: ocherk*. St. Petersburg, 1906.

Nikitin, N. V. *Peterburg noch'iu: bytovye ocherki*. St. Petersburg, 1903.

Novye peterburgskie trushchoby: ocherki stolichnoi zhizni. Nos. 1–4. St. Petersburg, n.d. (1909–10).

Ozerov, I. Kh. *Bol'shie goroda, ikh zadachi i sredstva upravleniia: publichnaia lektsiia*. Moscow, 1906.

Peterburg i ego zhizn'. St. Petersburg, 1914.

Peterburg noch'iu: premiia zhurnala Shut 1911 g. No 3. St. Petersburg, 1911.

Peterburg-Petrograd-Leningrad v russkoi poezii. Leningrad, 1975.

Peterburgskie vechera. 4 vols. St. Petersburg, 1912–14.

Peterburg v russkoi poezii, XVIII–nachala XX v: poeticheskaia antologiia. Leningrad, 1988.

Predvaritel'nyi svod statisticheskikh dannykh po g. S-Peterburgu za 1909 god. St. Petersburg. n.d. (1910?).

Ruadze, V. P. *K sudu!*. . . *Gomoseksual'nyi Peterburg*. St. Petersburg, 1908.

Samoubiistvo: sbornik obshchestvennykh, filosofskikh i kriticheskikh statei. Moscow, 1911.

Sinel'nikov, Mikhail, ed. *Sankt-Peterburg, Petrograd, Leningrad v russkoi poezii*. St. Petersburg, 1999.

Statisticheskii spravochnik po Petrogradu. Petrograd, 1919.

Sveshnikov, N. *Peterburgskie Viazemskie trushchoby i ikh obitateli: original'nyi ocherk s natury*. St. Petersburg, 1900.

Svirskii, A. "Peterburgskie khuligany (ocherk)." In *Peterburg i ego zhizn'*, 250–77. St. Petersburg, 1914.

Tastevin, Genrikh. *Futurizm (na puti k novomu simvolizmu)*. Moscow, 1914.
Vekhi: sbornik statei i russkoi intelligentsia. Moscow, 1909.
Zhivotov, N. N. *Peterburgskie profili*. 4 vols. St. Petersburg, 1894–95.

SECONDARY SOURCES

Selected Studies of St. Petersburg, Russian Cities, and Russian Modernity

Antsiferov, N. P. *Byl' i mif Peterburga*. Petrograd, 1924.
———. *Dusha Peterburga*. Petrograd, 1922.
———. "*Nepostizhimyi gorod . . .*": *Dusha Peterburga. Peterburg Dostoevskogo. Peterburg Pushkina*, ed. M. B. Verblovskaia. St. Petersburg, 1991.
———. *Peterburg Dostoevskogo*. Petrograd, 1923.
Banjanin, Milica. "Between Symbolism and Futurism: Impressions by Day and by Night in Elena Guro's City Series." *Slavic and East European Journal* 37, no. 1 (Spring 1993): 67–84.
———. "Elena Guro: From the City's Junkyard of Images to a Poetics of Nature." *Studia Slavica Finlandensia* 16, no. 1 (1999): 43–63.
———. "The Female 'Flâneur': Elena Guro in Petersburg." *Australian Slavonic and East European Studies* 11, no. 1–2 (1997): 47–63.
———. "The Prose and Poetry of Elena Guro." *Russian Literature Triquarterly* 9 (Spring 1979): 303–16.
Bater, James H. *St. Petersburg: Industrialization and Change*. Montreal, 1976.
Beer, Daniel. *Renovating Russia: The Human Sciences and the Fate of Liberal Modernity, 1880–1930*. Ithaca, 2008.
Bernstein, Laurie. *Sonia's Daughters: Prostitutes and their Regulation in Imperial Russia*. Berkeley, 1995.
Bespiatykh, Iu. N. *Fenomen Peterburga*. St. Peterburg, 2001.
Bonnell, Victoria. *Roots of Rebellion: Workers' Politics and Organizations in St. Petersburg and Moscow, 1900–1914*. Berkeley, 1983.
Bradley, Joseph. *Muzhik and Muscovite: Urbanization in Late Imperial Russia*. Berkeley, 1985.
Brower, Daniel. *The Russian City Between Tradition and Modernity, 1850–1900*. Berkeley, 1990.
Buckler, Julie. *Mapping St. Petersburg: Imperial Text and Cityshape*. Princeton, 2005.
Bunatian, G. G., and M. G. Charnaia. *Peterburg serebrianogo veka*. St. Petersburg, 2002.
Clark, Katerina. *Petersburg, Crucible of Revolution*. Cambridge, Mass., 1995.
Clements, Barbara Evans, Rebecca Friedman, and Dan Healy, eds. *Russian Masculinities in History and Culture*. New York, 2002.

Clowes, Edith, Samuel Kassow, and James West, eds. *Between Tsar and People: Educated Society and the Quest for Public Identity in Late Imperial Russia*. Princeton, 1991.

Cooper, Nancy L. "Images of Hope and Despair in the Last Part of Blok's 'Gorod'." *Slavic and East European Journal* 35, no. 4 (Winter 1991): 503–17.

Crone, Anna Lisa, *My Petersburg/Myself: Elegiac Identification, Mental Architecture, and Imaginative Space in Modern Russian Letters*. Bloomington, 2003.

Dolgopolov, L. K. "Obraz goroda v romane A. Belogo 'Peterburg'." *Izvestiia Akademii Nauk SSSR: seriia literatury i iazyka* 34, no. 1 (January–February 1975): 46–59.

Engelstein, Laura. *The Keys to Happiness: Sex and the Search for Modernity in Fin-de-Siècle Russia*. Ithaca, 1992.

Engelstein, Laura, and Stephanie Sandler, eds. *Self and Story in Russian History*. Ithaca, 2000.

Fanger, Donald, "Dostoevsky's Early Feuilletons: Approaches to a Myth of the City." *Slavic Review* 22, no. 3 (September 1963): 469–82.

Fink, Hillary L. *Bergson and Russian Modernism, 1900–1930*. Evanston, 1999.

Hamm, Michael F., ed. *The City in Late-Imperial Russia*. Bloomington, 1986.

Healey, Dan. *Homosexual Desire in Revolutionary Russia: The Regulation of Sexual and Gender Dissent*. Chicago, 2001.

———. "Masculine Purity and 'Gentlemen's Mischief': Sexual Exchange and Prostitution between Russian Men, 1861–1941." *Slavic Review* 60, no. 2 (Summer 2001): 233–65.

Hoffmann, David L., and Yanni Kotsonis, eds. *Russian Modernity: Politics, Knowledge, Practices*. New York, 1999.

Holquist, Michael. "St. Petersburg: From Utopian City to Gnostic Universe." *Virginia Quarterly Review* 48, no. 4 (1972): 557–37.

Hoy, David Couzens. *The Time of Our Lives: A Critical History of Temporality*. Cambridge, Mass., 2009.

Ignatova, Elena. *Zapiski o Peterburge: ocherk istorii goroda*. St. Petersburg, 1997.

Iukhneva, N. V. *Etnicheskii sostav i etnosotsial'naia struktura naseleniia Peterburga: vtoraia polovina XIX–nachalo XX veka*. Leningrad, 1984.

———, ed. *Etnografiia Peterburga-Leningrada: tridtsat' let uzucheniia, 1974–2004*. St. Petersburg, 2004.

Ivanov-Razumnik. *Peterburg Belogo*. Munich, 1972.

Jahn, Hubertus. *Armes Rußland: Bettler and Notleidende in der russischen Geschichte vom Mittelalter bis in die Gegenwart*. Paderborn, 2010.

Jensen, Kjeld Bjørnager. *Russian Futurism, Urbanism and Elena Guro*. Aarhus, 1977.

Johnson, Emily D. *How St. Petersburg Learned to Study Itself: The Russian Idea of Kraevedenie*. University Park, 2006.

Kaganov, G. Z. (Grigorii Zosimovich). *Images of Space: St. Petersburg in the Visual and Verbal Arts*, trans. Sidney Monas. Stanford, 1997.

———. *Sankt-Peterburg: obrazy prostranstva*. 2d ed. St. Petersburg, 2004.

Kazakova, N. Iu. V. V. *Rozanov i gazeta A. S. Suvorina "Novoe vremia."* Avtoreferat diss., Moscow, 2000.

Keller, E. E. *Prazdnichnaia kul'tura Peterburga: ocherki istorii*. St. Petersburg, 2001.

Kelly, Catriona, and David Shepherd. *Constructing Russian Culture in the Age of Revolution, 1881–1940*. Oxford, 1998.

Langen, Timothy. *The Stony Dance: Unity and Gesture in Andrei Bely's "Petersburg."* Evanston, 2005.

Lapin, V. V. *Peterburg: zapakhi i zvuki*. St. Petersburg, 2007.

Levitt, M., and A. Toporkov, eds. *Eros i pornografiia v russkoi kul'tury*. Moscow, 1999.

Lincoln, W. Bruce, *Sunlight at Midnight: St. Petersburg and the Rise of Modern Russia*. New York, 2000.

Lotman, Iu. M. "Blok i narodnaia kul'tura goroda." In *Izbrannye stat'i*, vol. 3, 185–200. Tallinn, 1993.

———. "Simvolika Peterburga i problemy semiotiki goroda." *Semiotika goroda i gorodskoi kul'tury—Peterburg (Trudy po znakovym sistemam XVIII)*, *Uchenye zapiski Tartuskogo gosudarstvennogo universiteta*, no. 664 (1984): 30–45.

Matich, Olga. *Erotic Utopia: The Decadent Imagination in Russia's Fin de Siècle*. Madison, 2005.

———, ed. *Petersburg/Petersburg: Novel and City, 1900–1921*. Madison, 2010.

McReynolds, Louise. *The News Under Russia's Old Regime: The Development of a Mass Circulation Press*. Princeton, 1991.

———. *Russia at Play: Leisure Activities at the End of the Tsarist Era*. Ithaca, 2003.

———. "St. Petersburg's 'Boulevard' Press and the Process of Urbanization." *Journal of Urban History* 18, no. 2 (February 1992): 123–40.

McReynolds, Louise, and Joan Neuberger, eds. *Imitations of Life: Two Centuries of Melodrama in Russia*. Durham, N.C., 2002.

Metafizika Peterburga. Peterburgskie chtenie po teorii, istorii i filosofii kul'tury, no. 1. St. Petersburg, 1993.

Mitchell, Rebecca. "Nietzsche's Orphans: Music and the Search for Unity in Revolutionary Russia 1905–21." Ph.D. diss., University of Illinois at Urbana-Champaign, 2011.

Morrissey, Susan. "Suicide and Civilization in Late Imperial Russia." *Jahrbücher für Geschichte Osteuropas* 43 (1995): 201–17.

———. *Suicide and the Body Politic in Imperial Russia.* Cambridge, 2006.

Nathans, Benjamin. *Beyond the Pale: The Jewish Encounter in Late Imperial Russia.* Berkeley, 2002.

Neuberger, Joan. *Hooliganism: Crime, Culture, and Power in St. Petersburg, 1900–1914.* Berkeley, 1993.

Orlov, Vladimir Nikolaevich. *Poet i gorod: Aleksandr Blok i Peterburg.* Leningrad, 1980.

Paperno, Irina. *Suicide as a Cultural Institution in Dostoevsky's Russia.* Ithaca, 1997.

Paperno, Irina, and Joan Delaney Grossman, eds. *Creating Life: the Aesthetic Utopia of Russian Modernism.* Stanford, 1994.

Peterburg kak fenomen kul'tury: sbornik statei. St. Petersburg, 1994.

Pinnow, Kenneth M. *Lost to the Collective: Suicide and the Promise of Soviet Socialism, 1921–1929.* Ithaca, 2010.

Rosenthal, Bernice Glatzer. "Eschatology and the Appeal of Revolution: Merezhkovsky, Bely, Blok." *California Slavic Studies* 11 (1980): 105–39.

———, ed. *Nietzsche and Soviet Culture.* Cambridge, 1994.

———, ed. *Nietzsche in Russia.* Princeton, 1986.

Ruane, Christine. *The Empire's New Clothes: A History of the Russian Fashion Industry, 1700–1917.* New Haven, 2009.

Sahadeo, Jeffrey. *Russian Colonial Society in Tashkent, 1865–1923.* Bloomington, 2007.

Sankt-Peterburg: okno v Rossiiu, 1900–1935. Gorod, modernizatsiia, sovremennost'. St. Petersburg, 1997.

Sankt-Peterburg v ob"ektive fotografov kontsa XIX–nachala XX veka. St. Petersburg, 2003.

Schlögel, Karl. *Petersburg: Das Laboratorium der Moderne, 1909–1921.* Munich and Vienna, 2002; originally published Berlin, 1988.

Seifrid, Thomas. "'Illusion' and Its Workings in Modern Russian Culture." *Slavic and East European Journal* 45, no. 2 (Summer 2001): 205–15.

Semiotika goroda i gorodskoi kul'tury—Peterburg (Trudy po znakovym sistemam XVIII), Uchenye zapiski Tartuskogo gosudarstvennogo universiteta, no. 664 (Tartu, 1984).

Sindalovskii, Naum. *Peterburg v fol'klore.* St. Petersburg, 1999.

Soboleva, Olga. *The Silver Mask: Harlequinade in the Symbolist Poetry of Blok and Bely.* Bern, 2008.

Steinberg, Mark D. *Proletarian Imagination: Self, Modernity, and the Sacred in Russia, 1910–1925.* Ithaca, 2002.

Steinberg, Mark D., and Heather Coleman, eds. *Sacred Stories: Religion and Spirituality in Modern Russia*. Bloomington, Indiana, 2007.

Steinberg, Mark D., and Boris Kolonitskii, eds. *Kul'tury gorodov rossiiskoi imperii na rubezhe XIX-XX vekov*. St. Petersburg, 2009.

Steinberg, Mark D., and Valeria Sobol, eds. *Interpreting Emotion in Russia and Eastern Europe*. DeKalb, 2011.

Stroud, Gregory. "Retrospective Revolution: A History of Time and Memory in Urban Russia, 1903–1923." Ph.D. diss., University of Illinois at Urbana-Champaign, 2006.

Sylvester, Roshanna. *Tales of Old Odessa: Crime and Civility in a City of Thieves*. DeKalb, 2005.

Tomei, Christine D. "'Landsafty Fantazii, Slysimoj Molca za Slovom': Dis/Juncture as a Patterning Principle in Andrej Belyj's *Peterburg*." *Slavic and East European Journal* 38, no. 4 (Winter 1994): 603–17.

———. "On the Function of Light and Color in Andrej Belyj's *Peterburg*: Green and Twilight." *Slavic and East European Journal* 36, no. 1 (Spring 1992): 57–67.

Toporov, V. N. *Peterburgskii tekst russkoi literatury: izbrannye trudy*. St. Petersburg, 2003.

Tsivian, Yuri. *Early Cinema in Russia and Its Cultural Reception*, trans. Alan Bodger. London, 1994.

———. "Russia 1913: Cinema in the Cultural Landscape." In *Silent Film*, ed. Richard Abel, 194–216. New Brunswick, N.J., 1996.

Vinitskii, I. Iu. *Utekhi melankholii*. Issue 2 of *Uchenye zapiski Moskovskogo kul'turologicheskogo litseia, Seriia: Filologiia*, no. 1310, 107–289. Moscow, 1997.

Volkov, Solomon. *Petersburg: A Cultural History*. New York, 1995.

Youngblood, Denise Jeanne. *The Magic Mirror: Moviemaking in Russia, 1908–1918*. Madison, 1999.

Zasosov, D., and V. Pyzin, *Povsednevnaia zhizn' Peterburga na rubezhe XIX-XX vekov*. Moscow, 2003.

Zorkaia, N. M. *Na rubezhe stoletii: u istokov massovogo iskusstva v Rossii 1900–1910 gg*. Moscow, 1976.

SELECTED COMPARATIVE STUDIES OF CITIES AND MODERNITY

Alter, Robert. *Imagined Cities: Urban Experience and the Language of the Novel*. New Haven, 2005.

Appadurai, Arjun. *Modernity at Large: Cultural Dimensions of Globalization*. Minneapolis, 1996.

Barta, Peter. *Bely, Joyce, and Döblin: Peripatetics in the City Novel.* Gainesville, 1996.

Baudrillard, Jean. *The Illusion of the End,* trans. Chris Turner [1992]. Stanford, 1994.

———. *Simulacra and Simulation,* trans. Sheila Faria Glaser [1985]. Ann Arbor, 1994.

Bauman, Zygmunt. *Modernity and Ambivalence.* Cambridge, 1991.

Benjamin, Walter. *The Arcades Project,* trans. Howard Eiland and Kevin McLaughlin. Cambridge, Mass., 1999.

———. *One-Way Street* [1928]. In Benjamin, *Selected Writings,* vol. 1, 444–88.

———. *Das Passagen-Werk,* ed. Rolf Tiedemann. 2 vols. Frankfurt am Main, 1982.

———. *Selected Writings,* ed. Michael Jennings, et al. 4 vols. Cambridge, Mass., 1996–2003.

Berman, Marshall. *All That Is Solid Melts Into Air: The Experience of Modernity.* New York, 1982.

Buck-Morss, Susan. *The Dialectics of Seeing: Walter Benjamin and the Arcades Project.* Cambridge, Mass., 1989.

———. *Dreamworld and Catastrophe: The Passing of Mass Utopia in East and West.* Cambridge, Mass., 2002.

Buse, Peter, Ken Hirschkop, Scott McCracken, and Bertrand Taithe. *Benjamin's Arcades: An UnGuided Tour.* Manchester, 2005.

Calhoun, Craig, ed. *Habermas and the Public Sphere.* Cambridge, Mass., 1992.

Calinescu, Matei. *Five Faces of Modernity.* Durham, N.C., 1987.

Carrol, Peter J. *Between Heaven and Modernity: Reconstructing Suzhou.* Stanford, 2006.

Çelik, Zeynep, Diane Favro, and Richard Ingersoll. *Streets: Critical Perspectives on Public Space.* Berkeley, 1994.

Certeau, Michel de. *The Practice of Everyday Life.* Berkeley, 1984.

Chaney, Leo, and Vanessa R. Schwartz. *Cinema and the Invention of Modern Life.* Berkeley, 1995.

Clark, T. J. *The Painting of Modern Life: Paris in the Art of Manet and His Followers.* Princeton, 1984.

Crary, Jonathan. *Suspensions of Perception: Attention, Spectacle, and Modern Culture.* Cambridge, Mass., 2000.

Felski, Rita. *The Gender of Modernity.* Cambridge, Mass., 1995.

Flatley, Jonathan. *Affective Mapping: Melancholia and the Politics of Modernism.* Cambridge, Mass., 2008.

Frisby, David. *Fragments of Modernity: Theories of Modernity in the Work of Simmel, Kracauer and Benjamin.* Cambridge, 1986.

Fritzsche, Peter. *Reading Berlin, 1900.* Cambridge, Mass., 1996.

———. *Stranded in the Present: Modern Time and the Melancholy of History*. Cambridge, Mass., 2004.

Gilloch, Graeme. *Myth and Metropolis: Walter Benjamin and the City*. Cambridge, 1996.

Gluck, Mary. *Popular Bohemia: Modernism and Urban Culture in Nineteenth-Century Paris*. Cambridge, Mass., 2005.

Hofmann, Andreas R., and Anna Veronika Wendland, eds. *Stadt und Öffentlichkeit in Ostmitteleuropa, 1900–1939: Beiträge zur Entstehung moderner Urbanität zwischen Berlin, Charkiv, Tallinn und Triest*. Stuttgart, 2002.

Hunt, Lynn. *Measuring Time, Making History*. Budapest, 2008.

Kern, Stephen. *The Culture of Time and Space, 1880–1918*. Cambridge, Mass., 1983.

Koselleck, Reinhart. *Futures Past: On the Semantics of Historical Time*. Cambridge, Mass., 1985.

———. *The Practice of Conceptual History: Timing History, Spacing Concepts*. Stanford, 2002,

Kostof, Spiro. *The City Assembled: The Elements of Urban Form Through History*. London, 1992.

Lehan, Richard. *The City in Literature: An Intellectual and Cultural History*. Berkeley, 1998.

Lefebvre, Henri. *The Urban Revolution*, trans. Robert Bononno. Minneapolis, 2003.

Löwy, Michael. *Fire Alarm: Reading Walter Benjamin's 'On the Concept of History'*. London, 2005.

Micale, Mark. *Hysterical Men: The Hidden History of Male Nervous Illness*. Cambridge, Mass., 2008.

Micale, Mark, and Paul Frederick Lerner, eds. *Traumatic Pasts: History, Psychiatry, and Trauma in the Modern Age, 1870–1930*. Cambridge, 2001.

Mumford, Lewis. *The City in History*. New York, 1961.

Nead, Lynda. *Victorian Babylon: People, Streets and Images in Nineteenth-Century London*. New Haven, 2000.

Nochlin, Linda. *The Body in Pieces: The Fragment as a Metaphor of Modernity*. London, 1994.

Pick, Daniel, *Faces of Degeneration: A European Disorder, c. 1848–1918*. Cambridge, 1989.

Pike, Burton. *The Image of the City in Modern Literature*. Princeton, 1981.

Pippin, Robert. *Modernism as a Philosophical Problem*. 2d ed. Oxford, 1999.

Reddy, William. *The Navigation of Feeling: A Framework for the History of Emotions*. Cambridge, 2001.

Joachim Schlör, *Nights in the Big City: Paris, Berlin, London, 1840–1930*. London, 1998.

Schorske, Carl E. *Fin-de-Siècle Vienna: Politics and Culture*. New York, 1981.

Schwartz, Vanessa. *Spectacular Realities: Early Mass Culture in Fin-de-Siècle Paris*. Berkeley, 1998.

Simmel, Georg. "The Metropolis and Mental Life" [1903]. In *The Sociology of Georg Simmel*, trans. and ed. Kurt Wolff. Glencoe, 1950.

Walkowitz, Judith. *City of Dreadful Delight: Narratives of Sexual Danger in Late-Victorian London*. Chicago, 1992.

Wilson, Elizabeth. *The Sphinx in the City: Urban Life, the Control of Disorder, and Women*. Los Angeles, 1992.

Wood, Nathaniel D. *Becoming Metropolitan: Urban Selfhood and the Making of Modern Cracow*. DeKalb, 2010.

Index

15

violence as, 53, 74, 123–24, 126, 130. *See also* crowd; street; visuality

spirit of the age, 159–66

spiritualism, 115, 212–13, 217, 218. *See also* religion

Spiritualist Society, 213

Staël, Germaine de (Madame de), 239, 241–42

Stolypin, Petr, 128

St. Petersburg: contradictory journalistic views of, 34–46; contrasted to Moscow, 12, 19, 23, 37; ethnic diversity of, 15–17; founding of, 10, 20; history of literary representations of, 17–34; physical history of, 10–17. *See also specific topics*

St. Petersburg Theological Academy journal. *See Tserkovnyi vestnik*

strangers, 13, 30, 142, 164, 239; and con games, 93–95, 97, 100–101, 108; crowd as, 19, 32, 47, 50–51, 82; and masks, 84–85, 89–90, 92, 111–12, 116–18; and violence, 123–25, 132, 171–72. *See also* crowd

Stray Dog cabaret, 208, 221–22

street, 23, 36, **47–83**, 157, 161, 222, 228, 232, 234; and advertising, 54, 74; as aesthetic fashion, 55–56; as animal, 51; art as, 34; in Belyi's *Petersburg*, 30, 92; as cinematograph, 56, 79; as compression of time, 48; contradictions of, 18–19, 40; as decadent, 169–70; as defined by journalists and theorists, **47–56**; and disgust, 82–83; as embodied by crowd, 32, 51–54; fun celebrations on, 224–25; and hooliganism, 171–76, 178; and masks, 91–93, 106, 109, 112; modernity as, 30, 49, 268; as moral space, 50–51, 63; as mystery and melancholy, 24–27, 29–30, 33; newspapers as, 68–69, 75; as noise, 70–72; physical history of, 10–12, 17, 20–21, 54; *pritony* as, 75–77; and prostitution, 189, 197; and provincials, 53–54; and

sex, 179, 186, 188–91; as spectacle, 13, 15, 56, 58, 81–82; suicide on, 135, 139; trams as symbol of, 73; as university for crime, 60; violence epidemic on, 72, 122–26. *See also* children; crime; crowd; flâneurs; mapping; noise; spectacle

streetcars. *See* trams

street literature. *See* boulevard literature

strike, general (1905), 245

sueta, 23, 45, 49, 67, 226

suicide, 46, 54, 106, **133–56**, 185, 188, 222, 228, 246, 269; causes of, 136–38, 149–52; clubs of, 141; as disenchantment, 146–47, 148, 150; and hooliganism, 174, 176; as illness of modernity, 2, 144–50, 155–56, 158, 160–62, 257; interpretations of, 126, **142–56**; of Kal'mansons, 140–41; and *lichnost'*, 151–53; in literature, 27, 127; and masquerade, 99, 117; as performance, 139–41, 146; as physical illness, 143; and prostitution, 191, 194; and religion, 147–49, 151; as reported in press, 35, 36, 50, 58, 64, 73, 79, 119, **133–42**; sham, 99–100; as spectacle, 141–42; statistics and rates of, 134–35; and *toska*, 248; unknowability of, 85, 154–55

Sumarokov, Aleksandr, 21

Summer Garden, 52, 63, 186

Sveshnikov, Nikolai, 36

Svirskii, Aleksei, 175

Svobodnye mysli (Free Thoughts), 244

swindling. *See* confidence games; performance; pretenders

symbolism, 32, 84, 127, 169, 202

syphilis, 168, 184, 228

Tal'nikov, N., 214, 216, 218

tango, 180–82

Tarnovskii, Veniamin, 197

Tastevin, Genrikh, 33

Tauride Gardens, 52, 63, 174, 186

technology, 37–38, 41–44, 204, 215, 263